SOFTWARE RELIABILITY
Measurement, Prediction, Application

McGraw-Hill Series in Software Engineering and Technology

Consulting Editor
Peter Freeman, *University of California, Irvine*

Cohen: *Ada as a Second Language*
Fairley: *Software Engineering Concepts*
Howden: *Functional Program Testing and Analysis*
Jones: *Programming Productivity*
Kolence: *An Introduction to Software Physics: The Meaning of Computer Measurement*
Musa, Iannino, Okumoto: *Software Reliability: Measurement, Prediction, Application*
Pressman: *Software Engineering: A Practitioner's Approach*

SOFTWARE RELIABILITY

Measurement, Prediction, Application

John D. Musa

Anthony Iannino

Kazuhira Okumoto

AT&T Bell Laboratories
Whippany, NJ

McGraw-Hill Book Company

New York   St. Louis   San Francisco   Auckland   Bogotá   Hamburg
London   Madrid   Mexico   Milan   Montreal   New Delhi
Panama   Paris   São Paulo   Singapore   Sydney   Tokyo   Toronto

To MARILYN   J.D.M.
To MY PARENTS   A.I.
To LILLIE   K.O.

This book was set in Times Roman by Publication Services.
The editor was Karen M. Jackson;
the production supervisor was Diane Renda;
the cover was designed by John Hite.
Project supervision was done by Publication Services.
Arcata Graphics/Halliday was printer and binder.

SOFTWARE RELIABILITY
Measurement, Prediction, Application

3 4 5 6 7 8 9 0   HALHAL   8 9 2 1 0 9 8 7

ISBN 0-07-044093-X

Library of Congress Cataloging-in-Publication Data
Musa, John D.
    Software reliability.
    (McGraw-Hill series in software engineering and
technology)
    Bibliography: p.
    Includes indexes.
    1. Computer software—Testing.   2. Computer software—Reliability.   I. Iannino, Anthony.
II. Okumoto, Kazuhira.   III. Title.   IV. Series.
QA76.76.T48M87   1987   005.1'4   86-27510
ISBN 0-07-044093-X

ABOUT THE AUTHORS

John D. Musa is Supervisor of Software Quality at AT&T Bell Laboratories, Whippany, N.J. He has been involved in the field of software reliability since 1973, developing two models (one with Okumoto) and making many theoretical contributions. Musa has published over 40 papers. A manager of a wide variety of software projects, he has been a leader in the practical application of software reliability measurement and prediction to guiding engineering and management decisions. He has created two courses at AT&T to integrate this extensive experience in both theory and practice and impart it to software practitioners. This book has benefited greatly from that effort.

Musa brings a wealth of experience in software engineering to his writing. As chairman of the IEEE Technical Committee on Software Engineering, he won a Meritorious Service Award for innovative leadership. His wide participation and leadership in a range of conferences and publications results in an unusual breadth of perspective and depth of technical judgment. He has been Chair of the Steering Committee for the International Conferences on Software Engineering. He is currently a member of the editorial boards of *IEEE Software, IEEE Spectrum*, and *IEEE Proceedings*. He has served as Vice President for Publications and is currently Vice President for Technical Activities and 2nd Vice President of the IEEE Computer Society. He is a fellow of the IEEE, cited for his "contributions to software engineering, in particular, software reliability."

Anthony Iannino is currently a Member of Technical Staff in the Computer Measurements and Capacity Planning Group at AT&T Bell Laboratories. He received his Ph.D. in Computer Science from Stevens Institute of Technology, where he was holder of the Robert Crooks Stanley Fellowship. He has been an active researcher in the field of software reliability for over seven years and has published several papers in professional journals and conference proceedings. He has consulted on software reliability with numerous projects, both internal and external to Bell Laboratories. He is a member of Tau Beta Pi.

Kazuhira Okumoto is a Distinguished Member of Technical Staff at AT&T Bell Laboratories, where he has been involved in various research and development activities such as software reliability, computer performance evaluation and capacity planning. He received his Ph.D. in Industrial Engineering and Operations Research from Syracuse University. He has been an active researcher in the field of software reliability for over ten years, including work toward his Ph.D. dissertation which was partly supported by the Air Force Systems Command's Rome Air Development Center. While he was an Assistant Professor at Rutgers University, he wrote a research proposal on software reliability modeling, which was accepted by NSF. He has published over 25 papers in professional journals and conference proceedings in the field and related topics, and has presented technical papers at numerous national conferences and workshops. He is a member of Alpha Pi Mu and was a committee member of the 5th Minnowbrook workshop on software performance evaluation.

CONTENTS

Part II   Practical Application

PREFACE

HOW TO USE THIS BOOK

Three large general groups of people need information on software reliability measurement. These needs have been carefully and systematically analyzed, and this book has been organized to meet them.

The first and largest group consists of those who need to develop a general understanding of software reliability measurement and what it can be used for, even though they may not directly apply it. This category includes high-level managers, engineers who use or whose designs interface with software, and people who purchase, lease, or use software. Part I of the book has been written for them. This part treats the basic concepts and illustrates a number of uses. The treatment is graphically oriented and can be understood in those terms. We have emphasized this approach, finding that about three-fourths of our readers prefer it. You can look at the plots, ignoring the symbols, and clearly understand the relationships. However, symbols are provided for the other one-fourth who understand a mathematical presentation more clearly. We also provide them with formulas illustrated with examples.

The second and also large group of people involves those who will be using and applying software reliability measurement. It also includes practitioners in related disciplines such as risk analysis, management decision sciences, and quality assurance. Part II has been written for this group (of course, they should also read Part I). Members of this group may play different roles, as noted in Chapter 3. The introduction to Part II indicates which topics are important to which roles. We present formulas when needed for calculation, but there are no derivations. Procedures are explained in step-by-step fashion, and examples are liberally provided.

The third group of people includes researchers and students in reliability, software engineering, applied statistics, operations research, and related disciplines and anyone who wants a deeper understanding of software reliability. Part III focuses on these needs by presenting the theoretical background of the field. It assumes that the reader has previously completed Parts I and II. Practitioners may find Chapters 9 and 13 of particular interest. Chapter 9 is generally nonmathematical. It enhances the depth of one's conceptual understanding substantially. It also provides a historical and logical perspective on most published models. Chapter 13 presents criteria for comparing models and makes some comparisons.

A "road map" for the book is presented in Figure P.1, based on questions on the reader's background and interests. Those readers needing reviews of probability, statistics, and random processes or hardware reliability theory before reading Part III will find them in Appendices A and B, respectively. It should be noted that our objective has been that the reader with no background in probability and statistics can read Parts I and II with nearly complete understanding. Such a reader should be able to comprehend most of Part III after mastering Appendices A and B. If a reader lacks technical background in computers, the brief overview of Appendix C should be read. The reader who is unfamiliar with how software is developed should begin with Section 4 of Appendix C. Otherwise, readers should start with the Overview, Part I. The short introductory summaries for Parts I, II, and III are important for placing the individual chapters in perspective.

The reader who wants a comprehensive treatment might consider the foregoing "three pass" approach to the subject illogical or inefficient. However, we believe that he or she will quickly find it is indeed superior for the following reasons. The overview of Part I rapidly creates a structure in which the rest of the material can be understood. The practical application section, Part II, provides the rich fabric of experience that gives meaning to the theory that follows. Then Part III unites and organizes the theoretical essence of the subject area. Part IV provides an analysis of the state of the art for all readers. The reader who has read only parts of the book should be able to follow the general sense of this analysis but not necessarily all details.

Professors and instructors will find this structure extremely flexible. The book can be easily adapted to the needs of widely varying courses. Courses that treat the areas of software engineering, computer science, management sciences, and reliability in a survey fashion will find Part I well-suited to their needs. Courses involving more depth in practical application will wish to add Part II as well. Finally, courses treating software reliability in depth in both practical and theoretical aspects will want to use the entire book. Although recommended directions for further research may be found throughout the book, Chapter 16 may be particularly useful in suggesting potential dissertation topics to doctoral students.

Examples, case studies, and problems have been provided to illustrate the concepts and give the background needed to develop judgment. They were included because identifying problems and determining which are worth solving is usually much more difficult than solving the problems themselves. Immersion in a wide variety of realistic experiences in a field is necessary to develop the former capabilities. Some of the problems are essentially thought questions, designed to deepen and expand one's understanding of the material. You may not always find them directly answered in the preceding text. However, solutions are always discussed in Appendix H. Although much "how to do it" information is provided, the value of practically oriented insight is recognized throughout as well. There has been a conscious effort to avoid theoretical exuberance in conveying this in-

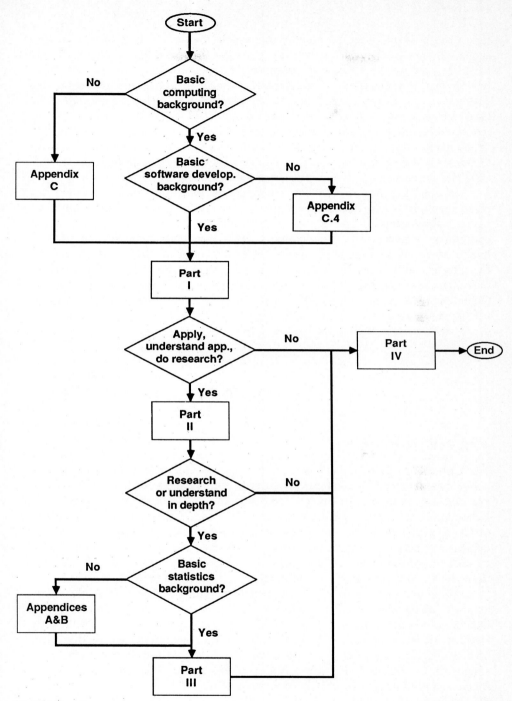

FIGURE P.1
Guide to reading the book.

sight. The book has been thoroughly indexed so that it can serve as a reference, and a glossary of terms (Appendix F) and a glossary of notation (Appendix G) have been provided for this same purpose. The glossary of terms includes those few probability terms used in Parts I and II. Terms used in the book reflect present standard usage. In most cases they are in conformance with the *IEEE Standard Glossary of Software Engineering Terminology* [IEEE (1983)], which is also an ANSI (United States) standard. The practitioner will find a summary of all the formulas likely to be needed for hand calculations in one place, Appendix E. In certain cases, detailed discussions of topics that might otherwise interrupt the flow of a chapter are placed at the end just before the summary.

In concentrating on software reliability *measurement*, the authors do not mean to imply that investigation of the *causes* and means of reducing software faults is unimportant. However, it is helpful to know how bad a situation is before one attacks it and just what economic benefits can be obtained from improving things, so that one knows how hard to attack. A discussion of the causes and cures for software faults would be a book (or books) in itself. Fault introduction and removal are related to such topics as cognitive psychology and software engineering technology. Reliability is obviously related to many characteristics of the software product and development process. It is hoped that this book will be a stimulus to other researchers to explore them *quantitatively*.

John D. Musa
Anthony Iannino
Kazuhira Okumoto

ACKNOWLEDGMENTS

The authors are most appreciative of the many people who contributed to this book. They received innumerable suggestions and reactions (which also led to improvements) from the instructors and students in 11 classes at AT&T Bell Laboratories in which the book was used. The book was also used at University of California at Berkeley with further helpful feedback. In addition, the authors gained invaluable experience by testing and refining the book's ideas on a large number of software projects at AT&T and throughout the world. We are indebted to the many software engineers and managers that worked with us.

We would like to thank the many people who provided thorough and incisive reviews, including Bharat Bhargava, Purdue University; Richard E. Fairley, Wang Institute of Graduate Studies; Daniel V. Ferens, Air Force Institute of Technology; Herbert Hecht, Sohar Incorporated; Way Kuo, Iowa State University; J.A. McCall, Science Applications International Corporation; C.V. Ramamoorthy, University of California at Berkeley; Roger S. Pressman, R.S. Pressman and Associates; and Martin Shooman, Polytechnic Institute of New York. We would also like to thank the following identified colleagues: S.J. Amster, W. Chen, L.H. Crow, W.K. Ehrlich, W.W. Everett, L.T. Frase, M.R. Garzia, D.A. James, N.K.

Kester, C.J. Keyser, W. Kremer, C.L. Mallows, J.D. Patterson, N.D. Prabhakar, J. Vizcarrondo, A. von Mayrhauser, and A.S. Wang (all from AT&T Bell Laboratories), C. Brehmer (China Lake Naval Weapons Center), R. Cairone (Grumman Aircraft), C.J. Dale (National Centre of Systems Reliability, United Kingdom Atomic Energy Authority), E. Girard and P. Saunier (both of CIMSA), and S. Sherer (Wharton School, University of Pennsylvania). We are appreciative of the efforts of M.A. Brana, S. Cole, C. Hubner, and D. Nolte, who helped coordinate the orderly revision of the book through its many drafts. Our special thanks go to C.A. Lopata, our indefatigable, efficient, and dedicated word processor, and her several colleagues who have helped at various times.

ONE

OVERVIEW

This part of the book has three principal objectives:

1. to demonstrate the great potential value of software reliability measurement in engineering and managing software,
2. to convey enough basic concepts such that the reader will be able to communicate intelligently with software reliability measurement practitioners and interpret the results of their studies, and
3. to increase awareness of possible uses for software reliability measurement.

Some material is also presented on how to plan and organize for applying these ideas to a project or a system in operation.

Chapter 1 focuses on general introductory material and basic concepts. Chapter 2 presents two selected software reliability models and discusses how the model parameters are determined. Chapter 3 discusses a range of potential uses and includes a section on overall planning and organization for application.

ONE

INTRODUCTION TO SOFTWARE RELIABILITY

This chapter places software reliability in the context of software engineering and shows its importance. A comparison with hardware reliability will be made. Then we will present basic definitions and concepts. Availability, a measure related to reliability, will be defined. There will be a general discussion of software reliability modeling. Finally, we will discuss some of the uses of software reliability measurement and prediction.

1.1 IMPORTANCE

Information processing is probably the most significant industry in the world economy today and in the foreseeable future. It has expanded and continues to expand at a rapid rate. This expansion is, in part, related to the increase in cost-effectiveness of computer hardware. Cost-effectiveness has increased by a factor of about 1000 every decade [Musa (1985)]. As long as this rate of change continues, the range of tasks that can be handled most economically by computing is likely to grow rapidly. Since software is the major part of most computer systems, the field of software engineering can expect similar rapid growth.

The major forces affecting the software engineering field today include:

1. the increasing level and truly international nature of business competition,
2. the increasing cost of both information system development and information system failure,
3. the increasing pace of change in computing technology, and
4. the increasing complexity of managing information system development.

Most information system customers are, in turn, businesses. The increasing level of business competition that they face makes them acutely aware of their needs in regard to software products. Since there is also more competition among software producers, software customers are more aware of the products and services available to them. These customers, once relatively naive and dependent on their suppliers, have become increasingly sophisticated and demanding. Software producers must understand their needs thoroughly and precisely. Three of the most significant needs are level of quality required, time of delivery, and cost.

At the same time, both the development and operational cost of software have increased substantially. The size, complexity, and degree of distribution of systems are increasing. We have many multicomputer systems linked by networks. They may have many diverse pieces of software that run simultaneously and interact. Consequently, development costs are becoming higher. The proliferation of information system applications has increased the heavy dependence of institutions on such systems. This dependence is extending to smaller organizations and down to lower levels of organizations. A growing proportion of the systems operate in real time. The operational effects of failure are large and often critical. For example, consider the effects of breakdowns of airline reservations, banking, automatic flight control, military defense, and nuclear power plant safety control systems, to name just a few. The economic results can be large and even catastrophic. Costs of failure include not only direct expenses but also product liability risks and damage to a company's reputation. The latter can have a dramatic impact on a company's market share and profitability.

The increasing pace of change in computing technology means that information systems become economically obsolete more rapidly. Software can become obsolete either as the result of new hardware technology or new software technology. The time of delivery of a system has become increasingly crucial. The *market window,* or time period available for the introduction of a new product before that product is surpassed in capability or cost by another, has shortened.

With the cost and schedule pressures we have discussed, it is becoming increasingly impossible to create a software product that is "generous" in the sense of simultaneously providing high quality, rapid delivery, and low cost. The view that such characteristics are simply desired objectives to be achieved is obsolete. For example, it would be nice to have programs that are "correct," but in this real world we must settle for something less. The need for trade-offs is pressing, and the characteristics of the software must be carefully selected to meet customer needs. This means that measurement and prediction of software product characteristics is essential.

The management of information system development has become more complex as the size and complexity of the systems have increased. Many systems are now divided into components that are developed by different companies. A definite need exists for the clear identification of the characteristics of the system and its components and for indicators of progress during development. Such identification is important from managerial, contractual, and legal viewpoints. Again, the result is that measurement and prediction of software product characteristics and the current status of those characteristics during development has become increasingly important.

We have indicated that three of the most important software product characteristics are quality, cost, and schedule. Note that these are primarily user-oriented rather than developer-oriented attributes. Quantitative measures exist for the latter two characteristics, but the quantification of quality has been more difficult. It is most important, however, because the absence of a concrete measure for software quality generally means that quality will suffer when it competes for attention against cost and schedule. In fact, this absence may be the principal reason for the well known existence of quality problems in many software products.

Reliability is probably the most important of the characteristics inherent in the concept "software quality." It is intimately connected with defects, and as Jones (1986) points out, defects represent the largest cost element in programming. Software reliability concerns itself with how well the software *functions* to meet the requirements of the customer. We define software reliability precisely in Section 1.3, but simply, it is the probability that the software will work without failure for a specified period of time. "Failure" means the program in its functioning has not met user requirements in some way. "Not functioning to meet user requirements" is really a very broad definition. Thus reliability subsumes, totally or partially, many properties that are often quoted as aspects of quality. One example is correctness. Another is program *behavior* that is not user-friendly. Some properties like software safety are actually specialized aspects of software reliability. Two of the few aspects of quality that probably cannot be related to reliability are modifiability and understandability of documentation. In addition to its preeminent importance, software reliability has proved to be the most readily quantifiable of the attributes of software quality.

Reliability represents a user-oriented view of software quality. Initial (and many present) approaches to measuring software quality were based on *attempting* to count the faults or defects found in a program. This approach is developer-oriented. Also, what was usually counted were either failures (the occurrences of malfunction) or repairs (for example, maintenance or correction reports), neither of which are equivalent to faults. Even if faults found are correctly counted, they are not a good status indicator (is a large number good or bad?). Faults remaining may be. Faults found can only be used to make rough comparisons with other projects. Such comparisons are commonly made in terms of faults per 1000 developed source lines of code. Reliability is a much richer measure. It is customer- or user-oriented rather than developer-oriented. It relates to operation rather than design of the program, and hence it is dynamic rather than static [Saunier (1983)]. It takes account of the frequency with which problems occur. It relates directly to operational experience and the influence of faults on that experience. Hence, it is easily associated with costs. It is more suitable for examining the significance of trends, for setting objectives, and for predicting when those objectives will be met. It permits one to analyze in common terms the effect on system quality of both software and hardware, both of which are present in any real system. Thus, reliability measures are much more useful than fault measures.

This does not mean that some attention to faults is without value. But the attention should be focused on faults as predictors of reliability and on the nature of faults. A better understanding of faults and the causative human error processes should lead to strategies to avoid, detect and remove, or compensate for them.

Understanding software reliability measurement and prediction has become a vital skill for both the software manager and software engineer. This knowledge is also important to managers and engineers of products that include software, and to users of these products. Fortunately, in the past 15 years a body of knowledge has been developed to help meet this need. Software reliability measures and models have been developed, and much practical knowledge has been gathered by applying them to actual projects. This history is recounted in Chapter 9. Since this area appears ripe for exploitation, it seemed desirable to organize the information and disseminate it. Some problems remain, but further progress in solving them is dependent on confronting them in real project situations and gathering relevant data. The models are sufficiently accurate (see Chapter 13) and useful (see Chapters 3 and 7) that the benefits in using them exceed their costs.

Experience with the application of software reliability measurement and prediction on projects indicates a cost of implementation of around 0.1 to 0.2 percent of project development costs. This includes the cost of education, the cost of data collection and processing, and the cost of studies. On many projects some of the costs are already being incurred. For example, many projects have formal mechanisms for reporting troubles. Also, many projects already conduct studies of the kind that we will describe, but decisions are arrived at in a less quantitative and a less satisfactory way. These costs, therefore, should represent an upper bound for the incremental costs involved.

A primary objective of this book is to help the engineer, manager, or user of software learn to make more precise decisions. A strong secondary objective is to make everyone more concretely aware of software quality by focusing attention on its most important characteristic, software reliability. Better decisions can save money on a project or during the life cycle of a piece of software in many ways. We will discuss some of these in the next section. In general, the total savings that we expect are more than 10 times greater than the cost of applying these ideas. Consider the following simple example for illustrative purposes. A 2-year software project with a system test period of about 6 months is fairly typical. The amount of testing is usually highly correlated with reliability, although it is not the only factor. Suppose you could establish that only 5 months of test are needed to get the reliability that is required for the particular application. Then you might well be able to save 4 percent of the development cost of the project. Compare this with the cost of application noted above. The cost effectiveness of the methodology is high.

1.2 SOFTWARE RELIABILITY AND HARDWARE RELIABILITY

The field of hardware reliability has been established for some time. Hence, you might ask how software reliability relates to it. In reality, the division between hardware and software reliability is somewhat artificial. Both may be defined in the same way. Therefore, you may combine hardware and software component reliabilities to get system reliability. Both depend on the environment. The source of failures in software is design faults, while the principal source in hardware has generally been physical deterioration. However, the concepts and theories developed for software reliability could really be applied to any design activity, including hardware design. Once a software (design) defect is properly fixed, it is in general fixed for all time. Failure usually occurs only when a program (design) is exposed to an environment that it was not developed or tested for. Although manufacturing can affect the quality of physical components, the replication process for software (design) is trivial and can be performed to very high standards of quality. Since introduction and removal of design faults occur during software development, software reliability may be expected to vary during this period.

The "design reliability" concept has not been applied to hardware to any extent. The probability of failure due to wear and other physical causes has usually been much greater than that due to an unrecognized design problem. It was possible to keep hardware design failures low because hardware was generally less complex logically than software. Hardware design failures had to be kept low because retrofitting of manufactured items in the field was very expensive. The emphasis in hardware reliability may be starting to change now, however. Awareness of the work that is going on in software reliability, plus a growing realization of the importance of design faults, may be having an effect. This growing awareness is strengthened by the parallels that people are starting to draw between software engineering and chip design.

A final characteristic of software reliability is that it tends to change continually during test periods. This happens either as new problems are introduced when new code is written or when repair action removes problems that exist in the code. Hardware reliability may change during certain periods, such as initial burn-in or the end of useful life. However, it has a much greater tendency than software toward a constant value.

Despite the foregoing differences, we can develop software reliability theory in a way that is compatible with hardware reliability theory. Thus system reliability figures may be computed using standard hardware combinatorial techniques [Shooman (1986) and Lloyd and Lipow (1977)]. Hardware and software reliability share many similarities and some differences. One must not err on the side of assuming that software always presents unique problems, but one must also be careful not to carry analogies too far.

1.3 BASIC CONCEPTS

We need to first thoroughly understand the basic terms and concepts of software reliability modeling before specific models or practical applications can be addressed. The reader will then find that the task of mastering software reliability will be much easier. This modeling background is frequently essential to making intelligent decisions in practical applications. For example, how do we model software reliability for a multiprocessor or a distributed system? This background will be deepened in Part II, when it is related to the application of software reliability models and to the analysis of system reliability as well. Finally, it will be thoroughly developed in Part III, since a solid conceptual underpinning is essential in understanding the basic theory. We will build up to the concept of software reliability in several steps, introducing some other concepts en route.

1.3.1   Failures and Faults

What do we mean by the term *software failure*? It is the departure of the external results of program operation from requirements (requirements are discussed in detail in Chapter 4). So our "failure" is something dynamic. The program has to be executing for a failure to occur. The term failure relates to the behavior of the program. Note that a failure is not the same thing as a "bug" or, more properly, "fault." This very general definition of failure is deliberate. It can include such things as deficiency in performance attributes and excessive response time.

A *fault* is the defect in the program that, when executed under particular conditions, causes a failure. There can be different sets of conditions that cause failures, or the conditions can be repeated. Hence a fault can be the source of more than one failure. A fault is a property of the program rather than a property of its execution or behavior. It is what we are really referring to in general when we use the term "bug." A fault is created when a programmer makes an *error*. It's *very* important to make the failure-fault distinction! This may not be apparent to you now, but hopefully it will be after you have delved more deeply into the field. There has been, and frequently remains, much confusion because these terms were mixed up and erroneously used interchangeably. If you get them clear in your mind, you will avoid much trouble that has bedeviled people trying to learn software reliability measurement.

Consider this simple example. A user requests a display at program start-up. It does not appear. That departure from how the program should behave is a failure. The fault associated with the failure might be that an initialization instruction for a variable was not provided. Note, however, that a fault does not have to be localized in nature. The fault could be an inefficient routine that has to be rewritten.

Reliability quantities have usually been defined with respect to time, although it would be possible to define them with respect to other variables. We are concerned with three kinds of time. The *execution time* for a program is the time that is actually spent by a processor in executing the instructions of that program. The second kind of time is *calendar time*. It is the familiar garden variety of time that we normally experience. Execution time is important, because it is now generally accepted that models based on execution time are superior. However, quantities must ultimately be related back to calendar time to be meaningful to engineers or managers. Sometimes the term *clock time* is used for a program. It represents the elapsed time from start to end of program execution on a running computer. It includes wait time and the execution time of other programs. Periods during which the computer is shut down are not counted. If computer utilization by the program, which is the fraction of time the processor is executing the program, is constant, clock time will be proportional to execution time. As an example of these three types of time, consider a word processing system serving a group of secretaries. In 1 week of calendar time, there may be 50 hr of clock time during which the system is running. There might be 25 hr of execution time for the word processing program itself. Note that when either execution time or clock time is used, any down time of a system is excluded. In this book, general descriptions of models, estimation, and techniques for adapting models to specific projects will be formulated in terms of a generic time t, so that they will have the widest possible applicability. However, when specific execution time models or outputs of programs using these models are described, discussions will be in terms of execution time τ and calendar time t.

There are four general ways of characterizing failure occurrences in time:

1. time of failure,
2. time interval between failures,
3. cumulative failures experienced up to a given time, and
4. failures experienced in a time interval.

These are illustrated in Tables 1.1 and 1.2.

Note that all the foregoing four quantities are random variables. By "random," we mean that the values of the variables are not known with certainty. There are many possible values, each associated with a probability of occurrence. For example, we don't really know when the next failure will occur. If we did, we would try to prevent or avoid it. We only know a set of possible times of failure

TABLE 1.1
Time-based failure specification

Failure number	Failure time (sec)	Failure interval (sec)
1	10	10
2	19	9
3	32	13
4	43	11
5	58	15
6	70	12
7	88	18
8	103	15
9	125	22
10	150	25
11	169	19
12	199	30
13	231	32
14	256	25
15	296	40

TABLE 1.2
Failure-based failure specification

Time (sec)	Cumulative failures	Failures in interval
30	2	2
60	5	3
90	7	2
120	8	1
150	10	2
180	11	1
210	12	1
240	13	1
270	14	1

occurrence and the probability of each. The probability of each time of occurrence is the fraction of cases for which it occurs. Note that "random" does not carry any connotation of true irrationality or unpredictability, as some mistakenly assume. "Random" means "unpredictable" only in the sense that the exact value is not known. However, the average value and some sense of the dispersion *are* known. It does not mean "unaffected by other variables." Although failure occurrence is random, it is decidedly affected by such factors as test strategy and the operational profile. Neither does "random" imply any specific probability distribution, which some mistakenly assume as "uniform."

There are at least two principal reasons for this randomness. First, the commission of errors by programmers, and hence the introduction of faults, is a very complex, unpredictable process. Hence the locations of faults within the program are unknown. Second, the conditions of execution of a program are generally unpredictable. For example, with a telephone switching system, how do you know what type of call will be made next? In addition, the relationship between program function requested and code path executed, although theoretically determinable, may not be so in practice because it is so complex. Since failures are dependent on the presence of a fault in the code *and* its execution in the context of certain machine states, a third complicating element is introduced that argues for the randomness of the failure process.

Table 1.3 illustrates a typical probability distribution of failures that occur within a time period of execution. Each possible value of the random variable of number of failures is given along with its associated probability. The probabilities, of course, add to 1. Note that here the random variable is discrete, as the number of failures must be an integer. We can also have continuous random variables, such as time, which can take on any value. Note that the most probable number of failures is 2 (probability 0.22). The mean or average number of failures can be computed. You multiply each possible value by the probability it can occur and add all the products, as shown. The mean is 3.04 failures.

A random process can be viewed as a set of random variables, each corresponding to a point in time. We can have a discrete or continuous time random

TABLE 1.3
Typical probability distribution of failures

Value of random variable (failures in time period)	Probability	Product of value and probability
0	0.10	0
1	0.18	0.18
2	0.22	0.44
3	0.16	0.48
4	0.11	0.44
5	0.08	0.40
6	0.05	0.30
7	0.04	0.28
8	0.03	0.24
9	0.02	0.18
10	0.01	0.1
Mean failures		3.04

process. One characteristic of a random process is the form of the probability distributions of the random variables. For example, one common form for failure random processes is Poisson. The other principal characteristic is the variation of the process with time.

We will look at the time variation from two different viewpoints, the mean value function and the failure intensity function. The *mean value function* represents the average cumulative failures associated with each time point. The *failure intensity function* is the rate of change of the mean value function or the number of failures per unit time. For example, you might say 0.01 failure/hr or 1 failure/100 hr. Strictly speaking, the failure intensity is the derivative of the mean value function with respect to time, and is an instantaneous value.

Table 1.4 illustrates an example of the random process of failures in simplified fashion, showing failure distributions of the cumulative number of failures experienced at two different time points. Note that the random variables are given at elapsed time t_A of 1 hr and elapsed time t_B of 5 hr. A random process whose probability distribution varies with time is called *nonhomogeneous*. Most failure processes during test fit this situation. Figure 1.1 illustrates the mean value and the related failure intensity functions at times t_A and t_B. Note that the mean failures experienced increases from 3.04 to 7.77 between these two points, while the failure intensity decreases.

Failure behavior is affected by two principal factors:

1. the number of faults in the software being executed, and
2. the execution environment or operational profile of execution.

TABLE 1.4
Probability distributions at times
t_A **and** t_B

Value of random variable (failures in time period)	Probability	
	Elapsed time t_A = 1 hr	Elapsed time t_B = 5 hr
0	0.10	0.01
1	0.18	0.02
2	0.22	0.03
3	0.16	0.04
4	0.11	0.05
5	0.08	0.07
6	0.05	0.09
7	0.04	0.12
8	0.03	0.16
9	0.02	0.13
10	0.01	0.10
11	0	0.07
12	0	0.05
13	0	0.03
14	0	0.02
15	0	0.01
Mean failures	3.04	7.77

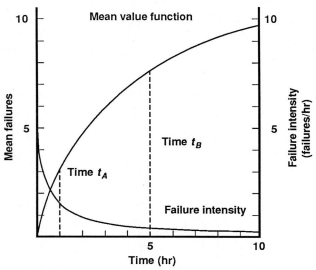

FIGURE 1.1
Mean value and failure intensity functions.

12

The number of faults in the software is the difference between the number introduced and the number removed.

Faults are introduced when the code is being developed by programmers. They may introduce the faults during original design or when they are adding new features, making design changes, or repairing faults that have been identified. The term *developed code,* defined as instructions that have been created or modified, is used deliberately. In general, only code that is new or modified results in fault introduction. Code that is *inherited* from another application does not usually introduce any appreciable number of faults, except possibly in the interfaces. It generally has been thoroughly debugged in the previous application. Note that the process of fault removal introduces some new faults because it involves modification or writing of new code. Hopefully (if you have a programming staff of reasonable competence!), the new faults entered are fewer than the faults being removed. Data on the introduction of faults is presented in Tables 5.2 to 5.4.

Fault removal obviously can't occur unless you have some means of detecting the fault in the first place. Thus fault removal resulting from execution depends on the occurrence of the associated failure. Occurrence depends both on the length of time for which the software has been executing and on the execution environment or operational profile. When different functions are executed, different faults are encountered and the failures that are exhibited tend to be different—thus the environmental influence. We can often find faults without execution. They may be found through inspection, compiler diagnostics, design or code reviews, or code reading.

Fault removal is also dependent on the efficiency with which faults are found and removed. For example, a failure correction team may remove 95 faults for every 100 failures reported. The efficiency depends on factors such as how well the circumstances surrounding the failure are documented and the degree of structuring and clarity of the program.

Finally, the failure process and hence software reliability is directly dependent on the environment or the operational profile for the program. For example, you can expect that an electronic switching system that is being used in a business district will have a software reliability different from that in a residential area.

We have seen that the failure process depends on the *system* being built, the nature of the development process for a particular *project,* and the *use* of the system. Since the system and the project are so closely associated, they are often used interchangeably in naming a particular failure process.

1.3.2 Environment

Let us scrutinize the term *environment*. The environment is described by the operational profile. We need to build up to the concept of the operational profile through several steps. It is possible to view the execution of a program as a single entity. The execution can last for months or even years for a real time system. However, it is more convenient to divide the execution into runs. The definition of *run* is somewhat arbitrary, but it is generally associated with some function that the program performs. Thus, it can conveniently describe the functional environment of the program. Runs that are identical repetitions of each other are said to form a *run type*. The proportion of runs of various types may vary, depending on the functional environment. Examples of a run type might be:

1. a particular transaction in an airline reservation system or a business data processing system,
2. a specific cycle in a closed loop control system (for example, in a chemical process industry), or
3. a particular service performed by an operating system for a user.

During test, the term *test case* is sometimes used instead of run type.

We next need to understand the concept of the *input variable*. This is a variable that exists external to the program and is used by the program in executing its function. For an airline reservation system, "destination" might be an input variable. One generally has a large quantity of input variables associated with the program, and each set of values of these variables characterize an *input state*. In effect, the input state identifies the particular run type that you're making. Therefore, runs can always be classified by their input states. Again, taking the case of the airline reservation system, the input state might be characterized by particular values of origin, destination, airline, day, and flight number. The set of all possible input states is known as the *input space,* illustrated in Figure 1.2.

Similarly, an *output variable* is a variable that exists external to a program and is set by it. An *output state* is a set of values of all output variables associated with a run of a program. In the airline reservation system, an output state might be the set of values of variables printed on the ticket and on different reports used in operating the airline. It can now be seen that a failure involves a departure of the output state from what it is expected to be.

The run types required of the program by the environment can be viewed as being selected randomly. Thus, we define the *operational profile* as the set of run types that the program can execute along with the probabilities with which they will occur. In Figure 1.2, we show two of many possible input states, A and B,

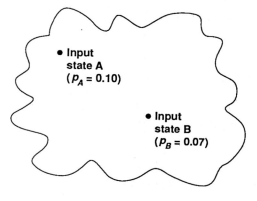

FIGURE 1.2
Input space.

with their probabilities of occurrence. The part of the operational profile for just those two states is shown in Figure 1.3. In reality, the number of possible input states is generally quite large. A realistic operational profile is illustrated in Figure 1.4. Note that the input states have been located on the horizontal axis in order of the probabilities of their occurrence. This can be done without loss of generality. They have been placed close together so that the operational profile would appear to be a continuous curve. The operational profile is an extremely useful concept. However, it may not always be practical to determine all the input states and their probabilities in full detail, because of the large number that can be involved. We can reduce the large number by the use of equivalence partitioning, as described in Chapter 4. With a reasonably small number of such classes, an operational profile based on the classes may be established in practice. One possible source of data for such an operational profile is a marketing study of the uses of a system.

1.3.3 Software Reliability

The definition that we will present here for *software reliability* is one that is widely accepted throughout the field. It is the probability of failure-free operation of a computer program for a specified time in a specified environment. For example, a time-sharing system may have a reliability of 0.92 for 8 hr when employed by the "average user." This system, when executed for 8 hr, would operate without failure for 92 of these periods out of 100. As a result of the general way in which we defined failure, note that the concept of software reliability incorporates the notion of performance being satisfactory. For example, excessive response time at a given load level may be considered unsatisfactory, so that a routine must be recoded in more efficient form.

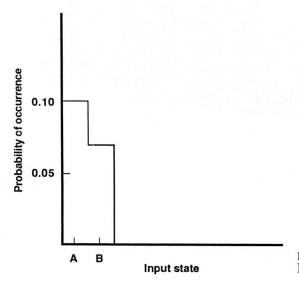

FIGURE 1.3
Portion of operational profile.

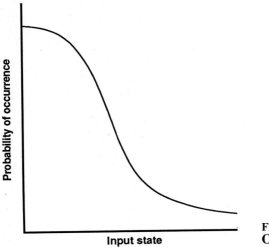

FIGURE 1.4
Operational profile.

This definition implies that you should, for accurate reliability measurement during test, select runs randomly with the same probability expected to occur in operation. Alternatively, if you use different probabilities, compensate for them as discussed in Chapter 6. The effect of selecting runs by plan rather than randomly depends on whether the instructions and machine states exercised are localized or not. If a localized part of the program is exercised, the failures that occur will only be the result of faults in that part. Removal of the faults will be more rapid than usual. Since the failure intensity curve will reflect just the part of the program examined, it will initially drop more rapidly than would be expected. When a transition to a new set of instructions and machine states occurs, the failure intensity curve will probably rise. This reflects the greater number of faults remaining in the new part of the program.

The definition also implies that the input space must be "well covered" for accurate reliability measurement. To measure input space coverage, take the sum of the probabilities in the operational phase associated with the test runs selected. The sum gives the probability that a run occurring during operation will have already been tested. Thus you will know whether it results in failure. The coverage can be small when the input space is very large. The number of tests in any practical test effort is limited. Equivalence partitioning, described in Chapter 4, is a technique for increasing the coverage. Assume equal run lengths. Then any error in reliability measurement due to insufficient coverage can not exceed the difference between 1 and the coverage. Thus we want input space coverage to be substantially closer to 1 than the level of reliability being measured. For example, one might attempt coverage of 0.9999 for a reliability measurement expected to be near 0.99. The probability that a run occurring in operation will not have been tested is 0.0001. If we assume equal run lengths, our reliability measurement will have an error of 0.0001 or less. This is about 1 percent.

Failure intensity is an alternative way of expressing reliability. We just gave the example of the reliability of a particular system being 0.92 for 8 hr of time. An equivalent statement, based on Equation (2.13), is that the failure intensity is 0.01 failure/hr. Each specification has its advantages. The failure intensity statement is more economical, as you only have to give one number. However, the reliability statement is better suited to the combination of reliabilities of components to get system reliability. If the risk of failure at any point in time is of paramount concern, failure intensity may be the more appropriate measure. This would be the case for a nuclear power plant. When proper operation of a system to accomplish some function with a time duration is required, reliability is often best. An example would be a space flight to the moon. Figure 1.5 shows how failure intensity and reliability typically vary during a test period, as faults are removed. Note that we define failure intensity, just like we do reliability, with respect to a specified environment. The relationship between failure intensity and reliability depends on the reliability model employed if these values are changing.

As faults are removed (for example, during a test phase), failure intensity tends to drop and reliability tends to increase. When faults are being introduced, they often accompany new features or design changes that are all made at one time. This situation can occur in test or operation. There tends to be a step increase in failure intensity and a step decrease in reliability in this situation. It is also common, particularly in the field, to introduce repairs in batches. There can be a step increase or decrease in failure intensity, depending on whether new code and its faults or repairs predominate. There will be a corresponding decrease or increase in reliability. If a system is stable (that is, the code is unchanging), both failure intensity and reliability tend to be constant. This might be the situation for a program that has been released to the field, with no changes in code and no repairs being made.

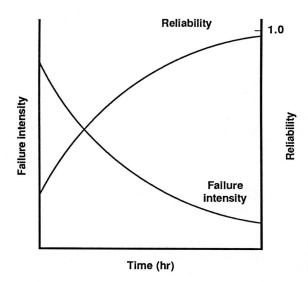

FIGURE 1.5
Reliability and failure intensity.

The term *mean time to failure (MTTF)* is used in the hardware reliability field and to a decreasing extent in software reliability. It is the average value of the next failure interval. The use of MTTF is attractive, in that "larger" indicates "better." However, there are many cases in software reliability in which MTTF is undefined. Failure intensity is preferred because it always exists. Also, failure intensities are simple to work with because they combine additively. In an approximate nonrigorous sense, the two are inverses of each other. The term *mean time between failures (MTBF)* is used in the hardware reliability field when repair or replacement is occurring. It is the sum of MTTF and *mean time to repair (MTTR)*.

1.4   AVAILABILITY

Software availability is usually defined as the expected fraction of time during which a software component or system is functioning acceptably. Assume that the program is operational and is not being modified by new features or repairs. Hence, it has a constant failure intensity. We can compute availability for software as we do for hardware. It is the ratio of up time to the sum of up time plus down time, as the time interval over which the measurement is made approaches infinity. The down time is the product of the failure intensity and the mean time to repair (MTTR). Usually the failure intensity applied here is a figure computed for serious failures and not those that involve only minor degradation of the system. It is generally not practical to hold up operation of the system while performing fault determination and correction in the field. Therefore, we ordinarily determine MTTR as the average time required to restore the data base for a program, reload the program, and resume execution.

A Markov model was developed by Shooman and Trivedi (1976) that depicts the concept of software availability. Okumoto and Goel (1978a) extended this model by assuming that a failure may be imperfectly repaired. A more recent paper by Laprie (1984) deals with the evaluation of availability during the operational phase.

Note that the term *maintainability* usually has somewhat different meanings for hardware and software. Hardware is considered "maintainable" if it can be repaired quickly so that its total down time is low. The term "maintainable" for software relates to the speed and ease with which a program can be corrected. However, since these repairs are not generally performed in a way that idles the program, software maintainability does not relate to down time.

1.5   MODELING

To model software reliability one must first consider the principal factors that affect it: fault introduction, fault removal, and the environment. Fault introduction depends primarily on the characteristics of the developed code (code created or modified for the application) and development process characteristics. The most significant code characteristic is size. Development process characteristics include software engineering technologies and tools used and level of experience of personnel. Note that code can be developed to add features or remove faults. Fault removal depends on time, operational profile, and the quality of the repair activity. The environment directly depends on the operational profile. Since some of the foregoing factors are probabilistic in nature and operate over time, software reliability models are generally formulated in terms of random processes. The models are distinguished from each other in general terms by the probability distribution of failure times or number of failures experienced and by the nature of the variation of the random process with time.

A software reliability model specifies the general form of the dependence of the failure process on the factors mentioned. We have assumed that it is, by definition, time-based (this is not to say that non-time-based models may not provide useful insights). The possibilities for different mathematical forms to describe the failure process are almost limitless. We have restricted ourselves to considering well-developed models that have been applied fairly broadly with real data and have given reasonable results. The specific form can be determined from the general form by establishing the values of the parameters of the model through either:

1. estimation—statistical inference procedures are applied to failure data taken for the program, or
2. prediction—determination from properties of the software product and the development process (this can be done before any execution of the program).

There is always some uncertainty in the determination of the specific form. This is generally expressed in terms of *confidence intervals* for the parameters. A confidence interval represents a range of values within which a parameter is expected to lie with a certain confidence. For example, the 0.75 confidence interval of total failures that will be experienced in infinite time may be 150 to 175.

Once the specific form has been established, many different characteristics of the failure process can be determined. For many models there are analytic expressions (see Chapters 10 and 11) for:

1. the average number of failures experienced at any point in time,
2. the average number of failures in a time interval,
3. the failure intensity at any point in time,
4. the probability distribution of failure intervals.

A good software reliability model has several important characteristics. It

1. gives good predictions[1] of future failure behavior,
2. computes useful quantities,
3. is simple,

---

[1] The term *prediction* has two different but commonly used meanings in this book, "prediction of parameter values" and "prediction of failure behavior." One must be careful to distinguish them.

4. is widely applicable, and

5. is based on sound assumptions.

We shall revisit these characteristics in Part III when different models are compared.

Prediction of future failure behavior assumes that the values of model parameters will not change for the period of prediction. If the net effect of the opposing influences of fault introduction and fault repair should change substantially, we must either compensate for the change or wait until enough new failures have occurred so that we can reestimate the model parameters. Incorporating such changes into the models themselves has generally been impractical due to the added complexity. In any event, the complexity is not worthwhile, considering the accuracy with which parameters are generally known.

In general, software reliability models are based on (although this is often not stated explicitly) a stable program executing in a constant environment. This means that neither the code nor the operational profile are changing. If the program and environment do change, they often do so and are usually handled in a piecewise fashion. Thus, the models focus mainly on fault removal. Most models can account for the effects of slow fault introduction, however. Some assume that the average net long-term effect must be a decrease in failure intensity. If neither fault introduction, fault removal, or operational profile changes are occurring, the failure intensity will be constant and the model should simplify to accommodate this. It is assumed that the behavior of the program is compared with the requirements with enough thoroughness that all failures are detected. It is possible to compensate for programs (Chapter 6) or environments that are changing.

For a program that has been released and is operational, it is common to defer installation of both new features and repairs to the next release. Assuming a constant operational profile, the program will exhibit a constant failure intensity.

In general terms, a good model enhances communication on a project and provides a common framework of understanding for the software development process. It also enhances visibility to management and other interested parties. These advantages are valuable, even if the projections made with the model in a specific case are not particularly accurate.

Developing a practically useful software reliability model involves substantial theoretical work, tool building, and the accumulation of a body of lore from practical experience. This effort generally requires several person years. In contrast, the application of a model that is well established in practice requires a very small fraction of project resources. Consequently, we will consider this factor as one of the criteria for selection in Chapter 2.

It has sometimes been suggested that a range of models be applied to each project. The ones that perform best (or some weighted combination of them) would be used. This approach may be suitable for research investigations. However, the authors consider the use of more than one or two models conceptually and economically impractical for real projects.

1.6 USES

Pressures have been increasing for achieving a more finely tuned balance among product and process characteristics, including reliability. Trade-offs among product components with respect to reliability are also becoming increasingly important. This has made "seat-of-the-pants" engineering increasingly unacceptable. Quantitative approaches are essential. Thus an important use of software reliability measurement is in system engineering. However, there are at least four other ways in which software reliability measures can be of great value to the software engineer, manager, or user.

First, you can use software reliability measures to evaluate software engineering technology quantitatively. New techniques are continually being proposed for improving the process of developing software, but unfortunately they have been exposed to little quantitative evaluation. Software engineers and managers greeted many of these innovations with enthusiasm at first, because of the strong need for them. This attitude often turned to skepticism when their cost seemed to outweigh their effectiveness. The inability to distinguish between good and bad new technology has often led to a general resistance to change that is counterproductive. Software reliability measures offer the promise of establishing at least one criterion for evaluating the new technology. For example, you might run experiments to determine the decrease in failure intensity (failures per unit time) at the start of system test resulting from design reviews. A quantitative evaluation such as this makes the benefits of good software engineering technology highly visible. This is likely to stimulate the investment of more money and effort in this field, in addition to making the investment more informed and efficient.

Second, a software reliability measure offers you the possibility of evaluating development status during the test phases of a project. Methods such as intuition of designers or test team, percent of tests completed, and successful execution of critical functional tests have been used to evaluate testing progress. None of these have been really satisfactory and some have been quite unsatisfactory. An objective reliability measure (such as failure intensity) established from test data provides a sound means of determining status. Reliability generally increases with the amount of testing. Thus, reliability can be closely linked with project schedules. Furthermore, the cost of testing is highly correlated with failure intensity improvement. Since two of the key process attributes that a manager must control are schedule and cost, reliability can be intimately tied in with project management.

Third, you can use a software reliability measure to monitor the operational performance of software and to control new features added and design changes made to the software. The reliability of software usually decreases as a result of such changes. A reliability objective can be used to determine when, and perhaps how large, a change will be allowed. The objective would be based on user and other requirements. For example, a freeze on all changes not related to debugging can be imposed when the failure intensity rises above the performance objective.

Finally, a quantitative understanding of software quality and the various factors influencing it and affected by it enriches your insight into the software product and the software development process. You are then much more capable of making informed decisions.

The following case study shows some of the uses of software reliability measurement.

CASE STUDY 1.1
THE DATCOM PROJECT

A bank desiring to set up the data network shown in Figure 1.6 hires an outside firm to design the hardware for the front end processor and system controller. In addition the firm is also contracted to develop the necessary software that will run on both of these processors. Wishing to monitor their progress toward a failure intensity objective for the system controller software, the firm decides to use a software reliability model. They will collect failure interval data during system test. In practice the firm would also monitor the reliability of the front end processor software. Combining the failure interval data with estimates for the amount of available resources and some project parameters, a report similar to that shown in Figure 1.7 can be generated.[2] The report shows the most likely value of the indicated quantity in the center. The lower and upper confidence bounds (for various confidence limits) are shown sandwiched around it. For example, we are 75 percent confident that the present failure intensity is between 0.079 and 0.125 failure/ CPU hr. The "completion date" refers to the date of meeting the failure intensity objective. It is in month-day-year format.

The 75 percent confidence interval has been found from experience to be a good compromise between a higher confidence and the resultant larger interval. Plots of estimated present failure intensity and completion date for this project are shown in Figures 1.8 and 1.9, respectively. The plots show running histories throughout the course of system test for the project, as indicated by the dates on the horizontal axis. They represent the behavior one expects on real projects. In both figures, the solid center curve is the most likely value and the dashed outer curves delineate the bounds of the 75 percent confidence interval. The jaggedness of the curves is a result of statistical fluctuations. Figure 1.8 is a plot of present failure intensity; it is useful for indicating progress toward the failure intensity objective. Note that failure intensity drops steadily throughout system test as the program is debugged. Figure 1.9 is a plot of the current estimate of project completion date. The left hand sides of the curves should be disregarded. Large fluc-

---

[2]The reports and plots for the DATCOM project were generated using Musa's (1975) basic execution time model. Hence we will be dealing with both execution time and calendar time.

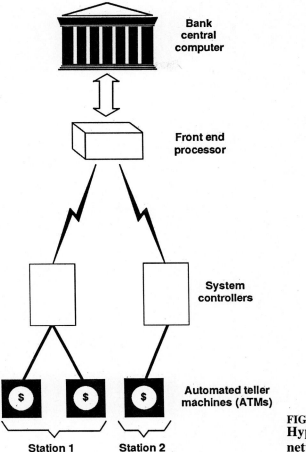

**Bank
central
computer**

**Front end
processor**

**System
controllers**

**Automated teller
machines (ATMs)**

Station 1   Station 2

**FIGURE 1.6
Hypothetical bank data
network.**

tuations are occurring because of the small size of the data sample in this time period. Note that they stabilize about halfway through system test.

A software reliability model can be used to help answer managerial questions relating to project status and scheduling. Three such questions are:

1. *Is* this software ready for release?
2. *When* will it be ready for release?
3. Should we regress to a previous version from the present one?

To answer the first question, compare the present failure intensity with the project's failure intensity objective. The report of Figure 1.7 is helpful, but plotting the recent history of the present failure intensity (Figure 1.8) will make additional information available for managerial judgments. The present failure intensity will normally exhibit steady (ignoring statistical fluctuations) improvement with time during testing. A sharp rise in failure intensity usually indicates new

SOFTWARE RELIABILITY PREDICTION
BASIC MODEL
DATCOM EXAMPLE

BASED ON SAMPLE OF 180 TEST FAILURES
EXECUTION TIME IS 450.57 HR
FAILURE INTENSITY OBJECTIVE IS .20e-03 FAILURES/CPU HR
CALENDAR TIME TO DATE IS 180 DAYS
PRESENT DATE 9/1/86

	CONF. LIMITS				MOST LIKELY	CONF. LIMITS			
	95%	90%	75%	50%		50%	75%	90%	95%
TOTAL FAILURES	190	191	193	196	199	204	208	213	217

FAILURE INTENSITIES (FAILURES/1000 CPU HR)

	95%	90%	75%	50%	LIKELY	50%	75%	90%	95%
INITIAL F.I.	850.1	878.6	924.1	968.8	1033	1099	1147	1197	1230
PRESENT F.I.	66.9	71.5	79.1	87.2	99.8	114.0	125.0	137.4	145.8

*** ADDITIONAL REQUIREMENTS TO MEET FAILURE INTENSITY OBJECTIVE ***

	95%	90%	75%	50%	LIKELY	50%	75%	90%	95%
FAILURES	10	11	13	15	19	24	28	33	37
EXEC. TIME (CPU HR)	899.6	939.5	1007	1080	1197	1336	1450	1586	1684
CAL. TIME (DAYS)	36.0	37.9	41.4	45.3	51.8	59.8	66.7	75.2	81.5
COMPLETION DATE	100786	100986	101386	101786	102386	103186	110786	111686	112286

FIGURE 1.7
Sample project status report.

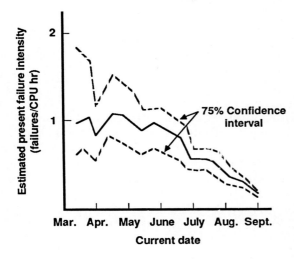

FIGURE 1.8
**Estimates of present failure
intensity for bank project.**

faults introduced by code change or exposed by extension of testing into new environments. If the system test phase is marked by many unforeseen new environments, test planning may have been inadequate. Unusually slow improvement in failure intensity usually indicates that a substantial number of faults remain. Alternatively, one could be introducing or exposing new faults at roughly the same rate that they are being corrected.

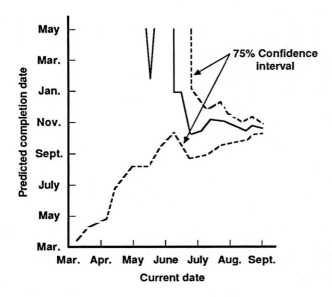

FIGURE 1.9
**Predicted completion
date for bank project.**

The question regarding when the software will be ready for release can be answered by observing the completion date line in Figure 1.7.

We can determine whether we should regress to a previous version by tracking present failure intensity for each version. If the new version is not meeting the failure intensity objective and the old one is, and the difference between the failure intensities is substantial, it will probably be worth the effort to regress.

The model can help the manager, through simulation, reach trade-off decisions among schedules, costs, resources, and reliability and can assist in determining resource allocations. One chooses several values of each parameter that is to be varied, applies the model to compute the effects, examines the results, and iterates this procedure as required. Usually one chooses the parameter values to include the extreme values that are reasonably possible, so that the influence of the parameters can be quickly determined.

To illustrate, consider the DATCOM project system test period report (Figure 1.7) for September 1, 1986. The project had a test team of 3 and a debugging team of 5 people. A failure intensity objective of 0.0002 failure/CPU hr for the system controller software was set originally. The estimated completion date was expected to be October 23, with a 75 percent confidence interval of October 13 to November 7. Assuming this date to be unsatisfactory, the effect of several different managerial actions on the schedule can be studied:

1. increasing the failure intensity objective,
2. working up to 50 percent overtime (as required to expedite the project),
3. increasing the size of the test team,
4. increasing the size of the debugging team, or
5. making more computer time available.

We will present the results of the studies here to show their usefulness. The explanation of how to conduct them will be given in detail in Part II. It is assumed that the increases of actions 3 and 4 are made by reallocating experienced people from other parts of the project so that negligible training time is involved.

The effect of increasing the failure intensity objective on the schedule is illustrated in Figure 1.10. The effect of varying the failure intensity objective on additional cost is illustrated in Figure 1.11. "Additional cost" represents the testing and debugging cost required to reach the objective.

The effects of resource changes are indicated in Figure 1.12. Overtime and additional personnel have negligible effect on schedules for this project at this point in its history. Making more computer time available has substantial effect. This indicates that this project is essentially though not completely limited by the computer time available. If the manager can make both more computer time available *and* back off on the failure intensity objective, it may be possible to change the estimated completion date even further. Note that we cannot generalize to other projects. Effects of resource changes are specific to a particular project and time.

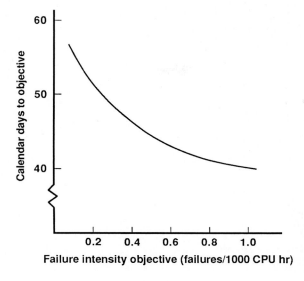

FIGURE 1.10
Effect of failure intensity objective on predicted completion date for bank project.

Options 3 through 5 do not affect costs because the total resources required will be the same. The resources will merely be expended at a more rapid rate (unless free time that occurs is not used on another task). Option 2 can affect costs only through the premium pay rates.

We have the capability to combine component reliabilities to determine system reliability. Consider the event diagram shown in Figure 1.13 for our bank data network system. It presents the view of a user at station 1 of how the functioning

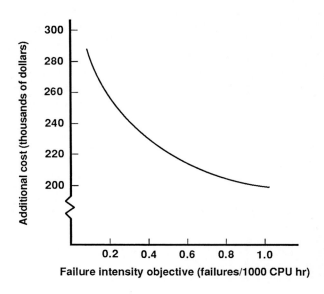

FIGURE 1.11
Effect of failure intensity objective on additional cost for bank project.

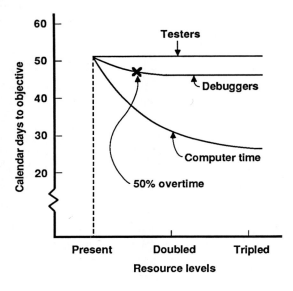

FIGURE 1.12
Effect of resource levels on predicted completion date for bank project.

of components affects the functioning of the system. The view from station 2 is similar except that there is only one ATM. This concept and the methods for combining reliabilities will be presented in Chapter 4. We will simply note that the calculation is easily performed and give the results. The bank's central computer is assumed to have a hardware reliability and software reliability of 1 for simplicity in presenting this example. The ATMs have a reliability of 0.995 for a 24-hr period. The front end processor and system controller hardware have 24-hr reliabilities of 0.99 and 0.995, respectively. The front end processor and system controller software each have a failure intensity in execution time of 0.004 failure/ CPU hr. The front end processor utilization is 0.95. The system controller utilization is 0.5. We wish to find the reliability of the system for a 24-hr period as seen from station 1 and from station 2 (see Figure 1.6).

The calendar time failure intensities for the front end processor and system controller software will be 0.0038 failure/hr and 0.002 failure/hr, respectively. The 24-hr reliabilities can be calculated, using a standard formula for relating failure

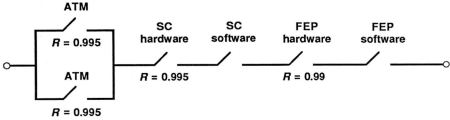

FIGURE 1.13
Bank data network failure event diagram (as seen from station 1).

intensity and reliability, as 0.913 and 0.953. The overall 24-hr period reliability as seen from station 1 is calculated to be 0.857 and that from station 2 turns out to be 0.853. If the bank considers this unacceptable, improvements should be made first in the front end processor software and then in the system controller software.

1.7 SUMMARY

Measurement is a vital element in the practice of software engineering. Good software engineering is important to the information industry. Reliability is one of the most important measurements. An understanding of the failure process is central to any effort to model and comprehend software reliability. Availability is closely related to and can be calculated from reliability.

PROBLEMS

1.1 The term "software reliability" is disturbing. Software doesn't wear out like hardware, so how can you apply a hardware concept?

1.2 How can you apply probability theory to software reliability? In hardware reliability it makes sense because there are a myriad of possible failure mechanisms operating on a microscopic level, and failures are essentially random. But aren't software failures deterministic, being the result of human error?

1.3 How can you talk of a failure intensity for software? It isn't the same situation as we have for hardware. You let me pick the tests and establish their sequence and I'll give any failure intensity estimate you want. For example, if one takes a run that operates without failure and repeats it endlessly, zero failure intensity will be obtained.

1.4 How can you view the usage of a system as a random process? If people learn the weaknesses of a system, they will avoid them.

1.5 If in testing we continually repeat the same set of test cases, will the accuracy of software reliability predictions be affected?

1.6 Aren't software failures due primarily to changes in the environment?

1.7 Are software reliability figures more usage-dependent than hardware reliability figures?

1.8 What is the meaning of mean time to repair (MTTR) for software?

1.9 What is meant when one says that for accurate reliability determination the entire input space must be covered?

1.10 Software reliability theory assumes that tests are selected randomly from the possible input space. This seems inefficient to us. We select the tests in an order that corresponds to our estimate of the likelihood they will occur during use. This removes faults most rapidly and economically. Can the theory be applied in our case?

TWO

SELECTED MODELS

In Chapter 1 the characteristics of a good software reliability model were summarized. In this chapter we select two models for presentation and application in detail throughout this book. We present the models from which the two were selected in Chapters 9 to 11 and compare them in Chapter 13. Two models were chosen because each has certain advantages not possessed by the other. However, the effort required to learn the lore associated with the application of a model makes presenting more than two a question of sharply diminishing returns. The models are the basic execution time model and the logarithmic Poisson execution time model. We consider first why we selected them; then they are described. You will see that both models have two components, named the execution time component and the calendar time component. Each component will be described with respect to both models. The determination of parameters will also be discussed.

2.1 MODEL SELECTION

Both models were developed with special regard to the needs of the engineers and managers who would use them. Consequently, both yield particularly useful quantities, such as the date for attaining a failure intensity objective. In addition, there were five primary reasons for selecting the basic execution time model:

1. It generally predicts satisfactorily.
2. It is simple and easy to understand.
3. It is the model that is most thoroughly developed and has been most widely applied to actual projects. Several programs have been developed to aid in implementing it.
4. Its parameters have a clear physical interpretation and can be related to information that exists before the program has been executed. The information in-

cludes characteristics of the software such as size and characteristics of the development environment. The foregoing property is important for system engineering studies.

5. It can handle evolving systems (systems that change in size) by adjusting the failure times to estimates of what they would have been if all the code had been present (see Chapter 6).

The logarithmic Poisson execution time model [Musa and Okumoto (1984b)] has high predictive validity, which it attains early in the system test phase. It is a relatively new model, initially published in March 1984. There is less experience with it than with the basic execution time model. However, it is almost as simple. At present, its parameters have not been related to software and development environment characteristics which exist prior to execution. The failure intensity is generally larger for large values of execution time than that of the basic model. The model may be somewhat pessimistic as compared to the basic model with regard to estimating the time, resources, and cost required to reach small failure intensity objectives. However, the nature of the prediction errors is not currently well known.

Both execution time models use an effective dual approach for characterizing failure behavior. Initial modeling is done in terms of execution time, the processor time used by the program. Then the models convert execution time to the more familiar calendar time. Quantities expressed in calendar time are more meaningful to most engineers and managers. The conversion is done through a second component of the model that characterizes the way in which human and computer resources are applied to the project.

Presently, a lot of evidence has accumulated that demonstrates the superiority of execution time over calendar time for initial modeling [Trachtenberg (1985), Musa and Okumoto (1984a), and Hecht (1981)]. This fact is generally accepted in the field. The reason that execution time is preferable is that it best characterizes the failure-inducing stress placed on software. Consider two different facilities associated with an operating system, an editor and a matrix manipulation package. Each is activated by input states that occur randomly in accordance with their operational profiles. The editor, perhaps executing 2 to 3 CPU hr daily, is certainly more stressed than the matrix package, which might execute for only a few CPU minutes. Both of the two models described previously were developed as execution time models. We currently have an interesting phenomenon. Some models, originally developed as calendar time models or without consideration of the kind of time involved, are being interpreted as execution time models.

In evaluating the basic execution time model, Dale (1982) states, "This is arguably the most practical model of all. It is a statistical model, and has been developed to the extent that it takes into account various personnel and resource constraints." Ramamoorthy and Bastani (1982) note that, "(the Musa model) . . . is better developed and is the first model to insist on execution time."

Managers involved in the projects on which these two models have been applied have observed benefits beyond the quantitative measures. They noted that the models provided an intuitively appealing and well-structured conceptual framework that gave a new perspective on the testing process. Developers and their customers were stimulated to think more carefully about just what should be considered a failure for the system involved. Also, they gave more careful consideration to what their reliability objective should be.

Before we leave the subject of model selection, we need to examine why we did *not* choose a number of other models. First, the other models do not use the execution time component–calendar time component approach that has proved so fruitful. Generally, reliability modeling is performed in calendar time, resulting in severe disadvantages, or the time domain is unspecified. If you interpret one of these models in terms of execution time, you may not have a way of relating execution time to calendar time, although it may be possible to generalize the approach used in Chapter 14. The calendar time capability is most important for engineers and managers. Most models do not provide many of the useful quantities that the basic execution time and logarithmic Poisson execution time models do. An example of one of these useful quantities is the calendar time required to reach a failure intensity objective. Concepts from several of the models [Goel and Okumoto (1979b), Jelinski and Moranda (1972), and Shooman (1972)] have been incorporated in the basic execution time model. Consequently, you can enjoy most of their advantages and those of the basic model itself when you use it. Some models such as the Littlewood-Verrall general model [Littlewood and Verrall (1973)] are very complex. They are difficult to understand and visualize physically and relatively difficult and costly to implement on a computer for practical and economical use. Finally, none of the other models match the basic execution time model in the extent of the practical experience that has been gained with it.

In general, it appears that these models can be applied to any type or size of software project, with the following exception. Very small projects (less than about 5000 lines of code) may not experience sufficient failures to permit accurate estimation of execution time component parameters and the various derived quantities. Some kind of estimate can usually be made, however, yielding a result of the form "present failure intensity is at least X failures/CPU hr."

We'll now take a look at each component in turn. The component will be described for both models and we will discuss parameter determination. We will provide both graphical and mathematical descriptions. However, any derivations will be covered only in Part III. The model descriptions and various useful formulas will be grouped in Appendix E for ready reference.

2.2 EXECUTION TIME COMPONENT

2.2.1 Description

The execution time component for both models assumes that failures occur as a random process, to be specific, a nonhomogeneous Poisson process.[1] Don't be

---

[1]The basic execution time model was not at first described as a nonhomogeneous Poisson process.

frightened by the term "nonhomogeneous Poisson process." "Poisson" simply refers to the probability distribution of the value of the process at each point in time. The term "nonhomogeneous" indicates that the characteristics of the probability distributions that make up the random process vary with time. This is exhibited in a variation of failure intensity with time. You would expect that, since faults are both being introduced and removed as time passes.

The two models have failure intensity functions that differ as functions of execution time. However, the difference between them is best described in terms of slope or decrement per failure experienced (Figure 2.1).[2] The decrement in the failure intensity function remains constant for the basic execution time model whether it is the first failure that is being fixed or the last. By contrast, for the logarithmic Poisson execution time model, the decrement per failure becomes smaller with failures experienced. In fact, it decreases exponentially. The first failure initiates a repair process that yields a substantial decrement in failure intensity, while later failures result in much smaller decrements.

The failure intensity λ for the basic model as a function of failures experienced is

$$\lambda(\mu) = \lambda_0 \left[1 - \frac{\mu}{\nu_0} \right]. \tag{2.1}$$

---

[2]In this discussion, since failures occur randomly, we are referring to "average failures experienced."

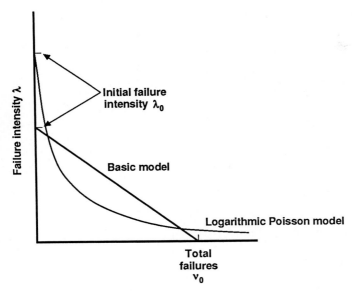

FIGURE 2.1
Failure intensity functions.

The quantity λ_0 is the initial failure intensity at the start of execution. Note that μ is the average or expected number of failures experienced at a given point in time. The quantity ν_0 is the total number of failures that would occur in infinite time.

Example 2.1. Assume that a program will experience 100 failures in infinite time. It has now experienced 50. The initial failure intensity was 10 failures/CPU hr. The current failure intensity is:

$$\lambda(\mu) = \lambda_0 \left[1 - \frac{\mu}{\nu_0} \right]$$

$$= 10 \left[1 - \frac{50}{100} \right]$$

$$= 5 \text{ failures/CPU hr} . \qquad \blacksquare$$

The failure intensity for the logarithmic Poisson model is

$$\lambda(\mu) = \lambda_0 \exp(- \theta\mu) . \tag{2.2}$$

The quantity θ is called the failure intensity decay parameter. Suppose we plot the natural logarithm of failure intensity against mean failures experienced. Then we can see by transforming (2.2) that the failure intensity decay parameter θ is the magnitude of the slope of the line we have plotted. It represents the relative change of failure intensity per failure experienced.

Example 2.2. Assume that the initial failure intensity is again 10 failures/CPU hr. The failure intensity decay parameter is 0.02/failure. We will assume that 50 failures have been experienced. The current failure intensity is:

$$\lambda(\mu) = \lambda_0 \exp(- \theta\mu)$$

$$= 10 \exp[- (0.02)(50)]$$

$$= 10 \exp(- 1)$$

$$= 3.68 \text{ failures/CPU hr} . \qquad \blacksquare$$

The slope of failure intensity, $d\lambda/d\mu$, is given by

$$\frac{d\lambda}{d\mu} = - \frac{\lambda_0}{\nu_0} \tag{2.3}$$

for the basic model.

Example 2.3. In Example 2.1, the decrement of failure intensity per failure is given by:

$$\frac{d\lambda}{d\mu} = - \frac{\lambda_0}{\nu_0}$$

$$= - \frac{10}{100}$$

$$= -0.1/\text{CPU hr}. \qquad \blacksquare$$

It is

$$\frac{d\lambda}{d\mu} = -\lambda_0 \, \theta \, \exp(-\theta\mu) = -\theta\lambda \qquad (2.4)$$

for the logarithmic Poisson model.

Example 2.4. In Example 2.2, the decrement of failure intensity per failure is given by:

$$\frac{d\lambda}{d\mu} = -\lambda_0\theta \, \exp(-\theta\mu)$$

$$= -10(0.02) \, \exp(-0.02\mu)$$

$$= -0.2 \, \exp(-0.02\mu)/\text{CPU hr}.$$

When no failures have been experienced, we have a decrement of $-0.2/\text{CPU}$ hr, greater than that for the basic model. After 50 failures have been experienced, the decrement is $-0.0736/\text{CPU}$ hr. Note the decrease to an amount smaller than the corresponding amount for the basic model. The *relative* change in failure intensity per failure experienced is constant at 0.02. In other words, the failure intensity at a given number of failures experienced is 0.98 of that at the preceding failure. $\qquad \blacksquare$

The basic model implies a uniform operational profile. Studies by both Downs (1985) and Trachtenberg (1985) demonstrate the association of the basic model with a uniform operational profile. They also show that highly nonuniform operational profiles yield failure intensity curves that are convex (of decreasing slope) with respect to number of failures experienced. The logarithmic Poisson model may be superior for highly nonuniform operational profiles, where some functions are executed much more frequently than others. The first occurrences of the input states will, on the average, be in the same order as the frequency rank. If a particular input state stimulates a fault and thus results in a failure, that failure will occur on the first instance of that input state being executed. Once the failure has been identified, the fault will in general be repaired. Then you won't see the failure recurring on subsequent instances of the particular input state. If the repair happens to be imperfect, the failure could return. In general, however, the failures tend to occur only on the early occurrences of the input states. Thus, the early failures that you tend to experience during a period of execution are associated with the frequently occurring input states. Consequently, when you repair the early failures, you tend to have a greater reduction in failure intensity. With a highly nonuniform operational profile, the early failures result in sharp decreases in failure intensity and the later failures show much smaller ones. Thus a highly nonuniform operational profile yields a failure intensity history that tends to be more suitably modeled by the logarithmic Poisson execution time model. We emphasize the point *highly* nonuniform because the basic execution time model appears to be quite tolerant to a substantial degree of nonuniformity. This fact has been demonstrated by both Downs (1985) and Trachtenberg (1985).

Note that failure intensity eventually decreases very slowly for the logarithmic Poisson model. This results from the very infrequent execution of the input states that still contain faults. This may be unrealistic with respect to system test. Often the operational profile is deliberately transformed by the test planners to reduce the system test execution time required to expose the problems. One could adjust for the transformed operational profile. It may be easier, however, to handle the situation indirectly by employing the less pessimistic basic model.

The curve for the logarithmic Poisson model may or may not cross the straight line characterizing the basic model, depending on its parameter values (see Figure 2.1). Each failure that is experienced will generate some repair activity and the result of this repair activity is a decrement in failure intensity. Neither model makes any assumption about the quality of the repair process (debugging may be imperfect). They both can allow for possible introduction of new faults during repair. Both models assume that the correction of faults following failures is immediate. In actuality, there is always some delay, but the effects of the delay are not serious and can easily be accounted for, as discussed in Chapter 4.

One might be concerned that a potential failure would be masked by a previous failure and that this behavior might affect the validity of the software reliability model. This is not likely. It occurs more frequently in unit test than in subsystem test or later, where software reliability models are commonly applied. The failures that mask other failures tend to have been eliminated by this point.

We can obtain some interesting relationships with some straightforward derivation (see Chapter 11). The expected number of failures experienced as a function of execution time is illustrated for both models in Figure 2.2. Whether the curve for the logarithmic Poisson model crosses that for the basic model depends on its parameter values. Note that the expected number of failures for the logarithmic Poisson model is always infinite at infinite time. This number can be and

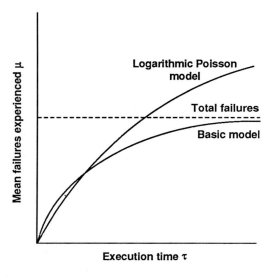

FIGURE 2.2
Mean failures experienced versus execution time.

usually is finite for the basic model during test, although it is usually infinite during the operational phase. The curve for the former model is logarithmic, hence the name. The curve for the latter is "negative" exponential, approaching a limit. Infinite failures can occur for the logarithmic Poisson model, even though the number of faults may be finite, because the model assumes decreasing effectiveness of the repair action, as explained in Chapter 11.

Let execution time be denoted by τ. We can write, for the basic model:

$$\mu(\tau) = \nu_0 \left[1 - \exp\left(-\frac{\lambda_0}{\nu_0}\tau \right) \right] . \tag{2.5}$$

Example 2.5. Let's again consider a program with an initial failure intensity of 10 failures/CPU hr and 100 total failures. We will look at the failures experienced after 10 and 100 CPU hr of execution. We have, for 10 CPU hr:

$$\mu(\tau) = \nu_0 \left[1 - \exp\left(-\frac{\lambda_0}{\nu_0}\tau \right) \right]$$

$$= 100 \left\{ 1 - \exp\left[-\frac{10}{100}\,(10) \right] \right\}$$

$$= 100[1 - \exp(-1)]$$

$$= 100(1 - 0.368)$$

$$= 100(0.632)$$

$$= 63 \text{ failures}.$$

For 100 CPU hr, we have:

$$\mu(\tau) = 100 \left\{ 1 - \exp\left[-\frac{10}{100}(100) \right] \right\}$$

$$= 100[1 - \exp(-10)]$$

$$= 100(1 - 0.0000454)$$

$$= 100 \text{ failures (almost)}. \qquad \blacksquare$$

For the logarithmic Poisson model, we have

$$\mu(\tau) = \frac{1}{\theta} \ln(\lambda_0\theta\tau + 1) . \tag{2.6}$$

Example 2.6. Use the same parameters as Example 2.2. Let's find the number of failures experienced for the logarithmic Poisson model at 10 and 100 CPU hr of execution. We have:

$$\mu(\tau) = \frac{1}{\theta} \ln(\lambda_0\theta\tau + 1)$$

$$= \frac{1}{0.02} \ln[(10)(0.02)(10) + 1]$$

$$= 50 \ln (2 + 1)$$

$$= 50 \ln 3$$

$$= 50(1.099)$$

$$= 55 \text{ failures.}$$

This is smaller than the number of failures experienced by the basic model at 10 CPU hr. At 100 CPU hr we have:

$$\mu(\tau) = \frac{1}{0.02} \ln [(10)(0.02)(100) + 1]$$

$$= 50 \ln (20 + 1)$$

$$= 50 \ln 21$$

$$= 50(3.045)$$

$$= 152 \text{ failures.}$$

Note that we now have more failures than the basic model. In fact, the number exceeds the total failures that the basic model can experience. ∎

The failure intensity as a function of execution time for both models is shown in Figure 2.3. Again, the curves for the two models may or may not cross, depending on the parameter values. This relationship is useful for determining the present failure intensity at any given value of execution time. Compare Figure 2.3 with Figure 2.1. Since intervals between failures increase as failures are experienced, the curves of Figure 2.1 are stretched out to the right when plotted against execution time. For the same set of data, the failure intensity of the logarithmic Poisson model drops more rapidly than that of the basic model at first. Later, it

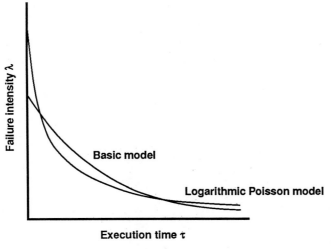

Basic model

Logarithmic Poisson model

Failure intensity λ

Execution time τ

FIGURE 2.3
Failure intensity versus execution time.

drops more slowly. At large values of execution time, the logarithmic Poisson model will have larger values of failure intensity than the basic model.

We have, for the basic model,

$$\lambda(\tau) = \lambda_0 \exp\left[-\frac{\lambda_0}{\nu_0}\tau\right]. \qquad (2.7)$$

Example 2.7. We will look at the failure intensities at 10 and 100 CPU hr, using the parameters of Example 2.1. We have, at 10 CPU hr:

$$\lambda(\tau) = \lambda_0 \exp\left[-\frac{\lambda_0}{\nu_0}\tau\right]$$

$$= 10 \exp\left[-\frac{10}{100}(10)\right]$$

$$= 10 \exp(-1)$$

$$= 10 (0.368)$$

$$= 3.68 \text{ failures/CPU hr}.$$

At 100 CPU hr we have:

$$\lambda(\tau) = 10 \exp\left[-\frac{10}{100}(100)\right]$$

$$= 10 \exp(-10)$$

$$= 10 (0.0000454)$$

$$= 0.000454 \text{ failure/CPU hr}. \qquad \blacksquare$$

We can write, for the logarithmic Poisson model,

$$\lambda(\tau) = \frac{\lambda_0}{\lambda_0 \theta \tau + 1}. \qquad (2.8)$$

Example 2.8. Consider the failure intensities for the logarithmic Poisson model at 10 CPU hr and 100 CPU hr, using the parameters of Example 2.2. We have for 10 CPU hr:

$$\lambda(\tau) = \frac{\lambda_0}{\lambda_0 \theta \tau + 1}$$

$$= \frac{10}{10(0.02)(10) + 1}$$

$$= \frac{10}{2 + 1}$$

$$= \frac{10}{3}$$

$$= 3.33 \text{ failures/CPU hr.}$$

This is slightly lower than the corresponding failure intensity for the basic model. At 100 CPU hr we have:

$$\lambda(\tau) = \frac{10}{10(0.02)(100) + 1}$$

$$= \frac{10}{20 + 1}$$

$$= \frac{10}{21}$$

$$= 0.476 \text{ failure/CPU hr}.$$

The failure intensity at the higher execution time is larger for the logarithmic Poisson model. ∎

As we have seen, the execution time components of both models are characterized by two parameters. They are listed in Table 2.1. The significance of changes in their values is shown in Figures 2.4 to 2.7 with respect to mean failures experienced. Both models have initial failure intensity as one parameter. It affects the "scale" (overall vertical positioning) of the failure intensity curve with respect to mean failures experienced. The basic model has total failures (failures expected in infinite time) as the second parameter; the logarithmic model, failure intensity decay parameter. Both of these parameters relate to how fast the failure intensity changes. If initial failure intensity is held constant, a larger value for total failures means that failure intensity becomes smaller less rapidly with the number of failures experienced. A larger value for the failure intensity decay parameter means that failure intensity and the failure intensity decrements become smaller more rapidly with the number of failures experienced.

The significance of changes in parameter values for relationships between failure intensity and execution time is shown in Figures 2.8 through 2.11. They are a little more complicated than you might think at first look. The initial failure intensity affects the shape (nature of variation) of each curve as well as the scale. The shape depends on the quantity λ_0/ν_0 for the basic model, and $\lambda_0\theta$ for the

TABLE 2.1
Execution time component parameters

Parameter	Basic	Logarithmic Poisson
	Model	
	Basic	**Logarithmic Poisson**
Initial failure intensity	λ_0	λ_0
Failure intensity change:		
Total failures	ν_0	—
Failure intensity decay parameter	—	θ

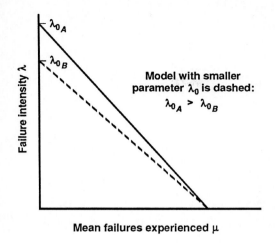

FIGURE 2.4
Variation of failure intensity versus mean failures experienced with initial failure intensity parameter—basic execution time model.

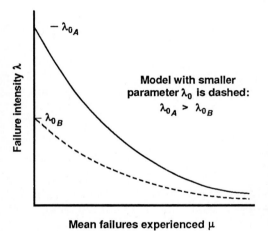

FIGURE 2.5
Variation of failure intensity versus mean failures experienced with initial failure intensity parameter—logarithmic Poisson execution time model.

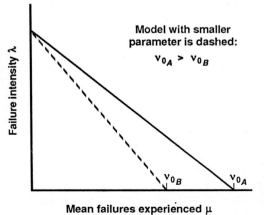

FIGURE 2.6
Variation of failure intensity versus mean failures experienced with total failures parameter—basic execution time model.

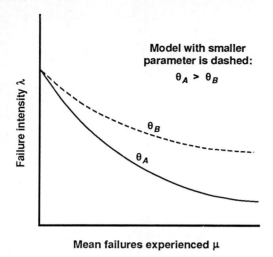

FIGURE 2.7
Variation of failure intensity versus mean failures experienced with failure intensity decay parameter — logarithmic Poisson execution time model.

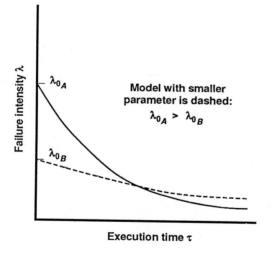

FIGURE 2.8
Variation of failure intensity versus execution time with initial failure intensity parameter — basic execution time model.

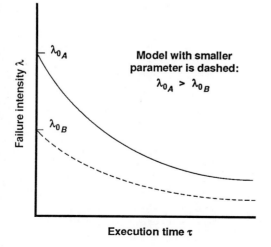

FIGURE 2.9
Variation of failure intensity versus execution time with initial failure intensity parameter — logarithmic Poisson execution time model.

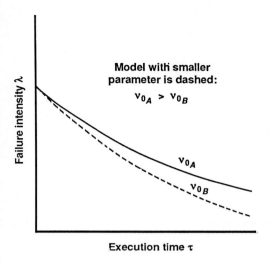

FIGURE 2.10
Variation of failure intensity versus execution time with total failures parameter — basic execution time model.

logarithmic model. Recall that λ_0 is initial failure intensity, ν_0 is total failures, and θ is the failure intensity decay parameter. If the shape quantities are held constant while λ_0 is varied, then the λ_0 variations affect only the scale of the curves.

DERIVED QUANTITIES. Assume that you have chosen a failure intensity objective for the software product being developed. Suppose some portion of the failures are being removed through correction of their associated faults. Then you can use the objective and the present value of failure intensity to determine the additional expected number of failures that must be experienced to reach that objective. The process is illustrated graphically in Figure 2.12. Equations describing the

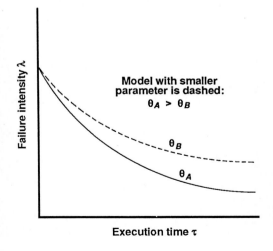

FIGURE 2.11
Variation of failure intensity versus execution time with failure intensity decay parameter — logarithmic Poisson execution time model.

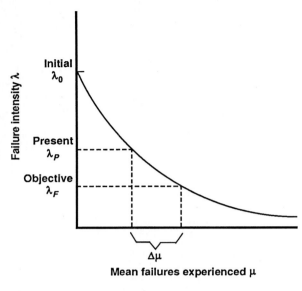

Failure intensity λ

Initial λ_0

Present λ_P

Objective λ_F

$\Delta\mu$

Mean failures experienced μ

FIGURE 2.12
Additional failures to
failure intensity objective.

relationships in closed form may be derived for both models (see Chapter 11) so that manual calculations can be performed. They are

$$\Delta\mu = \frac{\nu_0}{\lambda_0} (\lambda_P - \lambda_F) \tag{2.9}$$

for the basic model and

$$\Delta\mu = \frac{1}{\theta} \ln \frac{\lambda_P}{\lambda_F} \tag{2.10}$$

for the logarithmic Poisson model. The quantity $\Delta\mu$ is the expected number of failures to reach the failure intensity objective, λ_P is the present failure intensity, and λ_F is the failure intensity objective.

Example 2.9. For the basic model, we will determine the expected number of failures that will be experienced between a present failure intensity of 3.68 failures/CPU hr and an objective of 0.000454 failure/CPU hr. We will use the same parameter values as in Example 2.1. Thus:

$$\Delta\mu = \frac{\nu_0}{\lambda_0} (\lambda_P - \lambda_F)$$

$$= \frac{100}{10} (3.68 - 0.000454)$$

$$= 10 (3.68)$$

$$= 37 \text{ failures}.$$

Note that this result cross-checks with the results of Examples 2.5 and 2.7. ■

Example 2.10. We will find, for the logarithmic Poisson model, the expected number of failures experienced between a present failure intensity of 3.33 failures/CPU hr and an objective of 0.476 failure/CPU hr. The parameter values will be the same as in Example 2.2. We have:

$$\Delta\mu = \frac{1}{\theta} \ln \frac{\lambda_P}{\lambda_F}$$

$$= \frac{1}{0.02} \ln \frac{3.33}{0.476}$$

$$= 50 \ln 6.996$$

$$= 50 \, (1.945)$$

$$= 97 \text{ failures}.$$

This result cross-checks with the results of Examples 2.6 and 2.8. ■

Similarly, you can determine the additional execution time $\Delta\tau$ required to reach the failure intensity objective for either model. This is

$$\Delta\tau = \frac{\nu_0}{\lambda_0} \ln \frac{\lambda_P}{\lambda_F} \tag{2.11}$$

for the basic model and

$$\Delta\tau = \frac{1}{\theta} \left[\frac{1}{\lambda_F} - \frac{1}{\lambda_P} \right] \tag{2.12}$$

for the logarithmic Poisson model. This is illustrated in Figure 2.13.

Example 2.11. For the basic model, with the same parameter values used in Example 2.1, we will determine the execution time between a present failure intensity of 3.68 failures/CPU hr and an objective of 0.000454 failure/CPU hr. We have:

$$\Delta\tau = \frac{\nu_0}{\lambda_0} \ln \frac{\lambda_P}{\lambda_F}$$

$$= \frac{100}{10} \ln \frac{3.68}{0.000454}$$

$$= 10 \ln 8106$$

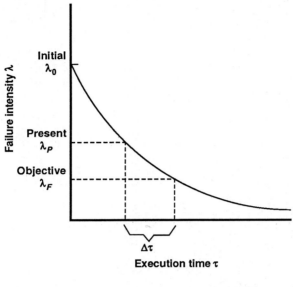

FIGURE 2.13
Additional execution time to failure intensity objective.

$$= 10 \ (9)$$

$$= 90 \ \text{CPU hr}.$$

This result checks with the results of Example 2.7. ∎

Example 2.12. For the logarithmic Poisson model, with the same parameter values used in Example 2.2, we will find the execution time between a present failure intensity of 3.33 failures/CPU hr and an objective of 0.476 failure/CPU hr. We have:

$$\Delta\tau = \frac{1}{\theta}\left[\frac{1}{\lambda_F} - \frac{1}{\lambda_P}\right]$$

$$= \frac{1}{0.02}\left[\frac{1}{0.476} - \frac{1}{3.33}\right]$$

$$= 50 \ (2.10 - 0.30)$$

$$= 50 \ (1.80)$$

$$= 90 \ \text{CPU hr}.$$

The result checks with the results of Example 2.8. ∎

The foregoing quantities are of interest in themselves. The additional expected number of failures required to reach the failure intensity objective gives some idea of the failure correction workload. The additional execution time indicates the remaining amount of test required. However, even more importantly, they are both used in making estimates of the additional calendar time required to reach the failure intensity objective. More about that in the next section.

In most situations for the logarithmic Poisson model, an alternative formulation is also possible. The MTTF exists for this model in most circumstances (it does not for the basic model). We can set a MTTF objective instead of a failure intensity objective. The additional expected number of failures that must be experienced and the additional execution time required to reach that objective may be determined in terms of the present and objective MTTFs.

We will see later in this chapter that we can never determine the values of the parameters precisely. We will always have some range of uncertainty. It is expressed through confidence intervals, discussed in Section 2.2.2. This uncertainty results in corresponding uncertainty in the derived quantities described above. One can visualize the effects of confidence intervals for the parameters on confidence intervals for the derived quantities by thinking of the model curves being expanded to bands in Figures 2.12 and 2.13.

2.2.2 Parameter Determination

Model parameters may be divided into two categories, execution time component and calendar time component parameters. If you are not concerned with determining calendar time, resource expenditures, or costs, there is no need to be concerned with the calendar time component parameters.

For the two models just described, the values of two parameters must be determined for the execution time components. We need the value of initial failure intensity λ_0 in both cases, total failures experienced ν_0 for the basic execution time model, and failure intensity decay parameter θ for the logarithmic Poisson model. Initially, we can *predict* (determine before program execution) the parameter values for the basic model from characteristics of the program itself. There will be some degree of uncertainty associated with these predictions. Once a program has executed long enough so that failure data are available, we can *estimate* these parameters. Maximum likelihood estimation or other methods may be used. Maximum likelihood estimation yields that set of parameters that make it most likely that the observed data could have occurred. The accuracy with which they are known generally increases with the size of the sample of failures, for small and moderate size samples. The accuracy may be characterized by estimating confidence intervals (Chapter 12). The confidence intervals represent that range of parameters that could possibly "explain" the data experienced, at some level of confidence (for example, 75 percent). Parameter determination procedures are described in detail in Chapter 5. Theoretical background is given in Chapter 12.

PREDICTION. Prediction of parameters is needed whenever system engineering studies are required in project phases before failure data are available. Procedures for predicting the values of the execution time component parameters are currently developed for the basic execution time model. They have not yet been developed for the logarithmic Poisson model. They are established from the size and perhaps other characteristics of the program and the average instruction execution rate of the computer on which the program is running. At present, the accuracy of prediction is limited because little work has been done in this area and only a small amount of data has been collected. However, since system engineering studies can be very significant in realizing substantial cost savings for a project, further work in this area is vital. Limited accuracy is not a handicap for studies in which only the *relative* values of quantities are important. Even where absolute quantities are needed, limited accuracy is usually preferable to making no study at all.

ESTIMATION. Estimation is generally accomplished either in subsystem or system test or in the operational phase. It is usually more accurate than prediction. Estimation is a statistical method that is based on either on the failure times or the number of failures per time interval (for example, failures per hour). The two formulations of the method are essentially equivalent theoretically. However, we are going to focus on the use of failure times. This approach often simplifies program implementation. There is no need to concern yourself with different intervals over which failures are counted. Furthermore, it is easy to convert failures per time interval into failure times and hence handle a mix of both kinds of data. This is simply done by randomly assigning the failures in the interval in which they are experienced. For example, if you have three failures in an hour, you would assign those three failures randomly within that time interval.

Estimation and the computation of derived quantities is straightforward, however, the calculations required are tedious. Consequently, it makes sense to develop computer programs to do the dirty work. We will discuss desirable characteristics of such programs in Chapter 5. However, their usefulness is illustrated in the following example.

> **Example 2.13.** A sample output from a software reliability program, taken during the system test phase of an actual project, is illustrated in Figure 2.14. Maximum likelihood estimates and 50, 75, 90, and 95 percent confidence intervals for each item are provided. The two confidence bounds are placed on either side of the maximum likelihood ("most likely") estimate in the figure. Clearly, the higher the confidence required, the larger the width of the interval. In practice, we have generally found that a reasonable compromise is to use 75 percent confidence intervals. The range of the present failure intensity is printed along with a range of projected completion dates based on the calendar time component. The dates are predictions of when a specified failure intensity objective will be reached. Note that failure intensities are specified as failures per thousand CPU hr. The expected number of additional failures that must be experienced $\Delta\mu$ and the additional execution time $\Delta\tau$ required to reach the failure intensity objective are given. The foregoing results are very useful for planning schedules, estimating status and progress, and determining when to terminate testing. In Figure 2.14 we have highlighted the maximum likelihood estimates and the 75 percent confidence interval of the quantities we have just been talking about. ∎

2.2.3   Operational Phase

If a program has been released and is operational, and no features are added or repairs made between releases, the failure intensity will be constant, as noted in

SOFTWARE RELIABILITY PREDICTION
BASIC MODEL
SYSTEM T2

BASED ON SAMPLE OF   54 TEST FAILURES
EXECUTION TIME IS   32.78 HR
FAILURE INTENSITY OBJECTIVE IS   .36e-01 FAILURES/CPU HR
CALENDAR TIME TO DATE IS   74 DAYS
PRESENT DATE   5/31/74

	CONF. LIMITS				MOST LIKELY	CONF. LIMITS			
	95%	90%	75%	50%		50%	75%	90%	95%
TOTAL FAILURES	55	55	55	55	56	57	58	60	61
FAILURE INTENSITIES (FAILURES/1000 CPU HR)									
INITIAL F.I.	4004	4258	4670	5077	5671	6282	6721	7183	7480
PRESENT F.I.	84.0	97.3	122.4	152.1	205.4	275.1	336.4	412.3	468.0

*** ADDITIONAL REQUIREMENTS TO MEET FAILURE INTENSITY OBJECTIVE ***

	95%	90%	75%	50%	MOST LIKELY	50%	75%	90%	95%
FAILURES	0	0	1	1	2	3	4	5	7
EXEC. TIME (CPU HR)	6.18	7.58	10.0	12.7	17.2	22.9	27.8	34.2	39.2
CAL. TIME (DAYS)	2.67	3.30	4.40	5.64	7.78	10.6	13.1	16.4	19.1
COMPLETION DATE	60574	60674	60774	61074	61274	61774	62074	62574	62874

FIGURE 2.14
Sample output—software reliability estimation program.

Chapter 1. Then both models, as nonhomogeneous Poisson processes, reduce to homogeneous Poisson processes with the failure intensity as a parameter. The number of failures in a given time period follows a Poisson distribution. The failure intervals follow an exponential distribution. The reliability R and failure intensity λ are related by

$$R(\tau) = \exp(-\lambda\tau) \ . \tag{2.13}$$

Note that the reliability is dependent not only on the failure intensity but also on the period of execution time. The reliability (probability of no failures in a period of execution time τ) is lower for longer time periods as is illustrated in Figure 2.15.

The operational phase of many programs consists of a series of releases. The reliability and failure intensity will then be step functions, with the levels of the quantities changing at each release. If the releases are frequent and the trend of failure intensity is decreasing, one can often approximate the step functions by one of the software reliability models we have presented. Alternatively, one may apply the software reliability models directly to reported unique failures (not counting repetitions). Note that the model now represents the failure intensity that will occur when the failures have been corrected. This approach is analogous to the one commonly taking place during system test of ignoring the failure correction delay, except that the delay is much longer here. Of course, if the failures are actually corrected in the field, then the operational phase should be handled just like the system test phase.

2.3 CALENDAR TIME COMPONENT

2.3.1 Description

The calendar time component relates execution time and calendar time by determining the calendar time to execution time ratio at any given point in time. The ratio is based on the constraints that are involved in applying resources to a pro-

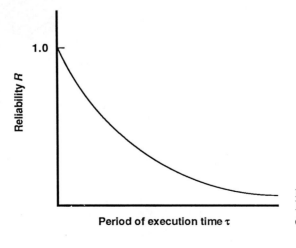

FIGURE 2.15
Reliability versus period of execution time.

ject. To obtain calendar time, you integrate this ratio with respect to execution time. The calendar time component is of greatest significance during phases where the software is being tested and repaired. During this period one can predict the dates at which various failure intensity objectives will be met. The calendar time component "exists" during periods in which repair is not occurring and failure intensity is constant. However, it reduces in that case to a constant ratio between calendar time and execution time.

In test, the rate of testing at any time is constrained by the failure identification or test team personnel, the failure correction or debugging personnel, or the computer time available.[3] The quantities of these resources available to a project are usually more or less established in its early stages. Increases are generally not feasible during the system test phase because of the long lead times required for training and computer procurement. At any given value of execution time, one of these resources will be limiting. The limiting resource will determine the rate at which execution time can be spent per unit calendar time. A test phase may consist of from one to three periods, each characterized by a different limiting resource.

The following is a common scenario. At the start of testing one identifies a large number of failures separated by short time intervals. Testing must be stopped from time to time to let the people who are fixing the faults keep up with the load. As testing progresses, the intervals between failures become longer and longer. The time of the failure correction personnel is no longer completely filled with failure correction work. The test team becomes the bottleneck. The effort required to run tests and analyze the results is occupying all their time. That paces the amount of testing done each day. Finally, at even longer intervals, the capacity of the computing facilities becomes limiting. This resource then determines how much testing is accomplished.

The calendar time component is based on a "debugging process" model. This model takes into account:

1. resources *used* in operating the program for a given execution time and processing an associated quantity of failures,
2. resource quantities *available,* and
3. the degree to which a resource can be *utilized* (due to bottlenecks) during the period in which it is limiting.

Table 2.2 will help in visualizing these different aspects of the resources, and the parameters that result.

RESOURCE USAGE. In Chapter 14 we show that resource usage is linearly proportional to execution time and mean failures experienced. Let χ_r be the usage of

---

[3]The calendar time component can readily be generalized to handle additional limiting resources.

TABLE 2.2
Calender time component resources and parameters

Resources	Usage parameters — requirements per:		Planned parameters	
	CPU hr	**Failure**	**Quantities available**	**Utilizations**
Failure identification personnel	θ_I	μ_I	P_I	1
Failure correction personnel	0	μ_F	P_F	ρ_F
Computer time	θ_C	μ_C	P_C	ρ_C

resource r. Then

$$\chi_r = \theta_r \, \tau + \mu_r \, \mu \, . \tag{2.14}$$

Note that θ_r is the resource usage per CPU hr. It is nonzero for failure identification personnel (θ_I) and computer time (θ_C). The quantity μ_r is the resource usage per failure. Be careful not to confuse it with mean failures experienced μ. It was deliberately chosen to be similar to suggest the connection between resource usage and failures experienced. It is nonzero for failure identification personnel (μ_I), failure correction personnel (μ_F), and computer time (μ_C).

Consider a test team that is running tests on a particular piece of software. If they conduct 2 hr of testing rather than 1, they will have twice the amount of work to be done. They will have approximately twice the amount of output to examine and they will spend twice as much time conducting the tests. The work effort related to failures experienced will be dependent on the number. A failure report will have to be written whenever a failure occurs. Some time will be needed to establish whether each suspected failure really is one, by checking the requirements. The test team may have to record some information, and perhaps make a couple of runs to get all the pertinent facts about the particular failure. Note that mean failures is used to estimate effort, so that mean resource requirements are obtained.

Example 2.14. Suppose the test team runs test cases for 8 CPU hr and identifies 20 failures. The effort required per hr of execution time is 6 person hr. Each failure requires 2 hr on the average to verify and determine its nature. The total failure identification effort required, using Equation (2.14), is

$$\chi_r = \theta_r \, \tau + \mu_r \mu$$

$$= 6(8) + 2(20)$$

$$= 48 + 40$$

$$= 88 \text{ person hr.} \qquad \blacksquare$$

For failure correction (unlike identification), resources required are dependent only on the mean failures experienced. However, computer time is used in both identification and correction of failures. Hence, computer time used will usually depend on both the amount of execution time and the number of failures.

Note that since "failures experienced" is a function of execution time, resource usage is actually a function of execution time only. The intermediate step of thinking in terms of failures experienced and execution time is useful in gaining physical insight into what is happening. Also, it permits data to be collected and fitted in a model-independent fashion, so that it has maximum applicability. Cumulative resource usage as a function of execution time is illustrated in Figure 2.16. In Example 2.14, if we eliminate failures experienced as the intermediate variable, we have an average of 11 person hr of effort used per hour of execution time. Alternatively, we may consider resource usage to be a function of failures experienced only. With execution time eliminated as a variable in the example, we have 4.4 person hr of effort used per failure.

Computer time required per unit execution time will normally be greater than 1. In addition to the execution time for the program under test, additional time will be required for the execution of such support programs as test drivers, recording routines, and data reduction packages.

Consider the change in resource usage per unit of execution time. This is shown in Figure 2.17. It can be obtained by differentiating Equation (2.14) with respect to execution time. We obtain

$$\frac{d\chi_r}{d\tau} = \theta_r + \mu_r\lambda \ . \tag{2.15}$$

Since the failure intensity decreases with testing, the effort used per hour of execution time tends to decrease with testing. It approaches the execution time coeffi-

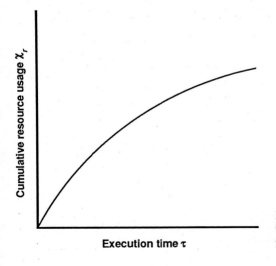

FIGURE 2.16
Cumulative resource usage as a function of execution time.

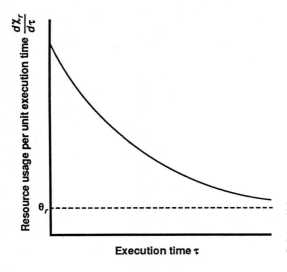

FIGURE 2.17
Variation of resource usage per unit execution time with execution time.

cient of resource usage asymptotically as execution time increases. Let's now look at the change in resource usage per failure. This is shown in Figure 2.18. It can be obtained by differentiating Equation (2.14) with respect to failures. We have

$$\frac{d\chi_r}{d\mu} = \mu_r + \theta_r \frac{d\tau}{d\mu} . \tag{2.16}$$

Note that the execution time between failures tends to increase with testing. Thus, failure identification effort and computer time required "for each failure" tend to increase throughout the test period as well.

CALENDAR TIME TO EXECUTION TIME RELATIONSHIP. Resource quantities and utilizations are assumed to be constant for the period over which the model is

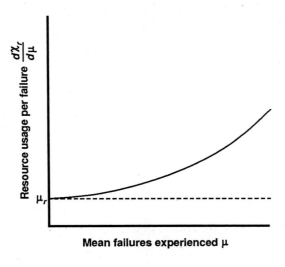

FIGURE 2.18
Variation of resource usage per failure with mean failures experienced.

being applied. This is a reasonable assumption, as increases are usually not feasible. Once a project is underway, there is a real limitation as to how fast personnel can be added without making the situation worse [Brooks (1975)]. Also, it's a well known fact that it's difficult to make substantial changes in computer resources rapidly. Orders for computers require a lead time and installation time is also long.

The instantaneous ratio of calendar time to execution time can be obtained by dividing the resource usage rate of the limiting resource by the constant quantity of resources available that can be utilized. Let t be calendar time. Then

$$\frac{dt}{d\tau} = \frac{1}{P_r \rho_r} \frac{d\chi_r}{d\tau}.$$

(2.17)

The quantity P_r represents resources available. Note that ρ_r is the utilization. The above ratio must be computed separately for each resource-limited period. Since χ_r is a function of τ, we now have a relationship between t and τ in each resource-limited period.

Example 2.15. Consider our previous test team illustration in Example 2.14. Assume that failure identification personnel are the limiting resource. Recall that 88 person hr were required to test for 8 CPU hr and identify 20 failures. Note that 11 person hr of effort were used per hour of execution time, on the average. Suppose there are 2 members of the test team and both are fully utilized. Then the calendar time to execution time ratio, averaged over the period, is 5.5. We can compute the elapsed calendar time as 44 hr. Assuming a standard work week, this is slightly longer than a week. ∎

The form of the instantaneous calendar time to execution time ratio for any given limiting resource and either model is shown in Figure 2.19. It is readily obtained from Equations (2.15) and (2.17) as

$$\frac{dt}{d\tau} = \frac{\theta_r + \mu_r \lambda}{P_r \rho_r}.$$

(2.18)

The shape of this curve will parallel that of the failure intensity. The curve approaches an asymptote of $\theta_r / P_r \rho_r$. Note that the asymptote is 0 for the failure correction personnel resource. At any given time, the maximum of the ratios for the three limiting resources actually determines the rate at which calendar time is expended; this is illustrated in Figure 2.20. The maximum is plotted as a solid curve. When the curve for a resource is not maximum (not limiting), it is plotted dashed. Note the transition points *FI* and *IC*. Here, the calendar time to execution time ratios of two resources are equal and the limiting resource changes. The point *FC* is a potential but not true transition point. Neither resource *F* nor resource *C* is limiting near this point.

Let's look at the general shape of the plot of calendar time against execution time for both models (Figure 2.21). This curve is composed of segments, each of which represents a period in which a different resource is limiting. Each segment represents the integral of the instantaneous calendar time to execution time ratio with respect to execution time. This ratio always decreases with execution time,

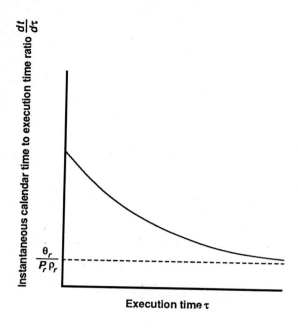

FIGURE 2.19
Instantaneous calendar time to execution time ratio.

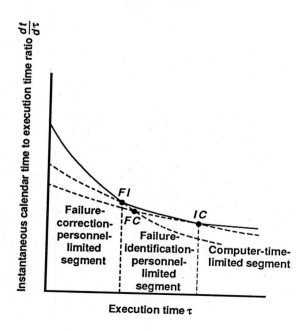

FIGURE 2.20
Calendar time to execution time ratio for different limiting resources.

56

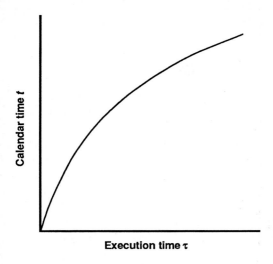

Execution time τ

FIGURE 2.21
Calendar time versus execution time.

hence the shape of the curve. The value of the ratio is continuous at the boundaries between different limiting resource periods. Hence the plot of calendar time against execution time is smooth with respect to these boundaries and the boundaries are not evident.

The calendar time component allows you to estimate the calendar time in days required to meet the failure intensity objective. The value of this interval is particularly useful to software managers and engineers. You may determine it from the additional execution time and additional number of failures needed to meet the objective that we found for the execution time component. Second, you now determine the date on which the failure intensity objective will be achieved. This is a simple variant of the first quantity that takes account of things like weekends and holidays. However, it is a useful quantity because it speaks in terms managers and engineers understand. If the foregoing prediction is not required, however, there is no need to be concerned with the calendar time component or the determination of its parameters. Note that uncertainty in determining model parameters will result in a corresponding uncertainty in the previous quantities.

2.3.2 Parameter Determination

There are two categories of parameters that must be established for the calendar time components of the two models. The parameters are the same and have the same values for both models. The categories are: planned and resource usage. Planned parameters are those that are established by managerial decisions on the project or by project conditions and policies. The decisions involve resource quantities. Resource quantity parameters include things such as the size of the test team and the number of failure correction personnel employed on the project. Conditions and policies affect the degree of resource utilization during the resource-limiting period for that resource. The resource usage parameters relate to the resources required for failure identification and correction. They are generally stated in terms of resources required per hour of execution time and per failure experienced. The resources are, as noted earlier in this chapter, failure identification personnel, failure correction personnel, and computer time. Note that computer usage is not the same quantity as execution time of test or operation. Computer usage includes the latter time, but also includes computer time devoted to collecting data related to a failure, debugging, demonstrating the fix, and performing regression testing.

Resource quantities available are readily ascertained from managers or project planners. Resource utilization expected is generally determined by formula or experience (Section 5.2.2). You can best establish resource usage parameter values at present by the collection of data for a particular project. Fit the data in a least squares fashion as described in Chapter 5. Some information on values of resource usage parameters is currently available (Section 5.2.3). It is hoped that ultimately these values can be determined for all software projects or for large classes of projects. It may eventually be unnecessary to actually collect and fit data. If you don't have information from a similar project available and cannot or do not wish to collect data on your own project, it is best to rely on experience. However, this is not the preferable approach. The values of the resource usage parameters may be related to such factors as:

1. batch debugging versus interactive debugging,
2. debugging aids available,
3. computer used,
4. language used, and
5. administrative and documentation overhead associated with corrections.

Herndon and Keenan (1978) have investigated some of these factors.

Uncertainties in determining the foregoing parameter values occur primarily for resource usage parameters. The range of uncertainty depends on a number of factors. The effects of these uncertainties on the prediction of the date for reaching the failure intensity objective can be established by calculating this date for different sets of values.

2.4 MODEL CHOICE

The choice of which of the two models to use in any given application depends on several factors. These are summarized in Table 2.3. If you desire to conduct studies or make reliability predictions before the program is executed and failure data taken, you will lean toward the basic model. The basic model would also be used when studying the effects of a new software engineering technology *if* this is done by looking at the effect of the new technology on faults. In that case, faults must be related to failure intensity. At present, only the basic model has this capability. If the size of the program is changing continually and substantially as fail-

TABLE 2.3
Choice between models

Purpose of application or existence of condition	Basic	Logarithmic Poisson
Studies or predictions before execution	X	
Studying effects of software engineering technology (through study of faults)	X	
Program size changing continually and substantially	X	
Highly nonuniform operational profile		X
Early predictive validity important		X

ure data is collected, then the basic model would again be the choice. This situation could occur due to design changes or to the program being integrated stage by stage. Moderate rates of program evolution do not affect the choice of model. Neither has been shown to be superior in the foregoing situation.

If the program is expected to be used with a decidedly nonuniform operational profile, the logarithmic Poisson model may be better. Note that efficiently run test phases generally employ input state (test case) selection without replacement. In this situation, as will be noted in Chapter 4, the test phase operational profile is, in effect, uniform. If high predictive validity is needed early in the period of execution, the logarithmic Poisson model will probably be preferable. The margin of superiority is greatest for small samples of failures (that is, after a short time of execution). For larger samples of failures, the superiority may be small, so that any other factors that exist should play the predominant role. The better predictive validity during early execution may occur primarily in the case of a highly nonuniform operational profile. The rapidly changing slope of failure intensity during this period can be fit better with the logarithmic Poisson than the basic model. This will be clear from Figure 2.1. In a number of circumstances, the choice between the two models may not be critical. In others, one may be preferable for just part of the period of application. One option may be to employ the basic model for pretest studies and estimates and periods of evolution. You would switch to the logarithmic Poisson model when integration is complete.

2.5 SUMMARY

The basic and logarithmic Poisson execution time models were selected for detailed exposition in this book. The basic model represents an arithmetic change of failure intensity with mean failures experienced; the logarithmic Poisson model, geometric. The two models have many advantages, and substantial practical experience has been gained with them. Modeling is initially performed in execution time. Results are then converted to calendar time. The determination of model parameters was discussed.

PROBLEMS

2.1 The same data have been fit with both the basic and logarithmic Poisson models. The parameters obtained are:

Basic	Logarithmic Poisson
$\lambda_0 = 20$ failures/CPU hr	$\lambda_0 = 50$ failures/CPU hr
$\nu_0 = 120$ failures	$\theta = 0.025$/failures

Note that the logarithmic Poisson usually has higher initial failure intensity. At first, recall that this falls off more rapidly than the failure intensity for the basic model, but finally it falls off more slowly. We will examine some consequences of this behavior.

First, determine the additional failures and additional execution time required to reach a failure intensity objective of 10 failures/CPU hr, using both models. Then repeat this for an objective of 1 failure/CPU hr. Assume in both cases that you start from the initial failure intensity.

2.2 Why do you speak of "failures that must be experienced to reach the failure intensity objective?" How will experiencing failures improve the failure intensity and permit an objective to be reached, unless the associated faults are corrected?

2.3 How can one determine the number of additional failures that must be experienced and removed to achieve a given reliability level (for an operating period of a specified duration)?

2.4 Does the ratio of calendar time to execution time approach 1 with increasing execution time?

2.5 Your basic model doesn't make sense. Suppose you have a program that runs for 1000 sec and has 100 evenly-spaced faults in it. After starting test, the first failure will occur at 10 sec. If you correct it and resume testing, the next failure will also occur after a 10 sec interval. This will continue right up to the last failure, which will also occur after a 10 sec interval. Where is the change in failure intensity that is supposed to occur as testing progresses?

THREE

APPLICATIONS

This chapter looks generally at how software reliability measurements can be used. The detailed procedures involved in application and some of the more advanced uses will be presented in Chapter 7.

It is convenient to classify applications into four groups, each of which we will treat in more detail:

1. system engineering,
2. project management during development and particularly test,
3. operational phase software management, and
4. evaluation of software engineering technologies.

Finally, we will discuss how to do overall planning for application of software reliability methods to projects. Table 3.1 summarizes some of the applications. It evaluates their potential value and current quality of results. Some applications are not presented until Chapter 7.

Software reliability measurement techniques are of great value in the evaluation of software engineering technology and in operational software management. The results of applying software reliability measurement to software project management are good but capable of improvement. Most of the project management applications relate to subsystem or system test phases. However, there is a reasonable possibility that they can be extended to the unit test phase.

The quality of the results of many of the studies in the system engineering phase is dependent on the quality of parameter prediction. The "fair" rating we have given these results may improve markedly if parameter prediction can be improved. In any case, the things that can be done now are beyond the pure research

TABLE 3.1
Summary and evaluation of applications

Development phase	Applications	Potential value of application	Current quality of results
System engineering	Product feasiblity studies	Very high	Fair−
	Trade-off studies	High+	Fair+
	Cost studies	High	Fair
	Scheduling studies	High+	Fair
	Reliability allocation	High−	Fair+
	Reliability specification	High−	Fair
Test	Status tracking	High	Good+
	Project completion estimation	High	Good−
	Redoing system engineering studies	High	Good
	Investigating management alternatives	High	Good
Operation	Reliability demonstration	High−	Excellent
	Change control	High	Excellent
	Preventive maintenance control	High−	Excellent
All	Evaluating software engineering technology	High−	Excellent

stage. We should be attempting practical applications. You should be judicious in doing so, of course. However, application to system engineering problems may be one of the most promising áreas. Decisions are made at this time that can have great financial, schedule, and other impacts on a project. Hence one is in greatest need of quantitative tools at this stage. Do not undervalue making applications in this area, even though the techniques may not be totally perfected. The significance of the general comments we have just made should become clearer after you have explored the details of this chapter.

The fact that software reliability measurement is better developed for the later stages of the software life cycle is not a problem. About two-thirds of the total costs occur after release. On many projects system test represents 40 to 50 percent of prerelease costs. Thus 80 percent or more of total life cycle costs occur after the start of system test. Improved decision making in this period can indeed have an impact! On the other hand, some of this money is committed (even if not spent) somewhat earlier in the life cycle. Consequently, any guidance that can be given to early decisions (even if imprecise) can be of great value.

3.1   SYSTEM ENGINEERING

Let us consider some typical system engineering applications (this is not an exhaustive list):

1. specifying reliability to a designer,
2. estimating costs of failure for an operational system,

3. pricing a service,
4. helping establish the market window for a software product (or product containing software),
5. investigating trade-offs between reliability and resources, cost, and schedules,
6. selecting the failure intensity objective, and
7. determining the amount of system testing required.

Reliability specification may be used internally within an organization to give concrete guidance or direction to a design team vis-à-vis other desired characteristics of a software product. It may be used similarly with external organizations (for example, subcontractors). It can even be employed as a contractual requirement with legal standing. An example of what you might do here is to state that the reliability of the program delivered from a particular subcontractor must be 0.99 for 10 CPU hr of execution. You would also specify this in terms of the operational profile that one would use to make this measurement.

How do we go about determining the costs of failure for an operational system? This can involve restoration costs such as reloading the program and cleaning up the data base. Even if recovery is automated, there will be an interruption in service, resulting in lost revenue and possible lost customers, among other things. Hence there is some average amount of resources expended or revenue lost each time a failure occurs. We multiply this by the number of failures for the period being studied. Let's look at an example. Suppose we have a system that has a failure intensity of 0.025 failure/CPU hr. Now let's also assume that the system works for 40 CPU hr/week. Suppose it requires an average of 4 person hr/failure to do restoration, including travel, at a cost of $25/hr loaded salary. On the average we'll be getting 1 failure per week per system, each requiring 4 hr of work and costing $100. That's $400/month per system.

When pricing a service, we first compute failure costs as above. Then we add other costs and a reasonable rate of return, based on financial considerations and market conditions. Suppose in the example given that our other system costs are $500/month. We would price this particular service at $900/month plus some reasonable rate of return.

Failure intensity estimates can help determine the market window for a software product or product containing software. Most of you probably know that the market window is the time period within which you can introduce a new product and have it be profitable. The main concern is the "late" limit of the market window. That is, if you should introduce a product too late, your competitors may have captured most of your expected market share. They can now reduce prices because of their volume. It is extremely difficult for you to compete. For software products particularly, there is likely to be a trade-off between the time of introduction of a product and its reliability. If you introduce the product too early, it may be unreliable, gain a bad reputation, and hence not sell well. And, of course you don't want it to be late either.

Here is an example of the application of software reliability measurement to this problem. Suppose you expect your competitor to introduce a product on June 17. You look at the trade-off between reliability and product introduction by running simulations with a software reliability program. You find you have the option of beating out your competitor by introducing a product on May 15, about a month ahead, with 0.02 failure/CPU hr. On the other hand, you may decide that you will compete on reliability. You could introduce your product at the same time as your competitor on June 17. Then you would have a failure intensity of 0.001 failure/CPU hr. This reliability improvement comes from more testing. You may feel that the 0.001 failure/CPU hr you can attain on June 17 will be superior to anything your competitor will be putting out. In your judgment, this margin of quality may be important for your market. The simulation clarifies the alternatives so you can apply external factors to the decision.

Let us now consider the topic of making trade-offs between reliability and resources, costs, and schedules. We will speak in terms of a failure intensity objective rather than a reliability objective as the analysis is simpler. The two are alternative forms of each other. Details on trade-offs are presented in Section 7.2.3. The trade-offs are usually straightforward if the range of possible values of failure intensity objective is moderate. We then typically involve only one limiting resource. Increasing reliability is equivalent to reducing the failure intensity objective or increasing the ratio of initial failure intensity to failure intensity objective. An increase in this ratio is associated with an increase in the limiting resource usage required and hence an increase in project cost. If the quantity of the limiting resource available is fixed, then increasing the failure intensity ratio lengthens the schedule.

If the range of possible values of failure intensity objective is sufficiently large such that more than one limiting resource is involved, the situation becomes more complex. Resource usages, cost, and project duration all still increase with failure intensity ratio. Making more resources available can reduce schedule durations. However, each resource can only affect the duration of its associated limiting period. Thus the effect of adding resources is limited. Clearly, cost provides one possible basis for selecting the failure intensity objective. Other bases will be discussed in Chapter 7.

If we can establish the failure intensity objective and the initial failure intensity at the start of system test, the execution time required for system test can be determined. This can be seen in Figure 2.13. The relationships are given by Equations (2.11) and (2.12) for the basic and logarithmic Poisson execution time models, respectively. The calendar time component of the selected model can then be used to find the length of system test in terms of calendar time.

3.2 PROJECT MANAGEMENT

Some typical project management applications include:

1. progress monitoring,

2. scheduling, and

3. investigation of alternatives.

These applications occur during time periods when the program is being executed and at least some repair action is being taken on the failures. Most commonly, this is the system test period. Estimates are made from failure data, generally using one or more of the programs described in Chapter 5.

A plot from a representative project, using the basic execution time model, is shown in Figure 3.1. The plot is a project history of present failure intensity. It is useful for indicating progress toward the failure intensity objective. The solid center curve is the maximum likelihood estimate and the dashed outer curves delineate the bounds of the 75 percent confidence interval. The report of Figure 3.2 could have been used to evaluate progress. However, plotting the recent history of the present failure intensity (Figure 3.1) will make additional information available for managerial judgments.

Scheduling involves determining when a program will be ready for release. When will the failure intensity objective be met as the result of the failure intensity decreasing due to repair actions? The date can be obtained from the completion date line in the tabular report in Figure 3.2. It is January 29, with a 75 percent confidence interval of January 16 to February 15. Figure 3.3 is a plot of the history of project completion date predictions.

The investigation of alternatives is a reopening of the question of trade-offs made during system engineering. The methods of Section 7.2.3 apply, with the

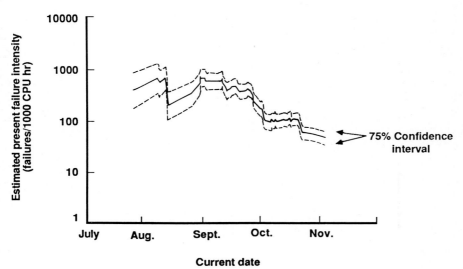

FIGURE 3.1
History of estimates of present failure intensity.

SOFTWARE RELIABILITY PREDICTION
BASIC MODEL
SYSTEM T1

BASED ON SAMPLE OF 136 TEST FAILURES
EXECUTION TIME IS   25.34 HR
FAILURE INTENSITY OBJECTIVE IS   .24e-02 FAILURES/CPU HR
CALENDAR TIME TO DATE IS   96 DAYS
PRESENT DATE   11/9/73

	CONF. LIMITS				MOST LIKELY	CONF. LIMITS			
	95%	90%	75%	50%		50%	75%	90%	95%
TOTAL FAILURES	139	139	140	141	142	144	145	147	149
FAILURE INTENSITIES (FAILURES/1000 CPU HR)									
INITIAL F.I.	953.0	988.1	1044	1098	1177	1258	1315	1376	1415
PRESENT F.I.	28.6	31.3	35.9	41.0	49.2	59.0	66.8	75.9	82.3

*** ADDITIONAL REQUIREMENTS TO MEET FAILURE INTENSITY OBJECTIVE ***

	95%	90%	75%	50%	MOST LIKELY	50%	75%	90%	95%
FAILURES	3	3	4	5	6	8	9	11	13
EXEC. TIME (CPU HR)	33.7	35.4	38.2	41.1	45.8	51.2	55.7	60.9	64.7
CAL. TIME (DAYS)	41.9	44.0	47.4	51.1	56.9	63.8	69.3	75.9	80.5
COMPLETION DATE	10874	11074	11674	12174	12974	20774	21574	22474	30474

FIGURE 3.2
Project status report.

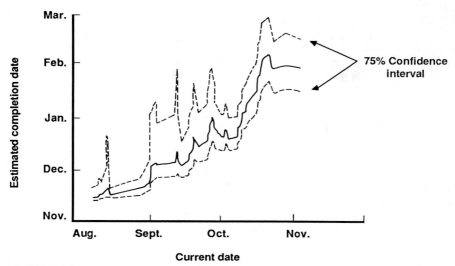

FIGURE 3.3
History of completion date predictions.

execution time parameters being estimated from failure data. An example has already been presented in Section 1.6.

3.3 MANAGEMENT OF OPERATIONAL PHASE

Failures continue to occur and new features (hence new code) continue to be added for virtually all software systems of any size during the operational phase. Usually the introduction of new features and fixes for discovered faults is handled by scheduled releases, perhaps on the order of months apart. In that case, we have a piecewise constant failure intensity. Each release has a failure intensity associated with it. The value of failure intensity changes when a new release is installed. In some situations, however, the incorporation of fault repairs occurs much more frequently, perhaps weekly or more often. Then the behavior of failure intensity looks more like that occurring during system test. Also, the manager of a particular operational installation may have discretion as to when a release with new features is installed. The failure intensity of the system exhibits a general stability about some value over the long term. However, there are many swings about this value. This behavior is generally due to the periodic incorporation of newly developed features that increase the failure intensity, followed by periods of fault removal, during which the failure intensity decreases.

In this situation, the manager is often faced with conflicting demands. He or she has some users and managers who are insisting that the new features that they value be introduced as soon as possible. On the other hand, there will be people who are running production programs, or other sorts of programs on which they're highly dependent, who insist that the reliability be as high as possible. They can't afford to have their functions interrupted. A good example of this would be the situation in a computation center that's also used by the payroll department. You may have some engineers who want changes made in the operating system to accommodate new things that they want to do. On the other hand, payroll is insistent that the operating system be as reliable as possible, since they have to get the checks out every week. The data processing manager is often caught in the middle of a tug of war between these conflicting interests. Suppose we let these interests slug it out and establish a level of service. This would be a failure intensity objective that is reasonable when all factors are taken into account. Once this has been established, the manager's job is vastly simplified, because he or she then controls the particular software system to maintain this particular level of service. This is done by freezing new feature changes to the system when the failure intensity level climbs above the objective. New features are introduced into the system only when the failure intensity is below the objective. The manager may use the amount of margin below the service objective as a guide to the size of the change to be permitted at any given time.

Figure 3.4 shows this sort of control, using data taken on a real operational software system. We have applied the basic execution time model, taking estimates of the parameters and then computing failure intensity at a number of points in time. The center line indicates the most likely value of the failure intensity estimate as a function of time. The dashed lines indicate the 75 percent confidence interval. A service objective of 0.05 failure/CPU hr is indicated. If the system is running 40 CPU hr/week, this means two failures per week. You will note periods of sharply rising failure intensity estimates where new features have been introduced into the system. You will also see the slow but steady drop during periods where the system is being debugged. Suppose we decide that we want to meet the service objective level with 75 percent confidence. Then every time the upper 75 percent confidence limit exceeds that level, we have a signal for stopping change to the system. And every time it drops below, we have an indication that now we can afford to make some changes. In actuality, you might first want to be sure that the failure intensity estimate drops an amount equal to the expected increment caused by the changes. Then the introduction of the changes would be allowed. In Chapter 7 we will consider how to estimate this increment.

3.4 EVALUATION OF SOFTWARE ENGINEERING TECHNOLOGIES

Many of you, either from reading the literature or attending conferences, have been bombarded by ideas, techniques, or tools for improving software productivity and software quality. Many ideas are presented with much fanfare but, unfortunately, not much solid evidence. We should be obtaining quantitative measures of the values of the techniques that are suggested. Obviously, improvement in productivity is one value. However, with today's emphasis on quality, improvement in reliability is very important also.

Software reliability measurements play an essential role in determining the value of new software engineering technologies, such as design methodologies,

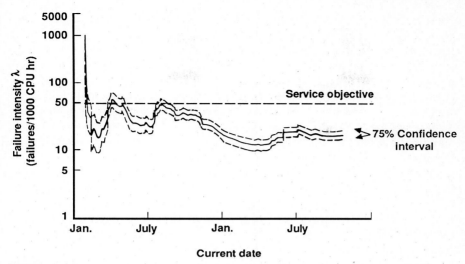

FIGURE 3.4
Failure intensity used for change management of operational software.

development tools, test methodologies, and inspections. Reliability and cost of a product are probably its two most important characteristics. Reliability is important in itself and it plays a major role in determining what the total cost of operating the product is. Thus it has a major effect on the customer. Any new software engineering technology should be considered at least in terms of its effects on reliability and cost.

The measurements of reliability in the operational phase of the software product are easily established by taking failure data. This should be done for software developed both with and without the new technology. The comparison should be made for releases occurring after the same amount of testing. An example of this might be to look at the technology of design inspections. We could collect data on failure intensities for releases occurring 100 CPU hr after the start of system test. We might obtain a result like "failure intensity is improved from 0.04 failure/CPU hr to 0.02 failure/CPU hr." In other words, we have cut in half the failure intensity experienced. This should be valuable in gaining an idea of the usefulness of design inspections. Suppose you compute the effect on operational phase cost of this failure intensity change. If you know the cost of the new technology, you now have a simple economic decision.

In doing the foregoing evaluation, it is important to establish confidence intervals. One must then see if the difference due to the new technology is significant in comparison with the uncertainty.

3.5 PLANNING FOR APPLICATION

Hopefully, the reader has at this point developed an interest in trying out the material presented in this book on an actual project. How should one go about it? It is probably best to start with some planning, even if the plans need to change later. Laner (1985) has pointed out that, "A plan is only a common base for changes. Everyone needs to know the plan so they can change easily." It may be desirable, if you have one or a few major customers for a product, to involve them in the planning of reliability objectives. The perceived quality of a product to a customer is usually higher when the customer has participated in the development in some way. In any case, the customer is likely to gain a better appreciation of the costs of quality and the trade-offs that can be made with other characteristics. Overall planning is presented in this chapter and implementation planning in Chapter 8. There are several steps involved in overall planning.

First, a thorough analysis should be made of project needs against possible applications. Possible applications are suggested in this chapter and Chapter 7. This is probably the most important step. It is important to establish the key problems engineers and managers are facing that might be helped with quantitative software reliability techniques. In making the analysis, one good approach is to poll managers and lead engineers on the project about their needs. Their responses will be most useful if they are made in the context of awareness of the possible applications. Another good method is to use a consultant who is knowledgeable in the possible applications to look at the situation in which the project finds itself. The needs should be scrutinized in the hard light of reality. Each activity that arises from a need will have a cost, and the expected benefit should justify that cost. You should be particularly skeptical of unplanned approaches like, "We'll collect data on everything and decide how to use it later."

Applications, such as those described in this chapter, are usually carried out in the context of a development project or in an operations organization. There are five roles that are commonly involved. Note that, depending on the organization concerned, a person may play one or more roles. The tasks usually associated with each role are presented in Table 3.2. Note that some tasks are divided between several roles. In practice, the details of this division must be clearly established.

The five roles are:

1. managers,
2. systems engineers,
3. quality assurance engineers,
4. test teams, and
5. debuggers.

The managers involved are the project or operations managers. They are most frequently at low or middle levels, but can be at relatively high levels for large projects. They are most commonly software managers, but large numbers are system managers, hardware managers, or data processing operations managers. Some of the functions they perform in which software reliability measurement can help are:

1. monitoring the status of projects that include software,
2. predicting the release date of software,

TABLE 3.2
**Common tasks and possible assignments to roles in application of
software reliability measurement.**

	Roles				
Tasks	Managers	Systems engineers	Quality assurance engineers	Test team	Debuggers
System analysis & tailoring procedures to project		X			
Data collection Failures		X	X	X	
Resource usage			X	X	X
Parameter determination			X		
Run programs		X	X		
System studies		X			
Supervision	X				

3. judging when to allow software changes in operational systems,

4. deciding on what software engineering technologies to apply to a project, and

5. deciding whether to accept delivery of subcontracted software.

Managers must have sufficient background to make intelligent decisions in these areas *in the context of their projects or organizations.* They must be able to evaluate the information generated for them to aid such decisions. Managers, aided by systems engineers, choose and revise schedules, budgets, system and component reliability goals, and development resource quantities. Finally, they must supervise the people performing the other roles in the information-gathering and decision-making processes.

The systems engineers have primary responsibility for thoroughly under- standing the nature of the system to which software reliability measurement is being applied. They adopt, adjust, and tune models and tailor processing rules and procedures to the system. They must define what a "failure" is for the system and continually interpret it as failure data is collected. They study trade-offs between reliability, resources, and schedules. They investigate different options for alloca- tion of reliability between components of the system. They may estimate opera- tional failure costs for the system. The results can be used for maintenance plan- ning and pricing of service based on the system. They can develop information on different software engineering technology options for managers to consider for use on a project. Systems engineers may estimate the impact of a proposed design change on reliability. In general, systems engineers perform studies and interpret results for management.

The quality assurance engineers are responsible for developing the data col- lection procedures that are needed to measure software reliability for the project or organization. They oversee the collection of data and process the data to yield useful results. They receive some direction from the systems engineers and provide some direction for the test team and the debuggers. They identify initial parameter values with the help of the systems engineers. They collect and process resource expenditure and failure data, operating various software reliability programs in doing so. They test the achieved failure intensity for programs that are being validated. Note that they do not have to have the depth of understanding of the system that the systems engineers do.

Test team members and debuggers have relatively simple roles. The test team member must identify when a failure has occurred and record the execution time of occurrence and other pertinent data. The debugger records when correction of the failure is complete. For both roles, resource expenditures must be recorded. The relative simplicity of these functions does *not* imply that the persons performing them need not have much understanding of software reliability measurement. On the contrary! The data that the test team members and debuggers collect is the ultimate source of the information generated as input to decision making. The quality of this data is vitally dependent on the intelligence and understanding that they apply in interpreting the real world conditions and complexities that they encounter. They must assist in planning the process of data collection. They need to be able to recognize problems and communicate them to quality assurance engineers, systems engineers, and managers.

Once the analysis of needs has been made, you should develop a list of all the tasks that must be done. The list will arise out of a consideration of the applications to be implemented and the characteristics of the project. It will often be a subset of the tasks listed in Table 3.2. Then assign responsibilities for the tasks. Table 3.2 will provide helpful guidance in making the assignments.

You then should consider what tools will be needed. Probably the most important tools will be the computer programs described in Chapter 5. Tool selection will depend on the tasks to be done, the form of the input failure data, and the form desired for the output of the programs. Certain additional tools may be required such as least squares fit programs for handling resource usage data. The programs must be acquired and tested on the machines on which they are to be used.

Training must be planned for project personnel. Most will need a broad view of what is happening so that they can intelligently help collect data and interpret the results of data analysis. Preferably, this involves educating the entire or a major portion of the project to at least the level given by Part I of this book. We have used a 1-day course for this. In addition, anyone who is *actively* involved in collecting and processing data and interpreting results needs further training that includes at least Part II as well. An additional 2-day course, supplemented by reading from this book and familiarization with program tools, can achieve this objective. There will also probably be some project-specific information to be conveyed such as system configuration, special conditions, and data collection and processing procedures. This might involve doing something as simple as providing a memorandum or a sheet of instructions.

Finally, it should be appreciated that projects can ultimately help themselves by helping to advance the general state of software reliability knowledge. Planning should take this need into account. Collection of failure data for both test and operational phases will permit models to be tested over a wide variety of projects. More resource usage data is needed, along with knowledge of the project characteristics that affect it. If special problems are encountered, they need to be clearly identified so that researchers can address them. Close liaison between a project and a researcher can often be particularly productive.

3.6 SUMMARY

Software reliability measurements can be used to guide managerial and engineering decisions on projects involving software. They can also guide customers and users of systems that have software components in purchasing and operating these systems. They can help focus software engineering research and its application by determining those methods that are most effective in enhancing reliability. Before applying software measurement techniques, a prospective user should analyze needs and plan for the most effective implementation.

TWO

PRACTICAL APPLICATION

This part of the book assumes that the reader has already considered the advantages to be gained in using software reliability measurement. It also assumes that the reader understands the basics of software reliability models, as covered in Part I. Consequently, we will proceed directly to the "how to do it." Specifically, the reader will learn how to conduct studies to support managerial and engineering decisions. In doing this, it is necessary to learn how to tailor the approach and procedures to the project involved. The reader will gain general familiarity with the features that we have found useful in software reliability estimation programs. Finally, implementation planning for application to actual projects will be discussed.

The models applied will be the basic and logarithmic Poisson execution time models. However, the techniques described can be applied to other models with appropriate modification. We will consider the most general case and assume that the software system being studied is part of a larger system that involves hardware and possibly other software components.

The steps to be taken in the process of practical application, in approximate logical order, may be outlined as follows:

1. failure definition (Section 4.1),
2. system description and decomposition (Section 4.2),
3. test run selection (Section 4.3),
4. determination of parameters for both execution time and calendar time components of the model (Chapter 5),
5. performance of studies and computation of useful quantities (Chapter 7).

Step 4 is very involved because of many practical considerations for different systems and circumstances; the latter are covered in Chapter 6. The implementation planning of the effort is discussed in Chapter 8.

In general, steps 1, 2, and 5 are principally performed by systems engineers. Step 3 is the province of the test planners. Step 4 is primarily organized and directed by quality assurance engineers. However, managers, test team members, and debuggers all get involved to varying degrees in the different steps. Thus a good overall understanding of all steps by all parties is highly desirable.

FOUR

SYSTEM DEFINITION

System definition is the first step in applying software reliability measurement and prediction. The definition of a system for reliability purposes has three principal aspects. The first of these is the specification of just what "failure" means for the system, and perhaps the categorizing and classification of failures. The second is the definition of the system configuration and its decomposition into components. The third is the interpretation of the system definition through test selection. In Chapter 5 we will discuss how the reliability parameters of the model(s) for the software part(s) of the system are established.

4.1 FAILURE DEFINITION

In this section we will determine what will be considered "failures" for the system whose reliability is being studied. The definition of failures sharpens the system definition by providing the perspective of what the system should *not* be doing. We will do this for various kinds of systems and circumstances. We will consider the classification and categorization of failures. Our discussions will apply to both software and hardware, unless otherwise noted.

Recall that a "failure" is a departure of operation from requirements, conveniently described for software in terms of the output state of a run. Note that "failure" implies operation of the system. A software failure must occur during execution of a program. Potential failures found by programmers as the result of design inspections, code reading, and other methods do not count.

A "fault" is a program defect that has caused or can potentially cause a failure (see Chapter 9 for a full discussion of failure and fault concepts). Some projects have included documentation faults in the count of program faults. This is generally *incorrect*, because documentation does not directly affect the execution of the program. Documentation faults may well lead to operator or user failures, as the operators and users will receive incorrect information on the use of the program. However, users and operators should be considered as a separate system component with regard to failures and reliability.

"Requirements," in hardware as well as software systems, are somewhat subject to interpretation. They may be restricted to being explicit or may involve implicit needs as well. For legal purposes, requirements should be explicit. Also, explicit requirements generally result in lower development costs. They reduce the number of failures due to misunderstanding of customer requirements. Hence you want to make the requirements as explicit as possible. However, the explicit requirements never include all the requirements important to the customer because neither the customer nor designer understanding of customer needs is perfect. Hence, it may be reasonable to allow for implicit requirements. In effect these are faults of omission in the explicit requirements.

The exact nature of "requirements" is further delimited and interpreted by considering what variations in operational behavior are tolerable. In establishing requirements, you provide a *positive* specification of a system. In defining failures, you supply a *negative* specification. You describe what the system must not do. Engineers using software reliability concepts have found that this negative specification is an extremely valuable system engineering technique. It adds another dimension of communication with the customer.

The definition of failure is really project-specific and must be established in consultation with the customer. For example, you may define "failure" as a program crash requiring interruption of processing and program reload. On the other hand, a very small variation in operation (for example, an incorrect title on a report) may be considered as a failure. Systems engineers will generally find themselves involved in establishing the definition of failure for their project. They will also interpret the definition during test. This fact makes it desirable for the systems engineers to work closely with the system test team, perhaps even as members. They are likely to receive some direct questions from the test team about whether a certain behavior is a failure or not. Does it violate system requirements? Members of the test team can't always resolve exactly what the requirements are, hence the systems engineers are looked on as the final arbiters. However, it is also recommended that systems engineers review at least some fraction, if not all, of the trouble reports. They need to determine if the test teams are interpreting requirements correctly.

The process of establishing the requirements for a system involves a consideration of the environment the system will operate in, that is, the operational profile. Although you may not completely quantify this profile, you usually have a general idea of the input states that will be presented to the program and their relative frequencies. This information should be used in test planning, so that testing represents expected operational use or so that differing operational profiles are compensated for in estimating reliability. It should also be used in design. The designer should consider the possibility of unexpected input states occurring due to failure in some other system. It is necessary to provide an appropriate response that minimizes performance degradation, data corruption, or undesirable outputs. Systems that respond rationally to nonfunctional input states are said to be *robust*.

When comparing the output state that results from a particular run with the required output state, note that extraneous output variables can occur. Some of these may be significant in that they cause data corruption that ultimately leads to failure. Variables that are members of the input states of future runs can be unintentionally changed, resulting in unexpected input states for which the program was not designed. Hence there can be a tendency for the program failure intensity to increase as it operates. There is a particular danger of missing unwanted extraneous output variables and hence missing failures when testing is automated. Normally in automated testing, checks are run for only a fixed set of output variables. If extraneous output variables cause data corruption during test, the tester may lose control of input state selection unless the system data is reinitialized before each run. Such loss of control is not necessarily a bad thing. It may realistically represent the operational environment.

There are at least two techniques for dealing with data corruption. First, a system may be made data corruption tolerant. This is done by designing the system to behave rationally for the additional input states that can result from data corruption. Second, data correction can be employed. Simple data correction schemes employ reinitialization of all or part of the data. Reinitialization can be periodic or generated in response to detection of a problem by an auditing program. Reinitialization can result in a failure or some loss of capability over the short term. However, the total set of reinitializations that occur in a consistent approach to countering data corruption has a positive average effect on reliability over the long haul. The results are automatically incorporated when you estimate reliability based on failure data. Sophisticated data correction involves techniques of redundancy (error correcting codes, checksums, etc.). Such corrections are expensive, but they can prevent failure and loss of capability.

4.1.1 Classification

Failures usually differ in their impact on the operations of an organization. Therefore, you may wish to classify them by severity and come up with the failure intensity or reliability for each classification. This can be particularly true for critical systems such as nuclear power plants, where serious failures may be rare but have an enormous impact. You must be careful not to confuse failure severity with the complexity or subtlety of the fault, and the difficulty and effort required to identify and correct it. The cost of repairing a fault is usually small with relation to the operational cost impact of the failure. Failure severity classification results in a slight effect on the data requirements, since you must determine and note the classification.

At least three classification criteria are in common use: cost impact, human life impact, and service impact. Cost impact is particularly applicable to any sys-

TABLE 4.1
Failure severity classification—service impact example

Class	Service impact
A	Basic service interruption
B	Basic service degradation
C	Inconvenience, correction not deferrable
D	Minor tolerable effects, correction deferrable

tem that is operating in the business world. What does this failure cost in terms of repair, recovery, lost business, and disruption? Human life impact is appropriate for nuclear power plants, air traffic control systems, military systems, or any kind of a system where safety or defense is paramount. Service impact might be appropriate for an interactive data processing service or a telephone switching system. It would probably be preferable to use the criterion of cost impact for systems such as this, but you may have situations where the cost impact is difficult to quantify. Also, service impact may be more relevant to the user. An example of service impact classification is given in Table 4.1 [Bardsley (1984)]. The most severe or Class A failure is one in which basic service is interrupted. An example of this would be the inability of a telephone switching system to process calls. Class B failures involve degradation of basic service. In the same system, excessive waits for dial tone would be considered Class B. Class C failures cause inconvenience, but not degradation of basic service. For example, suppose that an enhanced service such as call forwarding malfunctions. Class D failures are those that have effects that are minor and tolerable, such that repair can be deferred. An example would be slightly mistimed ringing.

An important question that must be answered with regard to any type of impact, but particularly cost impact, is "impact to whom?" A developer who delivers a product but has little continuing responsibility for it will have one viewpoint. A developer who will use the product to provide a service will have a different view. Experience indicates that it is generally best to establish your severity classes on the basis of orders of magnitude of the criterion being measured, since the measurement usually can't be that precise. Even when you use cost impact, many quantities such as lost business or good will are difficult to quantify and hence approximate.

In practice, severity classifications of failures are often made by more than one person. Consequently, to avoid variability in results, it is desirable to have objective (quantitative, if possible) rather than subjective classification criteria. Even if the judgment of the quantitative criteria is prone to error, their existence enhances the likelihood of understanding and reducing differences.

There appear to be three principal approaches to handling severity classifications in estimating reliability and related quantities:

1. Classify the failures and estimate failure intensity and other quantities separately for each class.

2. Classify the failures, but lump the data together, weighting the time intervals between failures of different classes according to the severity of the failure class.

3. Classify the failures, but ignore severity in estimating the overall failure intensity. Develop failure intensities for each failure class by multiplying the overall failure intensity by the proportion of failures occurring in each class.

The first method is the most precise approach, but it suffers from the problem of dividing the sample of failures into several groups. Consequently, the time required to build up a reasonable sample size for good statistical estimation is longer. It is much later during the project that you get the information that you want with reasonable accuracy. The second method does not have the drawback of the small sample sizes that the first does, but the resultant "weighted present failure intensity" has little physical significance. For example, what would be the meaning of "failure intensity weighted by dollars?" Consequently, reliability and other quantities computed from this failure intensity would also have little meaning. The third approach appears to be the best. It takes advantage of the largest possible sample size. The validity of this procedure depends on the proportion of failures in each class remaining constant with time. It appears that most projects have this experience. For example, on the Space Shuttle Ground System, failures were classified into critical, major, and minor severities [Misra (1983)]. There were only 4 critical failures. Hence, we will look at critical and major failures taken together. The proportions of these failures to total failures are 0.33, 0.36, 0.38, and 0.36 at the four "quarter" points of the data collected.

Example 4.1. Consider a system whose failures will be classified by cost impact. The overall failure intensity, determined by estimation from *all* failure data, is 0.1 failure/hr. The number of failures in each class is shown, and the class failure intensities have been calculated.

Class	Failure cost impact range	Failures observed	Class failure intensity (failure/hr)
A	>$100,000	10	0.01
B	$10,000–$100,000	20	0.02
C	$1,000–$10,000	40	0.04
D	<$1,000	30	0.03

Sometimes it is useful to work with *categories* of failures to focus attention on particular aspects of reliability. Also, many systems that would appear to have requirements of ultrahigh reliability actually have these requirements only for certain categories of failures. Failure categorization makes it possible for the reliability goals of these systems to be achieved at costs that are economic and with schedules that are reasonable.

One example of the foregoing is illustrated by the area of *software safety* [Leveson (1986)]. We consider a software safety failure to be any software system behavior that involves risk to human life, risk of injury, or risk of equipment damage. We can determine a "safety" failure intensity, based on failures of this category. In one sense, software safety imposes less stringent requirements than software reliability. We do not consider all departures from requirements as failures, but only those departures that have output states that are unacceptable because they are unsafe.

Another example is that of the electronic switching system for telecommunications. Ultrahigh reliability requirements are specified for the category of failures that would effectively prevent all communication in the area served by the system. The categories of failures that would delay some communication or interrupt some communication in progress are related to less stringent requirements.

4.1.2 Counting

Sometimes you must give careful consideration as to whether and how to count certain failures.

First, you may deliberately decide not to repair the fault causing a failure. The failure impact may not be severe. The cost of distributing the fix may be high. There can be schedule pressures. A *deliberate* decision not to fix a fault is really a redefinition of the system requirements. You are now saying that the associated failure(s) can be accepted. Hence, they should not be counted.

Second, people often ask how to handle repeated identical failures. By "identical" we mean that when the same run is made, the same deviation of program behavior from requirements occurs. These can occur at the same site or at different sites. They occur because the fault underlying the failure has not yet been repaired. Repeated failures primarily arise during the operational period. Since one principle of efficient testing is to avoid repeating the same input states, failure recurrences in test should be rare. The delay in correction can be the result of the normal delay involved in identifying and correcting the fault. Alternatively, it may result from a deliberate policy of holding the installation of repairs for a later software release.

The effect is illustrated in Figure 4.1. Instantaneous failure correction yields the failure intensity curve shown by the solid line. The dashed line indicates the actual failure intensity curve that results from delaying the installation of fault repairs until the next release. The failure intensity estimates that are made in the presence of such recurrences are accurate. However, they are higher than the failure intensity estimates that would be obtained if the failure recurrences were not counted. The offset of the curve to the right is due to the delay between failure identification and the associated fault correction. The discontinuous, stepped effect results from the grouping of fault corrections into releases. The horizontal length of the steps varies with the delay time for installation of the fault repairs.

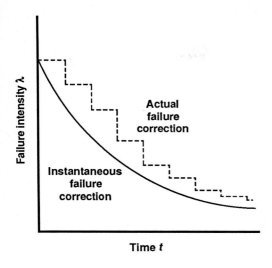

FIGURE 4.1
Actual failure intensity compared to instant repair failure intensity.

The vertical height of the steps varies with the number of fault repairs being delayed and their effect on failure intensity.

When we do not count recurrences, we obtain a failure intensity estimate based on unknown remaining faults (the solid line) rather than all remaining faults (the dashed line). This is a better indicator of progress and status if repair action is going on. An analogy would be a checking account. You are more interested in knowing the amount of uncommitted funds (balance minus outstanding checks) than the actual balance. Thus, if you are in the test phase, it is probably best *not* to count the recurrences. Since testing is in practice a fairly centralized and controlled activity, it is generally not difficult to recognize repeated failures of the same type.

On the other hand, in the operational phase, it probably is best to count *all* failures, including repetitions of the same type. Repairs are generally made back at the test site and batched and delivered in a new release. Therefore, the failure intensity will be constant for the duration of the present release. A release may remain in operation for a period of a few weeks to 2 or 3 years. It makes sense to measure what is actually being experienced over the life of the release. It is generally not practical to try to identify and "eliminate" repetitions anyway. Operational personnel generally have less system knowledge than testers and may not recognize the repetitions. Furthermore, the system is usually installed at multiple sites. Communication between sites is usually not good enough for most of the repetitions to be jointly identified. Finally, documentation of the failures is usually not thorough enough for the "elimination" to be done back at the central site with high confidence.

Suppose you want to obtain data during test on the effect of different operational profiles on failure intensity. Then the counting of repeated failures during test will be significant. Testing must be partitioned, and the selection of input states for each partition must be representative of the corresponding operational profile. Alternatively, the test and operational profiles could differ, if enough information were available to permit adjustment of the results.

Third, some failures may result from defects in the *tools* used to design and develop a system. This is not a common occurrence. It can occur when tools are developed in parallel with or only slightly ahead of the systems they are to be used on. Examples are compilers (for software) or computer-aided design/computer-aided manufacturing (CAD/CAM) systems (for hardware). Consider the final use of the tool for the product before delivery. If the tool is then expected to be reliable, do not count these failures when making estimates of failure intensity or reliability. If it will probably still be unreliable, you may wish to make your estimates twice. The tool-caused failures should be included in one and excluded in the other. You will then have a range of failure intensities or reliabilities. The extreme values will represent a reliable tool and an unreliable one.

Fourth, there may be some question of what a failure is in fault-tolerant systems. Fault-tolerant systems include design features (either hardware or software, but frequently software) that counter the effects of hardware or software faults. They are called *hardware-fault-tolerant* or *software-fault-tolerant* in accordance with the faults they defend against. In interpreting failure for a fault-tolerant system, note that we are always concerned with variations of *external* and not internal behavior from requirements. Thus, an internal component failure may occur but be counteracted by fault-tolerant features of the system. In that case, there is no system failure. On the other hand, a malfunction of a fault-tolerant feature that affects program output *will* represent a system failure. A fault-tolerant feature is a requirement that a system defend against certain faults. Another view of a fault-tolerant system is that it is a system that is insensitive to defects, physical defects if hardware-fault-tolerant and design defects if software-fault-tolerant. Note that this fault-tolerance is purchased at a cost. Usually fault-tolerant software contains extra code. Two common fault-tolerant techniques applied to software are audits and recovery blocks.[1] The extra code induces additional faults into the system that must be found and removed, increasing the development time and costs.

Data in a system can degrade with time as they are affected by failures. Once a fault causes a failure to occur, further deviations from required behavior on the same run due to data degradation *are not counted as additional failures*. Sometimes a fault acting during a run causes a data item that can be an input to other runs to be degraded. The effect is that each later run is made with a different input state than what it otherwise would have been. One frequent attribute of software-fault-tolerant systems is that they constrain what the outputs resulting from all or some of such "degraded" input states can be. Thus, such systems are, in effect, more tightly and broadly specified than are systems without such tolerance. Finally, failures identified during subsystem test should usually not be com-

---

[1]For a thorough survey of this topic, see Anderson and Lee (1981). A method of reliability modeling of recovery blocks is given in Laprie (1984).

bined with those found during system test. The exception would be if subsystem test is viewed as a stage in the evolution of the overall system. Then appropriate techniques for evolving systems are applied (Chapter 6).

4.2 SYSTEM CONFIGURATION

The next step in the practical application of software reliability modeling is to gain a full understanding of the hardware-software system whose reliability is to be studied. You need to know exactly what is included in the system. Ordinarily you will be concerned with the deliverable product, and not tools or "scaffolding" unless they are part of the delivered product. Sometimes tools introduce faults into a system (for example, a compiler). You may want to account for this phenomenon, as noted in Section 4.1.

The system should be divided into a set of components, each of whose reliabilities is known or is easy to estimate or measure. We then deal with the relationships between the reliabilities of components and the reliability of the system. One uses these relationships to predict or evaluate system reliabilities from component reliabilities and to allocate or budget a system's reliability to its components.

4.2.1 Components and Operational Modes

Division into components is often dependent on the physical nature of the system or the nature of previously collected data. For example, what sets of similar elements of known reliabilities exist? However, other important considerations are the need to track a particular component for project management purposes and the amount of effort required for data collection. Tracking many separate components can be expensive, although the cost probably increases somewhat less than linearly with the number of components. Further, an excessive number of components results in a division of the failure sample among the components to the extent that accuracy suffers. If a system is integrated in stages, the code included in each stage may suggest the best way to divide the system into components.

The determination of what constitutes a software component requires a clear understanding of the term "program" in the definition for software reliability. A *program* is defined as a set of complete machine instructions (operations with operands specified) that executes within a single computer and relates to the accomplishment of some major function. In any particular situation, the identification of the specific program(s) in question is important. Many other definitions such as "input state," "output state," "failure," and "execution time" are dependent on the delineation of exactly what is included in the program. For example, an application program may or may not be considered separately from the operating system with which it runs. That depends on the objectives and method of analysis adopted for the study being undertaken.

Some systems operate in several different *operational modes*, or characteristic operational profiles. The proportion of time spent in each mode varies from installation to installation, or as a function of time. Here it may be desirable to determine the reliability for each mode, so that the different overall reliabilities at different installations can be determined. An example of the foregoing is a telephone switching system, which may operate in either a business customer mode or a residential customer mode. This is illustrated in Figure 4.2, with operational mode A representing the business customer mode and operational mode B, the residential customer mode. Operational mode A has a wide variety of types of calls such as conference calls, credit card calls, and international calls. Operational mode B has fewer of the special calls, hence the operational profile shows more of a peak. At any given site, the proportions of time devoted to the two modes will vary. Further, a given installation may operate primarily in the business customer mode in the daytime and the residential customer mode at night.

It may be possible to determine the different reliabilities for different operational modes by analysis of the effect of operational profile on reliability. However, different operational modes are often associated with the employment of different parts of the system. For example, at one installation, only certain functions are implemented. At another, a set of different functions is implemented. If so, it will probably be easiest to use this information to divide the system into components and analyze the different operational modes as different combinations of components.

Note that when we have different operational modes, we do increase the data requirements. When we record data, we must record the operational mode in which the data are being taken. Alternatively, if operational modes are correlated with components, we must record component information with all our failure data.

Example 4.2. The program for a space vehicle has two operational modes, prelaunch checkout and flight. In the prelaunch checkout mode, the system uses a

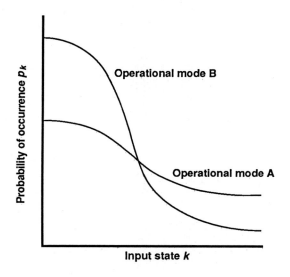

FIGURE 4.2
**System with different
operational modes.**

driver, a functional component that performs all the in-flight tasks, and a display module. The display module interfaces with the astronaut and tells him or her what is going on. The flight mode uses only the functional and display modules. Let us assume that the driver module is going to be developed by a separate contractor. How should you analyze this system?

There may be more than one answer to this situation, since much engineering judgment is involved. However, the solution that many people would choose is to define two subsystems. One subsystem would consist of the driver and the other, of the functional and display modules. You now have a situation where the prelaunch checkout mode uses subsystems A and B and the flight mode uses just subsystem B. Thus, you have things set up in such a way that you can apply combinatorics to get the appropriate reliabilities for each of these different operational modes. You also have the driver module isolated by itself. That is probably desirable since it is being delivered by a subcontractor. You will want to know the reliability of the code that this subcontractor is delivering to you. Furthermore, you will want the contractor to be collecting data on this module. It is probably better to have that data collected separately, with the subcontractor using his own procedures, than to try to have a mixed multicompany data collection system.

Why not three subsystems? This would be satisfactory, but the factor that pushes us to two subsystems is simply economy and simplicity of data collection. ∎

For the purposes of this chapter, we will assume that component reliabilities can be determined. Literature on the reliability of hardware components is extensive [see, for example, Shooman (1986)]. Reliability of software components was initially discussed in Chapter 2 and is developed in more detail in many other chapters.

Since we have divided the overall system into hardware and software components, it is necessary to be able to attribute a failure to a particular component. Although experience indicates that perhaps 95 percent or more of failures can be readily classified on examination as software or non-software (hardware, operator, etc.), occasionally the choice is not certain. Then we recommend that you classify a failure as non-software if it doesn't recur when you run the program with all software and known non-software inputs exactly the same.

Recall from Chapter 1 that "requirements" should be interpreted very broadly. There are cases where the requirements that must be met by a system include performance figures, such as response time for a specified load. Thus, system reliability depends not only on our conventional concept of reliability, based on failures of functionality, but also reliability based on failures of performance. For example, it may be required that response time under a certain load be less than 0.2 sec. Determination of the frequency the system fails to meet such an objective depends on an analysis of performance which may involve load studies and queueing theory. A convenient way to handle systems of this kind is to consider the performance requirement as a pseudocomponent. This component would have a "reliability" equal to the probability with which the performance requirement is met (see Figure 4.3). Note that this approach implicitly assumes that performance is independent of the "conventional reliability" of the system. This may not be precisely true, but it is adequate as an approximation. The performance analysis is

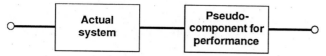

FIGURE 4.3
Use of pseudocomponent to represent performance.

then conducted separately and the probability that the performance requirement is met is calculated. This reliability of performance is combined with the conventional reliability of the actual system to determine the system reliability with performance requirements accounted for.

There are two basic types of system relationships considered in the combinatorial analysis of reliability, concurrent and sequential. *Concurrent* systems consist of components that function at the same time, for example, a computer and its operating system. *Sequential* systems consist of components that function at different times, with only one component functioning at a time. An example of a sequential system is a set of software routines that function as a subsystem, with only one routine executing at a time. Strictly speaking, software components executing on the same processor do so sequentially, although they may have the appearance of being concurrent. They can generally be analyzed as a concurrent system, however, as will be shown in Example 4.4. Further, it is often more convenient to do so.

4.2.2 Concurrent Systems

The most general approach to analyzing concurrent systems is known as Failure Modes and Effects Analysis [Lawson (1983)]. It provides for the consideration of different types of failures and usually involves a complex, computerized analysis. It generally proceeds forward from components to the system. It is often preceded by fault tree analysis. This analysis works backward from the system to the components, with the purpose of determining which combinations of component failures can lead to system failures. Fault tree analysis based on the existence or nonexistence of a specific fault is feasible but probably not practical for software. If you knew what the specific fault was, you would fix it. However, fault tree analysis at the module level can identify the modules that are most critical. These modules must operate properly for critical functions of the system to work. Hence they need the most attention. This may be of particular value for analysis of safety of critical systems. Note, however, that a given module can have a range of faults, some of which may be catastrophic in effect and others negligible. Thus we are only identifying criticality in an average sense.

If it is assumed that all failures are of the same type or if we conduct a separate analysis for each type, then the problem is considerably simplified. Further, many systems can be described in terms of certain types of combinations for which simple combinatoric rules hold. The simplest types of combinations are AND and OR.

AND-OR CONFIGURATION. The AND-OR configuration of components with independent failures represents many common situations and it is easy to analyze. Hence, it is one of the most useful. It consists solely of subconfigurations of two types, AND and OR. It can be identified from its event diagram or event expression. Sometimes the subconfigurations are called *series* or *parallel* systems, respectively, based on electrical circuit analogies to the event diagram.

The *event diagram* is an analog of an electrical circuit with each component represented as a switch (see Figure 4.4). If the component is functioning, the switch is viewed as being closed and if not functioning, as open. System success occurs if there is a continuous path through the configuration. An AND-OR configuration exists if each component appears only once on the diagram and the diagram is composed solely of components in parallel and in series.

The *event expression* is the Boolean expression that relates the event of system success to the events of component successes. An AND-OR configuration exists if the event expression contains only ANDs and ORs and component success events appear only once. For example, in the AND-OR configuration of Figure 4.4, we have the event expression $S = (A + B + C)DE$, where S represents system success.

An example of a configuration that is *not* AND-OR is a set of three components, any two of which must be functioning for the system to function.

The following combinatoric rules apply, based on the failures in Q_P different components being independent of each other.

1. If *all* Q_P components must function successfully for system success (AND condition), or the failure of any of the Q_P components will cause system failure, the system reliability R is given by

$$R = \prod_{k=1}^{Q_P} R_k,$$ (4.1)

where R_k are the component reliabilities.

2. If successful functioning of *any* of Q_P components will result in system suc-

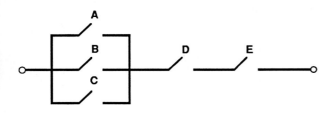

S = (A + B + C) DE   **S = System success**

FIGURE 4.4
Event diagram for AND-OR configuration.

cess (OR condition), or the failure of all Q_P components is required for system failure, the system reliability is given by

$$R = 1 - \prod_{k=1}^{Q_P} (1 - R_k) .$$ (4.2)

This formula is derived from the principle that the overall failure probability is equal to the product of the individual failure probabilities.

Suppose we have Q_P components with constant failure intensities. Their reliabilities are measured over a common calendar time period. Assume that *all* must function successfully for system success. Then the system failure intensity λ is given by

$$\lambda = \sum_{k=1}^{Q_P} \lambda_k ,$$ (4.3)

where λ_k are the component failure intensities.

K-OUT-OF-N STRUCTURE. Let us consider a system with Q_P components. At least Q_E components must operate for the system to work. Such a system is commonly said to have a *k-out-of-n structure* (in our notation, it is Q_E-out-of-Q_P). The reliability evaluation of such a system is, in general, difficult, except for the case where all the component reliabilities are the same.

If it is assumed that all components have the same reliability R_0 the system reliability R is given by

$$R = \sum_{k=Q_E}^{Q_P} \begin{bmatrix} Q_P \\ k \end{bmatrix} R_0^k (1 - R_0)^{Q_P - k} ,$$ (4.4)

which is a partial sum of the binomial probabilities.

Note that a Q_E-out-of-Q_P structure reduces to an AND structure when all the components must be operating (that is, $Q_E = Q_P$). Thus, the system reliability is obtained from Equation (4.4) for $Q_E = Q_P$ as

$$R = R_0^{Q_P} .$$ (4.5)

If at least one component must be operating (that is, $Q_E = 1$), the structure becomes an OR structure. The system reliability is obtained as

$$R = \sum_{k=1}^{Q_P} \begin{bmatrix} Q_P \\ k \end{bmatrix} R_0^k (1 - R_0)^{Q_P - k}$$

$$= 1 - (1 - R_0)^{Q_P} .$$ (4.6)

The last equation was obtained using the fact that the sum of all the binomial probabilities is one.

TIME BASIS. Implicit in the rules for combining reliabilities of software and hardware components is the assumption that the reliabilities are all based on the same calendar time period. Since hardware component reliabilities are commonly stated with respect to operating time, we actually want to work with reliabilities based on the same clock time period. After combination of component reliabilities, the resultant system reliability will be established in terms of the same clock time period.

Software reliabilities are usually stated in terms of periods of execution time. Hence, before combining software and hardware components, conversion of software reliabilities will be necessary. To do this, it will be most convenient to convert reliability R of each software component to failure intensity. We will use the notation λ_τ to distinguish this failure intensity as being with respect to execution time. We use the equation

$$\lambda_\tau = -\frac{1}{\tau} \ln R, \qquad (4.7)$$

obtained from Equation (2.13), where τ is the execution time period for which the reliability was specified. Note that combinatoric analyses are generally done for some specified state of the software (for example, at release to the field). Hence reliability change is not occurring, and Equation (4.7) is valid. This does not rule out the possibility of looking at the combination at several different points in time.

Let ρ_C be the average utilization by the program of the machine it runs on. Assume that this average utilization, taken over a period comparable to the failure intervals, does not vary significantly. Such is often the case. Then the failure intensity with respect to clock time λ_t is given by

$$\lambda_t = \rho_C \lambda_\tau. \qquad (4.8)$$

Note that the failure intensity with respect to clock time is always the same or lower than that with respect to execution time, since $\rho_C \leq 1$. Utilization can be measured by recording processor clock (CPU) time expended in a given clock time interval. Many operating systems have the capability to do this readily. If the computer is running continuously, then Equation (4.8) also yields calendar time.

Once the failure intensities with respect to the "reference" period of clock time are established for all components, we can compute the corresponding reliabilities. We have

$$R = \exp(-\lambda_t t). \qquad (4.9)$$

Note that the system failure intensity λ_t for an AND combination of Q_P software components, using Equations (4.3) and (4.8), is

$$\lambda_t = \sum_{k=1}^{Q_P} \rho_{C_k} \lambda_{\tau_k}. \qquad (4.10)$$

The quantity ρ_{C_k} is the utilization of the machine on which it runs by software component k. The quantity λ_{τ_k} is the failure intensity with respect to execution time of the same component.

Adjustment of failure intensities and hence reliabilities when a program is moved to a different machine is readily done. Suppose a program is moved from computer 1 of average instruction execution rate r_1 to computer 2 of average instruction execution rate r_2. Then the failure intensity λ_2 on computer 2 is given by

$$\lambda_2 = \frac{r_2}{r_1}\lambda_1 ,\qquad (4.11)$$

where λ_1 is the failure intensity on computer 1.

> **Example 4.3.** This example will illustrate some of the foregoing points. Consider a system made up of two software components, 1 and 2, as illustrated in the event diagram of Figure 4.5. Both operate concurrently, and both must operate without failure for the system to operate without failure. Assume that all hardware components have reliability 1. The components have reliabilities, respectively, of 0.670 and 0.527 for a period of 8 hr of execution time. It will be seen from Equation (4.7) that these correspond to failure intensities of 5 failures/100 CPU hr and 8 failures/100 CPU hr, respectively.
>
> Consider the case where both software components run on the same machine, each taking up half the execution time. Then, using Equation (4.8), we get failure intensities with respect to clock time of 2.5 failures/100 hr and 4 failures/100 hr, respectively. The corresponding reliabilities for 8 hr of clock time are 0.819 and 0.726. System reliability for this period is thus 0.595. Alternatively, you can add the failure intensities with respect to clock time from both components, yielding 6.5 failures/100 hrs, and use Equation (4.9) to obtain 0.595 for system reliability. Note from Equation (4.10) that the system failure intensity with respect to clock time can also be obtained directly. Each component failure intensity is weighted by the average utilization of the machine by that component. Here we obtain $0.5(0.05 + 0.08) = 0.065$ failure/hr as the system failure intensity with respect to clock time.
>
> If software components run on *different* machines, we have a different situation. Assume that both machines have the same average instruction execution rate and are fully utilized by these components. Each software component experiences a greater amount of execution time and thus more failures in the same amount of clock time. Thus, failure intensities in clock time are now higher: 5 failures/100 hr and 8 failures/100 hr. Corresponding reliabilities are, for 8 hr of clock time, 0.670 and 0.527, and system reliability is 0.353. ∎

INDEPENDENCE OF SOFTWARE FAILURES IN REDUNDANT PROGRAMS.
The rules for combination of AND-OR and k-out-of-n component structures assume that failures in the different components are independent of each other. This means that there can be no failures that result from the same cause. [For a survey of the topic of common-cause failures, see Watson (1981).] Reliability is often increased in hardware systems by providing redundant components. It is hence

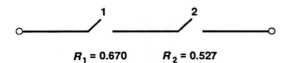

1   2

$R_1 = 0.670$ $R_2 = 0.527$

FIGURE 4.5
Event diagram for system with two AND software components.

tempting to apply the same principle to software, but usually *it does not work*. The causes of failure associated with physically individual but functionally identical hardware components are frequently independent of each other. This is not true for software, because copies of a program are identical not only with respect to function but also with respect to the faults that can cause failures.

There is a possible exception. If programs are developed in separate versions by separate teams, following the same requirements, there is some possibility that many of the faults introduced may be independent of each other. Experiments in multiversion programming [for example, Knight and Leveson (1986)] seem to indicate that failures in different versions are clearly not completely independent of each other. They do not appear to all be common either, however. The amount of correlation remains to be determined. Hence multiversion programming may well improve the reliability level, but not to the extent totally independent components would. Having totally independent components may be cost effective for critical modules of systems with ultrahigh reliability requirements, such as nuclear power reactors, air traffic control, and space missions. Typical failure intensity requirements for such systems are in the range of 10^{-7} to 10^{-9} failure/CPU hr.

CASE STUDY 4.1
HANDLING REDUNDANT SOFTWARE
IN SYSTEM RELIABILITY CALCULATIONS

Suppose a chain of department stores wants to set up a computerized transaction processing system. They set a reliability objective of 0.90 for an 8-hr shift. Several different system configurations are being considered. We will take a look at each of these and in the process determine the reliability required of the transaction processor software to meet the overall reliability objective. The cost of each alternative will also be considered. In addition, several of the proposed system configurations illustrate some important points about "redundant" software.

Each configuration is composed of a front-end processor (FEP) whose job is to assign incoming transactions to one or more transaction processors (TP). The load is such that the utilization of one TP is 0.4. FEP utilization is 1. The FEP has an 8-hr reliability of $R_{fh} = 0.99$ for its hardware and $R_{fs} = 0.95$ for its software. The 8-hr reliability of the TP hardware is $R_{th} = 0.98$. These reliabilities can be related to failure intensities by using Equation (4.10). Table 4.2 summarizes the reliabilities and failure intensities for these components.

The reliability of the TP software is to be determined. The cost of developing this software is shown in Figure 4.6 as a function of the failure intensity (expressed in terms of execution time). As is seen, the cost increases as the delivered failure intensity decreases. The transaction processor hardware costs $250,000 per unit.

In computing costs, we will ignore constant factors and calculate software development cost plus any hardware costs beyond a single transaction processor

TABLE 4.2
Summary of component reliabilities

Component	8-hr reliability	Failure intensity (failures/hr)
FEP hardware (fh)	0.99	0.00126
FEP software (fs)	0.95	0.00641
TP hardware (th)	0.98	0.00253

system. For the purposes of this study each of the following configurations is said to have failed if the processing of any transaction is incorrect or made impossible for any reason.

ALTERNATIVE A

The first alternative is a single transaction processor being fed by a front-end processor, as shown in Figure 4.7(a). In this situation, the event diagram is as shown in Figure 4.8(a), where we have denoted the unknown TP software reliability as R_x. Applying the formula for AND events, Equation (4.1), we have for the system reliability (0.99) (0.95) (0.98) R_x = 0.922 R_x. Setting this equal to our objective and solving for R_x results in R_x = 0.976. Since it is known that the utilization of the TP will be 0.4, an 8 hr shift corresponds to 3.2 hr of execution time. Using Equation (4.9), we can write

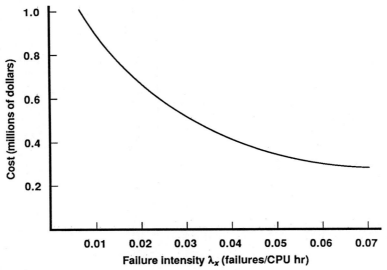

FIGURE 4.6
TP software development cost as a function of failure intensity.

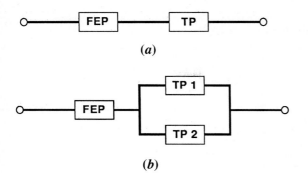

(a)

(b)

FIGURE 4.7
Different system configura-tions. (*a*) Alternative A. (*b*) Alternatives B, C, and D.

$$R_x = \exp(- 3.2\lambda_x),$$ (4.12)

where λ_x is the failure intensity of the TP software expressed in execution time. Solving, $\lambda_x = 0.0076$ failure/CPU hr. The cost of developing this software, from Figure 4.6, is about \$940,000. This is also the "total" cost.

ALTERNATIVE B

The second alternative is an attempt to save some of the TP software development costs. We try to trade off a lower component reliability (higher failure intensity) with the greater expense of added redundancy. The proposed processor configura-tion is shown in Figure 4.7(b). The front-end processor assigns every incoming transaction to each processor, that is, each transaction will get processed twice. Successful system operation occurs if either transaction processor correctly processes the transaction. The event diagram for this case is shown in Figure 4.8(b). It is not difficult to apply our AND-OR rules to determine the overall sys-tem reliability, that is, $(0.99)(0.95) \{ - [1 - (0.98)R_x]^2\}$. Setting this equal to the system reliability objective and solving, $R_x = 0.809$. This translates into a failure intensity of $\lambda_x = 0.0662$ failure/CPU hr. This latter figure is almost 10 times less stringent than that required by the first alternative. The software development cost is about \$290,000. An additional cost of \$250,000 will be incurred because of the second TP, giving a very attractive total cost of \$540,000. *But this is wrong!* We have fallen into a common trap, as we shall see below.

A failure in one TP software component would also occur in the other since they are identical. Both copies contain identical faults. Since the software compo-nents are not independent of each other in regard to failure behavior, software re-dundancy does not improve reliability. *This is a commonly occurring and very im-portant point for software components.*

In hardware reliability theory where multiple components fail due to a single cause, a *common-cause* failure is said to have occurred. This can be easily ex-tended to software components. A straightforward method to incorporate these common-cause failures in our analysis is given in Dhillon (1983). Define γ as the fraction of component failures that are common-cause. Each component's failure

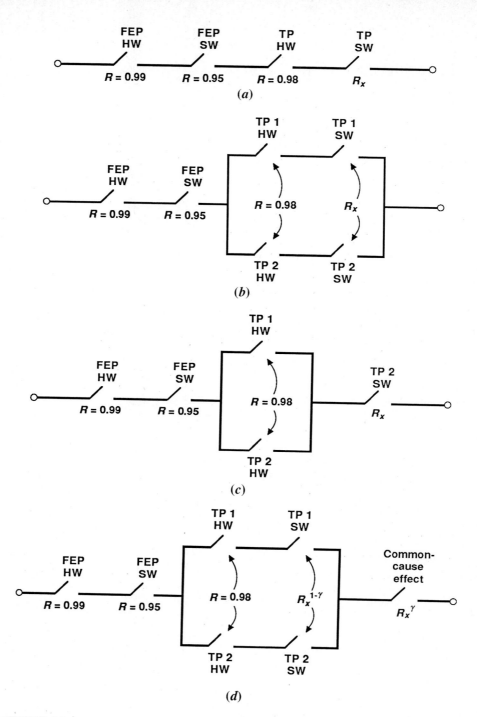

FIGURE 4.8
Event diagrams. (*a*) **Alternative A.** (*b*) **Alternative B.** (*c*) **Alternative B (corrected).** (*d*) **Alternative C.**

96

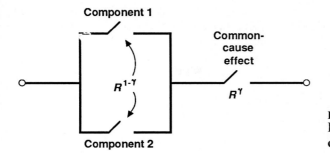

FIGURE 4.9
Event diagram for
common-cause model.

intensity λ is the sum of an independent failure intensity $(1 - \gamma)\lambda$ and a common-cause failure intensity $\gamma\lambda$.

Suppose two components subject to common-cause failures are in a parallel configuration. The event diagram is shown in Figure 4.9. Our model will yield as the system reliability $[1 - (1 - R^{1-\gamma})^2] R^{\gamma}$. The overall effect of common-cause failures is displayed in Figure 4.10. Shown in this figure is the percent increase in reliability achieved using two independently developed components instead of a single component as a function of the fraction of common-cause failures. The reliability of a single component is given by R. Thus, when all failures are common-cause, $\gamma = 1$ and there is no improvement in system reliability. When there are no common-cause failures, $\gamma = 0$ and maximum improvement $[100(1 - R)$ percent$]$ is achieved.

Now, let us apply the common-cause model to the configuration of Figure 4.7(b). Here $\gamma = 1$, that is, all TP software failures are common-cause and the model for the TP software degenerates into a single component with reliability R_x. The correct event diagram is shown in Figure 4.8(c). Solving for R_x results in a value of 0.957 (or $\lambda_x = 0.0137$ failure/CPU hr), which represents some but not

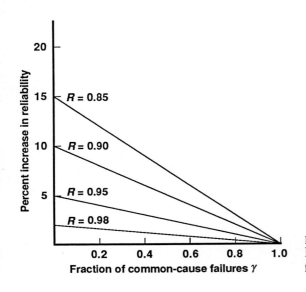

FIGURE 4.10
Effect of common-cause
failures on reliability.

the significant reduction in reliability requirement hoped for. The software development cost now is $780,000 as opposed to the incorrect value of $290,000. Total cost is $1,030,000.

ALTERNATIVE C

The store's third approach, one that is potentially expensive, is to have two completely separate development teams produce two independent versions of the TP software. We assume that each copy of the software has attained the same reliability. The system operates just like the previous alternative, that is, a front-end processor is used to assign every incoming transaction to *each* processor. System success is obtained if either transaction processor correctly processes the transaction. The event diagram using our common-cause model is shown in Figure 4.8(d). The system reliability is $(0.99)(0.95)\{1 - [1 - (0.98)R_x^{1-\gamma}]^2\}R_x^\gamma$. If there are no common-cause failures then $\gamma = 0$ and R_x becomes 0.809 ($\lambda_x = 0.0662$ failure/CPU hr). This is, of course, the value of R_x we determined in our original analysis of alternative B. However, chances are that γ is relatively large, that is, similar errors are made by each team. If $\gamma = 0.5$, then $R_x = 0.922$ ($\lambda_x = 0.0254$ failure/CPU hr).

If $\gamma = 0$ the development cost for the TP software will be about $580,000 ($290,000 for each copy of the software). Similarly, if $\gamma = 0.5$ the software development cost will be about $1,150,000. As with alternative B an additional $250,000 will be incurred for the second unit of TP hardware. Total cost will be $830,000 or $1,400,000, depending on the value of γ.

ALTERNATIVE D

The final and most difficult alternative to analyze is a dual transaction processor with the front-end processor assigning transactions to the *next* transaction processor that becomes available. Each transaction is only processed once. This type of parallel system is sometimes referred to as a *shared load* system [Kapur and Lamberson (1977)]. In normal operation, each TP equally shares the load. Upon failure of the hardware component of one TP, the surviving processor must sustain an increased load, which can be limited by the capacity of the processor. Thus, the failure intensity, measured in clock time, of the software component of the surviving processor will increase. The failure intensity expressed in execution time will remain unaltered.

A system transition diagram is shown in Figure 4.11. Three states can be identified. State S represents a fully operational system, that is, both TPs are functioning. State P represents a partially operational system, that is, the hardware component of one TP has failed. State F represents the failed system. The indicated failure intensities represent the rates at which the system goes from one state to another.

We need to make two assumptions before giving an expression for system reliability. These are:

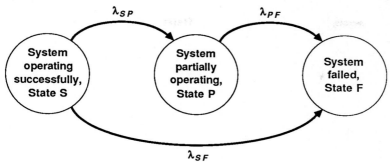

FIGURE 4.11
System transition diagram.

1. System failures are statistically independent.
2. Both TP hardware components cannot fail simultaneously.

Given these assumptions it can be shown [Dhillon (1983)] that the system reliability, defined as the probability of being in state S or P, is given by

$$R(t) = \exp[-(\lambda_{SP} + \lambda_{SF})t]$$

$$+ \frac{\lambda_{SP}}{\lambda_{SP} + \lambda_{SF} - \lambda_{PF}} \left\{ \exp(-\lambda_{PF}t) - \exp[-(\lambda_{SP} + \lambda_{SF})t] \right\}. \quad (4.13)$$

What remains to be done is to determine the values of λ_{SP}, λ_{SF}, and λ_{PF}. The system goes from operating normally to operating partially if one TP hardware component fails but not both. The transition diagram for the transition from state S to state P is shown in Figure 4.12(a). Thus, $\lambda_{SP} = 2\lambda_{th}$. The system goes from normal operation to a failed state if the FEP hardware or software fails or if either TP software component fails. The transition diagram for the transition from state S to state F is shown in Figure 4.12(b). Let ρ_{C_0} be the utilization of a TP when the system is operating normally. Then, from Equation (4.8), the failure intensity of the TP software expressed in calendar time is $\rho_{C_0}\lambda_x$. Thus, $\lambda_{SF} = \lambda_{fh} + \lambda_{fs} + 2\rho_{C_0}\lambda_x$. Finally, the system goes from operating partially to a failed state if the FEP hardware or software fails, the TP software fails, or the remaining unit of TP hardware fails. The transition diagram for the transition from state P to state F is shown in Figure 4.12(c). Let ρ_{C_1} be the utilization of the TP hardware when only one processor is operating. Then, $\lambda_{PF} = \lambda_{fh} + \lambda_{fs} + \lambda_{th} + \rho_{C_1}\lambda_x$.

The system reliability for an 8-hr shift can be found by substituting the values of λ_{SP}, λ_{SF}, and λ_{PF} into $R(t)$ with $t = 8$. Carrying this out and making use of relationships such as $\exp(-8\lambda_{th}) = R_{th}$ results in

$$R_{th}^2 R_{fh} R_{fs} R_x^2 + \frac{2\lambda_{th} R_{th} R_{ts} R_{fh}}{\lambda_{th} + (2\rho_{C_0} - \rho_{C_1})\lambda_x} \left[R_x^{\frac{\rho_{C_1}}{\rho_{C_0}}} - R_{th} R_x^2 \right]. \quad (4.14)$$

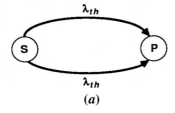

(a)

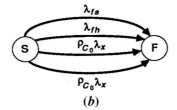

(b)

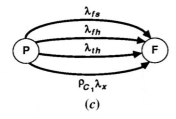

(c)

FIGURE 4.12
Transition diagrams for alternative D. (a)
Transition from state S to state P. (b) Transition
from state S to state F. (c) Transition from state
P to state F.

Since ρ_{C_1} is the utilization for a single processor doing the work that was previously done by two processors, its value is given by min $(2\rho_{C_0}, 1)$. Note that ρ_{C_1} cannot exceed 1. Thus, if $\rho_{C_0} = 0.6$ and one TP fails, the remaining processor will be worked to the limit. In fact, the responsiveness of the system to the user may be intolerable at this point. This may be outweighed by the fact that system availability is more critical.

In our store example $\rho_{C_0} = 0.2$ and $\rho_{C_1} = 0.4$. If the system is operating partially, it is equivalent to alternative A. Solving for the TP software reliability results in $R_x = 0.978$. This value is actually somewhat larger than R_x for alternative A! It seems we have wasted a TP for nothing. Actually, since the utilization of each processor is half of the utilization in alternative A, the required failure intensity with respect to execution time for the TP software is correspondingly larger. In fact, it is $\lambda_x = 0.0139$ failure/CPU hr. The software development cost will be about \$770,000. Total cost will be \$1,020,000.

SUMMARY

Several examples were presented that illustrated the important concepts of common-cause failures and shared-load systems. The development of system reliability figures when these conditions are present was also shown. For our specific examples the results are summarized in Table 4.3. These should not be taken to endorse any particular configuration over another. The value of γ may be difficult to

TABLE 4.3
Summary of results for each alternative

Alternative	Failure intensity (failures/CPU hr)	Cost (millions of dollars)
A	0.0076	0.94
B	0.0137	1.03
C ($\gamma = 0$)	0.0662	0.83
C ($\gamma = 0.5$)	0.0254	1.40
D	0.0139	1.02

quantify a priori. If it is only moderately large, then alternative C will cost a great deal in comparison to the other alternatives. Other factors, such as the cost of of slow response time to the users of the system, were not considered. If this is a major factor, then alternative D has a distinct advantage.

4.2.3 Sequential Systems

We will consider the case of a series sequential system, illustrated in Figure 4.13. The satisfactory operation of the system is dependent on the satisfactory functioning of each component *when it is active*. This type of system is characteristic of most software. It does not include the case of software with recovery features. In such software, one routine can cause recovery from a failure experienced in another routine and hence effectively cancel it out.

Littlewood (1976) has developed a model for such systems. The model assumes that the system consists of Q_P components among which control is switched randomly according to transition probabilities that depend only on the two components involved. Typically a component is a segment or branch of a program. Thus, it would consist of a sequence of instructions without branches or loops. The branching and looping structure is expressed by the transition probabilities. Failures for the kth component are assumed to occur in accordance with a Poisson process with failure intensity λ_k. If the λ_k are small, then the system failure process is Poisson with failure intensity λ given by

$$\lambda = \frac{\displaystyle\sum_{k=1}^{Q_P} \sum_{l=1}^{Q_P} \rho_k p_{kl} \mu_{kl} \lambda_k}{\displaystyle\sum_{k=1}^{Q_P} \sum_{l=1}^{Q_P} \rho_k p_{kl} \mu_{kl}}. \tag{4.15}$$

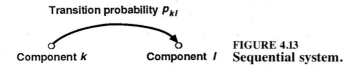

Transition probability p_{kl}

Component k   **Component l**

FIGURE 4.13
Sequential system.

The transition probability from component k to component l is given by p_{kl}. The quantity μ_{kl} is the mean duration (sojourn time) spent in component k before switching to component l. Note that no assumption regarding the probability distribution of the sojourn times has to be made. The ρ_k are the probabilities of control residing in each component. They are given by

$$\rho_k = \sum_{l=1}^{Q_P} \rho_l p_{lk} ,$$ (4.16)

where the sum of all ρ_k must be 1.

Let us try to understand the two foregoing equations conceptually. Note that Equation (4.16) states that the probability of control residing in a target component is equal to the sum of the probabilities of control residing in each component *and* switching to the target component. Now consider Equation (4.15). Note in the numerator that $\mu_{kl}\lambda_k$ represents the average number of failures experienced in component k in the case where there is a transition to component l. Now $\rho_k p_{kl}$ is the probability of control residing in component k and switching to component l. Thus for each term in the numerator we have the number of failures experienced in a particular situation multiplied by the probability of being in that situation. Since the double sum covers all possible situations, the numerator is the total number of failures experienced. Each term of the denominator represents the average time spent in component k when a switch to component l occurs, multiplied by the probability of being in that situation. Thus the denominator represents total time elapsed. Note that the transition between components is assumed to be instantaneous. Hence Equation (4.15) yields total failures divided by total time, or overall failure intensity.

It is possible to generalize Equation (4.15) to handle the possibility of failures occurring during transition [Littlewood (1979)]. This would be done by replacing $\mu_{kl}\lambda_k$ in the numerator by $\mu_{kl}\lambda_k + q_{kl}$, where q_{kl} is the probability of a failure occurring during the transition from component k to component l. Usually failures during transition are erroneous transitions. You should not also count these situations as transitions in their own right.

The application of sequential system formulas requires knowledge of transition probabilities p_{kl}, sojourn times μ_{kl}, and component failure intensities λ_k. Transition probabilities and sojourn times can be determined most accurately by instrumenting the program to measure them. Many software development environments have execution trace facilities that could be modified to collect the foregoing statistics. Before execution, you would have to predict these quantities from knowledge of software system functions (the expected operational profile) and software system architecture. Component failure intensities can be determined by estimation if the program can be executed. To do this, failures and execution times would have to be separated by component. Prior to execution, component failure intensities would be predicted from component characteristics, especially size.

It will be seen that practical measurement and analysis problems increase rapidly with the number of components involved. Hence, the formulas given are most useful *in practice* when the number of components is small. However, they are a valuable conceptual tool independent of the number of components.

Note that when two software components execute on the same processor, a sequential configuration exists. However, this type of analysis is complex. The combination can generally be analyzed as a concurrent configuration, provided that the "dwell time" in each component is small compared to the interval between failures. Here the transfer of control is so rapid that it appears as if the components were operating concurrently. However, each component is operating in a slowed-down fashion since it is only operating part of the time. Analysis as a concurrent configuration is much simpler. This is illustrated by the following example, a sequential configuration analysis of the system presented in Example 4.3.

> **Example 4.4.** The system of Example 4.3 may be viewed as consisting of components 1 and 2. Each component has a transition probability of 0.5 to itself and 0.5 to the other component. The state transition diagram is shown in Figure 4.14. The steady state probabilities of execution in the components are given by, using Equation (4.16):
>
> $$\rho_1 = \rho_1 p_{11} + \rho_2 p_{21} = 0.5(\rho_1 + \rho_2) \,, \tag{4.17}$$
>
> $$\rho_2 = \rho_1 p_{12} + \rho_2 p_{22} = 0.5(\rho_1 + \rho_2) \,. \tag{4.18}$$
>
> Thus, since $\rho_1 + \rho_2 = 1$,
>
> $$\rho_1 = \rho_2 = 0.5 \,. \tag{4.19}$$
>
> In Example 4.3 the overall time spent in the two components is equal. For simplicity we will assume that this results from dwell times in each component that are equal and independent of the component from which control is transferred. Then Equation (4.15) becomes
>
> $$\lambda = \frac{\rho_1 p_{11} \lambda_1 + \rho_1 p_{12} \lambda_1 + \rho_2 p_{21} \lambda_2 + \rho_2 p_{22} \lambda_2}{\rho_1 p_{11} + \rho_1 p_{12} + \rho_2 p_{21} + \rho_2 p_{22}}$$
>
> $$= \frac{\lambda_1 + \lambda_2}{2} \,. \tag{4.20}$$
>
> Note that this is the same result as obtained in Example 4.3. ∎

4.2.4 Simplified Approach for Distributed Systems

The concurrent system combinatoric approach represents a straightforward approach for handling distributed computing systems. However, it has certain practical disadvantages. First, data collection is complicated. Failure data must be kept separated by component and the failure intensity of each component must be tracked separately. Second, execution times must be measured on each machine and referred to a common base. Third, the process of setting failure intensity objectives is made more difficult, since the overall system failure intensity objective

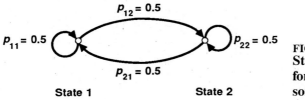

FIGURE 4.14
**State transition diagram
for system with two
software components.**

must be allocated among the components. Finally, computation of calendar time to overall failure intensity objective for the system is complicated, since each component must be considered and then results for the overall system derived.

A simplified approach is possible if:

1. It is only desired to track system and not component reliability behavior.
2. The system fails if any software component fails.
3. The ratios of execution time intervals between each component and an arbitrarily chosen reference component are constant, for intervals of size comparable to the failure intervals.

Constant ratios of execution times among software components imply that the various processors in the system work together in some approximately synchronous manner.

This approach permits the software components to be considered as *one* software system. A failure in any component is also a system failure, hence the union of the sets of component failures is identical with the set of system failures. Even though the components may be executing on different machines with different average instruction execution rates, they are running together synchronously (on the average). You measure failures with respect to the execution time of a reference component, and all failure intervals are determined on that basis. The total system execution time will be proportional to that of the reference component. The foregoing does *not* imply that the hardware components can be lumped together.

Consider the example of the bank data network given in Case Study 1.1. It is likely that the firm hired by the bank will use different processors for the front-end processor and system controller. This, coupled with the fact that the functions and hence the software differ between processors, would lead to the disadvantages described previously if the full combinatoric approach were taken.

Instead, we will take the simplified approach. Let the average instruction execution rates of the front-end processor and system controller be r_F and r_S, respectively. The utilization of the front-end processor is ρ_{C_F} and that of the system controller is ρ_{C_S}. In a given period of clock time the execution time τ_S of the system controller is related to the execution time τ_F of the front-end processor by

$$\tau_S = \frac{\rho_{C_S}}{\rho_{C_F}} \tau_F . \tag{4.21}$$

We will consider the front-end processor as the reference. An execution time τ_S on the system controller is equivalent to an execution time of $(r_S/r_F)\tau_S$ on the front-end processor. Hence the execution time of the system controller referred to the front-end processor, using Equation (4.21), is $(r_S/r_F)(\rho_{C_S}/\rho_{C_F})\tau_F$. Then the total execution time, referred to the front-end processor, is

$$\tau_F \left[1 + \frac{r_S}{r_F} \frac{\rho_{C_S}}{\rho_{C_F}} \right].$$

Note that the factor in parentheses can be determined from measurements of r_F, r_S, ρ_{C_S}, and ρ_{C_F} made at one time. For our example, this factor is taken to be 3.63. Table 4.4 shows the first few operating execution times of the front-end processor between software failures (which may occur anywhere) and the resulting system failure intervals.

In some complex systems, it may be impractical to determine all the execution time ratios among the various software components. There may be another measure that is representative of the total software workload of the system. The measure should be proportional to the sum of all instructions executed in all system processors. The average proportionality factor, when averaged over a time comparable to the failure intervals, should be approximately constant. Then this measure can be used as an approximation to execution time. One example of such a measure is the number of scheduling messages flowing in the distributed system. The scheduling messages represent the assignment of tasks to processors. If the average task size in instructions, where the average is taken over a time comparable to a failure interval, is constant, then the measure approximates execution time.

4.2.5 Standby Redundant Systems

Redundant systems, such as OR systems discussed in Section 4.2.2, represent one approach to improving system reliability. A standby redundant system is another

TABLE 4.4
Failure data for distributed system example

Failure number	Front-end processor execution time	System failure interval[1]
1	148	537
2	1	4
3	1631	5920
4	1422	5162
⋮	⋮	⋮

[1]System failure time = 3.63 × FEP execution time

method that is frequently used to achieve high reliability. Spare parts and back-up systems are examples of standby redundancy.

Consider a system that has Q_P components, where only one component is in operation. If the operating component fails, then another component is brought into operation. Time to system failure is therefore a sum of operation times of Q_P components. Suppose that all components have a constant failure intensity of λ. Then, the distribution of time to system failure is given by the sum of Q_P exponential random variables, which is a Gamma distribution with the shape parameter Q_P and the scale parameter λ. Hence, the reliability function of the standby redundant system is given by

$$R(t) = \exp(-\lambda t) \sum_{i=0}^{Q_P-1} \frac{(\lambda t)^i}{i!}. \tag{4.22}$$

4.2.6 Procedure for Analyzing System Configuration

Let us now summarize the procedure for analyzing the system configuration. If the system has different operational modes, this question must be addressed first. Assuming that this question has been settled, you must determine what kind of a system you have from a combinatorial viewpoint. The two principal kinds to consider are the concurrently functioning system and the sequentially functioning system. If you have a concurrently functioning system, you will develop an event diagram to describe the system. If you have a sequentially functioning system, you will use a transition diagram.

Now you have to determine the different components that you are going to track. In making your reliability predictions and estimates, there are in general four principal things to consider. First, you may want to consider your operating modes. If operating modes are correlated with components, this could influence the division into components. Second, you should address the question of system evolution, which is covered in Chapter 6. Sometimes you have systems that are integrated as major blocks or major subsystems. If that is the situation, you may want to track the reliability of these separately, because this will be the most appropriate approach to handling the evolution. The third thing to consider is that your project may have particular needs for tracking the reliabilities of certain components. For example, certain components may be critical from either a cost, schedule, or development risk point of view. The three initial factors that we talked about here are all factors that tend to drive you in the direction of more components. The fourth and countervailing factor is the complexity and difficulty of data collection and the possible loss of statistical significance when failure samples are divided among many components. Thus, you must reach a trade-off here. Finally, if you have a distributed system, you can handle the analysis of system configuration in a simplified fashion under certain conditions.

4.3   TEST RUN SELECTION

A set of requirements for a software system only achieve true validity when the performance of the system designed to satisfy them has been verified. Thus, verification is an aspect of system definition. Although there are many approaches to verification, sooner or later the system must be tested. To the best of our knowledge, there currently is no economically viable or perhaps even technically feasible methodology that *guarantees* that user requirements for useful program products can be met without test. The quality and efficiency of testing depend largely on how the test runs are selected. Hence testing must be carefully planned. Of course, there are other considerations such as adequacy of data recorded, and quality of data reduction and diagnostic tools available. But the foregoing are to little avail if test selection is poorly done.

4.3.1   Selection Strategy

Input state selection during test can, of course, be deterministic, since the tester and not the external environment is in control. Test selection is *deterministic* if each test case and its order in the test sequence is specified with certainty. It is *random* if more than one test case is possible at any point, and each test case has a probability of occurrence at that point associated with it. Estimated reliability status can be manipulated almost at will by picking the "right" input states. You must, of course, have previously executed the run corresponding to that input state, so you know whether a failure occurs. Completely arbitrary selection of input states is undesirable, however, from the viewpoints of test realism, optimum testing strategy, and characterization of reliability status.

The optimum test strategy at any point during test is the one that yields the greatest reduction in operational failure "cost" per unit of test cost. "Cost" usually is economic, but it can represent human life lost, service degradation, or other operational impacts. Test cost at any given level of failure intensity is primarily affected by execution time. The operational cost of failures is, on the average, proportional to the failure intensity. Hence, the optimum average test strategy will be to select input states in a way that will reduce failure intensity most rapidly with respect to execution time. Suppose we select input states randomly with probabilities equal to those that occur during operation. Then, on the average, the first executions of the input states will occur in the order of their occurrence probabilities. Hence, failures associated with the most frequently occurring input states tend to be found and removed first, reducing the failure intensity the most rapidly. Note that this approach also yields a failure intensity at each point in test that would be equal to that experienced in operation if the program were released at that time. This is because the operational profiles would be the same. You will recall that our test selection strategy is based on average operational cost of failures. Sometimes it may be possible to identify particular input states which, if faulty, would lead to exceptionally costly failures. In that case, it might be wise to test them first. This situation might occur for life-critical systems. Fault tree analysis can be useful in identifying the critical input states.

You must be careful to have the entire input space open to selection at all times. This does not mean that every input state must be selected at least once. That is usually impossible to accomplish in any reasonable length of time. However, sometimes testers concentrate on one part of the input space and then move to another. This approach is likely to yield misleading software reliability figures and *late, unpleasant* surprises about problem areas in the software. Following a fixed, deterministic sequence of testing is particularly dangerous if different functions tend to each have their own code. Then you obtain no information at all about the condition of certain parts of the software until late in test. It may then be too late to take expeditious corrective action. Sometimes the localization of input selection mentioned is unavoidable when the system is integrated in phases. In that case, however, the special techniques for handling evolving systems described in Chapter 6 should be employed. They may reduce, but probably not eliminate, the reliability figure errors caused by localization.

Testing can be more efficient if one recognizes that once an input state has been selected, it does not have to be repeated. Sometimes this is referred to as *test selection without replacement*, a reference to classic sampling problems in statistics. Repetition should not be necessary, because any failure that would occur would be observed and corrected on the first execution of the input state. This is the principle behind the concept of test compression, discussed in Chapter 6. If repetition is prevented, failure intensities should be adjusted as described there. When test selection without replacement occurs, we in effect obtain a uniform operational profile in test. However, the sequence of input states selected will be, on the average, in the order of their occurrence probabilities. In practice, some repetitions of input states are made. These are known as *regression tests*. Regression testing is necessary because the principle of "first execution fault removal" is not totally met in practice. It depends on the program being stable (no changes), all failures being observed, and all corrections being perfectly carried out.

Some testers criticize random selection of input states as being inefficient. This may be because they have taken advantage of test selection without replacement when selecting tests deterministically but not when choosing them randomly. Such an approach leads to an obviously unfair basis of comparison. Recent studies [Duran and Ntafos (1984)] have shown that random testing is an effective strategy for many programs, both for minimizing test cost and finding faults. This is seen both from direct measures and the fact that random testing performs well with respect to branch and path coverage. Often, it is superior to *partition testing* or dividing input space into sections (partitions) and taking one input state from each section. Note that path testing is a special case of partition testing, since input space can be partitioned by program structure as well as function. Partitions have the effect of forcing a certain planned diversity on testing. A recent study [Currit, Dyer, and Mills (1986) interpreting data of Adams (1980)] points to the superiority of random testing. It shows that random testing based on the operational profile would have been 30 times more effective than structural testing for nine large

IBM products. Structural testing is testing based on knowledge of a program's structure. It is oriented toward executing as many different program branches or paths as possible.

The tester who is trying to truly represent the operational phase by random selection is not constrained in selection by the correlations between input states that can occur during operation. This is because input states can be set by manual intervention. As long as the operational period is sufficiently long such that input state selection probabilities can be characterized by the steady state, random testing using these probabilities but independent selection will be representative of the operational environment.

Testers often pick input states to test that they think are fault-prone. These states may lie at the boundaries of the expected range of inputs or appear to be ones that the designers may not have considered. This strategy is seductive, because the likelihood of finding a fault and enjoying the resultant satisfactions *is* frequently higher. However, often these input states do not occur with high probability in the operation of the program. Consequently, the strategy is inefficient when evaluated against the proper objective of reducing failure intensity rapidly. Do not confuse the inappropriate strategy of specially selecting input states that may be fault prone but infrequently executed with the good strategy of specially selecting input states that may have severe costs associated with them *if* faulty.

It could conceivably be worthwhile to try to identify frequently occurring input states that are fault-prone. This is much more difficult than picking rarely occurring ones. There is no proven way to do this now. There is great risk that overconfidence of a tester in ignoring certain input states could lead to disaster. The risk is akin to that of betting your life savings on a "sure thing" in the stock market.

There is some indication that some *modules* may be more fault-prone than others. The fault-proneness may relate to the function implemented, the development methodology employed, or the capability of the designer. However, single modules usually do not correspond to single input states. Virtually any program product with any substantial function will be quite complex in the pattern of modules executed during a run. Consequently, we cannot take advantage of the possible existence of fault-prone modules in predicting fault-prone input states.

It has been suggested [Budd et al. (1979)] that *mutation testing* may be an efficient approach to identifying fault-prone input states. It is based on the concept that certain patterns of faults are likely to occur, and that these result in certain types of mutations in a program. You then try to design tests so that they are most efficient in stimulating the failures connected with these mutations. Work in this area has generally concentrated on designing the tests, given that the particular types of mutations occur. Further studies of the error process in software engineering are necessary to establish mutation patterns. If mutation testing is to be cost effective, the patterns identified must represent types of faults that will occur even though designers are aware of their likelihood and are taking precautions against them. It is not at all clear that this is the case.

We have implicitly assumed that test selection is primarily a question of selecting individual input states. In some circumstances, it may be important to select sequences of input states. One such circumstance is that of systems in which there is substantial undetected corruption of data. This would typically occur for systems that access and modify large and complex data bases such as those used by CAD/CAM systems. A run may function quite properly except for an erroneous change in the data base. We may not consider that a failure has occurred, since the immediate function meets customer needs. Or, if data corruption is specified as a violation of a requirement, we may not be able to completely examine the many dimensions of the output state and detect the failure. As a result, it may be desirable to include sequences of runs in test to uncover failures that would result from data corruption. Unfortunately, this approach has its own problems. The number of sequences is so large that it is difficult to enumerate them and/or establish their probabilities of occurrence. A compromise test plan involving some sequence testing may be feasible.

4.3.2 Equivalence Partitioning

Equivalence partitioning is a useful technique that can increase the efficiency of testing. The key to the technique lies in the fact that many input states are very similar to one another, differing in only a few aspects. For example, two deposit transactions in a banking program may differ only in the amount of the deposit. If one functions correctly, it is extremely (but not perfectly!) likely that the other will also. One can perform a grouping or *equivalence partitioning* [Cox (1981) and Myers (1979)] of the input space. You select only one input state from each group, with a probability equal to the total probability of occurrence of all states in the group. This drastically reduces the number of input states that you must select from and speeds up testing, since input states that are unlikely to expose new failures are not executed. This increase in testing efficiency is achieved with added risk, however, in that the ignored states may indeed be associated with failures, which are then missed. In reality, the practicality of limited time available for test often forces an implied equivalence partitioning. The test phase may consist of a few hundred or few thousand test cases, but the input space may be much larger.

Equivalence partitioning may be performed on the basis of either functional similarity or structural coverage. More attention has been paid to the latter approach. The basic philosophy of the structural coverage approach is to select input states to most rapidly "cover" the program in some fashion, avoiding redundant coverage. In order of increasing capability to find potential failures, you may cover the execution of all instructions, all segments or branches, or all paths. Note that the coverage of all paths still does not insure that all failures are found, since failures may be data-dependent. Structural testing at the path level is very lengthy because loops vastly increase the possible number of paths (each additional iteration represents one or more additional paths). In practice, it is usually feasible to test only some random sample of paths. Studies by Howden (1980) suggest that overall, structural testing is not as effective as functional testing in uncovering faults. However, each method finds certain faults more effectively than the other. Incidentally, Howden's work also shows that static analysis is more effective than testing for finding about half the faults. It may be difficult to take into account the various frequencies with which input states (functions) can be executed. Relating structural elements executed to input states can be complicated from a practical point of view. The use of equivalence partitioning does not require any adjustment to failure intensity figures. The failure intensity figures obtained in test will directly reflect and incorporate the more rapid reduction obtained through this technique.

One way to lessen the risk inherent in equivalence partitioning is to select a new input state within an input state group whenever a regression test must be performed for that group. If the test fails, you will not know whether the failure is due to poor partitioning or the introduction of a new fault due to program change. There is even a very minor risk that a newly introduced fault would be detected by a run with the initial input state but not by another run in the same partition group. The foregoing effects are very small, however, compared with the overall advantage gained.

4.4 SUMMARY

The definition of "failure" really involves the thorough elucidation of system requirements. This elucidation comes about because of the different perspective taken when thinking about failures and their varying impacts on the use of a system.

The way in which we think about the configuration of a system is strongly influenced both by the analytical tools available to us and the purposes of our analysis. Both must be clearly understood before attempting to establish a system decomposition. Finally, the reliability figures obtained for a system during test are dependent on the tests selected. Hence, this process is very important.

PROBLEMS

4.1 A computing center has a reliability objective of 0.90 for an 8-hr shift for its interactive service. The system requirement is simply that service be provided, regardless of the response time involved. All reliabilities are measured with respect to this shift. It has a dual processor configuration fed by a front-end processor, as shown in Figure 4.15. The front-end processor has a reliability of 0.99 and its operating system, 0.95. The reliability of each mainframe processor is 0.98. What must the reliability of the mainframe operating system be to meet the overall reliability objective?

4.2 Figure 4.16 represents the event diagram for a time-sharing system running on a multiprocessor machine with two processors. The time-sharing system runs under a general purpose operating system, and both run on both processors. The reliabilities of the hardware for a 10-hr prime shift are labeled. The operating and time-sharing sys-

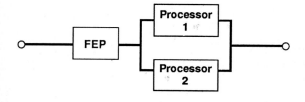

FIGURE 4.15
Computing center configuration.

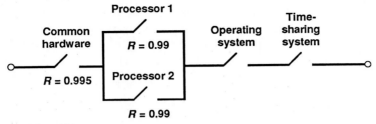

FIGURE 4.16
Event diagram for interactive computing service.

tems have failure intensities measured in *execution time* of 0.05 and 0.025 failure/ CPU hr, respectively. Each runs about 20 percent of the time and the other 60 percent of the processor capacity is used by application programs. Find the prime shift reliability of the entire extended machine (reliability of application programs is not considered).

4.3 We are working with a compiler that is not fully debugged. Consequently, we often find that a failure is the result of incorrect compilation rather than erroneous programming. Should we account for this in any way?

4.4 When you experience a failure in testing, can you continue testing or must you restart from scratch? If the former, how do you account for the fact that degraded data may cause another failure?

4.5 Would complex or subtle faults be more likely to be uncovered toward the end of the test period?

4.6 We find in testing that we tend to locate the most severe failures first and the failures with less impact later. Note that "severity of failure" is not the same thing as "complexity of fault" in that severity relates to impact on the user. Does this affect the application of the theory?

4.7 If a program and its associated data are reloaded, won't this affect the length of the failure interval just afterward, since degraded data will be cleaned up by the reload?

4.8 Are there cases where it is difficult to determine whether a failure is due to hardware or software?

4.9 What is the difference between hardware-fault-tolerance, software-fault-tolerance, and robustness?

4.10 Does the reliability of test drivers have an impact on a software reliability model?

4.11 Do we have different failure types when the same software is run on two different machines and fails in the same way on the same runs?

4.12 Derive Equation (4.3).

4.13 Can a deficiency in performance of a software component (for example, excessive response time at a given traffic level) be a failure?

4.14 Many operating systems can recover from certain kinds of software malfunctions and continue to process work. Are these malfunctions failures?

4.15 You define "failure" as an unacceptable departure of program operation from program requirements. Does this rule out the possibility of failures resulting from requirement faults?

4.16 How do you handle multiple failures resulting from the same fault on a single run during test?

4.17 How do you handle failures found by unit test that continues in parallel with system test?

FIVE

PARAMETER DETERMINATION

We have defined the system we are working with in Chapter 4. We must now determine the parameters for the model(s) of the software part(s) of the system. The determination of parameters was first discussed in Chapter 2. In this chapter, we will deepen our understanding of this process, particularly with respect to its practical aspects. A summary of methods for the determination is presented in Table 5.1. Finally, we will discuss some of the features of programs we have found helpful in experience with estimating parameters and computing other useful quantities. In Chapter 6 we will look at a number of project-specific techniques.

5.1 EXECUTION TIME COMPONENT

You will recall that execution time component parameters for the basic model can be determined by prediction from characteristics of the software and the development process. This can be done before any execution of the software. Once the software is executed and failure data is available, the parameters can be estimated statistically from the data. The parameters are summarized in Table 2.1.

5.1.1 Prediction

The basic execution time model has two parameters we must predict, total failures ν_0 that would be experienced in infinite time and initial failure intensity λ_0.

5.1.1.1 TOTAL FAILURES. The net number of faults removed is only a portion of the failures experienced, expressed by the fault reduction factor B. Thus the total

113

TABLE 5.1
Method of parameter determination

Parameter	Method				
	Prediction	Estimation	Identification	Formula and/or experience	Data
Execution time component					
Basic model	X	X			
Logarithmic Poisson model		X			
Calendar time component (both models)					
Planned					
Resource quantity			X		
Resource utilization				X	
Resource usage					X

failures ν_0 may be estimated, before test, from the number of inherent faults ω_0 and the fault reduction factor B, since

$$\nu_0 = \frac{\omega_0}{B}. \tag{5.1}$$

Faults. You can theoretically determine the number of inherent faults in coded programs by an empirical method, variously called "fault seeding," "error seeding," or "bebugging" [Gilb (1977), Rudner (1977), Basin (1973), and Mills (1972)]. Introduce artificial faults into the program in some suitable random fashion, unknown to the people who will be trying to find program faults. It is assumed that these seeded faults are equivalent to the inherent faults in the program in terms of difficulty of detection. Inspect the code and count separately the inherent and seeded faults discovered. The proportion of seeded faults found to total seeded faults is noted. You can then predict the number of inherent faults in the program. The reasoning is based on the concept that with equal difficulty of discovery, the same proportions of both types of faults will have been uncovered at any point in time.

For example, suppose that 100 faults are seeded into a program that contains an unknown number of inherent faults. After a period of debugging, 20 seeded and 10 inherent faults have been discovered. The seeded faults discovered represent 20 percent of the total number of seeded faults. We assume that 20 percent of the inherent faults have been discovered also. Therefore, the total number of inherent faults must be 50. Actually, the situation is a bit more complex than this. We are dealing with random samples, and we are estimating the number of inherent faults and its confidence interval.

Unfortunately, it has proved difficult to implement seeding in practice. It is not easy to introduce artificial faults that are equivalent to inherent faults in difficulty of discovery. It is generally *much* easier to find the seeded faults. Consequently, the number of inherent faults is usually underestimated with this technique. Hence, we usually determine the number of faults from program characteristics.

It has long been assumed that the size of a program has the most effect on the number of inherent faults it contains. At least several researchers [Feuer and Fowlkes (1979), Motley and Brooks (1977), Thayer (1976), and Akiyama (1971)] have verified this hypothesis. It appears that for *modules*, there may be a constant inherent fault component unrelated to size [Shen et al. (1985)], although its existence is in dispute [Card, Church, and Agresti (1986)]. A possible source of this component is interface faults, which are likely to be size-independent [Basili and Perricone (1984)]. In any case, we are interested in estimating the number of inherent faults in *systems*, usually of appreciable size, or in increments to systems. The constant inherent fault component for modules should not be significant in either of these situations.

Inherent fault density. Data can be collected on average inherent fault densities (faults per instruction) at the start of various phases of testing. These data will permit the number of inherent faults ω_0 to be estimated by simply multiplying predicted inherent fault density by program size. Implicit in this approach is the assumption that the number of inherent faults is linearly related to program size. The validity of this assumption is supported by Basili and Hutchens (1983) and strongly backed by Takahashi and Kamayachi (1985). The latter found less than 0.03 correlation between inherent fault density and program size over 30 projects, ranging from 4K to 130K lines of developed (new or modified) code. The Basili and Hutchens study also presented evidence to indicate uniform inherent fault distribution across the code. Metrics based only on specific parts of the code were less effective in predicting the number of inherent faults.

Experience has indicated that inherent fault quantities are more closely correlated with source than object instructions. Hence we count *deliverable executable source instructions* developed during the project. Thus, we do not count drivers or support programs. Data statements, declarations, and comments are not counted. When the project involves program changes rather than program creation, we do not count instructions/statements that are left alone or deleted. The incidence of inherent faults associated with such statements is much less than that associated with those that are created or modified. In studies of mathematically oriented FORTRAN routines for space applications, 98 percent of the modules that were reused without change were fault-free. In practice, the number of *instructions* is highly correlated with the number of *lines* of code. As the latter is easier to count, it is most often used.

A summary of available data on the density of inherent faults found in different phases of a number of projects is presented in Table 5.2. The data vary in quality because of differences in the care with which the terms were defined and the data were collected. Individual references are presented so that the user of these data may investigate them. Possibly, one might make better predictions than those

TABLE 5.2
Density of faults found during different life cycle phases for various projects

Reference	System identifier	Developed code (K source lines)	Faults/K source lines	Phases[1]
Basili and Perricone (1984)		90	44.1[2]	C, UT, SS, S
Stover (1977)		4.0	71.3	C, UT, SS, S
Albin and Ferreol (1982)		27.6	21.0[2]	C, UT, SS, S
Boehm (1981)		2	75	C, UT, SS, S
Rubey, Dana, and Biché (1975)	multiple[3]	9	113	C, UT, SS, S
Ostrand and Weyuker (1982)		10	16.0	UT, SS, S
Akiyama (1971)		17.1	20.3	UT, SS, S
Schafer et al. (1979)	4	115.3	36.2	SS, S
Mendis (1981)		28	4.6	S
Motley and Brooks (1977)	S	181	19.5	S
	T	115	17.4	S
Akiyama (1971)		17.1	3.2	S
Schafer et al. (1979)	1	120	17.0	S
	2	610	12.8	S
	3	96.9	3.78	S
	7	1317	2.69	S
	14	32.2	15.6	S
	15	32.4	13.8	S
	16	123.7	10.8	S
Angus, Bowen, and VanDenBerg (1983)		330	10.6	S
Weiss (1981)	SEL 1	46.5	3.87	S
	SEL 2	31.1	3.83	S
	SEL 3	78.6	3.91	S
	ARF	21.8	6.56	S
Bendick (1976)	1	217	4.8	S
	2	31.5	9.8	S
	4	32	5.2	S
	5	73	5.1	S
	6	36	3.6	S
Endres (1975)	DOS/VS	86	6.0	S
Rubey, Dana, and Biché (1975)	multiple[4]	18.3	4.5	S
Walston and Felix (1977)	multiple[5]	20	3.1	S
Inglis et al. (1986)	multiple[6]	-	4.20	S
Inglis et al. (1986)	multiple[7]	-	1.44	OP
Walston and Felix (1977)	multiple[8]	103	1.4	OP
Schafer et al. (1979)	5	115.3	3.9	OP

[1]Phases: C = coding, UT = unit test, SS = subsystem test, S = system test, OP = operation

[2]Likely to be low because of way data were collected.

[3]Average of 12 systems, with size ranging from 3 to 16 K source lines and faults from 13 to 320 faults/K source lines.

[4]Average of 8 systems, with size ranging from 1.5 to 27 K source lines and faults from 1.7 to 20 faults/K source lines.

[5]Data from 46 systems. Median size is 20 K source lines and lower and upper quartiles are 10 and 59 K source lines. Median fault density is 3.1 faults/K source lines and lower and upper quartiles are 0.8 and 8.0 faults/K source lines.

[6]Carefully defined data from 55 systems, with fault density ranging from 0.01 to 80.39 faults/K source lines. Sizes extended from 4.1 to 564.9 K source lines of developed code.

[7]Carefully defined data from 50 systems, with fault density ranging from 0 to 10.95 faults/K source lines. Average time in operational phase is 11 months, ranging from 0 to 41 months. Sizes ran from 4.1 to 523.8 K source lines of developed code.

[8]Data from between 3 to 11 projects (exact number not reported). Median size is 103 K source lines and lower and upper quartiles are 56 and 474 source lines. Median period of operation is 18 months; lower and upper quartiles are 11 and 31 months. Median code changed is 4 percent. Median fault density is 1.4 faults/K source lines and lower and upper quartiles are 0.2 and 2.9 faults/K source lines.

obtained from averages if one matched product and development process characteristics with those of the recorded projects.

There are three likely sources of error in these data:

1. The data usually are taken for all faults repaired, not just inherent faults. Thus, they include the repair of faults that were themselves spawned in the repair process. This factor results in estimates that are probably about 1 to 7 percent high, as we will discuss shortly.
2. The data generally represent corrections reported rather than faults repaired. Some faults will be repaired by means of multiple corrections, each correction representing a partial fault repair. This factor results in estimates that are high by some unknown amount.
3. Data collection does not usually continue until all faults are repaired. Hence estimates are low, probably by not more than 15 percent and perhaps around 8 percent.

Although the effects of these error sources are not well known at present, there appears to be substantial cancellation between them. Hence the net error can probably be ignored.

When data are specified for the coding phase, they include all semantic but no syntactic faults. *Semantic faults* are defects arising from programmer error in communicating the *meaning* of what is to be done. An example would be specifying the wrong variable for an operation. *Syntactic faults* result from errors in following the rules of the language in which the program is written. For example, one might not establish the end of a loop properly. Syntactic faults are generally discovered by the compiler or assembler. They usually must be removed before successful compilation or assembly can occur. Semantic faults are hence the faults that are left after successful compilation or assembly. Coding phase inherent faults represent inherent faults found by inspection, since inherent faults found in unit test are noted separately. Subsystem test represents that phase in which developers, working individually or as a team, perform tests that involve more than one unit or module but not the entire system. Testing is generally functional rather than structural in system test. It is usually performed by an independent test team. Ordinarily, the code is under configuration control and a formal failure reporting system is in use. Operation is, of course, the phase after release to the customer. The number of inherent faults found in a phase varies with the length of the phase. Of all life-cycle phases, the operational phase exhibits the greatest variation in length. Hence we potentially have the most severe problem in specifying these data. One possibility would be to define a period such as 2 years after release as the duration for which inherent fault data should be collected. A standard period has not been defined for the data presented here. Fortunately, the proportion of inherent faults found during operation is small compared to that of other phases, so the effect of any variation is considerably moderated.

If we average the data presented in Table 5.2, we obtain the results shown in Table 5.3. The data for the subsystem and system test phases combined are proba-

TABLE 5.3
Means and ranges of fault density data

Phase (or group of phases)	Number of systems providing data	Faults/K source lines	
		Range	Average
C, UT, SS, S	16	13–320	98.0
UT, SS, S	2	16.0–20.3	18.2
SS, S	1	36.2	36.2
S	131	0.01–80.4	4.53
OP	51	0–11.0	1.48

bly unreliable. The data for the system test phase are probably good, since they represent 131 projects. Although operational phase data come from 51 systems, there is some variation due to the length of the phase. If a standard is established for this, the variation will be reduced. The average value will probably not change by more than 1 fault/K lines. In Table 5.4, we have estimated mean inherent fault density remaining at the beginning of several different life-cycle phases. The difference in inherent fault density between the start of coding and the start of unit test is believed to be due to desk checking and code inspections.

Possibly, measures of program complexity can improve the prediction of number of inherent faults. Complexity measures form an active current research area. However, most of the complexity metrics developed to date show a high correlation with program size. They provide little improvement over just program size alone in predicting inherent faults remaining at the start of system test [Sunohara et al. (1981)]. The metrics considered were:

1. McCabe's cyclomatic number [McCabe (1976)],
2. Halstead's effort [Halstead (1977)],
3. a statement count weighted by data references and branches from each statement, and
4. a data flow metric.

TABLE 5.4
Mean fault density remaining at beginning of various phases

Phase	Faults/K source lines
Coding (after compilation/assembly)	99.5
Unit test	19.7
System test	6.01
Operation	1.48

Typical coefficients of determination relating program size and inherent faults range between 0.5 and 0.6, so there is room for predictability improvement. The foregoing conclusions are supported by similar findings by Basili and Hutchens (1983) and Gremillion (1984).

Takahashi and Kamayachi (1985) have studied the effects of other factors on improving inherent fault prediction, based on data taken for 30 projects. After normalizing the inherent fault data by program size (the most important predictive factor) to obtain inherent fault density, they found three significant additional factors:

1. specification change activity, measured in pages of specification changes per K lines of code,
2. average programmer skill, measured in years, and
3. thoroughness of design documentation, measured in pages of developed (new plus modified) design documents per K lines of code.

Greater specification change activity increases the inherent fault density. Greater programmer skill and more thorough design documentation decrease inherent fault density. The effect of all three factors accounts for about 60 percent of the variation in inherent fault density experienced for the projects. In another study [Basili and Hutchens (1983)], it has been shown that use of a disciplined development methodology in a team setting reduces inherent fault density. Most of this current research on inherent fault density has been empirical. At this point, adding insight coming from studies of human problem-solving activity to this empiricism may result in inherent fault density models with greater predictability.

Belady and Lehman (1976) have observed a growing "unstructuredness" in systems that undergo a series of releases. The unstructuredness probably results from several factors such as:

1. different people modifying or repairing the system,
2. the tendency of modifications and repairs to be made locally and cheaply, degrading the global conceptual integrity of the system, and
3. deficiencies in documenting modifications.

It appears likely that the inherent fault density of developed code in multirelease systems will increase from release to release, unless deliberate system restructuring activities are undertaken. We are not aware of presently existing data that indicate the magnitude of the foregoing effect.

The inherent fault density at the start of system test will probably show the least variation from project to project. Earlier measurements will be subject to uncertainties in determining the size of the program until it is well developed and at least partially tested. Later measurements will reflect the fact that reliability goals of different projects vary, hence there will be considerable variation in remaining inherent fault density at release to the field.

Several researchers [for example, Jones (1986)] have raised the issue of the validity of counting instructions or lines of code. However, this question has arisen in the context of *productivity*. This may well be a valid concern, because a software engineer can write a lengthy program and appear more productive, while providing no more function than the more concise designer. This is much less of a problem regarding reliability, since we are only interested in predicting the number of faults introduced. This relates to human error processes and thus appears to be strongly related to the amount of design work done. Hence, a longer program with the same function probably *will* have a larger number of inherent faults. Whatever the disadvantages of instructions or lines of code, they comprise, when clearly defined, an objective, readily determinable metric. It is a metric that can be fully automated. Finally, despite much effort, no one has been able to develop another metric that is consistently superior.

Fault reduction factor. The fault reduction factor B is the ratio of *net* fault reduction to failures experienced as time of operation approaches infinity. Expected values are taken for both the faults and the failures. If this weren't done, the result would depend on the particular realization of input states executed rather than the operational profile. The *total* number of faults corrected is frequently larger than the net number. As a simple example, 100 failures may occur for a system. Let us assume that insufficient information is available to permit the faults that caused 2 of them to be found. However, 98 faults are removed. In the correction process, assume that 5 new faults are spawned. The *total* number of faults corrected is 98 but the *net* number is 93. The fault reduction factor B would be 0.93.

A long period of operation is necessary for obtaining a good count of faults corrected. Correction actions are often only partial in nature. A fault may be repaired only for certain input states (see Chapter 9). The factors that must be considered in estimating B are:

1. the degree to which relationships between failures that are the product of the same underlying fault are recognized,
2. detectability (the proportion of failures whose faults can be found, which depends on the amount of information recorded about the failure),
3. the extent to which code inspection independent of test is performed,
4. the degree to which relationships between faults are discerned, and
5. the extent to which new faults are spawned during fault correction.

The proportion of failures whose faults can be identified depends on the amount of information recorded about the failures. It is close to 1 during test phases, although variable during operation. Since we are ordinarily applying B in the period before operation, the latter situation is generally not significant. Independent code inspection during test does not occur for most projects. The first, fourth, and fifth factors probably will not vary much from project to project. There is evidence [Miyamoto (1975) and Musa (1975)] that the fifth one does not. Thus, there is a good possibility that a project-independent value of B can be found, although the value is not known at present.

Some data are currently available that indicate the values of B that typically result from just new fault spawning alone. This is shown in Table 5.5. The range of values is 0.925 to 0.993 and the average is 0.955.

5.1.1.2 INITIAL FAILURE INTENSITY. The initial failure intensity parameter λ_0 may be predicted from

$$\lambda_0 = fK\omega_0. \qquad (5.2)$$

The quantity f is the linear execution frequency of the program. This is the average instruction execution rate r divided by the number of *object* instructions I in the program,

$$f = \frac{r}{I}. \qquad (5.3)$$

The linear execution frequency is the number of times the program would be executed per unit time if it had no branches or loops. Then it would simply execute all instructions in a linear sequence. If the size of the program has been measured in source instructions I_S, an estimate of the number of object instructions I can be made by multiplying by the average expansion ratio Q_X. For a table of approximate expansion ratios, see Jones (1986), p. 49. The fault exposure ratio K relates failure intensity to "fault velocity." The fault velocity $f\omega_0$ is the average rate at which faults in the program would pass by if the program were executed linearly. The concept of fault velocity is illustrated in Figure 5.1.

Fault exposure ratio. The fault exposure ratio K represents the fraction of time that the "passage" results in a failure. It accounts for the following facts:

1. Programs are not generally executed in "straight line" fashion, but have many loops and branches.

TABLE 5.5
Values of fault reduction factor B due to faults spawned while correcting other faults

Reference	System	System size (K source lines)	B
Basili and Perricone (1984)		90	0.94
Weiss (1981)	SEL 1	50.9	0.98
	SEL 2	75.4	>0.925
	SEL 3	85.4	0.952
	ARF	21.8	0.993
Fries (1977)		120	0.939

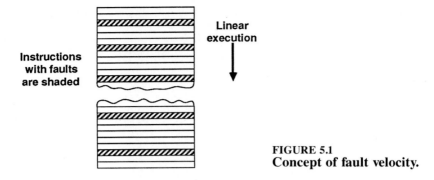

Instructions with faults are shaded

Linear execution

FIGURE 5.1
Concept of fault velocity.

2. The machine state varies and hence the fault associated with an instruction may or may not be exposed at one particular execution of the instruction.

The effect of machine state in exposing a fault is illustrated in Figure 5.2. Note that when X has a value larger than 25, the faulty program executes correctly by performing A. It also executes correctly by performing B if X is 20 or less. A failure occurs, exposing the fault of the incorrect conditional statement, only if X is larger than 20 but less than or equal to 25. Since faults such as this can cover narrow ranges of data, it is no surprise that K can be small.

At present, K must be determined from a similar program. It may be possible in the future to relate K to program structure in some way. Another possibility is that the range of values of K over different software systems may be small, allowing an average value to be used without excessive error. This could be due to program dynamic structure averaging out in some fashion for programs of any size. The small range would require that the average "structuredness" or decision density not vary from one large program to another. This appears to be the case. It has been shown that cyclomatic complexity, a measure of the number of decisions in a program, is highly correlated with program size [Basili and Hutchens (1983)]. It may be possible to more accurately determine a value for K as a function of some program characteristic. Values of K for several different systems are given in Table 5.6. The systems are described in Table 13.1, except for systems P7, P9, P10, and P15. Systems P7 and P9 are identical copies of an operating system running in different environments. System P10 is a different operating system and P15 is a large real-time system. For details, see Musa (1979b), systems SS1A, SS1C, SS4, and 14C, respectively. The average value of K is 4.20×10^{-7} failures/fault and the values cover a total range of 7.5 to 1. It will be seen from the values of K that intervals between failures typically represent cycling through the program a large number of times.

Correct program   **Faulty program**

        IF x > 25   IF x > 20 ---- Fault
           THEN A   THEN A
           ELSE B   ELSE B

FIGURE 5.2
Effect of machine state in exposing a fault.

TABLE 5.6
Fault exposure ratio
on different projects

System designator	K ($\times 10^{-7}$)
T1	1.87
T2	2.15
T3	4.11
T4	10.6
T5	4.2
T6	3.97
P7	4.43
P9	5.64
P10	1.41
P15	2.09
T16	3.03
T19	4.54
T20	6.5

To evaluate K for other projects for which data may be available, we require only four items of information:

1. a set of failure data sufficient to permit $B\phi = \lambda_0/\nu_0$ to be estimated,
2. the fault reduction factor B,
3. program size in object instructions, and
4. average instruction execution rate.

Care must be taken to insure that the failure data are true execution time data or that appropriate adjustments are performed to make them so. You can find execution time intervals from clock time intervals by multiplying the clock time intervals by the average computer utilization ρ_C. If failure intervals are from the test phase, they must be adjusted to the operational phase by multiplying by the testing compression factor (Chapter 6). Data in the form of failures per time interval are adjusted by dividing by the average computer utilization and the testing compression factor. Estimation of the quantity λ_0/ν_0 of the basic execution time model is now done. The linear execution frequency f is computed from the average instruction execution rate and program size. The value of K can now be determined from Equations (5.1) and (5.2) as

$$K = \frac{1}{Bf} \frac{\lambda_0}{\nu_0}. \tag{5.4}$$

Example 5.1. A health insurance claim processing program, involving 50,000 deliverable executable source instructions, has just been turned over to the system test group. Previous experience in this development environment for similar programs indicates a fault density of 6 faults/1000 delivered executable source instructions. The fault reduction factor is 1. We have a fault exposure ratio of 2×10^{-7} failure/fault. The code expansion ratio (object instructions per source instruction) is 4. The instruction execution rate of the target machine is 3.33 million object instructions/CPU sec. If we apply the basic execution time model, what values of the total failures and initial failure intensity parameters can we expect?

We compute the inherent faults ω_0 from

$$\omega_0 = \omega_I \Delta I . \tag{5.5}$$

Note that ΔI is the number of developed source instructions and ω_I is the fault density. Thus

$$\omega_0 = \left[\frac{6 \text{ faults}}{1000 \text{ inst}} \right] (50{,}000 \text{ inst})$$

$$= 300 \text{ faults.}$$

From Equation (5.1) we have

$$\nu_0 = \frac{\omega_0}{B}$$

$$= \frac{300}{1}$$

$$= 300 \text{ failures.}$$

Now

$$I = I_S Q_X , \tag{5.6}$$

where Q_X is the code expansion ratio. Thus

$$I = (50{,}000 \text{ inst}) (4)$$

$$= 200{,}000 \text{ inst.}$$

The linear execution frequency f is

$$f = \frac{r}{I}$$

$$= \frac{3.33 \times 10^6 \text{ inst/CPU sec}}{0.2 \times 10^6 \text{ inst}}$$

$$= 16.7 \text{ cycles/CPU sec.}$$

Using Equation (5.2) we have

$$\lambda_0 = f K \omega_0$$

$$= (16.7 \text{ cycles/CPU sec}) (2 \times 10^{-7} \text{ failure/fault}) (300 \text{ faults})$$

$$= 10^{-3} \text{ failures/CPU sec.} \qquad \blacksquare$$

5.1.2 Estimation

We can use estimation to determine the execution time component parameters of either the basic or logarithmic Poisson execution time models as execution progresses. For the basic model, estimation can be used to refine the values established by prediction. We will use maximum likelihood estimation, although other methods are also possible (see Chapter 12). It is most efficient to use a program to do the calculations. Hence, we will not discuss them in detail but will take a graphical view.

The essential data required for estimation are the failure times or failures per time interval (grouped data) experienced during execution. The process is illustrated schematically for the basic model in Figure 5.3. A set of failure intensities has been plotted against execution time. They represent number of failures in a time interval divided by that time interval. The basic execution time model provides the basis for plotting the dashed line of anticipated failure intensity against execution time. Two parameters determine this line, the initial failure intensity λ_0 and the total expected failures ν_0. The first parameter is represented by the vertical axis intercept. Values of the parameters are chosen to maximize the likelihood of occurrence of the set of failure intensities that have been experienced. In an approximate sense, the curve is being fit to the data indicated. Some derived quantities are also illustrated on the plot.

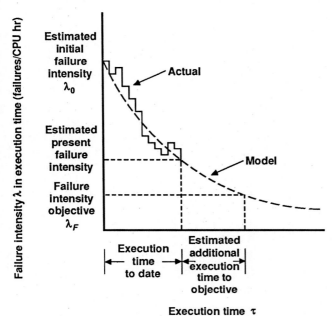

FIGURE 5.3
Conceptual view of parameter estimation.

The foregoing parameters were selected to describe the basic model because they had the most immediate connection with the characteristics of the product and the development process. We can also define a parameter ϕ, the per-fault hazard rate, given by

$$\phi = \frac{\lambda_0}{\omega_0} . \tag{5.7}$$

The quantity ω_0 is the number of faults inherent in the code. Note that the decrement in failure intensity per failure is given by $\lambda_0/\nu_0 = B\phi$, where B is the fault reduction factor or ratio of net fault reduction to failures experienced. We can describe the model in terms of ν_0 and $B\phi$. This alternative formulation of the model simplifies parameter estimation and will be used in Chapter 12. Conversion between different parameters is readily accomplished.

Since estimation of the parameters is a statistical process, you will also wish to determine confidence intervals. The curve should now be viewed as a band. The width increases with the magnitude of the confidence interval. A 90 percent confidence interval requires a wider band than a 75 percent one. The confidence interval for λ_0 is given by the range of vertical axis intercepts.

The process of estimating the parameters of the logarithmic Poisson model, initial failure intensity λ_0 and failure intensity decay parameter θ, is analogous.

To obtain some idea of the accuracy with which model parameters are being estimated, look at plots of the estimates as functions of execution time. The values should be constant if the program is stable except for repairs. A confidence interval estimated late in the period of execution will be a reasonable approximation to the range of values in which the parameter actually lies. Hence, a confidence interval estimated earlier can be compared with it to check the quality of the estimation.

Example 5.2. We will look at how use of calendar time as the basis for modeling can lead to results that are not useful. In Figure 5.3, we have an increasing spacing of failures or decreasing failure intensity in execution time, as more and more faults are removed. For execution time, you will obtain a finite estimate for total failures. Assume that the project is in the failure-correction-personnel-limited phase. This resource can handle, on the average, a fixed number of failures per day. Therefore, testing will be paced such that failures will have an approximately constant spacing or constant failure intensity in calendar time. This is shown in Figure 5.4. With no trend in the failure intensities, the estimate of total failures is undefined or infinite. It is not possible to predict when various failure intensity objectives will be reached, as it is when failure intensity is expressed in execution time. ∎

During the initial use of estimation, accuracy can be low (generally indicated by large confidence intervals) because of the small failure samples available. Note that accuracy is primarily related to number of failures in the sample. If data are in the form of failures per interval, you can have an adequate sample size even though the number of intervals may be small. We can sometimes improve accuracy by taking a weighted average of previous parameter predictions along with parameter estimates. The weights would be functions of the sample

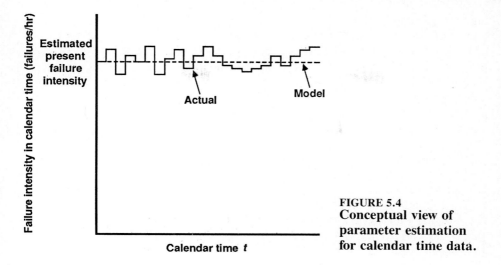

**FIGURE 5.4
Conceptual view of
parameter estimation
for calendar time data.**

size. It is probably best that the weights for the estimates be zero until the estimates have an accuracy within an order of magnitude of that of the predictions. We would then set the relative weights proportional to the relative estimated accuracies. The weights for the predictions would be set to zero when the estimates become superior in accuracy by about an order of magnitude. Adjust the confidence intervals as well as the parameter values proper by this technique.

The refinement of parameters raises many practical issues relating to the collection of failure data. Project-specific techniques are discussed in Chapter 6. We will cover general data collection planning and procedures in Chapter 8.

GROUPED FAILURE DATA. Many projects collect grouped failure data (failures in some time interval) rather than individual failure times or intervals. This is slightly easier to do, involving somewhat less data collection effort, particularly if the time interval is a natural unit like a day. The disadvantage is decreased accuracy in estimating parameters, which we will examine. We will treat this topic in more detail in the Discussion at the end of this chapter. A summary is given here of grouping for fixed time periods. We will consider both the basic and logarithmic Poisson execution time models. Estimation of the parameter that affects the rate of failure intensity reduction is examined in each case ($B\phi$ or $\lambda_0\theta$, respectively). The initial failure intensities and all derived quantities depend on the foregoing parameters and their accuracies in the cases of both models. Note that the study is based on a representative rather than an exhaustive set of parameter values. The accuracy depends on the parameter values. Hence, our results will convey general effects rather than precise behavior.

The effect of grouping will be quantified by comparing the observed information in the grouped data to that in the failure time data. Observed information affects the accuracy of the estimates. More information leads to greater accuracy. Let I_g be the ratio of the observed information in the grouped data to that in the failure time data. Values of I_g which are less than 1 show that our estimates are more variable for grouped data. Values of I_g greater than 1 indicate otherwise. It is *expected* that I_g will generally be less than 1 since there will inevitably be some loss of information in neglecting the actual failure times.

Results are presented in Tables 5.7 and 5.8 for the basic and logarithmic Poisson models. Note that the quality of the estimates for the basic model is excellent if the number of groups is, say, 10 or more. Quality of estimates for the logarithmic Poisson model is markedly inferior. It does not even become satisfactory until there are at least 200 groups or so.

If data have been gathered in grouped form, there are situations where it may be desirable to convert them to failure times or failure intervals. The most realistic method for doing this is to assign the failure times randomly within the interval in which the data have been collected. We use a uniform distribution, which reflects the fact that we have no knowledge that would favor assignment to any particular part of the collection interval. Let us consider the error introduced into the estimation of the parameter $B\phi$ or $\lambda_0\theta$. The amount of error will vary with the values of the parameters. We will consider representative cases, illustrated in Tables 5.9 (simulated data) and 5.10 (real project data). Randomization does not cause errors in estimation of $B\phi$ or $\lambda_0\theta$ greater than about 15 percent for either model, even when there are as few as five groups.

5.2   CALENDAR TIME COMPONENT

Parameters have the same values for the calendar time component of both the basic and logarithmic Poisson execution time models. Refer to Table 2.2 to obtain

TABLE 5.7
Values of I_g for equal time groupings for the basic execution time model

Number of failures	Number of groups	I_g
100	4	0.899
	8	0.969
	15	0.992
	29	0.995
	48	0.999
	72	0.999
50	5	0.941
	11	0.992
	21	0.997
	42	0.999
25	8	0.987
	16	0.999
	32	1.002

TABLE 5.8
Values of I_g for equal time groupings for the logarithmic Poisson execution time model

Number of groups	I_g
10	0.118
19	0.163
47	0.104
94	0.411
156	0.538
312	1.032

a good overview of these parameters. Usually, the failure correction personnel resource has the greatest effect on calendar time prediction. This is particularly true for a system released to the field with moderate failure intensity.

Only the computer time and failure identification personnel resources can be simultaneously limiting. It is not a frequent occurrence, since it is required that

$$\frac{\mu_C}{\mu_I} = \frac{\theta_C}{\theta_I} = \frac{P_C \rho_C}{P_I} \tag{5.8}$$

for the situation to occur. When two resources are simultaneously limiting, the ratios of calendar time to execution time for both resources are identical. Hence either can be used to compute calendar time.

On some projects, separate failure identification and failure correction personnel are not used. Each person does both jobs. If these resources are thus com-

TABLE 5.9
Results of randomizing grouped data for some simulated data sets

Model group	Number of failures	Number of groups	Maximum likelihood estimate of $B\phi$ or $\lambda_0\theta$ using		
			Original data	Randomly converted data	Uniformly converted data
Exponential ($B\phi = 0.3 \times 10^{-4}$)	100	4	0.293×10^{-4}	0.266×10^{-4}	0.257×10^{-4}
		15	0.287×10^{-4}	0.284×10^{-4}	0.275×10^{-4}
	50	5	0.347×10^{-4}	0.401×10^{-4}	0.268×10^{-4}
		11	0.327×10^{-4}	0.326×10^{-4}	0.265×10^{-4}
Geometric ($\lambda_0\theta = 0.25 \times 10^{-3}$)	100	10	0.283×10^{-3}	0.253×10^{-3}	0.244×10^{-3}
		20	0.307×10^{-3}	0.301×10^{-3}	0.321×10^{-3}
	50	10	0.246×10^{-3}	0.241×10^{-3}	0.210×10^{-3}
		20	0.249×10^{-3}	0.257×10^{-3}	0.213×10^{-3}

TABLE 5.10
Results of randomizing grouped data for systems T38 and T39

		Maximum likelihood estimate of $B\phi$ or $\lambda_0\theta$ using		
Model group	**System**	**Original data**	**Randomly converted data**	**Uniformly converted data**
Exponential	T38	0.105×10^{-1}	0.122×10^{-1}	0.089×10^{-1}
	T39	0.664×10^{-6}	0.661×10^{-6}	0.641×10^{-6}
Geometric	T38	0.207×10^{-1}	0.227×10^{-1}	0.170×10^{-1}
	T39	0.377×10^{-5}	0.354×10^{-5}	0.341×10^{-5}

bined, you must merge them and the resource requirements as far as the calendar time model is concerned.

The question may arise of the effect of deviations in the values of calendar time component parameters from the values we have predicted for them. Deviations are most likely to occur for the resource usage parameters, since we may be using values taken from another project or averages over a group of projects. The effect can be determined by doing a sensitivity study. One chooses parameter values on either side of the estimated values in accordance with the range of variation expected. The resultant calendar time, resource use, and cost variations can then be determined. It is usually easiest to do this with a simple simulation, but there may be times when an analytic study is possible.

5.2.1   Interpretation of Resource Definitions

Failure identification involves the activity of testing, the determination of what failures have occurred, and the documentation of the nature of the failures. Failure correction starts from the point where failures are identified. It includes fault identification, which is the determination of the fault that caused the failure, and fault correction. The process ends when the fault has been corrected. The person performing the fix must prove through appropriate testing, to the satisfaction of the test team, that the input state that previously caused the failure no longer does so. It may also be necessary to run certain regression tests to show that the fix, to a reasonable degree of confidence, did not adversely affect other input states. The failure correction activity includes the task of program change documentation *if* required to be completed during test rather than after.

Computer time is the measure that is used for allocating computer resources; it is not necessarily the same as execution time. In a dedicated facility that is allocated to a single user at a time, it may be clock time. Frequently, it is the residence time of the program in the machine (perhaps divided by the number of programs in the case of multiprogramming).

The key concept in determining what resource quantities should be counted under special conditions that may exist on different projects is the idea of a resource being *limiting*. Does the resource limit the pace at which test and failure correction for the program can proceed? For example, support staff such as programming librarians and technical writers are not counted because they do not directly constitute a limiting resource. Of course, the amount of support available may affect the environment in which the project operates, so that the *resource usage parameters* (μ_C, μ_F, μ_I, θ_C, θ_I) may be a function of the support level. That is, a higher level of support may reduce the amount of work done by the failure identification and failure correction personnel.

The failure identification activity usually includes the generation of trouble reports. This task must be performed by failure identification personnel for each failure before other activities related to the failure can take place and is thus limiting. Tasks associated with test planning and test case development are usually (but not always) completed before the test effort and not included. Including the foregoing tasks improperly in making resource usage estimates can lead to appreciable error because of their substantial size. One large project [Angus, Bowen, and VanDenBerg (1983)] reported 15 percent of test activity devoted to test planning and 35 percent to test case development. Only 50 percent was used for test conduct and analysis and could be considered limiting.

Test planning or replanning or test procedure debugging may be performed by failure identification personnel *as part of the test effort*. Often they require work proportional to the amount of testing (execution time) or the number of failures or both. We adjust the debug environment parameters μ_I (failure identification work per failure) and θ_I (failure identification work per unit execution time) to reflect this fact. At other times, the work is not proportional to these factors but does require effort by failure identification personnel. Then the number available should be reduced to reflect the time taken by these tasks.

As another example of interpretation of limiting resources, one project created test cases by recording data in the field and then processing them. The rate at which the cases could be generated was limited, and this paced the testing effort. The project determined the execution time associated with the tests that could be generated per week. The available computer time was then set at the minimum of the actual and foregoing values.

Generally a problem review board is not a limiting resource in the sense that failure identification or correction personnel are. Ordinarily you wouldn't halt testing so that the review board could catch up on a backlog of problems. The board causes a fixed delay that should be added to the total test period. Visualize test as a pipeline of a fixed length that represents the amount of processing done on each failure. A certain number of failures must be corrected or flow through the pipe before the failure intensity objective is reached. One determines calendar time primarily by flow rate through the pipe and number of failures processed. Limiting resources appear as bottlenecks that slow the flow. The problem review board appears as an added fixed length of pipe. You should add the *maximum* expected delay.

5.2.2 Planned Parameters

The planned parameters of the calendar time component of the model are easily determined. These parameters consist of resource quantities available and their utilizations. They are:

P_C: available computer time (measured in terms of prescribed work periods),

P_F: number of available failure correction personnel,

P_I: number of available failure identification personnel,

ρ_C: computer utilization factor during the computer-limited period, and

ρ_F: failure correction personnel utilization factor during the failure-correction-personnel-limited period.

RESOURCE QUANTITIES. The project manager is usually faced with the task of determining the proper resource quantities. This is really a system engineering problem of trade-offs between reliability, schedules, and resources, as described in Chapter 7. We obtain the resource quantities available by identification (that is, asking the person responsible). Note that "available" is not the same thing as "used." Personnel are simply counted, regardless of the length or time of their working hours. These two factors are considered only:

1. in counting computer time available, because computer time is measured in terms of prescribed work periods,
2. in converting calendar time hours to calendar time days, and
3. in converting calendar time days to dates.

The parameter P_C represents available computer time in terms of prescribed work periods. For example, if available computer time per week is 80 hr and the prescribed work week is 40 hr, then $P_C = 2$. This unit was chosen so that computer resources would be stated in the same units as personnel.

The prescribed work period represents "available time" or the total amount of time that the average member of the project can work *upon request*. In general, you establish available time by company policy or the practical consideration of the maximum time one can reasonably request a person to work. Normally, any one person will not work at the limit for an extended period, but it can happen. "Available" also implies reasonably short notice. It does not imply that the project member must be standing by for the available time. It *does* imply, for example, that he or she must be able to work 2 hr overtime sometime before the next day, when requested at 4 P.M. It also implies that the persons involved are not partially allocated to other tasks that take priority over the limiting resource activity. If they are, that time (in terms of prescribed work periods) must be subtracted from the number of persons available.

To calculate available computer time, determine the number of hours the computer is ready for use from a policy viewpoint. For example, although a computer may be available 24 hr/day, 7 days/week from a physical viewpoint, it may be operated for only 2 shifts on 6 days. Determine the maximum part of this time that *can* be allocated to your project, though you may not use all the time unless pressed. Subtract unavailable periods such as maintenance time, down time, and file backup time. The result is hours of availability, which should be expressed in terms of prescribed work periods. Consider the effect of work hours and procedures on availability. For example, suppose that all work to be done on the computer is interactive. If the machine is operated for 16 hr/day but personnel work one shift of 8 hr, availability is really only 8 hr. Availability in this case could be expanded to 16 hr by dividing personnel into 2 shifts or staggering their work hours in various ways. Alternatively, use of the machine for 8 hr in a noninteractive mode would accomplish the same objective. The calculation is normally made on a weekly basis, with the prescribed work period equal to the product of the workday and the workweek. The workday is the average hr per day personnel are available to work. The workweek is the average days per week personnel are available to work.

We obtain the best estimate of the number of failure correction personnel P_F by counting the number of programmers available who were occupied full time in coding the units of the system under test. The parameter P_I represents the number of members of the test team. This is the number of personnel familiar with system requirements and test plans and available for executing tests, verifying proper operation of the system, and identifying departures from proper operation.

We assume that each person involved in failure identification can run and examine the results from any test that is made. Failure correction personnel are assumed to work only on failures that have been attributed to their respective design areas. A person who can and does work at either failure identification or failure correction, depending on where staff is required, should be included in *both* counts. This does not represent duplication, at least to a first approximation, because only one resource at a time can be limiting. Inaccuracy arises only if there aren't enough people to perform the nonlimiting function.

Personnel who are not being fully utilized may be assigned other tasks without violating the assumptions of the calendar time component of the model. However, they must be *available* for their primary task when needed. For example, failure correction personnel may be transferred to other projects in the latter stages of a project. Infrequent but priority demands will be made on them for correction of failures on the original project. Availability may be taken care of with "suitable" replacements, suitable meaning having the same skill level and experience with respect to the project as the original personnel.

When programs are executed at multiple sites, some adjustments are necessary. Add personnel and computer resources P_F, P_I, and P_C for all sites. Note that in making this addition, we are implicitly assuming that the *location* of the resources is unimportant. This is generally true if the failure identification personnel are reasonably well distributed among the sites. If they can be redistributed when necessary, or if they can run tests remotely, then it is also true. It is correct to add P_C's from computers of different power, since the power differences are accounted for by adjusting execution times. The parameters μ_F, μ_I and θ_C will normally be the same for all sites.

RESOURCE UTILIZATIONS. Resource utilizations are generally estimated from formula or practical experience. We are interested in their maximum practical values for the limiting period of the resource. This is not necessarily the same as the values that may actually occur.

The resource utilization of failure identification personnel ρ_I is 1. It is not restricted by any queueing constraints.

The computer utilization factor ρ_C is often either implicitly or explicitly controlled to maintain satisfactory turnaround time. If testing is scheduled and organized, and there are few unpredictable demands for computer time, the computer utilization factor may approach 1. However, even in a scheduled testing situation, demands for computer time for failure correction often occur at unpredictable times. The most likely situation is one in which the demand for computer time is dependent on many complex factors. Thus it is essentially unpredictable and can best be modeled as being random. One approach to controlling utilization is to provide sufficient hardware to maintain the utilization at an economic optimum. We minimize the sum of computing costs and and wait time (for response) costs of software engineers. When utilization is high, response is poor and salary costs (due to waiting) will be high, although direct computing costs will be low. When utilization is low, response will be excellent and salary costs will drop. However, direct computing costs will be high. The minimum overall cost will occur at some intermediate value. This approach is described in more detail in Chapter 14.

The resource utilization to be selected for failure correction is based on preventing an excessive backlog of failures awaiting correction from building up in any area of code. Such a backlog might hamper further testing in that area. Note that the area of code will generally be associated with a particular person responsible. We compute the failure correction personnel utilization factor ρ_F using

$$\rho_F = (1 - P_{m_Q}^{1/P_F})^{1/m_Q}, \tag{5.9}$$

where P_{m_Q} is the probability that the number of failures awaiting correction by any debugger does not equal or exceed m_Q. In Figure 5.5, curves of utilization are plotted against number of failure correction personnel for various values of queue length. The plot is constructed such that 90 percent of the queues that occur are less than the specified value. Data taken on projects T1, T2, T3, and T4 (projects described in Table 13.1) showed that the 90 percent points for queue lengths occurred at 7, 4, 5, and 5 failures, respectively. Thus it appears reasonable for the present to assume that the failure queue length is controlled so that it does not equal or exceed 5 with probability 0.9. The control is not usually conscious. However, the test team generally has some sense of the backlog of failures and paces testing accordingly. The queue lengths that you observe have a fair amount of consistency, as indicated. It may be possible to refine the values with more knowledge of the effect of backed-up failures on the debugging process. The foregoing computation can be incorporated in software reliability estimation programs.

The foregoing relationship assumes that the assignment of failures for correction can be modeled by random assignment among all failure correction person-

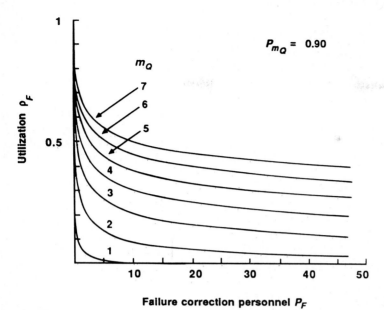

FIGURE 5.5
Failure correction personnel utilization.

nel. This is a reasonable approximation if each programmer has code in the ₊art of the system that is being tested. If this is not the case, it may still be possible to handle the situation with an appropriate correction. For example, we can adjust the number of failure correction personnel to the average number to whom failures can be assigned. One common case in which the foregoing situation occurs is that of a program that is highly modular in terms of function. Such a program is often tested in a modular fashion so that only some of the failure correction personnel are involved at any given time. Note, however, that it is possible to tolerate a somewhat longer failure queue for each programmer because a backlog of failures has less effect on another function. Hence, the actual effect on calendar time may not be large.

5.2.3 Resource Usage Parameters

The resource usage parameters describe resource usage as a function of execution time and failures experienced. They are:

θ_C: average computer time expended per unit execution time,

θ_I: average failure identification work expended per unit execution time,

μ_C: average computer time required per failure,

μ_F: average failure correction work required per failure, and

μ_I: average failure identification work required per failure.

The values of the resource usage parameters of the calendar time model represent *average* values of resource expenditure. They appear to be dependent on the factors of programmer skill level, level of task difficulty, and development environment. By "environment" we are referring to characteristics such as batch debugging versus interactive debugging, debugging aids available, computer used, language used, and administrative and documentation overhead associated with corrections. The values are accurate if measured for the project on which they are used, and there are no major changes in the factors after the measurements are taken. Values from another project can be applicable if it is similar to the project on which they will be used in the foregoing three aspects. If both projects are of reasonable size, differences in the first two factors tend to become small, and applicability is dependent primarily on the similarity of development environment. This averaging effect has been noticed on projects as small as 5 programmers and 5000 instructions. When there is a marked difference in, say, programmer skill level between two small projects, it still may be possible to apply parameter values from one project to the other. One estimates appropriate multiplicative factors. If failure correction is not done on the test machine (and there is sufficient time for it on another machine), the parameter μ_C will be 0.

ESTIMATION FROM DATA. The resource usage parameters may be evaluated by collecting data on failure identification work, failure correction work, and computer usage at various values of execution time. We also record failures experienced. Then we fit the data with a transformation of the resource usage model expressed in incremental terms,

$$\frac{\Delta\chi_r}{\Delta\tau} = \theta_r + \mu_r \frac{\Delta m(\tau)}{\Delta\tau}, \tag{5.10}$$

using a least squares criterion. Note that $\Delta\chi_r$ represents usage of the generic resource r. The subscript r becomes C for computer time, F for failure correction work, or I for failure identification work. The quantity $\Delta\tau$ is execution time; Δm, failures identified (for resource I), corrected (for F), or an average of the two (for C). Note that Δm and $\Delta\tau$ are not independent of each other, since they are related through the execution time component of the model.

A relatively painless approach to collection of the data for the estimation of the resource usage parameters μ_C, μ_F, μ_I, θ_C, and θ_I is to obtain weekly resource expenditure totals from each person involved in testing. It is also possible to collect data on a per-failure basis. This will be more accurate but will require much more data collection effort. Note that time spent in proving suspected failures false is included in either approach and thus will be apportioned among real failures. In cases where only one person is identifying the failures, the data gathered will be individual-dependent unless we average data for several "one identifier" projects involving different persons. The least squares fit to Equation (5.10) is unweighted. We treat all data points equally. Usually measurements made of the parameters will represent net times. The measures must be increased by a suitable overhead factor to account for overhead such as vacations, holidays, absences, training, and administrative activities. A common value is 1.67. This is based on typical figures of 15 percent for vacations, holidays, and absences and 25 percent for training and administrative activities.

If you can obtain better estimates of the resource usage parameters as the test period proceeds, you should use them. A "jump change" may occur in many of the quantities being computed as a result, but the quantities should henceforth be more accurate.

DELPHI AND OTHER ESTIMATION METHODS. If determination from data is not feasible, a "Delphi" survey of the members of the project may be useful. The Delphi survey involves taking an average of informed judgments. It appears to work best when periods of full communication between participants alternate with independently developed judgments [Boehm (1981)]. A coordinator should explain the purpose of the survey, define all the parameters carefully, and make sure everyone understands what they involve. This is best done in a meeting, so questions can be asked. Then each person writes down *independently* his or her best estimates of what the parameters should be, based on experience and careful consideration. The coordinator summarizes and presents the distribution of estimates for each parameter. The group discusses the results, focusing on the reasons for any wide variations in estimates. Then another round of independent estimation ensues, usually resulting in less variation. The process continues until little further convergence occurs. The mean of the estimates is used for each parameter value. These estimates are often surprisingly reasonable! It appears that people can estimate work time best in direct hours expended (that is, *you* should compute and apply overhead factors).

It appears likely that some or all of the resource usage parameters will prove to be constant over wide varieties or classes of projects. As more data are collected, we may gain a deeper understanding of what ranges of values these parameters can have and on what factors they are dependent. This knowledge should make it possible to establish appropriate parameter values from previously collected data for projects with similar characteristics. It may not be necessary to collect data for the project in question.

We currently have some data available for the failure correction work per failure μ_F. The data are illustrated in Table 5.11. Two components of this work are recorded. *Fault identification* is the work to diagnose the fault, given the identified failure. *Fault correction* is the work to design, install, and test the fix for a known fault. We also have total failure correction work. All the values except the Musa and Iannino ones come from data collected on a per-failure basis. The latter values were obtained from resource expenditure data [Musa (1979b)] that were recorded weekly, along with number of failures and execution time. The data were fit by Iannino, using Equation (5.10) in a least squares sense. The systems on which the Musa data were taken are described in Table 13.1. The values are net, without provision for any overhead factor. Means are given, and also means adjusted by an overhead factor of 1.67.

TABLE 5.11
Failure correction effort per failure (in system test unless noted)

Reference	System	Fault identification (person hr)	Fault correction (person hr)	Failure correction (person hr)
Ostrand and Weyuker (1982)				5.5[1]
Weiss (1981)	SEL 1	4	1.8	5.8
	SEL 2	4	3	7
	SEL 3	1	2	3
Presson (1981)	A1	3.3	2.6	5.9[2]
	A2	2.4	2.4	4.8[2]
	B1	3.5	3.1	6.6
	B2	4.5	3.3	7.8[3]
	C	2.9	2.2	5.1
Musa and Iannino (Table 14.3)	T1			4.42
	T2			6.88
	T3			0.58
	T4			0.68
Shooman and Bolsky (1975)		2.46	1.98	4.44
Mean value (system test)				4.54
Mean value with overhead (system test)				7.58

[1]For unit test and system test

[2]First and second halves of system test for same project

[3]Test prior to system test

There are also some values available for the other resource expenditures, failure identification effort and computer time. These values also come from data of Musa (1979b), fit by Equation (5.10) in a least squares sense. They are given in Tables 5.12 and 5.13, respectively, along with the means. The values for the failure identification work parameters with an overhead factor of 1.67 are given also. Note that all four systems in each table were run on a computer with an average instruction execution rate of 280,000 object instructions/CPU sec. The failure

TABLE 5.12
Failure identification effort (in person hr)

Reference	System designator	Effort per CPU hr component[1]	Effort per failure component
Musa (1979b)	T1	9.92	0.23
	T2	3.24	3.89
	T3	4.77	0.53
	T4	5.70	0.24
	Mean value	5.91	1.22
	Mean value with overhead	9.87	2.04

[1]Based on machine with instruction processing rate of 280,000 object instructions/CPU sec.

TABLE 5.13
Computer time (in CPU hr) used in failure identification and correction

Reference	System designator	Computer time per CPU hr component	Computer time per failure component[1]
Musa (1979b)	T1	4.80	1.56
	T2	1.73	1.73
	T3	1.06	0.38
	T4	2.13	0.63
	Mean value	2.43	1.08

[1]Based on machine with instruction processing rate of 280,000 object instructions/CPU sec.

identification work per CPU hr may be a function of the computer on which the application is run, but this is not known for certain at present. The computer time per failure probably will be less for faster machines. It may be inversely proportional to the average instruction execution rate, as the function that has to be performed per failure may be almost constant.

SPECIAL CONSIDERATIONS. Poor computer turnaround time can affect the pace at which failures are corrected. Suppose that the total nonproductive wait time involved in correcting each failure is substantial in comparison with average failure work time required per failure. Then μ_F should be increased by the ratio of failure correction work plus wait time to failure correction work time. Note that there is usually only one approach to the machine for each failure identification. Hence, turnaround time has little effect on that process.[1]

If the fault reduction factor B is substantially different from 1, then it may be necessary to adjust the μ_C and μ_F parameters that would ordinarily be employed by multiplying by B. This is done because resources required for the repair work tend to be most closely related to the number of faults removed. However, for practicality they are measured in terms of failures experienced.

5.3 SUPPORTING COMPUTER PROGRAMS— RECOMMENDED FEATURES AND USE

5.3.1 Features

Experience with many projects and their needs over more than 10 years has indicated at least four computer programs that are useful in the *application* of software

---

[1]Shooman and Bolsky (1975) have collected data that indicate an average of 0.61 runs per failure for failure identification and 1.35 runs per failure for failure correction.

reliability measurement and prediction. This experience, and the construction and use of various versions of these programs, has led to some considerations regarding the *features* of these programs. The features are discussed here, and the *design*, in Appendix I. Of course, there are additional programs that may be useful for research purposes, but we are not discussing them.

The programs should be designed as a compatible set so that they can function with each other. When they have the same inputs, the formats should be identical. Human interfaces should be as similar as possible, using the same commands, command formats, and input variable names. The programs should allow for data input as failure times or grouped data (failures per time interval) to accommodate the varying practices of different projects. Failure times are preferred, because they retain the most information and are therefore most likely to yield accurate estimates and predictions. In any case, it is easy to convert from one form to the other. In general, programs of this kind can be used for any project phase in which the program is executing and experiencing failures. Also, they can ordinarily be used for hardware as well as software. Failure trends and predictions are not usually dependent on the source of the failures.

One program [Musa, Hamilton, and Hollander (1983) and Musa and Hollander (1983)] has been found to be essential. We shall call it a *tabular program* because of the form of its output. This program accepts failure intervals and calendar time component parameters as inputs. The output is a snapshot of status for a software system at a point in time. The program should estimate execution time component parameters for either the basic or logarithmic Poisson execution time models. It computes present failure intensity. It also computes the additional failures, execution time, and calendar time required to reach whatever failure intensity objective the user may specify. The date of reaching this objective is also computed. The foregoing quantities and their 50, 75, 90, and 95 percent confidence intervals are computed for whichever model has been selected. The output is illustrated in Figure 5.6. Various control variables provide the capability to select different program options and input a title. Defaults are taken if they are not specified. The program includes the capability to adjust failure times for evolving programs (Section 6.3) and can both use the resulting intervals for computation and output them to other programs. When this capability is used, information on total code and developed code at each failure is required.

Although not as essential, it is very useful to have a plotting program as well, since it provides a running history of a project and can highlight trends. It plots the data that would be obtained by running the tabular program again and again as the failure intervals available for estimation increase one at a time. This program has the same inputs as the tabular program. In addition, it has a set of plot control variables (with defaults) to let you select the plots you desire and the detailed format of the plots. You should be able to plot any of the quantities that are computed for the table of the tabular program. They can be plotted against either execution time, calendar time, date, or number of failures. It is also often useful to be able to plot total execution time. This is the time from start of execution to time predicted for meeting the failure intensity objective. The usefulness of

SOFTWARE RELIABILITY PREDICTION
LOG POISSON MODEL
SYSTEM T2

BASED ON SAMPLE OF   54 TEST FAILURES
EXECUTION TIME IS   32.78 HR
FAILURE INTENSITY OBJECTIVE IS   .36e−01 FAILURES/CPU HR
CALENDAR TIME TO DATE IS   74 DAYS
PRESENT DATE   5/31/74

	CONF. LIMITS				MOST LIKELY		CONF. LIMITS		
	95%	90%	75%	50%		50%	75%	90%	95%
FAILURE INTENSITY DECAY	.0426	.0456	.0503	.0548	.0611	.0675	.0720	.0767	.0796
FAILURE INTENSITIES (FAILURES/1000 CPU HR)									
INITIAL F.I.	6440	7185	8563	10172	13054	16856	20260	24600	27873
PRESENT F.I.	377.8	391.5	415.0	440.1	480.5	527.9	566.5	611.8	643.8

*** ADDITIONAL REQUIREMENTS TO MEET FAILURE INTENSITY OBJECTIVE ***

	95%	90%	75%	50%	MOST LIKELY	50%	75%	90%	95%
FAILURES	30	31	34	37	42	49	55	62	68
EXEC. TIME (CPU HR)	315.5	329.0	352.3	377.8	420.2	472.5	517.2	573.1	614.9
CAL. TIME (DAYS)	142.1	148.4	159.2	171.0	190.8	215.2	236.1	262.3	281.9
COMPLETION DATE	121874	122674	11075	12875	22375	33175	42975	60375	63075

FIGURE 5.6
Sample project status report as generated by program.

this plot is described in Section 6.3. To avoid clutter on the plot, you should be able to determine whether confidence intervals should be plotted, and if so, which ones. A capability to "window" and blow up on a separate page any section of the plot you want to examine on a more detailed basis is frequently valuable. Early values of quantities plotted can sometimes be noisy. Consequently, it should be possible to select the point at which plotting starts to reduce excessive clutter. Finally, you should have some control over the labeling of the plot and be able to furnish an appropriate title. A sample plot is shown in Figure 5.7. This program should also be able to adjust failure times for evolving programs.

A simulation program is useful for system studies. It permits various parameters to be varied so that "what if" questions can be answered. It performs a function equivalent to that of running the tabular program repetitively, with different values of parameters. The results are most readily interpretable if plotted. For example, you can look at the effect of changes in failure intensity objective on program release date (that is, date of meeting the failure intensity objective). It is possible to either estimate the execution time component parameters from failure intervals or input them as parameters that can be varied.

A failure log conversion program has frequently proved to be helpful. Such a program processes failure information as recorded in failure logs or trouble reports and converts it to failure intervals. It handles time uncertainties (Section 6.2.2) and multiple copies of programs (Section 6.2.3), including those running on machines with different instruction execution rates. It can also sort out data from different subsystems that have been recorded together, weighting each time interval by its utilization. This program functions independently of the particular software reliability model being used. The output can be used as the input to any of the foregoing programs. Sometimes the failure intervals needed for input to the foregoing programs have been recorded directly and no adjustment is necessary. Then you do not need to run the log conversion program.

Many projects record or could record (with minor modifications) failure data in their software change management systems. A direct link between such a system and software reliability estimation programs through a failure log conversion program may be very advantageous for a project.

Finally, you may wish to have a standard least squares fit package. This will be needed if you determine resource usage parameters by collecting data.

5.3.2 Interpretation of Results
and Special Problems

The 75 percent confidence interval has been found from experience to be the most useful from the manager's viewpoint. However, the 50, 90, and 95 percent confidence intervals contribute some added insight. The 75 percent interval provides a level of confidence comparable to that with which many other managerial decisions are made. Higher levels of confidence result in intervals for many quantities that are too large to be useful.

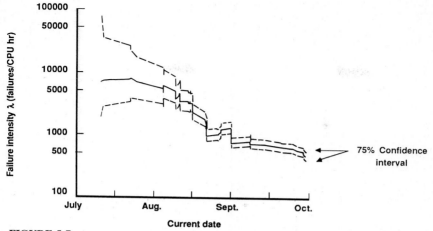

FIGURE 5.7
Sample plot of history of present failure intensity estimates.

To obtain an estimate of total remaining failures rather than failures to reach the failure intensity objective, set the failure intensity objective to zero.

Sometimes you may wish to determine the present failure intensity of a program that is released to the field with some faults not corrected. This, of course, depends on the particular faults that are not corrected. However, a first approximation to the present failure intensity may be obtained by running the software reliability estimation program with a number of the latest failure intervals removed. This number should correspond to the faults outstanding.

Occasionally, you may not be able to obtain a good estimate of the confidence interval for the completion date of a project. This may occur because the confidence interval for total failures has an upper bound of infinity. The estimation algorithm may not be able to discern a trend in failure intervals with high confidence. Here, other available information may be used to estimate an upper bound for the 75 percent confidence interval for total failures. One possibility is faults found per 1000 lines of delivered executable source code from system test onward. This information is applied to find additional failures required to achieve the failure intensity objective. To obtain the completion date bound to a first approximation, use linear interpolation or extrapolation between two additional failures-completion date pairs for different confidence bounds in the tabular output from the software reliability estimation program.

5.4 DISCUSSION: FAILURE GROUPING AND RANDOMIZATION

We will use two case studies to look more closely at the effects of the grouping of and the randomization of data.

CASE STUDY 5.1
EFFECT OF GROUPING DATA

Failure data are often available only in grouped form. Here we wish to compare the relative precision with which model parameters are estimated when using failure time data to the estimates obtained using the equivalent grouped data. Our focus will be on the basic and logarithmic Poisson execution time models.

In Chapter 12 we will see that maximum likelihood inference for the basic execution time model is centered around the parameter representing the product $B\phi$. For the logarithmic Poisson execution time model, inference is centered around the parameter representing the product $\lambda_0\theta$. Although $B\phi$ and $\lambda_0\theta$ have somewhat different meanings, they both affect the rate of reduction in failure intensity. The rate increases as the parameter increases in both cases. Since all the other model parameters and derived quantities depend on our estimates of these two parameters and their associated accuracies, our study will focus on them.

The simplest way to do the comparison is via simulation (analytic results being too difficult to obtain). A sequence of failure time data can easily be generated according to a known model. It can then be converted into grouped data in many ways depending on how we define the duration of each group. Two of these ways, studied here, are fixed time per group and equal number of failures per group.

BASIC EXECUTION TIME MODEL

A sequence consisting of 100 failure times from the model defined by

$$\mu(t) = 150\{1 - \exp[-(0.3 \times 10^{-4})t]\},$$

where $\mu(t)$ is the mean number of failures in time t and $B\phi = 0.3 \times 10^{-4}$/sec, is used as our illustrative example. Table 5.7 contains the values of I_g resulting from various equal time groupings and several different sample sizes. It is apparent from an examination of this table that grouping has minimal effect when there is a moderate amount of failure data on hand. When grouping is based on an equal number of failures per group the results shown in Table 5.14 are obtained. The results are almost as good as before. Of the two types of groupings it appears that equal length is to be preferred, but equal number groups are acceptable in practice.

LOGARITHMIC POISSON EXECUTION TIME MODEL

Data for the illustrative example used in this section were generated from the model specified by

$$\mu(t) = 20 \ln[1 + (0.25 \times 10^{-3})t],$$

where $\lambda_0\theta = 0.25 \times 10^{-3}$/sec.

TABLE 5.14
Value of I_g for equal number of failures per group for the basic execution time model

Number of groups	Number of failures	
	100	50
	I_g	I_g
5	0.901	0.94
10	0.975	0.977
15	0.957	0.984
20	0.984	0.989

Consider first grouping based on an equal amount of time per group. Results analogous to those given in Table 5.7 are shown in Table 5.8 for a sample size of 100 failures. Note that we can have more groups than failures. Some groups will have zero failures associated with them. We conclude that this method of grouping is very detrimental to the estimation of model parameters unless the number of groups is large (many times the number of failures). If, on the other hand, we group the failure time data based on an equal number of failures per group, the results shown in Table 5.15 are obtained. The improvement in the value of I_g is substantial. I_g indicates that there is still a 10 to 20 percent loss of information.

General conclusions should not be drawn from a limited study as this. However, it does appear that the basic execution time model is robust to grouping in general. Also, it appears that some care must be exercised when the logarithmic Poisson execution time model is used with grouped failure data. Specifically, the results shown in Tables 5.8 and 5.15 indicate that equal time groups should be avoided unless the number of failures per group is almost uniform.

TABLE 5.15
Values of I_g for equal number of failures per group for the logarithmic Poisson model

Number of groups	Number of failures	
	100	50
	I_g	I_g
5	0.395	1.2
10	1.115	0.854
15	0.833	0.794
20	0.894	0.821
50	0.84	0.761

CASE STUDY 5.2
EFFECT OF RANDOMIZING GROUPED DATA

In Case Study 5.1 we examined the effects of grouping failure time data. Here we will briefly look at the reverse process, that is, taking a set of grouped data and "converting" it into failure time data. We do this primarily because it may be convenient to implement software reliability estimation programs to accept just failure times as inputs.

Both simulated and actual failure data will be employed. The simulated data are the same as those from Case Study 5.1.[2] The actual failure data represent two projects, T38, given in Table 12.3, and T39, given in Table 5.16. For these projects, data were collected weekly. The number of failures occurring and the amount of execution time during each week are shown.

Grouped data can be converted into failure time data in several ways. Two of these are random and uniform assignments. The latter is the easiest to implement. Failure times are equally spaced in each group. The former is somewhat more complicated to implement but should be more realistic. In this method failure times are randomly assigned (according to a uniform distribution) in each group. The assumption used in random assignment is that the failure intensity varies slowly and can be considered constant for the duration of a group.[3]

As we did in Case Study 5.1, attention will be focused on the parameters $B\phi$ and $\lambda_0\theta$. In particular, we will consider the maximum likelihood estimate, the information content being of little use in this context. Results of the study are shown in Table 5.9 and 5.10 for simulated and actual data, respectively. The reader can see that for a reasonable number of groups the amount of error introduced by the random conversion can be neglected, in practice. The uniform conversion, while not necessarily bad, is never as good as the random conversion.

5.5 SUMMARY

Determination of the values of many parameters is straightforward. You must *predict* the values of the execution time component parameters from characteristics of the software product and the development process in the period before the pro-

---

[2]Groups for the simulated data for the basic execution time model were based on an equal amount of time per group. For the logarithmic Poisson execution time model, they were based on an equal number of failures per group.

[3]This assumption implies a homogeneous Poisson process where, conditioned on the number of failures experienced in a group, the times of the failures are independently and uniformly distributed over the period of the group [Cox and Lewis (1966)].

TABLE 5.16
Grouped failure data for system T39

Group no.	Group duration, CPU hr	No. of failures
1	62	5
2	63	25
3	66	10
4	24	7
5	8	4
6	206.5	4
7	60	0
8	65	2
9	59	0
10	163	1
11	62.5	0
12	60	6
13	61.5	0
14	66	5
15	64	0
16	109	5
17	186	1
18	51	0
19	180	2

gram can be executed. Afterwards, you can *estimate* them from failure data. Ordinarily, the estimation process should be automated. The means for determination of calendar time component parameters depends on the particular parameters, but it can involve data collection, use of historical data, and current project estimates.

PROBLEMS

5.1 Which of the following activities utilize limiting resources?
(*a*) Writing a user manual.
(*b*) Generating test cases based on test results.
(*c*) Filling out trouble reports.
(*d*) Attending a meeting of a trouble review board.
(*e*) Documenting a program correction.

5.2 What values will you get for total failures ν_0 and failure intensity decay parameter θ during the operational phase?

5.3 Can the software reliability estimation programs be used for hardware?

5.4 Can software reliability measurement be applied to a situation where a program is released to the field with some failures not yet addressed?

5.5 Can we apply a software reliability model when we run formal system tests at widely spaced intervals during the test period? Interval data are recorded for the formal tests but not otherwise, except that number of failures and total execution time per day or week is noted.

5.6 Can software reliability models be applied to individual programmers who are testing subsystems?

5.7 Nonoperating time can affect hardware failures because aging can occur even without operation. Can this happen for software?

5.8 We log our failures in real times against a "clock" that keeps track of cumulative execution time. Since determining that a failure really occurred involves a delay, all the failures are logged at a time later than they actually occurred. Does this cause a problem in estimation during system test?

5.9 Do we count a fault found by a programmer on his or her own without testing?

5.10 We are examining our output data from testing by using a computerized analysis program. This makes location of failures much easier. Should the computer time used by this program be accounted for in any way?

5.11 We seem to be getting results with the basic execution time model that do not make sense. We removed some closely spaced failures from the failure interval data because we thought they were not true failures. Predictions of total failures expected increased. What is wrong?

5.12 What is the effect on the basic model parameter estimates of a failure that keeps occurring, can't be fixed, and is still counted?

5.13 How can corrected faults be proportional to identified failures? What you correct depends on what it is profitable to correct or what the customer pays for.

5.14 Can two or more resources be simultaneously limiting?

5.15 How can total failures of the basic execution time model be a finite value? If you run a program for an infinite time, won't you get an infinite number of failures?

5.16 The definition of the fault reduction factor B states that it relates *total* failures experienced to *net* faults corrected. Why is this distinction made?

5.17 Are any assumptions made about specialization of failure identification or failure correction personnel?

5.18 Are support staff (program librarians, etc.) counted in applying the theory?

5.19 Must all P_F failure correction personnel be retained on the project for the entire system test phase?

5.20 How do you calculate hours of availability for a computer?

5.21 Do the utilization factors ρ_C and ρ_F that are used hold for the entire system test phase?

5.22 How do you handle vacations and absences in computing calendar time durations?

5.23 If you obtain better data on your parameters during the test period, should you change them or will this adversely affect the results?

5.24 Is it necessary to establish the values of all the parameters when you are applying software reliability measurement during the period of field test?

5.25 Our test teams are required to do a substantial amount of test planning or replanning and test procedure debugging while testing is going on. Should these activities be taken into account in making calendar time predictions?

5.26 Would a program that is highly modular in terms of function affect the length of the failure queue that would be acceptable for each programmer?

5.27 We use different failure diagnosis tools during different phases of test. As a result, some new failures may be found that were missed during an earlier phase. How should this be handled?

5.28 In our project, failure identification and correction are done on different computers. What adjustments must be made in applying a software reliability model?

5.29 Why does the occurrence of a number of failures separated by short time intervals (compared to the intervals previously experienced) often lead to a *decrease* in the estimate of initial failure intensity? This seems counterintuitive.

5.30 Can the quality of the parameter predictions being made be checked by looking at a project history of such predictions?

5.31 We plot total (present plus the prediction of the additional amount required to meet the failure intensity objective) execution and calendar times against either present execution or calendar time. How should we interpret them?

5.32 During testing we record much data on tape and then examine these data interactively on a display afterwards. What is the significance of the examination time?

5.33 Every failure reported for our project goes to a problem review board before it is assigned to a programmer for correction. Sometimes the customer must approve before the failure is corrected. The process can add 1 to 4 days delay. Must predictions of additional calendar time required to meet the failure intensity objective be altered to account for this?

5.34 In our project, test cases are created by recording data in the field and then processing them. The rate at which these cases can be generated is limited, and this really paces our testing effort. Can this consideration be incorporated in the software reliability model?

5.35 How should regression testing be handled when doing software reliability modeling?

5.36 Is prediction of the initial failure intensity machine-dependent?

5.37 It appears that the accuracy of determining when a failure intensity objective will be reached will get worse for smaller objectives because the slope of failure intensity with respect to execution time is decreasing. Is this true?

5.38 A program with 50,000 source instructions and a source to object expansion ratio of 4 will be executed on a machine with an average instruction execution rate of 333,333 instructions/CPU sec. On similar projects, a fault exposure ratio of $K = 1.67 \times 10^{-7}$ has been experienced, along with a fault density of 6 faults per 1000 source instructions. The fault reduction factor $B = 1$. Estimate the initial failure intensity at the start of system test.

5.39 Our computer has a utilization of about 0.3. How should I set the value of the computer utilization factor?

5.40 It is difficult for us to obtain the cooperation necessary to collect resource expenditure data. We want to reduce data collection requirements to a basic minimum. What resource expenditure data are most important?

5.41 Our failure correction personnel and failure identification personnel use different computers. Does this mean that we may have four limiting resources?

5.42 All corrections made to our system must pass through a "software manufacturing" process. In this process, corrected source routines are recompiled and bound into a new system. Then the new system is formally tested by the test team. Is the software manufacturing process a limiting resource in the sense of affecting the calendar time component of the model?

5.43 Suppose that failures can be assigned to one of several people for correction rather than just one person. How do you account for this in the utilization factor for failure correction personnel?

5.44 During test we find a number of faults (and hence implied failures) by code reading.

How can we reflect these in our software reliability estimates?

5.45 How can the parameter θ_C, computer time used per unit execution time, be greater than 1?

5.46 We do program testing on one machine, correct faults on another, and verify that the faults have been removed on yet another. How do we apply the calendar time component of the model?

5.47 Do you really count *all* testing during system test in determining total execution time that has occurred?

SIX

PROJECT-SPECIFIC TECHNIQUES

In Chapter 5 we looked at the problem of parameter determination. In this chapter we will present ways of dealing with various special problems that have arisen from experience with a variety of projects. Interestingly enough, these problems generally do not result from advances in software engineering technology. Such advances may change values (for example, faults per delivered source instruction at the start of system test) but generally do not affect assumptions and basic concepts. In Chapter 7 we will see how to use all the techniques of Chapters 4 to 6 for specific applications.

6.1 UNOBSERVED FAILURES

A common problem that must be dealt with is the fact that some failures may not be observed. This occurs most frequently with less severe failures, and particularly failures that do not stop the execution of the program. Failures can be missed in hardware just as easily as software systems, provided the two are analogous in the strictness with which "failure" is defined. Even if the failures are observed, you often get incomplete reporting from the field. Sometimes this is just carelessness or lack of interest or motivation. At other times it may simply be due to the fact that field personnel are not as highly trained and sensitive to the importance of reporting failures as development personnel. The fact that some failures are not being observed or reported means that in general failure intensity is going to be underestimated. The saving grace is that usually the customers miss more failures than the system testers. In other words, any underestimating of failure intensity by the system test personnel is less than that the customers will underestimate. Thus, the customers will generally think the system is more reliable than the system testers do. This will be the case if the observation and reporting difference is greater than the change of environment in going from test to operation. Occasionally it may happen that things look worse in the field. If so, this may be due to rather poor system test planning. If system test doesn't represent the conditions that will be encountered in the field, then indeed you may see an increase in failure intensity when the program is released. This increase occurs when the effect of the change in environment is greater than the pseudo "improvement" you see because the customers are not observing some of the failures.

If you think it is desirable to adjust for unobserved and unreported failures, you can. However, it is a bit of a risky endeavor. You need good data on a similar project that indicate the proportion of failures that are missed. To find out how many failures are missed, you have to do a comprehensive analysis of the history of failure observations. You don't know how many have been missed until they are ultimately found. So it is best to do this on a project with a long operational history. You would look for "late" failures that "must" have occurred earlier and been missed. Earlier occurrence could be inferred if you know that the same input states were exercised earlier during the operational history.

Some projects use correction reports as well as trouble or failure reports. Correction reports close out failure reports for which repairs have been made and note the program changes. Other projects have reports of program changes available from automated configuration control systems. One might think that comparison of failure reports with correction reports could yield valuable clues about missing reports of failures. Unfortunately, they do not indicate the proportion of failures not observed. They only represent failures that have been observed and fixed, but not reported for some reason.

You should be careful to ascertain whether unobserved failures are significant. The fact that they are not observed *may* be a clue to a misunderstanding between developer and customer about what the system requirements really are. A large proportion of unobserved failures may indicate that inadequate attention has been given in system design to failure recording functions and procedures. This can particularly be a problem for unattended systems.

Special care must be exercised for failures identified by automated reporting systems. Since these systems must be programmed with respect to recognizing what behaviors constitute failures, there is a substantial risk that some failures will be missed. Frequently, the unexpected failures are the most significant ones; if they were known, they might have been eliminated in the design.

CASE STUDY 6.1
EFFECTS OF FAILURE OBSERVABILITY
ON FAILURE INTENSITY ESTIMATE

Let us consider how failure intensity estimates are affected when some failures are not observed. The basic and logarithmic Poisson execution time models will be used to investigate the effects at various times during testing.

The basic execution time model has been applied to an actual software project for which it is believed that some proportion (increasing with time) of failures were missed. Project personnel indicated that after a function was tested, less attention was paid to looking for failures associated with it, and therefore some failures may have gone unnoticed. Also a good portion of the latter data was collected by the end user of the product, who was known to have paid less attention to program behavior. Thus a higher proportion of failures probably was missed. The results for this project suggested that the model tended to underpredict the failure intensity.[1] In the following we present results that emanate from these observations.

Denote the probability that the ith failure goes unnoticed as $P(i)$. Many forms for $P(i)$ are possible but for simplicity we consider only the linear case (Figure 6.1), that is,

$$p(i) = p_1 + \frac{i}{a}(p_2 - p_1); \quad i < a \qquad (6.1)$$

$$= p_2; \quad i \geq a .$$

At the start of system test the probability of not observing any particular failure will be p_1. As testing progresses this probability changes linearly to its final value of p_2. The rate of change is governed by the constant a. When p_2 is set equal to p_1, the proportion of missed failures is constant throughout the test phase.

BASIC EXECUTION TIME MODEL

The *expected* failure intensity at time t for the basic execution time model is given by

$$\lambda(t) = v_o \phi B \exp(-\phi Bt) . \qquad (6.2)$$

Simulations were conducted to see how closely the *estimated* failure intensity at time t follows the value given by Equation (6.2) when failures are missed according to Equation (6.1). The model parameters used in the following simulations were $v_0 = 250$ failures, $\phi = 0.005$/sec, and $B = 1$. One thousand different failure time sequences for this model were randomly generated. Then, failures were randomly removed with probability given by Equation (6.1). For each resulting failure time sequence, $\hat{\lambda}(t)$ was determined at various values of t and the ratio of $\hat{\lambda}(t)$ to $\lambda(t)$ was determined. Finally, the average value of this ratio was calculated using the results of all 1000 failure time sequences. Values of this ratio near 1 tell us that our estimation is about what is expected. Values less than 1 indicate an underestimation and values greater than 1, an overestimation. This entire process was repeated for different values of p_1 and p_2.

---

[1]This is entirely reasonable since the number of failures observed is less than normal. It appears that fewer failures are occurring in the same amount of time. Thus, the lower failure intensity.

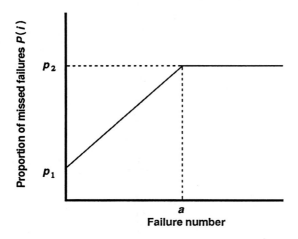

FIGURE 6.1
Probability that ith failure goes unnoticed.

Figure 6.2 shows how the ratio varies with t for some different values of (p_1, p_2). The results show that:

1. If $P(i)$ is constant ($p_1 = p_2$), then estimates for failure intensity are low.[2]
2. If $P(i)$ increases with time, the estimate for failure intensity is low and becomes lower still as time passes.

---

[2]We would expect the value of the ratio to be about equal to $1 - p$, since this is the fraction of failures actually observed. The data do bear this out.

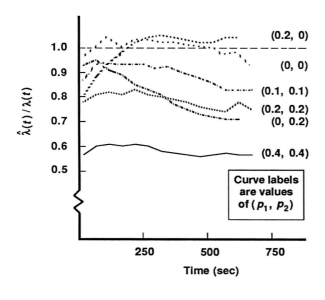

FIGURE 6.2
Effect of unobserved failures: estimated-actual failure intensity ratio for basic execution time model.

3. If $P(i)$ decreases with time the estimate for failure intensity is initially low but becomes better as time passes.

In summary, a simple correction [just divide by $(1 - p_1)$] to the estimated failure intensity can be applied if the proportion of missed failures does not change over time. When the proportion decreases over time, one of two things can be done. First, you can ignore the problem since the missed early failures do not significantly impact estimates made later. The second option is to divide the estimated failure intensity by the current probability of observing a failure. This option is only feasible if the mentioned probability can be estimated. When the proportion increases over time care must be exercised. Here the missed failures occur late during testing and they are the ones having the greatest impact on the estimated failure intensity.[3]

LOGARITHMIC POISSON EXECUTION TIME MODEL

The same simulations were conducted using a logarithmic Poisson execution time model with $\theta = 0.05$/failure and $\lambda_0 = 0.005$ failure/sec. Figure 6.3 shows how the ratio of $\hat{\lambda}(t)$ to $\lambda(t)$ varies with t for some different values of (p_1, p_2). The results show that the estimated failure intensity is low under a broad range of condi-

---

[3]In all this we are assuming that the missed failures do not constitute an implicit redefinition of what a failure really is.

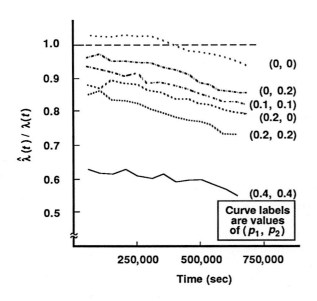

FIGURE 6.3
Effect of unobserved failures: estimated-actual failure intensity ratio for logarithmic Poisson execution time model.

tions. For a constant $P(i)$, dividing the estimated failure intensity by $1 - p_1$ will result in values not far from those obtained when all failures are observed. The correction here is not as good as that for the basic model.

6.2 FAILURE TIME MEASUREMENTS

When making failure time measurements in execution time, there will sometimes be questions of interpretation to be resolved. The most basic principle is that the execution time is measured on the processor on which the program is running. This would mean, for example, that the time required to perform input-output functions on peripheral processors or controllers is not counted. Of course, if we are measuring the reliability of the peripheral processor software, then its run time *is* the quantity to measure. Care must be taken so that we only measure the execution of those functions that would be included in the deliverable product and normally operated by the customer. For example, the execution of utility programs that analyze or display data recorded from the output of the program for the purpose of failure identification should not be included in measuring the failure intervals.

Other considerations include approximations to execution time, failure time uncertainties, and handling of multiple installations of the same program.

6.2.1 Approximations to Execution Time

It certainly is best to collect failure data in terms of execution time if possible. However, there may be some situations where it is difficult to do this. Rather than give up, there are approximations that are possible. There are at least three different kinds of approximations that have been used: clock time, weighted clock time, and natural units.

If the average utilization of the system over a period comparable to a failure interval is almost constant, then clock time is a good approximation to execution time. What does this mean? Suppose failures are occurring hourly. If the average utilization over one hour is 0.60 and over another, 0.63, the approximation is good. If the average utilization is varying, then the weighted clock time approximation should be used.

For the weighted clock time approximation, you multiply short segments of clock time by utilization or some approximation to utilization. The products are then added. One example would be an interactive time sharing system where it is easy to get data on the number of users. You could approximate execution time by the product of clock time and fraction of maximum possible users.

Example 6.1. A time sharing system has a maximum feasible load of 40 users. This is defined for the particular system as the number that yields 0.8 utilization. Above this number, response time on this system becomes intolerable, although more users are physically possible. We sample the number of users at a randomly chosen instant within a 5-minute period. The 12 periods occurring in an hour are averaged to give users for that hour. The following table gives the figures. The fraction of maximum feasible users, multiplied by 0.8, yields an approximation to utilization.

Hour	Number of users	Approximation of utilization
8–9 A.M.	16	0.32
9–10 A.M.	36	0.72
10–11 A.M.	40	0.8
11–12 A.M.	36	0.72
12–1 P.M.	20	0.4
1–2 P.M.	36	0.72
2–3 P.M.	40	0.8
3–4 P.M.	40	0.8
4–5 P.M.	36	0.72
5–6 P.M.	24	0.48

If a failure occurs at 10 A.M. and another at 2 P.M., we may approximate the execution time interval by summing the utilizations in the intervening hours. This approach yields an interval of 2.64 CPU hr. ∎

The third kind of approximation is natural units. A natural unit would be some quantity that is easy to measure and that represents a constant average number of instructions executed. Some examples of natural units would be transactions, such as reservations in an airline or hotel reservation system, calls in a telephone switching system, or copies in a reproduction system.

Note that failure intensity values are now specified in terms of the new quantity. This may be an advantage if the quantity is a natural one for the application. However, adjustment of the failure intensity objective λ_F may be necessary. Also, two of the resource usage parameters may have to be adjusted. These are the computer time and the failure identification effort per unit execution time. Since these parameters are measured with respect to true execution time, they can be different when we are using approximations to it that differ by a proportionality factor.

Example 6.2. A microcomputer-controlled laser printer produces 1 copy/sec (3600 copies/hr). There is no convenient means for measuring the execution time of its software in the field. However, the number of copies produced is easily determined and recorded. We will determine failure events in terms of copies generated rather than time.

Let us consider the parameter adjustments required to model in this domain. We want the system to operate without failure for an extended working day of 10 hr. This particular system is utilized about half the time. Assume that the hardware is highly reliable and that the system reliability is determined by the software. We can establish a conveniently measured software failure intensity objective of 1 failure/18K copies. This would represent 1 failure/day. Note that we must measure computer time and failure identification effort required for system test in terms of number of copies and number of failures rather than execution time and number of failures. The per-copy component of computer time might be 0.001 CPU hr, and failure identification effort, 0.002 person hr. ∎

Some special methods exist for approximating execution time in distributed systems. These were covered in Chapter 4.

6.2.2 Time Uncertainties

The time of a failure or start or end of a period of execution may be uncertain due to either limitations in data recording or in record keeping and reporting. To handle this situation, first determine the window during which the event must have occurred. Then choose the event time randomly (assuming a uniform distribution) within that window. The foregoing procedure will yield more accurate results than ignoring the failures and test periods that are not accurately recorded. The effect of the uncertainty can be determined by making estimates using the extreme values of the possible range of failure intervals.

A common application of the procedure is to situations where we only know the number of failures per day and the hours of run time for each day. The failures are assigned randomly within the window of the day's run time. This approach is readily generalized to the situation where m_W failures occur in a specified period of uncertainty t_W. All the failures are assigned randomly within this window. An alternative method is to divide the window into $m_W + 1$ segments of length $t_L = t_W/(m_W + 1)$ and assign the failures at t_L, $2t_L$, $3t_L$, and so on. However, this latter approach yields inferior results when model parameters are estimated, as shown in Case Study 5.2. If run time is not recorded, an estimate of average run time can be used, although this will cause a deterioration in accuracy and ability to predict. Note that data on a failures-per-day basis that are mixed with failure interval data can be handled with the preceding procedure.

Example 6.3. The following log of a day of testing was recorded. We have decided to use clock time as an approximation to execution time.

Event	Calendar time
Start test	8 A.M.
Failure 1	8:30 A.M.
Failure 2	9:30–10:20 A.M.
Failure 3	11 A.M.
Stop test for lunch	12 noon
Start test	1 P.M.
Failures 4, 5	1:00–4:20 P.M.
Stop test	5:00 P.M.

We convert the times of the events to minutes of clock time for convenience. We then select numbers from a random number table. We multiply these numbers by whatever constant is necessary to adjust their range of variation to the range of uncertainty of times. The failure times are thus established and the intervals calculated. The procedure is illustrated in the table below.

Event	Clock time (min)	Random number	Adjustment factor	Assigned clock time (min)	Clock time interval since last failure (min)
Start test	0			0	
Failure 1	30			30	30
Failure 2	90–140	67557	0.0005	63.8	33.8
Failure 3	180			180	116.2
Stop test	240			240	
Start test	240			240	
Failure 4	240–440	26446	0.002	292.9	112.9
Failure 5	240–440	97159	0.002	434.3	141.4
Stop test	480			480	

Sometimes (although this is undesirable) the time reported for a failure is the time of identification rather than the time of occurrence. This adds to inaccuracy, but it may not be too serious if the mean execution time lag between failure occurrence and identification is relatively constant with time.

You must beware of the natural tendency of people to "save time" by logging closely occurring failures as happening at the same time. Doing this would result in an excessive number of zero failure intervals, which would yield an overly pessimistic estimate of potential failures in the system. If data have already been logged in this fashion, it is probably best to correct them as follows. Assume there are k identical times between the unequal times t_i and t_{i+k+1}. Pick k random time *points* (for example, from a random number table) in the range $[t_i, t_{i+k+1}]$ and order them as $t_{i+1}, t_{i+2}, \ldots, t_{i+k}$. The *intervals* that will replace the zero intervals will be found as

$$t'_{i+1} = t_{i+1} - t_i \ ,$$

$$t'_{i+2} = t_{i+2} - t_{i+1} \ , \qquad\qquad (6.3)$$

$$\vdots$$

$$t'_{i+k} = t_{i+k} - t_{i+k-1} \ ,$$

and t_{i+k+1} must be changed to $t_{i+k+1} - t_{i+k}$.

Time uncertainties can affect the accuracy of parameter estimates, as noted in the following case study.

**CASE STUDY 6.2
EFFECT OF UNCERTAINTY WINDOW ON ESTIMATION**

Failure time data are often rounded off to some degree. Just what effect this has on the maximum likelihood estimates (see Chapter 12) of the model parameters for the basic and logarithmic Poisson execution time models will be briefly investigated. Actually only the parameter $B\phi$ for the basic model and $\lambda_0\theta$ for the logarithmic Poisson model need be considered. This is because maximum likelihood inference for all other parameters and derived quantities for both models is based on $B\phi$ and $\lambda_0\theta$, as will be seen later in Chapter 12. We can let $B = 1$ for simplicity without loss of generality.

Suppose failure intervals that are recorded as t' actually lie in the interval $[\max(0, t' - \gamma/2), t' + \gamma/2]$, where γ is the uncertainty or precision of measurement. Consider an interval of testing lasting until t_e with m_e failures experienced. As the number of failures increases in this interval more precision in recording the time will be required. In fact, if the number increases sufficiently, it may be better to treat the data as grouped data (number of failures in a given time interval).

Define the relative accuracy of estimation as the ratio of $\hat{\phi}$ to ϕ, that is, the ratio of the estimated to true value. Also, let $\bar{t}'$ denote the average failure interval (AFI). Since we are considering a nonhomogeneous Poisson process, this quantity will increase with time.

Figure 6.4 shows the results of a simulation study based on the basic execution time model. Note that the relative accuracy is always less than 1.0. This means ϕ is underestimated. Consider a case where we are willing to accept at

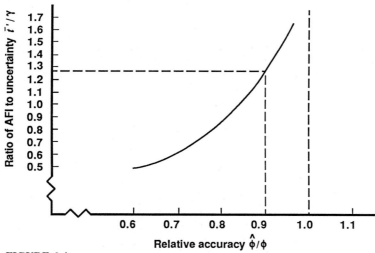

**FIGURE 6.4
Required time measurement precision for specified parameter estimation accuracy: basic execution time model.**

most a 10 percent loss in relative accuracy. The precision required to achieve this goal can be determined from Figure 6.4. Here γ must be no larger than $\bar{i}'/1.28$ or $0.78\,\bar{i}'$. Since AFI increases as time goes by, the precision requirement becomes less strict. A little thought tells us that this is not entirely unexpected.

As a further illustration consider the case where $\nu_0 = 150$ failures and $\phi = 0.25 \times 10^{-4}$/sec. Then at $t_e = 40{,}000$ sec (11.1 hr), the expected number of failures would be $\mu(40{,}000) = 150\{1 - \exp[-(0.25 \times 10^{-4})(40{,}000)]\} = 94.8$. This results in $\bar{i}' = 40{,}000/94.8 = 421.9$ sec. Therefore, each failure interval must be measured to within $\gamma = 0.78\,\bar{i}' = 329$ sec in order to not suffer more than 10 percent loss in accuracy in the estimation of ϕ. At $t_e = 80{,}000$ sec it is only necessary to measure to within $\gamma = 481$ sec. Note that our measurements can be less precise in this case.

Some projects have recorded time of failure to the nearest day. Is this sufficiently accurate to give satisfactory parameter estimates for the basic execution time model? Note from Figure 6.4 that accuracy is generally within 15 percent if AFI is greater than γ. That is, recording to the nearest day is probably satisfactory only if there is less than 1 failure per day on the average. This requirement becomes easier to satisfy as testing progresses.

Figure 6.5 shows similar results for the logarithmic Poisson model. Here the situation is more complicated, as the results depend on the value of $\lambda_0\theta t_e$. Once again, assume we are willing to tolerate at most a 10 percent loss in accuracy. If the value of $\lambda_0\theta t_e$ is 5, then γ must be no larger than 71 percent of the AFI. When $\lambda_0\theta t_e$ increases to 10, then γ must be less than or equal to 50 percent of the AFI. As $\lambda_0\theta t_e$ increases, the required percentage of the AFI is decreasing. However, the AFI itself is increasing. These two factors nearly cancel. This results in a roughly constant precision requirement. For example, let $\theta = 0.01$/failure and

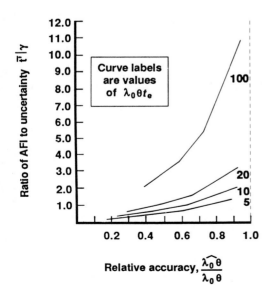

FIGURE 6.5
Required time measurement precision for specified parameter estimation accuracy: logarithmic Poisson execution time model.

$\lambda_0 \theta = 0.25 \times 10^{-3}/\text{sec}$. If $t_e = 20,000$ sec, the expected number of failures is $\mu(20,000) = (1/0.01) \ln [1 + (0.25 \times 10^{-3})(20,000)] = 179$. We have $\overline{\tau}' = 20,000/179 = 112$ sec. Thus, the required precision γ is $0.71 \overline{\tau}' = 79.5$ sec. If $t_e = 80,000$ sec, then $\gamma = 87$ sec.

6.2.3 Multiple Installations

When there are multiple computers running the same program, you should inter-leave the failures from the different computers in the order in which they oc-curred. Then add the concurrently running execution times. This procedure is used because all you are really doing is exposing the same program to more testing. When a failure is found on one computer, all copies of the program on the other computers are normally corrected sooner or later. Consider the following example with CPU utilization of 1 for each of two systems. Both have the same average instruction execution rate (see Table 6.1). You will note that installation A starts executing at 8 A.M. We have a failure at 9 A.M. On installation B, we start at 8:30 and experience a failure at 9:30. We compute that failure 1 occurs after 90 CPU min, 60 CPU min of execution on installation A and 30 CPU min of execution on installation B. Failure number 2 occurs after 30 CPU min of execution on installa-tion A and another 30 CPU min of execution on installation B. Thus failure inter-val 2 is 60 CPU min in length.

You might argue that times should be considered separately for each pro-gram and failure intervals computed for that program as a separate entity. Such an approach would indeed apply to hardware where wear is occurring and the differ-ent accumulated operation times for each system are significant. It *does not* apply to software! Remember that the program is only the logic and not the physical machine it is running on. The nature of that machine or its condition is *immate-*

TABLE 6.1
Example of interleaving failures from multiple installations (CPU utilization $= 1$)

Event	Calender time	Cumulative execution time (min)			Time between failures (min)
		Installation A	Installation B	All Installations	
Start of program execution on installation A	8:00 A.M.	0	0	0	0
Start of program execution on installation B	8:30 A.M.	30	0	30	0
Failure on installation A	9:00 A.M.	60	30	90	90
Failure on installation B	9:30 A.M.	90	60	150	60

rial. If the software copies are presented with the same operational profile, the runs for these copies may be different but the probability of a given run for any copy is identical. Hence whether execution time is experienced on one copy or many *does not matter*, and time periods may be grouped together.

In fact, there is another significant difference from the hardware situation. When a failure occurs and the fault that causes it is repaired, it is repaired for *all* copies at the same time. In actuality, there may be variations in repair time, but simultaneous repair is a good approximation. Thus the nature of the software changes with calendar time, and it is necessary to keep failure data synchronized between different copies with respect to calendar time. Hence the interleaving approach we have described.

The foregoing simple interleaving method assumes that all the computers have the same average instruction execution rate. If not, choose a "reference computer" and adjust all execution times and failure intensities to that machine. Let r_1 be the average instruction execution rate of computer 1 and r_2, that of computer 2. If computer 1 is chosen as the reference, then execution times on computer 2 are adjusted to the reference by multiplying them by r_2/r_1. Suppose machine 1 executes 1 million instructions/sec and machine 2 executes 2 million instructions/sec. Then execution time intervals on machine 2 would be multiplied by a factor of 2 when they were referred to machine 1. Obviously, that makes sense. Since machine 2 is twice as fast, intervals on machine 1 have to be twice as long to be equivalent in terms of instructions executed. It is really instructions executed that is related to the failure inducing stress placed on the software. However, it is more practical to work with execution time and adjust it when necessary. Note that the failure intensity objective should, of course, be specified in terms of the reference.

Example 6.4. A computer game is being tested on personal computers A and B. Machine A has an average instruction execution rate of 0.8 million instructions/sec; machine B, 1.6 million. Part of the test log for each machine is reproduced below. We want to refer all failure intervals to machine B and interleave both sets. We expect to end up with clock times in minutes.

Machine A		Machine B	
Event	**Time**	**Event**	**Time**
Start test A	8:00 A.M.	Start test B	9:20 A.M.
Failure A1	9:00 A.M.	Failure B1	9:50 A.M.
Failure A2	9:30 A.M.	Failure B2	10:00 A.M.
Failure A3	10:20 A.M.	Failure B3	10:50 A.M.
Stop test A	11:00 A.M.	Failure B4	12:00 noon
		Stop test B	12:30 P.M.

Time intervals on machine A must be referred to machine B by multiplying them by

$$\frac{r_A}{r_B} = \frac{0.8}{1.6} = 0.5 \ .$$

The process of interleaving and adjustment is illustrated below.

Interleaved list

| | | Clock time interval (min) | | | | Cumulative adjusted clock time—both machines (min) |
| | | Machine A | Machine B | Machine A adjusted to B | Both machines (adjusted) | |
Event	Time					
Start test A	8:00 A.M.	—	—	—	—	0
Failure A1	9:00 A.M.	60	—	30	30	30
Start test B	9:20 A.M.	20	—	10	10	40
Failure A2	9:30 A.M.	10	10	5	15	55
Failure B1	9:50 A.M.	20	20	10	30	85
Failure B2	10:00 A.M.	10	10	5	15	100
Failure A3	10:20 A.M.	20	20	10	30	130
Failure B3	10:50 A.M.	30	30	15	45	175
Stop test A	11:00 A.M.	10	10	5	15	190
Failure B4	12:00 noon	—	60	—	60	250
Stop test B	12:30 P.M.	—	30	—	30	280 ∎

The resource usage parameters μ_C and θ_I depend on the average instruction execution rate of the computer to which they are referred. This is because the first deals with computer resource usage per failure and the second is a personnel resource usage per unit execution time. Thus, if measured on computer 2, they may be referred to machine 1 as follows: multiply μ_C by r_2/r_1 and divide θ_I by this ratio. In the example given, suppose the computer time μ_C required on machine 2 for failure identification and correction per failure is 1 hr. Then the parameter μ_C adjusted to machine 1 will be 2 hr. The necessary work per failure will take longer on the slower machine (essentially the same average number of runs must be made). If the failure identification effort per unit execution time is 4 person hr/ CPU hr on machine 2, it will be 2 person hr/CPU hr on machine 1. The same amount of work must be done in both cases, but the execution time for machine 1 is twice as large. Hence, the effort per unit execution time is half as much. No adjustment for θ_C is necessary because a change in throughput affects computer time used and execution time equally. If failure correction or identification occurs on more than one machine, a reasonable approach may be to take a weighted average of each parameter in question. Each parameter would be measured on or referred to each machine in use, weighted by the appropriate resources (P_C or P_I) associated with that machine.

Example 6.5. In Example 6.4, resource usage parameter μ_C was measured for machine A at 1.2 hr/failure. Parameter θ_I was measured (also on machine A) at 20 person hr/CPU hr. The parameters must be adjusted to machine B. Denote the adjusted parameters with tildes. We have

$$\tilde{\mu}_C = \frac{r_A}{r_B} \mu_C = \frac{0.8}{1.6}(1.2) = 0.6 \text{ hr/failure}$$

and

$$\tilde{\theta}_I = \frac{r_B}{r_A} \theta_I = \frac{1.6}{0.8}(20) = 40 \text{ person hr/CPU hr.}$$ ∎

Large systems that are installed in many locations may have several versions or releases of the program in the field at one time. This can be the result of the need to spread the installation of a new release over a period of time. Other possibilities are differing needs of different locations as to the issue of new features versus reliability, or perhaps economic factors. Later releases usually have fixes for at least some of the failures experienced in the earlier releases, but they also typically have new features and performance improvements that introduce new faults. Sometimes, you may want to establish the failure intensity for each version. However, variation in failure intensity from release to release is often not great since the economic, marketing, customer need, and competition factors that caused the first version to be released at a certain reliability level may still be operative for the later versions. We are usually most interested in determining the status of the latest release. This can be done by using any of the techniques for evolving systems, as described in the next section. However, if the differences between versions are not great, it may be satisfactory and much simpler to pool all the data. This can be done immediately, or the failure intensities can be estimated for the separate versions and then an average taken.

Example 6.6. An electronic switching system is installed in 1000 central offices around the country. There are currently three different releases of software involved, as shown in the following table.

Release	Number of installations	Failure intensity (per K hr)
5	300	2.0
6	500	1.5
7	200	3.0

All failures are included in the failure intensity data, although only a very small proportion have a sufficiently severe impact to cause service interruption. You can find the overall failure intensity by taking an average of the separate versions, weighted by the proportion of installations of each. This is 1.95 failures/K hr. ∎

6.3   EVOLVING PROGRAMS

Reliability models assume that the program being executed is stable (not changing, except for those changes that result from failure correction). This is often not the case in reality. Programs can evolve due to either requirements changes or integration of parts during development. Requirements changes may occur to provide *enhancement* of the features of the system, in response to competition, changing customer needs, and other factors. They may be necessary for *adaptation* of the system to changing hardware and software. Frequently the latter changes occur because of the opportunity to reduce operating costs provided by technological progress. Finally, requirements may be changed to provide necessary or desirable system *performance improvement*. Such improvement might involve redesign for faster operation or program restructuring to improve maintainability (ease with which program can permit future evolution). Evolution also occurs naturally as part of the development process itself. It is quite common to test a system as it is integrated. Since evolution is essentially independent of the failure correction process, it must be dealt with separately.

There are two additional situations that are analogous to program evolution and can be handled in the same way:

1. A program is fully integrated but it is tested in a step-by-step fashion. One subsystem is turned on, then another, then another, and so on. Many systems undergo what is called "feature testing," where one feature after another is verified in sequence. If the features are highly correlated with modules that are disjoint, the effect is the same as if the program evolved sequentially.

2. A program is fully integrated and active but the observation of the subsystems for failures is handled in a step-by-step fashion. You start with a narrow focus of observation and then widen it subsystem by subsystem. This can happen when new failure diagnosis tools (usually diagnostic software) are added at intervals during test.

One clue to the presence of program evolution or an analogous situation may be provided by plotting total predicted execution time (from start of execution to attainment of failure intensity objective) against execution time. Assuming parameter estimation is of good quality, total execution time should be constant if the program is stable. A changing value suggests that it may not be.

There are three general approaches to handling evolution or its analogs:

1. View program change in terms of component configuration changes (that is, addition or removal of independent subsystems).

2. Ignore change, letting the model adapt its parameters to account for it.

3. Adjust times of failures to what they would have been if the complete final program had been present. Then process the failure times as you would for a stable program.

A summary of the approaches, the situations to which each is best suited, and the advantages and disadvantages of each is given in Table 6.2.

TABLE 6.2
Approaches to handling evolving systems

Approach	Best areas of application	Advantages	Disadvantages
Component configuration change	Small number of changes, each an independent subsystem	Reliability of each component and associated function known, making adjustments to different usage easier	Extra data collection

Allocation of failures, execution time, resources, reliability objectives required

Less accurate prediction |
| Ignoring change | Many small changes

Different operational versions running simultaneously | Simple, minimum effort | Estimation and prediction errors |
| Failure time adjustment | Many changes of medium size | Good combination of reasonable accuracy and reasonable effort | Limited to one path of evolution

Pure growth (or much extra work) required

Final program size must be known (total and developed code) |

6.3.1   Component Configuration Change

The component configuration changes approach generally works best when you have a small number of large changes, each resulting from the addition of an independent component. Each component should be substantial in size with relation to the overall program. If you have this situation, then you have one in which the system changes by virtue of adding subsystems. You estimate reliability of each component separately and then you combine the reliabilities to get overall system reliability, using the rules of Section 4.2. It will usually be best to use the same software reliability model for all software components. Execution times and failures must be assigned to each subsystem. Note that to assign execution times, you must know the average percentage of time each subsystem is executing.

The following quantities are determined separately for each subsystem:

1. model parameters,
2. initial failure intensity,
3. present failure intensity,
4. additional failures required to reach failure intensity objective,

5. additional execution time required to reach failure intensity objective, and

6. additional calendar time required to reach failure intensity objective.

The failure intensity objective of the system must be allocated among the subsystems by allocating reliability objectives. The determination of the additional calendar time required to reach the failure intensity objective will require an allocation of resources (failure identification and correction personnel and computer time) among subsystems. To determine overall system figures, the estimates of (4) and (5) are added, respectively. Quantities (2) and (3) are combined (also respectively) using standard combinatorial rules on their associated reliabilities. The rules applied depend on the structure that relates subsystem failures to overall system failure. The maximum of the subsystem values for quantity (6) is taken.

The approach can theoretically be extended to any number of subsystems. However, the increasing complexity of data collection and processing restricts the number. Also, the quality of statistical estimation may suffer at some point if the subsystems become too small to yield good samples of failures. Hence, this approach is best suited to the situation where a program grows in a small number of steps, each the addition of a large independent function. One example of this situation is that of an application program added to a special operating system. The two are designed to work together for a particular application. The operating system is developed before the application program.

The disadvantages of this approach are:

1. the extra data collection required because of the multiple components,

2. the need to allocate failures and execution time among the components,

3. less predictive validity (or later achievement of a specified degree of accuracy in predictive validity) due to smaller sample sizes, and

4. the extra effort required to allocate resources and reliability goals.

> **Example 6.7.** A word processing program is to be built from two major independent, equal size subsystems. Both must function for the system to operate. One is a special purpose operating system used for other products. The other is the application subsystem. When working together, each executes 50 percent of the time. We will apply the basic model to both subsystems. The special purpose operating subsystem is tested first by itself. It has an initial and present failure intensity of 1 failure/CPU hr. Total failures expected is 100. The application subsystem has an initial and present failure intensity of 10 failures/CPU hr. Total failures expected is 1000. The failure intensity objective for the overall system is 2 failures/100 CPU hr. We will simplify the example we are presenting by assuming that both subsystems will always be in the failure-correction-personnel-limited period. We have 25 debuggers. Average failure correction personnel effort per failure is 8 person hr. The workday is 8 hr. We want to find for the overall system:
>
> **1.** total failures,
> **2.** initial failure intensity,
> **3.** present failure intensity,
> **4.** additional failures required to reach failure intensity objective,

5. additional execution time required to reach failure intensity objective, and
6. additional calendar time required to reach failure intensity objective.

   Total failures for the system is determined by adding those for the two subsystems to obtain 1100. The system initial and present failure intensities are identical here. They are obtained by adding the subsystem failure intensities, weighted by their utilizations, as per Equation (4.10). We have 5.5 failures/CPU hr.
   Since the two subsystems have equal utilizations, they must run for equal amounts of additional execution time to reach their failure intensity objectives. Thus the choices of subsystem failure intensity objectives are constrained. Of course, together they must yield the system objective. We have

$$\lambda_F = 0.5\,\lambda_{F_1} + 0.5\,\lambda_{F_2} = 0.02 \,, \tag{6.4}$$

where λ_F is the system objective, and λ_{F_1} and λ_{F_2} are the subsystem objectives. Hence

$$\lambda_{F_1} = 0.04 - \lambda_{F_2} \,. \tag{6.5}$$

   The additional execution time is obtained for the operating subsystem, using Equation (2.11), as

$$\Delta\tau = \frac{\nu_0}{\lambda_0}\,\ln\,\frac{\lambda_P}{\lambda_F}$$

$$= \frac{100}{1}\,\ln\,\frac{1}{\lambda_{F_1}}$$

$$= -\,100\,\ln\,\lambda_{F_1}\,. \tag{6.6}$$

For the application subsystem we have

$$\Delta\tau = \frac{1000}{10}\,\ln\,\frac{10}{\lambda_{F_2}}$$

$$= 100\,(\ln\,10 - \ln\,\lambda_{F_2})$$

$$= 230 - 100\,\ln\,\lambda_{F_2}\,. \tag{6.7}$$

Since the execution times are equal we have

$$\ln\,\lambda_{F_1} = \ln\,\lambda_{F_2} - 2.30 \,. \tag{6.8}$$

Now, substituting Equation (6.5) we obtain

$$\ln\,(0.04 - \lambda_{F_2}) = \ln\,\lambda_{F_2} - 2.30 \,. \tag{6.9}$$

The solution is $\lambda_{F_2} = 0.036355$ failure/CPU hr. Thus $\lambda_{F_1} = 0.003645$ failure/CPU hr. The additional execution time, using Equation (6.6), is $\Delta\tau = 561.4$ CPU hr.
   The number of additional failures to reach the failure intensity objective for the operating subsystem is, using Equation (2.9),

$$\Delta\mu = \frac{\nu_0}{\lambda_0}\,(\lambda_P - \lambda_{F_1})$$

$$= \frac{100}{1} \, (1 - 0.003645)$$

$$= 99.6 \text{ failures}. \tag{6.10}$$

For the application subsystem we have

$$\Delta \mu = \frac{1000}{10} \, (10 - 0.036355)$$

$$= 996 \text{ failures}. \tag{6.11}$$

The additional system failures and execution time required to reach the system failure intensity objective are obtained by adding the respective subsystem quantities. We obtain 1096 failures and 1122.8 CPU hr.

Consider the calendar time required for each subsystem. It may be seen from Equation (2.18) that the calendar time to execution time ratio is

$$\frac{dt}{d\tau} = \frac{\mu_F \lambda}{P_F \rho_F} = \frac{8}{P_F \rho_F} \lambda \, . \tag{6.12}$$

The subscript "F" denotes the failure correction personnel resource. If we integrate Equation (6.12), we obtain the calendar time required to meet the failure intensity objective. We have

$$t = \frac{8}{P_F \rho_F} \, \Delta \mu \, . \tag{6.13}$$

The calendar time required for each subsystem depends on the resources allocated to it. One tries to allocate resources for proper balance, so that the calendar times are approximately equal. Assume that two people are assigned to the operating subsystem and 23 to the application subsystem. From Figure 5.5 we estimate failure correction personnel utilizations for each of these subsystems. We have 0.55 and 0.365, respectively. From Equation (6.13), we obtain for the operating subsystem

$$t = \frac{8(100)}{2(0.55)} = 727 \text{ hr} = 91 \text{ days}. \tag{6.14}$$

We have, for the application subsystem

$$t = \frac{8(996)}{23(0.365)} = 949 \text{ hr} = 119 \text{ days}. \tag{6.15}$$

The calendar time required by the system will be the maximum of the subsystem times or 119 days. Note that a shift of one person either way between the subsystems would create a greater imbalance between subsystems and a longer total calendar time. ∎

6.3.2 Ignoring Change

The second approach of ignoring change is appropriate when the program is changing slowly and in a continuous fashion (or at least in relatively small steps). The continual reestimation of parameters, based on the latest data, will reflect the fact that they are changing due to program change. The parameters of some software reliability models may adapt more rapidly than others to change, although this is not known definitively at present. The estimates will be somewhat in error, since they are made by combining data from the execution of slightly different programs. Since recent data is weighted most heavily, the error will not be substantial unless the program is changing rapidly. The obvious advantage of this approach is that no extra data collection or other effort is required.

An extreme example of what happens when change is ignored is shown in Figure 6.6. Code changes were introduced in this system amounting to about 21 percent of total system size. The basic execution time model was applied. The plot shows the history of estimates of total failures and their 75 percent confidence interval as a function of calendar time. Note that the estimate of total failures increased by a factor of about 3. The actual total failures for the system increased immediately and discontinuously when the new code was added. However, there is a time lag in the estimates and possibly some tendency for them to overshoot. Note that the confidence interval increases in size during the period of greater uncertainty when the estimation algorithm recognizes it is dealing with data from a changed system. It then decreases, as the proportion of new data increases and the dimensions of the change become more evident. It will be seen that, except for the transition period, the estimation algorithm is quite robust with respect to even large program changes.

For a sudden and substantial change, you might consider discarding all the data on the old phase of the program. Estimates would be based on the new phase only. The disadvantage (a strong one) of this approach is the sometimes substantial period of time that can elapse before a large enough sample of data is in hand to make estimates of reasonable accuracy. The old data, when combined with the new, often yield a better estimate than no data at all. Whether you should discard old data depends on the size of the design change being made. Finally, the technique of failure time adjustment described in the next section may be superior to either using or not using old data, although it involves more effort.

The "ignore" approach is probably best if one is dealing with several different operational versions of a program that exist in the same time frame but on different computers. You could estimate reliability for each version separately. However, the effort required to do this is probably not justified if they do not differ from each other substantially and are all about equally debugged.

6.3.3 Failure Time Adjustment

The third approach is best when a program cannot be conveniently divided into separate independent subsystems. Also, the program should be changing rapidly enough to produce unacceptable errors in estimating model parameters. The errors are commonly exhibited as follows:

1. Present failure intensity tends to be underestimated in the early stages of a project, resulting in overly optimistic status evaluations. These are followed by long periods in which *apparent* progress is slight.
2. Completion date predictions are undefined or unstable.

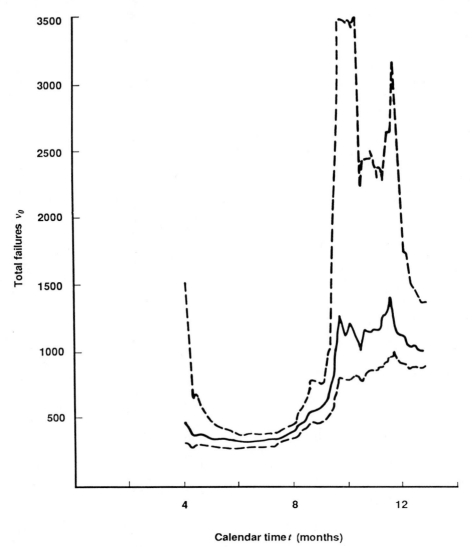

FIGURE 6.6
Effect of substantial code changes.

The approach of adjusting failure times to what they would have been if the complete program had been present is fully developed theoretically in Chapter 15. The programs described in Section 5.3 can do the adjustment. Hence, the description of the approach here will be brief and nonmathematical. The method of failure time adjustment is dependent on being able to obtain a good estimate of the final size of the program.

There are three principal assumptions that are made in developing failure time adjustment:

1. **The program evolves sequentially.** This means that at any one time there is only one path of evolution of the program for which you are trying to estimate software reliability quantities. Sequential evolution is not a significant restriction. Several versions of a program may exist at one time in the field, each installed in a different set of sites. However, each version can be dealt with separately. In test, sequential evolution is characteristic of most projects, except possibly those with multiple test teams.

2. **There is pure growth.** The system changes by adding, not removing, code. Experience indicates that most design changes do not involve the removal of code. Those that do usually involve small reductions that can be neglected. It is possible to remove the restriction of pure growth in the case where there are substantial removals of code. You must carefully identify all failures that would not have occurred if the code had not been there and remove them from the data base. Thus, the cost of this greater generality is extra data analysis that is probably not worthwhile unless code removals are appreciable.

3. **The number of faults introduced by program change is proportional to the developed code.**

By *developed code*, we mean the sum of the new plus modified deliverable executable instructions.[4] In actuality, the number of faults is not totally dependent on size. If a better metric that relates to faults can be established, then we can substitute this improved metric into our procedure. An example might be a complexity metric. We use instructions because, with the present state of the art, it appears that this quantity does as good a job of predicting faults as anything available. Complexity metrics currently available do not add anything in terms of better prediction.

Let's look now at the effects of missing code and see what we do to compensate for them in failure time adjustment. The two effects we will describe counteract each other but do not necessarily exactly cancel. When the system is not yet at its final size, it executes faster and thus failures will be closer together in time. Adjustment spreads them apart again, as a function of the total object code ratio. The second effect that you observe is that with missing code, there are fewer faults. Hence failures tend to be farther apart and the failure intensity drops faster with execution time. To compensate for this effect with failure time adjustment, you reduce the failure spacing as a function of the developed source code ratio and the failure number. Depending on the relative sizes of the two effects, the spacing between two particular failures may either be increased or decreased by adjust-

---

[4]Code that is reused without change from a previous project or version is called *inherited code*.

ment. Although we have specified *object* code ratio and developed *source* code ratio, it is actually immaterial in each case whether you use object or source instructions since ratios are involved. Similarly, since *lines* of code generally have a high correlation with *instructions*, they may be used instead. They may be more readily available on some projects.

> **Example 6.8.** We are developing an application program for a personal computer whose final length will be 10,000 object instructions. At present, part of the program has been integrated and is being tested. This part has 5000 object instructions. Assume that this is a very simple program with no branches or loops. Faults have been introduced into the program every 100 instructions. The program executes at 1,000,000 instructions/sec. The program fails every time it encounters a fault. The final program will cycle at 100 repetitions/sec; the partial program, at 200. Thus the partial program has more opportunities to fail. However, the final program will have 100 faults; the partial program, 50. With fewer faults, the partial program will fail less often. Note that, without repair, both programs have a failure intensity of 10,000 failures/sec. The two effects we described have precisely canceled each other.
>
> Now look at the situation after 10 faults have been corrected in each case. The final program will have 90 faults and a failure intensity of 9000 failures/sec. The partial program will have 40 faults and a failure intensity of 8000 failures/sec. Note that with the partial program, repairs cause the failure intensity to decrease more rapidly than it would with the entire program present.
>
> Admittedly, this example is artificial. However, the oversimplification does not affect the principle.   ■

Failure time adjustment is dependent on being able to relate failure intensity to quantity of developed code or some other measurable characteristic(s) of the software. At present, this can be done only for the basic execution time model. In addition to failure times, you must supply information on the size of the program and the amount of developed code it contains at each failure. The adjustment calculation is generally too lengthy for manual computation, but it is straightforward in concept.

Failure time adjustment is done by stages. A *stage* is a period of execution during which the total code and the developed code remain constant. First you estimate the per-fault hazard rate ϕ based on stage 1 data. Then you adjust the stage 1 failure times, using that estimate, to the values they would have had if they had occurred with all the code present that is in stage 2. You estimate the per-fault hazard rate again. Then you adjust the failure times now associated with stage 2 (originally or by adjustment) to the values they would have had if they had occurred with all the code of stage 3 being present. This procedure continues until finally you adjust the failure times now associated with the next to last stage to the values they would have had if they had occurred in the last stage. Now you estimate total failures and initial failure intensity with all the code being present and all the failure times.

The formula for adjusting failure time t_i of stage k to stage l is derived in Chapter 15 as

$$\tilde{t}_i = -\frac{I_l}{\phi_k I_k} \ln\left\{1 - \frac{\Delta I_k}{\Delta I_l}\left[1 - \exp(-\phi_k t_i)\right]\right\}, \tag{6.16}$$

when $\tilde{t}_i$ is the adjusted time. The quantities I_k and I_l are the numbers of object instructions in stages k and l, respectively. Similarly, ΔI_k and ΔI_l are the numbers of developed source instructions in stages k and l. The quantity ϕ_k is the per-fault hazard rate for stage k. Once the times have been adjusted to the last stage, normal estimation procedures can be applied. It should be noted, however, that the adjustment procedure is model-dependent. Hence, it is important to be consistent in the use of models for adjustment and for estimation.

For each stage we must measure the numbers of executable object and developed executable source instructions. However, measurement is often easiest in total source "lines" (comments, data statements, line continuations, etc., counted). Note that Equation (6.16) depends only on code ratios. As long as the ratio of executable object or source instructions to source lines is relatively constant throughout the program, lines can be used instead of instructions when necessary. Other quantities may also be used. The only characteristics that a substitute quantity must have are that:

1. It measures disjoint items.
2. Failures may be associated with the items.
3. Failures are distributed uniformly with respect to the items.

Some examples of alternative quantities are:

1. fraction of fields being processed in a file that is the exclusive output of a program, and
2. fraction of functions integrated.

It should be made clear that when a failure occurs, it must be associated with a unique stage, and that this association is fixed. Often a transition between stages does not coincide with a failure. Some execution time may have accumulated without a failure occurring. This accumulated execution time must be recorded and associated with the proper stage. After appropriate adjustment, it is added to the first failure time (which also has been properly adjusted) from the following stage.

You may ask how strongly the final adjusted failure times are affected by the number of stages. In fact, the number of stages is not important. It is the difference in the characteristics between the stages (I and ΔI) that determines the effect on the failure times. Ideally, a new stage is defined whenever I or ΔI change. However, ignoring small changes in I and ΔI and defining new stages only for the major changes will result in a smaller number of stages. This will simplify data collection requirements without materially degrading the quality of the adjustment.

It is assumed that the operational profile (possible input states for runs with their probabilities of being executed) is affected only by evolution because of the absence of code. That is, the selection of a run during a certain stage may not be possible because the required code has not yet been added (by plan). This can become a problem for systems in which the operational profile is highly nonuniform *and* the probabilities of occurrence of the most frequent input states are markedly different for different stages of integration. In that case, the adjustment procedure accounts for code being absent but does not completely compensate for the difference in operational profile. Note, however, that variation of the operational profile between stages of integration implies that these profiles do not represent the use of the program in the field. Either better test planning or compensation for the difference is required. Hence this "problem" is not really a problem related to the failure time adjustment.

The calendar time component of the model assumes that failures are randomly assigned among all the failure correction personnel for repair. Partial integration can conceivably upset the assignment, when the responsibility for the code being tested does not involve all of the members of the failure correction team. If each programmer doing failure correction "owns" a part of the integrated code, random assignment among all programmers will occur and partial integration will have little effect. If some programmers do not, the number of failure correction personnel should be appropriately reduced. The latter situation will yield satisfactory short-term predictions, but long-term predictions will have greater error since the number of personnel will not be constant.

To illustrate failure adjustment, consider the bank network of Case Study 1.1. Assume that the firm, during the first part of the test phase, is testing the system controller code necessary to perform all the interface functions implied by the system. It is also verifying the programs for deposits and withdrawals of cash by bank customers. Later during the test phase, the code necessary to allow transactions such as credit card payments and transfer of funds between accounts is integrated and tested along with the previous code. To adjust the failure data, the number of executable object and executable developed source instructions is measured before and after the latter code is integrated. For our example, assume that two-thirds of the code developed by the firm is tested initially in stage 1. Furthermore, all code is developed. No inherited code is used. This will lead to the adjusted failure interval data shown in Table 6.3. The adjusted times will then be used to obtain better estimates of the quantities shown in Figures 1.8 and 1.9.

6.4   CHANGES IN ENVIRONMENT

It has been noted that software reliability has been defined in terms of the environment in which a program executes. This refers to the operational profile or set of probabilities associated with the set of possible input states. Hence, if a program is executed in a different environment, the reliability can be expected to change. The determination of the changed reliability is perhaps best analyzed in terms of failure intensities. Let λ_1 be the failure intensity for the input states that the old

TABLE 6.3
Failure data for sequentially
integrated system example

Failure number	Unadjusted failure time	Adjusted failure time
1	537	537
2	541	541
3	6461	6451
4	11623	11591
.	.	.
.	.	.
.	.	.

and new environments have in common. Let λ_2 be the failure intensity for the unique input states of the new environment. Let p_1 be the probability of being in an input state of the old environment; p_2, the new. Then the failure intensity λ in the new environment is

$$\lambda = p_1\lambda_1 + p_2\lambda_2 . \tag{6.17}$$

The foregoing is based on the assumption that the failures for any part of the input space for a stable program can be characterized by a homogeneous Poisson process. To determine p_2 and hence $p_1 = 1 - p_2$, you must know to what extent the environment has changed. For λ_1, you would use the present failure intensity for the old program. For λ_2, you would estimate the failure intensity for the new input states in the environment. In the absence of better information, it probably would be reasonable to use the initial failure intensity of the old program. It represents the failure intensity of input states that have not been executed before.

> **Example 6.9.** A program has a failure intensity of 1 failure/hr when executing with the operational profile for which it was designed. When the program was originally tested, its initial failure intensity was 20 failures/hr. We expect that new conditions will occur for the program 1 percent of the time. We estimate the new failure intensity by assuming a failure intensity of 20 failures/hr for the new conditions. Using Equation (6.17) we have
>
> $$\lambda = 0.99(1) + 0.01(20)$$
> $$= 0.99 + 0.2$$
> $$= 1.19 \text{ failure/hr} . \qquad \blacksquare$$

It would be theoretically possible to analyze two operational profiles on a microstructure level, looking at probabilities of occurrence and failure intensities for each input state. You could then compute the effect of a change in operational profile in a detailed fashion. However, this would require an enormous amount of data collection and computation. In practice, it would appear to offer little advantage over the vastly simpler and more economical approach just described.

Sometimes the input space expands at a rate that can be modeled. For example, after a new software product is released, users may try to apply the product in ways for which it was not designed. The rate at which the input space expands may be proportional to the execution time for the program, taken over all installations.

It is possible for the operational environment to be changing in such a way that the observed failure intensity remains approximately constant for a substantial period of time. This can occur during a system test period, for example, when a series of functions is being executed without repetition. This is sometimes called *feature test*, in contrast with the term *load test* that is used to describe testing for the normal operational environment that is expected for the program. If each function is associated with different code, then any correction that occurs after a failure does not affect succeeding runs. We thus pass from function to function and routine to routine, all having approximately the same fault density and hence the same failure intensity. The result is that we observe constant failure intensity for the period of the test. Frequently, this situation can be handled by using one of the techniques developed for evolving programs (see Section 6.3).

An example of a program that was executed in two different environments is given in Hamilton and Musa (1978). The program was an operating system that was installed on two essentially identical but physically separate computers. The two computers were kept in step with regard to software releases. The operating system on the first machine was being used primarily to provide batch service; on the second, time sharing service. The failure intensity at a common point in time was computed for the first use as 0.0201 failure/CPU hr, and the second use as 0.0163 failure/CPU hr. The foregoing represents a variation of about 19 percent.

There is a special change in environment that is of particular interest—the change from the test phase to the operational phase. The change results solely from the fact that input states are not generally repeated during the test phase.

We will define the *testing compression factor* C as the ratio of execution time required in the operational phase to execution time required in the test phase to cover the input space of the program. Let's first consider a simple example to clarify the concept, before making a more general formulation. Assume that a program has only two input states, A and B. Input state A occurs 90 percent of the time; B, 10 percent. All runs take 1 CPU hr. In operation, on the average, it will require 10 CPU hr to cover the input space, with A occurring nine times and B, one. In test, the coverage can be accomplished in 2 CPU hr. The testing compression factor would be 5 in this case.

A more general formulation of the testing compression factor is derived in Chapter 9 as

$$C = \frac{\sum\limits_{k=1}^{Q_I} \dfrac{p_k}{p_{\min}} \tau_k}{\sum\limits_{k=1}^{Q_I} \tau_k}. \tag{6.18}$$

Here Q_I is the total number of input states in the input space. The quantity p_k is the probability of occurrence of input state k. Note that p_{min} is the probability of occurrence of the input state that is least probable. Finally, τ_k is the run time for run type k. It is shown in Section 9.1.2 that this expression simplifies to

$$C = \frac{1}{Q_I \, p_{min}} \qquad (6.19)$$

if all runs are of equal length. If the probability of occurrence of input state k is inversely proportional to its rank (that is, number) then Equation (6.19) becomes

$$C = \psi(Q_I + 1) - \psi(1) . \qquad (6.20)$$

The function ψ is the psi or digamma function [Davis (1962)]. A plot of C as a function of the number of input states Q_I for this situation is shown in Figure 6.7. It is interesting to note that C changes very slowly with Q_I. Hence the range of values of C to be expected is probably relatively small.

Equivalence partitioning increases the testing compression factor. This will be seen if you note that only one test need be run per input state *group* rather than input state. Thus the denominator in Equation (6.19) becomes smaller and the test compression factor larger.

The name *testing compression factor* comes from the fact that an amount of execution time in test can represent a larger amount of execution time in operation. This concept is analogous to that of stress testing for hardware. It offers promise in permitting the testing of high reliability systems in reasonable amounts of execution time, particularly if equivalence partitioning is employed. Note that equivalence partitioning must not be used to the point where the risk of missing failures increases substantially. The extra care required in test planning when equivalence partitioning is employed increases test planning costs substantially. However, the shorter test period required usually results in a net reduction in test costs.

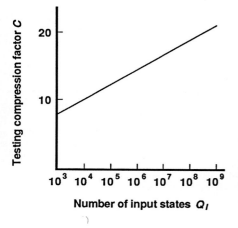

FIGURE 6.7
Testing compression factor versus number of input states for equal run lengths and occurrence probability inversely proportional to rank.

Execution times experienced in test should be multiplied by the testing compression factor. They can then be processed by software reliability estimation programs. Alternatively, the failure times obtained in test can be used to estimate test phase failure intensities, using the programs. These failure intensities should then be *divided* by the testing compression factor C to obtain the corresponding failure intensities to be expected in operation. The testing compression factor computed by formula may overestimate the actual testing compression factor achieved. In many test phases, some repetition of input states may occur, often deliberately due to regression testing. The computed testing compression factor should be divided by the average number of occurrences of each input state expected.

Sometimes testing is carried out at multiple sites, with one site maximizing test efficiency. The others conduct actual field tests in accordance with the operational profile expected in the field. When test data are combined from these sites, execution times from the "efficient" site should be multiplied by the testing compression factor for that site. Execution times from the other sites do not need adjustment, since these sites will have testing compression factors of 1.

6.5   OTHER CONSIDERATIONS

If testing starts before integration is complete, then there may be periods of inactivity in testing and debugging due to waits for programs not yet ready. These periods must be estimated separately and added to estimates of remaining t, or else t must not be viewed as "running" when they occur. Note that severe computer outages (one day or more) and delays due to requirements changes have not been included in the estimate of remaining test phase length. They must be added if expected.

6.6   SUMMARY

In this chapter we have absorbed a rich lore of experience gained from actual software projects. We have dealt with real world problems such as incomplete and inaccurate data collection, multiple installations, evolving programs, and changing environments. Reasonable solutions to these problems are available.

PROBLEMS

6.1 We plan to test our program first with a software environment simulator and later in the real environment. Would you expect present failure intensity to increase or decrease in making the transition?

6.2 Can software reliability measurement be applied to systems that are designed and tested "top down?"

6.3 Is there some way we can determine failure intervals in the situation where we only know that the failure occurred at some time during a period of uncertain length?

6.4 Does it make sense to handle substantial design changes made at one time by separating the pre- and post-change estimation procedures and then later combining the estimates in some way?

6.5 We are testing at multiple sites. Because of time lags in communicating and fixing problems, failures encountered at one site are often repeated at another. Does this cause any problem?

6.6 We are testing at two different sites, the development site and a field site. There is a time lag in releasing new versions of the program to the field site. Consequently, the field site is always testing an earlier release than the one we are testing at the development site. The later version does not have many new features but it does have fault corrections not included in the previous release. How can we handle this?

6.7 Can you account for a situation where the actual operating environment is much more demanding than the test environment?

6.8 How do we combine failure intervals from projects with several different versions of software simultaneously in test?

6.9 It is difficult for us to measure execution time associated with a tester running a particular test. Several tests are usually running simultaneously and they may all be serviced by some common processes. We *can* measure elapsed time and pinpoint the occurrence of failures with respect to it. We can also measure total execution time for the system at various elapsed times (for example, hourly). How can we convert elapsed time between failures into execution time? The number of users on the system varies, so utilization (the ratio of execution time to elapsed time) is not constant.

6.10 We are trying to determine the interval between failures for an interactive system with a varying number of users in which measuring execution time is difficult. Is there a better way of doing this than measuring clock time?

6.11 Suppose a known number of failures occur in a time window at unknown times. When you assign the failure times randomly within the window, why not assume a trend to the failure intervals?

SEVEN

APPLICATION PROCEDURES

A survey of typical uses of software reliability measurement was presented in Chapter 3. Now that we have armed the reader with a deeper understanding of the practical aspects of software reliability measurement in Chapters 4, 5, and 6, we will revisit the sphere of applications. We will describe the procedures to be employed and touch on some more advanced topics. We will not repeat the material presented in Chapter 3, so you may want to refer back to it. You will recall that Table 3.1 gives a summary of applications. Before we deal with the applications, however, we will examine three types of calculations that are common to many of the applications to gain some insight. These include the computation of:

1. system test duration,
2. system test resource requirements and cost, and
3. operational cost of failures.

Usually we have found it best to implement calculations in computer programs (Section 5.3). However, sometimes it is more convenient to perform short calculations manually, especially if one wants to gain some insight. A summary of the most useful formulas is provided for reference in Appendix E. We will group the applications to be discussed into several broad categories. These include system engineering, project management, management of operational phase, and evaluation of software engineering technologies.

7.1 BASIC DURATION AND COST CALCULATIONS

In computing costs, we will be dealing with only the reliability-dependent components, not total costs. This is satisfactory because other costs are readily calculated and added if total costs are needed. Many applications, however, are concerned mainly with finding the reliability that minimizes cost, and the foregoing components are totally satisfactory for this. When we say "reliability dependent" we refer to the differences in reliability obtained by varying the amount of testing. Reliability is affected by the support environment and methodologies used on the project. However, these factors are not easily varied while the project is underway.

The time required, resources needed, and costs associated with testing are mainly dependent on the initial reliability of the design and code and the reliability goal to be attained. Although program size influences the two foregoing quantities, it is far from the sole factor. Hence "person months per K lines of code" estimating is not generally appropriate, and a reliability-related approach must be taken.

Note that we can calculate system test duration and system test cost using the simulation program described in Chapter 5. This is the recommended procedure, but another approach is presented here to give the reader insight. Also, some may prefer quick hand calculations or may not have ready access to the program. The procedure is, for the most part, independent of the particular execution time component used. For illustration, we will use the basic model.

7.1.1 System Test Duration

To compute system test duration (excluding the test planning effort), we first determine the values of the execution time component parameters as described in Chapter 5.

The calendar time interval t consists of the sum of one to three periods. In each period, a different resource is *limiting*. This means that the resource produces the maximum ratio of calendar time to execution time for that period. That resource is indicated by the value of the index r: C is computer time, F is failure correction personnel, and I is failure identification personnel. We compute the duration of each period separately, based on its limiting resource. Then the durations are summed. We have

$$t = \sum_r \frac{\Delta \chi_{rr}}{P_r \rho_r} . \tag{7.1}$$

The quantity $\Delta \chi_{rr}$ is the requirement for resource r during the period for which it is limiting. For example, it might be 100 person days. Note that it is generally not the same as the total resource requirement to meet the failure intensity objective $\Delta \chi_r$. Note that P_r is the quantity of resource r *available* (for example, 5 persons). The quantity ρ_r is the utilization factor for resource r. The resource utilization factor reflects the possibility that all of an available resource cannot be usefully employed.

Each resource requirement during its limiting *period* is given by

$$\Delta \chi_{rr} = \theta_r \Delta \tau_r + \mu_r \Delta \mu_r . \tag{7.2}$$

Note that θ_r is the resource expenditure per unit execution time. The quantity μ_r is the resource expenditure per failure. The symbol $\Delta\tau_r$ represents the execution time interval for the *period*. The quantity $\Delta\mu_r$ is the number of failures experienced in the *period*.

To obtain the expected number of failures experienced in the period for the basic model, we use

$$\Delta\mu_r = \nu_0 \frac{\lambda_{r_1} - \lambda_{r_2}}{\lambda_0} . \tag{7.3}$$

The quantities λ_{r_1} and λ_{r_2} are the failure intensities at the boundaries of the limiting resource period. The execution time interval is determined from

$$\Delta\tau_r = \frac{\nu_0}{\lambda_0} \ln \frac{\lambda_{r_1}}{\lambda_{r_2}} . \tag{7.4}$$

The boundaries of the different resource-limited periods λ_{r_1} and λ_{r_2} are the present and objective failure intensities and the transition points (derived in Chapter 14) λ_{rs} that lie within the range. We have for the potential transition points

$$\lambda_{rs} = \frac{P_s\rho_s\theta_r - P_r\rho_r\theta_s}{P_r\rho_r\mu_s - P_s\rho_s\mu_r} . \tag{7.5}$$

The subscripts (r, s) have the values (F, C), (F, I), and (I, C). You must determine which resource-limited periods actually occur from an examination of the boundaries and a determination of the maximum calendar time to execution time ratio for each period. To find the maximum calendar time to execution time ratio for each period we compute

$$\frac{dt}{d\tau}\bigg]_{max} = max \left(\frac{\theta_r + \mu_r\lambda}{P_r\rho_r} \right) . \tag{7.6}$$

The quantity λ is any failure intensity in the range $[\lambda_{r_1}, \lambda_{r_2}]$.

Example 7.1. The resource usage parameters (with overhead included) for a software project to build an inventory control system are the following:

	Resource usage	
Resource	Per failure	Per CPU hr
Failure identification personnel (person hr)	3	5
Failure correction personnel (person hr)	8	0
Computer time (CPU hr)	1	1

The test team has 4 people and there are 12 debuggers. Everyone works a normal 8-hr day. The computer operates 16 hr/day, 5 days/week. Work hours and procedures are organized so that this time can be used. Thus $P_C = 2$. Computer utilization is 0.75. Failure correction personnel utilization is 0.333. Failure identification personnel utilization, as always, is 1. The initial and present failure intensity is 10 failures/CPU hr. The failure intensity objective is 0.1 failure/CPU hr. The number of total failures is 100. We want to determine the calendar time required to reach the objective, using the basic execution time model.

We must first establish the extent of each resource-limited period. We compute the potential transition point between the failure-correction-personnel-limited and failure-identification-personnel-limited periods as follows, using Equation (7.5):

$$\lambda_{FI} = \frac{P_I \rho_I \theta_F - P_F \rho_F \theta_I}{P_F \rho_F \mu_I - P_I \rho_I \mu_F}$$

$$= \frac{4(1)(0) - 12(0.333)(5)}{12(0.333)(3) - 4(1)(8)}$$

$$= \frac{-20}{12 - 32}$$

$$= 1 \text{ failure/CPU hr.}$$

The potential transition point between the failure-identification-personnel-limited and computer-time-limited periods is

$$\lambda_{IC} = \frac{P_C \rho_C \theta_I - P_I \rho_I \theta_C}{P_I \rho_I \mu_C - P_C \rho_C \mu_I}$$

$$= \frac{2(0.75)(5) - 4(1)(1)}{4(1)(1) - 2(0.75)(3)}$$

$$= \frac{7.5 - 4}{4 - 4.5}$$

$$= -7 \text{ failures/CPU hr.}$$

This potential transition point clearly falls outside the range of failure intensities (10 to 0.1 failures/CPU hr) we are concerned with. The potential transition point between the failure-correction-personnel-limited and computer-time-limited periods is

$$\lambda_{FC} = \frac{P_C \rho_C \theta_F - P_F \rho_F \theta_C}{P_F \rho_F \mu_C - P_C \rho_C \mu_F}$$

$$= \frac{2(0.75)(0) - 12(0.333)(1)}{12(0.333)(1) - 2(0.75)(8)}$$

$$= \frac{-4}{4 - 12}$$

$$= 0.5 \text{ failure/CPU hr.}$$

There are three potential resource-limited periods: 10 to 1, 1 to 0.5, and 0.5 to 0.1 failures/CPU hr. We must evaluate the derivative of calendar time with respect to execution time for each resource at some point in each of these periods, using Equation (7.6). At $\lambda = 10$ failures/CPU hr we have

$$\frac{dt}{d\tau}\bigg]_I = \frac{\theta_I + \mu_I \lambda}{P_I \rho_I} = \frac{5 + 3(10)}{4(1)} = \frac{35}{4} = 8.75 \,,$$

$$\frac{dt}{d\tau}\bigg]_F = \frac{\theta_F + \mu_F \lambda}{P_F \rho_F} = \frac{0 + 8(10)}{12(0.333)} = \frac{80}{4} = 20 \,, \text{ and}$$

$$\frac{dt}{d\tau}\bigg]_C = \frac{\theta_C + \mu_C \lambda}{P_C \rho_C} = \frac{1 + 1(10)}{2(0.75)} = \frac{11}{1.5} = 7.33 \,.$$

The period from 10 to 1 failures/CPU hr is failure-correction-personnel-limited. At $\lambda = 0.8$ failure/CPU hr we have

$$\frac{dt}{d\tau}\bigg]_I = \frac{5 + 3(0.8)}{4(1)} = \frac{7.4}{4} = 1.85 \,,$$

$$\frac{dt}{d\tau}\bigg]_F = \frac{0 + 8(0.8)}{12(0.333)} = \frac{6.4}{4} = 1.6 \,, \text{ and}$$

$$\frac{dt}{d\tau}\bigg]_C = \frac{1 + 1(0.8)}{2(0.75)} = \frac{1.8}{1.5} = 1.2 \,.$$

The period from 1 to 0.5 failures/CPU hr is failure-identification-personnel-limited. At $\lambda = 0.1$ failure/CPU hr we have

$$\frac{dt}{d\tau}\bigg]_I = \frac{5 + 3(0.1)}{4(1)} = \frac{5.3}{4} = 1.325 \,,$$

$$\frac{dt}{d\tau}\bigg]_F = \frac{0 + 8(0.1)}{12(0.333)} = \frac{0.8}{4} = 0.2 \,, \text{ and}$$

$$\frac{dt}{d\tau}\bigg]_C = \frac{1 + 1(0.1)}{2(0.75)} = \frac{1.1}{1.5} = 0.733 \,.$$

The potential transition point at $\lambda_{FC} = 0.5$ failure/sec is not real, since failure identification personnel are still limiting at 0.1 failure/sec. You might also have concluded this from the fact that failure identification personnel were limiting just above 0.5 failure/sec. Consequently, a transition *from* a failure-correction-personnel-limited period could not have occurred. Then, the period from 1 to 0.1 failure/CPU hr is failure-identification-personnel-limited.

Next, we will calculate the expected number of failures experienced and execution time elapsed for each period, using Equations (7.3) and (7.4). For the failure-correction-personnel-limited period we have

$$\Delta\mu_F = \nu_0 \frac{\lambda_{F_1} - \lambda_{F_2}}{\lambda_0} = 100 \frac{10 - 1}{10} = 90 \text{ failures}$$

and

$$\Delta\tau_F = \frac{\nu_0}{\lambda_0} \ln \frac{\lambda_{F_1}}{\lambda_{F_2}} = \frac{100}{10} \ln \frac{10}{1} = 23.0 \text{ CPU hr.}$$

For the failure-identification-personnel-limited period we have

$$\Delta\mu_I = \nu_0 \frac{\lambda_{I_1} - \lambda_{I_2}}{\lambda_0} = 100 \frac{1 - 0.1}{10} = 9 \text{ failures}$$

and

$$\Delta\tau_I = \frac{\nu_0}{\lambda_0} \ln \frac{\lambda_{I_1}}{\lambda_{I_2}} = \frac{100}{10} \ln \frac{1}{0.1} = 23.0 \text{ CPU hr.}$$

The failure correction effort required during the failure-correction-personnel-limited period is, from Equation (7.2)

$$\Delta\chi_{FF} = \theta_F \Delta\tau_F + \mu_F \Delta\mu_F$$

$$= 0(23.0) + 8(90)$$

$$= 720 \text{ person hr.}$$

The failure identification effort during the failure-identification-personnel-limited period is

$$\Delta\chi_{II} = \theta_I \Delta\tau_I + \mu_I \Delta\mu_I$$

$$= 5(23) + 3(9)$$

$$= 142 \text{ person hr.}$$

The calendar time expended during the failure-correction-personnel-limited period is, from Equation (7.1),

$$t_F = \frac{\Delta\chi_{FF}}{P_F \rho_F} = \frac{720}{12(0.333)} = \frac{720}{4} = 180 \text{ hr.}$$

The calendar time expended during the failure-identification-personnel-limited period is

$$t_I = \frac{\Delta\chi_{II}}{P_I \rho_I} = \frac{142}{4(1)} = 35.5 \text{ hr.}$$

Thus the total calendar time is

$$t = t_F + t_I = 180 + 35.5 = 215.5 \text{ hr.}$$

Dividing by the 8-hr day, we obtain 27 days.   ∎

7.1.2   System Test Resource Requirements and Cost

The starting point for computing resource requirements and cost is also the determination of the values of the execution time component parameters. Then find the expected number of failures

$$\mu = \nu_0 \left[1 - \frac{\lambda_F}{\lambda_0} \right] \qquad (7.7)$$

that must be experienced and the associated execution time

$$\tau = \frac{\nu_0}{\lambda_0} \ln \left[\frac{\lambda_0}{\lambda_F} \right] \qquad (7.8)$$

to decrease the failure intensity from λ_0 to the failure intensity objective λ_F. Normalized values of these quantities are plotted in Figures 7.1 and 7.2 as a function of the failure intensity ratio λ_0/λ_F. In Figure 7.1, the fraction μ/ν_0 of total failures that must be experienced to reach the failure intensity objective is plotted. Note that as the failure intensity ratio approaches infinity, the fraction of total failures that must be experienced approaches 1. In Figure 7.2, we plot a normalized execution time increment $B\phi\rho$, where B is the fault reduction factor and ϕ, the per fault hazard rate. As the failure intensity ratio approaches infinity, the normalized (and hence actual) execution time increment approaches infinity. Each of the three *total* resource expenditures χ_r is given by

$$\chi_r = \theta_r \tau + \mu_r \mu , \qquad (7.9)$$

where r has the values C, F, and I. As the failure intensity ratio approaches infinity, the failure identification and computer resource expenditures approach infinity logarithmically. The general shape of the curves is shown in Figure 7.3. The failure correction resource expenditure approaches the product of total failures and failure correction effort per failure. The general shape of the curve is the same as that shown in Figure 7.1. To get overall cost, multiply each χ_r by its cost rate and

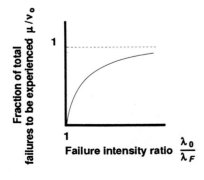

FIGURE 7.1
Variation of fraction of total failures to be experienced with failure intensity ratio— basic execution time model.

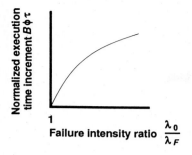

FIGURE 7.2
Variation of normalized execution time increment with failure intensity ratio—basic execution time model.

total the results. Note that cost approaches infinity as the failure intensity ratio approaches infinity. The general shape of the cost curve is shown in Figure 7.3. For large failure intensity ratios, the cost curve approaches a logarithmic shape. Suppose you decrease the failure intensity objective or increase the failure intensity ratio by a factor of 2. Then the cost of achieving the more stringent goal is less than twice as much. This might seem counterintuitive. However, with the basic model, the removal of "later" faults in a system reduces failure intensity by a larger factor than removal of "early" faults. The reduction factor is $\omega/(\omega-1)$, where ω is the number of faults remaining. Thus, although the execution time between failures and consequent costs are increasing rapidly, the foregoing countervailing factor makes the relationship between cost and failure intensity sublinear.

The foregoing approach implicitly assumes that idle time for all resources during the project can be profitably employed in other activities and should not be charged as a cost. If this is not true for any resource, the cost for that resource should be determined as follows. Multiply t from Equation (7.1) by the total number of personnel (or dedicated computers) and the resource rate.

Example 7.2. We will calculate the resource requirements and cost of system test for the inventory control software project of Example 7.1. The personnel cost (including loading or overhead) is $75/hr. The computer cost is $500/CPU hr. We will first use Equation (7.7) to compute the expected number of failures that must be experienced to reach the failure intensity objective. We have

$$\Delta\mu = \nu_0 \left[1 - \frac{\lambda_F}{\lambda_0} \right]$$

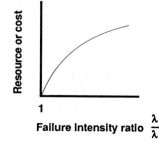

FIGURE 7.3
General form of failure identification effort, computer time, and cost curves with failure intensity ratio—basic execution time model.

$$= 100 \left[1 - \frac{0.1}{10} \right]$$

$$= 99 \text{ failures.}$$

The associated execution time, using Equation (7.8), is

$$\Delta\tau = \frac{\nu_0}{\lambda_0} \ln \left[\frac{\lambda_0}{\lambda_F} \right]$$

$$= \frac{100}{10} \ln \left[\frac{10}{0.1} \right]$$

$$= 10 \ln 100$$

$$= 46.0 \text{ CPU hr.}$$

The failure identification personnel effort is, from Equation (7.9),

$$\chi_I = \theta_I \tau + \mu_I \mu$$

$$= 5(46.0) + 3(99)$$

$$= 527 \text{ person hr.}$$

We have, for the failure correction personnel effort

$$\chi_F = \theta_F \tau + \mu_F \mu$$

$$= 0(46.0) + 8(99)$$

$$= 792 \text{ person hr.}$$

The computer time is

$$\chi_C = \theta_C \tau + \mu_C \mu$$

$$= 1(46.0) + 1(99)$$

$$= 145 \text{ CPU hr.}$$

The total personnel effort is 1319 hr. Multiplying by the cost rate of $75/hr, we obtain a personnel cost for system test of $98,925. The computer cost, using a rate of $500/CPU hr, is $72,500. Thus total system test cost is $171,425.

Note from Example 7.1 that the failure correction effort during the failure-correction-personnel-limited period was 720 person hr. Subtracting this figure from the total effort of 792 person hr, you will see that 72 person hr were expended during the failure-identification-personnel-limited period. Similarly, the failure identification effort during the failure-identification-personnel-limited period was 142 person hr. Subtracting this from the total effort of 527 person hr, you will see that 385 person hr were used during the failure-correction-personnel-limited period.   ∎

7.1.3 Operational Cost of Failures

The first step in computing reliability-dependent cost for the operational period is to establish the cost of each failure. You should consider factors such as the cost of disrupted service on operations, the cost of restoring the system to operation, the impact of lost customers, and the cost of possible product liability actions. Restoration involves such activities as:

1. making a service call,
2. terminating an unsatisfactorily operating program in an orderly fashion,
3. reconstructing relevant data bases,
4. reloading and restarting the program, and
5. documenting the circumstances of failure.

Usually the underlying fault is not repaired in the field but is corrected in the next release of the software. However, field repairs may be undertaken for critical failures or critical systems. In that case, the costs of fault detection and correction at the central site *and* repair distribution and installation must be added to operational period costs. We generally assume a cost per failure that is independent of failure intensity. This appears to be generally valid, but the cost can increase nonlinearly when failure intensities are large. A greater than linear increase can arise from increased costs of restoration when closely spaced failures interact with each other. An even more likely source of nonlinearity is the impact of lost customers. Customer defections may increase markedly after some level of tolerance is exceeded.

The expected life of the release of the system must be estimated, and the number of systems installed must be determined. The product of the two foregoing factors gives total operational hours expected for all installed systems for this release. If we multiply operational hours by failure intensity objective and cost per failure, we obtain an expression for total operational cost of failures for the release. Implicit in the calculation is the assumption that failure intensity per CPU hour is constant over the life of the release. In general, this is true because usually there are no substantial changes (enhancements or repairs) to a program between releases. Sometimes reported failures per calendar period (day, week, etc.) vary with time, but this is due to variations in operating time and number of installations.

We have focused on software failure intensity and software-failure-caused costs. However, in many cases we will want to take a broader view. We will determine computer *system* failure intensity and account for costs resulting from all aspects of system failure.

> **Example 7.3.** Consider a securities portfolio tracking and evaluation program that is installed at 1000 locations. It is considered to have a useful life of 2 years. It operates 250 days/year. On the average, we can expect 2 CPU hr of execution time per

day. The total execution time of each program copy is thus 1000 hr. The total operational hours over all copies is 1,000,000. Suppose the failure intensity objective is 2 failures/1000 hr. Then we can expect 2000 failures. If the cost of a failure averages $1000, then the total operational cost of failure for this system is $2,000,000. ∎

7.2 SYSTEM ENGINEERING

You may be concerned about the accuracy with which parameters on a particular project can be estimated. If this is a problem, you should note that inaccuracies usually affect absolute rather than relative values. Many and perhaps most system engineering decisions are concerned with relative values of alternatives. In any case, we can and should perform calculations with different values of a parameter to determine the sensitivity of a decision to parameter inaccuracy. As experience is gained and more data is available, it should be possible to determine parameters more accurately and hence improve the *absolute* accuracy with which costs, schedules, and other quantities can be estimated.

7.2.1 Reliability Specification

Specification of reliability to a designer involves the determination of a system reliability objective, which we will consider shortly. It also involves "allocation" of the reliability to the system components, if the designer is responsible for just a component. Good allocation depends primarily on gaining a good technical understanding of the relative difficulties of achieving different levels of reliability for the components in question. "Difficulty" should be considered particularly in economic and schedule terms. Example 7.7 provides a simple illustration of the allocation process. An example of a specification placed on a designer would be "Software subsystem X must have a reliability of 0.99 for a 10-hr period."

7.2.2 Failure Restoration Resource Requirements and Costs

Predictions of failure restoration resource requirements and costs are closely related. Both depend on determination of the failure intensity that will be experienced in the operational phase. The following examples should be illustrative.

> **Example 7.4.** A software-based system that operates 40 hr/week was released with a failure intensity of 0.025 failure/hr. The average time (including travel) required for a repair person to restore the system after a failure is 4 hr. How many systems can one repair person maintain?
>
> Note that the expected number of failures in one week will be one, requiring 4 hr for restoration. Thus one repair person can theoretically handle 10 systems. In actuality, each repair person should be assigned fewer systems, perhaps seven. This would allow for variations in the occurrence of failures that could result in a backlog of failures awaiting restoration. Such a backlog might be unacceptable from a system availability viewpoint. Apply queueing theory to find the utilization factor for repair

personnel that is acceptable. An alternative strategy would be to operate at a higher utilization factor and handle backlogs with overtime. ∎

Example 7.5. Assume in Example 7.4 that the loaded salary of the repair person is $25/hr. Since 4 hr/week of restoration work are required on a system, the monthly cost for this effort is $433, based on 4¹/₃ weeks/month. However, if a lighter load is assigned to each repair person to ensure rapid response and good system availability, the cost would be $619/month. ∎

7.2.3 Reliability-Schedules-Resources-Cost Trade-offs

The investigation of trade-offs among reliability, schedules, resources, and cost involves the following general procedure. You choose several values of each parameter that is to be varied. Apply either execution time model to compute the effects of parameter variations. Examine the results and iterate this procedure as required. Usually you choose the parameter values to include the extreme values that are reasonably possible, so that the influence of the parameters can be quickly determined. Reliability and failure intensity vary with the average instruction execution rate of the machine on which a program is running. Hence you may consider function and performance as additional factors in making a trade-off. For example, assume that a retail store online transaction processing program A, developed for machine A, has half the failure intensity of program B, developed for machine B. But suppose that program B runs five times as fast. The failure intensity with respect to transactions is 2¹/₂ times better for program B.

It is possible to develop an initial project schedule for the system test period *before testing begins* by use of the equations given in Section 7.1.1. Alternatively, one may use the simulation program (Chapter 5), which implements these equations. We can predict the number of failures that must be experienced (and the associated execution time required) to attain the failure intensity objective. Predictions of system test cost may be made, using the equations of Section 7.1.2 (or again, the simulation program). The accuracy of the foregoing *pretest* predictions depends on how well the parameters can be predicted. At present, limited data from a few projects are available to answer this question. Much more data are required. However, pretest predictions may be of substantial value if looked at *relative* to one another. Examining the changes induced by varying different parameters may be helpful in deciding on project trade-offs.

Since the execution time component parameters may be continually refined by *reestimation* during test, it is easy to continually reestimate derived quantities (with confidence intervals). Recall that the derived quantities include:

1. the present failure intensity,
2. the additional number of failures that must be experienced in order to reach the project failure intensity objective, and
3. the associated additional execution and calendar times and completion date.

We can also calculate resource requirements and costs, giving us the capability to relook at reliability-schedule-resource-cost trade-offs at any time during test. Programs for making these calculations were discussed in Chapter 5.

7.2.4 Setting a Failure Intensity Objective

The first question one must ask in setting a failure intensity objective is, "*Who* is the customer?" The second is, "What does the customer want?" And third, "Which objective is best for you, in the broadest sense, in your particular competitive environment?" Consider a delivered product with a rapid rate of technological obsolescence. The approach taken may be different from that for a stable product delivered internally within a company for use in providing external service. For example, when computing costs in a cost-based approach to setting the objective, it is necessary to know "costs to whom?"

There are at least three principal methods used in establishing the failure intensity objective for a system:

1. system balance,
2. release date, and
3. life cycle cost optimization.

The first approach, system balance, is primarily used in allocating reliabilities among components of a system. It is particularly applicable to systems in which the development is especially challenging. This could be because the system uses state-of-the-art technology or because the reliability requirements are severe ones. Hence we often use it for military systems. The basic principle to be followed is to *balance* the difficulty of development work on different components. The components that have the most severe functional requirements or are most advanced technologically are assigned less stringent reliability requirements. In the case of software, functions never implemented before or based on untried algorithms might fall in this category. Components that are relatively standard and that are used in common practice are assigned more stringent reliability requirements. For software, this might include previously tested routines that will be reused. This approach generally leads to the least costly development effort in the minimum time.

The second approach, release date, is used when product release date is particularly critical. Schedule criticality can result from military requirements or market window necessities. Alternatively, the product may be a component of a larger system with severe delivery date requirements. This approach involves keeping the release date fixed. The failure intensity objective is either established by the resources and funds available, or is traded off against these quantities.

In the release date approach, it is desirable to have some sense of how failure intensity trades off with release date. First, we determine how failure intensity trades off with execution time. We then convert to dates. The failure intensity at the start of system test may be assumed to have been established by the nature of the project and the programming environment. We obtain the relationship between the ratio of failure intensity change in system test λ_0/λ_F and execution time τ for the basic execution time model from Equation (2.11) as

$$\tau = \frac{\nu_0}{\lambda_0} \ln \frac{\lambda_0}{\lambda_F} . \tag{7.10}$$

For the logarithmic Poisson execution time model, it is obtained from Equation (2.12) as

$$\tau = \frac{1}{\theta \lambda_0} \left(\frac{\lambda_0}{\lambda_F} - 1 \right) . \tag{7.11}$$

Since the quantities ν_0, λ_0, and θ are fixed in any given case, the comparative variations of execution time τ with failure intensity ratio λ_0/λ_F will be as shown in Figure 7.4. Note that the increase in execution time with larger ratios of failure intensity is greater for the logarithmic Poisson model (linear rather than logarithmic).

Example 7.6. Use the failure data for system T1 (provided in Table 12.1)   estimate parameters for both the basic and logarithmic Poisson models. The following results are obtained, if the testing compression factor $C = 1$ (in other examples using system T1 in the book, it is 15.1).

Basic	Logarithmic Poisson
$\lambda_0 = 17.8$ failures/CPU hr $\nu_0 = 142$ failures	$\lambda_0 = 39.9$ failures/CPU hr $\theta = 0.0236$/failure

By using Equations (7.10) and (7.11) we can determine the length of the system test period for various failure intensity improvement factors.

	Execution time (CPU hr)	
Improvement factor	Basic	Logarithmic Poisson
10	18.4	9.56
100	36.7	105.1
1000	55.1	1060.9
10,000	73.5	10,619

∎

The relationship of calendar time to execution time will vary with the values of the calendar time component parameters. However, the general shape will be as shown in Figure 2.21. If we "combine" this figure with Figure 7.4, we obtain the general shape of the relationship of calendar time with failure intensity ratio, shown in Figure 7.5. The relationship can be used to determine the failure intensity ratio and hence the objective, given the release date and the resources available.

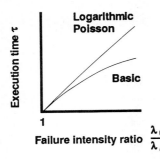

FIGURE 7.4
Comparative variation of execution time with failure intensity ratio—basic and logarithmic Poisson execution time models.

The third approach, life cycle cost optimization, applies particularly to the software component of a system, although it can readily be adapted to the overall system as well. The basis for optimization is the assumption that reliability improvement is obtained by more extensive testing, which of course affects costs and schedules. Costs and schedules for other phases are assumed to be constant. This assumption is reasonable. Reliability improvement techniques such as structured programming and design reviews are commonly implemented on a "yes-no" basis dependent on their cost effectiveness. You do not ordinarily trade off the degree to which structured programming is employed with reliability. The part of development cost due to testing decreases with higher failure intensity objectives, while operational cost increases (Figure 7.6). Thus total cost has a minimum.

To find this minimum, you must first compute the system test cost. This can be done manually (Section 7.1.2) or by using a simulation program (Chapter 5). Sometimes, you may wish to add an "opportunity cost" to system test cost [Mittermeir (1982)]. This is the cost of profits lost or expenses incurred because the release date of the program must be delayed for additional testing. Then the operational cost can be computed as noted in Section 7.1.3. We can now add system test cost and operational cost of failures to obtain the *reliability-dependent component* of total system life cycle costs. Note that there will also be development and operational costs that are independent of reliability but that add to total system life cycle costs. Suppose that the reliability-related component of total system life cycle costs can be expressed analytically as a function of failure intensity objec-

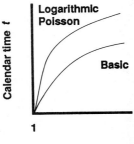

FIGURE 7.5
Variation of calendar time with failure intensity ratio—basic and logarithmic Poisson execution time models.

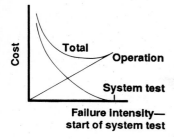

Cost

Total

Operation

System test

Failure Intensity—
start of system test

Failure Intensity objective λ_F

FIGURE 7.6
Life cycle cost optimization.

tive λ_F. Then we can use calculus to find the value of λ_F that minimizes the expression. Otherwise, a search process is used to find the value.

7.2.5 Reliability Allocation

Reliability allocation deals with the setting of reliability goals for individual components such that a specified system reliability goal is met *and* the component goals are "well balanced" among themselves. Well balanced usually refers to approximate equality of development time, difficulty, or risk or to the minimization of overall system development cost. The first step in the allocation process is to describe the system configuration, as discussed in Chapter 4. Next, trial component reliability allocations are selected, using best engineering judgment. Compute system reliability for this set of component reliabilities. Compare the result against the goal. Adjust component reliabilities to move system reliability toward the goal, and component reliabilities toward better balance. Repeat the process until the desired goal and good balance are achieved.

> **Example 7.7.** A space vehicle will use three identical onboard computers, each with an independently designed and developed program that performs the identical function. The overall reliability goal for this vehicle is 0.999 for a 100-hr mission. Development costs are estimated as follows for different alternatives.

Program		Computer	
Reliability (100 hr)	Cost	Reliability (100 hr)	Cost
0.91	$ 3M	0.91	$ 300K
0.92	$ 3.25M	0.93	$ 400K
0.93	$ 3.5M	0.95	$ 500K
0.94	$ 3.75M	0.96	$ 600K
0.95	$ 4M	0.97	$ 800K
0.97	$ 4.5M	0.98	$ 1.5M
0.99	$ 5M	0.99	$ 5M

The computers operate simultaneously. Outputs are subjected to a sanity check. If any output passes, the system is considered operational. The sanity checking routine is considered to have a reliability of 1. Note that if a computer fails, the sanity checker cannot run and the output from that machine is considered to have failed. How should we allocate reliability goals to the computer and the program to minimize total development cost?

This is a concurrently functioning system with the event diagram of Figure 7.7. R_C denotes the reliability of the computer; R_P, the program. Let R_{sys} be the overall system reliability. Applying the rules for AND and OR event logic, we have

$$R_{\text{sys}} = 1 - (1-R_C R_P)^3 \ .$$

For $R_{\text{sys}} = 0.999$, we have $R_C R_P = 0.9$.

Try $R_C = 0.95$ and $R_p = 0.95$. This will give the requisite system reliability. Note that cost of achieving this hardware reliability is relatively low and the total cost is \$4.5M.

Try a more difficult goal for the hardware: $R_C = 0.96$. Note that $R_P = 0.94$ will provide the proper overall reliability. Now the total cost is \$4.35M.

It is apparent we are headed in the right direction. A trial of $R_C = 0.97$ and $R_P = 0.93$ yields the proper overall reliability and a cost of \$4.3M.

A trial of $R_C = 0.98$ and $R_P = 0.92$ indicates we have gone too far. Improving the hardware this much is getting costly. The overall cost is now up to \$4.75M.

Thus we choose $R_C = 0.97$ and $R_P = 0.93$.   ∎

7.2.6 System Simulation

A system simulator can be used to predict reliability of a software system before it is constructed. You must be able, from the system design, to determine the segments of the system and the transition probabilities between them. Also, we must know the size of the segments (executable source instructions) and the fault rate. Some estimate of the proportion of time for which the execution of a fault leads to a failure is required. You can now establish for each segment the probability it will fail when executed.

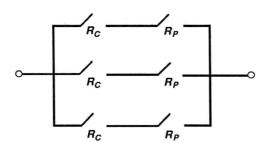

FIGURE 7.7
Event diagram for reliability allocation.

A Monte Carlo simulation is now conducted. For each run, use a random number generator to determine which transitions between branches are made and whether a failure occurs in a branch. Record all failures with their times. A large number of runs are made. Use the set of failure intervals to estimate model parameters, present failure intensity, and software reliability. Obviously, the determination of the last two quantities is based on the assumption of a particular model.

7.3 PROJECT MANAGEMENT

First, we should note that many of the studies done in the system engineering phase are often repeated during development. Conditions change, and project management needs guidance to adapt.

At present, software reliability measurement has been applied during development primarily to the *system* test phase of projects. However, we can also apply it to subsystem testing. The subsystem should have a size of approximately 5000 source instructions or greater. It may prove possible to extend use of the theory to unit testing by grouping of units. When systems are small, estimates are likely to have wide confidence intervals for a large part of the test period and hence be of limited value. Also, if the number of people involved is small, performance (in terms of resources required for debugging) may depart substantially from the average, yielding inaccurate calendar time predictions. We can handle this by replacing average resource requirement values for debugging by individualized values obtained through measurement or estimation.

Estimates of test period duration may be combined with estimates of the length of system requirements analysis, design, and program unit coding phases to produce overall project estimates. An approach to elapsed time estimation that can be applied to either individual phases of a project or the entire project has been developed by Putnam (1976). It is based on a Rayleigh personnel profile. Substitution of an execution time model for the Rayleigh model in the test phases should yield better results. More information (for example, the failure intensity objective, initial failure intensity, and total expected failures) is taken into account.

The present failure intensity will normally exhibit steady (ignoring statistical fluctuations) improvement with time during testing. A sharp rise in failure intensity usually indicates new faults introduced by code modification or exposed by extension of testing into new environments. The latter case may indicate inadequate test planning. An unusually slow decrease in failure intensity usually indicates that a substantial number of faults remain. Another possibility is that we are introducing or exposing new faults at roughly the same rate that faults are being corrected.

One question that occasionally occurs when an unreliable release is encountered in a multirelease project is, "Should we regress to a previous version from the present one?" This question can be answered by tracking present failure intensity for each version. Suppose that the new version is not meeting the failure intensity objective and the old one is. If the difference between the failure intensities is substantial, it will probably be worth the effort to regress.

The tracking of the failure intensities of different subsystems of an overall system is sometimes useful. You might want to determine the relative priorities to be given to the subsystems with respect to failure correction. The relative criticalities of the functions implemented by the subsystems may affect the decision. Also, knowledge of how system failure is related to failures of the individual subsystems can be important.

Another application of software reliability modeling relates to the use of overtime. Consider how use of *selective* overtime for those debuggers who have a failure backlog affects the calendar time required for the testing effort. Let α be the overtime fraction (ratio of overtime to standard time for each work day). Now the effective *available* personnel are increased by the factor $(1 + \alpha)$ and hence the calendar time for the failure-correction-personnel-limited segment of the test phase is reduced by that factor.

It is shown in Section 14.4.1 that the probability for each debugger that there are one or more failures awaiting correction or being corrected is ρ_F. Only those debuggers who have failures to work on will be assigned overtime. Hence the *actual* fraction of overtime work is $\alpha\rho_F$ for the failure-correction-personnel-limited segment. For example, suppose $\rho_F = 0.2$ and $\alpha = 0.2$. Assume that the entire test phase is failure-correction-personnel-limited. Then calendar time is reduced by a factor of $1 + \alpha = 1 + 0.2 = 1.2$. The actual overtime fraction is $\alpha\rho_F = 0.2\,(0.2) = 0.04$. With 50 percent premium pay, this represents a 2 percent increase in cost. The premium pay is the only extra cost. No extra work is required. It is merely shifted in time. The value of *selective* overtime is clearly shown. Note the importance, however, of applying overtime only for the limiting resource. There will be no beneficial effect if applied to a nonlimiting resource.

There is a graphical method for determining when (in execution time) a failure intensity objective will be reached for the basic execution time model. This approach may be useful for quick and dirty calculations. Taking the logarithm of both sides of Equation (2.7) we obtain

$$\ln \lambda = \ln \lambda_0 - \frac{\lambda_0}{\nu_0}\,\tau\,. \tag{7.12}$$

If we plot the model on semilogarithmic paper, it becomes a straight line. It has now become an easy matter to project the model to where it intersects the failure intensity objective, and read off the execution time.

A control chart is a useful tool for management to monitor, control, and predict the quality (or the failure intensity) of a software system being tested. The control chart is constructed based on confidence limits for the future failure intensity. If the future failure intensity data conform to a pattern of random variation within the control limits, the process will be judged as being in control. Departures from the pattern are investigated and assignable causes tracked down.

Example 7.8. To illustrate the method, we use the first 100 failures of System T1 (Table 12.1). Failure intensities are computed for 20 data points, with each data point based on 5 failures. Each failure intensity is computed from times of failures spaced 4 failures apart. We determined the 95 percent confidence limits for various values of failure intensity. Figure 7.8 shows the observed failure intensity along with the confidence limits. The failure intensity data beyond 100 failures are plotted on the control chart developed based on the first 100 failures. As can be seen from Figure 7.8, these new failure intensity data points continue to fall within the limits on the chart. Therefore, with 95 percent confidence the failure intensity process may be judged to be in a state of statistical control. We will describe the method for constructing confidence limits for future failure intensity in detail in Section 12.3. ∎

7.4 MANAGEMENT OF OPERATIONAL PHASE

7.4.1 Reliability Demonstration Testing

The situation frequently arises where it is desirable or necessary to prove that a given level of reliability has been achieved. This situation occurs particularly when software is being developed by a subcontractor. You may be involved in such a demonstration either as a party letting the contract or as a subcontractor.

The purpose of a reliability demonstration is to determine if the failure intensity objective is met with high confidence or not. In conducting a demonstration, you assume that the proper operational profile has been executed. It must represent actual operation. You also assume that there will not be any repair of the software. You are testing the product as it has been delivered to you or as you are delivering it. Our reliability demonstration approach is based on sequential sampling theory. Sequential sampling theory provides an efficient approach to testing a hypothesis by taking just enough data and no more. The data points are added one by one and you stop as soon as you can reach a decision.

We have constructed a chart (Figure 7.9) which tests whether or not the failure intensity objective you have established is met within a factor of 2 (discrimination ratio). There is a 10 percent risk of falsely saying that the objective is not met when it *is*. Similarly, there is a 10 percent risk of falsely saying that the objective is met when it is *not*. We have chosen for you what we feel to be a reasonable discrimination ratio and reasonable risk levels to simplify the approach. If different discrimination ratios or risk levels are desired, a different chart must be constructed.

Let's go through the steps for conducting a reliability demonstration. First, you have to establish what the failure intensity objective is that you are testing. We now run the test and record the time of the next failure that is experienced. The failure time is then normalized by multiplying it by the failure intensity objective. The normalized failure time is then located on the reliability demonstration chart. If it falls in the "accept" region, then the failure intensity objective is considered met with high confidence. If it falls in the "reject" region, there is little possibility of meeting the objective. It is not worth testing further. If it falls in the "continue"

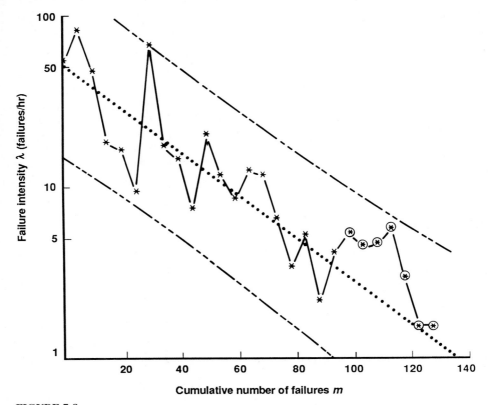

FIGURE 7.8
Observed failure intensity data along with the control chart constructed from the first 100 failure intervals of the data set T1.

region, the result is uncertain. You should continue to test. It is legitimate to keep testing as long as you are in the "continue" region. However, in some practical cases "reject" is assumed after a specified period of normalized time if "accept" has not occurred.

> **Example 7.9.** A personal computer manufacturer wishes to know if the software house furnishing the operating system for a new machine has met the failure intensity objective of 0.1 failure/CPU hr. A series of tests are applied and failure data are recorded.
>   The first failure occurs at 8 CPU hr or 0.8 normalized time units. This falls in the "continue" region of Figure 7.9. The second failure occurs at 19 CPU hr or 1.9 normalized time units. Again, we are in the "continue" region. The third failure occurs at 60 CPU hr or 6.0 normalized time units. Now, we clearly fall in the "accept" region. We can stop testing and assume with high confidence that the failure intensity objective must be within a factor of 2 of the specification.   ■

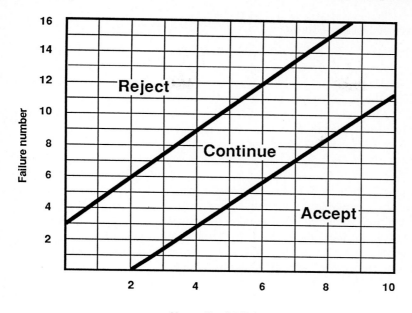

Normalized failure time

FIGURE 7.9
Reliability demonstration chart.

The construction of a different chart is not difficult [Grant and Leavenworth (1980)]. Let γ be the discrimination ratio. The quantity α is the risk (probability) of falsely saying that the objective is not met when it *is*. The quantity β is the risk of falsely saying that the objective is met when it is *not*. Define

$$A = \ln \frac{\beta}{1 - \alpha} \tag{7.13}$$

and

$$B = \ln \frac{1 - \beta}{\alpha}. \tag{7.14}$$

Then the boundary between the "reject" and "continue" regions of the chart is given by

$$\frac{A - n \ln \gamma}{1 - \gamma}, \tag{7.15}$$

where n is the failure number. The boundary between the "continue" and "accept" regions is given by

$$\frac{B - n \ln \gamma}{1 - \gamma}. \tag{7.16}$$

7.4.2   Impact of Design Change

Determining the effect of a proposed design change on the failure intensity of a program can be particularly useful for software managers who are managing operational programs. If they can establish what the new failure intensity would be after the change, they can determine whether this failure intensity meets the service objective for the system. If it doesn't, they can defer the change. When the failure intensity is low enough so that the proposed change does not push failure intensity above an acceptable level, it can be installed.

The impact of a design change on a program may be predicted, assuming the basic model, by predicting the number of faults introduced by the change. This is most easily done by determining the size of the change in terms of developed (new or modified) executable deliverable source instructions (or lines). Then we apply known data on average faults per source instruction (line) at the appropriate point in time. This is usually the start of system test. We assume that the change has been thoroughly tested by itself before introduction, in a fashion akin to unit or subsystem test. Hence the "start of system test" data are appropriate. Compute the number of faults that remained in the program at release by multiplying the remaining failures by the fault reduction factor B. Remaining failures are usually estimated by one of the programs in Chapter 5. The basic model assumes that failure intensity is proportional to the faults present. Hence we may predict the failure intensity λ_A just after the design change as

$$\frac{\lambda_A}{\lambda_B} = \frac{\omega_A}{\omega_B} . \tag{7.17}$$

Note that λ_B is the failure intensity just before the design change. The quantities ω_B and ω_A are the expected faults remaining just before and after the change, respectively.

The impact of the design change on resource expenditures, cost, and schedules may be determined by computing these quantities for both λ_B and λ_A. We can do this for either a fixed objective or a fixed schedule. The former case is appropriate when product quality level is paramount. The latter is better when meeting a deadline or getting a product to market rapidly is most important.

In the foregoing calculation, we implicitly ignored, for simplicity, any effect the change might have on failure intensity by lengthening the program and hence reducing its execution frequency. Usually the effect is negligible.

We utilized the assumption that the failure intensity is proportional to the faults present. Note that we are implicitly assuming that the code of the design change will be executed with the same frequency as that of the existing program, on the average. We could have a special situation, however. For example, suppose that the design change is in a routine that is executed very frequently. Then the ratio of failure intensities after to before the change should be multiplied by the ratio of average execution frequency of the change to average execution frequency of the existing program. Ordinarily the foregoing situation will occur only for a small and hence localized design change.

Example 7.10. The latest run of the software reliability estimation program on a word processing program indicates 500 total failures expected. It shows 485 already experienced. The basic model is being applied. The fault reduction factor is 1. The same program indicates a present failure intensity of 0.06 failure/CPU hr. If a change of 2000 developed source instructions is introduced, what will be the effect on failure intensity? Assume that inherent faults per source instruction have been measured at 0.005.

There are 15 remaining faults. The change will introduce 10 new faults. The failure intensity after the change λ_A will be, using Equation (7.3):

$$\lambda_A = \frac{\omega_A}{\omega_B} \lambda_B = \frac{15 + 10}{15} (0.06) = 0.10 \text{ failure/CPU hr}. \qquad \blacksquare$$

7.4.3 Measuring Ultrahigh Reliability

There is great interest in measuring reliability at ultrahigh levels. The measurement is important for systems where failure is of a life critical nature. Examples of such systems include nuclear power reactors, aircraft control and air traffic systems, and space vehicle control. The following evaluation was performed for a component of one of these systems.

CASE STUDY 7.1
NUCLEAR POWER AGENCY

A nuclear power agency uses a computer-based monitoring system for its reactors. The operating system (which we denote "P38") for the computer is employed for this and other applications in an estimated 5000 installations throughout the world. It is desired to evaluate the reliability of the system. Failure data collected on a per-month basis are shown in Table 7.1. A total of 17 failures have occurred in 43 calendar months of operation. Each system runs 24 hr/day. Computer utilization is constant. Coupled with the fact that 5000 systems are in operation, this translates into 1.57×10^8 hr of operation.

Failure time data are required as input for the estimation program. The raw data were converted into this format by randomly selecting the failure times in each appropriate month. The resulting failure times are listed in Table 7.2. Note also that the total time of operation is greater than the time of the last failure. This denotes failure-free time, that is, 3906 years of failure-free execution has accumulated since the last failure. Note also that the data in this table and the following results pertain to a *single copy* of the software system.

Two sets of results are presented. The first consists of estimates of the lower confidence limit of the expected number of total failures (Table 7.3) using the basic execution time model. For example, we are 95 percent certain that at least 20 failures (3 more in addition to the 17 that have already been experienced) will

TABLE 7.1
Monthly failure data for system P38

Month[1]	Number of failures
8/79–9/79	0
10/79	1
5/80	1
7/80	2
11/80	2
2/81	1
3/81	1
6/81	1
8/81	1
9/81	1
10/81	1
12/81	2
1/82	1
3/82	1
5/82	1
6/82–2/83	0

[1]Missing months had no failures.

TABLE 7.2
Converted failure time data for system P38

Failure number	Failure time (yr)	Months from start of operation
1	932	3
2	4035	10
3	4696	12
4	4893	12
5	6369	16
6	6524	16
7	7882	19
8	8170	20
9	9339	23
10	10400	25
11	10542	26
12	11036	27
13	11696	29
14	11905	29
15	12266	30
16	12954	32
17	14000	34

Note: Total time of operation is 17,906 yr.

TABLE 7.3
**Lower confidence limit on
the expected total failures**

Confidence level	Confidence limit
95%	20
90%	21
75%	25
50%	33

occur at some time. Estimates of the upper confidence limit are not reliable due to the small sample size.

The second set of results (Table 7.4) concerns the failure intensity of the software system. The results show that the most likely value for the failure intensity is 0.867 failure/1000 yr using the basic model. It is 0.895 failure/1000 yr using the logarithmic Poisson model. Results for both models are compatible until we reach the higher confidence limits (that is, 90 and 95 percent). Larger failure intensities are predicted by the logarithmic Poisson model.

7.4.4 Controlling Level of Preventive Maintenance

Many organizations generate fixes for software in the field in response to failure reports and then ship these fixes to the various installations. Responses are not made to all failures, nor are fixes necessarily sent to all sites. Local managers frequently exercise considerable discretion over whether the fixes are installed or not. How should we select which repairs should be implemented?

Software reliability concepts provide some guidance. Each fault has associated with it a set of failures that it can cause. Each failure is the result of a particular run being made. The sum of the probabilities of occurrence of these different runs represents the contribution that the fault makes to the overall failure in-

TABLE 7.4
Confidence intervals for present failure intensity

Confidence level	Failure intensity (failures/1000 yr)	
	Basic model	Logarithmic Poisson model
Most likely value	0.867	0.895
50%	0.638–1.143	0.689–1.197
75%	0.506–1.372	0.579–1.494
90%	0.394–1.633	0.492–1.908
95%	0.333–1.810	0.445–2.24

tensity. Thus the failure intensity contribution of the fault depends on the operational profile.

The failure intensity contribution has an effect on the operation of the program, with each failure resulting in some financial cost. The preparation, dissemination, and installation of fixes have definite financial costs also. In addition, there is some risk that the installation of a repair to a fault may introduce other faults as well. A reasonable approach to deciding which faults one should concentrate on would be to conduct a brief analysis of the foregoing cost impacts.

Adams (1984) notes that usually a system has a relatively small number of faults that have large contributions to failure intensity. These are usually found early in the use of the system. One should vigorously pursue development and installation of fixes for these faults. It may, however, be wise for a local site manager *not* to install fixes on a preventive basis for all faults that have been found. The better strategy may be to observe which failures occur frequently for your own operational profile (your local profile may differ from the system average global one). You can then install corrections for just those faults that are causing those failures.

7.5 EVALUATION OF SOFTWARE ENGINEERING TECHNOLOGIES

Evaluation of a new software engineering technology requires that you first establish a technology base (that is, the "old" technology) or a "control" technology. We will then compare the new technology with it. The technique to be evaluated must be carefully described and defined. What appears to be a single technique may actually turn out to be a complex of related techniques. It is proper to evaluate such a complex. However, there is more risk of difficulty in this evaluation. All members of the complex may not be applied with equal vigor in all circumstances. A suitable experiment to compare the new technique with its control is then devised. The statistical theory of experimental design may be helpful in guiding the experimenter toward efficient investigation. Efficiency is often very important in view of the large cost of many software engineering experiments.

We have two common alternatives to use in making comparisons, a fixed schedule and a fixed objective approach. In the fixed schedule approach, one measures failure intensity for both the experimental and the control method after equal amounts of test. We judge any improvement in failure intensity against the cost of applying the technique. This method is best when the release data are constrained (as they might be, for example, by marketing considerations). In the fixed objective approach, you test in both cases until the same failure intensity is reached and then compute the saving in cost involved, if any. The saving is the reduction in test costs due to a shorter test period, with the cost of applying the technique subtracted.

A common result of new software engineering technologies applied during phases before test, if they are effective, is to reduce the number of inherent faults. Assume the basic model. A 10 percent reduction (for example) in inherent faults will reduce ν_0, the total number of failures in infinite time, by 10 percent, per Equation (5.1). It will also decrease λ_0, the initial failure intensity at the start of test, by 10 percent, per Equation (5.2). The failure intensity curve is described by

$$\lambda = \lambda_0 \exp\left(-\frac{\lambda_0 \tau}{\nu_0}\right), \tag{7.18}$$

where τ is execution time. Thus the principal overall effect is to lower the curve, the amount being 10 percent at $\tau = 0$.

Now, reaching a given failure intensity objective λ_F from the initial failure intensity λ_0 requires that $\Delta\mu$ failures be experienced and $\Delta\tau$ of execution time expended. We have

$$\Delta\mu = \nu_0\left(1 - \frac{\lambda_F}{\lambda_0}\right) \tag{7.19}$$

and

$$\Delta\tau = \frac{\nu_0}{\lambda_0} \ln\left(\frac{\lambda_0}{\lambda_F}\right). \tag{7.20}$$

Both $\Delta\mu$ and $\Delta\tau$ will be reduced by the new technology in this example, but by less than 10 percent. Let $\lambda_F = 0.01 \lambda_0$. Then $\Delta\mu$ will be reduced by almost 10 percent and $\Delta\tau$ by slightly over 2 percent. The net effect on the duration and cost of the test period will depend on various resource and cost parameters, but will probably fall somewhere between 2 and 10 percent. A slightly different view is that with a fixed failure intensity objective, a successful software engineering technology reduces the failure intensity ratio that must be attained over the test period. Thus duration and cost of test can be reduced as shown in Figures 7.2 and 7.3.

Sometimes the new technology may affect the size of the program as well as the number of faults it contains. For example, writing a program in structured form may result in a somewhat longer program. Here the linear execution frequency (average instruction execution rate divided by size) will be reduced. The analysis of the effect of the new technology will be slightly more complicated, since it affects two parameters.

7.6 DOCUMENTATION DEBUGGING AND OTHER APPLICATIONS

It appears that we can generally apply software reliability concepts, methodologies, and tools to products of certain systematic creative processes and to the processes themselves. This becomes apparent when you realize that software development is one of a number of such creative processes. These processes are characterized by an initial implementation followed by a period of "failure" detection through "test" and fault correction. Hardware design is one example of such a potential application. Another is writing.

Note that a draft of a paper, article, or document receives its "system test" through reading by reviewers. We do the reading against the "system requirements" of conveying information to meet particular needs. Needs might be diagnosing a software failure or determining how to add a change. The test "runs" represent attempts to attain information to meet these needs. The "operational profile" represents the range and relative frequencies of these needs. It is reasonable to assume that any particular run occurs randomly with a probability expressed by the operational profile. A "failure" is any situation in which the reading of the text does not convey the information required to meet the need. The fault is the particular deficiency in the text that is responsible for the failure. The failure intensity will decrease with time as the document is "repaired." Software reliability models can be applied to this situation. We can establish an objective for the document such as "0.95 'reliability' in obtaining the required information for various needs per hour of reading." The foregoing may be a useful approach to the evaluation of user manuals and program documentation. It might also conceivably be applied to the evaluation of requirements or design specifications.

7.7   SUMMARY

A wide range of applications in four major areas has been presented. You need to keep these possibilities in mind, along with the data and effort required to implement them, as you analyze a project's needs. This will permit the establishment of a sound basis for the implementation of software reliability measurement and prediction on a project.

PROBLEMS

7.1 The Soft Landing software service company has won a service contract to provide recovery service for a patient control and billing system. The service is provided to doctors in a region who own personal computers. It has a failure intensity of 1 failure/100 CPU hr. The average system runs 10 CPU hr/week and there are 600 doctors to be serviced. The average service person can make 2 service calls daily, including travel and allowing for enough spare personnel to prevent excessive service backlogs from building up.

How many service personnel do we need? Assuming a cost of $200/call, what annual contract fee must we charge each doctor to achieve 20 percent profit on sales?

7.2 A software project manager desires to evaluate the cost effectiveness of design reviews on a project. The program has 50,000 source instructions. Previous experience indicates 8 faults/1000 instructions and an initial failure intensity of 10 failures/CPU hr when design reviews are not conducted. These data were collected for a similar program of the same size on a machine of the same speed at the start of system test. It is found that design reviews reduce the fault figure to 6.

Assume that the fault reduction factor $B = 1$. For simplicity, assume that the entire system test period is failure-correction-personnel-limited and that all resources are profitably employed (none are idle at any time). Loaded salary is $50/hr and computer (CPU) time is $1000/CPU hr. The system at delivery must have a failure intensity of 1 failure/10 CPU hr.

Data taken in similar environments indicate that 6 person hr are required for failure correction per failure. This effort is independent of amount of execution time. We require 5 person hr of system test team effort and 2 CPU hr of chargeable computer time per hr of execution time. Also, we need 3 person hr of system test team effort and 0.5 CPU hr of computer time per failure.

The design reviews require 3 meetings, each attended by 10 people and lasting 6 hr. Follow-up activities require 200 person hr of time.

Does the design review pay off? If so, what is the saving?

7.3 A program has an initial failure intensity of 10 failures/CPU hr. We want to test and debug this program until a failure intensity of 1 failure/10 CPU hr is achieved. Assume the following resource usage parameters.

Resource usage	Per hr	Per failure
Failure identification effort	3 person hr	2 person hr
Failure correction effort	0	6 person hr
Computer time	1.5 CPU hr	1 CPU hr

(a) What resources must be expended to achieve the reliability improvement required? Use the logarithmic Poisson execution time model. Assume a failure intensity decay parameter of 0.05.

(b) If the failure intensity objective is cut in half, are the resources required doubled?

7.4 A company is planning an online order processing system. It will process orders received and generate bills. It breaks down the work involved into tasks, writes work orders on those tasks, and orders materials. We wish to establish the failure intensity objective for the system that will minimize total system cost over an estimated lifetime of 2 years. Faults are not to be corrected in the field for this system. They will be fixed at the next release. Assume for simplicity that the hardware components of the system are much more reliable than the software and hence may be neglected in this analysis. Also, for simplicity, assume that the entire system test period is failure-correction-personnel-limited. All resources are profitably employed. None are idle at any time. The system is expected to operate 250 days/yr, 8 CPU hr/day. The average total cost impact of a failure (in terms of reduced efficiency, extra supervisory time and other work required to "straighten out the mess," etc.) is $10,000. The cost of the requirements, design, code, and unit test phases is independent of the failure intensity achieved.

The software consists of 100,000 source (400,000 object) instructions. Programmer loaded salary is $50/hr and computer (CPU) time is $1000/CPU hr. There are 25 program designers available for debugging. Testing is to be paced so that no debugger has more than 2 failures awaiting correction, with 90 percent probability. Average instruction execution rate is one million object instructions per CPU second. On similar projects, a value of fault exposure ratio $K = 2.222 \times 10^{-7}$ has been experienced. We can estimate the average fault density at 5 faults/1000 source instructions. Assume that the fault reduction factor $B = 1$. Data taken in similar environments indicate that 5 person hr are required for failure correction per failure. This effort is independent of amount of execution time. Similarly, 4 person hr of system test team effort and 1 CPU hr of chargeable computer time are required per hr of execution time. We need 2 person hr of system test team effort and 1/2 CPU hr of computer time per failure.

What is the failure intensity objective that minimizes total life cycle cost? What is the minimum cost of system test and operational failures? What is the length of the system test period (in calendar time) for the minimum failure intensity objective? What is the reliability of the optimum system for 1 day of operation?

7.5 The following problem will use the basic execution time model. We are conducting a system analysis for the proposed software system COMPROD to determine the range of cost choices available as a function of failure intensity objective. We wish to investigate costs for failure intensity objectives ranging from 1 to 5 failures per 100 CPU hr. The following system test costs (with ranges of variation) have been determined.

Failure intensity objective (per 100 CPU hr)	System test cost (K $)	Range of system test cost (K $)
1	1585	1230–1840
2	1490	1160–1710
3	1440	1100–1650
4	1400	1070–1600
5	1360	1040–1560

Compute the overall component of system cost that is dependent on reliability (failure intensity objective). Assume that the system will operate for 4 years, 250 days/yr, 10 CPU hr/day. There will be 5 installations of the system. The total cost impact of a failure is estimated to be $100. What is the optimum value for the failure intensity objective? What range of values does this objective take on as a result of inaccuracies in the knowledge of total failures and initial failure intensity?

7.6 A program has a failure intensity objective of 0.1 failure/CPU hr. It is run for 50 CPU hr with no failures occurring. How confident are we that it has met its objective?

7.7 A change to 2000 source instructions is being made in a program of 100,000 source instructions. The fault density of the base program at the start of system test was 5 faults/1000 source instructions. Assume that the fault reduction factor $B = 1$. The initial failure intensity of the base program was 2 failures/CPU hr. It was released with a failure intensity of 6 failures/100 CPU hr. Fixes of faults are not made during the operational phase. What is the expected impact on failure intensity of the operational program?

7.8 Can we use a software reliability model to help establish the priority with which different subsystems should be tested?

7.9 Assume that we can make overtime available to failure identification personnel (as a percentage of regular work time) to be used whenever it will expedite the work in progress. How much can be profitably used?

7.10 What is the impact of inefficient programs on failure intensity? Couldn't an inefficient program give a spuriously low failure intensity?

7.11 Should we try to balance failure intensities between different components of a system so that they are *equal*?

7.12 What are the effects of better testing on the variation of failure intensity with execution time?

7.13 How would you determine the effect of built-in tests (audits) on software reliability?

7.14 How can you rapidly (without substantial calculations) make predictions of the execution time required to reach various failure intensity objectives?

EIGHT

IMPLEMENTATION PLANNING

In Chapter 3 we discussed overall planning on how to apply software reliability measures to your project. We would now like to continue this effort to the detailed planning stage. There are some general detailed planning steps that you should consider. You may wish to augment these steps with steps that are specific to your project as well.

You should realize that one always encounters resistance when introducing new ideas in an institution or project. Some of this is desirable. It serves to protect the organization against uncritically considered ideas and hasty decisions. It prevents disruption of processes that are functioning well. Some of the resistance is undesirable but natural. Change disturbs people, forcing them to learn new knowledge and skills, adapt, and invest extra efforts. Hence you can expect some hostility. You may feel it is unjustified. However, if you can see things from the viewpoint of the people affected, you will usually be more effective. It is important to try to understand the existing system before introducing change. Then you will retain its good features. Also, you are giving the project members the implicit message that you are interested in their problems and respect the competence they have exhibited in solving them in the past.

One thing that you must consider is the definition of failure for your project. Do you want explicit definition through requirements documents or do you want to consider any program behavior that may be unsatisfactory to customers as a failure? You should also think about whether you wish to classify failures by severity. If so, how many classes do you want to have and how will you establish them?

After this, you need to determine whether your system will be operating in different modes. Then you need to think about your system, and determine what its configuration is and how you will be breaking it down into components. If you expect the system to evolve, then you need to determine how this is going to take place. What, if anything, should you do about taking the evolution into account?

You must choose which model or models you will apply. You need to plan how you will go about determining parameters for the model. How will you select a failure intensity objective? How will you establish the parameters for resource usage? You should anticipate any special problems regarding resource quantities or utilizations that may require some special adjustments to the parameters.

You have established many of the basics of your detailed plan. Consideration now has to be given to the process of data collection. To what extent will you collect data? Will you be collecting data during both test and operation? Will you be collecting data during subsystem test as well as system test? What types of data do you need to collect? Will you be collecting failure data? Resource usage data? What general project information will you need? Think about any special considerations. Will you be able to measure execution time or must you make an approximation to it? Are there multiple installations? If so, will there be different computers with different average instruction execution rates? How are you going to motivate and train your data takers? What recording procedures will you use? How will you be going about the process of data scrubbing? How will you feed back results to members of the project, particularly the data takers and managers? Do you plan to conduct a prototype experiment? How are you going to go about this?

Finally, you need to think about the tools that you will need, such as programs for conveniently handling calculations. Some useful programs are suggested in Chapter 5. Which of these will you need? Where will you obtain them? Or will you develop them? What has to be done to install and use them? What machine and operating system will you be running them on? Are there any changes that need to be made to adapt these programs to that machine?

8.1 DATA COLLECTION

Careful planning and organization are necessary if one is to collect data of high quality. You need to identify a project contact who is interested in the data collection effort and will take charge of it.

It may seem obvious to tell you that you need to spend some time thinking about what data you are going to collect. Unfortunately, this step is frequently ignored, with undesirable results. You should have a clear purpose in mind for each piece of data and a clear understanding of how the data will be processed to achieve that purpose. Establishing this linkage will expose weaknesses in your plans that need correction (or perhaps it will show that a certain objective isn't feasible) and avoid wasted effort. Is the data item that you plan to collect worth the cost of collecting it? Many people seem to take the approach that if the data might be of any potential value whatsoever, they should be collected. The problem with this approach is that it places such a burden on the data collectors that they soon become weary and disillusioned. Then you get a real deterioration in all the data that you are trying to collect, including the important data. Also, there is a definite cost in collecting data and the more data you collect the greater the cost.

You can impose a substantial overhead on a project, which will then discourage project managers and members in the future from cooperation with you.

Look carefully at possible alternatives for each piece of data that you are thinking of collecting. One might be the possibility of approximating data. Approximate data, if satisfactory in quality, may be easier, less expensive, and less burdensome to collect than precise data. Another alternative you should consider is collecting the data at a lower frequency. You may not really need the amount of data that you are planning to take. Finally, look hard for multipurpose data. Perhaps by slightly changing some of your requirements, a data item that you collect can serve several purposes. Maybe it doesn't serve all of them perfectly, but it is good enough, and it reduces the collection burdens considerably.

Probably the most important issue, however, is how to obtain the cooperation of personnel on the project in collecting the data. One approach to this problem is to obtain the support of the manager of the data takers and have that manager order them to do the things that you require. "Management by machismo" may secure for you a blizzard of paper, but these data will generally be provided grudgingly and without much consideration or thought. Consequently, they will usually be of questionable quality.

We believe that the following approach is generally more fruitful:

1. Obtain the motivated participation of the data takers.
2. Make the collection mechanism as easy as possible.
3. Collect and scrub the data in real time.
4. Provide feedback of results obtained from the data on a regular and timely basis.

8.1.1   Motivating Data Takers

The first question that needs to be tackled is how one can motivate the data takers. Analyze why you are collecting the data, and how your goals can be related to those of the data takers. It is usually most effective to appeal to the strongest motivations of the data takers. In order, these are typically: direct personal benefit, project benefit, and benefit to the profession. Thus, if you can show any direct personal benefit from collecting the data, do so. For example, you may be giving the people involved in the data collection effort some feedback on the software product they have produced. This can be particularly helpful if it is from a different perspective than the usual feedback they receive. People are usually very interested in getting feedback on their performance, as long as it is done in a nonjudgmental way. The feedback helps them to improve and grow in their profession. The second best approach is to show that the data collection effort will be of direct project benefit. Most people realize that if they cooperate in something that benefits the project they are working on, their colleagues and their management will notice this, and it will be to their credit. Third, many professionals are truly interested in advancing the state of their field. If you can show that what you are doing will help achieve this, they are often willing to go to a certain amount of trouble to help you. However, you really have to be honest with them in showing what you are trying to accomplish. If they think that the data are of poor quality for the objective or that the research effort is meaningless, you will not appeal to them.

Enlist the participation of the data takers in planning how the data collection effort will be applied to their project. The sense of participation engendered will usually materially improve the degree of cooperation attained. Furthermore, letting the data takers plan the details of the effort will actually result in concrete benefits. They will usually know many details about the project that would elude you. We have found it helpful to explicitly ask the data takers to give us the benefit of their experience. We have tried several formats in working with data collection personnel on a project. They are usually the members of the test and development teams and are professional software engineers. The approach of coming in with a totally organized plan and informing people how to carry it out does not seem to work. On the other hand, the approach of sitting down and saying we have a problem and how are we going to solve it generally does not work too well either. Most of the people involved are not willing to devote a large amount of time to solving your problem. The approach that seems to work best is to start with a first draft of a data collection plan. Provide it to the data collection personnel to read if they desire. Then call a meeting and present its main features. Ask the participants to identify problems and to suggest improvements. Generally you will then have a small number of problems to deal with. You elicit the participation of the attendees at the meeting in solving the problems. Hopefully you go away from the meeting with a set of suggested changes to your plan. Sometimes you may have some action items that have to be resolved, and perhaps another meeting may be required before things stabilize. Finally, you modify and issue the plan. Generally, we have found that the group in any given meeting should not be larger than 15 or so. It is difficult to have a participative session with a larger group.

Once the plan has been established, it must be disseminated. Data takers should be given a clear technical understanding of the purpose of the data collection, if it isn't already obvious to them from the planning session. This is important. They must be able to make intelligent decisions when confronted with the many special problems that can occur in trying to reduce reality to a box on a form. We have found that an oral presentation is usually best for this purpose rather than written material. A meeting affords attendees the opportunity to ask questions and test their understanding of the material presented. The written material may be useful as an adjunct for later reference, however.

It is, of course, highly desirable to convince project management as well as the data takers of the value of the collection effort. However, convincing the data takers is probably most important, provided project management at least acquiesces in what you are doing. Attention to detail is more important than organization or coordination in this activity.

8.1.2   Making Data Collection Easy

Data collection is at best an annoying and burdensome chore that often gets in the way of one's primary work. Hence, every effort must be bent toward reducing this chore as much as possible. Can you reduce the number of people involved in collecting a particular data item? For example, one person might be able to estimate a quantity with satisfactory accuracy. It may be unnecessary to collect data individually from five people and average them.

Try to integrate your data collection activities with other data collection activities and with the primary work that is proceeding in parallel. Combine forms whenever feasible. Automate the collection (that is, make human intervention unnecessary) if possible, building appropriate tools into the software development environment. The advantages of automated data collection are the reduced burden and greater accuracy. The principal disadvantage is that this mode is generally unsatisfactory when interpretation is needed in establishing the data values. Sometimes online data collection, perhaps in a conversational mode with a menu or "fill in the blanks" template that is presented to the person entering the data, is appropriate. This is particularly true when the activity for which you are collecting data is also being operated online. Many people prefer talking to writing. Consider the possibility of telephone reporting of your data if it is feasible. Probably the best thing here is to have someone that will record the data live, so he or she can straighten out any difficulties. The second best alternative would be to have a recording device to which the data taker can dictate. If you are using forms, invest some effort in designing them for ease of use and ease of computer entry. The form should provide enough space to record the information required and should elicit the information in the natural order in which the person would provide it. A simple matter such as providing someone to collect the forms and answer questions about filling them out may make a big difference.

It is important to make a trial run of your data collection procedures. No amount of planning can predict all the snags you will encounter, since many of these will result from human misunderstanding, misinterpretation, or miscommunication. Definitions of data items to be collected may not be clear, important data may be missed, collection systems may malfunction, computer programs may not work in all situations, and special unanticipated cases may arise. It is desirable to have a meeting of the participants in the trial to critique it and uncover and solve the problems. One possible time for the trial run is during subsystem test prior to system test, perhaps for one subsystem.

8.1.3   Collecting and Scrubbing Data in Real Time

It becomes more and more difficult to correct data as they age, since people's memories fade rapidly. Consequently, the project must collect data promptly as events occur and it needs to have a knowledgeable person reviewing all data as they are collected. You must be careful about how much of this function is delegated to a clerk. Even if the clerk is well trained, there should never be complete delegation. There will always be important nonroutine aspects of the data whose significance can be appreciated only by persons with a software engineering background. Pursue missing reports and missing data promptly. This will increase the quality of the data indirectly as well as directly. The data takers will know that someone is interested, that their input is being used, and that it is easier to submit data correctly in the first place than to subject themselves to pestering. Question the data actively. Apply the data promptly for your purposes (for example, generate reports), and see if the results appear correct. Involve project personnel in looking at the reports for reasonableness. Identify data collection problems.

There are three problems that commonly occur with failure reports. First, trouble or maintenance reports do not always imply program failures. They may be used to request new features. The user may be dissatisfied with some program characteristic and report it as a failure. They may represent failures, but they are failures in documentation rather than failures of the program. For example, the user manual is not clear on something. Therefore, what someone thinks is a program failure really is not. A second consideration is that the time that is recorded on a trouble report may not be the actual time that a failure really occurred. There have been some instances where the date that is recorded happens to be the date at which the person recording the trouble wrote it down or even perhaps the date at which the trouble report was received by the data collection group. Finally, data takers sometimes record multiple failures that occurred close together as happening at the same time. This can result in multiple zero failure intervals. A failure intensity that was steadily decreasing suddenly exhibits a discontinuous jump to infinity. Multiple zero failure intervals can substantially distort the estimation of model parameters.

If it appears that there is widespread misunderstanding of the meaning of certain items or if serious data collection problems exist, hold an additional meeting with your data takers to clear up these difficulties. Request their participation and the benefit of their experience in resolving these problems. However, we have found it usually not wise to hold general meetings to discuss localized problems. It is better to discuss them only with the people involved. Otherwise, people who are collecting data correctly will resent the implied criticism and the waste of their time.

8.1.4   Results Feedback

It is strongly recommended that you provide feedback of derived results to participants on a regular and timely basis. You should particularly make sure that the promised benefits from the data collection effort are not missing due to poor follow-through. Certainly, you cannot always guarantee that the expected benefits from the data collection effort will materialize. However, do not guarantee that the results will not be useful by neglecting to provide timely reports or any reports at all, providing inaccurate reports, or supplying reports that do not present material well. Scrutinize the reports to be sure that they are well organized, incorporate useful material, and are in a format that is easily grasped. Present material in graphical form (color is nice) whenever appropriate and possible. Ask your data takers and project managers what they think of the reports. If they are using them, how are they using them, and for what purpose? Do they appear valid? Is the format convenient and readable? Modify them if they can be improved to better satisfy the needs of the project. In addition to other benefits, this approach helps maintain the sense of participation and motivation of the data takers.

Interpret the meaning and describe the possible uses of the reports to the managers involved. If they use them and find them helpful, their backing will make the data collection effort easier. Further, you will show them that the resources and money devoted to data collection are paying dividends.

Personally analyze the format of the reports and what they are used for. Your extra experience may suggest improvements and uses not seen by the users. Users often do not see future possibilities in a report, even when they understand present needs. They may not appreciate that the possibility exists for changing their method of operating and doing things they never thought of before.

8.1.5 Record Keeping

Records should be kept in such a fashion that information is not lost when project personnel are transferred. They should be readily interpretable so that the information is available for use on similar projects in the future. One convenient way of recording failure times is to note them on the trouble reports or failure reports that many projects use for all formal testing and that are commonly used in the field during operation. It may be possible to automatically record time at regular intervals during test along with the output quantities one is monitoring for the purpose of locating failures. Then time of failure can be established precisely.

Another approach is to take run-time data in a log. A log can also be used for recording (possibly interactively) any occurrence that might be a failure. An example of a form used to log testing activities and failures is provided in Figure 8.1. The event code differentiates failures from beginning and end of test and changes in program size. The system code permits events to be separated by component or system. One purpose of separation is to permit adjustment of execution times for software components running on machines of different average instruction execution rates. The window is used to bound events whose precise time is uncertain. A time can then be selected randomly within those bounds. The information on instructions and developed instructions is used for failure time adjustment.

Observation of failures may occur at the time of program operation or when analyzing program output afterwards. Therefore, it has proved best to allow 1 or 2 days to elapse after a test run before using the failure interval data. Then false failures can be weeded out and the results thoroughly analyzed to minimize missed failures. Experience indicates that after analysis one is more likely to miss failures than to report false ones. Faults found by a programmer without test (by code reading or other means) during the test period should not be counted as failures. They

FAILURE DATA COLLECTION FORM

(Left justify)															(Left justify)
Event Code	System Code	Date			Event Time or Window Start Time			Window End Time			Instructions	Developed Instructions	Comments
		Mo	Day	Yr	Hr	Min	Sec	Hr	Min	Sec			
1-8	9-16	17-18	19-20	21-22	23-24	25-26	27-28	29-30	31-32	33-34	41-48	49-56	57-80

(Right justify)

Event Code: Presence of number indicates a failure event; B, begin test; E, end test; G, program growth. If event is known only within a window, window start and end times are filled in.

FIGURE 8.1
Sample testing activity and failure log.

are not "failures" by definition. When the development environment is such that test is accompanied by extensive code reading, the value of the fault reduction factor may be affected.

8.2 USE OF CONSULTANTS

We have mentioned the use of consultants in Chapter 3 to assist in implementing software reliability measurement in an organization. Consultants frequently play an important role in technology transfer. This includes both professional external consultants and individuals inside an organization, who by virtue of their technical leadership and initiative have a seminal impact throughout the organization. In order for consulting to be effective, consultant and consultee must each understand both roles. Sometimes one person may take on both roles during a project. For example, you might engage a consultant to advise in applying software reliability measurement to a project. You might then take on the role of consultant yourself in trying to disseminate the consultant's ideas to your project team.

8.2.1 Consultee

Engaging a consultant, of course, involves the expenditure of resources by the consultee. Frequently, compensation and expenses of the consultant are outweighed by the cost of effort expended by other project personnel. A substantial investment of effort by project personnel is usually desirable, so that they can learn from the consultant and apply this knowledge in the future. The potential benefits from effective consulting generally dwarf the resources expended. For all the foregoing reasons, we will concentrate on maximizing the effectiveness rather than minimizing the costs of the consultant. In fact, the cost-cutting strategy usually backfires. A generous attitude toward the consultant will often result in extra efforts and benefits for the project.

The consultee should place great importance on the process of selecting the consultant. The extra cost of a consultant of superior quality is negligible with respect to the likely greater benefits. It is important for you to realize that you are not just "buying" expertise from the consultant but trying to apply expertise effectively in the solution of project problems. Therefore, you must be open and honest in providing the consultant with information. It is desirable to truly incorporate the consultant as a part of your team. Invest some effort in determining the needs and problems of your project and conveying them to the consultant. Provide any technical background information that may be relevant to the problem, and give the consultant some guidance about which information is likely to be most important. If you provide a set of reports and memoranda, a rank ordering of the value of this material is useful.

One area of information that is frequently overlooked, but that is vital, is that of organizational power structure and politics. The consultant may develop good ideas, but it is likely that they will wither on the vine without this knowledge. You need to help the consultant help you by identifying the key people on the project with respect to the particular area being addressed. These may be people with power in either the formal structure (for example, managers) or the informal structure (for example, people generally recognized as technical innovators, initiators, or mentors among their peers).

It usually pays to devote some effort to determining and understanding the motivations of the consultant. It is often possible to relate these motivations to the goals of the project. Then you multiply both the effectiveness of the consultant to the project and the achievement of the consultant's goals. There are many consultants "with a mission" who are more interested in spreading a set of ideas than in their compensation. An organization can profit by helping. Positive feedback, when appropriate, to the consultant, to your management and project, and to potential "customers" of the consultant can be especially productive.

Finally, feedback of all kinds is important. The consultant usually has only a short time to learn the needs of the project and the appropriate background, develop appropriate recommendations, and help implement them. Hence, a high level of interaction is essential. It is particularly important for the consultant to be able to report problems that are interfering with the ability to work. A consultant needs to be told when he or she is on the wrong track. Honesty with tact on both sides will usually be most effective.

8.2.2   Consultant

The role of the consultant is demanding, in that he or she must work rapidly and efficiently to be effective. The first order of business is to define project needs and problems. Next, the consultant must identify information sources and evaluate their relative importance. Third, the consultant develops plans about what should be done.

At this point, it is necessary to gain an understanding of the formal and informal power structures of the organization and the organizational politics. The key people should be identified. It is desirable to concentrate one's efforts on them and to gain an understanding of their attitudes and motivations. The plans of what should be done are considered in the light of the reality of the organization. They should then be modified into a set of objectives that have a realistic chance of success. An approach that has frequently worked has been to search for project objectives that are also likely to satisfy the objectives of the individual key players. The consultant must then seek strategies that will sell them on this synergy. In the case of software reliability measurement where new concepts must be disseminated, the consultant should look for high visibility activities that will make as many project personnel aware of the concepts as possible. He or she should also look for "multiplier" activities that enlist other people in the cause and spawn other activities.

Once a plan of action has been developed, project members must be sold on the plan. Here, the help and ideas of the key people that have been cultivated can be vital. It usually helps if the consultant has developed a thorough understanding of the needs of the project and its environment *and* exhibits this understanding with high visibility. It is desirable to fit new approaches into the existing ones. Use of terminology, concepts, and approaches already familiar to project members and in use on the project is helpful. The consultant should be generous with praise and credit for good aspects of the project and good performance of its members. The praise should be provided directly to the people involved, to their managers, and to people on other projects with whom he or she may come in contact. Positive feedback is important not only as a strategy for getting ideas accepted, but also as a way of making sure that the project team understands which things are being done right and should not be changed. Negative aspects must be dealt with honestly, privately, and with tact, but not avoided. The consultant must maintain project confidentiality when he or she deals with several projects. However, when the consultant has obtained the necessary permission, he or she is in an excellent position to spread good ideas. Ensuring that the idea originators get proper credit will strengthen relationships.

8.3   SUMMARY

In this chapter you have learned how to plan and implement software reliability measurement and prediction for your project. Particular attention was paid to the collection of data and to how to work with a consultant in this field.

THREE

THEORY

This part of the book is designed for anyone who wants a deeper understanding of the theory that supports Parts I and II of the book. Their objectives may be:

1. solution of practical problems that have occurred during application,
2. examination of the applicability of various techniques to certain projects or circumstances,
3. extension of applications into new areas,
4. further research in the field, or
5. simple intellectual curiosity.

Although the level of treatment in this part is somewhat more difficult than that of Parts I and II, special efforts have been made to render it understandable to the software engineer with an elementary knowledge of probability and statistics. It should be possible to follow the general structure, the significant concepts, and the important steps in reasoning even if you do not have all the background to understand the mathematical and statistical details.

Chapter 9 revisits software reliability modeling concepts in much greater depth. It discusses them, both from historical and general viewpoints, and presents a model classification scheme. Chapter 10 is a generalized treatment of Markovian models. Almost all published models are Markovian or can be approximated by such models. Specific models are covered in Chapter 11, with many of the relationships being developed as special cases of those presented in Chapter 10. Chapter 12 covers estimation of parameters for the models. Models are evaluated and compared in Chapter 13, and justification for the recommended models employed in Parts I and II of the book is presented. The topic of calendar time modeling, applicable to execution time models, is discussed in Chapter 14. Chapter 15 is the presentation of the theory upon which failure time adjustment for evolving programs is developed.

SOFTWARE RELIABILITY MODELING

Software failure and software reliability concepts were first addressed in Chapter 1. We further developed the subject of the meaning of "failure" in Chapter 4. Software reliability modeling was discussed in Chapter 2 and model parameter determination in Chapter 5. We will now take a thorough and broad look at these ideas as a basis for understanding software reliability theory. Note that the terms and concepts described in this chapter have evolved over time. Many of the earlier models do not use them and considerable development in the concepts has occurred to resolve various practical problems. We will first carefully examine concepts related to the failure process. Then we will look at some general model characteristics. The third section of this chapter will recount some of the historical development of models. Finally, we will present a model classification scheme that will help organize the further discussion of models in Part III.

9.1 CONCEPTS

Recall that the generally accepted definition of *software reliability* is the probability of failure-free operation of a computer program in a specified environment for a specified time. We will examine several significant terms in this definition in detail to gain greater insight, after taking note of the relationship of reliability to certain other associated quantities. In Chapters 9, 10, 12, and 15 we will generally be conducting our discussions in terms of generic time. In Chapters 11, 13, and 14 we will use both execution time and calendar time as appropriate.

The following relationships apply to reliability generally (hardware or software). Reliability, denoted $R(t)$, is related to failure probability $F(t)$ by

$$R(t) = 1 - F(t) \ . \tag{9.1}$$

The failure probability is the probability that the time of failure is less than or equal to t. If $F(t)$ is differentiable, then the failure density $f(t)$ is the first derivative of $F(t)$ with respect to time t. The hazard rate $z(t)$ is the conditional failure density, given that no failure has occurred in the interval between 0 and t. It is given by

$$z(t) = \frac{f(t)}{R(t)} \ , \tag{9.2}$$

and it is also related to the reliability by

$$R(t) = \exp\left[- \int_0^t z(x)dx \right] \ . \tag{9.3}$$

The mean time to failure (MTTF) Θ is related to the reliability by

$$\Theta = \int_0^\infty R(x)dx \ , \tag{9.4}$$

where the integration is performed with respect to the operating time of the system.

A software reliability model describes software failures as a random process, which is characterized in either times of failures or the number of failures at fixed times. We denote by T_i and T_i' the random variables representing times to the ith failure and between the $(i-1)$th and ith failures, respectively. The realizations of T_i and T_i' will be denoted by t_i and t_i', respectively. Time can be specified in either calendar time, the actual chronological period, or execution time, the processor (CPU) time accumulated. Sometimes clock time is used as an approximation to execution time. Let $M(t)$ be a random process representing the number of failures experienced by time t. The realization of this random process will be denoted $m(t)$. Then $\mu(t)$, the mean value function, is defined as

$$\mu(t) = E[M(t)] \ , \tag{9.5}$$

which represents the expected number of failures at time t. The function $\mu(t)$ will be nondecreasing and is assumed to be a continuous and differentiable function of time t. The failure intensity function of the $M(t)$ process is the instantaneous rate of change of the expected number of failures with respect to time. It is defined by

$$\lambda(t) = \frac{d\mu(t)}{dt} \ . \tag{9.6}$$

The question of time was previously addressed in Chapters 2 and 6. It was pointed out that execution time was fundamental in regard to the failure-inducing stress placed on software. You might argue that "instructions executed" is even more fundamental. Hence you might speak of failure intensity in terms of failures per trillion (10^{12}) instructions executed. Note that a machine executing 1 million instructions/sec executes this number in less than 2 weeks. The "more fundamental" contention is probably valid. It takes account of the fact that software can execute on machines of different instruction execution rates. No compensation is necessary for different machines. However, there are serious problems with the foregoing approach. Most engineers have a better physical grasp of time. But more important, hardware reliability is defined in terms of time. It is essential that we be able to combine hardware and software reliabilities to get system reliability. Consequently, we use execution time and make adjustments where necessary.

Other approaches that have sometimes been advocated are based on measuring reliability in terms of the proportion of *runs* or of *input states* that execute without failure. The problem with these approaches is that many systems have runs of widely varying lengths, so the proportion may give an inaccurate reliability picture. Further, the latter approach is poorly associated with the user's viewpoint. It does not take into account the substantially different frequencies with which different input states may be selected. Finally, note that both of the foregoing approaches result in measures that are incompatible with the time-based measures used for hardware. Thus, we would lose the important capability of determining system reliability.

9.1.1 Program

We will first examine exactly what we mean by the term "program." A *program* will be defined as a set of complete machine instructions (operations with operands specified) that executes within a single computer and accomplishes a specific function. More than one program can execute "simultaneously" on a single computer if the machine is multiprogrammed. A program is generally assumed to be stable (not changing in size or content with time) for the purpose of software reliability modeling. However, techniques have been developed to compensate for change (Chapter 15).

A program may be designed (especially if written in assembly language) for a particular computer. Hence a version for another computer is really a separate program insofar as reliability attributes are concerned. Conversely, you can design a program to be machine-independent or highly portable. Then the reliability attributes are independent of the computer used, except for adjustment for instruction execution rate.

A program can consist of one or more logical instruction streams. A logical instruction stream is a set of instructions that must be executed in a prescribed sequence. When there is more than one logical instruction stream, the program is said to be *multitasked*. The computer on which the program is running may be a multiprocessor, in which case there are multiple physical instruction streams executing simultaneously. The computer can be a vector or array processor, in which case there are multiple data streams. Each instruction accesses one or more data elements. A sequence of related data elements may be viewed as a data stream. A matrix manipulation program running in an array processor would have multiple data streams. Note that distributed systems or networks are considered to have separate programs executing in each of their computers.

The concept of what is included within a computer is somewhat arbitrary in these days of distributed systems and networks. It may even differ from application to application, but the objective is to draw the boundaries in such a way that:

1. The hardware included may be treated as a unit for analyzing overall system reliability.
2. The time associated with the execution of the program or programs, the values of time at which failures occur, and the processing speed of the computer are readily measured.

9.1.2 Environment and Runs

We can view the execution of a program as a single entity, lasting for months or even years for real-time systems. However, as we noted in Chapter 2, it is easier to characterize the environment if the execution is divided into a set of *runs*. Runs that are identical repetitions of each other are said to form a *run type*. Then the *environment* is specified by the *operational profile*. This is the set of relative frequencies of occurrence of the run types, usually expressed as fractions of the total set of runs (in which case, we have probabilities). Note that the software reliability model proper is not dependent on the "run type" concept, only on the description of the environment in which the software executes. During operation, the factors that cause a particular run to occur are very numerous and complex. Hence we can view the run types required of the program by the environment as being selected randomly in accordance with the probabilities just mentioned. Note that "*randomly*" *does not* imply "with equal probability."

A run type should ordinarily be associated with the accomplishment of a user function. Variations in the environment can usually be characterized by variations in the relative probabilities of demand for different user functions. Examples of such user functions or run types would be a particular banking transaction, missile flight trajectory, operating system command, or a cyclic operation in process control. Sometimes we refer to user functions as "features."

A run type is specified by its *input state* or set of values for its input variables that it receives. Recurrent runs have the same input state. We judge the reliability of a program by the output states (sets of values of output variables created) of its runs. Note that a run type represents a transformation between an input state and an output state. Multiple input states may map to the same output state, but a given input state can have only one output state. The input state uniquely determines the particular instructions that will be executed and the values of their operands. Thus it establishes the *path* of control taken through the program. Whether a particular fault will cause a failure for a specific run type is predictable in theory. However, the analysis required to determine this might be impractical to pursue.

The input state is of more than just theoretical interest. It is important to understand exactly what the input variables to a run are and to record them for diagnostic purposes. Many failures that are difficult to diagnose result from "hidden" input variables. These may be data items in a data base that were corrupted by a previous run. The program may not function properly for the particular values.

An *input variable* for a program run is any data item that exists external to the run and is *used* by the run. There doesn't have to be a physical input process. The input variable may simply be located in memory, waiting to be accessed. Correspondingly, an *output variable* for a program run is any data item that exists external to the run and is *set* by the run. It is not necessary that the output variable actually be used, printed out, or physically moved. An output variable can be a control signal, command, printout, display, or item of transmitted data, among other possibilities. An input variable cannot also be an output variable but the two can occupy the same memory location at different times. A data item consists of an associated set of one or more data elements. A data element is a scalar such as a numerical quantity, logical variable, character string, or even abstract data type. "Association" is determined by the functional use of the data elements. Multiple data elements that relate to a single external condition would be considered associated. An example would be the elements of a vector that locates an aircraft in an air traffic control system. A data item may be a scalar, array, or structure. The "value" of a data item is the set of values of its elements.

A data element can have only one value with respect to a run. Therefore, each use or setting of a quantity that is varying must be considered as a separate data element. Suppose the time relative to the start of the run at which a quantity is used or set can change and is therefore significant. Then the data item that describes the quantity should include the time as an element. Consequently, each activation of an interrupt of a given type is a separate data item. Since the number of interrupts occurring during a run can vary, different input states may have different numbers of input variables and hence dimensions. Note that a data element is not a physical or symbolic memory location. The same physical or symbolic location can be associated with multiple data elements by "time sharing" them through dynamic storage allocation.

Externally initiated interrupts such as interrupts generated by the system clock, by operator actions, and by other components of the system outside the program are considered as input variables. Intermediate data items computed by the program during a run and not existing external to the program are considered neither input nor output variables. Hence, interrupts generated directly by a run or interrupts that are determined from other input variables (for example, overflow and underflow) are not input variables.

All runs will terminate sooner or later as a consequence of the input state selected. "Termination" may mean that the program completes a task and searches a task queue for a new one. Some terminations may be premature in the sense that no useful function is completed. If a run is terminated early by operator action, the termination action represents an interrupt that signifies a different input state from a run with a normal termination.

The *input space* for a program is the set of input states that can occur during the operation of the program. An input space is discrete (it is assumed that interrupt times can be stated only to some quantization level). Thus we can identify a given input state by an index number. The number of dimensions of the input space is equal to the sum of the dimensions of the input variables. The input space may change if the program changes.

The *environment* or *operational profile* of a program is established by enumerating the possible input states and their probabilities of occurrence. It can change with time. This change generally either actually occurs or is recognized to occur in definite steps (that is, piecewise) rather than continuously. Hence it is best and simplest to assume that the environment is homogeneous or time invariant until it changes, when a different homogeneous environment occurs.

If the run types are independent, it is relatively easy to determine their probabilities of occurrence. However, a run may be dependent on a previous run. For example, this may be true of a control system for which we define a run as one cyclic operation. In this case, one may ignore the dependencies and use the probabilities of occurrence of each run computed over a long period of time. This procedure is acceptable because one can set input states by manual intervention. A particular run in a dependent sequence can be made in test without actually executing the run that normally precedes it during operation.

The validity of the foregoing approach may be explained in statistical terms. You can view the sequence of input states of successive runs as a Markov chain, with the relationships between the states being expressed in terms of transition probabilities. A transition probability is the conditional probability that a system in a given state will transfer to some specified state. We will assume a homogeneous environment as noted previously. Then the transition probabilities will be stationary. It is reasonable to assume that every input state is reachable from every other input state.[1] Consequently, the probabilities of the various states of the Markov chain occurring will approach a steady state, given enough time. The steady-state probabilities may thus be used to characterize the environment.

There is an alternative approach to the operational profile for characterizing the environment [Cheung (1980)]. You may specify the sequence of program modules executed instead of the input state to characterize a run. There is a many-to-one mapping between input states and module sequences. The analog of the operational profile is the set of all possible module sequences and their associated probabilities of occurrence. Instead of these probabilities, however, it is more convenient to use the transition probabilities between modules. If the transition probabilities are dependent only on the two modules involved and are homogeneous, in time the system will reach a steady state. Each module will have a probability

---

[1] In some applications there will be sequences of input states that are limited in length. Nevertheless, they will be connected by the action of the tester in selecting the start of a sequence of input states. The selection probabilities become the transition probabilities of the connecting links.

of being executed. We can obtain the overall program reliability from the reliabilities of the modules and the transition probabilities. The foregoing approach emphasizes the structural characteristics of the program. Sensitivity coefficients are developed to indicate which modules are most critical in affecting system reliability. Identification of critical modules could be useful in suggesting the most efficient testing and evolution strategies. In the former case, one would test to cover modules in descending order of criticality. In the latter, one would try to avoid changes in critical modules when adding new features.

In reality, the foregoing approach is much less practical than the operational profile approach. Probabilities of occurrence of input states are the natural and original information related to program usage. Transition probabilities between modules would have to be determined from the input state probabilities through program instrumentation and extensive execution. The latter would be essentially equivalent to doing input-state-based testing. Estimation of component reliabilities would usually be difficult because the failure samples associated with modules would be small. Hence the module sequence approach is mainly of conceptual value.

TESTING COMPRESSION FACTOR. During test, you usually do not repeat input states. To predict the failure intensity that will occur during operation, we must adjust failure intensity figures for the different operational profiles that will exist in test and in operation. As mentioned in Chapter 6, this compensation is handled by dividing the failure intensity experienced in test by the testing compression factor C. This quantity is the ratio of execution time required in the operational phase to execution time required in the test phase to cover the input space of the program.

Let τ_k be the execution time for the run corresponding to input state k. Assume that this input state occurs with probability p_k during operation. Let Q_I be the total number of input states. The quantity $p_{\min}$ is the probability of the input state that occurs most rarely. Note that if the input space is to be covered during the operational phase, the rarest input state must be executed at least once. Then the expected frequency of execution of input state k is $p_k/p_{\min}$. The expected total time of execution to cover the input space is $\sum_{k=1}^{Q_I}(p_k/p_{\min})\tau_k$. Since only one execution of each input state is required in test, the time of execution to cover the input space in that phase is $\sum_{k=1}^{Q_I}\tau_k$. Thus we have

$$C = \frac{\displaystyle\sum_{k=1}^{Q_I} p_k\tau_k}{p_{\min}\displaystyle\sum_{k=1}^{Q_I}\tau_k}. \tag{9.7}$$

The foregoing expression simplifies, if all runs are of equal length, to

$$C = \frac{1}{Q_I p_{\min}}. \tag{9.8}$$

Let us assume that the probability p_k has the form

$$p_k = ak^b .$$
(9.9)

Note that $b \leq 0$, since typically we rank order the input states, without loss of generality. We have selected a very general function that should be capable of representing a wide range of operational profiles satisfactorily. Since $\sum_{k=1}^{Q_I} p_k = 1$, we have

$$a = \frac{1}{\sum_{k=1}^{Q_I} k^b} .$$
(9.10)

Input state Q_I will occur with probability p_{min}. If we evaluate Equation (9.9) for $k = Q_I$ and substitute Equation (9.10) we obtain

$$p_{min} = \frac{Q_I^b}{\sum_{k=1}^{Q_I} k^b} .$$
(9.11)

Substituting Equation (9.11) in Equation (9.8) we obtain

$$C = \frac{\sum_{k=1}^{Q_I} k^b}{Q_I^{b+1}} .$$
(9.12)

One possibility is that the probability of selection is inversely proportional to rank order. Then $b = -1$ and

$$C = \sum_{k=1}^{Q_I} \frac{1}{k} .$$
(9.13)

The sum can be written in terms of the psi or digamma function [Davis (1962)]. Hence we have

$$C = \psi(Q_I + 1) - \psi(1) ,$$
(9.14)

where ψ is the psi function and $\psi(1) = -0.57722$. The psi function is defined as

$$\psi(x) = \frac{1}{\Gamma(x)} \frac{d\,\Gamma(x)}{dx} ,$$
(9.15)

where $\Gamma(x)$ is the gamma function. The value of C changes very slowly with the number of input states Q_I, as shown in Figure 6.7. Hence in practice C will probably be found in a relatively narrow range.

9.1.3   Failure

The reader may find reference to Figure 9.1 helpful as we explain the important concepts relating to failures and faults. The set of bars at the left represents the run types (U, V, W, X) for a program. The length of the bar represents the execution time for that run type. As execution proceeds, the same run types can be re-selected, yielding different runs.

A *failure* is a departure of the external results of program operation from program requirements on a run. Thus, it represents a defect in a transformation. A "departure" is the occurrence of a discrepancy between the desired output state specified by the requirements for the particular run and the actual output state. The *output state* is the set of values of output variables the run generates.

A *discrepancy* may be more precisely defined as a difference between the actual value of an output variable, resulting from a run, and the value prescribed by the requirements. However, differences that have propagated from a previous difference during the run are not considered as additional discrepancies. Thus, we do not consider data corruption to cause additional failures within the same run. It can operate to cause failures for other runs. Note that the requirements frequently do not specify the values of all output variables since some may not be significant. You can see that multiple failures for a given run imply multiple discrepancies. The time of a failure is the time at which the discrepancy first occurs. Discrepancies are noted in Figure 9.1 as circled numbers.

We will define the *type* of a failure as the conjunction of both run type or input state and discrepancy. Failure types have been labeled U_A, V_A, W_A, W_B, X_A,

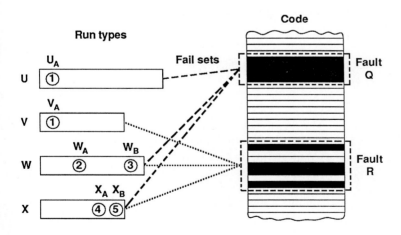

① Discrepancy 1

U_A Failure type

FIGURE 9.1
Failure and fault concepts.

and X_B in Figure 9.1. Thus, two failures have the same type if they occur for the same run type and are characterized by the same discrepancy. Otherwise, they have different types. If run type U is executed twice, there will be two failures, but they will have the same failure type U_A. But the failures occurring for run types U and V are of different failure types, U_A and V_A, even though they are associated with the same discrepancy, 1. It will be seen that repeated failures of the same type will occur when the same run type recurs, if effective repair action is not taken. In Chapter 4 we discussed when one should and should not count repeated failures. This issue arises only when the failures have the same *type*. Failures can have the same *discrepancy* and appear to be the same. However, unless they have the same *type*, they are not.

More than one failure can occur for a particular run type, but each will be associated with a different discrepancy and hence have a different type. Note that run type W has failure types W_A and W_B, arising from discrepancies 2 and 3. Obviously, failures occurring for different run types will have different failure types.

9.1.4   Fault

Software reliability depends heavily on the defects in a software product and the repair activity undertaken to correct them. Consequently, we want an entity to characterize these defects. Generally we have used the fault to do this. The program is executed and faults are counted by observing the repair actions taken in response to failures. However, there are several complex issues related to the definition and practical use of the concept of the "fault." These complexities have not generally been discussed or appreciated. The result is that the concept of a fault is less precise and more variable than that of a failure.

DEFINITION. In considering possible approaches to defining the term "fault," it is instructive to view two widely differing concepts—the absolute and the operational. The absolute concept views the fault as an independent entity that can be defined without reference to failures. The operational concept views the fault as an entity that exists only with reference to actual or potential failures. "Potential" refers to the fact that the failure will occur for an input state if that state is executed. In the operational view, we would define the fault as the defect that is the cause for a particular failure type. A fault and a failure type would relate one-to-one. Both of these concepts represent polarizations that do not fully represent the intuitive notions of practitioners and that are not fully useful in some sense.

The absolute concept makes it necessary to postulate a "perfect" program to which an actual program can be compared. Then the fault is a defective, missing, or extra instruction or set of instructions. It may be an instruction (set) in the perfect program that is not matched in the proper sequence in the actual program. Alternatively, it may be an extra instruction (set) in the actual program.

Unfortunately, there are many possible "perfect" programs or programs that could meet the program requirements. In theory, you might select the perfect program that the designer was intending to produce and compare the actual program to that. However, this is not possible in practice because this program is not completely defined and known until it has been achieved through repair activity. If the perfect program were known from the start, we would use it and have zero faults.

The operational concept conflicts with the sense of software engineering practitioners that a fault has *some* reality on its own. It is an implementation defect and the implementation has physical reality. Furthermore, a number of failure types (not just one) may stem from the same implementation defect.

We will take a middle road in defining faults. It will be assumed that there is a perfect program that the designer is intending to produce. The full definition of this program comes about only after its imperfections have been discovered and corrected. Thus faults have an independent reality, but it is one that is not fully known until the program has been thoroughly inspected and executed. The discovery of faults usually occurs through observation of potential failures by code inspection (and imagined execution) or actual failures by execution (and output state inspection). In some cases, faults may be observed directly by code inspection and related activities.

We will thus define a *fault* as a defective, missing, or extra instruction or set of related instructions that is the cause of one or more actual or potential failure types. Note that *by definition* there cannot be multiple faults causing a failure. The entire set of defective instructions that is causing the failure is considered to be the fault. The requirement that the instructions be "related" is specified so that the count of the number of faults cannot be arbitrarily changed by a regrouping of instructions. The right side of Figure 9.1 illustrates a section of code with faults Q and R. The instructions comprising the faults are shaded. Note that for fault R, not all instructions are adjacent. The faults are designated by the dashed boxes. The set of input states that produces failures for a fault at any point in time will be called its *fail set*. The fail set for each fault is designated by the dashed or dotted lines connecting each fault with run types. Fault Q causes failure types U_A, W_B, and X_A. Hence its fail set is U, W, and X. Fault R causes failure types V_A, W_A, and X_B. Its fail set is V, W, and X.

How does one determine exactly which instructions should be included in a fault? Some judgment is involved. At first glance, when a failure occurs, you would include in the fault all the instructions that must be modified, added, or removed to prevent the failure from recurring. However, if repairing a few *related* instructions would also prevent additional failures from occurring, then these instructions should also be included in the fault. Consider the following simple example. Suppose a segment of code must generate values of G corresponding to values of I as shown in Table 9.1. Assume that the code has been erroneously written as shown in Figure 9.2. If the program is run with I = 320, it will fail by giving an output of 1000. The output should be 100. The obvious definition of the extent of the fault would be line 10. However, it doesn't take much looking to see that there are several related lines, another of which, line 30, is also defective. It makes sense to define the fault as encompassing lines 10 and 30. Note that the extent defined for a fault depends somewhat on your perspective. It is likely that

TABLE 9.1
Program specification

I	G
>360	1000
60–360	100
<60	0

faults found in unit test or unit inspection will be confined to that unit. However, faults discovered in design review or subsystem test may extend past module boundaries.

Repair activity involves changing (hopefully reducing!) the size of the fail set. A fault is considered removed or completely repaired when the fail set is null. A partial repair has occurred when the size of the fail set changes but does not reach zero. For example, consider a situation where the branching of control of a program depends on the testing of a variable against a value that has been incorrectly established. We might reset the value so that the failure just observed doesn't recur, but the value may still be incorrect. In Figure 9.1, this might be illustrated by the removal of run type X from the fail set of fault Q. The sum of the probabilities associated with the input states in a fail set for a fault represents the probability of occurrence of a failure caused by that fault. If it is large, then that fault will be more likely to be uncovered [Ramamoorthy and Bastani (1982)].

Note that it was necessary to define failure type in terms of discrepancy *and* run type. If it had been defined solely in terms of discrepancy, we could not have defined fault to incorporate the possibility that different faults can cause, for different run types, the same discrepancy. In Figure 9.1, note that faults Q and R both caused discrepancy 1, but the discrepancy occurred on different run types, U and V. The same discrepancy can result when the same desired and actual output states exist for different run types.

As noted, there are two fault detection processes that occur during the development and evolution of software: direct and indirect. We can detect faults directly as a result of procedures that do not involve actual execution of the program. The approaches that fall in this category are:

1. requirements reviews,
2. design reviews,

Line Number	Code
10	IF I > 300
20	THEN G = 1000
30	ELSE IF I ≥ 0
40	THEN G = 100
50	ELSE G = 0

FIGURE 9.2
Program that illustrates extent of fault.

3. code reviews, and

4. use of compiler diagnostics.

Repair of faults found through direct detection prevents the occurrence of potential failures.

We detect faults indirectly through detection of failures. Failures are detected by executing the program, either in test or regular operation. The symptoms of the failure suggest the areas of code to be searched for the fault that is causing it.

Inherent faults are the faults that are associated with a software product as originally written or modified. Faults that are introduced through fault correction (spawned faults) or design changes are not included.

COUNTING. Often, attempts have been made to count faults by counting each occasion on which a program module was changed. This is an approximation that is probably proportional to the number of faults if all changes that reflect requirements or design changes are excluded. The difference between the two counts would be due to changes that repair multiple faults, changes that constitute only partial repair to faults, and faults that span multiple modules. In other cases, the number of faults has been assumed to be equal to the number of failures. The latter is a highly inaccurate assumption, although the number of faults is probably proportional to the number of failure types.

It has not been generally noted that the number of changes does not yield a stable approximation of the number of faults until the execution time becomes very large. The proportions of changes that repair multiple faults and faults that span multiple modules do not appear to change with time. However, when partial repairs occur, the number of changes per fault increases with time. It approaches a stable value after most repairs have been completed. Often the full nature of a fault and the extent of its fail set are not known until failures of several different types have been experienced. This can require a large amount of execution time.

You might attempt to assign fractional values to faults repaired as testing or use proceeds, based on the degree to which the fail set is reduced. However, this is not practical because the size of the fail set is not known until the program has been extensively executed. Thus it will be seen that it is not feasible to keep a current count of faults repaired or to approximate this quantity by counting changes. However, total faults repaired or total changes made over a long period of time can be counted. The extensive history available at this point makes it likely that we can identify partial repairs of the same fault. Thus we can determine the correct total number of faults. Hence, if spawned faults are identified, it is possible to determine the number of inherent faults associated with a program. It is given by the net (total minus spawned) number of faults repaired as time approaches infinity. Then we can relate the number of inherent faults to characteristics of the program and the process of its development. Similarly, if total changes are counted, one is reasonably certain that this quantity is proportional to the total number of faults repaired.

You will note that it *is* feasible to keep a running count of failures experienced. A failure is a clearly defined event. Consequently, we need to determine if number of failures experienced is sufficiently related to repair activity that it may be used to characterize it. When repair is occurring, each failure experienced will "on the average" stimulate effort that will result in a change in the fail set of its associated fault. The fail sets of related faults may change as well. Usually, the change will be a reduction. However, it could represent the aggravation of a fault or the spawning of a new fault (in the latter case, a fail set is created). The fail sets of other faults can be reduced when the designer recognizes a pattern or relationship among the faults. For example, if the fault involves incorrect limits on a loop, the designer may check other loops and find similar faults. There may be a partial reduction of the fail set, as has been discussed before. Frequently, there may be no change in the fail set for a particular failure. For example, the information recorded about the failure may be inadequate to determine anything about the fault. It is even possible for fail sets to be reduced when no failure (and perhaps even no execution of the program) has occurred. Repair may be undertaken solely as the result of program inspection.

Taking a macroscopic view over a number of failures, the total of the changes in the fail sets for all faults will be a function of the number of failures experienced. Consider the failure intensity. Let p_k represent the execution probability of input state k and τ_k the associated run time. Denote the fail set of fault a as Y_a. Now the failure intensity λ of the program is given by

$$\lambda = \frac{\sum\limits_{a} \sum\limits_{k \epsilon Y_a} p_k}{\sum\limits_{k} p_k \tau_k}, \tag{9.16}$$

where ϵ means "is a member of." Note that the same input state may appear in different fail sets if it is associated with multiple failures. The amount of change in the expected failure intensity will be related to the total of the changes in the fail sets and thus also to the number of failures experienced. Since the effect of repair activity is measured by changes in the expected failure intensity, it is clear that we may characterize repair activity in terms of failures experienced.

It was noted before that a good count or approximation of inherent faults can be obtained when the program has been executed for a very long time. It is desirable to determine how inherent faults vary with program size and other characteristics and variables that characterize the development process over a range of systems. Note that faults represent a natural entity in which to describe the results of the human error process in program creation. We can estimate inherent faults during the program development phases before test, based on program and development environment characteristics. The procedure is described in Chapter 5.

9.1.5   Error

We have been talking about fault detection and correction. We should also give attention to fault *avoidance*. This is best approached by looking at the errors that produce faults. Errors can arise from many causes, but most of them can be grouped in one of four categories:

1. communication,
2. knowledge,
3. incomplete analysis, or
4. transcription.

Communication errors probably form the largest group, and the proportion can be expected to increase with the size of the project. They are generally of one of three types:

1. interrole: between customer and designer, designer and coder, designer and tester;
2. intrarole: among designers, coders, testers; or
3. temporal: between different times for the same person.

The principal factors in improving communication are comprehensive, continually updated documentation, accuracy, and clarity. Clarity is principally a matter of matching information organization to human information processing capabilities. Because of the limitations of human short-term memory, you must limit the number of objects and relationships between objects that must be considered simultaneously. Thus the virtues of hierarchical organization, structured design, modularity and locality, abstraction (exclusion of anything irrelevant), and clustering. Clustering of objects or primitive relationships into objects or relationships with greater information richness increases the level of abstraction and efficiency of information communication. An example of clustering is the use of abstract data types. Note that it is also important for clarity to use, as much as possible, objects and relationships whose meanings are standardized and well known.

Defective knowledge results in another category of errors. These errors are particularly prevalent when project personnel are inexperienced. They include errors arising from defective knowledge of the application area, the design methodology, and the programming language.

Errors can result from incomplete analysis. These errors are often exhibited in a lack of recognition of all the possible conditions that can occur at a given point in the program. Finally, one has the transcription errors that occur between mind and paper or machine.

9.2 GENERAL MODEL CHARACTERISTICS

A *software reliability model*, as previously noted, usually has the form of a random process that describes the behavior of failures with time. Specification of the model generally includes specification of a function of time such as the mean value function (expected number of failures) or failure intensity. The parameters of the function are dependent on repair activity and program change[2] and properties of the software product and the development process. Properties of the product include size, complexity, and structure. Properties of the development process include, among others, software engineering technologies and tools used and level of experience of personnel. The "time" involved in the characterization of the models is a cumulative time. The origin may be arbitrarily set. It is frequently the start of system test.

Software reliability models almost always assume that failures are independent of each other. They may do this through assuming that failure times are independent of each other or by making the Poisson process assumption of independent increments. This condition would appear to be met for most situations. Failures are the result of two processes: the introduction of faults and their activation through selection of the input states. Since both of these processes are random, the chance of influence on one failure by another is small. Influence would require two conditions. One fault would have to affect the introduction of another during development. Further, an input state that results in failure for the first fault would have to cause the selection of an input state that results in failure for the second fault. The independence conclusion is supported by a study of correlograms of failure data from 15 projects [Musa (1979d)]. No significant correlation was found.

The reason that independence is sometimes disputed is that the "two process" situation is not recognized. For example, it may be argued that programmers tend to have patterns of errors (that is, one error may influence the next one). The possibility that this might create related faults does not by itself imply the existence of related failures. Similarly, it is sometimes stated that one failure can prevent another failure from occurring because the failure prevents access to or "hides" certain code. Prevention of access to code may occur occasionally in unit test but it is much less common in practice in system test or in the operational phase. In any case, it will be a much rarer situation in which the introduction of the fault causing the first failure causes a second fault to be introduced into the "hidden" code.

It is possible to develop both macromodels and micromodels of software reliability. We have concentrated on macromodels. They generally have the greatest usefulness per unit effort required to apply them. They deal with the major factors and effects that are the principal concerns of software engineers and managers. Data collection for such models is usually easy. Micromodels may be more accurate in certain circumstances, since they may deal with particular factors that are important in those circumstances. However, they usually attain the accuracy through added complexity and a limited sphere of applicability. They may some-

---

[2]Program change is often handled separately by applying models in a piecewise fashion or by adjusting failure times to what they would have been if the entire program had been there. The adjustment is based in part on the inherent faults introduced by program change.

times have the potential of providing theoretical insight into underlying processes. For example, Shooman (1983) presents a path decomposition model that is related to program structure. Unfortunately, the theory is usually very difficult to verify because of the complex data collection and analysis involved.

One example of microbehavior that has been observed in certain circumstances is clustering of failures [Crow and Singpurwalla (1984)]. The most likely cause of clustering is localization of input state selection to an area of the input space associated with a high fault density. Localization typically occurs when successive input states are related to one another. This frequently happens in cyclic systems like feedback control systems. An example would be an aircraft control system. A common reason for entering a region of input space associated with high fault density is the effect of data corruption. Data corruption can drive you into an area of input space for which the system was not designed. Thus clustering might occur for a cyclic system in which the data had been corrupted beyond the point at which the system could handle them properly.

Most published models use calendar time or do not specify the type of time. The basic and logarithmic Poisson execution time models employ execution time. Execution time has been shown to be superior [Musa and Okumoto (1984a) and Hecht (1981)]. These models have calendar time components associated with them (Chapter 14). The components convert execution time into calendar time, yielding a time scale that is generally more meaningful to managers and engineers. Other models can sometimes be transformed into execution time models, and appropriate calendar time components developed (Chapter 14).

9.2.1 Random Process

Both the human error process that introduces defects into code and the run selection process that determines which code is being executed at any time are dependent on an enormous number of time-varying variables. The use of a random process model is appropriate for such a situation. There are two equivalent ways of describing the failure random process: the times of failures or the number of failures in a given period.

It is possible that the selection of runs could be planned or manipulated during test. The tester has at least partial control of the environment, and this could make random selection of input states a poor model. However, a random process is still a reasonable model of failure behavior. The introduction of faults into code and the relationship between input state and code executed are usually both sufficiently complex processes to make deterministic prediction of failure impractical. In other words, you can not predict which input states are more likely to yield failures. Consequently, a deterministic selection of input states will not have a deterministic effect on reliability. Of course, if the relative frequencies of selection have changed, then the operational profile has changed and that will affect the reliability.

There is one case in which manipulation of the characteristics of the random process can occur. It requires that:

1. The relationship of program segments executed with respect to input states is disjoint.
2. There are clear differences in fault density between different program segments.

"Disjoint" means that each input state maps to a different set of program segments executed and there are no program segments executed in common by different input states. The clear differences may occur when some segments may be tested code from previous programs and some may be newly written. In this situation, it is possible to manipulate reliability figures to somewhat higher or lower figures by biasing the selection of input states. You select input states that exercise code that has either high or low fault density. Note that the essential character of failures as a random process is unchanged. You can not predict when the next failure will occur, even if you can manipulate average behavior. One example of manipulation would be to select input states deterministically in such a way that no code segments are reexecuted. If fault density is the same for all segments, the observed failure intensity would tend to be constant. Fault repair would show no effect on failure intensity. In reality, failure intensity based on random selection of input states would be decreasing.

9.2.2   With and Without Repair

Software reliability models must cover two situations, the situation of programs that are being repaired when failures occur and the situation of programs that are not. These situations can occur in either the test or the operational phase, but "no repair" is usually associated with the latter. The situation of "no repair" is simple and will be covered in this section. The situation of "with repair" is the subject of most of this book. When we say "no repair" we really mean "deferred repair." Failures are noted but repairs of the underlying faults are not incorporated into the program until the next release.

Thus, as far as the program is concerned, the failure intensity is constant for the duration of the release. Hence, the failure process is conveniently modeled by a homogeneous Poisson process. This implies that the failure intervals are exponentially distributed and that the number of failures in a given time period follows a Poisson distribution. If the failure intensity is λ and the period of execution of the program is τ, then the number of failures during this period is distributed Poisson with parameter $\lambda\tau$.

As mentioned previously, a principal factor that causes reliability to vary with time is the correction of faults that have caused failures. In general, the time of correction does not coincide with the time of original failure. This could lead to substantial complication in characterizing the failure process. However, it can be handled by assuming instantaneous repair and not counting the reoccurrence of the same failure. It would be recounted, however, if the recurrence were due to inability to locate and repair the fault. Although the result is not precisely equivalent, it is a very good approximation. All the leading models take this approach.

9.2.3 Particularization

The model specifies the general form of the dependence of the failure process on the variables mentioned. The specific form can be determined from the general form, at least in theory, through determination of parameters. For the execution time component, this can occur in one of two ways [Hecht (1977)]:

1. Prediction—properties of the software product and the development process are used to particularize the model by determination of its parameters (this can be done prior to any execution of the program).
2. Estimation—inference (for example, parameter estimation) procedures are applied to failure data.

A model and an inference procedure are commonly associated. Together, they provide projection through time. Without a model, you could not make inferences about reliability outside the time period for which failure data have been taken. In fact, you could not make inferences at all, because the size of the failure sample would be one. The model provides the structure that relates behavior at different points in time. It thus, in effect, provides for a sample of reasonable size to be taken.

Note that the inference procedure that has historically been associated with a model is not necessarily the "best." You may wish to consider alternatives. Inference also generally includes the determination of the range of uncertainty. We either establish confidence intervals for the parameters or determine posterior probability distributions for significant quantities in the case of Bayesian inference. The determination of ranges of uncertainty is generally extended to quantities that are derived from the models as well.

Failure data are most commonly available in the form of times of failures or number of failures in a given time interval. The time of failure form is the most precise and contains the most information, although sometimes the difference may be small (see Case Study 5.1). Time can be specified in either calendar time, the actual chronological period that has passed, or execution time, the processor (CPU) time accumulated. Note that for a multiprocessor, execution time may be larger than calendar time for a given interval that has passed.

9.2.4 Other Information

We have seen that in addition to the basic description of the failure process, the term "software reliability model" usually also connotes an inference procedure. For execution time models, it also includes a calendar time component. To this we must add the derivation of associated useful quantities. For example, we can compute execution time required to reach a failure intensity objective. There is also the lore developed as the result of experience in applying the model to the wide variety of situations that can occur in actual practice.

9.3 HISTORICAL DEVELOPMENT OF MODELS

This section presents the historical development of software reliability models. Our purpose is to indicate to researchers which concepts have been tried, which have been more successful and which less, and which have been modified and adapted. This historical information should help the researcher looking at a new problem in the field evaluate proposed solutions for their degree of promise.

There are a number of major themes in the historical development:

1. the creation of various models relating reliability to time, failures experienced, and other variables,
2. the discovery that measurement with respect to execution time simplifies models substantially,
3. the clarification of the distinction between "fault" and "failure" and the development of a rich conceptual base that amplified our understanding of just what we mean by "software reliability,"
4. a concern with how to estimate model parameters,
5. an interest in comparison of models, which led to the development of comparison criteria,
6. the classification of models,
7. an increasing concern with collecting better data,
8. the development of a "lore" of techniques in using and adapting models for the particular circumstances of various applications, and
9. the transition from use of mean time to failure in characterizing status to failure intensity.

This section will concentrate mainly on the first theme, but it will touch on the others. We will group related developments, which will result in departures from strict chronology. For an interesting perspective by one of the pioneers, see Shooman (1984).

The first study of software reliability appears to have been conducted by Hudson (1967). He viewed software development as a birth and death process (a type of Markov process). Fault generation (through design changes, faults created in fixing other faults, etc.) was a birth, and fault correction was a death. The number of faults existing at any time defined the state of the process. The transition probabilities related to the birth and death functions. He generally confined his work to pure death processes, for reasons of mathematical tractability. He assumed that the rate of detection of faults was proportional to the number of faults remaining and a positive power of the time. In other words, the rate of fault detection was assumed to increase with time. It was shown that the number of faults detected follows a binomial distribution whose mean value as a function of time has the form of a Weibull function. Data from the system test phase of one program were presented. Reasonable agreement between model and data is obtained if the system test phase is split into three overlapping subphases and separate fits made for each.

The next major steps were made by Jelinski and Moranda (1972) and Shooman (1972). Both assumed a hazard rate for failures that was piecewise constant and proportional to the number of faults remaining. The hazard rate changes at each fault correction by a constant amount, but is constant between corrections. Jelinski and Moranda applied maximum likelihood estimation to determine the total number of faults in the software and the constant of proportionality between number of faults remaining and hazard rate. Shooman postulated that the hazard rate was proportional to the fault density per instruction, the number of unique instructions executed per unit time, and a bulk constant. The bulk constant represented the proportion of faults that cause failures. The fault density is the difference between the inherent or original fault density and the faults corrected per instruction. The profile of the latter quantity as a function of time was assumed to be related to the project personnel profile in time. Several different fault correction profiles were proposed. The choice would depend on the particular project one was working with. The fault density and instruction execution rate concepts contributed to the development of Equation (5.2). Shooman and Natarajan (1976) have also proposed more complex models of the fault generation and correction process.

Another early model was proposed by Schick and Wolverton (1973). The hazard rate assumed was proportional to the product of the number of faults remaining and the time. Hence the size of the changes in hazard rate (at fault correction) increases with time. Wagoner (1973) suggested a model in which the hazard rate was proportional to the number of faults remaining and a power of the time. This power could be varied to fit the data.

Schick and Wolverton (1978) also proposed a modified model. It can be shown that the hazard rate for this model is a parabolic function instead of a linear function in time. Although this hazard rate is close in form to that of the Weibull distribution, it is clearly different.

Schneidewind (1972) initially approached software reliability modeling from an empirical viewpoint. He recommended the investigation of different reliability functions and selection of the distribution that best fit the particular project in question. Suggested candidates were the exponential, normal, gamma, and Weibull distributions. In looking at data, Schneidewind found that the best distribution varied from project to project. He indicated the importance of determining confidence intervals for the parameters estimated rather than just relying on point estimates.

In a later paper Schneidewind (1975) viewed fault detections per time interval as a nonhomogeneous Poisson process with an exponential mean value function. He applied either least squares or maximum likelihood estimation to the determination of the parameters of the process. Schneidewind also suggested that the time lag between failure detection and correction be determined from actual data and used to correct the time scale in forecasts.

Moranda (1975) has also proposed two variants of the Jelinski-Moranda model. In the "geometric de-eutrophication process," the hazard rate decreases in steps that form a geometric progression (rather than being of constant amount). The second, called the "geometric Poisson" model, has a hazard rate which also decreases in a geometric progression. However, the decrements occur at fixed intervals rather than at each failure correction.

Shortly after some of the early work, Musa (1975) presented an execution time model of software reliability (referred to as the "basic execution time model" in this book). This theory built on earlier contributions, but also broke new ground in several ways. He postulated that execution time, the actual processor time utilized in executing the program, was the best practical measure of the failure-inducing stress that was being placed on the program. Hence, he concluded that software reliability theory should be based on execution time rather than calendar time. Calendar time does not account for varying usage of the program in either test or operation. The removal of this confounding factor greatly simplifies modeling. An execution time model is superior in ability to model the failure process simply, in conceptual insight, and in predictive validity.

Musa also had observed that when rates were taken *with respect to execution time*, the fault correction rate was generally proportional to the fault detection or hazard rate. This observation made consideration of debugging personnel profiles unnecessary.

These concepts were tested in real time on four development projects with excellent results. With this formulation, the variability in models from project to project noted by Schneidewind and Shooman did not occur. Thus the modeling approach became universal and much easier to apply. Hecht (1981) has independently verified the simplification resulting from looking at software reliability as a function of execution time rather than calendar time.

A calendar time component was developed for the model that related execution time to calendar time, allowing execution time predictions to be converted to dates. The calendar time component is based on the fact that available resources limit the amount of execution time that is practical each calendar day.

A Bayesian approach to software reliability measurement was taken by Littlewood and Verrall (1973). They viewed software reliability as a measure of strength of belief that a program will operate successfully. This contrasts with the classical view of reliability as the outcome of an (possibly hypothetical) experiment to determine the number of times a program would operate successfully out of, say, 100 executions. Almost all published models assume that failures occur randomly during the operation of the program. However, while most postulate simply that the value of the hazard rate is a function of the number of faults remaining, Littlewood and Verrall modeled it as a *random variable*. One of the parameters of the distribution of this random variable is assumed to vary with the number of failures experienced. It thus characterizes reliability change. Littlewood and Verrall proposed various functional forms for the description of this variation. The values of the parameters of each functional form that produce the best fit for that form are determined. Then the functional forms are compared (at the optimum values of the parameters) and the best fitting form is selected.

The concept of the hazard rate as a random variable reflects uncertainty in the effectiveness of the fault correction process. Note that the hazard rate changes discontinuously at each failure detection and correction and varies continuously with the cumulative execution time. The heights of the discontinuities usually, but not necessarily, decrease with failures experienced. The continuous decrease of hazard rate with time reflects one's subjective ideas of how reliability should change in a failure-free environment.

Keiller et al. (1983) investigated a model similar to the Littlewood-Verrall general model. It characterizes the randomness of the hazard rate with the same distribution. However, it uses a different parameter of that distribution to express reliability change.

The differential fault model proposed by Littlewood (1981) may be viewed as a variant of the general Littlewood-Verrall model. It is similar in viewing the hazard rate as a random variable and in using Bayesian inference. Reliability growth is modeled through two mechanisms. One is the number of faults remaining. The second is the variation of the per-fault hazard rate with time. The second source follows from the hypothesis that failures occur with different frequencies due to the variation in frequency with which different input states of the program are executed. The most frequently occurring faults are detected and corrected first. Littlewood considers that uncertainties in reliability growth probably result more from uncertainties in the relative frequencies of execution of different input states than uncertainties in fault correction.

Goel and Okumoto (1978) developed a modification of the Jelinski-Moranda model for the case of imperfect debugging. It is based on a view of debugging as a Markov process, with appropriate transition probabilities between states. Several useful quantities can be derived analytically, with the mathematics remaining tractable. Kremer (1983) developed this idea further, including the possibility of introducing a new fault due to the repair activity.

In another paper, Goel and Okumoto (1979b), reasoning from assumptions similar to those of Jelinski and Moranda, described failure detection as a nonhomogeneous Poisson process (NHPP) with an exponentially decaying rate function. The cumulative number of failures detected and the distribution of the number of remaining failures are both found to be Poisson. Maximum likelihood estimation methods were developed for both the cases when failure data are given in terms of failure intervals and failures per interval. A simple modification of the NHPP model was investigated by Yamada, Ohba, and Osaki (1983), where the cumulative number of failures detected is described as an S-shaped curve.

Crow (1974) proposed a model for reliability estimation of hardware systems during development testing. It is a nonhomogeneous Poisson process with a failure intensity function that is a power function in time. It can be applied to software with certain ranges of parameter values.

It will be seen from the foregoing that much of the early history of software reliability modeling involved looking at different possible models. In the late 1970s and early 1980s, efforts began to focus on comparing software reliability models, with the objective of selecting the "best" one or ones. The initial efforts at comparison [Sukert (1979) and Schick and Wolverton (1978)] suffered from lack of good failure data and lack of agreement on the criteria to be used in making the comparisons. The publication by Musa (1979b) of a set of data of reasonably good quality stimulated comparison efforts. Several researchers worked out a consensus on the comparison criteria to be employed [Iannino et al. (1983)]. Examination of the basic concepts underlying software reliability modeling and development of a classification scheme [Musa and Okumoto (1983)] have helped to clarify and organize comparisons and to suggest possible new models. This work led to the development of the Musa-Okumoto logarithmic Poisson execution time model [Musa and Okumoto (1984b)], which combines simplicity with high predictive validity.

The logarithmic Poisson model is based on a nonhomogeneous Poisson process with an intensity function that decreases exponentially with expected failures experienced. This model reflects the situation where failures repaired in an early phase of execution reduce the failure intensity more than those in a later stage. It is called "logarithmic" because the expected number of failures is a logarithmic function of time. Validation of the model with actual data indicated that the model combines high predictive validity with great simplicity. The calendar time component of this model is analogous to that of the original Musa execution time model.

Interest in clarifying the distinction between "fault" and "failure" and developing the conceptual base for software reliability is recent. Much of this material appears for the first time in this book (Sections 4.1, 4.3, 9.1, 9.2). Practical experience obtained from application has been scattered through many papers too numerous to list. This experience has been collected and presented in an organized fashion in Parts I and II of this book.

9.4 MODEL CLASSIFICATION SCHEME

This section presents a classification scheme developed by Musa and Okumoto (1983) for software reliability models. The scheme permits relationships to be derived for groups of models. It highlights relationships among the models and suggests new models where gaps occur in the classification scheme. It reduces the task of model comparison.

Models are classified in terms of five different attributes:

1. *time domain*: calendar time or execution (CPU or processor) time,
2. *category*: the number of failures that can be experienced in infinite time is *finite* or *infinite*,
3. *type*: the distribution of the number of failures experienced by time t,
4. *class* (finite failures category only): functional form of the failure intensity in terms of time, and
5. *family* (infinite failures category only): functional form of the failure intensity in terms of the expected number of failures experienced.

The classification approach was chosen to be different for the two different categories because of greater analytical simplicity and physical meaning. For finite failures models of Poisson and binomial types, the class represents both the functional form of the failure intensity in terms of time and the failure time distribution of an individual fault. The classes take their names from these distributions. The distribution of the intervals between failures depends on both type and class. The families of the infinite failures models take their names from the functional form of the failure intensity in terms of expected failures.

Table 9.2 illustrates the classification scheme with respect to the last four attributes. It is identical for both kinds of time. The table notes where most of the

TABLE 9.2
Software reliability model classification scheme

Finite failures category models

Class[2]	Type[1]		
	Poisson	Binomial	Other types
Exponential	Musa (1975) Moranda (1975) Schneidewind (1975) Goel-Okumoto (1979b)	Jelinski-Moranda (1972) Shooman (1972)	Goel-Okumoto (1978) Musa (1979a) Keiller-Littlewood (1983)
Weibull		Schick-Wolverton (1973) Wagoner (1973)	
C1		Schick-Wolverton (1978)	
Pareto		Littlewood (1981)	
Gamma	Yamada-Ohba-Osaki (1983)		

Infinite failures category models

Family[3]	Type[1]			
	T1	T2	T3	Poisson
Geometric	Moranda (1975)			Musa-Okumoto (1984b)
Inverse linear		Littlewood-Verrall (1973)		
Inverse polynomial (2nd degree)			Littlewood-Verrall (1973)	
Power				Crow (1974)

[1]Type: Distribution of number of failures experienced.

[2]Class: Functional form of failure intensity (in terms of time).

[3]Family: Functional form of failure intensity (in terms of expected number of failures).

published models fit in the scheme. As can be seen, a larger portion of published models fall in the finite failures category. Poisson and binomial are the most important types. The references indicated in the table provide detailed descriptions of the models. A discussion of how the models fit into the classification scheme will be provided in Chapter 11. We will also derive functional relationships there for the failure intensity both with respect to time and the expected number of failures experienced. This will be done for each class of finite failures models and each family of infinite failures models. They are summarized in Table 11.1.

Note that only the Musa basic and Musa-Okumoto logarithmic Poisson execution time models have been explicitly defined as being in the execution time domain. The other models are either calendar time models or their time domain is not explicitly stated. However, execution time counterparts may be defined for most of them. Many special distributions can occur that do not have common names. They are denoted with letter-number codes (for example: T1, T2, T3, where "T" stands for "type"). Similarly, there is a class without a commonly named per-fault failure distribution; it is denoted C1. The Littlewood-Verrall general model can fall in different classifications depending on the form of the reliability change functions $\xi(i)$ for the ith failure (see Chapter 11). For the infinite failures category, a specified family may lead to a particular type of model. "Holes" in the table do not imply that models can always be developed to fill them. Some combinations of family and type or class and type may be impossible.

9.5 SUMMARY

Understanding the difference between "failure" and "fault" is crucial to a clear grasp of software reliability theory. The most useful software reliability models are macromodels. They characterize failure behavior as a random process. Classification of software reliability models by time domain, category, type, and class or family provides an organized way of viewing models.

PROBLEMS

9.1 Why don't you use percentage of program segments covered rather than execution time to characterize the failure stress placed on software?

9.2 Why don't you use "instructions executed" rather than "execution time" as the basic software reliability metric? It would seem to be more fundamental, since it would be independent of the particular computer used and its throughput.

9.3 Why do you talk about *faults* corrected but *failure* correction personnel?

9.4 Isn't it true that a fault can cause multiple different failures?

9.5 How can the number of faults in a program vary with the environment in which the program is used or tested? Isn't the number of faults a fixed number?

9.6 What is the difference between failure intensity and failure density, as used in software reliability models?

9.7 How should you view incorrect or inconsistent requirements in relation to defining failures?

9.8 If a fault is never detected is it still a fault?

TEN

MARKOVIAN MODELS

This chapter presents a generalized approach to the development of a large group of software reliability models that includes most published models. We will illustrate reduction of the generalized models to specific models. This approach is expected to help markedly in

1. unifying the field,
2. highlighting relationships among the models,
3. suggesting possible new models, and
4. making comparisons among the models.

We will present general concepts of Markov processes in Section 10.1 and examine basic assumptions and characteristics for a nonhomogeneous Poisson process in Section 10.2. We then discuss both binomial-type and Poisson-type models of the finite failures category using Markov processes in Sections 10.3 and 10.4, respectively. The assumptions and characteristics of the binomial-type and Poisson-type models are compared and expressions for important relationships are derived for specific models in Section 10.5.

It will be seen that most published models (see Table 9.2) can be described in terms of a Markov process, except for the geometric de-eutrophication model of Moranda (1975) and the Bayesian model of Littlewood and Verrall (1973). Miller (1986) examined characterizations, properties, and examples of various models using exponential order statistic models, which are a subset of Markov models.

253

10.1 GENERAL CONCEPTS

The concept of Markov processes is useful in modeling random behavior of software in time such as faults remaining at time t and failures experienced by time t. A Markov process has the property that the future of the process depends only on the present state and is independent of its history. The assumption may be reasonable for a software failure process, which is mainly dependent on faults remaining and the operational profile (the latter is not dependent on the past). Markov processes are, in general, characterized by the amount of time spent in a state and the transitions between states.

To illustrate the process, let us consider a computer program that has total faults u_0 at the start of the system test. A fault will cause a software failure when the program is executed for certain input states. Failures will occur randomly in time because of the random selection of input states and uncertainty of fault location. When a failure occurs, an attempt will be made to identify and remove the fault that caused the failure. However, because of possible imperfect debugging, the fault may not be removed with certainty. Furthermore, the repair activity may introduce a new fault.

In this example, the number of faults remaining at a future time will not be known with certainty. Such random behavior can be formulated as a Markov process. Let $U(t)$ denote a random variable representing faults remaining at time t. We assume that there are u_0 faults at time $t = 0$, that is, $U(0) = u_0$ with probability 1. Figure 10.1 shows a possible realization of the $U(t)$ process, where t_i represents the ith failure time. Note that one fault was removed at t_1 and another at t_3. The repair activity was imperfect at t_2 (that is, no fault was removed) and there was a new fault introduced at t_4 because of the repair process.

The Markov property for the $U(t)$ process can be stated as follows: For an interval Δt, faults remaining at time $t + \Delta t$ depends only on the present state at time t. In other words, the conditional probability

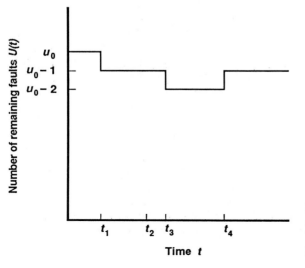

FIGURE 10.1
A possible realization of the number of faults $U(t)$ remaining at time t.

$$P[U(t + \Delta t) = j | U(t) = i]$$

describes the future behavior of the $U(t)$ process. The conditional probability, which is often called the transition function of the process, is usually dependent on both t and Δt (in addition to i and j). If we denote the transition function by $P_{ij}(t, \Delta t)$, the probability that $U(t + \Delta t)$ is equal to j is given by

$$P[U(t + \Delta t) = j] = \sum_i P_{ij}(t, \Delta t)P[U(t) = i] \ . \tag{10.1}$$

It should be pointed out that Goel and Okumoto (1978, 1979a) and Shanthikumar (1981) studied the $U(t)$ process with imperfect debugging. Kremer (1983) further incorporated the possibility of introducing a new fault because of the repair action. The approach is interesting because of the insight it provides. Expressions for reliability and other quantities of interest are, however, complex and it is difficult to apply this approach in practice. Also, the $U(t)$ process cannot be clearly observed (see Chapter 9). Note that binomial-type models assume perfect debugging (see Section 10.3 for a detailed discussion).

Another way of looking at the problem from the practical point of view is to formulate failures experienced by time t as a Markov process. We can actually observe failures experienced, whereas faults cannot be clearly observed in reality. Therefore, we will take the former approach. In Section 10.2, we will develop a nonhomogeneous Poisson process as a special case of a Markov process for studying random behavior of failures experienced in a computer program. Note that we can describe existing Poisson-type models of both finite and infinite failures category as special cases of the Poisson process. In Section 10.3 we will discuss binomial-type models as special cases of a Markov process. It is then shown in Section 10.4 how a generalization of binomial-type models leads to Poisson-type finite failures models. The latter are, of course, special cases of general Poisson-type models. We then compare Poisson-type models of the finite failures category with the binomial-type models in Section 10.5. Most of the derivations discussed here can be found in standard books on stochastic processes [for example, Cinlar (1975)].

10.2 GENERAL POISSON-TYPE MODELS

Poisson processes provide a good approximation to the occurrence of many real-world events such as telephone calls, orders to a factory, breakdown of machinery, arrivals on a queue, and insurance claims. In this section we will study the software failure process using a nonhomogeneous Poisson process (NHPP) with failure intensity $\lambda(t)$. We will describe existing Poisson-type models (of both finite and infinite failures category) as special cases of the underlying general NHPP (see Section 10.4). We first present basic assumptions and characteristics and then derive expressions for reliability and other performance measures.

10.2.1 Assumptions

Let $M(t)$ denote failures experienced by time t. Figure 10.2 shows a possible realization of the $M(t)$ process, where t_i represents the ith failure time. Note that the

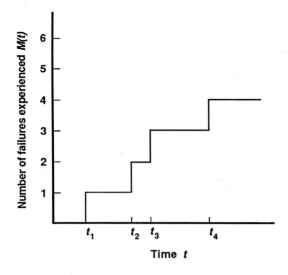

FIGURE 10.2
A possible realization of the number of failures $M(t)$ experienced by time t.

$M(t)$ process increases in value by 1 whenever a failure occurs. We will derive the $M(t)$ process for Poisson-type models based on the following assumptions:

1. There are no failures experienced at time $t = 0$, that is, $M(0) = 0$ with probability 1.
2. The process has independent increments. In other words, the number of failures experienced during $(t, t + \Delta t]$, that is, $M(t + \Delta t) - M(t)$, is independent of the history. Note that this assumption implies the Markov property that the future $M(t + \Delta t)$ of the process depends only on the present state $M(t)$ and is independent of its past $M(x)$ for $x < t$.
3. The probability that a failure will occur during $(t, t + \Delta t]$ is $\lambda(t) \Delta t + o(\Delta t)$, where $\lambda(t)$ is the failure intensity of the process. Note that the function $o(\Delta t)$ is defined as

$$\lim_{\Delta t \to 0} \frac{o(\Delta t)}{\Delta t} = 0 .$$

In practice, it implies that the second or higher order effects of Δt are negligible.
4. The probability that more than one failure will occur during $(t, t + \Delta t]$ is $o(\Delta t)$.

10.2.2 Failures Experienced and Remaining

Let's look at the properties of the random quantities failures experienced and failures remaining for the process that satisfies the four assumptions. These quantities are useful for a software project manager for answering:

1. How many failures will occur in a certain amount of time?
2. How many more failures remain (where "remain" means "would be experienced in infinite time") after testing for a certain amount of time?

Using assumptions 2, 3, and 4, we can identify the transition function for the $M(t)$ process as (assuming a transition from i to j)

$$P_{ij}(t, \Delta t) = \begin{cases} 1 - \lambda(t)\Delta t + o(\Delta t) & , j = i \\ \lambda(t)\Delta t & , j = i + 1, \\ o(\Delta t) & , \text{otherwise} . \end{cases} \quad (10.2)$$

Let $P_m(t)$ denote the probability that $M(t)$ is equal to m, that is,

$$P_m(t) = P[M(t) = m] . \quad (10.3)$$

Substituting Equation (10.2) into the general Markov process Equation (10.1) with $U(t)$ replaced by $M(t)$ yields the equation

$$P_m(t + \Delta t) = [1 - \lambda(t)\Delta t]P_m(t) + \lambda(t)\Delta t P_{m-1}(t) + o(\Delta t) , \quad (10.4)$$

which is then solved for $P_m(t)$. It can be shown that $M(t)$ is distributed as a Poisson random variable, that is,

$$P_m(t) = \frac{[\mu(t)]^m}{m!} \exp[-\mu(t)] , \quad (10.5)$$

where

$$\mu(t) = \int_0^t \lambda(x)dx . \quad (10.6)$$

The derivation (see Problem 10.1) is similar to that for a stationary process. Consult Appendix A for a detailed derivation of a stationary Poisson process. Note that the NHPP $[M(t), t \geq 0]$ has a mean and variance of $\mu(t)$, which is often called the mean value function of the process. It can be seen from Equation (10.6) that the failure intensity is the derivative of the mean value function. Therefore, the $M(t)$ process can be particularized by specifying the mean value function or the failure intensity function.

Suppose that we have observed m_e failures during $(0, t_e]$. The Poisson process $[M(t), t \geq 0]$ has independent increments and hence we obtain the conditional distribution of $M(t)$ given $M(t_e) = m_e$ for $t > t_e$ as

$$P[M(t) = m \mid M(t_e) = m_e] = P[M(t) - M(t_e) = m - m_e]$$

$$= \frac{[\mu(t) - \mu(t_e)]^{m-m_e}}{(m - m_e)!} \exp\left\{ -[\mu(t) - \mu(t_e)] \right\}, \quad (10.7)$$

which is the distribution of additional failures during $(t_e, t]$.

Let $Q(t)$ be a random variable representing failures remaining at time t, that is,

$$Q(t) = M(\infty) - M(t). \tag{10.8}$$

Then, substituting $t_e = t$ and $t = \infty$ into Equation (10.7) yields

$$P[Q(t) = q] = P[M(\infty) - M(t) = q]$$

$$= \frac{[\nu(t)]^q}{q!} \exp[-\nu(t)], \quad q = 0, 1, \cdots . \tag{10.9}$$

Note that $\nu(t)$ is the expected number of remaining failures at time t and is given by

$$\nu(t) = \mu(\infty) - \mu(t) . \tag{10.10}$$

10.2.3   Failure Times and Times Between Failures

We will now use the expressions derived in Section 10.2.2 to study the behavior of the random quantities failure times and times between failures for the Poisson-type models. These quantities will help a project manager to answer:

1. How long does it take to experience a certain number of failures?
2. What is the probability of failure-free operation during a certain amount of time (that is, reliability)?

Let T_i' $(i = 1, 2,...)$ be a random variable representing the ith failure interval and define $T_i (i = 1, 2,...)$ as a random variable representing the ith failure time, that is,

$$T_i = \sum_{j=1}^{i} T_j'$$

$$= T_{i-1} + T_i', \quad i = 1, 2, \cdots, \tag{10.11}$$

where $T_0 = 0$.

Consider the following two events:

E1: There are at least i failures experienced by time t, denoted by $[M(t) \geq i]$.
E2: Time to the ith failure is at most t, denoted by $[T_i \leq t]$.

Then, it can be shown that the events E1 and E2 are equivalent, that is,

$$[M(t) \geq i] <=> [T_i \leq t]. \tag{10.12}$$

Using Equations (10.5) and (10.12), we can obtain the cumulative distribution function of T_i as

$$P[T_i \leq t] = P[M(t) \geq i]$$

$$= \sum_{j=i}^{\infty} \frac{[\mu(t)]^j}{j!} \exp[-\mu(t)]. \tag{10.13}$$

Similarly, from Equation (10.7) we derive the conditional cumulative distribution function of T_i given $M(t_e) = m_e$, where $i \geq m_e$, as

$$P[T_i \leqslant t \mid M(t_e) = m_e] = P[M(t) \geqslant i \mid M(t_e) = m_e]$$

$$= \sum_{j=i}^{\infty} P[M(t) - M(t_e) = j - m_e] \qquad (10.14)$$

$$= \sum_{j=i}^{\infty} \frac{[\mu(t) - \mu(t_e)]^{j-m_e}}{(j - m_e)!} \exp\left\{-[\mu(t) - \mu(t_e)]\right\}.$$

Note that the event $T_{i-1} = t_{i-1}$ is equivalent to $M(t_{i-1}) = i - 1$. For $m_e = i - 1$ Equation (10.14) is the sum of Poisson probabilities except for one term. Hence

$$P[T_i \leqslant t \mid M(t_{i-1}) = i - 1] = 1 - \exp\left\{-[\mu(t_i) - \mu(t_{i-1})]\right\}. \quad (10.15)$$

Therefore, we obtain the conditional reliability of T_i' on the last failure time $T_{i-1} = t_{i-1}$ using Equation (10.15), as

$$R(t_i' \mid t_{i-1}) = P[T_i' > t_i' \mid T_{i-1} = t_{i-1}]$$

$$= 1 - P[T_i \leqslant t_i \mid M(t_{i-1}) = i - 1]$$

$$= \exp\left\{-[\mu(t_{i-1} + t_i') - \mu(t_{i-1})]\right\}, \quad i = 1, 2, \cdots. \quad (10.16)$$

Recall that reliability $R(t)$ is related to the failure distribution $F(t)$ by $R(t) = 1 - F(t)$ and that the failure density $f(t)$ is the derivative of $F(t)$. Hence, if we take the negative of the derivative of Equation (10.16) with respect to t_i', we obtain the conditional density function of t_i', that is,

$$f(t_i' \mid t_{i-1}) = \lambda\left(t_{i-1} + t_i'\right)\exp\left\{-[\mu(t_{i-1} + t_i') - \mu(t_{i-1})]\right\}, \quad i = 1, 2, \cdots. \quad (10.17)$$

Since the program hazard rate is related to the reliability and the failure density by $z(t) = f(t)/R(t)$, we have

$$z(t_i' \mid t_{i-1}) = \lambda(t_{i-1} + t_i'), \quad i = 1, 2, \cdots. \quad (10.18)$$

It can be seen from Equation (10.18) that the program hazard rate for the Poisson-type models is the same as the failure intensity function.

Table 10.1 provides a summary of the relationships that have been developed for a general Poisson model in Sections 10.2.2 and 10.2.3. It will be seen in Section 10.4 that the table is useful for obtaining relationships for a particular Poisson-type model.

10.3 BINOMIAL-TYPE MODELS

In Chapter 9 we classified finite failures category models by types (for example, Poisson and binomial), depending on how the failure quantity distribution was specified. Finite failures models are further subdivided into classes, based on the functional form of the failure intensity in terms of time. Note that for finite failure models of the binomial or Poisson type, the class represents not only the func-

TABLE 10.1
Derived relationships for a general Poisson model

Random quantities	General Poisson model
Failures experienced $P[M(t) = m]$	$\dfrac{[\mu(t)]^m}{m!} \exp[-\mu(t)]$
$E[M(t)]$	$\mu(t)$
$\mathrm{var}[M(t)]$	$\mu(t)$
Failures remaining $P[Q(t) = q]$	$\dfrac{[\mu(\infty) - \mu(t)]^q}{q!} \exp\left\{-[\mu(\infty) - \mu(t)]\right\}$
$E[Q(t)]$	$\mu(\infty) - \mu(t)$
$\mathrm{var}[Q(t)]$	$\mu(\infty) - \mu(t)$
Failure time $P[T_i \leqslant t]$	$\displaystyle\sum_{j=1}^{\infty} \dfrac{[\mu(t)]^j}{j!} \exp[-\mu(t)]$
Program hazard rate $z(t_i'\mid t_{i-1})$	$\lambda(t_{i-1} + t_i')$
Reliability $R(t_i'\mid t_{i-1})$	$\exp\left\{-[\mu(t_{i-1} + t_i') - \mu(t_{i-1})]\right\}$

tional form of the failure intensity but also the form of the failure time distribution of an individual fault. The classes take their names from these distributions. Table 10.2 shows some specific models in the classification scheme.

In this section we will develop a generalized approach to the binomial-type models as special cases of a Markov process. We will first present assumptions and characteristics and then derive expressions for reliability and other performance measures.

10.3.1 Assumptions

We develop binomial-type models based on the following assumptions:

1. Whenever a software failure occurs, the fault that caused it will be removed instantaneously.
2. There are u_0 inherent faults in the program.
3. Each failure, caused by a fault, occurs independently and randomly in time, according to the per-fault hazard rate $z_a(t)$. In other words, the hazard rates for all faults are the same.

TABLE 10.2
Classification of finite failures category models

| Class (per-fault failure distribution) | Type (failure quantity distribution) | |
	Binomial	Poisson
Exponential	Jelinski-Moranda (1972) Shooman (1972)	Musa (1975) Schneidewind (1975) Moranda (1975) Goel-Okumoto (1979b)
Weibull	Schick-Wolverton (1973) Wagoner (1973)	
C1	Schick-Wolverton (1978)	
Pareto	Littlewood (1981)	
Gamma		Yamada-Ohba-Osaki (1983)

Note that assumption 1 implies that the binomial-type models do not permit consideration of faults that cannot be located (that is, debugging is perfect), extra faults found through code inspection, or faults spawned as the result of correcting previous faults. Therefore, in the binomial-type models the net number $N(t)$ of faults corrected by time t is the same as the number $M(t)$ of failures experienced by t. The expected total failures experienced in infinite time, ν_0, will be equal to the inherent faults u_0. If we denote by $Q(t)$ a random variable representing failures remaining at time t, we have

$$Q(t) = u_0 - M(t). \tag{10.19}$$

Note that u_0 will vary with changes in the operational profile, the operational history of the program, and the effectiveness of repair actions. However, binomial-type models assume that the operational profile is established, and that from a macroscopic viewpoint there is an "average" history and average effectiveness of repair actions so that the number of failures can be viewed as a fixed constant.

Each failure is not in reality totally independent of every other failure. One failure can influence succeeding failures by its individual impact on the effectiveness of repair. For example, failure A could conceivably reveal the possibility of failure C occurring to a greater extent than failure B would. This could result in repairs that would more greatly reduce the probability that failure C would occur. Also, a failure may prevent another failure from occurring because it may prevent a particular code path from being executed. The latter situation is more likely to occur in unit test than in system test. However the effects are, on the average, secondary and will be neglected.

We can rewrite assumption 3 as follows: Let T_a denote a random variable representing time to failure of a fault "a," where $a = 1, 2,..., u_0$. Then, the random variables T_a are independently and identically distributed as $F_a(t)$ for all remaining faults. Note that we can obtain the cumulative distribution function $F_a(t)$

from the per-fault hazard rate $z_a(t)$. If we denote by $f_a(t)$ the probability density function of T_a, then by the definition of $z_a(t)$ we have

$$z_a(t) = \frac{f_a(t)}{1 - F_a(t)}, \qquad (10.20)$$

where

$$f_a(t) = \frac{dF_a(t)}{dt}. \qquad (10.21)$$

Note that the per-fault quantities $F_a(t)$, $z_a(t)$, and $f_a(t)$ are the same for all faults. Substituting Equation (10.21) into Equation (10.20) yields a differential equation which can easily be solved for $F_a(t)$, that is,

$$F_a(t) = 1 - \exp\left[-\int_0^t z_a(x)\,dx\right]. \qquad (10.22)$$

Therefore, for the binomial-type models the per-fault hazard rate $z_a(t)$ characterizes the distribution of T_a.

It should be pointed out that there are simple ways of deriving expressions for the underlying quantities. However, in each of the following sections we will first show how the problem can be formulated into a Markov process (discussed in Section 10.1) and then give alternative simpler methods (based on the concepts of a binomial distribution). This approach is taken for the purpose of consistency in describing different models.

10.3.2   Failures Experienced and Remaining

Recall from assumption 1 that the net number of faults corrected is the same as the number of failures experienced. If $m - 1$ failures have occurred by time t, there are $u_0 - (m - 1)$ faults remaining at time t and each fault has the hazard rate $z_a(t)$. The probability of a failure in $(t, t + \Delta t)$ is therefore given by $(u_0 - m + 1)z_a(t) \times \Delta t$. Similarly, when m failures have occurred by time t, there are $u_0 - m$ faults remaining at time t. Hence, the probability of no failures in $(t, t + \Delta t)$ is $1 - (u_0 - m)z_a(t)\Delta t$. Substituting these probabilities in Equation (10.1) with $U(t)$ replaced by $M(t)$ we obtain

$$P_m(t + \Delta t) = P[M(t + \Delta t) = m]$$

$$= P[\text{ a failure in } (t, t + \Delta t) \mid m - 1 \text{ failures in } (0, t)]P_{m-1}(t)$$

$$+ P[\text{no failures in } (t, t + \Delta t) \mid m \text{ failures in } (0, t)]P_m(t),$$

$$= (u_0 - m + 1)z_a(t)\Delta t P_{m-1}(t)$$

$$+ [1 - (u_0 - m)z_a(t)\Delta t]P_m(t), \quad m = 0, 1, \cdots, u_0. \qquad (10.23)$$

Finally, forming $[P_m(t + \Delta t) - P_m(t)]/\Delta t$ from Equation (10.23) and letting $\Delta t \to 0$, we obtain the differential equation:

$$\frac{dP_m(t)}{dt} = (u_0 - m + 1)z_a(t)P_{m-1}(t)$$

$$- (u_0 - m)z_a(t)P_m(t), \quad m = 0, 1, \cdots, u_0, \quad (10.24)$$

where $P_{-1}(t) = 0$. Equation (10.24) can easily be solved for $P_m(t)$ under the boundary conditions $P_0(0) = 1$ and $P_m(0) = 0$ for $m = 1, 2, \ldots, u_0$. Solving Equation (10.24) and substituting Equation (10.22) in the result, we obtain (see Problem 10.2)

$$P[M(t) = m] = \binom{u_0}{m}[F_a(t)]^m[1 - F_a(t)]^{u_0 - m}, \quad m = 0, 1, \cdots, u_0. \quad (10.25)$$

This is a binomial distribution with a mean of

$$\mu(t) = E[M(t)] = u_0 F_a(t) \quad (10.26)$$

and a variance of

$$\text{var}[M(t)] = u_0 F_a(t)[1 - F_a(t)]. \quad (10.27)$$

The failure intensity may be found by differentiating Equation (10.26) as

$$\lambda(t) = u_0 f_a(t). \quad (10.28)$$

Binomial-type models take their name from the fact that the number of failures experienced in time t is distributed binomially. We will extend this result in Chapter 12 to show that the numbers of failures $Y_1, Y_2, \ldots, Y_p$ in p intervals are distributed multinomially.

Example 10.1. To illustrate the behavior of $M(t)$, we choose the specific distribution $F_a(t) = 1 - \exp(-\phi t)$ (that is, the exponential class). Note that this is the de-eutrophication model of Jelinski and Moranda (1972). Suppose that $u_0 = 100$ faults and $\phi = 0.3$/hr. Then, we can obtain the mean value function from Equation (10.26) as

$$\mu(t) = 100[1 - \exp(-0.3t)].$$

From Equation (10.27) we have the variance

$$\text{var}[M(t)] = 100[1 - \exp(-0.3t)]\exp(-0.3t).$$

Figure 10.3 shows the mean value function $\mu(t)$ and the 90 percent bounds for $M(t)$ [approximated by $\mu(t) \pm \kappa_{0.95}\sqrt{\text{var}[M(t)]}$, where $\kappa_{0.95}$ is the 95th percentile of a standard normal distribution]. The upper bound is truncated at 100 if it exceeds 100. Note that since $F_a(0) = 0$ and $F_a(\infty) = 1$, we have from Equations (10.26) and (10.27) $\mu(0) = 0$, $\text{var}[M(0)] = 0$, $\mu(\infty) = u_0$, and $\text{var}[M(\infty)] = 0$. Therefore, as shown in Figure 10.3, failures experienced $M(\infty)$ in an infinite amount of time will be u_0 with probability 1 and the variation of $M(t)$ around $\mu(t)$ increases up to the time at which $F_a(t) = 0.5$, and then decreases, eventually becoming zero. ∎

We can find a simpler alternative derivation for Equation (10.25) based on assumption 3. Note that at any time t, a fault "a" will be removed with probability

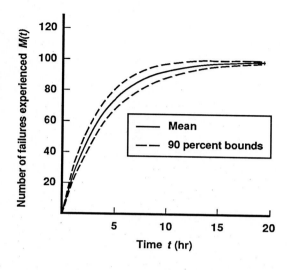

FIGURE 10.3
The mean value function and the 90 percent bounds for the number of failures $M(t)$ experienced by time t for a binomial-type exponential-class model. Parameter values are $u_0 = 100$ faults and $\phi = 0.3/hr$.

$F_a(t)$ and remain with probability $1 - F_a(t)$. There are u_0 independent faults at $t = 0$. Therefore, the probability that m of u_0 faults will be removed by time t is given by the binomial distribution derived previously. It should be pointed out that the situation is known as "life testing without replacement" in hardware reliability. The difference between software reliability and life testing is that total faults is an unknown parameter in software reliability whereas it is known in hardware reliability.

Using Equation (10.19) and the distribution of $M(t)$ given in Equation (10.25), we can derive the distribution of $Q(t)$ failures remaining at time t, as

$$P[Q(t) = q] = P[u_0 - M(t) = q]$$

$$= P[M(t) = u_0 - q]$$

$$= \binom{u_0}{q}[1 - F_a(t)]^q[F_a(t)]^{u_0 - q}, \quad q = 0, 1, \cdots, u_0. \quad (10.29)$$

This is a binomial distribution with a mean of

$$\nu(t) = E[Q(t)] = u_0[1 - F_a(t)], \quad (10.30)$$

and a variance of

$$\text{var}[Q(t)] = u_0 F_a(t)[1 - F_a(t)]. \quad (10.31)$$

Example 10.2. Consider the exponential-class model discussed in Example 10.1. Then we can find the expected number of failures remaining at time t from Equation (10.30) as

$$v(t) = 100 \exp(-0.3t)$$

and the variance from Equation (10.31) as

$$\text{var}[Q(t)] = 100 [1 - \exp(-0.3t)] \exp(-0.3t) .$$

Figure 10.4 shows the mean value function $v(t)$ and the 90 percent bounds for $Q(t)$. The lower bound is truncated at zero if it is less than zero. It should be pointed out that failures remaining in an infinite amount of time $Q(\infty)$ will be zero with probability 1 and the variation of $Q(t)$ around $v(t)$ increases up to the time at which $F_a(t) = 0.5$, and then decreases, eventually becoming zero. ∎

Suppose that we have observed m_e failures during $(0, t_e]$. Then, we wish to find the conditional distribution of $M(t)$ and $Q(t)$ for $t > t_e$. We can derive the conditional distribution of $M(t)$, given m_e failures by t_e, by solving Equation (10.24) under the boundary conditions $P_{m}(t_e) = 1$ and $P_m(t_e) = 0$ for all $m \geq m_e$:

$$P[M(t) = m \mid M(t_e) = m_e] =$$

$$\binom{u_0 - m_e}{m - m_e} [F_a(t \mid t_e)]^{m-m_e}[1 - F_a(t \mid t_e)]^{u_0 - m} , \quad (10.32)$$

where

$$F_a(t \mid t_e) = \frac{F_a(t) - F_a(t_e)}{1 - F_a(t_e)} . \quad (10.33)$$

Note that from Equation (10.22) we have

$$F_a(t \mid t_e) = 1 - \exp\left[\int_{t_e}^{t} z_a(x)dx\right]. \quad (10.34)$$

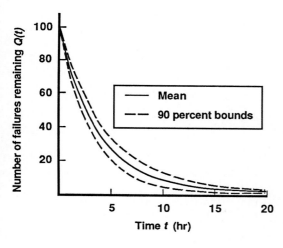

FIGURE 10.4
The mean value function and the 90 percent bounds for the number of failures $Q(t)$ remaining at time t for a binomial-type exponential-class model. Parameter values are $u_0 = 100$ faults and $\phi = 0.3$/hr.

Hence, $F_a(t \mid t_e)$ represents the cumulative distribution function of T_a conditional on $T_a > t_e$. It is the probability that a fault "a" will be removed by time t when it remains at time t_e.

Alternatively, we can derive the distribution as follows. There are $u_0 - m_e$ faults remaining at time t_e, each of which will be removed during $(t_e, t]$ with probability $F_a(t \mid t_e)$ and remain with probability $1 - F_a(t \mid t_e)$. Therefore, the probability that $m - m_e$ of $u_0 - m_e$ will occur during $(t_e, t]$ is given by Equation (10.32).

Now, the conditional distribution of $Q(t)$ given $M(t_e) = m_e$ can be derived from Equations (10.19) and (10.32) as follows.

$$P[Q(t) = q \mid M(t_e) = m_e]$$

$$= P[u_0 - M(t) = q \mid M(t_e) = m_e]$$

$$= P[M(t) = u_0 - q \mid M(t_e) = m_e]$$

$$= \binom{u_0 - m_e}{q} [1 - F_a(t \mid t_e)]^q [F_a(t \mid t_e)]^{u_0 - m_e - q}. \quad (10.35)$$

Note that Equations (10.25) and (10.29) are special cases of Equations (10.32) and (10.35), respectively, when $t_e = 0$.

10.3.3 Failure Times and Times Between Failures

In this section we deal with two more random quantities: failure times $\{T_i; i = 1, 2,...\}$ and times between failures $\{T_i'; i = 1, 2,...\}$. Note that the quantities to be studied in this section are also useful for estimating the model parameters, which will be discussed in Chapter 12.

We can obtain the cumulative distribution function of T_i from Equations (10.12) and (10.25) as

$$P[T_i \leqslant t] = P[M(t) \geqslant i] = \sum_{j=i}^{u_0} P[M(t) = j]$$

$$= \sum_{j=1}^{u_0} \binom{u_0}{j} [F_a(t)]^j [1 - F_a(t)]^{u_0 - j}. \quad (10.36)$$

Furthermore, using a derivation similar to that discussed in Section 10.2.3, we can obtain the conditional distribution of T_i given $T_{i-1} = t_{i-1}$ as (see Problem 10.3)

$$P[T_i > t_i \mid T_{i-1} = t_{i-1}] = [1 - F_a(t_i \mid t_{i-1})]^{u_0 - i + 1}. \quad (10.37)$$

If we further substitute Equation (10.34) into Equation (10.37), we obtain

$$P[T_i > t_i \mid T_{i-1} = t_{i-1}] = \exp[-(u_0 - i + 1) \int_{t_{i-1}}^{t_i} z_a(x) dx], \quad (10.38)$$

where $t_0 = 0$. Now, transforming T_i into T_i' through Equation (10.11) yields

$$R(t_i'|\ t_{i-1}) = \exp\left\{- (u_0 - i + 1) \int_{t_{i-1}}^{t_{i-1}+t_i'} z_a(x)dx \right\}. \qquad (10.39)$$

Therefore, the reliability for the binomial-type models will depend on faults remaining (that is, $u_0 - i + 1$) and the last failure time (that is, t_{i-1}). However, if a constant per-fault hazard rate is chosen [that is, $z_a(t) = \phi$], then the reliability depends only on the faults remaining. We can obtain the conditional hazard rate of the program as

$$z(t_i'|\ t_{i-1}) = - \frac{1}{R(t_i'\ |\ t_{i-1})} \frac{dR(t_i'|\ t_{i-1})}{dt_i'}$$

$$= (u_0 - i + 1)z_a(t_{i-1} + t_i')\ . \qquad (10.40)$$

Note that the program hazard rate will depend on the faults remaining and the last failure time. Hence, the program hazard rate for the binomial-type models has discontinuities of height $z_a(t)$ at each failure. When the per-fault hazard rate is constant, the program hazard rate depends only on the number of remaining faults and is unconditional. The program hazard rate given by Equation (10.40) is not equivalent to the failure intensity given by Equation (10.28). Note that expressions for the program hazard rate and failure intensity are exactly equal for Poisson-type models (see Section 10.2).

Example 10.3. Consider the exponential class model discussed in Examples 10.1 and 10.2. Substituting $u_0 = 100$ faults and $z_a(t) = \phi = 0.3$/hr into Equation (10.39), we have the reliability

$$R(t_i'\ |\ t_{i-1}) = \exp[- (101 - i)(0.3)t_i'\ ]\ .$$

From Equation (10.40) we find the program hazard rate

$$z(t_i'\ |\ t_{i-1}) = (101 - i)(0.3)\ .$$

Note that both the reliability and the program hazard rate depend only on the faults remaining.

Figure 10.5 shows the program hazard rate associated with a set of failures generated from a Monte Carlo simulation of the exponential-class binomial-type model. Note that the program hazard rate has a decrement of ϕ at each failure and it is a constant between failures. ∎

10.4 POISSON-TYPE MODELS (FINITE FAILURES)

In this section we discuss the analogs of the basic assumptions and characteristics derived for the binomial-type models presented in Section 10.3.1. It will be shown

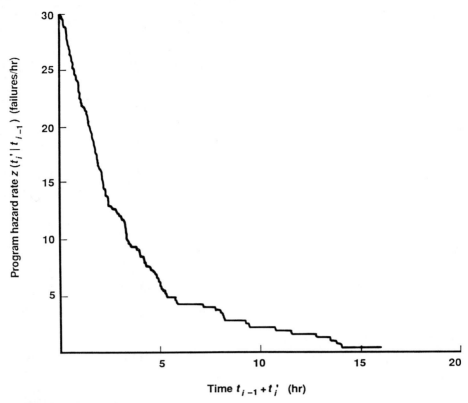

FIGURE 10.5
The program hazard rate $z(t_i' \mid t_{i-1})$ for a binomial-type exponential-class model. Parameter values are $u_0 = 100$ faults and $\phi = 0.3/\text{hr}$.

that Poisson-type models of the finite failures category can be developed directly from the binomial-type models. The development is necessary to relate the per-fault cumulative failure probability to the mean value function. Then expressions for various quantities of interest can be easily found from those developed for the general Poisson model discussed in Section 10.2.

10.4.1   Assumptions

Assumption 3 made for the binomial-type models is also applied here. Recall from assumption 2 that the binomial-type models assume a fixed number of faults remaining at $t = 0$, that is, $U(0) = u_0$ with probability 1. We now modify this assumption for developing Poisson-type models as follows:

2a. The total number of faults remaining in the program at $t = 0$ is a Poisson random variable with a mean of ω_0.

Since total faults is an extraordinarily complex function of many factors (for example, program size, complexity, and human performance), it is appropriate to consider it as a random variable. The Poisson distribution is a reasonable assumption, since the number of faults is a count of essentially independent events. It should be mentioned that Langberg and Singpurwalla (1985) took this approach to derive an exponential-class Poisson-type model from a binomial-type model using a Bayesian point of view.

10.4.2 Failures Experienced and Remaining

In this section, we will study the random quantities failures experienced $M(t)$ and failures remaining $Q(t)$ under the assumptions made in Section 10.4.1. It will be shown that both $M(t)$ and $Q(t)$ form Poisson processes whose mean value functions are, respectively, similar to those for the binomial-type models.

We assumed that $U(0)$ follows a Poisson distribution with a mean of ω_0. Hence, we can obtain the distribution of $M(t)$ as

$$P[M(t) = m] = \sum_{x=0}^{\infty} P[M(t) = m \mid U(0) = x] P[U(0) = x], \quad (10.41)$$

which may be viewed as a mixture distribution. Note that the conditional probability of $M(t) = m$ given $U(0) = x$ is zero if $x < m$. For $x \geq m$ it is given by Equation (10.25), where $u_0 = x$. Therefore, Equation (10.41) becomes

$$P[M(t) = m] = \sum_{x=0}^{\infty} \binom{x}{m} [F_a(t)]^m [1 - F_a(t)]^{x-m} \frac{\omega_0^x}{x!} \exp(-\omega_0)$$

$$= \frac{[\omega_0 F_a(t)]^m}{m!} \exp(-\omega_0) \sum_{x=m}^{\infty} \frac{\{\omega_0[1 - F_a(t)]\}^{x-m}}{(x-m)!}. \quad (10.42)$$

Further noting

$$\sum_{x=m}^{\infty} \frac{\{\omega_0[1 - F_a(t)]\}^{x-m}}{(x-m)!} = \exp\{\omega_0[1 - F_a(t)]\}, \quad (10.43)$$

we obtain

$$P[M(t) = m] = \frac{[\omega_0 F_a(t)]^m}{m!} \exp[-\omega_0 F_a(t)]. \quad (10.44)$$

This is a Poisson distribution with a mean (and equivalent variance) of

$$\mu(t) = \omega_0 F_a(t). \quad (10.45)$$

Thus the failure process $M(t)$ is Poisson. Differentiating Equation (10.45) yields the failure intensity as

$$\lambda(t) = \omega_0 f_a(t). \tag{10.46}$$

As can be seen in the analysis, the principal difference between binomial-type and Poisson-type models is the way in which the number of remaining faults is treated (that is, a fixed number for the binomial-type and a Poisson random variable for the Poisson-type).

> **Example 10.4.** Figure 10.6 shows the mean value function $\mu(t)$ and the 90 percent upper and lower bounds [approximated by $\mu(t) \pm \kappa_{0.95}\sqrt{\mu(t)}$] for $M(t)$, based on the exponential-class model with $F_a(t) = 1 - \exp(-\phi t)$. We chose the same values for $\omega_0 = u_0$ and ϕ (that is, $\omega_0 = 100$ faults and $\phi = 0.3$/hr) as in Figure 10.3 so that a comparison can be made. The variation in $M(t)$ constantly increases with time t and eventually becomes a constant, that is, $\text{var}[M(t)] = \omega_0$. ■

We can find all quantities of interest for the Poisson-type models of the finite failures category simply by substituting Equation (10.45) or Equation (10.46) into appropriate equations derived in Section 10.2.

> **Example 10.5.** Using Equation (10.9), we can obtain the distribution of the number $Q(t)$ of failures remaining at time t, where the expected number $\nu(t)$ of remaining failures at time t is given by
>
> $$\nu(t) = \mu(\infty) - \mu(t)$$
>
> $$= \omega_0 - \mu(t)$$
>
> $$= \omega_0[1 - F_a(t)]. \tag{10.47}$$

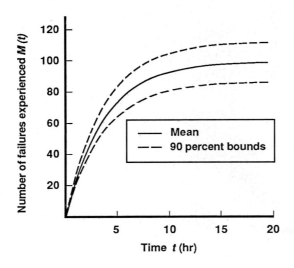

FIGURE 10.6
The mean value function and the 90 percent bounds for the number of failures $M(t)$ experienced by time t for a Poisson-type exponential-class model. Parameter values are $\omega_0 = 100$ faults and $\phi = 0.3$/hr.

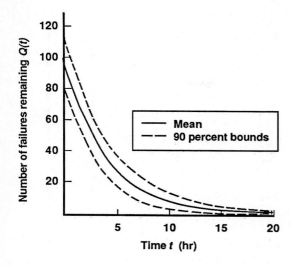

FIGURE 10.7
The mean value function and the 90 percent bounds for the number of failures $Q(t)$ remaining at time t for a Poisson-type exponential-class model. Parameter values are $\omega_0 = 100$ faults and $\phi = 0.3$/hr.

It can be seen from Equation (10.47) for $t = 0$ that the number of initial failures in the program is a Poisson random variable with the mean ω_0. Figure 10.7 shows the mean value function $\nu(t)$ and the 90 percent upper and lower bounds for $Q(t)$. We computed them in a similar fashion to that described in Example 10.4. ∎

10.4.3 Failure Times and Times Between Failures

Substituting Equation (10.45) into Equation (10.16) yields the conditional reliability as

$$R(t_i'\mid t_{i-1}) = \exp\left\{ -\omega_0[F_a(t_{i-1} + t_i') - F_a(t_{i-1})] \right\}. \tag{10.48}$$

Hence, as noted above, the reliability for the Poisson-type models depends on the last failure time t_{i-1}, but not on the failures remaining as for the binomial-type [see Equation (10.39)]. Also note that from Equation (10.48) we have

$$R(\infty\mid t_{i-1}) = \exp\left\{ -\omega_0[1 - F_a(t_{i-1})] \right\}. \tag{10.49}$$

Therefore, the Poisson-type models of the finite failures category allow nonzero probability of no failures in an infinite amount of time. Furthermore, substituting Equations (10.9) and (10.47) into Equation (10.49) yields

$$R(\infty\mid t_{i-1}) = P[Q(t_{i-1}) = 0]. \tag{10.50}$$

Note that the probability that no failure remains after the last experienced failure is 1, that is, the program is "perfect."

Substituting Equation (10.46) into Equation (10.18) yields the program hazard rate

$$z(t_i'|\ t_{i-1}) = \omega_0 f_a(t_{i-1} + t_i') ,\qquad (10.51)$$

which is a continuous function. Note that the binomial-type models differ from Equation (10.51) in that they have discontinuous hazard rates whose discontinuities occur at the failures [see Equation (10.40)].

> **Example 10.6.** Consider the exponential-class model discussed in Example 10.4. From Equation (10.48) we have the reliability
>
> $$R(t_i'|\ t_{i-1}) = \exp\left[-100 \left\{ \exp(-0.3t_{i-1}) - \exp[-0.3(t_{i-1} + t_i')] \right\} \right]$$
>
> We also obtain the program hazard rate from Equation (10.51) as
>
> $$z(t_i'|\ t_{i-1}) = 30 \exp[-0.3(t_{i-1} + t_i')] .$$
>
> Figure 10.8 shows the changes in the program hazard rate with respect to the ith failure time, $t_{i-1} + t_i'$. The program hazard rate for the ith failure interval can be determined if the last failure time t_{i-1} is given. ∎

10.5   COMPARISON OF BINOMIAL-TYPE AND POISSON-TYPE MODELS

In this section we will compare the characteristics of Poisson-type and binomial-type models of the finite failures category. Recall that we have summarized the basic assumptions in assumptions 1, 2, and 3 for the binomial-type and in assumptions 1, 2a, and 3 for the Poisson-type models, respectively.

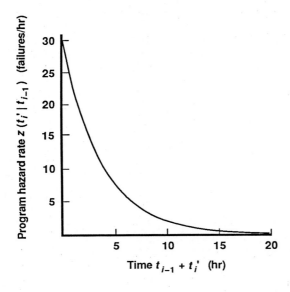

FIGURE 10.8
The program hazard rate
$z(t_i'\ |\ t_{i-1})$ **for a Poisson-type exponential-class model. Parameter values are** $\omega_0 = 100$ **faults and** $\phi = 0.3/\text{hr}$.

First, both binomial-type and Poisson-type models assume that the hazard rates are the same for all faults, as shown by assumption 3.

Assumptions 2 and 2a suggest that the Poisson-type models incorporate the case when the initial number of faults is not known with certainty. There is not a fixed number of initial faults as with the binomial-type models, but the expected value ω_0 of initial faults is known. The parameter ω_0 in the Poisson-type model is, therefore, not restricted to an integral number of faults. The number of faults in a program is dependent on many unpredictable factors besides the known factors of program characteristics (for example, size and complexity) and the development environment. Hence, it is reasonable to model initial faults as a random variable.

Poisson-type models also accommodate, in an approximate fashion, imperfect debugging and introducing new faults because of the repair action. For example, in the case of imperfect debugging discussed in Section 10.1, we may use a Poisson model with the mean value function given in Equation (10.45) (See Section 10.6).

We summarize the principal relationships derived for both binomial-type and Poisson-type models in Table 10.3, from which a comparison can easily be made. For example, we can compare the characteristics of the program hazard rates of Table 10.3. While the binomial-type models have discontinuous program hazard rates whose discontinuities occur at the failures, the Poisson-type models do not have discontinuities in the program hazard rate. Binomial-type models are more realistic in that repairs *do* cause discontinuities in the failure intensity. However, the repairs occur at some variable (perhaps reasonably modeled as "random") time *after* the failures. This fact favors Poisson-type models.

Note that as will be seen in Chapter 12, the estimation procedure for the Poisson-type models is the same as for the binomial-type. This suggests that binomial-type models can be closely approximated by the Poisson-type. The program hazard rates shown in Figures 10.5 and 10.8 confirm a close approximation. It should be pointed out that the parameter u_0 for the binomial-type models is assumed to be a real number in developing an estimation procedure. Based on the assumptions for the binomial-type models, however, u_0 must be an integer. For the Poisson-type models, on the other hand, such problems will not be encountered since ω_0 is assumed to be a real number. However, there is no difference in computation, since in practice for binomial-type models we use a real number and round it to the nearest integer for the estimate of u_0.

We have derived the relationships for the binomial-type models in Section 10.3 and for the Poisson-type models in Section 10.4, respectively. We obtained expressions for the relationships in a general form. The derived relationships can be applied to any specific finite failures category models. Note that the specific models are characterized by the class, which refers to the distribution $F_a(t)$ for the Poisson-type and binomial-type models (see Table 10.2). Furthermore, Table 10.3 shows the relationships for both binomial-type and Poisson-type models in terms of the per-fault quantities $z_a(t)$, $f_a(t)$, $F_a(t)$, and $R_a(t) = 1 - F_a(t)$. Table 10.4 shows such quantities for the exponential, Pareto, and Weibull classes. Table 10.5

TABLE 10.3
Derived relationships for binomial-type and Poisson-type models

Random quantities	Type (failure quantity distribution)	
	Binomial	**Poisson**
Failures experienced $P[M(t) = m]$	$\binom{u_0}{m}[F_a(t)]^m[R_a(t)]^{u_0-m}$	$\dfrac{[\omega_0 F_a(t)]^m}{m!}\exp[-\omega_0 F_a(t)]$
$\mu(t)$	$u_0 F_a(t)$	$\omega_0 F_a(t)$
$var[M(t)]$	$u_0 F_a(t) R_a(t)$	$\omega_0 F_a(t)$
Failures remaining $P[Q(t) = q]$	$\binom{u_0}{q}[F_a(t)]^{u_0-q}[R_a(t)]^q$	$\dfrac{[\omega_0 R_a(t)]^q}{q!}\exp[-\omega_0 R_a(t)]$
$\nu(t)$	$u_0 R_a(t)$	$\omega_0 R_a(t)$
$var[Q(t)]$	$u_0 R_a(t) F_a(t)$	$\omega_0 R_a(t)$
Failure time $P[T_i \leqslant t]$	$\displaystyle\sum_{j=1}^{u_0}\binom{u_0}{j}[F_a(t)]^j[R_a(t)]^{u_0-j}$	$\displaystyle\sum_{j=1}^{\infty}\dfrac{[\omega_0 F_a(t)]^j}{j!}\exp[-\omega_0 F_a(t)]$
Program hazard rate $z(t_i' \mid t_{i-1})$	$(u_0 - i + 1)z_a(t_{i-1} + t_i')$	$\omega_0 f_a(t_{i-1} + t_i')$
Reliability $R(t_i' \mid t_{i-1})$	$\exp\left[-(u_0 - i + 1)\displaystyle\int_{t_{i-1}}^{t_{i-1}+t_i'} z_a(t)\,dt\right]$	$\exp\left\{-\omega_0[F_a(t_{i-1} + t_i') - F_a(t_{i-1})]\right\}$
Failure intensity $\lambda(t)$	$u_0 f_a(t)$	$\omega_0 f_a(t)$

illustrates the derived relationships for the exponential class (which has been studied extensively by many researchers) for comparing the binomial-type with the Poisson-type. We will discuss each of the specific models in detail in Chapter 11.

10.6 FAULT REDUCTION FACTOR FOR POISSON-TYPE MODELS

Poisson-type models also permit consideration of faults that can't be located, extra faults found through code-inspection, and spawned faults. The fault removal process is characterized on an average basis by assuming that the fault correction rate

TABLE 10.4
Specific models and per-fault failure time distributions for each of three classes of finite failures category models

Item	Class (per-fault failure distribution)		
	Exponential	Pareto	Weibull
Specific models studied by	Jelinski-Moranda (1972) Shooman Musa (1975) Schneidewind (1975) Moranda (1975) Goel-Okumoto (1979b)	Littlewood (1981)	Wagoner (1973) Schick-Wolverton (1973)
Per-fault failure time distribution (alternative expressions)			
$z_a(t)$	ϕ	$\dfrac{\alpha}{t+\beta}$	$\phi\gamma t^{\gamma-1}$
$R_a(t)$	$\exp(-\phi t)$	$(1+\dfrac{t}{\beta})^{-\alpha}$	$\exp(-\phi t^{\gamma})$
$f_a(t)$	$\phi\exp(-\phi t)$	$\dfrac{\alpha}{\beta}(1+\dfrac{t}{\beta})^{-\alpha-1}$	$\phi\gamma t^{\gamma-1}\exp(-\phi t^{\gamma})$
$F_a(t)$	$1-\exp(-\phi t)$	$1-(1+\dfrac{t}{\beta})^{-\alpha}$	$1-\exp(-\phi t^{\gamma})$

is proportional to the hazard rate. Musa (1975) called this proportionality constant a fault reduction factor, denoted by B. The "average basis" is reasonable because the useful applications of software reliability theory are primarily macroscopic in nature.

For a given number of faults ω_0 the total expected number of failures will be $\nu_0 = \omega_0/B$. Denote the cumulative distribution function of time to remove a fault by $G_a(t)$. Since the fault correction rate is the product of the fault reduction factor B and the hazard rate $z_a(t)$, we have

$$G_a(t) = 1 - \exp\left[-B\int_0^t z_a(x)\,dx\right]. \qquad (10.52)$$

The exact expression for the distribution of $M(t)$ is difficult to obtain, but it may be approximated by the Poisson distribution:

$$P[M(t) = m] = \frac{[\nu_0 G_a(t)]^m}{m!}\exp[-\nu_0 G_a(t)], \quad m = 0, 1, \cdots. \qquad (10.53)$$

TABLE 10.5
Derived relationships for binomial-type and Poisson-type models of exponential class

Random quantities	Type (failure quantity distribution)	
	Binomial	**Poisson**
Failures experienced		
$P[M(t) = m]$	$\binom{u_0}{m}[1 - \exp(-\phi t)]^m \exp(-\phi t)^{u_0-m}$	$\dfrac{\{\omega_0[1 - \exp(-\phi t)]\}^m}{m!}\exp\{-\omega_0[1 - \exp(-\phi t)]\}$
$\mu(t)$	$u_0[1 - \exp(-\phi t)]$	$\omega_0[1 - \exp(-\phi t)]$
$\mathrm{var}[M(t)]$	$u_0[1 - \exp(-\phi t)]\exp(-\phi t)$	$\omega_0[1 - \exp(-\phi t)]$
Failures remaining		
$P[Q(t) = q]$	$\binom{u_0}{q}[1 - \exp(-\phi)]^{u_0-q}[\exp(-\phi t)]^q$	$\dfrac{[\omega_0 \exp(-\phi t)]^q}{q!}\exp[-\omega_0 \exp(-\phi t)]$
$\nu(t)$	$u_0 \exp(-\phi t)$	$\omega_0 \exp(-\phi t)$
$\mathrm{var}[Q(t)]$	$u_0 \exp(-\phi t)[1 - \exp(-\phi t)]$	$\omega_0 \exp(-\phi t)$
Failure time		
$P[T_i \leqslant t]$	$\displaystyle\sum_{j=i}^{u_0}\binom{u_0}{j}[1 - \exp(-\phi t)]^j[\exp(-\phi t)]^{u_0-j}$	$\displaystyle\sum_{j=i}^{\infty}\dfrac{\{\omega_0[1 - \exp(-\phi t)]\}^j}{j!}\exp\{-\omega_0[1 - \exp(-\phi t)]\}$
Program hazard rate		
$z(t_i\,\|\,t_{i-1})$	$(u_0 - i + 1)\phi$	$\omega_0\phi\,\exp[-\phi(t_{i-1} + t_i')]$
Reliability		
$R(t_i\,\|\,t_{i-1})$	$\exp[-(u_0 - i + 1)\phi t_i]$	$\exp\{-\omega_0\{\exp(-\phi t_{i-1}) - \exp[-\phi(t_{i-1} + t_i')]\}\}$
Failure intensity		
$\lambda(t)$	$u_0\phi\,\exp(-\phi t)$	$\omega_0\phi\,\exp(-\phi t)$

The mean value function is given by

$$\mu(t) = \nu_0 G_a(t) \tag{10.54}$$

and the failure intensity function is

$$\lambda(t) = \nu_0 g_a(t) , \tag{10.55}$$

where $g_a(t)$ is the probability density function associated with $G_a(t)$. The program hazard rate is then given by

$$z(t_i'|\ t_{i-1}) = \nu_0 g_a(t_{i-1} + t_i') . \tag{10.56}$$

Since the actual repair process occurs at times of failure, the Poisson-type model would not tend to fit as well as the binomial-type. However, the effectiveness of the repair action is often imperfect, and the degree of imperfection varies randomly from repair to repair. The Poisson-type model offers the promise of approximating reality more closely because of its capability for handling imperfect repair.

10.7 SUMMARY

We have discussed a large group of existing software reliability models using Markov processes. The generalized approach is intended to help unify the field, highlight relationships among the models, suggest possible new models, and make comparisons among the models.

PROBLEMS

10.1 Show that the distribution of $M(t)$ is given by Equation (10.5).

10.2 Solve the differential equations given in Equation (10.24) to show that $M(t)$ is distributed as the binomial given in Equation (10.25).

10.3 Show that the conditional distribution of T_i given $T_{i-1} = t_{i-1}$ for binomial-type models is given by Equation (10.37).

ELEVEN

DESCRIPTIONS OF SPECIFIC MODELS

We have given a unified treatment of a large group of models and developed many general relationships in Chapter 10. Now we will look at specific models, often using particular instances of the general relationships. Relationships of the failure intensity with respect to time and the expected number of failures experienced will be developed for each of the model groups. They are summarized in Table 11.1. Some models are simpler in one form and some in the other. Also, one form may be superior in providing a physical feel for an essential characteristic of the model. For example, finite failures models, when expressed in time, usually yield visible per-fault distributions. We will look first at finite failures and then at infinite failures models.

11.1 FINITE FAILURES CATEGORY MODELS

Finite failures category models have a number of failures experienced in infinite time that can be and usually is limited. Most published models fall in this category. The fault concept is often useful for developing finite failures category models because of the physical reality of defects in programs. The models are classified into types depending on how the failure quantity distribution is specified. Poisson and binomial are the most important types. Binomial-type models have a deterministic number of faults and failures, and one fault is removed for each failure. Poisson-type models have a random number of failures, and the number of faults removed for each failure is a random variable. Within each type we will divide the models into classes based on the functional form of the failure intensity in terms of time.

11.1.1 Binomial-Type Models

Binomial-type models assume that there is a fixed number u_0 of faults remaining in the program at $t = 0$. Each fault will generate a failure according to its own

TABLE 11.1
Functional relationships for failure intensity with respect to time t and expected number of failures experienced μ (ξ_0, ξ_1, ξ_2, ϕ_0, ϕ_1, ϕ_2 are constants)

Finite failures category (all types)

Class	$\lambda(t)$	$\lambda(\mu)$
Exponential	$\xi_0 \exp(-\xi_1 t)$	$\phi_0(\phi_1 - \mu)$
Weibull	$\xi_0 t^{\xi_2-1} \exp(-\xi_1 t^{\xi_2})$	$\phi_0 \left[-\ln\left[1 - \dfrac{\mu}{\phi_1}\right]\right]^{\phi_2} (\phi_1 - \mu)$
Pareto	$\xi_0(\xi_1 + t)^{-\xi_2}$	$\phi_0(\phi_1 - \mu)^{\phi_2}$
Gamma	$\xi_0 t \exp(-\xi_1 t)$	

Infinite failures category (all types)

Family	$\lambda(t)$	$\lambda(\mu)$
Geometric	$\xi_0(\xi_1 + t)^{-1}$	$\phi_0 \exp(\phi_1 \mu)$
Inverse linear	$\xi_0(\xi_1 + t)^{-1/2}$	$\dfrac{1}{\phi_0 + \phi_1 \mu}$
Inverse polynomial (2nd degree)	$\dfrac{\xi_0}{\sqrt{t^2 + \xi_1}} \left[\sqrt[3]{t + (t^2 + \xi_1)^{1/2}} - \sqrt[3]{t - (t^2 + \xi_1)^{1/2}} \right]$	$\dfrac{1}{\phi_0 + \phi_1 \mu^2}$
Power	$\xi_0 \xi_1 t^{\xi_1-1}$	$\phi_0 \mu^{\phi_1}$

hazard rate $z_a(t)$. When the failure occurs, the fault is removed. The hazard rates for the different faults are identical functions of time. The number of faults removed by time t is the same as the number of failures experienced by time t.

The distribution of the number of failures experienced by time t, denoted by $M(t)$, is given by the binomial distribution of Equation (10.25). The program hazard rate of the ith failure interval T_i' conditional on the last failure time $T_{i-1} = t_{i-1}$ is given by (see Chapter 10)

$$z(t_i' \mid t_{i-1}) = (u_0 - i + 1)z_a(t_{i-1} + t_i').$$ (11.1)

Hence, the binomial-type models have discontinuous hazard rates whose discontinuities occur at each failure. The heights of the discontinuities are $z_a(t)$. Note that $u_0 - i + 1$ represents the number of faults remaining.

It was shown in Chapter 10 that the expected number of failures by time t (or the mean value function) is given by

$$E[M(t)] = \mu(t) = u_0 F_a(t) ,$$ (11.2)

where $F_a(t)$ represents the cumulative distribution function corresponding to the per-fault hazard rate $z_a(t)$. Taking the derivative of Equation (11.2) yields the failure intensity function

$$\lambda(t) = u_0 f_a(t) ,\tag{11.3}$$

where $f_a(t)$ is the per-fault probability density function. From Equation (11.2) we have

$$t = F_a^{-1}\left(\frac{\mu}{u_0}\right).\tag{11.4}$$

Substituting Equation (11.4) into Equation (11.3) yields the functional relationship of the failure intensity function with the mean value function

$$\lambda(\mu) = u_0 f_a\left[F_a^{-1}\left(\frac{\mu}{u_0}\right)\right].\tag{11.5}$$

The models of this type are further classified by the choice for $z_a(t)$ into several classes.

EXPONENTIAL CLASS. The Jelinski-Moranda model (1972) and the Shooman model (1972) are both of the exponential class. We can show that the per-fault hazard rate is a constant, denoted by ϕ, that is,

$$z_a(t) = \phi .\tag{11.6}$$

If we substitute Equation (11.6) into Equation (11.1), we obtain the program hazard rate for the ith interval

$$z(t_i' | t_{i-1}) = (u_0 - i + 1)\phi,\tag{11.7}$$

which is a function of the remaining faults, $u_0 - i + 1$, alone. Therefore, all the discontinuities in the hazard rate are the same size, ϕ. There is no change in the program hazard rate between failures. Figure 11.1 illustrates typical behavior of the program hazard rate for a binomial-type exponential-class model.

Applying Equations (9.2) and (9.3) to Equation (11.6) and substituting the result into Equation (11.3) yields

$$\lambda(t) = u_0 \phi \exp(-\phi t).\tag{11.8}$$

Similarly, apply Equations (9.1), (9.2), and (9.3) to Equation (11.6) and substitute the result into Equation (11.5). We obtain the failure intensity in terms of the mean value function as

$$\lambda(\mu) = \phi(u_0 - \mu),\tag{11.9}$$

which is a linear function of μ.

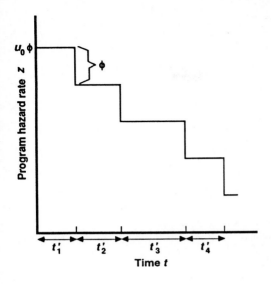

FIGURE 11.1
Program hazard rate for a binomial-type exponential-class model.

Shooman characterized the hazard rate $z(t')$ in terms of the inherent fault density of the program ω_I, the proportion of unique instructions processed β_1, a bulk constant β_2, and the faults corrected per instruction per unit time $\beta_3(t)$. The bulk constant represents the proportion of faults that cause failures. Thus

$$z(t') = \left[\omega_I - \int_0^{t'} \beta_3(x)\,dx\right]\beta_1\beta_2 . \tag{11.10}$$

WEIBULL CLASS. The per-fault hazard rate for a Weibull-class model may be shown to be $z_a(t) = \phi\gamma t^{\gamma-1}$, where $\gamma > 0$. Here the program hazard rate becomes

$$z(t_i'|\,t_{i-1}) = (u_0 - i + 1)\phi\gamma(t_{i-1} + t_i')^{\gamma-1} , \tag{11.11}$$

which has discontinuities of height $z_a(t)$ at each failure. As discussed in Appendix B, the per-fault hazard rate $z_a(t)$ may be a decreasing, constant, or increasing function of t, depending on the value of the shape parameter γ. That is, it is decreasing for $0 < \gamma < 1$, constant for $\gamma = 1$, and increasing for $\gamma > 1$. A typical behavior of the program hazard rate for a Weibull-class model with $0 < \gamma < 1$ is illustrated in Figure 11.2. The functional forms of $\lambda(t)$ and $\lambda(\mu)$ can be easily described, using an approach similar to that taken for the exponential class (see Problem 11.1). Wagoner (1973) suggested a Weibull model of the form of Equation (11.11), where u_0 was assumed to be known.

The Schick-Wolverton model (1973) may be interpreted as having a per-fault hazard rate of $z_a(t) = 2\phi t$. This is a special case of the Weibull class with $\gamma = 2$. The program hazard rate for this model becomes

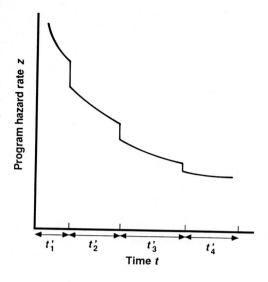

FIGURE 11.2
**Program hazard rate for a
binomial-type Weibull-class
model with $0 < \gamma < 1$.**

$$z(t_i'\mid t_{i-1}) = 2(u_0 - i + 1)\phi(t_{i-1} + t_i') ,\qquad (11.12)$$

which is illustrated in Figure 11.3.

C1 CLASS. Schick and Wolverton (1978) also proposed a more general model. It can be shown that the per-fault hazard rate for this model is a parabolic instead of a linear function in t, that is, $z_a(t) = (-\beta_1 t^2 + \beta_2 t + \beta_3)\phi$. Although this model

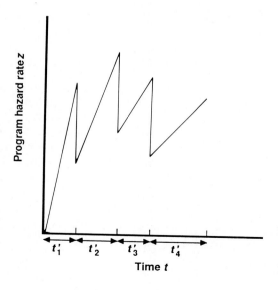

FIGURE 11.3
**Program hazard rate for a
binomial-type Weibull-class
model with $\gamma = 2$.**

is similar to those of the Weibull class, it is not a member of that class. The program hazard rate is given by

$$z(t_i' \mid t_{i-1}) = (u_0 - i + 1)\phi\left[-\beta_1(t_{i-1} + t_i')^2 + \beta_2(t_{i-1} + t_i') + \beta_3\right]. \quad (11.13)$$

This hazard rate does not represent a known probability distribution. Hence we have simply named it "C1."

Note that $\lambda(t)$ may be found, but $\lambda(\mu)$ will not be obtained explicitly in this case. This model is not included in Table 11.1 since it does not appear to have practical applicability. It is more complex than the other models, having more parameters. There is no evidence of superior properties that would justify the complexity.

PARETO CLASS. Littlewood (1981) proposed a differential model to account for the possibility that some faults are more likely to occur than others. These tend to be repaired first. The reduction in the program hazard rate is greater for the repair of more likely faults. Each fault is viewed as causing a failure at a time that is distributed exponentially, independently of the other faults. The hazard rate associated with each fault is a random variable Z_a. The random variable representing the hazard rate Z_i for the ith failure interval is a sum of hazard rates Z_a. Thus

$$Z_i = \sum_{a=1}^{u_0-i+1} Z_a. \quad (11.14)$$

Here u_0 represents the total number of inherent faults in the software. Since $i - 1$ represents the number of faults detected and corrected up to the present, $u_0 - i + 1$ is the number of faults remaining. The probability distributions of the hazard rates associated with the individual faults before any debugging are assumed to be identical and independent gamma distributions. The density function is given by

$$f_a(z) = \frac{\beta_1^{\beta_2} z^{\beta_2-1} \exp(-\beta_1 z)}{\Gamma(\beta_2)}, \quad z > 0. \quad (11.15)$$

Using Bayes' theorem, we can show that for this model the per-fault hazard rate is that of a Pareto distribution, that is, $z_a(t) = \beta_2/(t + \beta_1)$. Hence, from Equation (11.1), the program hazard rate is

$$z(t_i' \mid t_{i-1}) = \frac{(u_0 - i + 1)\beta_2}{t_{i-1} + t_i' + \beta_1}. \quad (11.16)$$

Note that there are discontinuities of height $z_a(t)$ at each failure. A typical behavior of the program hazard rate is illustrated in Figure 11.4. The discontinuities decrease in height from failure to failure because the hazard rate is decreasing with t. This corresponds to the supposition noted previously that the removal of faults that occur frequently (and hence early) in execution causes the greatest changes in

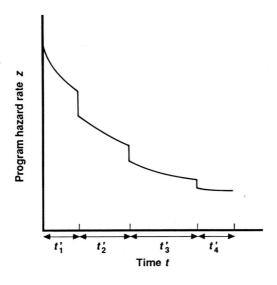

FIGURE 11.4
Program hazard rate for a binomial-type Pareto-class model.

the program hazard rate. Removal of infrequently occurring faults has much less effect. There is also a decreasing trend in the program hazard rate between failures. This latter property expresses the increased reliability you expect as a program operates without failure. The foregoing behavior is not restricted to the Pareto class of models. It holds for any decreasing per-fault hazard rate (for example, Weibull with $\gamma < 1$). Thus there are other possibilities besides the Pareto distribution for characterizing unequal contributions of faults to the program hazard rate and increased reliability as a program operates without failure. The functional forms of $\lambda(t)$ and $\lambda(\mu)$ can be easily described, using an approach similar to that taken for the exponential class (see Problem 11.2).

It is interesting to note (see Table 11.1) that the Pareto class is, in the sense of failure intensity, the generalization of three other classes or families. We can see this by comparing the failure intensity functions with respect to expected failures μ. Note that the exponential class is a subset of the Pareto class with $\phi_2 = 1$. Alternatively, if $\beta_1 \to \infty$ and $\beta_2 \to \infty$ such that β_2/β_1 is constant, Equation (11.16) reduces to the constant hazard rate of the exponential class. The Pareto class is related to the power family by translation in the amount ϕ_1. This is then followed by reflection about the axis $\mu = \phi_1$, which can be viewed as imposing the constraint that the total expected failures must be finite. Finally, if we compare the failure intensities with respect to time t we will see that the geometric family is a special case of the Pareto class with $\xi_2 = 1$. You could conceivably reduce the number of classes or families because of the general characteristics of the Pareto class. However, this was not done because the less general classes have the virtue of simplicity. Also, the exponential class is additionally a subset of the Weibull class.

11.1.2 Poisson-Type Models

For the Poisson-type models there is not a fixed number u_0 of total faults as with the binomial-type models. Total faults is a random variable with mean ω_0. The parameter ω_0 in the Poisson-type models is not restricted to an integer number of faults (although realizations of the random variable "number of faults" are, of course, integers).

The distribution of the number of failures experienced by time t is given by the Poisson distribution of Equation (10.44). Note that the mean value function is

$$\mu(t) = \omega_0 F_a(t). \tag{11.17}$$

The intensity function can be obtained by differentiating $\mu(t)$ as

$$\lambda(t) = \omega_0 f_a(t). \tag{11.18}$$

Also, the program hazard rate of T_i' conditional on $T_{i-1} = t_{i-1}$ can be shown (see Chapter 10) to be

$$z(t_i' \mid t_{i-1}) = \omega_0 f_a(t_{i-1} + t_i') . \tag{11.19}$$

As we can see from Equation (11.19), the program hazard rate in the Poisson-type models does not have discontinuities at each failure.

We must define a per-fault failure time distribution for the Poisson-type models, just as for the binomial-type models. Likely possibilities are the same as for binomial-type models: exponential, Weibull, and Pareto classes. Two of these classes include existing models and are discussed below.

EXPONENTIAL CLASS. The basic execution time model of Musa (1975) is best characterized as a Poisson-type model of the exponential class, although it was not originally described as such. Goel and Okumoto (1979b) later specifically addressed this kind of model and described it in terms of a nonhomogeneous Poisson process. Since this is an execution time model, its execution time component will be discussed in terms of execution time τ.

These models assume that time to failure of an individual fault has an exponential distribution, that is, $f_a(\tau) = \phi \exp(-\phi\tau)$. The per-fault hazard rate is constant at ϕ, that is, $z_a(\tau) = \phi$. Musa described ϕ, using additional elements, as

$$\phi = fK, \tag{11.20}$$

where f is the linear execution frequency of the program or the ratio of average instruction rate to program size in object instructions. Note that K is the fault exposure ratio. It accounts for the effects of program dynamic structure and data dependency on the hazard rate.

For a given fault reduction factor B, we can obtain the expected number of failures experienced by τ for the basic execution time model from Equations (10.52) and (10.54) as

$$\mu(\tau) = \nu_0[1 - \exp(-\phi B\tau)] . \tag{11.21}$$

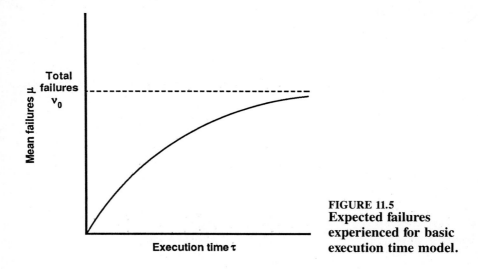

FIGURE 11.5
Expected failures
experienced for basic
execution time model.

This relationship is illustrated in Figure 11.5. Also, we can find the failure intensity by differentiating Equation (11.21) to yield

$$\lambda(\tau) = \nu_0 \phi B \exp(-\phi B \tau). \tag{11.22}$$

This is an exponentially decaying function of τ with the initial failure intensity $\lambda_0 = \nu_0 \phi B$. The relationship is illustrated in Figure 11.6.

Alternatively, we may derive these models from the postulate (noted in Chapter 2) that the failure intensity function has a constant slope with respect to

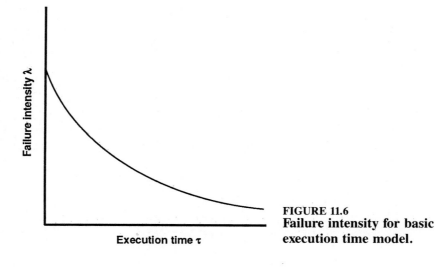

FIGURE 11.6
Failure intensity for basic
execution time model.

average failures experienced. We write

$$\lambda(\mu) = \phi B (\nu_0 - \mu) \tag{11.23}$$

or

$$\lambda(\tau) = \phi B \left[\nu_0 - \mu(\tau)\right] . \tag{11.24}$$

Since $\lambda(\tau)$ is the derivative of $\mu(\tau)$ we have

$$\frac{d\mu(\tau)}{d\tau} + \phi B \mu(\tau) = \phi B \nu_0 . \tag{11.25}$$

This differential equation has the solution given by Equation (11.21).

Expressions for various useful quantities can be found by substituting Equations (11.21) and (11.22) into appropriate equations derived in Section 10.2. Specifically, substituting Equation (11.21) into Equation (10.13) gives the cumulative probability distribution of time to the ith failure

$$P[T_i \leqslant \tau] = \exp\left\{-\nu_0[1 - \exp(-\phi B\tau)]\right\} \sum_{j=i}^{\infty} \frac{\nu_0^j [1 - \exp(-\phi B\tau)]^j}{j!} . \tag{11.26}$$

Substituting Equation (11.21) into Equation (10.16) yields the program reliability after the $(i - 1)$th failure

$$R(\tau_i' | \tau_{i-1}) = \exp\{ - [\nu_0 \exp(-\phi B\tau_{i-1})] [1 - \exp(-\phi B\tau_i')]\} \tag{11.27}$$

and substitution of Equation (11.22) into Equation (10.18) yields the program hazard rate

$$z(\tau_i' | \tau_{i-1}) = \nu_0 \phi \exp(-\phi B\tau_{i-1}) \exp(-\phi B\tau_i') . \tag{11.28}$$

If a failure intensity objective λ_F has been set for the program, then the additional number of failures that must be experienced to meet this objective can be derived from Equation (11.23) as

$$\Delta\mu = \frac{\nu_0}{\lambda_0} (\lambda - \lambda_F) . \tag{11.29}$$

Similarly, using Equation (11.22), the additional execution time is

$$\Delta\tau = \frac{\nu_0}{\lambda_0} \ln\left[\frac{\lambda}{\lambda_F}\right] . \tag{11.30}$$

The model has a calendar time component, which will be covered in Chapter 14.

There are two interesting models that are not developed as finite failures category models of the exponential type but turn out to have equivalent failure intensities at fixed intervals. These are the discrete-time nonhomogeneous Poisson process model of Schneidewind (1975) and the geometric Poisson model of Moranda (1975). Both models divide time into fixed intervals of length T. For both, the hazard rate is constant during the interval and changes at its end. The models thus represent piecewise homogeneous Poisson processes. Both models can be described by

$$\lambda(t) = \alpha \exp\left[- \theta \left\lfloor \frac{t}{T} \right\rfloor\right],$$ (11.31)

where $\lfloor\ \rfloor$ indicate "next lowest integer." Note that the set of values of $\lambda(t)$ for successive intervals of time form a geometric progression, since $\exp(-\theta)$ is a constant. Hence the name "geometric Poisson model."

GAMMA CLASS. The model of Yamada, Ohba, and Osaki (1983) assumes that time to failure of an individual fault follows a gamma distribution with a shape parameter of 2, that is,

$$f_a(t) = \phi^2 t \exp(- \phi t).$$ (11.32)

The failure intensity function is obtained from Equation (11.18) as

$$\lambda(t) = \omega_0 \phi^2 t \exp(- \phi t) .$$ (11.33)

It can be shown that both Equations (11.32) and (11.33) initially increase from $t = 0$ up to $t = 1/\phi$ and then gradually decrease, approaching zero (see Figure 11.7). Since the per-fault cumulative distribution function is the integral of Equation (11.32), it will be S-shaped. It is given by

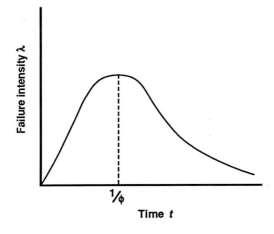

FIGURE 11.7
Failure intensity for a gamma-class Poisson-type model.

$$F_a(t) = 1 - (1 + \phi t) \exp(-\phi t). \tag{11.34}$$

Hence the mean value function given by Equation (11.17) will also be S-shaped.

11.2 INFINITE FAILURES CATEGORY MODELS

For infinite failures category models the number of failures in infinite time is unbounded. We can classify the models by type and family. We will review four models in this category, the second one of which can be a finite failures category model under certain conditions.

11.2.1 Poisson-Type Models

GEOMETRIC FAMILY: MUSA-OKUMOTO LOGARITHMIC POISSON EXECUTION TIME MODEL. The logarithmic Poisson execution time model [Musa and Okumoto (1984b)] has an intensity function that decreases exponentially with expected failures experienced:

$$\lambda(\tau) = \lambda_0 \exp[-\theta\mu(\tau)]. \tag{11.35}$$

Note that λ_0 denotes the initial failure intensity and θ, the failure intensity decay parameter, where $\theta > 0$. The quantity μ represents the expected number of failures. Again, the execution time component of this model will be described in terms of execution time τ.

Expressions for $\lambda(\tau)$ and $\mu(\tau)$ can be derived as follows. Since $\lambda(\tau)$ is the derivative of $\mu(\tau)$, we get the differential equation:

$$\frac{d\mu(\tau)}{d\tau} = \lambda_0 \exp[-\theta\mu(\tau)] \tag{11.36}$$

or

$$\frac{d\mu(\tau)}{d\tau} \exp[\theta\mu(\tau)] = \lambda_0. \tag{11.37}$$

Noting that

$$\frac{d \exp[\theta\mu(\tau)]}{d\tau} = \theta \frac{d\mu(\tau)}{d\tau} \exp[\theta\mu(\tau)], \tag{11.38}$$

we obtain from Equation (11.37)

$$\frac{d \exp[\theta\mu(\tau)]}{d\tau} = \lambda_0\theta. \tag{11.39}$$

Integrating Equation (11.39) yields

$$\exp[\theta\mu(\tau)] = \lambda_0\theta\tau + C \ . \tag{11.40}$$

where C is the constant of integration. Since $\mu(0) = 0$, we get $C = 1$. Hence, the mean value function is obtained as

$$\mu(\tau) = \frac{1}{\theta} \ln (\lambda_0\theta\tau + 1) \ , \tag{11.41}$$

which is a logarithmic function of τ. Furthermore, from the definition of $\lambda(\tau)$ the failure intensity function is given by

$$\lambda(\tau) = \frac{\lambda_0}{\lambda_0\theta\tau + 1} \ , \tag{11.42}$$

which is an inverse linear function of τ. This relationship is illustrated in Figure 11.8.

Expressions for various useful quantities can be found by substituting Equations (11.41) and (11.42) into appropriate equations derived in Section 10.2. Specifically, substituting Equation (11.41) into Equation (10.13) gives the cumulative probability distribution of time to failure

$$P[T_i \leqslant \tau] = (\lambda_0\theta\tau + 1)^{-\frac{1}{\theta}} \sum_{j=i}^{\infty} \frac{\ln (\lambda_0\theta\tau + 1)^j}{\theta^j \, j!} \ . \tag{11.43}$$

Substituting Equation (11.41) into Equation (10.16) yields the program reliability

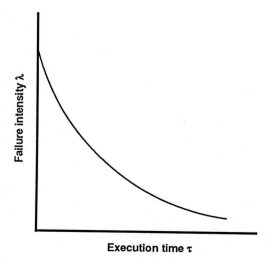

FIGURE 11.8
Failure intensity for the logarithmic Poisson model.

$$R\left(\tau_i'|\ \tau_{i-1}\right) = \left[\frac{\lambda_0\theta\tau_{i-1} + 1}{\lambda_0\theta(\tau_{i-1} + \tau_i') + 1}\right]^{1/\theta}. \tag{11.44}$$

Substitution of Equation (11.42) into Equation (10.18) yields the program hazard rate

$$z\left(\tau_i'|\ \tau_{i-1}\right) = \frac{\lambda_0}{\lambda_0\theta(\tau_{i-1} + \tau_i') + 1}. \tag{11.45}$$

The mean time to failure (MTTF) is defined only for $\theta < 1$, but θ generally satisfies this constraint for actual projects. It can be determined by substituting Equation (11.44) in Equation (9.4) and integrating. We obtain

$$\Theta\left[\tau_{i-1}\right] = \frac{\theta}{1 - \theta}\left[\lambda_0\ \theta\tau_{i-1} + 1\right]^{1 - \frac{1}{\theta}}. \tag{11.46}$$

If a failure intensity objective λ_F has been set for the program, then we can derive $\Delta\mu$ and $\Delta\tau$ required to meet the objective from Equation (11.42) as

$$\Delta\mu = \frac{1}{\theta}\ \ln\left[\frac{\lambda}{\lambda_F}\right] \tag{11.47}$$

and

$$\Delta\tau = \frac{1}{\theta}\ \left[\frac{1}{\lambda_F} - \frac{1}{\lambda}\right]. \tag{11.48}$$

The model has a calendar time component, which will be covered in Chapter 14.

The total number of failures for this model is infinite. It is very likely that the number of inherent faults in a program is finite. It would be unlikely for a development team to introduce an infinite number of inherent faults. The model should be able to accommodate simultaneously an infinite number of failures and a finite number of faults. We will show in Section 11.3 that we can do this by assuming a time-varying fault reduction factor of a specific form.

It would be very useful if we could relate the execution time component parameters of the model to characteristics of the software product, the development process, and the execution environment. This would enable prediction of these parameters before execution. Initial failure intensity may be a function of linear execution frequency f, number of inherent faults ω_0, and a "constant" analogous to the fault exposure ratio K for the basic model. The failure intensity decay rate θ could be a function of the initial (at $\tau = 0$) fault reduction factor, the number of inherent faults, and the shape of the failure intensity curve with respect to faults remaining. This issue is addressed in detail in Section 11.3.

The problem of parameter prediction for the logarithmic Poisson model will probably be more difficult than that for the basic model. We cannot accurately assess the degree of difficulty now. It will be seen in Section 11.3 that the prediction of initial failure intensity for the logarithmic Poisson model involves a power of the number of inherent faults. Hence, this prediction is likely to be less accurate. Thus, the basic model is likely to be superior for initial, approximate determination of behavior.

POWER FAMILY: WEIBULL PROCESS MODEL. Crow (1974), observing a failure intensity trend for hardware reported by Duane (1964), noted that the behavior could be represented by a Weibull process. The Weibull process is a nonhomogeneous Poisson process with the failure intensity function having the same form as the Weibull hazard rate:

$$\lambda(t) = \beta_1 \beta_2 t^{\beta_2 - 1} \tag{11.49}$$

The model was originally developed for the reliability estimation of hardware systems during development testing. However, it may also be applied to software reliability because of the decreasing failure intensity for $\beta_2 < 1$. This relationship is illustrated in Figure 11.9.

Note that the mean value function of this model is

$$\mu(t) = \beta_1 t^{\beta_2}. \tag{11.50}$$

We can easily show by combining Equations (11.49) and (11.50) that the failure intensity is a power function of the mean value function, that is,

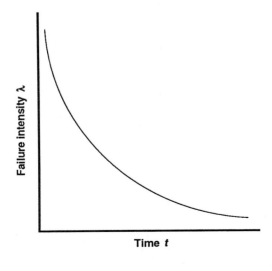

FIGURE 11.9
Failure intensity for a Weibull process model.

$$\lambda(\mu) = \beta_3 \mu^{\beta_4} .\tag{11.51}$$

In other words, the log-failure intensity is a linear function of the log-mean value function.

11.2.2 Other Types

LITTLEWOOD-VERRALL GENERAL MODEL (VARIOUS TYPES AND FAMILIES). Let $f(t_i')$ be the probability density function of T_i'. Littlewood and Verrall (1973) proposed a model in which T_i' has an exponential distribution conditional on the hazard rate, that is,

$$f(t_i'|z_i) = z_i \exp(-z_i t_i') .\tag{11.52}$$

The hazard rate itself is assumed to be a random variable which has a gamma distribution with the scale and shape parameters given by $\xi(i)$ and α, respectively. In other words, if we denote by $g(z_i)$ the probability density function of the hazard rate, then we have

$$g(z_i) = \frac{\xi(i)[\xi(i)z_i]^{\alpha-1} \exp[-\xi(i)z_i]}{\Gamma(\alpha)} .\tag{11.53}$$

Therefore, the unconditional distribution of T_i' is

$$f(t_i') = \int_0^\infty f(t_i'|z_i)g(z_i)dz_i$$

$$= \alpha \left[\frac{\xi(i)}{t_i' + \xi(i)} \right]^\alpha \frac{1}{t_i' + \xi(i)} ,\tag{11.54}$$

which is a Pareto distribution. The mean time to failure between the $(i-1)$th and ith failures, denoted by $\Theta(i)$, is

$$\Theta(i) = E[T_i']$$

$$= \frac{\xi(i)}{\alpha} .\tag{11.55}$$

We have, for the resulting program hazard rate,

$$z(t_i') = \frac{\alpha}{t_i' + \xi(i)} .\tag{11.56}$$

This relationship is illustrated in Figure 11.10.

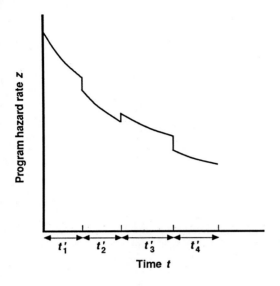

FIGURE 11.10
Program hazard rate for
Littlewood-Verrall general model.

The program hazard rate decreases continuously with t'_i and experiences discontinuities of various heights at each failure. The heights usually but not necessarily decrease with failures experienced. Littlewood and Verrall contend that the decrease in hazard rate between failures reflects the increasing confidence we have that the hazard rate is lower as long as the program runs without failures. Since we can choose the reliability growth function $\xi(i)$ arbitrarily, the model is general and flexible. However, it is also very complex and more difficult to apply than many of the others.

The model can fall in different classifications depending on the form of the reliability growth function $\xi(i)$. Two suggested by Littlewood and Verrall are:

$$\xi(i) = \beta_0 + \beta_1 i, \tag{11.57}$$

and

$$\xi(i) = \beta_0 + \beta_1 i^2. \tag{11.58}$$

For both cases there is no restriction on i. Hence infinite failures can be experienced. The families are inverse linear and inverse polynomial (2nd degree), respectively.

Values of parameters for a given growth function and comparisons determining which growth function is best are established by testing goodness of fit to the data. Littlewood and Verrall use the Cramer-von Mises statistic. This computation requires repeated sorting of the data and minimization of the statistic over a multidimensional surface. These calculations are unfortunately very expensive in computer time. Work by Iannino (1979) indicates that maximum likelihood estimation of parameters rather than a goodness of fit approach may reduce the difference in computation somewhat.

The functional forms of $\lambda(t)$ and $\lambda(\mu)$ for Equation (11.57) can be derived as follows. Without loss of generality, we assume $\alpha = 1$. From Equations (11.55) and (11.57), the mean time to failure for the inverse linear family is a linear function of i, that is,

$$\Theta(i) = \beta_0 + \beta_1 i. \tag{11.59}$$

To obtain expressions for $\lambda(t)$ and $\mu(t)$ for each family of models we use the following approximations:

$$\Theta(i) \approx \frac{1}{\lambda(t)} , \tag{11.60}$$

and

$$i \approx \mu(t). \tag{11.61}$$

Substituting Equations (11.60) and (11.61) into Equation (11.59) yields

$$\frac{1}{\lambda(t)} = \beta_0 + \beta_1 \mu(t). \tag{11.62}$$

Further substitution of Equation (9.6) into Equation (11.62) yields the differential equation

$$[\beta_0 + \beta_1 \mu(t)]d\mu(t) = dt. \tag{11.63}$$

Integrating both sides, we obtain

$$\beta_0 \mu(t) + \frac{\beta_1}{2} [\mu(t)]^2 = t + C, \tag{11.64}$$

where C is the constant of integration. Equation (11.64) is a quadratic function of $\mu(t)$ and hence it can be solved as

$$\mu(t) = \frac{1}{\beta_1} \left[-\beta_0 \pm \sqrt{\beta_0^2 + 2\beta_1(t + C)} \right]. \tag{11.65}$$

Noting that $\mu(t)$ is a nonnegative function and $\mu(0) = 0$, we have $C = 0$. Hence, the mean value function is given by

$$\mu(t) = \frac{1}{\beta_1} \left[-\beta_0 + \sqrt{\beta_0^2 + 2\beta_1 t} \right]. \tag{11.66}$$

We obtain the failure intensity by differentiating $\mu(t)$ with respect to t to yield

$$\lambda(t) = \frac{1}{\sqrt{\beta_0^2 + 2\beta_1 t}}. \tag{11.67}$$

Also, from Equation (11.62) we have

$$\lambda(\mu) = \frac{1}{\beta_0 + \beta_1 \mu}. \tag{11.68}$$

This is an inverse linear function of μ and hence this is a model of the inverse linear family. Note that the functional forms of the failure intensity and mean value function for the inverse polynomial family (2nd degree) can be easily found, using the similar approach (see Problem 11.3).

Musa (1979a) has suggested the use of a rational function for $\xi(i)$, based on the concept that the parameter should be inversely related to the number of failures remaining. The suggested function was

$$\xi(i) = \frac{\nu_0 \alpha}{\lambda_0(\nu_0 - i)}. \tag{11.69}$$

The quantity ν_0 is the number of failures expected in infinite time, λ_0 is the initial failure intensity, α is the parameter of the gamma distribution, and i is the index number of the failure. Note that this model belongs to the finite failures category.

Keiller et al. (1983) investigated a model similar to the general model with the exception that reliability growth is induced via the shape parameter, rather than the scale parameter as in Equation (11.53). We can find the resulting expressions for the unconditional distribution of T'_i, $\Theta(i)$, and program hazard rate by simply substituting a parametric family $\alpha(i)$ for α and β_1 for $\xi(i)$ into Equations (11.54), (11.55), and (11.56), respectively. Although the function $\alpha(i)$ may be chosen arbitrarily as with $\xi(i)$ of the general model, a linear function was suggested, that is,

$$\alpha(i) = \beta_2 + \beta_3 i . \tag{11.70}$$

Note that if we use the approximations (11.60) and (11.61), we get

$$\lambda(\mu) = \frac{\beta_2 + \beta_3 \mu}{\beta_1} . \tag{11.71}$$

We can easily observe from Equation (11.71) that the foregoing model has the same functional form as the exponential class of finite failures category model.

GEOMETRIC DE-EUTROPHICATION MODEL (TYPE T1, GEOMETRIC FAMILY). Moranda (1975) proposed a geometric de-eutrophication model in which the hazard rate decreases, after each failure is corrected, to a fraction k of the rate in

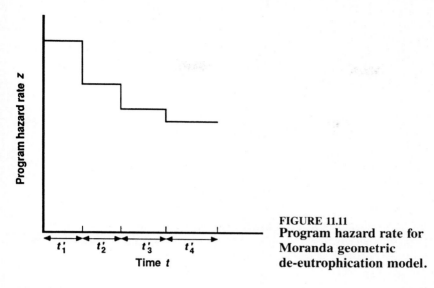

FIGURE 11.11
Program hazard rate for
Moranda geometric
de-eutrophication model.

effect before the failure. This fraction is assumed constant. As a result, the hazard rates form a geometric progression. That is, the program hazard rate for T_i' is given by

$$z(t_i') = z_0 k^{i-1}, \qquad (11.72)$$

where z_0 represents the initial hazard rate and $0 < k < 1$. This relationship is illustrated in Figure 11.11. Moranda claimed that this model alleviates some of the objections to models in which the hazard rate decreases by constant steps (with the implied equality of effect for all faults). Since the hazard rate given in Equation (11.72) is constant with respect to t_i', T_i' follows an exponential distribution whose mean value is given by

$$\Theta(i) = \frac{1}{z_0 k^{i-1}}. \qquad (11.73)$$

The functional forms of $\lambda(t)$ and $\lambda(\mu)$ can be easily obtained using an approach similar to that described for the inverse linear family (see Problem 11.4). Note that the model belongs to the geometric family. The geometric de-eutrophication model and the logarithmic Poisson model have similar failure intensity functions, the former of a stepped nature and the latter continuous.

11.3 DISCUSSION: INTERPRETATION OF MODEL PARAMETERS OF LOGARITHMIC POISSON EXECUTION TIME MODEL

As mentioned previously, we wish to relate the execution time component parameters of the logarithmic Poisson execution time model to characteristics of the

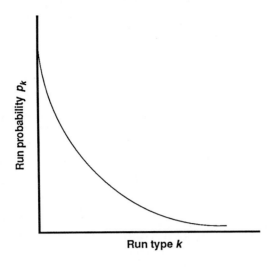

Run type _k_

FIGURE 11.12
Nonuniform operational profile.

software product, the development process, and the execution environment. We would also like to understand how an infinite quantity of failures can arise from a finite quantity of faults ω_0. The following derivation is not a proof but an attempt to provide a heuristic interpretation.

We will start by considering the operational profile of the program being executed. Recall that the operational profile is the set of probabilities of execution for the (finite) set of possible input states of the program. The probabilities may be arranged in order of decreasing size without loss of generality. We now have the situation of Figure 11.12, where the input states are plotted sufficiently close together on the horizontal axis that the operational profile appears as a continuous curve.

Some of the input states will have faults associated with them, and these will lead to failures. When these input states are executed, the potential for reducing the failure intensity through fault repair will depend on the sum of the frequencies of occurrence of the input states of the fault's fail set. On the average, these potential reductions will form a decreasing function with respect to the number of faults removed (or increasing with respect to the number of faults remaining ω). The latter relationship is illustrated in Figure 11.13. We will assume the very general function

$$\frac{d\lambda}{d\omega} = \beta_1 \omega^{\beta_2} , \tag{11.74}$$

where $\beta_2 \geq 0$. This should be capable of expressing a very wide range of possible forms of increasing functions.

Consider a generalization of the fault reduction factor B defined for the basic execution time model. Let

$$B(\tau) = \frac{d\eta(\tau)}{d\mu(\tau)} , \tag{11.75}$$

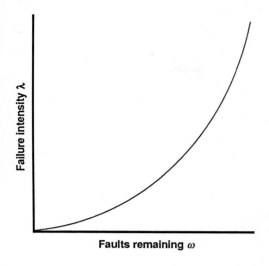

Failure intensity λ

Faults remaining ω

FIGURE 11.13
Behavior of change in failure intensity with respect to faults remaining.

when η is faults repaired and μ is failures experienced. For the logarithmic Poisson model, assume that $B(\tau)$ has the form

$$B(\tau) = B_0 \exp[-\beta_3\mu(\tau)], \qquad (11.76)$$

where B_0 is the initial fault reduction factor, and β_3 is the fault reduction factor decay parameter.

This assumption expresses the concept that repair effectiveness can drop as failures experienced increases. This can occur because:

1. It becomes more and more difficult to find faults. The hardest ones to find tend to remain in the program.

2. Often, for a given failure, the associated fault has only part of its fail set removed. The fraction removed becomes smaller with time, the more difficult repairs usually affecting a smaller part of the fail set.

3. Results of executing the program tend to be more poorly recorded as the program approaches the operational phase and in the operational phase itself. There are probably two reasons for this. First, the amount of recording per failure becomes more and more onerous as failures become less frequent. Second, the average level of experience and motivation of the personnel executing the program may drop, as we will note.

4. The average level of experience and motivation of failure correction personnel may drop, both in terms of overall experience and experience with the particular program. This can result from experienced personnel moving on to other projects during system test and being replaced by less experienced people. These people may feel less of a sense of "ownership" of the code since they didn't create it. This factor reduces net repair effectiveness both

through faults not corrected and a higher rate of new faults spawned during the correction process.

5. When fewer faults remain, the fault correction personnel may be less likely to recognize relationships among them. Hence the discovery of one fault would be less likely to lead to the discovery of others.

Note that the assumption implies that $B \to 0$ as $\tau \to \infty$. If $\beta_3 = 0$ we would have had the case of the basic execution time model (constant B).

We shall now find the form of the failure intensity function. First find the relationship between ω and μ. Note that we can write Equation (11.76) as

$$\frac{d\eta(\tau)}{d\mu(\tau)} = B_0 \exp[-\beta_3\mu(\tau)] . \tag{11.77}$$

Integrating, and noting that $\eta(0) = 0$ and $\mu(0) = 0$, we obtain

$$\eta(\tau) = \frac{B_0}{\beta_3} \{1 - \exp[-\beta_3\mu(\tau)]\} . \tag{11.78}$$

At $\tau = \infty$, $\mu(\tau) = \infty$ and $\eta(\tau) = \omega_0$. Thus

$$\omega_0 = \frac{B_0}{\beta_3} . \tag{11.79}$$

Note that

$$\omega = \omega_0 - \eta . \tag{11.80}$$

Now using Equations (11.79) and (11.80), we have

$$\omega(\tau) = \omega_0 \exp[-\beta_3\mu(\tau)] . \tag{11.81}$$

Note that we must have $\beta_3 > 0$ to have both infinite expected failures and finite expected faults.

Now consider the relationship between λ and ω. Substituting Equation (11.81) into Equation (11.74) we obtain

$$\frac{d\lambda}{d\omega} = \beta_1\omega_0^{\beta_2} \exp[-\beta_2\beta_3\mu(\tau)] . \tag{11.82}$$

Now, using Equations (11.81) and (11.82) we can show that

$$\frac{d\lambda}{d\mu} = -\beta_1\beta_3 \,\omega_0^{\beta_2+1} \,\exp[-(\beta_2 + 1) \,\beta_3 \,\mu(\tau)] . \tag{11.83}$$

Integrating and noting that $\mu(\infty) = \infty$ and $\lambda(\infty) = 0$, we obtain

$$\lambda(\tau) = \frac{\beta_1 \, \omega_0^{\beta_2+1}}{\beta_2+1} \, \exp[- \, (\beta_2 + 1) \, \beta_3 \, \mu(\tau)] \,. \tag{11.84}$$

Now Equation (11.84) has the form of Equation (11.35) with

$$\lambda_0 = \frac{\beta_1 \omega_0^{\beta_2+1}}{\beta_2 + 1} \tag{11.85}$$

and

$$\theta = (\beta_2 + 1) \, \beta_3 \,. \tag{11.86}$$

Consider the failure intensity decay parameter θ. From Equations (11.79) and (11.86) we obtain

$$\theta = \beta_2 \, \frac{B_0}{\omega_0} \,. \tag{11.87}$$

Note that β_2 describes the shape of the failure intensity against faults remaining curve, B_0 is the initial (at $\tau = 0$) fault reduction factor, and ω_0 is the number of inherent faults. It is probably often the case that B_0 is 1 or close to it.

Note from Equation (11.85) that λ_0 is related to ω_0 through the shape parameter β_2 and the scale parameter β_1 of the failure intensity against faults remaining curve. It is likely that β_1 is related to the linear execution frequency and perhaps a proportionality constant that may not vary between projects. If β_2 can be determined (it may be project-independent), the possibility is opened for predictions of reliability in the system engineering phase for the logarithmic Poisson execution time model. Note that if $\beta_2 = 1$, the initial failure intensity reduces to that for the basic model

$$\lambda_0 = \beta_1 \omega_0 \,. \tag{11.88}$$

11.4 SUMMARY

Finite failures models seem to have a natural affinity, from a credibility viewpoint, with situations in which there is a vigorous repair program. On the other hand, it would appear that infinite failures models might have an affinity for the weak repair situation. Note that infinite failures does not necessarily imply infinite faults. A situation of infinite faults appears improbable, since the amount of code is finite. The case of infinite failures is credible for a program executed for infinite time.

PROBLEMS

11.1 Show that the functional forms of $\lambda(t)$ and $\lambda(\mu)$ for a Weibull-class, binomial-type model are given by

$$\lambda(t) = \xi_0 t^{\xi_2 - 1} \exp(-\xi_1 t^{\xi_2})$$

and

$$\lambda(\mu) = \phi_0 [-\ln(1 - \frac{\mu}{\phi_1})]^{\phi_2}(\phi_1 - \mu),$$

respectively.

11.2 Show that the functional forms of $\lambda(t)$ and $\lambda(\mu)$ for a Pareto-class, binomial-type model are given by

$$\lambda(t) = \xi_0(\xi_1 + t)^{-\xi_2}$$

and

$$\lambda(\mu) = \phi_0(\phi_1 - \mu)^{\phi_2},$$

respectively.

11.3 Show that the functional form of $\lambda(t)$ for an inverse-polynomial-family model is given by

$$\lambda(t) = \frac{\xi_0}{\sqrt{t^2 + \xi_1}} \left[\sqrt[3]{t + \sqrt{t^2 + \xi_1}} - \sqrt[3]{t - \sqrt{t^2 + \xi_1}} \right].$$

11.4 Show that the functional forms of $\lambda(t)$ and $\lambda(\mu)$ for the geometric de-eutrophication model are given by

$$\lambda(t) = \frac{\xi_0}{\xi_1 + t}$$

and

$$\lambda(\mu) = \phi_0 \exp(\phi_1 \mu),$$

respectively.

TWELVE

PARAMETER ESTIMATION

Binomial- and Poisson-type models, as we have seen, occupy an important position in software reliability work. An entire chapter will be devoted to a discussion of basic inference procedures for them. Although the results in the following sections are specific to the above model types, the discussion illustrates several general points about inference for all models in general.

Parametric point and interval estimation will be the primary topics considered. Three popular methods will be presented. The first, *maximum likelihood* estimation, has in our experience been the best choice and is presented at great length in Section 12.2. The second method is that of *least squares*. It provides an excellent alternative to maximum likelihood and is described in Section 12.3. Finally, the *Bayesian* approach to estimation is briefly covered in Section 12.4.

Maximum likelihood estimation is considered for "failure time" (Section 12.2.1) and "grouped" data (Section 12.2.2). Results for binomial- and Poisson-type models (both finite and infinite failures categories for the latter) are given for both types of data. The exponential class and geometric family of these models are used throughout for illustrative purposes because of their practical importance (they include the two models covered most extensively in this book).

A least squares estimation approach is presented in Section 12.3. The approach can be applied to failure time data and grouped data. Point and interval estimation for model parameters and derived quantities is considered. Finally, the results of a simulation study comparing the least squares approach and the maximum likelihood approach are given for the logarithmic Poisson model.

An overview of Bayesian inference is given in Section 12.4. Only failure time data are considered, though the extension to grouped data is straightforward. Some examples are presented that compare the Bayesian approach to the maximum likelihood approach. However, no attempt is made to do a formal comparison of the methods.

Finally, the methods presented here will usually require the numerical optimization (possibly constrained) of a function. The algorithm that is employed is described in Appendix D.

12.1 PRELIMINARIES

The subject of parameter estimation will be treated shortly. However, before actually doing so, we will discuss some preliminary topics. This will result in a simpler and clearer presentation. The first topic concerns the types of failure data usually available and the associated notation. The second topic involves the notion of scaled mean value functions. The one-parameter subcase of these functions is of great theoretical interest. The final topic will be a look at two important (that is, practically useful) Poisson-type model groups: the exponential class and the geometric family.

12.1.1 Time and Grouped Failure Data

In order for any software reliability model to be of practical use during the test phase its parameters (which are assumed to be unknown) must be estimated using failure data. These data will usually be collected in one of two ways, depending on limitations or convenience in data recording or record keeping and reporting.

Usually the most detailed and desirable type of failure data, from an estimation point of view, results when the times of successive failures are recorded. Equivalently, the data may be recorded as intervals between failures and converted. Figure 12.1 illustrates a possible sequence of failures, with failures being experienced at times $t_1, \ldots, t_{m_e}$, for a total of m_e failures. The total time of observation or testing is denoted by t_e, which in this example does not correspond with the last failure. Table 12.1 contains some failure time data collected for system T1 [Musa (1979b)]. These data will be used throughout this chapter in some of our examples. Note that time for these data is execution time.

The other commonly collected type of data is called *grouped data*. This occurs in cases where we only know the number of failures that were experienced during an interval of testing. Table 12.2 illustrates a possible scenario for grouped data. At the end of the first interval of testing x_1 time units have elapsed, resulting in y_1' failures. Interval 2 ends with an additional $x_2 - x_1$ time units of testing and y_2' failures. This pattern continues until the end of the pth interval. Table 12.3 contains some grouped data collected for system T38. This will be used for illustrative purposes later. Like system T1, time in this case is execution time.

As we have stated, one would expect time or interval data to be more desirable for estimation than grouped data. That is, the precision with which model pa-

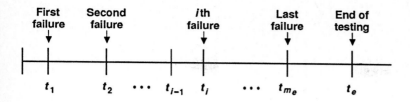

Time *t*

FIGURE 12.1
A failure time sequence.

TABLE 12.1
Failure time data for system T1

Time of failure for system T1 (CPU sec)					
3	2676	7843	16185	35338	53443
33	3098	7922	16229	36799	54433
146	3278	8738	16358	37642	55381
227	3288	10089	17168	37654	56463
342	4434	10237	17458	37915	56485
351	5034	10258	17758	39715	56560
353	5049	10491	18287	40580	57042
444	5085	10625	18568	42015	62551
556	5089	10982	18728	42045	62651
571	5089	11175	19556	42188	62661
709	5097	11411	20567	42296	63732
759	5324	11442	21012	42296	64103
836	5389	11811	21308	45406	64893
860	5565	12559	23063	46653	71043
968	5623	12559	24127	47596	74364
1056	6080	12791	25910	48296	75409
1726	6380	13121	26770	49171	76057
1846	6477	13486	27753	49416	81542
1872	6740	14708	28460	50145	82702
1986	7192	15251	28493	52042	84566
2311	7447	15261	29361	52489	88682
2366	7644	15277	30085	52875	
2608	7837	15806	32408	53321	

Note: End of test occurred at 91208 CPU sec.

TABLE 12.2
Grouped data

Interval number	Total test time at end of interval	Duration of test interval	Number of failures in interval	Cumulative number of failures
1	x_1	x_1	y_1'	y_1
2	x_2	$x_2 - x_1$	y_2'	y_2
⋮	⋮	⋮	⋮	⋮
p	x_p	$x_p - x_{p-1}$	y_p'	y_p

rameters can be estimated using the former data should be greater than that obtained using the latter data. Case Study 5.1 presented some results on this topic.

12.1.2 Scaled Mean Value Functions

The types of failure data just discussed can be used to estimate the unknown model parameters. These parameters will be denoted by the vector $\boldsymbol{\beta} = (\beta_0, ..., \beta_w)$. We will be treating the parameter β_0 in a special fashion. When necessary $\boldsymbol{\beta_A} = (\beta_1, ..., \beta_w)$ will be used to refer to all parameters except β_0.

The functional relationship of the failure intensity with respect to time for various models was given in Table 11.1. Let's apply a reparameterization from $\boldsymbol{\xi}$ to $\boldsymbol{\beta}$. The transformations we will use are indicated in Table 12.4. Table 12.5

TABLE 12.3
Grouped failure data for system T38

Interval number	Total test time at end of interval (CPU hr)	Duration of test interval (CPU hr)	Number of failures in interval	Cumulative number of failures
1	5	5	1	1
2	15	10	0	1
3	25	10	16	17
4	35	10	1	18
5	45	10	1	19
6	50	5	0	19
7	65	15	1	20
8	75	10	3	23
9	95	20	2	25
10	120	25	7	32
11	125	5	0	32

TABLE 12.4
Relationship between ξ and β

Category	Class or family	Parameter transformation ξ_0	ξ_1	ξ_2
Finite	Exponential	$\beta_0\beta_1$	β_1	—
	Weibull	$\beta_0\beta_1\beta_2$	β_1	β_2
	Pareto	$\dfrac{(\beta_2 - 1)\beta_0}{\beta_1^{1-\beta_2}}$	β_1	β_2
	Gamma	$\beta_0\beta_1^2$	β_1	—
Infinite	Geometric	β_0	β_1^{-1}	—
	Inverse linear	$\dfrac{\beta_0}{2}$	β_1	—
	Inverse polynomial	β_0	β_1	—
	Power	β_0	β_1	—

TABLE 12.5
Mean value and failure intensity functions[1]

Category	Class or family	$\mu(t;\boldsymbol{\beta})$	$\lambda(t;\boldsymbol{\beta})$
Finite	Exponential	$\beta_0[1 - \exp(-\beta_1 t)]$	$\beta_0\beta_1\exp(-\beta_1 t)$
	Weibull	$\beta_0[1 - \exp(-\beta_1 t^{\beta_2})]$	$\beta_0\beta_1\beta_2 t^{\beta_2-1}\exp(-\beta_1 t^{\beta_2})$
	Pareto	$\beta_0\left[1 - \left(\dfrac{\beta_1 + t}{\beta_1}\right)^{1-\beta_2}\right]$	$\dfrac{\beta_0(\beta_2 - 1)}{\beta_1^{1-\beta_2}}(\beta_1 + t)^{-\beta_2}$
	Gamma	$\beta_0[1 - (1 + \beta_1 t)\exp(-\beta_1 t)]$	$\beta_0\beta_1^2 t\,\exp(-\beta_1 t)$
Infinite	Geometric	$\beta_0\ln(1 + \beta_1 t)$	$\dfrac{\beta_0\beta_1}{1 + \beta_1 t}$
	Inverse linear	$\beta_0[(\beta_1 + t)^{1/2} - \beta_1^{1/2}]$	$\dfrac{\beta_0}{2(\beta_1 + t)^{1/2}}$
	Inverse polynomial	$3\beta_0(Q_1 + Q_2)$	$\dfrac{\beta_0}{\sqrt{t^2 + \beta_1}}(Q_1 - Q_2)$
	Power	$\beta_0 t^{\beta_1}$	$\beta_0\beta_1 t^{\beta_1-1}$

[1] $Q_1 = \sqrt[3]{t + (t^2 + \beta_1)^{1/2}}$; $Q_2 = \sqrt[3]{t - (t^2 + \beta_1)^{1/2}}$

shows the mean value and failure intensity functions after applying the re-parameterization to the various classes and families.

Referring to Table 12.5 we see that all the models are characterized by mean value functions that can be written in the form

$$\mu(t) = \mu(t; \boldsymbol{\beta}) = \beta_0 \mu_1(t; \boldsymbol{\beta}_A) . \tag{12.1}$$

Here $\mu_1(t; \boldsymbol{\beta}_A)$ can be any function that is either always nonnegative or always nonpositive. In the former case β_0 must be positive, while in the latter, β_0 must be negative to have a nonnegative mean value function. Figure 12.2 depicts one possible set of mean value functions. Alternatively, these models can also be characterized by the failure intensity function

$$\lambda(t) = \lambda(t; \boldsymbol{\beta}) = \beta_0 \frac{d}{dt}\mu_1(t; \boldsymbol{\beta}_A) \tag{12.2}$$
$$= \beta_0 \lambda_1(t; \boldsymbol{\beta}_A).$$

The mean value function given by Equation (12.1) in no way limits the type of model we can describe. There are three possibilities, shown in Figure 12.3. If β_0 is set equal to 1 then $\mu(t)$ specifies a general function and therefore a general model. If β_0 does not equal 1, and if $\mu_1(\infty)$ is finite, then $\mu(t)$ describes a finite failures model (including the binomial- and Poisson-types). From Equation (12.1) we have $\mu(\infty) = \beta_0 \mu_1(\infty)$. This must equal the expected number of failures ν_0 for Poisson-type models. Similarly, it must equal the number of failures u_0 for binomial-type models. For most practical forms of $\mu_1(t)$ we will have $\mu_1(\infty) = 1$ and β_0 will be identical to ν_0 or u_0 depending on the type of model. If this is not the case, we can always parameterize Equation (12.1) in such a way that it is. We will interpret the parameter β_0 as ν_0 or u_0, as appropriate, for finite failures models. If neither of the above two cases apply, we have an infinite failures model (including the Poisson-type) with scale parameter β_0. We will refer to all mean value functions with $\beta_0 \neq 1$ as *scaled mean value functions* with w parameters. Note that w

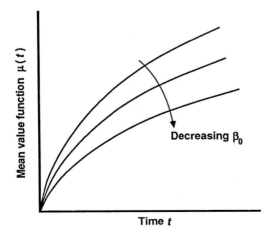

Decreasing β_0

Mean value function $\mu(t)$

Time t

FIGURE 12.2
A set of scaled mean value functions.

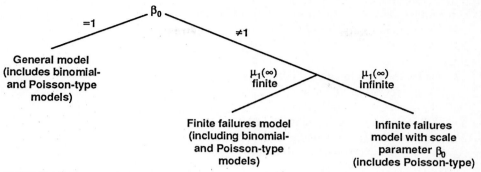

FIGURE 12.3
The set of models described by $\mu(t) = \beta_0\mu_1(t_i;\beta_A)$.

represents the number of parameters making up the function $\mu_1(t)$. The total number of parameters including β_0 is $w + 1$.

Great practical interest centers around scaled mean value functions where $w = 1$, that is, models that are characterized by the function

$$\mu(t) = \beta_0\mu_1(t; \beta_1) . \qquad (12.3)$$

As a practical matter the set of models that can be described by Equation (12.3) is not as restrictive as one might first think. Models that are described by a *one-parameter* scaled mean value function include (see Table 12.5)

1. the exponential and gamma classes of finite failures binomial- and Poisson-type models, and
2. the geometric, inverse linear, inverse polynomial (2nd degree), and power families of the infinite failures Poisson-type models.

12.1.3 Two Important Model Groups

We now discuss two important groups of models, the exponential and geometric Poisson. The two models that have been highlighted in this book belong to these groups. From our discussion we know that each group is characterized by a one-parameter scaled mean value function. The special cases of the basic and logarithmic Poisson execution time models are illustrated.

EXPONENTIAL POISSON GROUP. The exponential Poisson group is characterized by the mean value function

$$\mu(t) = \beta_0\mu_1(t; \beta_1) = \beta_0[1 - \exp(- \beta_1 t)] , \qquad (12.4)$$

or the failure intensity function

$$\lambda(t) = \beta_0\lambda_1(t; \beta_1) = \beta_0\beta_1\exp(- \beta_1 t) . \qquad (12.5)$$

Cox and Lewis (1966), Bartholomew (1963), and many others have discussed estimation procedures for this and closely related models. However, their formulations were not developed in the context of software reliability. Results that are of interest will be quoted as needed without proof (or with proofs left as exercises). The reader is urged to consult these references if greater detail is desired.

The exponential Poisson group can accommodate increasing and decreasing failure intensities. Figure 12.4 illustrates these types of behavior. When β_0 and β_1 are both less than 0 an increasing failure intensity model results. If β_1 equals 0 and the product $\beta_0\beta_1$ is nonzero,[1] a constant failure intensity (stationary Poisson process) results. And finally, when both β_0 and β_1 are greater than 0, a decreasing failure intensity model results. The basic execution time model falls into this category. When we refer to this model, we will interpret the parameter β_1 as $B\phi$, the product of the fault reduction factor and the per-fault hazard rate. It is worth noting here that there are no restrictions on the range of values that β_1 can take on. However, β_0 must be such that $\mu(t)$ and $\lambda(t)$ are nonnegative.

CASE STUDY 12.1
TEST FOR TREND FOR AN EXPONENTIAL-CLASS MODEL

A problem of some interest and one that provides insight into how sensitive the exponential Poisson group is to either an increasing or decreasing trend in the failure

---

[1]This can occur by letting $\beta_1 \to \infty$ and $\beta_0 \to 0$ in such a way that $\beta_0\beta_1 \to$ a constant.

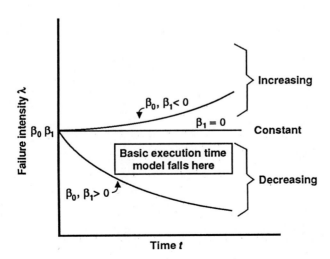

FIGURE 12.4
Behavior of exponential Poisson models.

intensity is to test the null hypothesis $\beta_1 = 0$ (remembering that this corresponds to a constant failure intensity). Suppose that there are a total of m_e failures experienced during a period of observation $(0, t_e)$. Bates (1955) showed that the statistic

$$U = \frac{\sum_{i=1}^{m_e} T_i - \frac{m_e}{2} t_e}{t_e \sqrt{\frac{m_e}{12}}}$$

tends rapidly to the standardized normal form. Large positive values of U indicate an increasing trend in the failure intensity (that is, $\beta_1 < 0$) or reliability decay, and large negative values of U indicate a decreasing trend in the failure intensity (that is, $\beta_1 > 0$) or reliability growth. A necessary condition for reliability growth, comes from the foregoing statistic:

$$\frac{1}{m_e} \sum_{i=1}^{m_e} T_i < \frac{1}{2} t_e \ ,$$

that is, reliability growth is present if the centroid of the failure times is less than the midpoint of the period of observation.

To see how this statistic varies with sample size, data for an exponential Poisson model with $\beta_0 = 200$ failures and $\beta_1 = 0.001$/sec were simulated (analytical results being difficult to obtain). A total of 1000 different failure time sequences were generated. The average value of U was computed as a function of m_e and is shown in Figure 12.5. It is quite apparent that reliability growth is difficult to detect until about $m_e = 100$ failures or halfway to the total number of expected failures ($\beta_0 = \nu_0 = 200$ failures). The simulation was repeated for other

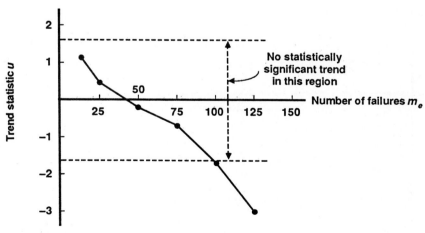

FIGURE 12.5
Value of trend statistic for a simulation.

values of β_0 and β_1 with similar results. Thus we conclude that when using this model class it is difficult to detect trends during the first half (based on the number of failures) of testing.

GEOMETRIC POISSON GROUP. The geometric Poisson group is characterized by the mean value function

$$\mu(t) = \beta_0\mu_1(t; \beta_1) = \beta_0 \ln (1 + \beta_1 t) , \tag{12.6}$$

or the failure intensity function

$$\lambda(t) = \beta_0\lambda_1(t; \beta_1) = \frac{\beta_0\beta_1}{1 + \beta_1 t} . \tag{12.7}$$

The group can accommodate decreasing and a certain type of increasing failure intensities. Figure 12.6 illustrates these types of behavior. When both β_0 and β_1 are greater than 0, a decreasing failure intensity model results. The logarithmic Poisson model falls here. When referring to this model we will interpret the parameter β_0 as θ^{-1}, where θ is the failure intensity decay parameter, and the parameter β_1 as $\lambda_0\theta$, where λ_0 is the initial failure intensity. If β_1 equals 0 and the product $\beta_0\beta_1$ is nonzero, then a constant failure intensity (stationary Poisson process) results. And finally when β_1 is greater than $-t_e^{-1}$ but less than 0 and β_0 is less than 0, an increasing failure intensity model is the result. In this latter case, the failure intensity will show explosive growth as the total test time approaches β_1^{-1}. Note that there are restrictions on the values that β_1 can take on. That is, β_1 must be greater than $-t_e^{-1}$ or else the mean value function given by Equation (12.6) will be undefined.

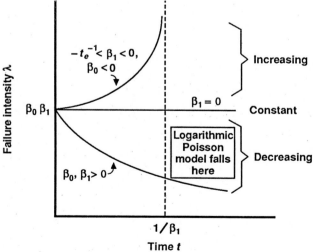

FIGURE 12.6
Behavior of geometric Poisson models.

12.2 MAXIMUM LIKELIHOOD ESTIMATION

The most important and widely used formal estimation technique is the method of *maximum likelihood*. Estimation by maximum likelihood is a general technique that may be applied when the underlying distributions of the data are specified or known. This section deals with a great many results for binomial- and Poisson-type models using failure time and grouped data. The overall organization of the section, which the reader can use as a "guide map," is pictured in Figure 12.7.

The foundation of the maximum likelihood method is the *likelihood function*. The function is defined as the joint density of the observed data, $L(\boldsymbol{\beta}; Y_D)$. This, in turn, is considered to be a function of the unknown set of $w + 1$ parameters, $\boldsymbol{\beta}$. Here Y_D represents a set of observations.

Figure 12.8 illustrates a typical likelihood function when there is only one unknown parameter (denoted β_k). In this example a small value of $L(\beta_k; Y_D)$ for a particular β_k could be interpreted to mean that observing Y_D is a rare event. It is reasonable to prefer the value of β_k which makes $L(\beta_k; Y_D)$ a maximum. That is, we would choose β_k so that the observed data are more probable than for any other choice.

Formalizing the notion, we have the definition of maximum likelihood estimators. For each data set, let $\hat{\boldsymbol{\beta}}$ be the values of the parameters that make $L(\boldsymbol{\beta};$

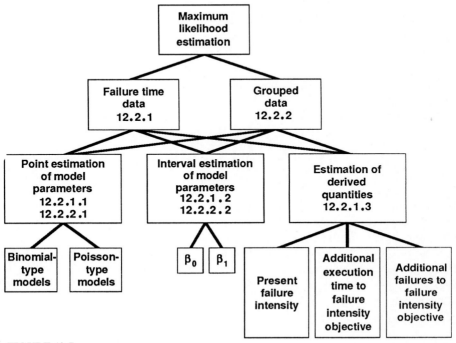

FIGURE 12.7
Organization of Section 12.2.

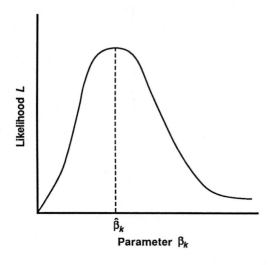

$\hat{\beta}_k$

Parameter β_k

FIGURE 12.8
Typical likelihood function with
only one unknown parameter.

Y_D) as large as possible. These maximizing values will, of course, be functions of the data. The functions themselves are called the maximum likelihood estimators. The values these functions take on are known as the maximum likelihood estimates. Figure 12.8 shows the maximum likelihood estimate of β_k as $\hat{\beta}_k$.

Maximum likelihood estimates can be obtained by solving the simultaneous equations (one for each β_k)[2]

$$\frac{\partial L(\boldsymbol{\beta}; Y_D)}{\partial \beta_k} = 0 \ , \ k = 0, \cdots, w \ . \tag{12.8}$$

In practice it is customary and often more convenient to work with $\ln L(\boldsymbol{\beta}; Y_D)$ instead of $L(\boldsymbol{\beta}; Y_D)$, the derivatives of both vanishing together. Thus, we will find our estimates by solving the simultaneous equations (which are called the *maximum likelihood equations*)

$$\frac{\partial \ln L(\boldsymbol{\beta}; Y_D)}{\partial \beta_k} = 0 \ , \ k = 0, \cdots, w \ . \tag{12.9}$$

Generally the maximum likelihood equations are highly complicated and a numerical solution will be possible only with a computer. An excellent iterative procedure for carrying out the solution is given in Appendix D.

Some of the β_k's may be such that they are restricted to discrete values; for example, they may only take on integer values. An important case occurs when β_0 equals u_0 for binomial-type models. When this happens we can treat β_0 as continu-

---

[2]One should also verify that a maximum and not a minimum or saddle point has been found.

ous for optimization purposes. This makes the maximization process simpler. After the result has been found the estimate is rounded off to the nearest allowable value. In the example given u_0 will be rounded to the nearest integer.

Maximum likelihood estimators possess many desirable optimum properties such as consistency, efficiency, and asymptotic normality [Kendall and Stuart (1961)]. An estimator is said to be *consistent* if its variance tends to zero and if its expectation tends to the true population parameter as the sample size tends to infinity. If two different estimators have the same expectation, then the one with the smaller variance is said to be more *efficient*. Furthermore, an estimator is called *asymptotically normal* if its distribution is almost normal for sufficiently large sample sizes. These properties "say" that for large sample size the maximum likelihood estimators are as good a set of estimators as there is.[3] That is, other estimators, such as the least squares estimators discussed in Section 12.3, might be just as good but not better. The asymptotic normality property of maximum likelihood estimators is important because it will often be the only alternative available to establish confidence intervals for the unknown parameters. We will have more to say on this a little later.

Finally, maximum likelihood estimators possess an important property that is often called the *invariance property*. This property means that the maximum likelihood estimator for any one-to-one function of $\boldsymbol{\beta}$, say Q, is given by a straightforward substitution as $Q(\hat{\boldsymbol{\beta}})$, where $\hat{\boldsymbol{\beta}}$ is the maximum likelihood estimator for $\boldsymbol{\beta}$. Thus, the maximum likelihood technique provides a simple way of finding estimators having "good" properties.

Point estimates are useful, yet it is often desirable to have them accompanied by some measure of the possible error of the estimate. For example, a point estimate might be accompanied by some interval in which the true value of the parameter lies with some measure of confidence. The likelihood function and the asymptotic normality property [Mood, Graybill, and Boes (1974) and Kendall and Stuart (1961)] enjoyed by maximum likelihood estimation can be used to establish these interval estimates under the appropriate conditions.

Consider first our one-parameter example. It can be shown [Kendall and Stuart (1961)] that the maximum likelihood estimator of β_k is asymptotically normally distributed with mean β_k and variance $1/I(\beta_k)$, where $I(\beta_k)$ is the expected, or Fisher, information given by

$$I(\beta_k) = E\left[-\frac{\partial^2 \ln L(\beta_k; Y_D)}{\partial \beta_k^2}\right]. \qquad (12.10)$$

Thus we can write

---

[3]By a large sample size we mean one in which the information content (defined later) approaches infinity. For small to medium sample size, other estimators (for example, least squares estimators) may be better.

$$\frac{\hat{\beta}_k - \beta_k}{\sqrt{\frac{1}{I(\hat{\beta}_k)}}} \sim N(0, 1) , \tag{12.11}$$

where $N(0, 1)$ denotes a normal distribution with zero mean and unit variance. From Equation (12.11) it can be shown that the upper and lower limits of an approximate $100(1 - \alpha)$ percent confidence interval for β_k are given by

$$\hat{\beta}_k \pm \frac{\kappa_{1-\alpha/2}}{\sqrt{I(\hat{\beta}_k)}} , \tag{12.12}$$

where $\kappa_{1-\alpha/2}$ is the appropriate normal deviate. Figure 12.9 illustrates a 95 percent confidence interval for β_k. Such an approximate confidence interval may include "impossible" values for β_k outside the range of permissible values. This problem, a frequent occurrence for small sample sizes, can be avoided by applying the asymptotic normal distribution to a transformation of β_k for which the range is unrestricted. For example, if β_k is restricted to positive values then ln β_k will have an unrestricted range.

One warning about an approximation like Equation (12.11) is that it may not be good for small to moderate sample sizes. The adequacy of the approximation must be checked for each particular application. When it is found to be inadequate, a search for some transformation of β_k whose distribution may be much more closely approximated by a normal distribution should be conducted. The transformation should be such that it does not have unnecessary range restrictions. Having found such a transformation and provided it is invertible, confidence intervals for β_k can then be easily established.

If the search for such a transformation fails, an alternate approximate procedure based on the likelihood ratio can be recommended. The likelihood ratio is de-

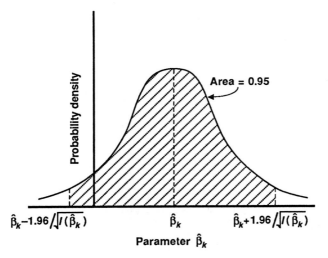

FIGURE 12.9
A 95 percent confidence interval for β_k.

fined as $- 2 \ln (\beta_k/\hat{\beta}_k)$ and is asymptotically distributed chi-square with one degree of freedom. To get a $100(1 - \alpha)$ percent confidence interval for β_k, one needs to find the set of values for which the likelihood ratio is less than or equal to $\chi^2_{(1),1-\alpha}$. This latter value is the $100(1 - \alpha)$ percentile of a chi-square distribution with one degree of freedom and can be determined using any standard set of statistical tables. The chi-square distribution that approximates the distribution of the likelihood ratio is often found to be accurate, even for small sample sizes [Lawless (1982)]. However, this approach requires considerably more computation than that needed by Equations (12.11) and (12.12).

An extension of this discussion on confidence intervals to more than one parameter is straightforward. The result is that $\hat{\boldsymbol{\beta}}$ is distributed approximately as the multivariate normal distribution with mean equal to $\boldsymbol{\beta}$ and covariance matrix that is the inverse of the Fisher information matrix whose entries are given as

$$I_{kl}(\boldsymbol{\beta}) = E\left[- \frac{\partial^2 \ln L(\boldsymbol{\beta}; Y_D)}{\partial \beta_k \, \partial \beta_l} \right], \quad k,l = 0, \cdots, w \, . \tag{12.13}$$

The diagonal elements of the covariance matrix give the variance of the respective parameters. The off-diagonal elements give the covariance between the corresponding elements.

A confidence interval for each β_k ($k = 0, \ldots, w$) can be established as before by using Equation (12.12) with $I(\hat{\beta}_k)$ replaced with $I_{kk}(\hat{\boldsymbol{\beta}})$. Warnings about the adequacy of the normal approximation apply here as well and will not be repeated. The likelihood ratio is still an excellent though computationally expensive alternative.[4]

Sometimes, especially when using one-parameter scaled mean value functions, it will be helpful to use a *conditional likelihood* function. The main reason for this is that the amount of computational effort is reduced. Side benefits of using a conditional likelihood function are:

1. the resulting estimators are the same or nearly the same as those obtained by using the unconditional likelihood function for binomial- and Poisson-type models, and
2. the substitution principle (see Section 12.2.1.2) may be used to establish confidence intervals in a straightforward fashion (for one-parameter scaled mean value functions).

Let E denote the event on which we are conditioning. The conditional likelihood can be obtained by dividing the unconditional likelihood function by the marginal probability of E equaling its observed value (denoted by e) for a discrete event or

---

[4]Here the ratio is asymptotically distributed chi-square with $w + 1$ degrees of freedom.

by the marginal density function of E for a continuous event. Thus, in the discrete case

$$L(\beta \mid E; Y_D) = \frac{L(\beta; Y_D)}{P[E = e; \beta]} . \tag{12.14}$$

To be of any gain over the use of the unconditional likelihood function Equation (12.14) must depend on fewer parameters, the missing parameters being estimated (if desired) in a different fashion.

The efficiency, consistency, asymptotic normality, and invariance properties of unconditional maximum likelihood estimators apply in this case. The adequacy of the normal approximation for generating confidence intervals must, of course, still be checked for each particular application. If it is inadequate, an appropriate transformation or the likelihood ratio should be used.

12.2.1 Failure Time Data

In the following subsections we will derive the necessary formulas to do point and interval estimation based on failure time data for both binomial- and Poisson-type models. We treat first the subject of point estimation for model parameters, followed by interval estimation for these same parameters. We conclude with a discussion on estimation for derived quantities, such as the present failure intensity.

12.2.1.1 POINT ESTIMATION OF MODEL PARAMETERS. Suppose that estimation is to be performed at a specified time t_e, not necessarily corresponding to a failure, and with a total of m_e failures being experienced at times $t_1, \ldots, t_{m_e}$. Figure 12.1 shows a possible sequence of failure times. The unconditional likelihood function in this case is, in complete generality,

$$L(\beta; t_1, \cdots, t_{m_e}) = f(t_1, \cdots, t_{m_e}) \, P[T_{m_e+1} > t_e \mid T_1 = t_1, \cdots, T_{m_e} = t_{m_e}] , \tag{12.15}$$

or equivalently (though less commonly expressed this way)

$$L(\beta; t_1, \cdots, t_{m_e}) =$$

$$\left[\prod_{i=1}^{m_e} f(t_i \mid t_1, \cdots, t_{i-1}) \right] P[T_{m_e+1} > t_e \mid T_1 = t_1, \cdots, T_{m_e} = t_{m_e}] , \tag{12.16}$$

where $f(t_1, \ldots, t_{m_e})$ is the joint density function of $(T_1, \ldots, T_{m_e})$, and T_i the random variable denoting the time of the ith failure. Note that $f(t_1 \mid t_0) = f(t_1)$.

A property of both binomial- and Poisson-type models that simplifies Equation (12.16) to some extent is that the conditional density function of T_i depends only on the previous failure time T_{i-1} [see Equations (10.17) and (10.37)], that is

$$f(t_i \mid t_1, \cdots, t_{i-1}) = f(t_i \mid t_{i-1}) . \tag{12.17}$$

Thus Equation (12.16) can be expressed as

$$L(\boldsymbol{\beta}) = \left[\prod_{i=1}^{m_e} f(t_i \mid t_{i-1}) \right] P[T_{m_e+1} > t_e \mid T_{m_e} = t_{m_e}], \qquad (12.18)$$

where, for simplicity, we have suppressed the explicit notation of the dependency of L on $(t_1, \ldots, t_{m_e})$.

As we mentioned in the introduction to Section 12.2, estimation can also be based on a conditional approach. This requires defining the conditioning event. Such a definition will depend on whether the testing process is observed for a predetermined time or the testing period is taken up to a preassigned number of failures.[5] The material presented here pertains solely to the former type of conditioning.

By selecting the time t_e as our basis of observation, the number of failures experienced in the interval $(0, t_e]$ will be a (discrete) random variable. The realization of this random variable is m_e and will be used as the conditioning event. Thus, the conditional likelihood function given by Equation (12.14) becomes

$$L(\boldsymbol{\beta} \mid m_e) = \frac{L(\boldsymbol{\beta})}{P[M(t_e) = m_e; \boldsymbol{\beta}]} . \qquad (12.19)$$

It is worthwhile at this point to discuss an interesting result that is obtained when using Equations (12.18) and (12.19) for binomial- and Poisson-type models. The result is this: Provided $\mu(t_e) = m_e$, unconditional and conditional estimation yields identical point and interval estimates for either type of model. Furthermore, the estimates for both model types will also be the same. That is, the two types of models are indistinguishable from each other using either type of estimation.[6] The details leading to this result can be found in the remainder of this section and Section 12.2.1.2.

This condition is intuitively appealing since m_e failures have been observed by time t_e (see Figure 12.10). In addition, for scaled mean value functions, $\mu(t_e) = m_e$ is the solution of the unconditional maximum likelihood equation for β_0 for Poisson-type models (see Table 12.6). It is approximately the solution obtained using the unconditional maximum likelihood equation for β_0 for binomial-type models.

Binomial-type models. Binomial-type models are of the finite failures category and as such are described by Equation (12.1) with $\beta_0 = u_0$ and $\mu_1(t; \boldsymbol{\beta}_A) = F_a(t; \boldsymbol{\beta}_A)$. For the sake of convenience, the notation $F_a(t; \boldsymbol{\beta}_A) = F_a(t)$, $f_a(t; \boldsymbol{\beta}_A) = f_a(t)$, and $z_a(t)$ will be adopted. In addition, because of the extreme importance of the

---

[5]In practice, we do not predetermine the total test time or the number of failures to be observed. Rather, estimation is performed at various times (as needed or on a regular basis) throughout testing. Cost and schedule may, in fact, influence the available time for system testing for some projects.

[6]The models are, of course, distinguishable from their other properties.

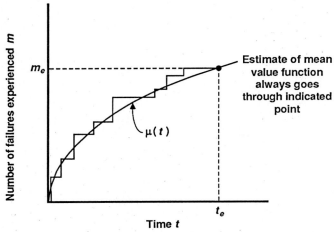

FIGURE 12.10
Relation of mean value function to failure data.

parameter u_0, the dependency of the likelihood function on this parameter and $\boldsymbol{\beta}_A$ will be noted explicitly. That is, $L(u_0, \boldsymbol{\beta}_A)$ will be used instead of $L(\boldsymbol{\beta})$.

First consider the unconditional likelihood approach. To particularize Equation (12.18) we must evaluate the two factors on the right side of the equation. Let us start with the first factor and one of its typical terms, that is, $f(t_i | t_{i-1})$. Using

$$f(t_i \mid t_{i-1}) = -\frac{d}{dt_i} P[T_i > t_i \mid T_{i-1} = t_{i-1}] \tag{12.20}$$

and Equation (10.38) we have

TABLE 12.6
Maximum likelihood estimates for β_0

Type of data	Estimate of β_0 for scaled mean value functions	
	Unconditional estimation[1]	Conditional estimation
Time	$\dfrac{m_e}{\mu_1(t_e; \hat{\boldsymbol{\beta}}_A)}$	Set equal to unconditional
Grouped	$\dfrac{y_p}{\mu_1(x_p; \hat{\boldsymbol{\beta}}_A)}$	estimate

[1] These estimates are approximate for binomial-type models and exact for Poisson-type models

$$f(t_i| t_{i-1}) = (u_0 - i + 1)z_a(t_i) \exp\left[- (u_0 - i + 1) \int_{t_{i-1}}^{t_i} z_a(x)dx\right]. \quad (12.21)$$

Combining Equations (10.20) and (10.22) we can express the above solely in terms of $f_a(t)$ and $F_a(t)$ as

$$f(t_i| t_{i-1}) = \frac{(u_0 - i + 1)f_a(t_i)}{1 - F_a(t_i)} \left[\frac{1 - F_a(t_i)}{1 - F_a(t_{i-1})}\right]^{u_0 - i + 1}. \quad (12.22)$$

It follows then that the first factor of Equation (12.18) becomes

$$\prod_{i=1}^{m_e} f(t_i| t_{i-1}) = [1 - F_a(t_{m_e})]^{u_0 - m_e} \prod_{i=1}^{m_e} (u_0 - i + 1)f_a(t_i). \quad (12.23)$$

The second factor is, starting with Equation (10.38) and using Equations (10.20) and (10.22),

$$P[T_{m_e+1} > t_e| T_{m_e} = t_{m_e}] = \left[\frac{1 - F_a(t_e)}{1 - F_a(t_{m_e})}\right]^{u_0 - m_e}. \quad (12.24)$$

The likelihood function after the appropriate substitutions and algebra is

$$L(u_0, \beta_A) = [1 - F_a(t_e)]^{u_0 - m_e} \prod_{i=1}^{m_e} (u_0 - i + 1)f_a(t_i). \quad (12.25)$$

The log-likelihood is

$$\ln L(u_0, \beta_A) = (u_0 - m_e) \ln [1 - F_a(t_e)]$$
$$+ \sum_{i=1}^{m_e} \ln (u_0 - i + 1) + \sum_{i=1}^{m_e} \ln f_a(t_i) \quad (12.26)$$

and from this the maximum likelihood equations become

$$\frac{\partial \ln L(u_0, \beta_A)}{\partial u_0} = \ln [1 - F_a(t_e)] + \sum_{i=1}^{m_e} \frac{1}{u_0 - i + 1} = 0, \quad (12.27)$$

and

$$\frac{\partial \ln L(u_0, \beta_A)}{\partial \beta_k} = - \frac{u_0 - m_e}{1 - F_a(t_e)} \frac{\partial F_a(t_e)}{\partial \beta_k}$$
$$+ \sum_{i=1}^{m_e} \frac{1}{f_a(t_i)} \frac{\partial f_a(t_i)}{\partial \beta_k} = 0, \quad k = 1, \cdots, w. \quad (12.28)$$

This latter set of equations may be rewritten in terms of the mean value and failure intensity functions by noting that $\mu(t) = u_0 F_a(t)$ and $\lambda(t) = u_0 f_a(t)$. The result is

$$- \frac{u_0 - m_e}{u_0 - \mu(t_e)} \frac{\partial \mu(t_e)}{\partial \beta_k} + \sum_{i=1}^{m_e} \frac{1}{\lambda(t_i)} \frac{\partial \lambda(t_i)}{\partial \beta_k} = 0, \quad k = 1, \cdots, w \ . \quad (12.29)$$

Conditional likelihood estimation can be performed by evaluating Equation (12.19). The denominator of this expression is given by Equation (10.25) as

$$P[M(t_e) = m_e] = \begin{pmatrix} u_0 \\ m_e \end{pmatrix} [F_a(t_e)]^{m_e} [1 - F_a(t_e)]^{u_0 - m_e} \ . \quad (12.30)$$

Substituting Equations (12.25) and (12.30) into Equation (12.19) we have the conditional likelihood

$$L(u_0, \boldsymbol{\beta}_A | m_e) = L(\boldsymbol{\beta}_A | m_e) = \frac{m_e! \prod_{i=1}^{m_e} f_a(t_i)}{[F_a(t_e)]^{m_e}} \ , \quad (12.31)$$

or since $\mu(t) = u_0 F_a(t)$ and $\lambda(t) = u_0 f_a(t)$ this is equivalent to

$$L(\boldsymbol{\beta}_A | m_e) = \frac{m_e! \prod_{i=1}^{m_e} \lambda(t_i)}{[\mu(t_e)]^{m_e}} \ . \quad (12.32)$$

It is apparent at this point that the parameter u_0 cannot be estimated from the conditional likelihood function. To estimate u_0 we use the fact that m_e failures have been observed by time t_e and hence we will write

$$\mu(t_e; \hat{\boldsymbol{\beta}}) = \hat{u}_0 F_a(t_e; \hat{\boldsymbol{\beta}}_A) = m_e \quad (12.33)$$

and solve for $\hat{u}_0$. It is left as an exercise to show that $\hat{u}_0$ given by Equation (12.33) is nearly equal to the unconditional maximum likelihood estimate from the solution to Equation (12.27).

The logarithm of the conditional likelihood function is, to an additive constant,

$$\ln L(\boldsymbol{\beta}_A | m_e) = \sum_{i=1}^{m_e} \ln \lambda(t_i) - m_e \ln \mu(t_e) \ , \quad (12.34)$$

and from this the maximum likelihood equations become

$$\sum_{i=1}^{m_e} \frac{1}{\lambda(t_i)} \frac{\partial \lambda(t_i)}{\partial \beta_k} - \frac{m_e}{\mu(t_e)} \frac{\partial \mu(t_e)}{\partial \beta_k} = 0 \ , \quad k = 1, \cdots, w \ . \quad (12.35)$$

It is clear that these equations and those for the unconditional likelihood, that is, Equation (12.29), will lead to the same $\hat{\boldsymbol{\beta}}$ if $\mu(t_e)$ is equal to m_e in both cases. For conditional estimation this is true because of Equation (12.33). For unconditional estimation it is only approximately true (see Problem 12.2), hence there will be a slight difference in $\hat{\boldsymbol{\beta}}$ resulting from the two types of estimation.

Exponential class. This class of binomial models is described with

$$\mu(t) = u_0[1 - \exp(-\beta_1 t)] \tag{12.36}$$

and

$$\lambda(t) = u_0 \beta_1 \exp(-\beta_1 t) \ . \tag{12.37}$$

The unconditional maximum likelihood estimates for u_0 and β_1 are given as the simultaneous solution to Equations (12.27) and (12.28) with $k = 1$ or

$$-\hat{\beta}_1 t_e + \sum_{i=1}^{m_e} \frac{1}{\hat{u}_0 - i + 1} = 0 \tag{12.38}$$

and

$$-t_e(\hat{u}_0 - m_e) - \sum_{i=1}^{m_e} t_i + \frac{m_e}{\hat{\beta}_1} = 0 \ . \tag{12.39}$$

Solving Equation (12.39) for $\hat{\beta}_1$ we have

$$\hat{\beta}_1 = \frac{m_e}{\sum\limits_{i=1}^{m_e} t_i + t_e(\hat{u}_0 - m_e)} \tag{12.40}$$

and on substitution into Equation (12.38) the maximum likelihood estimate for u_0 becomes the solution to

$$-\frac{m_e t_e}{\sum\limits_{i=1}^{m_e} t_i + t_e(\hat{u}_0 - m_e)} + \sum_{i=1}^{m_e} \frac{1}{\hat{u}_0 - i + 1} = 0 \ . \tag{12.41}$$

Example 12.1. As a numerical example of unconditional maximum likelihood estimation, suppose we use the failure time data from system T1 (see Table 12.1). Here $m_e = 136$ failures, $t_e = 91208$ CPU sec, and $\sum_{i=1}^{m_e} t_i = 3,365,955$ CPU sec. Using the procedure in Appendix D, Equation (12.41) is solved for $\hat{u}_0$ as 141 failures (rounded to the nearest integer since u_0 can only take on integer values). Substituting this value into Equation (12.40) we find that $\hat{\beta}_1 = 0.3555 \times 10^{-4}$/CPU sec. ∎

The conditional likelihood of β_1 given m_e failures is, after substituting Equations (12.36) and (12.37) into Equation (12.32) and manipulating,

$$L(\beta_1 | m_e) = \frac{m_e! \, \beta_1^{m_e} \exp(-\beta_1 \sum\limits_{i=1}^{m_e} t_i)}{[1 - \exp(-\beta_1 t_e)]^{m_e}} \ . \tag{12.42}$$

The point estimate for β_1, using Equation (12.35), is given as the solution to

$$\frac{m_e}{\hat{\beta}_1} - \frac{m_e t_e}{\exp(\hat{\beta}_1 t_e) - 1} - \sum_{i=1}^{m_e} t_i = 0 . \tag{12.43}$$

Example 12.2. Using the data from the previous example and solving for the conditional estimate of $\hat{\beta}_1$ using Equation (12.43) results in $\hat{\beta}_1 = 0.348 \times 10^{-4}$/CPU sec. By setting Equation (12.36) equal to m_e at $t = t_e$ we have

$$\hat{u}_0 = \frac{m_e}{1 - \exp(-\hat{\beta}_1 t_e)} = 142 \text{ failures},$$

where we have rounded $\hat{u}_0$ to the nearest integer value. The conditional estimates are of course close to the unconditional estimates. The difference resulting because $\mu(t_e) = m_e$ does not hold for unconditional estimation. ∎

Poisson-type models. Proceeding in a fashion similar to what we did for binomial-type models, we have the following results:

$$f(t_i \mid t_{i-1}) = \lambda(t_i) \exp\{-[\mu(t_i) - \mu(t_{i-1})]\} \tag{12.44}$$

and

$$P[T_{m_e+1} > t_e \mid T_{m_e} = t_{m_e}] = \exp\{-[\mu(t_e) - \mu(t_{m_e})]\} , \tag{12.45}$$

and on substitution of those expressions into Equation (12.18)

$$L(\boldsymbol{\beta}) = \left[\prod_{i=1}^{m_e} \lambda(t_i)\right] \exp[-\mu(t_e)]. \tag{12.46}$$

The logarithm of the likelihood function is found to be

$$\ln L(\boldsymbol{\beta}) = \sum_{i=1}^{m_e} \ln \lambda(t_i) - \mu(t_e) , \tag{12.47}$$

and from this the maximum likelihood equations become

$$\sum_{i=1}^{m_e} \frac{1}{\lambda(t_i)} \frac{\partial \lambda(t_i)}{\partial \beta_k} - \frac{\partial \mu(t_e)}{\partial \beta_k} = 0 , \quad k = 0, \cdots, w . \tag{12.48}$$

At this point it is interesting to compare Equation (12.48) with Equations (12.29) and (12.35). When the same mean value function is used for both types of models, the Poisson type, of course, becomes a finite failures model and β_0 can be interpreted as $\nu_0 = \omega_0/B$. We see from our comparison that estimates for $\hat{\boldsymbol{\beta}}_A$ will be identical provided $\mu(t_e; \hat{\boldsymbol{\beta}}) = m_e$ for binomial-type models.

It can be verified by direct substitution in Equation (12.48) with $k = 0$ that all scaled mean value functions yield the result $\mu(t_e; \hat{\boldsymbol{\beta}}) = m_e$, which in effect can be rewritten as

$$\hat{\beta}_0 = \frac{m_e}{\mu_1(t_e; \hat{\beta}_A)} \cdot \qquad (12.49)$$

The probability of observing m_e failures by time t_e for this type of model is given by Equation (10.5) as

$$P[M(t_e) = m_e] = \frac{[\mu(t_e)]^{m_e}}{m_e!} \exp[-\mu(t_e)], \qquad (12.50)$$

and thus after the appropriate substitutions the conditional likelihood is

$$L(\beta_A \mid m_e) = \frac{m_e! \prod_{i=1}^{m_e} \lambda(t_i)}{[\mu(t_e)]^{m_e}} \cdot \qquad (12.51)$$

This result is identical to the one for binomial-type models. The conditional likelihood function cannot be used to estimate β_0 (which is interpreted as ν_0 for finite failures models). However, if we use $\mu(t_e; \hat{\beta}) = m_e$ to estimate β_0, the conditional likelihood estimates are equivalent to the unconditional likelihood estimates.

The form of the likelihood function given by Equations (12.32) and (12.51) shows that the T_i's are the order statistics (positional values such as first, second, third of a random sample arranged in order of increasing magnitudes) of a random sample from the probability density function [see Mood, Graybill, and Boes (1974)]

$$f(t) = \frac{\lambda(t)}{\mu(t_e)}, \quad 0 \leqslant t \leqslant t_e. \qquad (12.52)$$

This may be useful for one-parameter scaled failure intensity functions in generating confidence intervals for β_1. An example of generating confidence intervals with Equation (12.52) will be illustrated shortly in Case Study 12.2.

Exponential class. Since the exponential class of Poisson-type models is characterized by a scaled mean value function, we can write the estimate of β_0 directly [using Equations (12.49) and (12.4)] as

$$\hat{\beta}_0 = \frac{m_e}{1 - \exp(-\hat{\beta}_1 t_e)} \cdot \qquad (12.53)$$

Also, we know that conditional estimation for Poisson-type models is equivalent to that for binomial-type models. Hence the estimate for β_1 is given by Equation (12.43), that is, as the solution to

$$\frac{m_e}{\hat{\beta}_1} - \frac{m_e t_e}{\exp(\hat{\beta}_1 t_e) - 1} - \sum_{i=1}^{m_e} t_i = 0. \qquad (12.54)$$

Geometric family. The geometric family is also characterized by a scaled mean value function. Thus, we write [using Equations (12.49) and (12.6)]

$$\hat{\beta}_0 = \frac{m_e}{\ln\,(1 + \hat{\beta}_1 t_e)}\,. \tag{12.55}$$

The conditional likelihood of β_1, Equation (12.51), after substituting Equations (12.6) and (12.7), is

$$L\,(\beta_1|\,m_e) = \frac{m_e!\,\beta_1^{m_e}\displaystyle\prod_{i=1}^{m_e}\frac{1}{1 + \beta_1 t_i}}{[\ln\,(1 + \beta_1 t_e)]^{m_e}}\,. \tag{12.56}$$

The maximum likelihood estimate for β_1, using Equation (12.35), is given as the solution to

$$\frac{1}{\hat{\beta}_1}\sum_{i=1}^{m_e}\frac{1}{1 + \hat{\beta}_1 t_i} - \frac{m_e t_e}{(1 + \hat{\beta}_1 t_e)\,\ln\,(1 + \hat{\beta}_1 t_e)} = 0\,. \tag{12.57}$$

Example 12.3. Using the T1 failure data, Equation (12.57) can be solved for $\hat{\beta}_1$, the value of which can then be substituted into Equation (12.55) to arrive at an estimate for β_0. The results for this case are $\hat{\beta}_0 = 42.3$ failures and $\hat{\beta}_1 = 0.262 \times 10^{-3}$/CPU sec. ∎

12.2.1.2 INTERVAL ESTIMATION OF MODEL PARAMETERS. As we have shown in the general discussion of maximum likelihood estimation, confidence intervals can be established using the likelihood function and the asymptotic normal distribution for maximum likelihood estimates. We will focus our attention on those models described by a one-parameter scaled mean value function. The reason for this is twofold. First, this type of function covers many of the more important models, including the two we have focused on in this book. Secondly, it is easier to describe what is taking place because of the smaller dimensionality.

Our discussion, for the reasons given in the introduction to Section 12.2, will concentrate on the conditional likelihood function that depends only on one parameter, namely, β_1. Based on this function, a confidence interval for β_1 can be generated as outlined in the introduction to Section 12.2. Then for a given $100(1 - \alpha)$ percent confidence interval for β_1, a $100(1 - \alpha)$ percent confidence interval can be obtained for a derived quantity $Q(\beta_1)$, if Q is a monotone function, by the *substitution principle*. A monotone function is one which is either always increasing or decreasing. The substitution principle is illustrated in Figure 12.11. Here Q is a monotone increasing function of β_1 and β_{low} and β_{high} are the lower and upper $100(1 - \alpha)$ percent confidence limits for β_1, respectively. Then $Q(\beta_{\text{low}})$ and $Q(\beta_{\text{high}})$ are the lower and upper $100(1 - \alpha)$ percent confidence limits for Q [Mood, Graybill, and Boes (1974)]. This property can generally be used to obtain confidence intervals for the parameter β_0, as well as derived quantities such as the initial and present failure intensity.

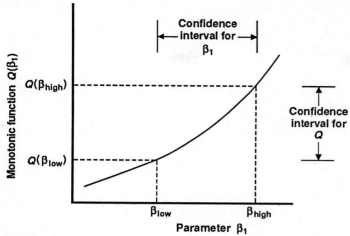

FIGURE 12.11
Illustration of the substitution principle.

An important point to remember before we continue is that the conditional likelihood function for binomial- and Poisson-type models is identical. This means that the following discussion about β_1 applies equally well to both model types.

Confidence interval for β_1. The conditional likelihood function Equation (12.51), after using Equations (12.1) and (12.2), becomes

$$L(\beta_1 \mid m_e) = \frac{m_e! \prod_{i=1}^{m_e} \lambda_1(t_i)}{[\mu_1(t_e)]^{m_e}} . \qquad (12.58)$$

The log-likelihood function (to within an additive constant) is

$$\ln L(\beta_1 \mid m_e) = \sum_{i=1}^{m_e} \ln \lambda_1(t_i) - m_e \ln \mu_1(t_e) . \qquad (12.59)$$

The first and second derivatives of this function are, respectively,

$$\frac{d \ln L(\beta_1 \mid m_e)}{d\beta_1} = \sum_{i=1}^{m_e} \frac{1}{\lambda_1(t_i)} \frac{d\lambda_1(t_i)}{d\beta_1} - \frac{m_e}{\mu_1(t_e)} \frac{d\mu_1(t_e)}{d\beta_1} \qquad (12.60)$$

and

$$\frac{d^2 \ln L(\beta_1 \mid m_e)}{d\beta_1^2} = \sum_{i=1}^{m_e} \frac{1}{\lambda_1(t_i)} \left\{ \frac{d^2\lambda_1(t_i)}{d\beta_1^2} - \frac{1}{\lambda_1(t_i)} \left[\frac{d\lambda_1(t_i)}{d\beta_1} \right]^2 \right\}$$
$$- \frac{m_e}{\mu_1(t_e)} \left\{ \frac{d^2\mu_1(t_e)}{d\beta_1^2} - \frac{1}{\mu_1(t_e)} \left[\frac{d\mu_1(t_e)}{d\beta_1} \right]^2 \right\} . \qquad (12.61)$$

The first derivative, when set equal to zero, is just the maximum likelihood equation and is solved to obtain $\hat{\beta}_1$, the maximum likelihood estimate of β_1. The second derivative is needed to obtain the information in the sample. The expected (or Fisher) information is given by

$$I(\beta_1) = E\left[-\frac{d^2 \ln L(\beta_1 \mid m_e)}{d\beta_1^2}\right]. \tag{12.62}$$

Usually this expectation is easy to determine. When it is not, an alternative is to use the asymptotically equivalent, observed information, that is

$$I_O(\hat{\beta}_1) = -\frac{d^2 \ln L(\beta_1 \mid m_e)}{d\beta_1^2}\Bigg|_{\beta_1 = \hat{\beta}_1}. \tag{12.63}$$

A confidence interval for β_1 can now be approximated by employing Equation (12.12) with k replaced by 1. The approximation should be checked to make sure it is appropriate. If it is not, either a transformation of $\hat{\beta}_1$ or the likelihood ratio should be used.

Confidence interval for β_0. Asymptotic properties of $\hat{\beta}_0$ assure us that the distribution of $\hat{\beta}_0$ will eventually approach normality. There are cases, however, where this approach to normality is extremely slow or where it can be shown that the approximation is invalid. Extreme care must be exercised. Care must also be exercised when using the substitution principle to establish a confidence interval for β_0.

The problems caused by the distribution of $\hat{\beta}_0$ can best be illustrated if we consider finite failures binomial-type models with scaled mean value functions, where we can write

$$\mu(t; \beta_0, \beta_1) = \beta_0 \mu_1(t; \beta_1). \tag{12.64}$$

The reader can compare Equations (12.64) and (10.26) and see that when $\beta_0 > 0$, it can be interpreted as u_0. From Equations (12.49), (10.22), and (10.26)

$$\hat{\beta}_0 = \frac{m_e}{F_a(t_e; \hat{\beta}_1)}$$

$$= \frac{m_e}{1 - \exp(-\int_0^{t_e} z_a(x; \hat{\beta}_1)dx)}. \tag{12.65}$$

The form of the denominator makes it possible for the right hand side of Equation (12.65) to have a pole (that is, division by zero may be possible) say, at $\hat{\beta}_1 = \beta_c$. Figure 12.12 shows a typical graph of the relationship between $\hat{\beta}_1$ and $\hat{\beta}_0$ when a pole at $\hat{\beta}_1 = \beta_c$ exists.

A possible distribution for $\hat{\beta}_1$ (from Figure 12.9) is superimposed on Figure 12.12. Note that the upper and lower confidence limits for a 95 percent confidence

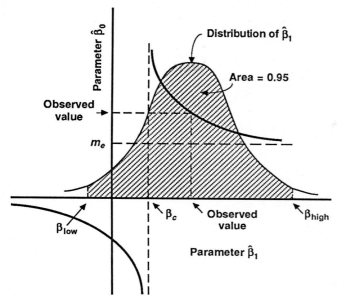

FIGURE 12.12
Relationship between $\hat{\beta}_0$ and $\hat{\beta}_1$ when a pole exists at β_c.

level are denoted as β_{high} and β_{low}, respectively, and that β_c lies within the interval. Since, in the case shown, $\hat{\beta}_0$ is confined to the intervals $-\infty \le \hat{\beta}_0 \le 0$ and $\hat{\beta}_0 \ge m_e$, its distribution cannot usually be approximated by the normal distribution. Also for the case shown, $\hat{\beta}_0$ is a monotonic function of $\hat{\beta}_1$ on either side of β_c. Thus we can say, using the substitution principle, that

$$P[-\infty < \beta_0 < \frac{m_e}{F_a(t_e; \beta_{\text{low}})} \text{ and } \frac{m_e}{F_a(t_e; \beta_{\text{high}})} < \beta_0 < \infty] \approx 0.95 . \quad (12.66)$$

See Figure 12.13a. This interval (or set of intervals) is not particularly useful for our purposes but it is technically correct. The reader may think that this is a special case that may not occur often enough to warrant this much attention. The results of Case Study 12.1, however, imply that for an exponential-class model we can expect this behavior (that is, $\beta_{\text{low}} < \beta_c < \beta_{\text{high}}$) for about the first half (based on the number of failures) of testing.

The normal approximation becomes better when most of the probability mass for $\hat{\beta}_1$ lies in a small interval on one side of β_c (which tends to happen when t_e is large), as illustrated in Figure 12.13b. Even here the adequacy of the normal approximation depends on the linearity of $\hat{\beta}_0$ with respect to $\hat{\beta}_1$. The more non-linear Equation (12.65) is, the worse the approximation. Figure 12.14 illustrates the skewness of the $\hat{\beta}_0$ distribution.

When $\hat{\beta}_0$ is a strictly monotonic function of $\hat{\beta}_1$ in the range given by the confidence limits of $\hat{\beta}_1$, then a confidence interval for $\hat{\beta}_0$ is given, by using the substitution principle, as

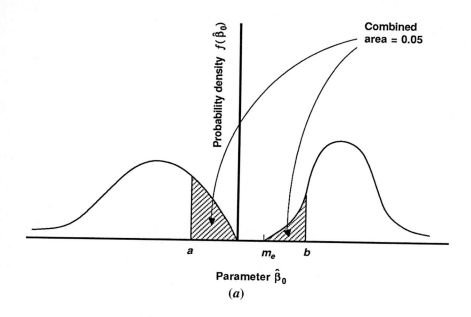

(a)

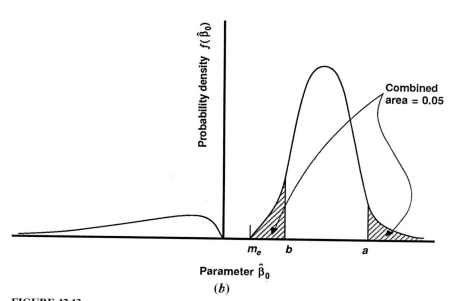

(b)

FIGURE 12.13
Normal approximation for $\hat{\beta}_0$. $a = m_e/F_a(t_e; \beta_{\text{low}})$ and $b = m_e/F_a(t_e; \beta_{\text{high}})$.
(a) Small sample. (b) Large sample.

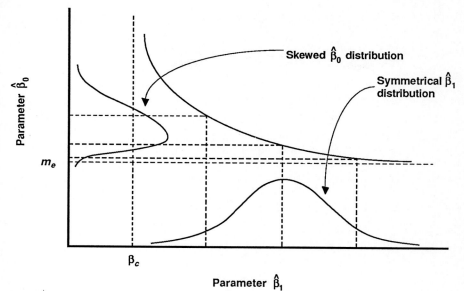

FIGURE 12.14
Skewness of $\hat{\beta}_0$ distribution.

$$\left[\frac{m_e}{F_a(t_e; \beta_{\text{high}})}, \frac{m_e}{F_a(t_e; \beta_{\text{low}})} \right].$$ (12.67)

Exponential class. Starting with Equation (12.54) the second derivative of the log-likelihood function is

$$\frac{\partial^2 \ln L(\beta_1 | m_e)}{\partial \beta_1^2} = -\frac{m_e}{\beta_1^2} + \frac{m_e t_e^2 \exp(\beta_1 t_e)}{[\exp(\beta_1 t_e) - 1]^2}.$$ (12.68)

Because t_e is considered not to be a random variable, the expected information is

$$I(\beta_1) = m_e \left[\frac{1}{\beta_1^2} - \frac{t_e^2 \exp(\beta_1 t_e)}{[\exp(\beta_1 t_e) - 1]^2} \right].$$ (12.69)

A confidence interval for β_1 can be established using the normal approximation Equation (12.12).

The maximum likelihood estimate for β_0 is given by Equation (12.53) as

$$\hat{\beta}_0 = \frac{m_e}{1 - \exp(-\hat{\beta}_1 t_e)}.$$ (12.70)

Since this is in the form of Equation (12.65), the previous discussion on confidence intervals applies and is not repeated here.

CASE STUDY 12.2
ADEQUACY OF THE NORMAL APPROXIMATION
FOR β_1 FOR EXPONENTIAL-CLASS MODELS

To show the extent to which the normal approximation gives appropriate confidence intervals in small samples, we will compare results with an approach based on a method proposed by Bartlett (1953), as well as with an exact method for $m_e = 2$ failures and $m_e = 3$ failures. The graphical method for testing the normal approximation that will be used later for the geometric family can be applied here. However, we wish to illustrate via this example the use of two alternative methods of generating confidence intervals that may be applied in other cases.

AN EXACT CONFIDENCE INTERVAL

The conditional probability density function of the T_i's is, from Equation (12.52),

$$f(t) = \frac{\beta_1 \exp(-\beta_1 t)}{1 - \exp(-\beta_1 t_e)} . \qquad (12.71)$$

The conditional probability density function of $X = \sum_{i=1}^{m_e} T_i$ is that of the sum of m_e independent random variables with the above density, since the T_i's are order statistics. In principle, if we knew the exact density function of X, we could easily establish confidence intervals for β_1 by employing the statistical method described in Mood, Graybill, and Boes (1974; pp. 387–393). The exact density function can be obtained (see Problem 12.17), but it is complicated and of practical use only for small to moderate m_e.

BARTLETT'S METHOD

Bartlett (1953) proposed a method for determining approximate confidence intervals that are asymptotically equivalent to those obtained from the maximum likelihood estimate, that is, Equation (12.12). The method is based on the sampling distribution of $\ln L(\beta_1 \mid m_e)$. This distribution is approximately normal with mean and variance known exactly to be 0 and $I(\beta_1)$. A correction for the asymmetry or skewness in this distribution is given below. The method used to derive this correction is also referenced in Kendall and Stuart (1961). Skewness is defined as the third moment about the mean.

Applying this method we can show (see Problem 12.19) that approximate $100(1 - \alpha)$ percent confidence limits for β_1 can be obtained by solving

$$\frac{\partial \ln L(\beta_1 \mid m_e)}{\partial \beta_1} - \frac{1}{6} \frac{\kappa_3}{I(\beta_1)} (\kappa_{1-\alpha/2}^2 - 1) = \pm \kappa_{1-\alpha/2}\sqrt{I(\beta_1)} \qquad (12.72)$$

for β_1, where κ_3 (the skewness) is given by

$$\kappa_3 = -\frac{2m_e}{\beta_1^3} + \frac{m_e t_e^3 \exp(-\beta_1 t_e)[\exp(-\beta_1 t_e) + 1]}{[1 - \exp(-\beta_1 t_e)]^2} . \qquad (12.73)$$

COMPARISON OF RESULTS

The confidence intervals generated by Bartlett's method are first compared to the exact confidence intervals for $m_e = 2$ and $m_e = 3$. This will establish the former method as providing an excellent approximation. Bartlett's method is then compared to Equation (12.12) to see how fast the two converge.

Some results of a simulation study are presented in Table 12.7. Results for 95 percent confidence intervals are shown for the exact method and Bartlett's method. The table shows that Bartlett's method provides excellent confidence intervals even for such small values of m_e. The method has been tested on many different types of problems with excellent results. Table 12.8 shows the results of another simulation where Equation (12.12) is compared to Bartlett's method. The two methods are seen to converge rapidly.

The adequacy of the asymptotic theory when m_e is small can also be investigated in another way. In Table 12.9 we give the coefficient of skewness of the distribution of $\ln L(\beta_1 \mid m_e)$ for various values of m_e and $\beta_1 t_e$. These may then be compared with the normal value of zero. The main conclusion that emerges from this table and the previous results is that it is justified to assume $\hat{\beta}_1$ is normally distributed even for small samples.

Example 12.4. The information contained in the T1 failure data for an exponential-class model is computed to be $I(0.348 \times 10^{-4}) = 6.07 \times 10^{10}$. The upper and lower limits of a 95 percent confidence interval for β_1 are then given by $0.348 \times 10^{-4} \pm 1.96/\sqrt{6.07 \times 10^{10}}$. That is, $(0.268 \times 10^{-4}, 0.427 \times 10^{-4})$ is an approximate 95 percent confidence interval for β_1.

Since $\hat{\beta}_0$ is a strictly monotonic function of $\hat{\beta}_1$ and is continuous in the range given by the confidence limits of $\hat{\beta}_1$, a 95 percent confidence interval can be established by the substitution principle. Thus, substituting each limit for $\hat{\beta}_1$ into Equation (12.70), we have as a 95 percent confidence interval for β_0 the range (138.8, 148.9). Given that $m_e = 136$, we are 95 percent certain that at least 3 and at most 13 more failures will occur. ■

Some care must be exercised when interpreting the maximum likelihood estimate and the confidence interval results for β_1 when the exponential class is par-

TABLE 12.7
Comparison of confidence limits for β_1 from Bartlett's method with exact values; $\beta_1 = 0.01$

Number of failures	β_0	Exact values		Bartlett's method	
		Lower	Upper	Lower	Upper
2	100	−3.65	0.56	−3.75	0.57
	200	−34.11	0.21	−35.00	0.15
3	200	−4.53	0.98	−4.57	1.02
	200	−2.93	1.21	−2.95	1.23

TABLE 12.8
**Comparison of confidence limits for β_1 from
Bartlett's method with those from the normal
approximation for $\hat{\beta}_1$: $\beta_0 = 200$, $\beta_1 = 0.01$**

Number of failures	Normal approximation		Bartlett's method	
	Lower	Upper	Lower	Upper
2	−27.89	4.79	−33.65	−0.21
5	−1.55	0.36	−1.66	0.32
25	−0.138	0.0586	−0.140	0.0585
50	0.0018	0.0712	0.0021	0.0718
100	0.0019	0.0256	0.0020	0.0257
150	0.0017	0.0105	0.0017	0.0105

ticularized as the basic execution time model. This model, being a finite failures model, requires $\beta_1 \geq 0$ (equality resulting in a stationary process suitable for modeling operational phase software). Thus, when $\hat{\beta}_1 < 0$ the appropriate procedure is to set $\hat{\beta}_1 = 0$. The same type of thing applies when the results of Equation (12.12) yield negative confidence limits for β_1. The appropriate procedure is to replace any negative confidence limit with zero. The maximum likelihood estimate and confidence limits for the parameter $\beta_0 = \nu_0$ generated using the substitution principle will automatically meet the requirement that they be greater than or equal to m_e by doing this.

Geometric family. The expected information for this family of models is given by (see Problem 12.16)

$$I(\beta_1) = m_e \left\{ \frac{2t_e}{\beta_1(1 + \beta_1 t_e) \ln (1 + \beta_1 t_e)} - \frac{1}{2\beta_1^2 \ln (1 + \beta_1 t_e)} \left[1 - \frac{1}{(1 + \beta_1 t_e)^2} \right] \right.$$
$$\left. - \frac{t_e^2[\ln (1 + \beta_1 t_e) + 1]}{[(1 + \beta_1 t_e) \ln (1 + \beta_1 t_e)]^2} \right\}. \quad (12.74)$$

TABLE 12.9
Coefficient of skewness

$\beta_1 t_e$	Number of failures m_e						
	2	5	10	20	30	40	50
0.05	−0.012	−0.008	−0.006	−0.004	−0.003	−0.003	−0.002
0.10	−0.025	−0.015	−0.011	−0.003	−0.006	−0.006	−0.005
0.20	−0.049	−0.031	−0.022	−0.016	−0.013	−0.011	−0.010
0.50	−0.122	−0.077	−0.055	−0.039	−0.032	−0.027	−0.025
1.0	−0.244	−0.154	−0.109	−0.077	−0.063	−0.054	−0.049

Confidence intervals can be established using Equation (12.12). However it can be shown that the approximation is poor unless the sample size is large, that is, the convergence to the normal distribution is slow in this case. Figure 12.15 shows a normal quantile-quantile plot for the estimated value of β_1 from 200 randomly generated failure time sequences.[7] This plot shows the sorted values of $\hat{\beta}_1$ plotted against the corresponding quantiles of the normal distribution. A plot with relatively large or systematic deviations from a straight line gives evidence of nonnormality. Each of the generated failure time sequences had the same value for t_e. This makes m_e a random variable, whose average value in this case was 162 failures. The quality of the approximation, even for so large a value for m_e, is clear from the figure. Similar behavior is shown over a range of values for β_1.

A much better alternative is available in that the distribution of

$$\hat{U} = \ln\,(1 + \hat{\beta}_1 t_e) \qquad (12.75)$$

is much more closely approximated by a normal distribution than is the distribution of $\hat{\beta}_1$, even in small samples. Note that $\hat{U}$ does not have restrictions on its range as does $\hat{\beta}_1$, and we should expect a better approximation. Figure 12.16 shows the improvement that results when applying Equation (12.75) to the data of Figure 12.15. Similar plots can be used to show that the distribution of $\hat{U}$ is approximately normal even for small samples. The mean and variance of this distribution are $\ln\,(1 + \hat{\beta}_1 t_e)$ and

$$\text{var}[\hat{U}] \approx \frac{1}{I(\hat{\beta}_1)} \left[\frac{t_e}{1 + \hat{\beta}_1 t_e} \right]^2 , \qquad (12.76)$$

respectively.[8] The procedure analogous to Equation (12.12) is to use the normal approximation

$$\frac{\hat{U} - U}{\sqrt{\text{var}[\hat{U}]}} \sim N(0, 1) . \qquad (12.77)$$

This approximation can be used to obtain confidence intervals for U, which are readily converted to confidence intervals for β_1. Thus, if $(U_{\text{low}}, U_{\text{high}})$ is a confidence interval for U then

$$\left[\frac{\exp\,(U_{\text{low}}) - 1}{t_e}, \frac{\exp\,(U_{\text{high}}) - 1}{t_e} \right] \qquad (12.78)$$

is one for β_1.

---

[7]The data were generated from the model $\mu(t) = \beta_0 \ln\,(1 + \beta_1 t)$ with $\beta_0 = 200$ failures, $\beta_1 = 0.00025/$ sec, and $t_e = 5000$ sec.

[8]For a function of a random variable X, say $g(X)$, approximate formulas for the mean and variance of g are given by $E[g] \approx g(E[X])$ and $\text{var}[g] \approx \text{var}[X] \{[\partial g(x)/\partial x] \mid_{x=E[X]}\}^2$, respectively [Mood, Graybill, and Boes (1974)].

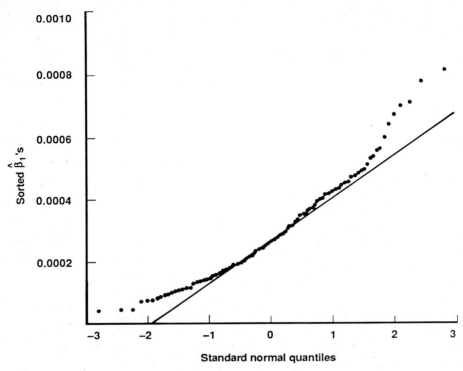

FIGURE 12.15
Normal quantile-quantile plot for $\hat{\beta}_1$.

The maximum likelihood estimate for β_0 is given by Equation (12.55) as

$$\hat{\beta}_0 = \frac{m_e}{\ln (1 + \hat{\beta}_1 t_e)} = \frac{m_e}{\hat{U}} \qquad (12.79)$$

Confidence intervals can be directly established by the substitution principle since this is a strictly monotonic function in the permissible range of $\hat{\beta}_1$.

It is worth noting here that when we speak of the logarithmic Poisson model, a parameter of interest is θ, which, in this framework, is given by β_0^{-1}. The maximum likelihood estimate of θ is given as

$$\hat{\theta} = \frac{1}{m_e} \ln (1 + \hat{\beta}_1 t_e) = \frac{\hat{U}}{m_e}, \qquad \hat{U} \geqslant 0 \qquad (12.80)$$

$$= 0, \qquad \hat{U} < 0 \,.$$

Confidence intervals for θ are given, directly, by

$$\left[\frac{U_{\text{low}}}{m_e}, \frac{U_{\text{high}}}{m_e} \right]. \qquad (12.81)$$

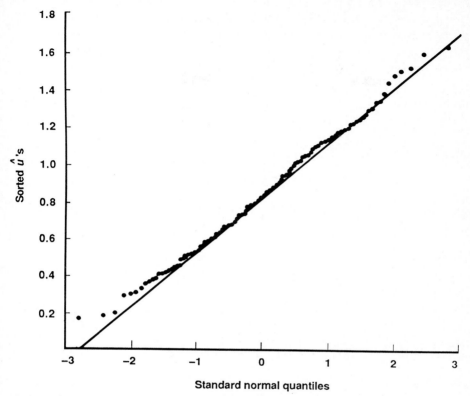

FIGURE 12.16
Normal quantile-quantile plot for $\hat{U}$.

As with the basic execution time model negative limits should be set equal to zero.

> **Example 12.5.** The information contained in the T1 failure data for a geometric-family model is computed to be $I(0.262 \times 10^{-3}) = 1.31 \times 10^{8}$. U has a value of 3.215 with a variance of 0.1024. The lower 95 percent confidence limit for U is $U_{\mathrm{low}} = 3.215 - 1.96\sqrt{0.1024} = 2.588$ and similarly the upper confidence limit is $U_{\mathrm{high}} = 3.842$. From Equation (12.78) the corresponding interval for $\hat{\beta}_1$ is $(0.135 \times 10^{-3}, 0.5 \times 10^{-3})$. The confidence interval for β_0 is $(35.4, 52.55)$. Using Equations (12.80) and (12.81) the point and interval estimates for θ are $\hat{\theta} = 0.024$ and $(0.019, 0.028)$, respectively. ∎

12.2.1.3 ESTIMATION OF DERIVED QUANTITIES. Up to now we have focused our attention on the model parameters β_0 and β_1. We now turn to inference about other useful quantities for those models described by one-parameter scaled mean value functions. These are (in the order in which they will be discussed):

1. the failure intensity (initial, present, and future),
2. the additional time required to meet a failure intensity objective, and
3. the additional number of failures to be experienced in order to meet the failure intensity objective.

The following development will be in terms of failure time data. It also applies equally well to grouped data if m_e and t_e are replaced with y_p and x_p, respectively.

Failure intensity. The failure intensity is given by Equation (12.2) as

$$\lambda(t) = \beta_0 \lambda_1(t; \beta_1) \, , \tag{12.82}$$

which upon substitution of the maximum likelihood estimates for β_0 and β_1 yields the maximum likelihood estimate

$$\hat{\lambda}(t) = \frac{m_e \lambda_1(t; \hat{\beta}_1)}{\mu_1(t_e; \hat{\beta}_1)} \, . \tag{12.83}$$

The failure intensity can be estimated for any value of time. When t is set equal to zero, the initial failure intensity $\hat{\lambda}_0$ will be estimated. Similarly, when t is set equal to t_e, the present failure intensity $\hat{\lambda}_P$ will be estimated. Finally, when t is set to some value greater than t_e, the failure intensity at some future time will be estimated. This is needed to make the control charts described in Chapter 7. The behavior of $\hat{\lambda}_0$ as a function of $\hat{\beta}_1$ is difficult to generalize for arbitrary λ_1. However, for exponential-class and geometric-family models it can be shown (see Problems 12.11 and 12.12) that $\hat{\lambda}_P$ is strictly monotonically increasing in $\hat{\beta}_1$. Thus, confidence intervals for λ_0 for these models can be directly established by substitution as shown in Figure 12.17. The reader should note that the values β_{low} and β_{high} take on are not the same for both models. However, for clarity, only one set is used in Figure 12.17. The behavior of $\hat{\lambda}_P$ is also difficult to generalize for arbitrary λ_1. Once again, for exponential-class and geometric-family models it can be shown (see Problems 12.11 and 12.12) that $\hat{\lambda}_P$ is a strictly monotonically decreasing function of $\hat{\beta}_1$. This allows confidence intervals for these models to be established by substitution in a way analogous to that shown in Figure 12.17.

Additional time to objective. The amount of time Δt required for the failure intensity to decrease from its current value of λ_P to some specified objective λ_F is sought. Given the value for λ, Equation (12.82) can be solved for the time. Thus,

$$t = \lambda_1^{-1} \left[\frac{\lambda}{\beta_0} \right] \, . \tag{12.84}$$

where λ_1^{-1} denotes the inverse of λ_1. From this it is straightforward to write

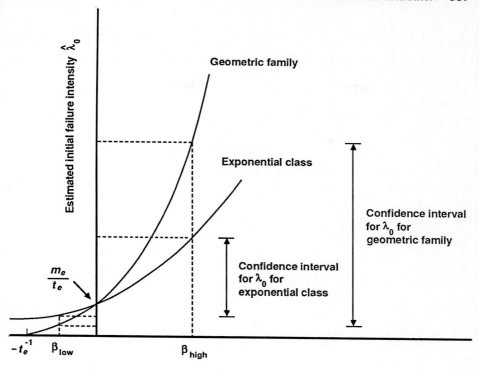

FIGURE 12.17
Initial failure intensity versus $\hat{\beta}_1$ for exponential-class and geometric-family models.

$$\Delta t = \lambda_1^{-1}\left(\frac{\lambda_F}{\beta_0}\right) - \lambda_1^{-1}\left(\frac{\lambda_P}{\beta_0}\right) \tag{12.85}$$

or equivalently,

$$\Delta t = \lambda_1^{-1}\left(\frac{\lambda_F}{\beta_0}\right) - t_e . \tag{12.86}$$

Substituting $\hat{\beta}_0$ as given by Equation (12.49) we have, for the latter expression,[9]

$$\hat{\Delta t} = \lambda_1^{-1}\left[\frac{\lambda_F \mu_1(t_e; \hat{\beta}_1)}{m_e}\right] - t_e . \tag{12.87}$$

---

[9]If, in evaluating $\hat{\Delta t}$, a negative value results, then $\hat{\Delta t}$ should be set equal to zero.

In general, Δt is not a monotonic function of $\hat{\beta}_1$ and confidence intervals cannot be established by direct substitution. However, for virtually all values of $\hat{\beta}_1$ that can be encountered in practice $\Delta \hat{t}$ is a monotonic function and thus we can use substitution to establish confidence intervals.

Additional number of failures. The expected additional number of failures $\Delta \mu$ experienced during the interval of length Δt is given simply as

$$\Delta \mu = \mu(t_F) - \mu(t_e) . \tag{12.88}$$

where t_F is the time at which the failure intensity reaches λ_F. Substituting the results from the previous section and noting that $\mu(t_e) = m_e$, the above becomes

$$\Delta \mu = \beta_0 \mu_1 \left\{ \lambda_1^{-1} \left[\frac{\lambda_F \mu_1(t_e; \beta_1)}{m_e} \right] \right\} - m_e . \tag{12.89}$$

The maximum likelihood estimate of $\Delta \mu$ can be found as before by substituting $\hat{\beta}_0$ and $\hat{\beta}_1$. We have[10]

$$\Delta \hat{\mu} = \frac{m_e}{\mu_1(t_e; \hat{\beta}_1)} \mu_1 \left\{ \lambda_1^{-1} \left[\frac{\lambda_F \mu_1(t_e; \hat{\beta}_1)}{m_e} \right] \right\} - m_e . \tag{12.90}$$

As with the additional time, Equation (12.90) is not a monotonic function of $\hat{\beta}_1$, but it can be treated as such in virtually all practical cases.

Example 12.6. Consider the exponential class. The failure intensity Equation (12.83) becomes, on substitution of Equations (12.4) and (12.5),

$$\hat{\lambda}(t) = \frac{m_e \hat{\beta}_1 \exp(- \hat{\beta}_1 t)}{1 - \exp(- \hat{\beta}_1 t_e)} . \tag{12.91}$$

The maximum likelihood estimate of λ_0 is

$$\hat{\lambda}_0 = \hat{\lambda}(0) = \frac{m_e \hat{\beta}_1}{1 - \exp(- \hat{\beta}_1 t_e)} \tag{12.92}$$

and that of λ_P is

$$\hat{\lambda}_P = \hat{\lambda}(t_e) = \frac{m_e \hat{\beta}_1 \exp(- \hat{\beta}_1 t_e)}{1 - \exp(- \hat{\beta}_1 t_e)} . \tag{12.93}$$

From the information given in Example 12.4 we can show that $\hat{\lambda}_0 = 0.49 \times 10^{-2}$ failure/CPU sec and $\hat{\lambda}_P = 0.21 \times 10^{-3}$ failure/CPU sec. Also, by substituting the

---

[10]If, in evaluating $\Delta \hat{\mu}$, a negative value results, then $\Delta \hat{\mu}$ should be set equal to zero.

upper and lower limits of the 95 percent confidence interval for β_1 we have the corresponding intervals for λ_0 and λ_P. These are $(0.40 \times 10^{-2}, 0.59 \times 10^{-2})$ for λ_0 and $(0.12 \times 10^{-3}, 0.35 \times 10^{-3})$ for λ_P.

Now suppose a failure intensity objective of 0.15×10^{-3} failure/CPU sec has been set for the project.[11] After determining the inverse of λ_1 [which turns out to be $\beta_1^{-1} \ln (\beta_1/\lambda)$] and substituting into Equation (12.87) we have for the additional time to reach the objective

$$\Delta \hat{t} = \frac{1}{\hat{\beta}_1} \ln \left\{ \frac{m_e \hat{\beta}_1}{\lambda_F [1 - \exp(-\hat{\beta}_1 t_e)]} \right\} - t_e . \qquad (12.94)$$

The maximum likelihood estimate and 95 percent confidence interval for Δt are 9205 CPU sec and (0, 31225) respectively. Note that when the lower limit for Δt is evaluated it actually comes out to be -5101 CPU sec. This was expected, since the lower limit for λ_P was below the objective.

The additional number of failures to reach the objective becomes, after some algebra,

$$\Delta \hat{\mu} = \frac{m_e}{\exp(\hat{\beta}_1 t_e) - 1} - \frac{\lambda_F}{\hat{\beta}_1} . \qquad (12.95)$$

The maximum likelihood estimate and 95 percent confidence interval are 2 failures and 0 to 7 failures, respectively.

The total set of results (from Examples 12.2, 12.4, and this example) for the exponential class of models is given in Table 12.10. ∎

Example 12.7. For the geometric family the failure intensity given by Equation (12.83) becomes

---

[11]This was deliberately chosen to lie within the confidence interval for λ_P.

TABLE 12.10
Parameter estimates and confidence limits for an exponential-class Poisson model[1] for system T1

| Parameter | Point estimate | 95 percent confidence limits | |
		Lower	Upper
β_1	0.348×10^{-4}	0.268×10^{-4}	0.427×10^{-4}
β_0	142	138.8	148.9
λ_0	0.49×10^{-2}	0.40×10^{-2}	0.59×10^{-2}
λ_P	0.21×10^{-3}	0.12×10^{-3}	0.35×10^{-3}
Δt	9205	0	31225
$\Delta \mu$	2	0	7

[1]For the basic execution time model $\beta_0 = \nu_0$ and $\beta_1 = \phi B$.

$$\hat{\lambda}(t) = \frac{m_e \hat{\beta}_1}{(1 + \hat{\beta}_1 t) \ln (1 + \hat{\beta}_1 t_e)} . \tag{12.96}$$

The maximum likelihood estimates for λ_0 and λ_P are

$$\hat{\lambda}_0 = \frac{m_e \hat{\beta}_1}{\ln (1 + \hat{\beta}_1 t_e)} , \tag{12.97}$$

and

$$\hat{\lambda}_P = \frac{m_e \hat{\beta}_1}{(1 + \hat{\beta}_1 t_e) \ln (1 + \hat{\beta}_1 t_e)} , \tag{12.98}$$

respectively.

The additional time required to reach the failure intensity objective is, after the appropriate substitutions and algebra (note that the inverse of λ_1 is $1/\lambda - 1/\beta_1$ in this case),

$$\Delta \hat{t} = \frac{m_e}{\lambda_F \ln (1 + \hat{\beta}_1 t_e)} - \frac{1}{\hat{\beta}_1} - t_e . \tag{12.99}$$

Similarly, the additional number of failures required to reach the objective is given by

$$\Delta \hat{\mu} = \frac{m_e}{\ln (\hat{\beta}_1 t_e + 1)} \left\{ \ln \left[\frac{m_e \hat{\beta}_1}{(\hat{\beta}_1 t_e + 1) \ln (1 + \hat{\beta}_1 t_e)} \right] - \ln \lambda_F \right\} . \tag{12.100}$$

Using the results of Examples 12.3 and 12.5 and the substitution principle we have the results shown in Table 12.11 (λ_F was set to the same value used in Example 12.6). ∎

12.2.2   Grouped Data

Estimation based on grouped failure data parallels that based on failure time data. The only difference between the two will be in the formulas regarding $\boldsymbol{\beta}$. For one-parameter scaled mean value functions β_1 is, once again, the basis for all inferences. Results from the previous sections regarding β_0 and derived quantities remain unchanged except that m_e should be replaced with y_p and t_e with x_p. Hence, the following sections will tend to be brief and will give the necessary formulas for the estimation of β_1.

12.2.2.1   POINT ESTIMATION OF MODEL PARAMETERS.

Suppose that estimation is to be performed using data such as those shown in Table 12.2. Let y_l ($l = 1, ..., p$) be the number of failures in $(0, x_l]$. Then the likelihood function is

$$L(\boldsymbol{\beta}; y_1, y_2, \cdots, y_p) = \prod_{l=1}^{p} P[M(x_l) = y_l]$$

$$= \prod_{l=1}^{p} P[M(x_l) = y_l \mid M(x_{l-1}) = y_{l-1}] P[M(0) = 0] , \tag{12.101}$$

TABLE 12.11
Parameter estimates and confidence limits for a geometric-family Poisson model[1] for system T1

Parameter	Point estimate	95 percent confidence limits	
		Lower	Upper
β_1	0.262×10^{-3}	0.135×10^{-3}	0.5×10^{-3}
β_0	42.3	35.4	52.55
λ_0	0.11×10^{-1}	0.71×10^{-2}	0.177×10^{-1}
λ_P	0.445×10^{-3}	0.380×10^{-3}	0.533×10^{-3}
Δt	187011	142799	251618
$\Delta \mu$	46	33	67

[1]For the logarithmic model $\beta_0 = \theta^{-1}$ and $\beta_1 = \lambda_0 \theta$.

where $x_0 = y_0 = 0$, and, by assumption, $P[M(0) = 0] = 1$.

The conditional likelihood when grouped data is used is given as

$$L(\boldsymbol{\beta}| y_p) = \frac{L(\boldsymbol{\beta})}{P[M(x_p) = y_p \, ; \boldsymbol{\beta}]} . \tag{12.102}$$

We will shortly see that if $\mu(x_p) = y_p$ the two forms of estimation given by Equations (12.101) and (12.102) and the two types of models (Poisson and binomial) are equivalent from an estimation point of view. The only exception is unconditional estimation for binomial-type models. Equivalence here requires the more restrictive $\mu(x_l) = y_l$; $l = 1, ..., p$. This will, in practice, never be satisfied. However, if the model fits well then the condition will be nearly satisfied. The maximum likelihood estimator of β_0 is given in Table 12.6 for various conditions. From this we see that $\mu(x_p) = y_p$ is the result of the maximum likelihood equation for β_0 for scaled mean value functions.

Binomial-type models. Each factor of the unconditional likelihood is given by Equation (10.32) if the obvious parameter variable translations (for example, using x_l in place of t) are made. Thus Equation (12.101) becomes[12]

$$L(u_0, \boldsymbol{\beta}_A) = \prod_{l=1}^{p} \binom{u_0 - y_{l-1}}{y_l'} [F_a(x_l| x_{l-1})]^{y_l'} [1 - F_a(x_l| x_{l-1})]^{u_0 - y_l} \tag{12.103}$$

where y_l' represents the number of failures in $(x_{l-1}, x_l]$, that is,

$$y_l' = y_l - y_{l-1} .$$

---

[12]Note that the joint density function forms a multinomial distribution.

The log-likelihood to within an additive constant is, after some algebra,

$$\ln L(u_0, \boldsymbol{\beta}_A) = \sum_{i=1}^{y_p} \ln (u_0 - i + 1) + \sum_{l=1}^{p} y_l' \ln [F_a(x_l \mid x_{l-1})]$$

$$+ \sum_{l=1}^{p} (u_0 - y_l) \ln [1 - F_a(x_l \mid x_{l-1})] . \quad (12.104)$$

From Equation (12.104) the maximum likelihood equations become

$$\frac{\partial \ln L(u_0, \boldsymbol{\beta}_A)}{\partial u_0} = \sum_{l=1}^{p} \ln [1 - F_a(x_l \mid x_{l-1})] + \sum_{i=1}^{y_p} \frac{1}{u_0 - i + 1} = 0 \quad (12.105)$$

and

$$\frac{\partial \ln L(u_0, \boldsymbol{\beta}_A)}{\partial \beta_k} = \sum_{l=1}^{p} \frac{y_l'}{F_a(x_l \mid x_{l-1})} \frac{\partial F_a(x_l \mid x_{l-1})}{\partial \beta_k}$$

$$- \sum_{l=1}^{p} \frac{u_0 - y_l}{1 - F_a(x_l \mid x_{l-1})} \frac{\partial F_a(x_l \mid x_{l-1})}{\partial \beta_k} = 0 . \quad (12.106)$$

The former likelihood equation reduces to

$$\ln [1 - F_a(x_p)] + \sum_{i=1}^{y_p} \frac{1}{u_0 - i + 1} = 0, \quad (12.107)$$

which is identical to Equation (12.27). It is left as an exercise to show that if $\mu(x_l) = y_l$ for $l = 1, \ldots, p$, then Equation (12.106) becomes

$$- \frac{\partial \mu(x_p)}{\partial \beta_k} + \sum_{l=1}^{p} \frac{y_l'}{\Delta \mu_l} \frac{\partial \Delta \mu_l}{\partial \beta_k} = 0 , \quad (12.108)$$

where $\Delta \mu_l = \mu(x_l) - \mu(x_{l-1})$.

For this model type the denominator of Equation (12.102) is given by Equation (12.30) if t_e is replaced with x_p and m_e is replaced with y_p. Then, substituting into Equation (12.102) and using Equations (12.103) and (10.33), we have

$$L(u_0, \boldsymbol{\beta}_A \mid y_p) = L(\boldsymbol{\beta}_A \mid y_p) = y_p! \prod_{l=1}^{p} \frac{1}{y_l!} \left[\frac{F_a(x_l) - F_a(x_{l-1})}{F_a(x_p)} \right]^{y_l'} . \quad (12.109)$$

This can be rewritten in terms of the mean value function as

$$L(\boldsymbol{\beta}_A \mid y_p) = \frac{y_p!}{[\mu(x_p)]^{y_p}} \prod_{i=1}^{p} \frac{1}{y_i!} (\Delta \mu_l)^{y_i'} . \quad (12.110)$$

The logarithm of this last function is, to within an additive constant,

$$\ln L(\boldsymbol{\beta}_A \mid y_p) = \sum_{l=1}^{p} y_l' \ln \Delta \mu_l - y_p \ln \mu(x_p) . \quad (12.111)$$

From Equation (12.111) the likelihood equations are

$$\sum_{l=1}^{p} \frac{y_l'}{\Delta\mu_l} \frac{\partial \Delta\mu_l}{\partial \beta_k} - \frac{y_p}{\mu(x_p)} \frac{\partial \mu(x_p)}{\partial \beta_k} , \quad k = 1, \cdots, w . \qquad (12.112)$$

Exponential class. For this class we have

$$F_a(x_l) = 1 - \exp(-\beta_1 x_l) , \qquad (12.113)$$

so that Equation (10.34) yields

$$F_a(x_l \mid x_{l-1}) = 1 - \exp[-\beta_1(x_l - x_{l-1})]. \qquad (12.114)$$

Substituting Equations (12.113) and (12.114) into Equations (12.106) and (12.107) yields for the unconditional maximum likelihood equations

$$-\hat{\beta}_1 x_p + \sum_{i=1}^{y_p} \frac{1}{\hat{u}_0 - i + 1} = 0 \qquad (12.115)$$

and

$$\sum_{l=1}^{p} \frac{y_l'(x_l - x_{l-1})}{\exp[\hat{\beta}_1(x_l - x_{l-1})] - 1} - \sum_{l=1}^{p} (\hat{u}_0 - y_l)(x_l - x_{l-1}) = 0 . \qquad (12.116)$$

The first of these equations is identical to Equation (12.38) if we note that $x_p = t_e$ and $y_p = m_e$.

> **Example 12.8.** As a numerical example, suppose we use the grouped data given in Table 12.3. Here $y_p = 32$ failures and $x_p = 125$ CPU hr. Using the procedure in Appendix D, Equations (12.115) and (12.116) are solved for the maximum likelihood estimates for u_0 and β_1. The results are $\hat{u}_0 = 43$ failures and $\hat{\beta}_1 = 0.0111$/CPU hr. ∎

The conditional maximum likelihood equation for β_1 is

$$\sum_{l=1}^{p} \frac{y_l'[x_l \exp(-\hat{\beta}_1 x_l) - x_{l-1} \exp(-\hat{\beta}_1 x_{l-1})]}{\exp(-\hat{\beta}_1 x_{l-1}) - \exp(-\hat{\beta}_1 x_l)} - \frac{y_p x_p}{\exp(\hat{\beta}_1 x_p) - 1} = 0 . \qquad (12.117)$$

> **Example 12.9.** Using the data from the previous example and solving for $\hat{\beta}_1$ in Equation (12.117) results in $\hat{\beta}_1 = 0.0105$/CPU hr. By using $\mu(x_p) = y_p$ we have
>
> $$\hat{u}_0 = \frac{y_p}{1 - \exp(-\hat{\beta}_1 x_p)} = 44 \text{ failures} \cdot \cdot$$
>
> The conditional estimates are close to the unconditional ones, as we expected. ∎

Poisson-type models. Since the Poisson process has independent increments Equation (12.101) may be written as

$$L(\beta) = \prod_{l=1}^{p} P[M(x_l) - M(x_{l-1}) = y_l - y_{l-1}]$$

$$= \prod_{l=1}^{p} P[M(x_l) - M(x_{l-1}) = y_l'] \, . \qquad (12.118)$$

It is easy to see [compare with Equation (10.7)] that

$$P[M(x_l) - M(x_{l-1}) = y_l'] = \frac{(\Delta\mu_l)^{y_l'}}{y_l'!} \exp(-\Delta\mu_l) \qquad (12.119)$$

and thus,

$$L(\beta) = \left\{ \prod_{l=1}^{p} \frac{(\Delta\mu_l)^{y_l'}}{y_l'} \right\} \exp\left[-\mu(x_p)\right] \, . \qquad (12.120)$$

The logarithm of the likelihood to within an additive constant is

$$\ln L(\beta) = \sum_{l=1}^{p} y_l' \ln \Delta\mu_l - \mu(x_p) \, . \qquad (12.121)$$

The maximum likelihood equations become

$$\sum_{l=1}^{p} \frac{y_l' \frac{\partial}{\partial\beta_k}\Delta\mu_l}{\Delta\mu_l} - \frac{\partial\mu(x_p)}{\partial\beta_k} = 0 \, , \qquad k = 0, \cdots, w \, . \qquad (12.122)$$

For scaled mean value functions, $\mu(t; \beta) = \beta_0\mu_1(t; \beta_A)$. Equation (12.122) yields for the equation for $\beta_0 (k = 0)$

$$\mu(x_p; \hat{\beta}) = y_p \, , \qquad (12.123)$$

which can in effect be rewritten as

$$\hat{\beta}_0 = \frac{m_e}{\mu_1(t_e; \hat{\beta}_A)} \, . \qquad (12.124)$$

As before, this is intuitively appealing. That is, the value of the mean value function at the end of test should equal the number of failures experienced.

Using Equations (12.50) and (12.120) and replacing t_e with x_p and m_e with y_p when necessary, the conditional likelihood of the observations, given y_p failures, is

$$L(\beta| y_p) = \frac{y_p!}{[\mu(x_p)]^{y_p}} \prod_{l=1}^{p} \frac{(\Delta\mu_l)^{y_l'}}{y_l'!} \, . \qquad (12.125)$$

Conditional and unconditional likelihood estimation result in identical estimates for $\boldsymbol{\beta}_A$ since it has been established that $\mu(x_p; \hat{\boldsymbol{\beta}}) = y_p$. Conditional likelihood estimation for binomial-type models is identical to that for Poisson-type models. It is also identical to the unconditional estimation for Poisson-type models provided $\mu(x_p; \hat{\boldsymbol{\beta}}_A)$ is set equal to y_p for the binomial case.

Exponential class. Since the exponential class is characterized by a scaled mean value function we can write the estimate of β_0 directly [using Equations (12.123) and (12.4)] as

$$\hat{\beta}_0 = \frac{y_p}{1 - \exp(- \hat{\beta}_1 x_p)} . \tag{12.126}$$

Also, we know that conditional estimation for Poisson-type models is equivalent to conditional estimation for binomial-type models, so the estimate for β_1 is given by Equation (12.117).

Geometric family. This family is also characterized by a scaled mean value function, so we write

$$\hat{\beta}_0 = \frac{y_p}{\ln (1 + \hat{\beta}_1 x_p)} . \tag{12.127}$$

The maximum likelihood equation (12.112) becomes, after some manipulation,

$$\sum_{l=1}^{p} \frac{y_l x_l}{(1 + \hat{\beta}_1 x_l)[\ln (1 + \hat{\beta}_1 x_l) - \ln (1 + \hat{\beta}_1 x_{l-1})]} - \frac{x_p y_p}{(1 + \hat{\beta}_1 x_p) \ln (1 + \hat{\beta}_1 x_p)}$$

$$- \sum_{l=1}^{p} \frac{y_l x_{l-1}}{(1 + \hat{\beta}_1 x_{l-1})[\ln (1 + \hat{\beta}_1 x_l) - \ln (1 + \hat{\beta}_1 x_{l-1})]} = 0 . \tag{12.128}$$

Example 12.10. Using the data in Table 12.3 and solving Equation (12.128) for $\hat{\beta}_1$ results in $\hat{\beta}_1 = 0.0207/\text{CPU hr}$, which on substitution into Equation (12.127) yields $\hat{\beta}_0 = 25.05$ failures. ∎

12.2.2.2 INTERVAL ESTIMATION OF MODEL PARAMETERS. Much, if not all, of what was said in Section 12.2.1.2 applies here. We will assume that $\mu(x_l) \approx y_l, l = 1,\ldots, p$, so that point and interval estimation is identical for both binomial-type and Poisson-type models.

The conditional likelihood function given by Equation (12.125), after using Equation (12.1), becomes

$$L(\beta_1 | y_p) = \frac{y_p! \prod_{l=1}^{p} \frac{1}{y_l} [\mu_1(x_l) - \mu_1(x_{l-1})]^{y_l}}{[\mu_1(x_p)]^{y_p}} . \tag{12.129}$$

The log-likelihood function (to within an additive constant) is

$$\ln L(\beta_1| y_p) = \sum_{l=1}^{p} y_l' \ln [\mu_1(x_l) - \mu_1(x_{l-1})] - y_p \ln \mu_1(x_p) . \quad (12.130)$$

The first and second derivatives of this function are, respectively,

$$\frac{\partial \ln L(\beta_1| y_p)}{\partial \beta_1} = \sum_{l=1}^{p} \frac{y_l'}{\mu_1(x_l) - \mu_1(x_{l-1})} \cdot \frac{\partial [\mu_1(x_l) - \mu_1(x_{l-1})]}{\partial \beta_1}$$

$$- \frac{y_p}{\mu_1(x_p)} \frac{\partial \mu_1(x_p)}{\partial \beta_1} \quad (12.131)$$

and

$$\frac{\partial^2 \ln L(\beta_1| y_p)}{\partial \beta_1^2} = \sum_{l=1}^{p} \frac{y_l'}{\mu_1(x_l) - \mu_1(x_{l-1})} \left\{ \frac{\partial^2 [\mu_1(x_l) - \mu_1(x_{l-1})]}{\partial \beta_1^2} \right.$$

$$- \frac{1}{\mu_1(x_l) - \mu_1(x_{l-1})} \left[\frac{\partial [\mu_1(x_l) - \mu_1(x_{l-1})]}{\partial \beta_1} \right]^2 \right\}$$

$$- \frac{y_p}{\mu_1(x_p)} \left\{ \frac{\partial^2 \mu_1(x_p)}{\partial \beta_1^2} - \frac{1}{\mu_1(x_p)} \left[\frac{\partial \mu_1(x_p)}{\partial \beta_1} \right]^2 \right\} . \quad (12.132)$$

The first derivative, when set equal to zero, is just the maximum likelihood equation for β_1 and is solved to obtain $\hat{\beta}_1$, the maximum likelihood estimate of β_1. The second derivative is needed to obtain the information in the sample. Usually in cases involving grouped data it is easier to use the observed information, that is,

$$I_O(\hat{\beta}_1) = - \frac{\partial^2 \ln L(\beta_1| y_p)}{\partial \beta_1^2} \bigg|_{\beta_1 = \hat{\beta}_1} . \quad (12.133)$$

This in turn can be combined with the normal approximation to generate an approximate confidence interval for β_1.

Exponential class. Starting with Equation (12.117), the second derivative of the log-likelihood function is

$$\frac{\partial^2 \ln L(\beta_1| y_p)}{\partial \beta_1^2} = \frac{y_p x_p^2 \exp(\beta_1 x_p)}{[\exp(\beta_1 x_p) - 1]^2}$$

$$- \sum_{l=1}^{p} \frac{y_l'(x_l - x_{l-1})^2 \exp[- \beta_1(x_l + x_{l-1})]}{[\exp(- \beta_1 x_{l-1}) - \exp(- \beta_1 x_l)]^2} . \quad (12.134)$$

A confidence interval for β_1 can be established by using Equations (12.134) and (12.133) and the normal approximation given by Equation (12.12).

Example 12.11. The observed information here is $I_O(\hat{\beta}_1) = 37,705$ which in turn yields an approximate 95 percent confidence interval for β_1 of $(0.366 \times 10^{-3}, 0.0205)$. This interval does not contain zero. Hence it will be seen that the right-hand side of Equation (12.126) is strictly monotone decreasing with respect to $\hat{\beta}_1$ and we may use substitution to establish the corresponding interval for β_0. Carrying this out results in (35, 716) being an approximate 95 percent confidence interval for β_0. ■

Geometric family. The second derivative of the log-likelihood function for the geometric family is, after some lengthy algebra,

$$\frac{\partial^2 \ln L(\beta_1 | y_p)}{\partial \beta_1^2} = \frac{y_p x_p^2}{(1 + \beta_1 x_p)^2 [\ln (1 + \beta_1 x_p)]^2} \left[1 + \ln (1 + \beta_1 x_p) \right]$$

$$+ \sum_{l=1}^{p} \frac{y_l' x_{l-1} \left\{ \dfrac{x_l - x_{l-1}}{1 + \beta_1 x_l} + x_{l-1} [\ln (1 + \beta_1 x_l) - \ln (1 + \beta_1 x_{l-1})] \right\}}{(1 + \beta_1 x_{l-1})^2 [\ln (1 + \beta_1 x_l) - \ln (1 + \beta_1 x_{l-1})]^2}$$

$$- \sum_{l=1}^{p} \frac{y_l' x_l \left\{ \dfrac{x_l - x_{l-1}}{1 + \beta_1 x_{l-1}} + x_l [\ln (1 + \beta_1 x_l) - \ln (1 + \beta_1 x_{l-1})] \right\}}{(1 + \beta_1 x_l)^2 [\ln (1 + \beta_1 x_l) - \ln (1 + \beta_1 x_{l-1})]^2}. \quad (12.135)$$

An approximate confidence interval for β_1 can be obtained by using Equations (12.76), (12.78), (12.133), and (12.135).

Example 12.12. The observed information in the T38 data for a geometric-family model is $I_O(\hat{\beta}_1) = 3642.29$. As with failure time data it becomes necessary to use the transformation given by Equation (12.75). In this particular case $\hat{U} = 1.2775$ with a variance given by Equation (12.76) of 0.333. The 95 percent confidence interval for U is (0.146, 2.409), which in turn yields the corresponding interval (0.0013, 0.0810) for β_1. By the substitution principle a 95 percent confidence interval for β_0 is given by (13.3, 212.5). ■

12.2.3 Summary

Unconditional and conditional maximum likelihood estimation for binomial- and Poisson-type models are essentially equivalent. General likelihood equations for both time and grouped data are summarized in Table 12.12. Equations necessary to perform maximum likelihood estimation based on failure time data for exponential-class and geometric-family models are given in Table 12.13 for easy reference.

TABLE 12.12
Likelihood equations for β

Model type	Failure data	Unconditional estimation	Conditional estimation
Binomial	Time	$-\dfrac{u_o - m_e}{u_o - \mu(t_e)} \dfrac{\partial \mu(t_e)}{\partial \beta_k} + \sum\limits_{i=1}^{m_e} \dfrac{1}{\lambda(t_i)} \dfrac{\partial \lambda(t_i)}{\partial \beta_k}$	$-\dfrac{m_e}{\mu(t_e)} \dfrac{\partial \mu(t_e)}{\partial \beta_k} + \sum\limits_{i=1}^{m_e} \dfrac{1}{\lambda(t_i)} \dfrac{\partial \lambda(t_i)}{\partial \beta_k}$
	Grouped	$\sum\limits_{l=1}^{p} \left[\dfrac{y_l}{F_a(x_l \mid x_{l-1})} - \dfrac{u_o - y_l}{1 - F_a(x_l \mid x_{l-1})} \right] \dfrac{\partial F_a(x_l \mid x_{l-1})}{\partial \beta_k}$	$-\dfrac{y_p}{\mu(x_p)} \dfrac{\partial \mu(x_p)}{\partial \beta_k} + \sum\limits_{l=1}^{p} \dfrac{y_l}{\Delta \mu_l} \dfrac{\partial \Delta \mu_l}{\partial \beta_k}$
Poisson	Time	$-\dfrac{\partial \mu(t_e)}{\partial \beta_k} + \sum\limits_{i=1}^{m_e} \dfrac{1}{\lambda(t_i)} \dfrac{\partial \lambda(t_i)}{\partial \beta_k}$	$-\dfrac{m_e}{\mu(t_e)} \dfrac{\partial \mu(t_e)}{\partial \beta_k} + \sum\limits_{i=1}^{m_e} \dfrac{1}{\lambda(t_i)} \dfrac{\partial \lambda(t_i)}{\partial \beta_k}$
	Grouped	$-\dfrac{\partial \mu(x_p)}{\partial \beta_k} + \sum\limits_{l=1}^{p} \dfrac{y_l}{\Delta \mu_l} \dfrac{\partial \Delta \mu_l}{\partial \beta_k}$	$-\dfrac{y_p}{\mu(x_p)} \dfrac{\partial \mu(x_p)}{\partial \beta_k} + \sum\limits_{l=1}^{p} \dfrac{y_l}{\Delta \mu_l} \dfrac{\partial \Delta \mu_l}{\partial \beta_k}$

TABLE 12.13
Summary of estimation equations for exponential-class and geometric-family models

Parameter or quantity	Estimation equations for exponential-class and geometric-family models[1]	
	Exponential class[2]	Geometric family[3]
β_1	$\dfrac{m_e}{\beta_1} - \dfrac{m_e t_e}{\exp(Q) - 1} - \sum_{i=1}^{m_e} t_i = 0$	$\dfrac{1}{\beta_1} \sum_{i=1}^{m_e} \dfrac{1}{1 + Q} - \dfrac{m_e t_e}{(1 + Q)\ln(1 + Q)} = 0$
β_0	$\dfrac{m_e}{1 - \exp(-Q)}$	$\dfrac{m_e}{\ln(1 + Q)}$
I	$m_e \left\{ \dfrac{1}{\beta_1^2} - \dfrac{t_e^2 \exp(Q)}{[\exp(Q) - 1]^2} \right\}$ Use m_e/β_1^2 for large Q	See (12.74) Use $\beta_0/2\beta_1^2$ for large Q
λ_0	$\dfrac{m_e \beta_1}{1 - \exp(-Q)}$	$\dfrac{m_e \beta_1}{\ln(1 + Q)}$
λ_P	$\dfrac{m_e \beta_1 \exp(-Q)}{1 - \exp(-Q)}$	$\dfrac{m_e \beta_1}{(1 + Q) \ln(1 + Q)}$
Δt	$\dfrac{1}{\beta_1} \ln \left\{ \dfrac{m_e \beta_1}{\lambda_F[1 - \exp(-Q)]} \right\} - t_e$	$\dfrac{m_e}{\lambda_F \ln(1 + Q)} - \dfrac{1}{\beta_1} - t_e$
$\Delta\mu$	$\dfrac{m_e}{\exp(Q) - 1} - \dfrac{\lambda_F}{\beta_1}$	$\dfrac{m_e}{\ln(1 + Q)} \ln \left[\dfrac{m_e \beta_1}{\lambda_F (1 + Q) \ln(1 + Q)} \right]$

[1] $Q = \beta_1 t_e$.
[2] $\beta_0 = \nu_0$ and $\beta_1 = B\phi$ for the basic execution time model.
[3] $\beta_0 = \theta^{-1}$ and $\beta_1 = \lambda_0\theta$ for the logarithmic Poisson model.

12.3 LEAST SQUARES ESTIMATION

The second method of statistical inference we will look at is the least squares approach. If you recall from Section 12.2, we said that no other estimators are better than maximum likelihood estimators for large sample sizes. So why consider least squares estimators? Well, for small or medium size samples least square estimators may be better. For example, they may have smaller bias or they may approach normality faster. Least squares estimation, like maximum likelihood estimation, is a fairly general technique which can be applied in most practical situations.

The approach we take is to estimate the model parameters by fitting the functional relationship of the failure intensity with respect to the mean value function to the observed failure intensity. This method will be discussed in detail for two-parameter model groups, especially the exponential class and geometric family.

We begin with a discussion on how to calculate the observed failure intensity (Section 12.3.1). Point and interval estimation of model parameters is discussed in Sections 12.3.2 and 12.3.3, respectively. Estimation of derived quantities is covered in Section 12.3.4.

12.3.1 Estimation of Failure Intensity

The determination of the observed failure intensity, using both failure time and grouped data, is a straightforward process. We begin by looking at failure time data. Let the observation interval $(0, t_e]$ be partitioned at every kth failure occurrence time so that there are p disjoint subintervals. (Note that p is the smallest integer greater than or equal to m_e/k.) The observed failure intensity r_l for the lth subinterval $(t_{k \times (l-1)}, t_{k \times l}]$ is given by

$$r_l = \begin{cases} \dfrac{k}{t_{k \times l} - t_{k \times (l-1)}}, & l = 1, \cdots, r - 1 \\[4mm] \dfrac{m_e - k(p-1)}{t_e - t_{k \times (l-1)}}, & l = p \end{cases} \tag{12.136}$$

where the subscript notation denotes the product of the two indices. For example, for $k = 5$ we can obtain the observed failure intensity for the second ($l = 2$) subinterval $(t_5, t_{10}]$ as $5/(t_{10} - t_5)$.

Note that the observed failure intensities as such are *independent* of each other since each subinterval is chosen to be disjoint with respect to the others. This independence of the data makes it possible to apply the least squares method, which will be discussed in Section 12.3.2. The ordinary least squares method cannot be applied if the relationship of the cumulative number of failures with time is used, because cumulative failures are dependent on the previous data.

The estimate of the mean value function for the lth subinterval is given by

$$m_l = k(l-1), \quad l = 1, \cdots, p . \tag{12.137}$$

It should be pointed out that the use of the midpoint was also investigated. That is, the mean value function could be estimated by taking the number of failures at the midpoint of the interval rather than at the end. A simulation study indicated that estimates of model parameters obtained based on the midpoint of each interval were biased. Specifically, the initial failure intensity λ_0 tends to be overestimated.

Grouping a small number of failures (a small value of k) will result in large variations in the observed failure intensity. On the other hand, grouping a large number of failures (a large value of k) will result in too much smoothing. A group of five failures (that is, $k = 5$) has been selected as a reasonable compromise in the following analysis. Although some information may be lost because of grouping failures, an advantage of this approach is that no specific model or distribution is assumed.

The observed failure intensity was computed using Equations (12.136) and (12.137) with k set equal to 5 for system T1. The resulting observed failure intensity data are plotted against the estimated mean value function in Figure 12.18. The data points are connected by a line.

Calculating the observed failure intensity using grouped data is even simpler. In this case the observed failure intensity for the lth subinterval (see Table 12.2) is given by $r_l = y_l'/(x_l - x_{l-1})$, where, you may recall, y_l' is the number of failures in the lth subinterval. The estimated mean value function is y_l. We will not consider grouped data further but will note that if the obvious parameter translations are made, results using failure time data can be readily applied to grouped data.

12.3.2 Point Estimation of Model Parameters

The functional relationship of the failure intensity with respect to the expected number of failures was given in Table 11.1. Let's reparameterize from ϕ to β for

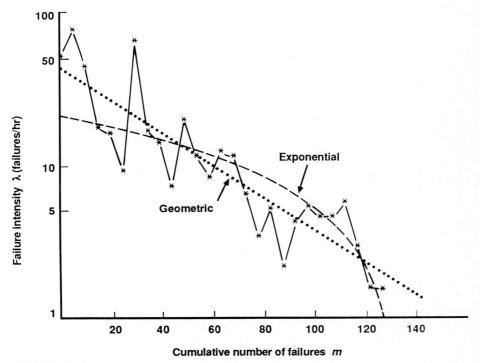

FIGURE 12.18
Plot of the observed failure intensity data and fitted curves for system T1.

TABLE 12.14
Relationship between ϕ and β

Category	Class or family	Parameter transformation		
		ϕ_0	ϕ_1	ϕ_2
Finite	Exponential	β_1	β_0	—
	Weibull	$\beta_1^{\beta_2^{-1}}\beta_2$	β_0	$\dfrac{\beta_2-1}{\beta_2}$
	Pareto	$\dfrac{\beta_2-1}{\beta_1}\beta_0^{(1-\beta_2)^{-1}}$	β_0	$\dfrac{\beta_2}{\beta_2-1}$
Infinite	Geometric	$\beta_0\beta_1$	β_0^{-1}	—
	Inverse linear	$\dfrac{2\beta_1^{1/2}}{\beta_0}$	$\dfrac{2}{\beta_0^2}$	—
	Power	$\beta_1\beta_0^{\beta_1^{-1}}$	$\dfrac{\beta_1-1}{\beta_1}$	—

consistency purposes. Table 12.14 contains the transformations and Table 12.15 the resulting failure intensity functions. The model parameters $\boldsymbol{\beta}$ can be estimated by fitting the functional relationship $\lambda(\mu; \boldsymbol{\beta})$ to the observed failure intensity $[(m_l, r_l), l = 1,\ldots, p]$. It should be pointed out that there are some other approaches to the least squares method. For instance, the functional relationship $\lambda(t; \boldsymbol{\beta})$ may be used instead of $\lambda(\mu; \boldsymbol{\beta})$. This approach will be discussed in Chapter 13. It is useful for investigating a general trend in the failure intensity.

TABLE 12.15
Relation of failure intensity function to mean value function

Category	Class or family	$\lambda(\mu; \boldsymbol{\beta})$
Finite	Exponential	$\beta_1(\beta_0 - \mu)$
	Weibull	$\beta_1^{\beta_2^{-1}}\beta_2[-\ln(1 - \dfrac{\mu}{\beta_0})]^{\frac{\beta_2-1}{\beta_2}}(\beta_0 - \mu)$
	Pareto	$\dfrac{\beta_2-1}{\beta_1}\beta_0^{(1-\beta_2)^{-1}}(\beta_0 - \mu)^{\frac{\beta_2}{\beta_2-1}}$
Infinite	Geometric	$\beta_0\beta_1 \exp(-\dfrac{\mu}{\beta_0})$
	Inverse linear	$\dfrac{\beta_0}{\dfrac{2\mu}{\beta_0} + 2\beta_1^{1/2}}$
	Power	$\beta_0^{\beta_1^{-1}}\beta_1\,\mu^{\frac{\beta_1-1}{\beta_1}}$

Let ϵ_l represent the logarithm of the ratio of the lth data point to the model value. Then, we have

$$\ln r_l = \ln \lambda(m_l; \boldsymbol{\beta}) + \epsilon_l . \tag{12.138}$$

It is assumed that all ϵ_l's are independent, identically distributed normal random errors with zero mean and a common variance σ^2. The normality assumption is not needed for obtaining the least squares estimates, but it is necessary for constructing confidence intervals. The validity of this assumption for the geometric family has been investigated by a simulation study, which is discussed in Case Study 12.3.

The estimates of the model parameters can be found so that the sum of the squares of ϵ_l's, that is,

$$S(\boldsymbol{\beta}) = \sum_{l=1}^{p} \epsilon_l^2 = \sum_{l=1}^{p} [\ln r_l - \ln \lambda(m_l; \boldsymbol{\beta})]^2 , \tag{12.139}$$

is minimized.

Note that this minimization is equivalent to the minimization of the sum of the squares of the *relative errors* (the absolute errors divided by the model values). The use of the relative errors yields the same weight for any level of failure intensity, that is, for all data points. On the other hand, if the absolute errors are used, the estimates will be significantly influenced by the data points with larger failure intensity. In tracking and predicting reliability, managers usually need a constant relative (rather than absolute) accuracy for failure intensity. In general, the approach described yields a nonlinear regression problem. The least squares estimates of the model parameters must be obtained using a numerical method such as that described in Appendix D because of the nonlinearity. The one exception, resulting in an analytic solution for $\boldsymbol{\beta}$, occurs for the geometric family of models.

EXPONENTIAL CLASS. The functional relationship of the failure intensity with the mean value function for the exponential class of models is given by (see Table 12.15)

$$\lambda(\mu; \boldsymbol{\beta}) = \beta_1(\beta_0 - \mu) . \tag{12.140}$$

Note that Equation (12.140) becomes a simple linear regression if the sum of the squares of the absolute errors is minimized. However, we will not take this approach because of the reason discussed above. Substituting Equation (12.140) with μ replaced with m_l into Equation (12.139) yields

$$S(\beta_0, \beta_1) = \sum_{l=1}^{p} [\ln r_l - \ln \beta_1 - \ln (\beta_0 - m_l)]^2 . \tag{12.141}$$

Minimizing this expression results in the least squares estimates $\hat{\beta}_0$ and $\hat{\beta}_1$ for the unknown parameters. Note that this is a nonlinear regression.

Example 12.13. For system T1 where a total of $m = 136$ failures were experienced during the test phase, there are $p = 27$ subintervals for which the failure intensities are estimated. Using the numerical method in Appendix D for the observed failure intensity data $[(m_l, r_l); l = 1, ..., p]$, we find the least squares estimates of β_0 and β_1 as $\hat{\beta}_0 = 137.2$ failures and $\hat{\beta}_1 = 0.156/\text{CPU hr} = 0.43 \times 10^{-4}/\text{CPU sec}$. These results can be compared to those obtained using maximum likelihood estimation (see Table 12.10). Note that for the basic execution time model, $\beta_1 = B\phi$ (the product of the fault reduction factor and the per-fault hazard rate) and $\beta_0 = \nu_0$ (total failures). Hence, the estimates imply that there will be a total of 137 failures and that the failure intensity is reduced by a constant of $0.156/\text{CPU hr}$ after every failure. Furthermore, the functional relationship of the failure intensity with the mean value function is estimated from Equation (12.140) as $\hat{\lambda}(\mu) = 0.1561 (137.2 - \mu)$ failure/CPU hr. This is shown in Figure 12.18, along with the observed failure intensity data.

∎

GEOMETRIC FAMILY. The functional relationship of the failure intensity with the mean value function for a geometric-family Poisson-type model is given by (see Table 12.15)

$$\lambda(\mu; \boldsymbol{\beta}) = \beta_0 \beta_1 \exp\left(-\frac{\mu}{\beta_0}\right). \tag{12.142}$$

The method of least squares is used to estimate β_0 and β_1 by fitting Equation (12.142) to the observed failure intensity $[(m_l, r_l); l = 1, ..., p]$. Substituting Equation (12.142) with μ replaced with m_l into Equation (12.138), we have

$$\ln r_l = \ln \beta_0 \beta_1 - \frac{m_l}{\beta_0} + \epsilon_l. \tag{12.143}$$

From Equations (12.139) and (12.143), we have

$$S(\beta_0, \beta_1) = \sum_{l=1}^{p} \epsilon_l^2 = \sum_{l=1}^{p} \left[\ln r_l - \ln \beta_0 \beta_1 + \frac{m_l}{\beta_0}\right]^2. \tag{12.144}$$

This expression may be minimized using ordinary calculus. The results for the least squares estimates of β_0 and β_1 are

$$\hat{\beta}_0 = -\frac{p\left(\sum_{l=1}^{p} m_l^2\right) - \left(\sum_{l=1}^{p} m_l\right)^2}{p \sum_{l=1}^{p} m_l \ln r_l - \left(\sum_{l=1}^{p} m_l\right)\left(\sum_{l=1}^{p} \ln r_l\right)} \tag{12.145}$$

and

$$\hat{\beta}_1 = \hat{\beta}_0^{-1} \exp\left[\frac{1}{p}\left(\sum_{l=1}^{p} \ln r_l + \frac{1}{\hat{\beta}_0} \sum_{l=1}^{p} m_l\right)\right], \tag{12.146}$$

respectively. Note that $\hat{\beta}_0$ is determined first and then used in determining $\hat{\beta}_1$. Substituting these estimates into Equation (12.143), the failure intensity can be estimated as

$$\ln \hat{r}_l = \ln \hat{\lambda}(m_l) = \ln \hat{\beta}_0 \hat{\beta}_1 - \frac{m_l}{\hat{\beta}_0} \tag{12.147}$$

or

$$\hat{r}_l = \hat{\lambda}(m_l) = \hat{\beta}_0 \hat{\beta}_1 \exp\left(-\frac{m_l}{\hat{\beta}_0}\right). \tag{12.148}$$

Example 12.14. The least squares estimates of β_0 and β_1 for system T1 are found from Equations (12.145) and (12.146) to be $\hat{\beta}_0 = 41.7$ failures and $\hat{\beta}_1 = 1.02/\text{CPU}$ hr $= 0.283 \times 10^{-3}/\text{CPU}$ sec, respectively. These results can be compared to those obtained using maximum likelihood estimation (see Table 12.11). The functional relationship of the failure intensity with the mean value function is estimated from Equation (12.148) as $\hat{\lambda}(\mu) = 42.5 \exp(-0.024\mu)$ failure/CPU hr. This is shown in Figure 12.18. It can be observed that the geometric family appears to fit better than the exponential class for this data set. This is also confirmed by examining the variance (see Examples 12.15 and 12.16). ∎

12.3.3 Interval Estimation of Model Parameters

The next step after obtaining the point estimates of the parameters is the computation of confidence intervals for the parameters. These will be useful in evaluating the accuracy of the estimates. The method for generating these intervals will be described for two-parameter model groups such as the exponential class and the geometric family. Modification of the method for a model with more than two parameters is straightforward.

In addition to the assumption that the ϵ_l's are independent random variables with zero mean, we also assume that they are normally distributed with a common variance σ^2. Then, we can estimate the common variance as

$$\hat{\sigma}^2 = \frac{S(\hat{\beta}_0, \hat{\beta}_1)}{p - 2}. \tag{12.149}$$

This reflects the variation about the regression line. We estimate the variance of $\hat{\beta}_j$ ($j = 0, 1$) as

$$\text{var}[\hat{\beta}_j] = \frac{\hat{\sigma}^2}{SS} \sum_{l=1}^{p} \left[\frac{\partial}{\partial \beta_{1-j}} \ln \lambda(m_l)\right]^2, \tag{12.150}$$

where

$$SS = \sum_{l=1}^{p} \left[\frac{\partial}{\partial \beta_0} \ln \lambda(m_l) \right]^2 \sum_{l=1}^{p} \left[\frac{\partial}{\partial \beta_1} \ln \lambda(m_l) \right]^2 -$$

$$\left\{ \sum_{l=1}^{p} \left[\frac{\partial}{\partial \beta_0} \ln \lambda(m_l) \frac{\partial}{\partial \beta_1} \ln \lambda(m_l) \right] \right\}^2 . \quad (12.151)$$

The estimated covariance of $\hat{\beta}_0$ and $\hat{\beta}_1$ is

$$\text{cov} [\hat{\beta}_0, \hat{\beta}_1] = - \frac{\hat{\sigma}^2}{SS} \sum_{l=1}^{p} \left[\frac{\partial}{\partial \beta_0} \ln \lambda(m_l) \frac{\partial}{\partial \beta_1} \ln \lambda(m_l) \right] . \quad (12.152)$$

In Equations (12.150) and (12.152) $\hat{\beta}_0$ and $\hat{\beta}_1$ are used to evaluate the expression.

Assuming that the least squares estimates β_0 and β_1 are normally distributed, a $100(1 - \alpha)$ percent confidence interval for the parameter $\beta_j (j = 0, 1)$ is given by

$$\hat{\beta}_j - t_{p-2; \, \alpha/2} \sqrt{\text{var}[\hat{\beta}_j]} \leqslant \beta_j \leqslant \hat{\beta}_j + t_{p-2; \, \alpha/2} \sqrt{\text{var}[\hat{\beta}_j]} , \quad (12.153)$$

where $t_{p-2; \alpha/2}$ is the upper $\alpha/2$ percentage point of the t distribution with $p - 2$ degrees of freedom. Note that the t distribution is used since the variance is estimated from the data.

EXPONENTIAL CLASS. For the exponential class we have

$$\ln \lambda(m_l) = \ln \beta_1 + \ln (\beta_0 - m_l) . \quad (12.154)$$

The required partial derivatives are

$$\frac{\partial}{\partial \beta_0} \ln \lambda(m_l) = \frac{1}{\beta_0 - m_l} \quad (12.155)$$

and

$$\frac{\partial}{\partial \beta_1} \ln \lambda(m_l) = \frac{1}{\beta_1} . \quad (12.156)$$

Substituting these two expressions into Equation (12.151) yields

$$SS = \frac{1}{\beta_1^2} \left[p \sum_{l=1}^{p} \left(\frac{1}{\beta_0 - m_l} \right)^2 - \left(\sum_{l=1}^{p} \frac{1}{\beta_0 - m_l} \right)^2 \right] . \quad (12.157)$$

Hence, from Equations (12.150) and (12.152),

$$\text{var} [\hat{\beta}_0] = \frac{\hat{\sigma}^2 p}{\hat{\beta}_1^2 \, SS} , \quad (12.158)$$

$$\text{var}[\hat{\beta}_1] = \frac{\hat{\sigma}^2}{SS} \sum_{l=1}^{p} \left[\frac{1}{\hat{\beta}_0 - m_l} \right]^2, \tag{12.159}$$

and

$$\text{cov}[\hat{\beta}_0, \hat{\beta}_1] = - \frac{\hat{\sigma}^2}{\hat{\beta}_1 SS} \sum_{l=1}^{p} \frac{1}{\hat{\beta}_0 - m_l}. \tag{12.160}$$

A $100(1 - \alpha)$ percent confidence interval can be obtained for each parameter from Equation (12.153).

Example 12.15. For the system T1, we compute $S(\hat{\beta}_0, \hat{\beta}_1) = 9.79$, $\hat{\beta}_0 = 137.2$ failures, and $\hat{\beta}_1 = 0.1561/\text{CPU hr}$. Substituting these estimates into Equation (12.149) yields the estimate of σ^2 as $\hat{\sigma}^2 = 9.79/25 = 0.392$ or $\hat{\sigma} = 0.626$. Furthermore, the variance and covariance of $\hat{\beta}_0$ and $\hat{\beta}_1$ are estimated as var $[\hat{\beta}_0] = 15.3$, var $[\hat{\beta}_1] = 5.83 \times 10^{-4}$, and cov $[\hat{\beta}_0, \hat{\beta}_1] = -5.92 \times 10^{-2}$, respectively. Using Equation (12.153) for $\alpha = 0.05$ ($t_{25; 0.025} = 2.06$), we compute the 95 percent confidence limits for β_0 as $137.2 \pm 2.06\sqrt{15.3}$ or $136 < \beta_0 < 145.2$. Note that the lower limit was truncated at 136 since this is the number of failures experienced to date. Similarly, we compute the 95 percent confidence limits for β_1 as $0.1561 \pm 2.06\sqrt{5.83 \times 10^{-4}}$ or $0.1064 < \beta_1 < 0.2058$. Converting the interval for β_1 from a per-CPU-hr basis to a per-CPU-sec basis yields $0.296 \times 10^{-4} < \beta_1 < 0.572 \times 10^{-4}$. This interval, as well as the one for β_0, can now be compared with those obtained using maximum likelihood estimation (see Table 12.10). ∎

GEOMETRIC FAMILY. For the geometric family we can derive closed form expressions for the variance and covariance. Starting with Equation (12.142) we have

$$\ln \lambda(m_l) = \ln \beta_1 + \ln \beta_0 - \frac{m_l}{\beta_0}, \tag{12.161}$$

$$\frac{\partial}{\partial \beta_0} \ln \lambda(m_l) = \frac{1}{\beta_0} \left[1 + \frac{m_l}{\beta_0} \right], \tag{12.162}$$

and

$$\frac{\partial}{\partial \beta_1} \ln \lambda(m_l) = \frac{1}{\beta_1}. \tag{12.163}$$

Substituting Equations (12.162) and (12.163) into Equation (12.151) yields

$$SS = \frac{1}{\beta_1^2 \beta_0^4} \left[p \sum_{l=1}^{p} m_l^2 - \left(\sum_{l=1}^{p} m_l \right)^2 \right]. \tag{12.164}$$

Hence, from Equations (12.150) and (12.152),

$$\text{var}[\hat{\beta}_0] = \frac{\hat{\sigma}^2 p}{\hat{\beta}_1^2 SS}, \tag{12.165}$$

$$\text{var}[\hat{\beta}_1] = \frac{\hat{\sigma}^2}{\hat{\beta}_0^2 SS} \left[p + \frac{2}{\hat{\beta}_0} \sum_{l=1}^{p} m_l + \frac{1}{\hat{\beta}_0^2} \sum m_l^2 \right], \tag{12.166}$$

and

$$\text{cov}\left[\hat{\beta}_0, \hat{\beta}_1\right] = - \frac{\hat{\sigma}^2}{\hat{\beta}_0 \hat{\beta}_1 SS} \left[p + \frac{1}{\hat{\beta}_0} \sum_{l=1}^{p} m_l \right]. \tag{12.167}$$

Example 12.16. For system T1, we compute $\hat{\beta}_0 = 41.7$ failures, $\hat{\beta}_1 = 1.02/\text{CPU}$ hr $= 0.283 \times 10^{-3}/\text{CPU}$ sec, $\Sigma_{l=1}^{p} m_l = 1755$, and $\Sigma_{l=1}^{p} m_l^2 = 155{,}025$. Substituting the least squares estimates $\hat{\beta}_0$ and $\hat{\beta}_1$ into Equation (12.144) yields $S(\hat{\beta}_0, \hat{\beta}_1) = 6.47$. Hence, the variance is estimated from Equation (12.149) as $\hat{\sigma}^2 = 6.47 / 25 = 0.259$ or $\hat{\sigma} = 0.509$. Furthermore, from Equations (12.165), (12.166), and (12.167), we estimate the variance and covariance of $\hat{\beta}_0$ and $\hat{\beta}_1$ as $\text{var}[\hat{\beta}_0] = 19.11$, $\text{var}[\hat{\beta}_1] = 6.53 \times 10^{-9}$, and $\text{cov}[\hat{\beta}_0, \hat{\beta}_1] = -0.33 \times 10^{-3}$, respectively. Using Equation (12.153) for $\alpha = 0.05$ ($t_{25;0.025} = 2.06$), we compute the 95 percent confidence limits for β_0 as $41.7 \pm 2.06\sqrt{19.11}$ or $32.7 \leq \beta_0 \leq 50.7$. Also, the 95 percent confidence limits for β_1 are obtained from Equation (12.153) as $0.283 \times 10^{-3} \pm 2.06\sqrt{6.53 \times 10^{-9}}$ or $0.117 \times 10^{-3} \leq \beta_1 \leq 0.449 \times 10^{-3}$ (on a per-CPU-sec basis). Similarly, $0.421 \leq \beta_1 \leq 1.616$ on a per-CPU-hr basis. ∎

12.3.4 Estimation of Derived Quantities

We now examine point and interval estimation of derived quantities such as future failure intensity and additional time required to achieve a failure intensity objective. Derived quantities are in general expressed as a function of the model parameters β_0 and β_1.

Let $g(\beta_0, \beta_1)$ represent a derived quantity of interest. We can then estimate this quantity by substituting the estimates $\hat{\beta}_0$ and $\hat{\beta}_1$ into the function as $\hat{g} = g(\hat{\beta}_0, \hat{\beta}_1)$. However, because of the statistical errors in estimating the parameters, a single estimate of g is always in error. It is therefore necessary to develop a confidence interval for g.

We can estimate the variance of $\hat{g}$ as [see Mood, Graybill, and Boes (1974), for example]

$$\text{var}[\hat{g}] = \text{var}[\beta_0] \left[\frac{\partial g}{\partial \beta_0} \right]^2 + \text{var}[\beta_1] \left[\frac{\partial g}{\partial \beta_1} \right]^2$$

$$+ 2 \text{ cov}[\beta_0, \beta_1] \left[\frac{\partial g}{\partial \beta_0} \frac{\partial g}{\partial \beta_1} \right], \tag{12.168}$$

where we use $\beta_0 = \hat{\beta}_0$ and $\beta_1 = \hat{\beta}_1$ to evaluate Equation (12.168). The estimate $\hat{g}$ is approximately normally distributed with mean $g(\hat{\beta}_0, \hat{\beta}_1)$ and variance var[$\hat{g}$]. Therefore, $100(1 - \alpha)$ percent confidence limits for g are given by

$$\hat{g} \pm t_{p-2;\,\alpha/2} \sqrt{\text{var}[\hat{g}]}, \tag{12.169}$$

where the t distribution is used since the variance is estimated from the data.

We will apply the method to estimate future failure intensity and additional execution time.

FUTURE FAILURE INTENSITY. We estimate the observed failure intensity r_0 at $m = m_0$ by $\hat{r}_0 = \hat{\lambda}(m_0)$ and the variance of $\ln \hat{r}_0$ is estimated as var[$\ln \hat{r}_0$] = $\hat{\sigma}^2$ + var[$\ln \hat{\lambda}(m_0)$], where $\hat{\sigma}^2$ is added for the error term ϵ_0. Hence, $100(1 - \alpha)$ percent confidence limits for $\ln r_0$ are given by

$$\ln \hat{r}_0 \pm t_{p-2;\,\alpha/2} \sqrt{\text{var}[\ln \hat{r}_0]}. \tag{12.170}$$

Exponential class. For the exponential class, we have

$$g = \ln \beta_1 + \ln (\beta_0 - m_0). \tag{12.171}$$

Then, we obtain the derivatives of g with respect to β_0 and β_1 as

$$\frac{\partial g}{\partial \beta_0} = \frac{1}{\beta_0 - m_0} \tag{12.172}$$

and

$$\frac{\partial g}{\partial \beta_1} = \frac{1}{\beta_1}. \tag{12.173}$$

The variance of g can be estimated from Equation (12.168). Hence, $100(1 - \alpha)$ percent confidence limits can be found from Equation (12.169).

Geometric family. For the geometric family, we have

$$g = \ln \beta_1 + \ln \beta_0 - \frac{m_I}{\beta_0}. \tag{12.174}$$

Here the required derivatives of g are

$$\frac{\partial g}{\partial \beta_0} = \frac{1}{\beta_0} \left[1 + \frac{m_0}{\beta_0} \right] \tag{12.175}$$

and

$$\frac{\partial g}{\partial \beta_1} = \frac{1}{\beta_1}. \tag{12.176}$$

After some straightforward manipulation we have

$$\text{var}[\ln \hat{r}_0] = \hat{\sigma}^2 \left[1 + \frac{1}{p} + \frac{\left(m_0 - \frac{1}{p} \sum\limits_{l=1}^{p} m_l \right)^2}{\sum\limits_{l=1}^{p} m_l^2 - \frac{1}{p} \left(\sum\limits_{l=1}^{p} m_l \right)^2} \right] . \tag{12.177}$$

Hence, we can find $100(1 - \alpha)$ percent confidence limits from Equation (12.169). See Example 7.8 for an application of Equation (12.177) for system T1.

ADDITIONAL TIME TO OBJECTIVE. Let t_P and λ_P represent the present time and failure intensity, respectively. If we denote a failure intensity objective by λ_F, then the time this objective will be reached t_F can be found by solving $\lambda(t_F) = \lambda_F$. That is,

$$t_F = \lambda^{-1}(\lambda_F) . \tag{12.178}$$

The additional time to reach the objective λ_F is given by $t_F - t_P$ since t_P is the present time (see Figure 12.19).

Exponential class. For the exponential class we have

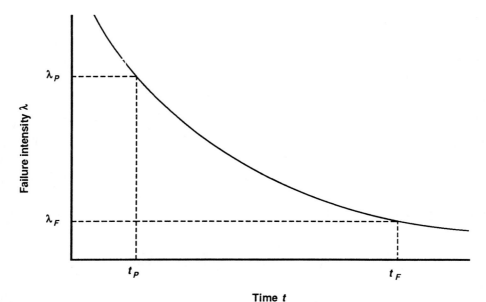

FIGURE 12.19
Plot of the failure intensity function versus execution time.

$$\lambda(t) = \beta_0\beta_1 \exp(-\beta_1 t) . \tag{12.179}$$

Hence,

$$t_F = -\frac{1}{\beta_1} \ln \frac{\lambda_F}{\beta_0\beta_1}$$

$$= \frac{1}{\beta_1} (\ln \beta_0\beta_1 - \ln \lambda_F) . \tag{12.180}$$

The derivatives of t_F with respect to β_0 and β_1 are given by

$$\frac{\partial t_F}{\partial \beta_0} = \frac{1}{\beta_0\beta_1} , \tag{12.181}$$

and

$$\frac{\partial t_F}{\partial \beta_1} = \frac{1}{\beta_1^2} (1 - \ln \beta_0\beta_1 + \ln \lambda_F) \tag{12.182}$$

respectively. Hence, we can estimate the variance of $\hat{t}_F$ from Equation (12.168) and $100(1 - \alpha)$ percent confidence limits can be found from Equation (12.169).

Geometric family. For the geometric family, we have

$$\lambda(t) = \frac{\beta_0\beta_1}{\beta_1 t + 1} . \tag{12.183}$$

Hence,

$$t_F = \frac{\beta_0}{\lambda_F} - \frac{1}{\beta_1} . \tag{12.184}$$

The derivatives of t_F with respect to β_0 and β_1 are given by

$$\frac{\partial t_F}{\partial \beta_0} = \frac{1}{\lambda_F} \tag{12.185}$$

and

$$\frac{\partial t_F}{\partial \beta_1} = \frac{1}{\beta_1^2} , \tag{12.186}$$

respectively. Hence, the variance of t_F can be estimated from Equation (12.168) and $100(1 - \alpha)$ percent confidence limits can be found from Equation (12.169).

Example 12.17. For system T1, we have $\hat{\beta}_0 = 41.7$ failures and $\hat{\beta}_1 = 1.02/\text{CPU}$ hr $= 0.28 \times 10^{-3}/\text{CPU}$ sec. At $t_P = 25.3$ hr the present failure intensity is estimated from Equation (12.183) as $\hat{\lambda}_P = 1.59$ failures/CPU hr or 0.44×10^{-3} failure/CPU sec. Suppose that the failure intensity objective is set to $\lambda_F = 1$ failure/CPU hr. Then, substituting $\hat{\beta}_0$, $\hat{\beta}_1$, and λ_F into Equation (12.184), the time the objective will be reached is estimated as $t_F = 40.7$ CPU hr. Hence, the additional execution time to reach the objective is $t_F - t_P = 15.4$ CPU hr. Also, from Equations (12.168), (12.185), and (12.186) the 95 percent confidence interval for t_F is computed as $32.2 \leq t_F \leq 49.1$. Therefore, with 95 percent confidence the additional time required to achieve this objective lies between 6.9 CPU hr ($= 32.2 - 25.3$) and 23.8 CPU hr ($= 49.1 - 25.3$). ∎

We conclude our discussion of least squares estimation with a case study. This study presents the results of a simulation conducted to see if the normality assumption for least squares estimators is suitable for a geometric-family model and to compare least squares with maximum likelihood estimation.

CASE STUDY 12.3
A SIMULATION STUDY

The primary purpose of this study is to see if the normality assumption for the least squares estimators of $\hat{\theta}$ and $\ln \hat{\lambda}_0$ for the logarithmic Poisson model is reasonable. A simulation of failure data is required to do this because of analytical difficulties. We first discuss a method for generating the necessary failure interval data. The actual results are then presented and analyzed. The study concludes by comparing the least squares estimators with the maximum likelihood estimators.

GENERATION OF FAILURE INTERVAL DATA

To generate failure interval data for the logarithmic Poisson model we first generate failure times for a stationary Poisson process with rate 1. This is equivalent to generating failure intervals that follow an exponential distribution with parameter 1. If we denote by $z_i(i = 1, \ldots, m)$ the ith random number of $(0, 1)$, then the exponential random value u_i' with rate 1 corresponding to z_i is given by

$$u_i' = - \ln (1 - z_i) , \qquad (12.187)$$

which is the ith failure interval for a stationary Poisson process with rate 1.

Let u_i be the ith failure time, that is, $u_i = \Sigma_{l=1}^{i} u_l'$. Then, we can convert this failure time u_i to a failure time for the logarithmic Poisson model, which is a nonstationary Poisson process with the mean value function given in Equation (11.41), by inverting the mean value function. Therefore, the ith failure time for the logarithmic Poisson model is given by

$$t_i = \mu^{-1}(u_i) \qquad (12.188)$$

$$= \frac{\exp(\theta) u_i - 1}{\lambda_0 \theta} .$$

[Consult Cinlar (1975) for a detailed description of the method.] The failure times t_i can be converted to failure intervals t_i' by taking differences between successive values.

The first step of the simulation study was to decide on suitable parameter values to be used to generate failure intervals. We have chosen the values $\lambda_0 = 50$ failures/CPU hr and $\theta = 0.05$/CPU hr for this study as a reasonable compromise based on estimates obtained from 15 sets of failure data collected from many software projects. We generated a total of 500 sequences of failure interval data, where each sequence contains 200 failure intervals.

RESULTS OF DATA ANALYSIS

Least squares estimates of λ_0 and θ can be obtained directly from $\hat{\beta}_0$ and $\hat{\beta}_1$ since $\theta = 1/\beta_0$ and $\lambda_0 = \beta_0\beta_1$. For each of the 500 sequences of failure data, we have computed estimates $\hat{\lambda}_0$ and $\hat{\theta}$ of the parameters λ_0 and θ based on the failure data up to $m_e = 20, 25, \ldots, 200$, using the methods described in this section.

To examine the behavior of the accuracy of the estimates $\ln \hat{\lambda}_0$ and $\hat{\theta}$ with respect to the number of failures experienced, interquartiles (25, 50, and 75 percent) of the relative errors $(\ln \hat{\lambda}_0 - \ln \lambda_0)/(\ln \lambda_0)$ and $(\hat{\theta} - \theta)/\theta$ were computed based on the 500 estimates at $m_e = 20, 25, \ldots, 200$. Note that if the errors are normally distributed, the median should be close to zero and the lower and upper quartiles symmetric about zero. The length between the lower and upper quartiles represents the accuracy of the estimates.

Figures 12.20 and 12.21 show the interquartiles (dashed lines) of the relative errors plotted against the cumulative number of failures m_e for $\ln \hat{\lambda}_0$ and $\hat{\theta}$ respectively. Note that the least squares method is denoted by "L." It can be observed from Figure 12.20 that the median (solid line) is stable around zero and the lower and upper quartiles are symmetric about zero. This implies that the normality assumption for $\ln \hat{\lambda}_0$ is good. The lower and upper quartiles do not change as the number of failures increases. Therefore, there would be no gain in the accuracy of the estimate $\ln \hat{\lambda}_0$ (and hence $\hat{\lambda}_0$) even if more failures are observed.

Figure 12.21 shows the reasonableness of the normality assumption for $\hat{\theta}$. Unlike $\ln \hat{\lambda}_0$, the length between the lower and upper quartiles decreases with the number of failures. The rate of decrease is significant up to roughly $m_e = 100$ and then the changes become negligible. Therefore, there is a significant gain in the accuracy of the estimate $\hat{\theta}$ up to $m_e = 100$.

It is evident from Figures 12.20 and 12.21 that both estimates $\ln \hat{\lambda}_0$ and $\hat{\theta}$ can be assumed to follow a normal distribution. After $m_e = 100$, the lower and upper quartiles are within ± 7 percent for both $\ln \hat{\lambda}_0$ and $\hat{\theta}$. We consider this accuracy to be reasonable from a practical point of view.

We also conducted a similar analysis using the method of maximum likelihood discussed in Section 12.2. Figures 12.20 and 12.21 show the results, where the maximum likelihood method is denoted by "M." Almost identical results were found. In other words, the maximum likelihood estimates (which are based on failure times rather than groups of failures) do not improve the accuracy in es-

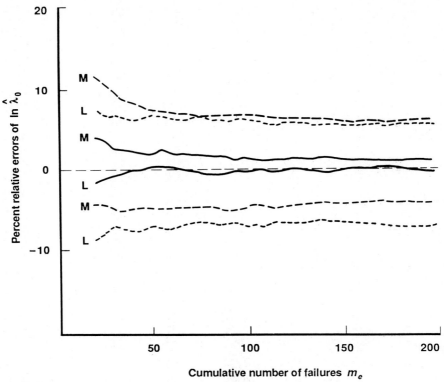

FIGURE 12.20
Plot of the interquartiles and median of the relative errors of ln $\hat{\lambda}_0$ versus cumulative number of failures based on 500 sets of simulated failure data for the logarithmic Poisson model ("M" represents the maximum likelihood method and "L" represents the least squares method).

timating the parameters. Note that the median is stable, but slightly away from zero. Therefore, the maximum likelihood estimates are biased.

12.3.5 Summary

The least squares method can be used to provide suitable parameter estimates from a practical point of view. In the special case of the logarithmic Poisson model the estimation is especially simple and effective.

12.4 BAYESIAN INFERENCE

The third and final method of statistical inference to be considered is the so-called Bayesian approach. Several authors including Langberg and Singpurwalla (1985),

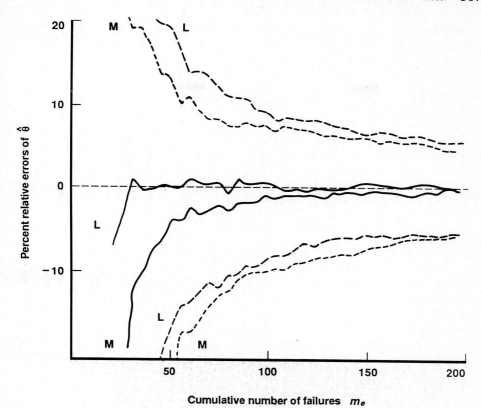

FIGURE 12.21
Plots of the interquartiles and median of the relative errors of $\hat{\theta}$ versus cumulative number of failures based on 500 sets of simulated failure data for the logarithmic Poisson model ("M" represents the maximum likelihood method and "L" represents the least squares method).

Meinhold and Singpurwalla (1983), Littlewood (1981), Okumoto and Goel (1978b), and Littlewood and Verrall (1973 and 1974) have developed or extended software reliability models based on the Bayesian viewpoint over the past 15 years or so. Here we will present a basic introduction to Bayesian inference. The Bayesian approach provides an efficient method for incorporating various subjective and objective data sources into the analysis. However, it is markedly inferior to maximum likelihood from a practical viewpoint. The analysis is more complex. Hence it is more difficult to convey the concepts. Also, computation is more complicated. Thus, no attempt will be made to be as comprehensive as we were with maximum likelihood estimation.

Like the two previous approaches the aim is to estimate the unknown parameters β based on the observed data Y_D. In maximum likelihood, least squares, and other classical methods of estimation β is treated as a vector of constants having unknown values. A major part of classical inference centers around determining estimators for $\boldsymbol{\beta}$ and their statistical properties (distribution, biasedness, efficiency, etc.). Confidence statements must be interpreted properly. For example, consider the $100(1 - \alpha)$ percent confidence interval for maximum likelihood estimation given by Equation (12.12). What the interval really means is that in repeated sampling the computed confidence intervals include the true value of β_k a proportion $(1 - \alpha)$ of the time. We cannot properly say that β_k lies within the interval with probability $1 - \alpha$. However, the Bayesian interpretation, while still considering $\boldsymbol{\beta}$ as unknown, treats the parameters as *random variables* with known distributions. All inference is based directly on these distributions. Questions on bias and efficiency no longer exist. Confidence statements directly represent valid probability statements on the model parameters. Thus, a statement such as

$$P[\beta_{\text{low}} \leqslant \beta_k \leqslant \beta_{\text{high}}] = 1 - \alpha \qquad (12.189)$$

gives the probability that β_k lies between β_{low} and β_{high}.

In the following development we will look at the case of one unknown parameter, say β_k. The generalization to two or more unknown parameters is straightforward and will be indicated later.

Bayes' theorem is the foundation of Bayesian inference [see, for example, Mood, Graybill, and Boes (1974)]. Suppose β_k has a density function given by $f(\beta_k)$. Then applying Bayes' theorem, given the observed data Y_D, the conditional density function of β_k is

$$f(\beta_k | Y_D) = \frac{f(Y_D | \beta_k)\, f(\beta_k)}{f(Y_D)}, \qquad (12.190)$$

where the marginal distribution $f(Y_D)$ may be obtained according to

$$f(Y_D) = \int f(Y_D | \beta_k)\, f(\beta_k) d\beta_k . \qquad (12.191)$$

The density function $f(\beta_k)$ is called the *prior* distribution of β_k. This function is supposed to represent what is known about β_k *before* the data are available. It plays an important role in Bayesian analysis, for it is used to represent prior knowledge or relative ignorance. Correspondingly, $f(\beta_k | Y_D)$ is called the *posterior* distribution of β_k given knowledge of the data, Y_D. This function represents what is known about β_k *after* the data have been made available. The denominator of Equation (12.190) is a normalizing constant which insures that $f(\beta_k | Y_D)$ integrates to 1.

Given the data, $f(Y_D | \beta_k)$ may be regarded as a function of β_k and not of Y_D. In so doing we can call it the likelihood function of β_k. Using the notation of Section 12.2 we have

$$f(Y_D | \beta_k) = L(\beta_k; Y_D) . \qquad (12.192)$$

Bayes' theorem can now be written as

$$f(\beta_k \mid Y_D) \propto L(\beta_k; Y_D) f(\beta_k) \,. \qquad (12.193)$$

This says that the posterior distribution of β_k is proportional to the product of the prior distribution of β_k and the likelihood function. The likelihood function plays an important role here as it does with maximum likelihood estimation. All the information about β_k coming from the data is contained in it. As the sample size increases the terms contributed by the likelihood function will tend to overwhelm the single term contributed by the prior. A typical relationship between the three functions of Equation (12.193) is shown in Figure 12.22. Note how the occurrence of the data Y_D increases the relative probability of certain values of β_k.

Now that we have the posterior distribution for β_k, what about point and interval estimation for β_k? For point estimation any measure of the central tendency of the posterior distribution will be adequate. Denote the Bayesian point estimate of β_k as β_k^*. Then three such estimates are

1. the posterior mean, that is,

$$\beta_k^* = \int \beta_k f(\beta_k \mid Y_D) \, d\beta_k \,, \qquad (12.194)$$

2. the posterior median, that is, the value of β_k^* such that

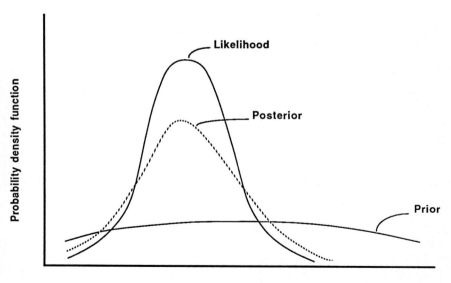

FIGURE 12.22
Typical relationship between the likelihood function and the prior and posterior distributions of β_k.

$$\int_{-\infty}^{\beta_k^*} f\left(\beta_k \mid Y_D\right) d\beta_k \geqslant 0.5$$

and $\qquad\qquad\qquad\qquad\qquad\qquad\qquad\qquad$ (12.195)

$$\int_{\beta_k^*}^{\infty} f\left(\beta_k \mid Y_D\right) d\beta_k \leqslant 0.5,$$

3. and the posterior mode or *generalized maximum likelihood estimator* [Martz and Waller (1982)], that is, the value of β_k^* that maximizes

$$f_k(\beta_k \mid Y_D) .$$

These three estimators are depicted in Figure 12.23.

The Bayesian approach to interval estimation is direct. A $100(1 - \alpha)$ percent probability interval for β_k is easily obtained once we know the posterior distribution of β_k. We need only solve the two equations

$$\int_{-\infty}^{\beta_{\text{low}}} f\left(\beta_k \mid Y_D\right) d\beta_k = \frac{\alpha}{2}$$

and $\qquad\qquad\qquad\qquad\qquad\qquad\qquad\qquad$ (12.196)

$$\int_{\beta_{\text{high}}}^{\infty} f\left(\beta_k \mid Y_D\right) d\beta_k = \frac{\alpha}{2}$$

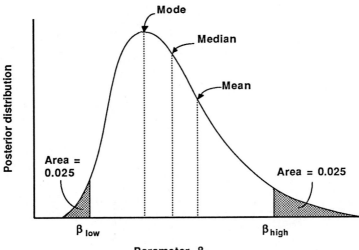

FIGURE 12.23
Three different Bayesian point estimators.

for the intervals' lower and upper limits, β_{low} and β_{high}, respectively. A 95 percent probability interval for β_k is also shown in Figure 12.23.

These integrals often cannot be expressed in closed form. This is also true (more so) when there is more than one unknown parameter. This does not present a problem since the integrals can be computed numerically with the use of computers.

Inference about some function of β_k, say $Q(\beta_k)$, can be made in a direct way. One good approach is to start with the posterior distribution of β_k and apply a change of variables to obtain the posterior distribution of Q. A point estimate of Q can now be obtained as before by using the posterior mean, median, or mode and an interval estimate by using Equation (12.196) with the appropriate notational changes.

A criticism and key difficulty in carrying out a Bayesian analysis is the identification of the prior distribution. Often mathematical simplicity and convenience and the ability to describe various distributional shapes are the key considerations. See Box and Tiao (1973) for a complete discussion on the identification of an appropriate prior. In this chapter we will assume that little or nothing is known a priori about β_k. Such a case can be handled using *a locally uniform* prior. A locally uniform prior is one that does not vary appreciably over the region in which the likelihood function is large. Outside this region a locally uniform prior also does not assume large values. Figure 12.22 shows what might be called a locally uniform prior. Such a prior can be approximated by a constant for all practical purposes. Doing this Equation (12.193) becomes

$$f(\beta_k \mid Y_D) \propto L(\beta_k; Y_D) \ . \qquad (12.197)$$

Thus the posterior distribution of β_k is directly proportional to the likelihood function.

The generalization to more than one unknown parameter is straightforward. If we let $f(\boldsymbol{\beta})$ denote the joint prior distribution of $\boldsymbol{\beta}$, then the joint posterior distribution of $\boldsymbol{\beta}$ is

$$f(\boldsymbol{\beta} \mid Y_D) \propto L(\boldsymbol{\beta}; Y_D) f(\boldsymbol{\beta}) \ . \qquad (12.198)$$

Point and interval estimates for each β_k ($k = 0,\ldots, w$) can be obtained using the marginal posterior distribution of β_k. For example, the distribution for β_k can be obtained from

$$f(\beta_k \mid Y_D) \propto \int \cdots \int f(\boldsymbol{\beta} \mid Y_D) \, \partial\beta_0 \cdots \partial\beta_{k-1} \, \partial\beta_{k+1} \cdots \partial\beta_w \ . \qquad (12.199)$$

All the previous discussion regarding point and interval estimation of β_k can now be applied. Inferences about a function of $\boldsymbol{\beta}$, say $Q(\boldsymbol{\beta})$, can be carried out by determining the posterior distribution of Q.

Finally, a locally uniform prior for multiple parameters is one that can be approximated by a constant for all practical values of $\boldsymbol{\beta}$. The posterior distribution of $\boldsymbol{\beta}$ when a locally uniform prior is used is directly proportional to the likelihood function.

12.4.1 Inference of Model Parameters

Inference about $\boldsymbol{\beta}$ for both binomial- and Poisson-type models will be discussed in this section. Only failure time data will be considered. The development is easily extended to grouped data. We assume little or no prior knowledge of $\boldsymbol{\beta}$ exists so that locally uniform priors can and should be used throughout.[13] Equivalently, we assume the posterior distribution of $\boldsymbol{\beta}$ is proportional to the likelihood function.

BINOMIAL-TYPE MODELS. The likelihood function for binomial-type models is given by Equation (12.25) as

$$L(u_0, \boldsymbol{\beta}_A) = [1 - F_a(t_e)]^{u_0 - m_e} \prod_{i=1}^{m_e} (u_0 - i + 1) f_a(t_i) . \qquad (12.200)$$

Using a locally uniform prior, the joint posterior distribution of u_0 and $\boldsymbol{\beta}_A$ becomes

$$f(u_0, \boldsymbol{\beta}_A | Y_D) \propto L(u_0, \boldsymbol{\beta}_A) . \qquad (12.201)$$

Exponential class. For this class $F_a(t) = 1 - \exp(-\beta_1 t)$ and the likelihood function becomes

$$L(u_0, \beta_1) = \frac{u_0!}{(u_0 - m_e)!} \beta_1^{m_e} \exp\left\{ -\beta_1 \left[\left(u_0 - m_e \right) t_e + \sum_{i=1}^{m_e} t_i \right] \right\}. \qquad (12.202)$$

To obtain a point or interval estimate of either u_0 or β_1 the posterior marginal distribution of the parameter must be obtained. Thus, using any table of standard integrals, the posterior marginal distribution of u_0 is

$$\int_0^\infty L(u_0, \beta_1) \, d\beta_1 \propto \frac{u_0!}{(u_0 - m_e)!} \frac{1}{[(u_0 - m_e)t_e + \sum_{i=1}^{m_e} t_i]^{m_e+1}} , u_0 \geqslant m_e . \quad (12.203)$$

Note that we have restricted the values that β_1 can take on through the limits of integration so that negative values (increasing failure intensities) are not allowed. Similarly, the posterior marginal distribution of β_1 is proportional to

$$\beta_1^{m_e} \exp\left[-\beta_1 \sum_{i=1}^{m_e} t_i \right] \int_{m_e}^\infty \frac{u_0!}{(u_0 - m_e)!} \exp[-\beta_1 (u_0 - m_e) t_e] du_0 , \beta_1 \geqslant 0 . \quad (12.204)$$

---

[13]Constraints will be placed on $\boldsymbol{\beta}$ so that a decreasing failure intensity model will always be obtained.

Numerical methods will be necessary when working with Equations (12.203) and (12.204).

> **Example 12.18.** As an example consider the data from system T1. The posterior marginal distributions of β_1 and u_0 are shown in Figures 12.24 and 12.25, respectively. Consider first Figure 12.24. The generalized maximum likelihood estimate of β_1 is 0.348×10^{-4}/CPU sec and the median estimate is 0.35×10^{-4}/CPU sec. A 95 percent probability interval is $(0.272 \times 10^{-4}, 0.432 \times 10^{-4})$. Comparing these results with those in Examples 12.1 and 12.4, we see that they are practically identical. Now consider Figure 12.25. The generalized maximum likelihood estimate of u_0 is 141 (rounded to nearest integer) and the median estimate is 142. A 95 percent probability interval is (137, 150). These results compare favorably with those obtained using maximum likelihood estimation. ∎

POISSON-TYPE MODELS. The likelihood function for Poisson-type models is given by Equation (12.46) as

$$L(\boldsymbol{\beta}) = \left[\prod_{i=1}^{m_e} \lambda(t_i) \right] \exp[-\mu(t_e)] , \qquad (12.205)$$

and, once again, if we use a locally uniform prior for $f(\boldsymbol{\beta})$ we have for the posterior distribution of $\boldsymbol{\beta}$

$$f(\boldsymbol{\beta}|\ Y_D) \propto L(\boldsymbol{\beta}) . \qquad (12.206)$$

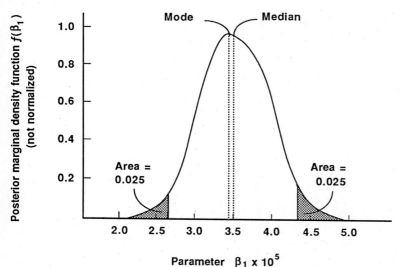

FIGURE 12.24
Posterior marginal distribution of β_1—exponential-class binomial model.

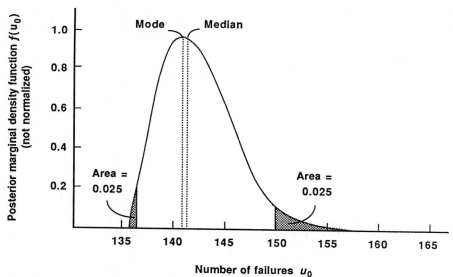

FIGURE 12.25
Posterior marginal distribution of u_0—exponential-class binomial model.

Exponential class. Using Equations (12.4) and (12.5) the likelihood function becomes

$$L(\beta_0, \beta_1) = (\beta_0\beta_1)^{m_e} \exp\left[-\beta_1 \sum_{i=1}^{m_e} t_i\right] \exp\{-\beta_0[1 - \exp(-\beta_1 t_e)]\} . \quad (12.207)$$

The posterior marginal distribution of β_1 is proportional to

$$\int_0^\infty L(\beta_0, \beta_1) \, d\beta_0 \propto \frac{\beta_1^{m_e} \exp\left[-\beta_1 \sum_{i=1}^{m_e} t_i\right]}{[1 - \exp(-\beta_1 t_e)]^{m_e+1}} , \quad (12.208)$$

while the posterior marginal distribution of β_0 is proportional to

$$\int_0^\infty L(\beta_0, \beta_1) \, d\beta_1 \propto \beta_0^{m_e} \exp(-\beta_0) \sum_{i=0}^\infty \frac{\beta_0^i}{i!} \left(\frac{\sum\limits_{i=1}^{m_e} t_i}{\sum\limits_{i=1}^{m_e} t_i + it_e}\right)^{m_e+1} , \quad \beta_0 \geqslant m_e . \quad (12.209)$$

A restriction on the posterior distribution of β_0 was imposed since in this treatment β_0 is equivalent to ν_0.

Example 12.19. Consider once again the system T1. The generalized maximum likelihood estimate for β_1 is 0.347×10^{-4}/CPU sec and the median estimate is 0.35

$\times$ 10^{-4}/CPU sec. A 95 percent probability interval is $(0.272 \times 10^{-4}, 0.432 \times 10^{-4})$. The results are nearly identical to those obtained in Example 12.18. Also note that the posterior marginal distribution of β_1 is almost identical to the conditional likelihood of β_1 [compare Equaions (12.42) and (12.208)]. As for β_0, the generalized maximum likelihood estimate and median estimate are 142 and 148, respectively. A 95 percent probability interval is (137, 171). These results show (at least for this example) that the distribution of β_0 $(= \nu_0)$ is more skewed than the corresponding distribution for a binomial-type model. ∎

Geometric family. For this family it will be slightly more convenient to reparameterize the mean value and failure intensity functions as

$$\mu(t) = \frac{\beta_2}{\beta_1} \ln (1 + \beta_1 t) \tag{12.210}$$

and

$$\lambda(t) = \frac{\beta_2}{1 + \beta_1 t}, \tag{12.211}$$

respectively. Comparing with Equations (12.6) and (12.7) we see that the new parameter β_2 is equal to $\beta_0 \beta_1$. This reparameterization leads to integrals that are slightly easier to evaluate using numerical methods. Using Equations (12.210) and (12.211) we can show that the joint posterior distribution of β_1 and β_2 is proportional to

$$\beta_2^{m_e} \left[\prod_{i=1}^{m_e} \frac{1}{1 + \beta_1 t_i} \right] \left[\frac{1}{1 + \beta_1 t_e} \right]^{\beta_2/\beta_1} \tag{12.212}$$

when using a locally uniform prior. The posterior marginal distribution of β_1 is proportional to

$$\frac{\beta_1^{m_e+1} \prod_{i=1}^{m_e} \frac{1}{1 + \beta_1 t_i}}{[\ln (1 + \beta_1 t_e)]^{m_e+1}} \tag{12.213}$$

and the posterior marginal distribution of β_2 is proportional to

$$\beta_2^{m_e} \int_0^\infty \left[\prod_{i=1}^{m_e} \frac{1}{1 + \beta_1 t_i} \right] \left[\frac{1}{1 + \beta_1 t_e} \right]^{\beta_2/\beta_1} d\beta_1 . \tag{12.214}$$

Example 12.20. The posterior marginal distribution for β_1 and β_2 are shown in Figures 12.26 and 12.27, respectively, for the T1 system data. Consider the distribution of β_1 shown in Figure 12.26. The generalized maximum likelihood estimate and median estimate of β_1 are 0.286×10^{-3}/CPU sec and 0.338×10^{-3}/CPU sec, respectively. A 95 percent probability interval for β_1 is given by $(0.156 \times 10^{-3}, 0.68 \times 10^{-3})$. These results can be compared with those given in Examples 12.3 and 12.5.

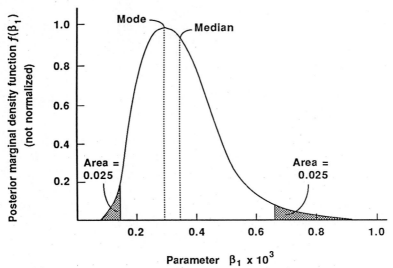

FIGURE 12.26
Posterior marginal distribution of β_1 — geometric family.

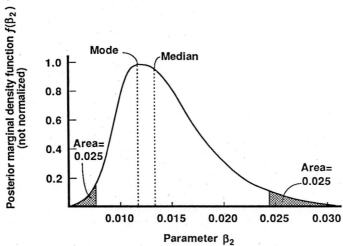

FIGURE 12.27
Posterior marginal distribution of β_2 — geometric family.

The generalized maximum likelihood estimate and median estimate of β_2 are 0.012 failure/CPU sec and 0.013 failure/CPU sec, respectively. A 95 percent probability interval for β_2 is given by (0.0077, 0.0242). ∎

12.4.2 Inference of Derived Quantities

We will not consider inference of derived quantities (such as additional time to reach the failure intensity objective) in any great detail here. Using an illustration we give the general approach one might use.

Consider the failure intensity functions resulting from one-parameter scaled mean value functions, that is, $\lambda(t) = \beta_0 \lambda_1(t; \beta_1)$. We wish to make inferences about $\lambda(t)$. Thus, we seek the posterior marginal distribution of $\lambda(t)$. Having this we can then set $t = 0$ or $t = t_e$ to make inferences about the initial failure intensity λ_0 and the present failure intensity λ_P respectively. Starting with $f(\beta_0, \beta_1)$ and applying a straightforward change of variables [see Mood, Graybill, and Boes (1974)] we can show that

$$f\left[\lambda(t)\right] \propto \int_0^\infty \frac{1}{\lambda_1(t; \beta_1)} f\left[\frac{\lambda(t)}{\lambda_1(t; \beta_1)}, \beta_1\right] d\beta_1 . \qquad (12.215)$$

Numerical procedures will almost certainly always be required to evaluate $f[\lambda(t)]$.

For an exponential-class Poisson-type model $\lambda_1(t; \beta_1) = \beta_1 \exp(-\beta_1 t)$. Using Equation (12.207) we have

$$f\left[\lambda(t)\right] \propto \left[\lambda(t)\right]^{m_e} \int_0^\infty \frac{1}{\beta_1} \exp\left\{\beta_1\left[(m_e + 1)t - \sum_{i=1}^{m_e} t_i\right]\right\}$$

$$\times \exp\left\{-\frac{\lambda(t)}{\beta_1} \exp(\beta_1 t) [1 - \exp(-\beta_1 t_e)]\right\} d\beta_1 . \qquad (12.216)$$

The posterior marginal distribution of λ_0 is given by setting $t = 0$ in Equation (12.216). We have

$$f(\lambda_0) \propto \lambda_0^{m_e} \int_0^\infty \frac{1}{\beta_1} \exp\left(-\beta_1 \sum_{i=1}^{m_e} t_i\right) \exp\left\{-\frac{\lambda_0}{\beta_1}[1 - \exp(-\beta_1 t_e)]\right\} d\beta_1 . \qquad (12.217)$$

A similar expression results for λ_P when $t = t_e$ is substituted in Equation (12.216).

For a geometric-family Poisson-type model $\lambda_1(t; \beta_1) = (1 + \beta_1 t)^{-1}$. Using Equation (12.212) the posterior marginal distribution of the failure intensity given by Equation (12.215) becomes

$$f\left[\lambda(t)\right] \propto \left[\lambda(t)\right]^{m_e} \int_0^\infty (1 + \beta_1 t)^{m_e+1} \left(\prod_{i=1}^{m_e} \frac{1}{1 + \beta_1 t_i}\right) \left(\frac{1}{1 + \beta_1 t_e}\right)^{\frac{\lambda(t)(1+\beta_1 t)}{\beta_1}} d\beta_1 . \qquad (12.218)$$

The posterior marginal distribution of the initial failure intensity is from Equation (12.218) with $t = 0$

$$f(\lambda_0) \propto \lambda_0^{m_e} \int_0^\infty \left\{ \prod_{i=1}^{m_e} \frac{1}{1 + \beta_1 t_i} \right\} \left(\frac{1}{1 + \beta_1 t_e} \right)^{\frac{\lambda_0}{\beta_1}} d\beta_1 . \qquad (12.219)$$

12.4.3 Summary

Bayesian analysis provides a way of incorporating prior knowledge into the estimation process. In the absence of any prior knowledge the use of ignorance priors is suggested. The results when these are used are usually close to the results obtained with maximum likelihood estimation since both methods depend heavily on the likelihood function.

12.5 SUMMARY

Three popular methods for point and interval estimation were discussed. Maximum likelihood estimation was given the most attention because of its widespread acceptance. The least squares method was seen to provide an excellent alternative to maximum likelihood. Finally, the Bayesian approach was outlined. This approach requires a great deal more computational effort than the other two.

   A comparison of results from these three methods using data from system T1 for an exponential-class Poisson-type model is shown in Table 12.16. Similarly, Table 12.17 shows the set of results for a geometric-family model. The three methods are seen to provide roughly equivalent results for this set of data.

PROBLEMS

12.1 Show that, for a fixed number of failures, the conditional likelihood function based on grouped data approaches that based on failure time data as the number of groups increases.

12.2 Show that $\hat{u}_0$ given by Equation (12.33) is nearly equal to the unconditional maximum likelihood estimate from the solution to Equation (12.27) for binomial models.

12.3 How much difference in $\hat{u}_0$ can be expected if we use Equation (12.33) instead of Equation (12.27) to do the estimation for binomial models?

12.4 What condition is sufficient to obtain a positive value for $\hat{\beta}_1$ for both the exponential class and geometric families? How does it relate to the condition given in Case Study 12.1?

12.5 As β_1 approaches 0 what value will the conditional likelihood function take on for exponential-class models? For geometric-family models?

12.6 What happens to our estimate for β_0 as our estimate for β_1 approaches 0 for exponential-class and geometric-family models? As a result what are the implications for these models?

TABLE 12.16
Comparison of point and interval estimates for system T1—exponential-class Poisson model

| Parameter | Point estimate | | | 95 percent interval estimates | | | | | |
| | Maximum likelihood | Least squares | Bayesian | Maximum likelihood | | Least squares | | Bayesian | |
				Lower	Upper	Lower	Upper	Lower	Upper
β_0	142	137.2	142	138.8	148.9	136	145.2	137	171
β_1	0.348×10^{-4}	0.43×10^{-4}	0.347×10^{-4}	0.268×10^{-4}	0.427×10^{-4}	0.296×10^{-4}	0.572×10^{-4}	0.272×10^{-4}	0.432×10^{-4}

TABLE 12.17
Comparison of point and interval estimates for system T1—geometric-family model

Parameter	Point estimate			95 percent interval estimates					
	Maximum likelihood	Least squares	Bayesian	Maximum likelihood		Least squares		Bayesian	
				Lower	Upper	Lower	Upper	Lower	Upper
β_0	42.3	41.7	—	35.4	52.5	32.7	50.7	—	—
β_1	0.262×10^{-3}	0.283×10^{-3}	0.286×10^{-3}	0.135×10^{-3}	0.5×10^{-3}	0.117×10^{-3}	0.449×10^{-3}	0.156×10^{-3}	0.68×10^{-3}

12.7 Derive the unconditional density function for T_i for Poisson-type models.

12.8 Suppose the testing process is observed for a preassigned number of failures, m. By selecting m as our basis of observation, the amount of time that has elapsed, T_m, will be a random variable. Use the result of Problem 12.7 to derive the conditional likelihood for Poisson-type models. How does this result compare with Equation (12.51)?

12.9 Redo Problem 12.8 for grouped data. The testing process is to be observed for p groups.

12.10 Show that if $\mu(x_l) = y_l$ for $l = 1, \ldots, p$ then Equation (12.106) becomes Equation (12.108).

12.11 Show for an exponential-class model that the maximum likelihood estimator for the initial failure intensity is a monotonically increasing function of $\hat{\beta}_1$. Also show that the maximum likelihood estimator for the present and future failure intensity are monotonically decreasing functions of $\hat{\beta}_1$.

12.12 Repeat Problem 12.11 for the geometric family.

12.13 What is the expected value of T_i for exponential class Poisson-type models?

12.14 Repeat Problem 12.13 for the geometric family showing that

$$E[T_i] = \frac{1}{\beta_1} \left[\left(\frac{\beta_0}{\beta_0 - 1} \right)^i - 1 \right],$$

provided $\beta_0 > 1$.

12.15 Consider the probability density function given by Equation (12.52) for the geometric family. Derive a formula for expected value of $(\beta_1 T + 1)^{-n}$, where n is an integer. This will be useful to help solve the following problem.

12.16 Derive the expected information given by Equation (12.74).

12.17 Obtain the conditional probability density function of $X = \sum_{i=1}^{m_e} T_i$. Consider the T_i's to be independent random variables distributed according to the truncated exponential distribution given by Equation (12.71). First, determine the Laplace transform of the truncated exponential distribution and hence also that of X. Then, invert the transform to obtain the probability density function of X.

12.18 To use the method described by Mood, Graybill, and Boes (1974; pp. 387–393) to establish confidence intervals for β_1 we need the cumulative density function for X. Obtain this function using the results of Problem 12.17.

12.19 Show that the skewness of $\partial \ln (\beta_1 \mid m_e)/\partial \beta_1$ is given by Equation (12.73).

12.20 Derive a simple formula involving the failure intensity function that can be used to determine where the pole(s) of Equation (12.65) occur.

12.21 Use the result of Problem 12.20 to determine where the pole(s) exist for an exponential-class and geometric-family model. Why does this cause a problem for the former and not the latter model?

12.22 Compare the confidence interval for β_1 in Example 12.4 with the one you would get using the likelihood ratio alternative.

12.23 Repeat Problem 12.22 for Example 12.5.

12.24 Show that the expected information in an exponential-class model approaches a constant value as the period of observation approaches infinity. Is the same true of a geometric-family model?

12.25 A decision has been made to use a constant failure intensity Poisson model during the *operational* phase of a software project. Is it more desirable from an estimation point of view to collect failure time data or grouped failure data? Use the unconditional likelihood function.

12.26 From the information contained in Table 12.9 determine if the distribution of $\partial \ln L(\beta_1 \mid m_e)/\partial \beta_1$ becomes more skewed or less skewed as m_e increases relative to $\beta_0 = \nu_0$.

THIRTEEN

COMPARISON OF SOFTWARE
RELIABILITY MODELS

We have described many published models in Chapter 11. This proliferation of models has been useful to the extent that many different approaches have been explored. However, software engineers and managers have been left adrift. They have had little guidance as to which models may be best or may be best for their application.

Some researchers [for example, Sukert (1979) and Schick and Wolverton (1978)] have attempted to compare some of the different models. Unfortunately, these efforts were handicapped by insufficient data of high quality and absence of standards about the comparison or evaluation criteria to be employed. Since then, more good quality failure data on a variety of software systems have become available [for example, Musa (1979b)]. Several researchers have jointly proposed comparison criteria, incorporating comments from many reviewers in the field [Iannino, Musa, Okumoto, and Littlewood (1984)]. To provide a sound and efficient basis for comparison, Musa and Okumoto (1983) have classified the various models. They have explored and examined the assumptions underlying software reliability theory.

In this chapter we will compare many existing models. We begin with a discussion of the evaluation criteria to be used in making the comparisons. The failure data used to compare the models are then described. After looking at the question of which time domain should be used for modeling, we will evaluate the important model attributes. Particularly promising models will be recommended.

13.1 COMPARISON CRITERIA

It is recommended that software reliability models be compared by the criteria discussed in this section. Note that these criteria have been proposed by Iannino,

Musa, Okumoto, and Littlewood (1984). Some of these criteria are general enough to apply to all types of models. However, we will describe and discuss them here in the specific context of software reliability. We have selected only "intrinsic" criteria. Attributes such as the documentation quality and the human interface quality of supporting tools are very important but they depend on the implementation. They are not characteristic of the model per se. It should be pointed out that functional validity and "insight gained" are valuable characteristics of models, even though not mentioned by Iannino, Musa, Okumoto, and Littlewood (1984).

We can use these criteria for assessment (determining the absolute worth of a model) as well as comparison. Comparison should be done with relation to a variety of software systems. It does not appear likely that the evaluation of the models will be application-dependent. However, one must watch for this possibility. We must, of course, collect the data with care. It would not be reasonable to compare models with poor quality data or, worse, data of unequal quality. However, as will be noted in Section 13.1.4, tolerance to or capability to compensate for certain types of poor data is a desirable quality in a model.

It is expected that comparisons will cause some models to be rejected because they meet few of the criteria discussed here. On the other hand, there may or may not be a clear choice between the more acceptable models. The relative weight to be placed on the different criteria may depend on the context in which the model is being applied. When comparing two models, we should consider all criteria simultaneously. We should not eliminate models by one criterion before considering other criteria, except if predictive validity is grossly unsatisfactory. It is not expected that a model must satisfy *all* criteria to be useful.

The proposed criteria include predictive validity, capability, quality of assumptions, applicability, and simplicity. We will discuss each of the criteria in more detail in the following sections.

13.1.1 Predictive Validity

Predictive validity is the capability of the model to predict future failure behavior from present and past failure behavior (that is, data). This capability is significant only when failure behavior is changing. Hence, it is usually considered for a test phase, but it can be applied to the operational phase when repairs are being regularly made. Note that "predictive validity" does not carry the connotation of "prediction" in referring to determination of parameters from program characteristics.

There are at least two general ways of viewing predictive validity. These are based on the two equivalent approaches to characterizing the failure random process, namely:

1. the number of failures approach and
2. the failure time approach.

We may apply various detailed methods, some representing approximations to predictive validity. It has not been determined if one is superior at the present time.

The number of failures approach may yield a method that is more practical to use than the failure time approach. In the former approach, we describe the failure random process by $[M(t), t \geq 0]$, representing failures experienced by time t. Such a counting process is characterized by specifying the distribution of $M(t)$, including the mean value function $\mu(t)$.

Assume that we have observed q failures by the end of test time t_q. We use the failure data up to time t_e ($\leq t_q$) to estimate the parameters of $\mu(t)$. Substituting the estimates of the parameters in the mean value function yields the estimate of the number of failures $\hat{\mu}(t_q)$ by t_q. The estimate is compared with the actually observed number q. This procedure is repeated for various values of t_e.

We can visually check the predictive validity by plotting the relative error $[\hat{\mu}(t_q) - q]/q$ against the normalized test time t_e/t_q. The error will approach 0 as t_e approaches t_q. If the points are positive (negative), the model tends to overestimate (underestimate). Numbers closer to 0 imply more accurate prediction and hence a better model. (See Section 13.3 for examples of this approach.)

The use of normalization enables one to overlay relative error curves obtained from different failure data sets. For an overall conclusion about the relative predictive validity of models, we may compare plots of the medians (taken with respect to the various data sets). We will consider a model to be superior if it yields the curve closest to 0. Note that one advantage of this approach is that normalized plots are project-independent. Hence they can be generated for inter-project comparisons.

In the failure time approach, we characterize the failure random process by failure times (execution or calendar). Assume that we have observed m failure times during testing, denoted by $T_1, T_2, \ldots, T_m$. The cumulative distribution function provides the most general (containing the most information) description of the random process. All other quantities such as mean time to failure (if it exists), failure intensity, and reliability may be obtained from this function. Typically, each model implicitly incorporates a procedure for making inferences about the parameters of the cumulative distribution function from the failure time data $t_1, t_2, \ldots, t_m$. The predictor distribution for the ith failure interval T_i', which incorporates model and inference procedure, may be written as $\tilde{F}_i(t_i' \mid t_1, \ldots, t_m)$.

Note that $i > m$, since we are concerned with prediction. We determine predictive validity by comparing predictor distributions of failure intervals from the model and its associated inference procedure with values experienced. This can be done based on the u-plot [Littlewood and Verrall (1973)], described in Chapter 16.

We will use m failure intervals to predict the ith failure interval. Let $k = i - m$. Then k signifies the prediction length or intervals we are predicting ahead. Since we need many data points to check the predictive validity of F_i, we can either hold m fixed and let k vary ($k > 0$) or hold k fixed and let m vary (i varies in both cases). In the former case, we are examining predictions of various lengths using a fixed sample size. In the latter case, we are examining prediction of a fixed length based on different sample sizes. Predictive validity should be checked from both viewpoints. If one model has equal predictive validity with another but attains this capability earlier (that is, for a smaller failure sample), it may be superior.

The sparseness of data (there is only one piece of data per predictor distribution) presents a problem. One must take advantage of functional relationships between distributions at different points in some way to evaluate predictive validity.

Although most models have been developed in association with a particular inference procedure (for example, maximum likelihood method or least squares method), we should consider other inference procedures if prediction is poor. We can examine the quality of inference by generating simulated failure intervals based on the model with assumed parameter values and using them in the prediction scheme (combination of model and inference procedure). This method removes any effects of the model. Any consistent differences between the predictor distribution and the actual distribution represent the effects of inference alone. Alternatively, we may compare the distributions of the parameter estimates with the observed values to evaluate inference quality. As will be seen in Section 13.3, however, it appears unlikely that different estimation methods will have a substantial effect on predictive validity.

13.1.2   Capability

Capability refers to the ability of the model to estimate with satisfactory accuracy quantities needed by software managers, engineers, and users in planning and managing software development projects or running operational software systems. We must gauge the degree of capability by looking at the relative importance of the quantities as well as their number. The quantities, in approximate order of importance, are:

1. present reliability, mean time to failure (MTTF), or failure intensity,
2. expected date of reaching a specified reliability, MTTF, or failure intensity objective,[1] and
3. human and computer resource and cost requirements related to the achievement of the objective.

Any capability of a model for prediction of software reliability in the system design and early development phases is extremely valuable because of the resultant value for system engineering and planning purposes. We must make these predictions through measurable characteristics of the software (size, complexity, structure, etc.), the software development environment, and the operational environment.

---

[1] It is assumed that the objective is variable and that dates can be computed for many objectives, if desired. If we cannot compute a date, we should at least be able to predict the achievement of the objective in terms of additional execution time or failures experienced.

13.1.3 Quality of Assumptions

The following considerations of quality should be applied to each assumption in turn. If it is possible to test an assumption, the degree to which it is supported by data is an important consideration. This is especially true of assumptions that may be common to an entire group of models. If it is not possible to test the assumption, we should evaluate its *plausibility* from the viewpoint of logical consistency and software engineering experience. For example, does it relate rationally to other information about software and software development? Finally, we should judge the clarity and explicitness of an assumption. These characteristics are often necessary to determine whether a model applies to particular software system or project circumstances.

13.1.4 Applicability

Another important characteristic of a model is its applicability. We should judge a model on its degree of applicability across software products that vary in size, structure, and function. It is also desirable that it be usable in different development environments, different operational environments, and different life cycle phases. However, if a particular model gives outstanding results for just a narrow range of products or development environments, we should not necessarily eliminate the model.

There are at least four special situations that are encountered commonly in practice. A model should either be capable of dealing with them directly or should be compatible with procedures that can deal with them. These are:

1. program evolution,
2. classification of severity of failures into different categories,
3. ability to handle incomplete failure data or data with measurement uncertainties (although not without loss of predictive validity),
4. operation of the same program on computers of different performance.

Finally, it is desirable that a model be robust with respect to departures from its assumptions, errors in the data or parameters it employs, and unusual conditions.

13.1.5 Simplicity

A model should be simple in three aspects. The most important consideration is that it must be simple and inexpensive to collect the data required to particularize the model. If this is not the case, we will not use the model. Second, the model should be simple in concept. Software engineers without extensive mathematical background should be able to understand the model and its assumptions. They can then determine when it is applicable and the extent to which the model may diverge from reality in an application. Parameters should have readily understood interpretations. This property makes it more feasible for software engineers to estimate the values of the parameters when data are not available. The number of parameters in the model is also an important consideration for simplicity. It should be pointed out that we need to compare the number of parameters on a common basis (for example, don't include calendar time component parameters for one model and not another).

Finally, a model must be readily implementable as a program that is a practical management and engineering tool. This means that the program must run rapidly and inexpensively with no manual intervention *required* (does not rule out *possibility* of intervention) other than the initial input.

It would seem that simplicity is just common sense. However, it is easy for all of us to get carried away with intellectual elegance and power. This appeal must be consciously resisted in modeling, whose purpose, after all, is pragmatic.

13.2   FAILURE DATA

The failure time data used for the evaluations in this chapter are composed of 15 sets of data and come from three sources [Miller (1980), Musa (1979b), and Sukert (1976)]. Table 13.1 shows the data source and system characteristics for each set of failure data. Note that in this chapter we have chosen the total time of testing to be the last failure time. The data represent a wide variety of applications (such as real time command and control, real time commercial, military, and space systems) and system sizes ranging from small (5.7K object instructions) to large (2.4M object instructions).

The failure data sets T1, T2, T3, T4, T5, T6, T16, T17, T18, T19, and T21 from Musa (1979b) are generally of the best quality. They were collected under Musa's supervision and carefully controlled to ensure their accuracy. All data represent execution time or clock time, which is generally proportional to and hence a good approximation for execution time. However, it was determined that for some data sets that were based on clock time [specifically, in Musa (1979b), data sets 14C and those prefixed by "SS"] there were probably some departures from proportionality because of diurnal load variations. These data sets were not included in the following study, since execution time may not have been accurately approximated.

The failure data sets T20 from Sukert (1976) and T22, T23, and T25 from Miller (1980) were developed from information on failures per day and clock time per day. The failure times were established randomly within the clock time window each day. A uniform distribution was assumed, since this is a "model free" assumption that is a good approximation for the short windows involved. Thus these data represent an approximation to execution time failure data, with a somewhat higher degree of noise.

These data sets were all taken during system test (except for T6, which was taken during subsystem test). The data represent complete test phases, except for T18. Data sets T1, T3, T4, and T18 are known to have had some data taken before

TABLE 13.1
Characteristics of software systems studied

System designator	System designator— reference source	Reference source	Delivered object instructions	Programmers	Total test time		Size of failure sample	Nature of system
					Execution time (hr)	Calendar time (days)		
T1	1	Musa (1979b)	21,700	9	24.6	92	136	Real time command and control
T2	2	Musa (1979b)	27,700	5	30.2	72	54	"
T3	3	Musa (1979b)	23,400	6	18.7	55	38	"
T4	4	Musa (1979b)	33,500	7	14.6	71	53	"
T5	5	Musa (1979b)	2,445,000	275	1785	173	831	Real time commercial
T6	6	Musa (1979b)	5,700	8	1.4	58	73	Commercial (subsystem)
T16	27	Musa (1979b)	126,100	8	1197.9	79	41	Military
T17	40	Musa (1979b)	180,000	8	5436.7	347	101	Military
T18	–	Musa (1979b)	?	8	9935.2	897	163	Military
T19	17	Musa (1979b)	61,900	8	64.9	56	38	Military
T20	–	Sukert (1976)	115,346	?	615.3	162	2191	Military command and control
T21	–	Musa (1979b)	25,000	?	32.3	89	75	Military
T22	ISEE-C	Miller (1980)	75,000*	4	8.2	42	118	Space
T23	AEM	Miller (1980)	50,000*	4	16.2	58	180	Space
T25	SMM	Miller (1980)	85,000*	7	21.6	216	213	Space

*High-level source statements, including comments

the respective systems were completely integrated (only 2 failure intervals for T3). Data set T2 is known to include only data taken after it was completely integrated. The remaining data sets probably involve systems that were completely integrated for all the data that were taken, but we do not know for certain.

13.3 COMPARISON OF PREDICTIVE VALIDITY OF MODEL GROUPS

To provide an efficient basis for comparison, we have classified software reliability models by five different attributes (see Table 9.2). We will now make comparisons of predictive validity using the following seven model groups (classes or families), which include most published models:

1. exponential class,
2. Weibull class,
3. Pareto class,
4. geometric family,
5. inverse linear family,
6. inverse polynomial (2nd degree only) family, and
7. power family.

We do not differentiate between binomial- and Poisson-type models because the mean value function is independent of type. It is this function that is the primary determinant of the model characteristics.

Although we may use various methods of evaluating predictive validity (as discussed in Section 13.1.1), we will take a relative error approach based on failures experienced, since it is especially practical to use. If a model is found to have the best predictive validity based on failures experienced, it will probably yield the best predictions of other reliability quantities. Consult Section 13.1.1 for a detailed description of this approach. We will apply the relative error approach for evaluating predictive validity for each of the model groups, using the 15 sets of failure data.

Note that execution time has proved to be a better time domain than calendar time (see Section 13.6 for a detailed discussion). Therefore, we will use execution time data in this comparison study.

We will consider the following two inference methods: maximum likelihood and least squares.

13.3.1 Maximum Likelihood Method

In Section 12.2 we described the maximum likelihood estimation method, using the general forms of $\lambda(\tau)$ and $\mu(\tau)$. We can easily particularize for each model group. Using maximum likelihood estimation yields an exact comparison for most models. It provides an approximate comparison for the Littlewood-Verrall model, which uses Bayesian inference.

To illustrate the comparison method, we will consider the predictive validity of the geometric family (logarithmic Poisson execution time model) for the data set T1. Note that the logarithmic Poisson execution time model has its mean value function given in Equation (11.41) and its intensity function given in Equation (11.42). We must first obtain estimates of the model parameters λ_0 and θ. We have found the estimates $\hat{\lambda}_0$ and $\hat{\theta}$ based on the failure data up to execution time values of τ_e. These values of τ_e range from 20 percent to 100 percent, in increments of 5 percent, of the total execution time $\tau_q = 24.6$ CPU hr. Table 13.2 summarizes the results.

For example, for the failure data up to 60 percent of the total execution time (that is, $\tau_e = 14.8$ CPU hr), we have $\hat{\lambda}_0 = 40$ failures/CPU hr and $\hat{\theta} = 0.0238/$ failure. We can then obtain the fitted mean value function by substituting these estimates into the mean value function as

$$\hat{\mu}(\tau) = \frac{1}{\hat{\theta}} \ln (\hat{\lambda}_0 \, \hat{\theta} \, \tau + 1)$$

$$= \frac{1}{0.0238} \ln \left[(40)(0.0238)\tau + 1 \right].$$

TABLE 13.2
Maximum likelihood estimates, predicted numbers of failures, and relative errors for system T1 based on the logarithmic Poisson execution time model

$\dfrac{\tau_e}{\tau_q}$ (percent)	$\hat{\lambda}_0$ (failures/CPU hr)	$\hat{\theta}$	$\hat{\mu}(\tau_q)$ (failures)	$\dfrac{\hat{\mu}(\tau_q) - q}{q}$ (percent)
20	39.7	0.0231	137	0.7
25	39.9	0.0232	137	0.7
30	44.0	0.0267	127	−6.6
35	43.1	0.0260	129	−5.1
40	45.6	0.0281	124	−8.8
45	44.7	0.0273	126	−7.4
50	42.6	0.0257	130	−4.4
55	42.1	0.0254	130	−4.4
60	40.0	0.0238	134	−1.5
65	36.4	0.0213	141	3.7
70	38.8	0.0229	137	0.7
75	36.8	0.0214	141	3.7
80	38.6	0.0227	137	0.7
85	38.8	0.0229	137	0.7
90	39.0	0.0230	136	0.0
95	39.3	0.0232	136	0.0
100	39.2	0.0232	136	0.0

Figure 13.1 shows the cumulative failures and the fitted curve plotted against the normalized execution time.

We can predict failures that will be experienced by the end of testing τ_q by evaluating the fitted mean value function at $\tau = \tau_q$. We obtain $\hat{\mu}(\tau_q) = 134$. Note that there were 136 failures experienced at the end of testing. Therefore, we compute the relative error in prediction as

$$\frac{\hat{\mu}(\tau_q) - 136}{136} = \frac{134 - 136}{136} = -0.015 \ .$$

In other words, for the 60 percent of the total failure data, the logarithmic Poisson execution time model, using the maximum likelihood estimation method, under-estimates by 1.5 percent.

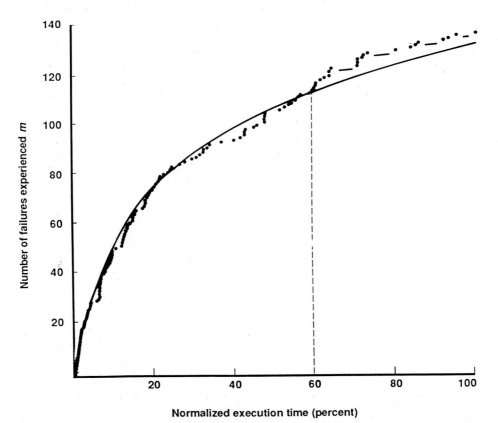

FIGURE 13.1
Cumulative number of failures for system T1: data and the fitted curve for logarithmic Poisson execution time model based on 60 percent of the total execution time.

Table 13.2 also shows the predicted values and relative errors for execution time values of τ_e that are from 20 percent to 100 percent of τ_q in increments of 5 percent. Figure 13.2 shows the relative errors plotted against the normalized execution time (that is, τ_e/τ_q). Note that the error will approach zero as τ_e approaches τ_q. Positive values of error indicate overestimation; negative, underestimation. Numbers closer to zero imply more accurate prediction. Figure 13.2 shows that the model predicts the future behavior well for this data set. The error curve is usually within ±5 percent.

The use of normalization enables us to overlay relative error curves obtained from different failure data sets. We overlay the relative error curves for the 15 failure data sets and summarize the results in Figure 13.3. The model again seems to predict the future behavior well since the error curves are, in general, within ±10 percent when prediction is made after 50 percent of the total execution time. Furthermore, there is no specific pattern such as overestimation or underestimation. This can be better seen in the median plot shown in Figure 13.4. Note that some of the dispersion in the prediction in Figure 13.3 may be because of different sizes

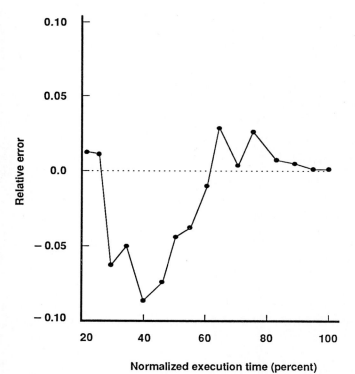

FIGURE 13.2
Relative error curve for logarithmic Poisson execution time model based on system T1 data set.

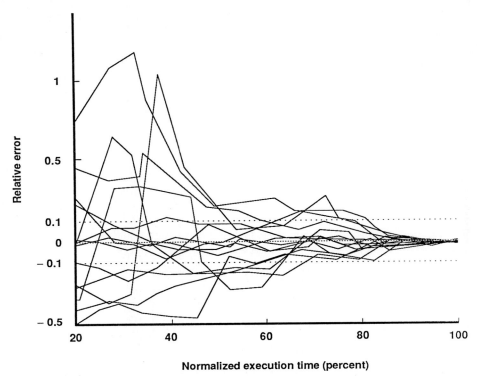

FIGURE 13.3
Relative error curves for logarithmic Poisson execution time model based on 15 failure data sets.

of data sets. Since prediction accuracy is related to the size of the sample of failures, we will achieve greater accuracy at the same normalized time for larger data sets.

Plots of the medians (taken with respect to the various data sets) are useful tools for drawing overall conclusions about the relative predictive validity of models. Figure 13.4 shows the median error curves for the model groups. Exponential, Pareto, and Weibull classes tend to underestimate whereas inverse linear and power families tend to overestimate. The geometric and inverse polynomial families on the whole yield the best prediction. However, the inverse polynomial family tends to be biased to the overestimation side, especially when prediction is made after 60 percent of τ_q. We can also confirm this pattern for the inverse polynomial family by examining its upper and lower quartile curves. We conclude that the geometric family is superior to the other software reliability model groups in predictive validity. Note that after 60 percent of the execution period, all model groups yield better than 10 percent accuracy. Hence after this point criteria other than predictive validity may be more important.

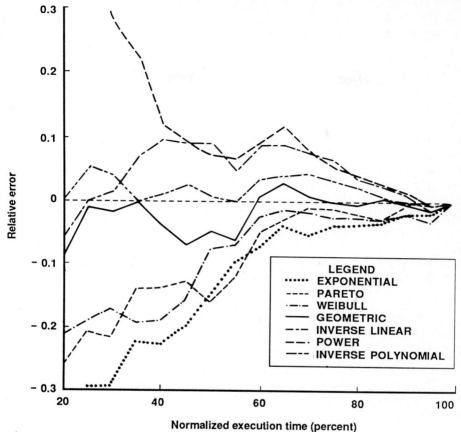

FIGURE 13.4
Median curves of relative error for seven model groups using the method of maximum likelihood.

It should be pointed out that most of the models fit the data sets when goodness of fit tests were applied. The prediction bias, therefore, is probably because of parameter estimation bias. Maximum likelihood estimates generally tend to be biased (see Case Study 12.3). It is possible to obtain unbiased or less biased estimates for some models [see Crow (1974) for the power family model and Joe and Reid (1985) for the exponential class], but for others this may be difficult. If prediction bias for a model can be removed by parameter estimation correction or improved parameter estimation, then the average relative error in prediction would tend to be near zero. A new technique under development, adaptive prediction (Chapter 16), appears to offer promise of reducing prediction bias substantially. If a method of reducing prediction bias is successful, dispersion of the prediction and the other comparison criteria will become more important. In our comparison study, the prediction bias was not removed, so that the comparison is on the degree of prediction bias with unadjusted parameter estimates.

13.3.2 Least Squares Method

We will now repeat the comparison among model groups for predictive validity using inference by least squares estimation. We first compute the observed failure intensity based on groups of failures. We then use the functional relationship to estimate the model parameters by fitting the function to the observed failure intensity.

Recall that the method of least squares discussed in Section 12.3 fits the functional relationship $\lambda(\mu)$ to the observed failure intensity [(m_l, r_l), $l = 1, \ldots, p$]. This method is attractive because of its simplicity and practicability. However, if we use the fitted mean value function to predict additional failures, it yields a result that is not always greater than or equal to 0. Since we use additional failures predicted by a model to evaluate predictive validity, we must modify the above method so that the fitted mean value function passes through the point (τ_m, m) that is,

$$\mu(\tau_m) = m \ . \tag{13.1}$$

In other words, to estimate the model parameters we will minimize the sum of the squares of relative errors under the condition given by Equation (13.1). Because of the nonlinear constraints, we cannot find an analytical solution but must obtain it numerically.

We now evaluate the predictive validity once more for the different model groups, using the same procedure as before but with the parameters obtained by least squares estimation. Figure 13.5 shows the results. These results, both relatively and in absolute terms, are similar to those for the case of maximum likelihood estimation. Thus, it appears unlikely that different methods of estimation will have a substantial effect on predictive validity of the models with which they are associated.

The studies discussed suggest that predictive validity is primarily affected by category and family or class (that is, the form of the failure intensity function). The model groups of the finite failures category tend to underpredict additional failures whereas those of the infinite category tend to overpredict or accurately predict. Predictive validity appears not to be affected by type (it isn't for least squares estimation, and binomial and Poisson types are almost equivalent for maximum likelihood estimation).

Based on the results presented in this section, it appears unlikely that different estimation methods will have a substantial effect on predictive validity.

13.4 EVALUATION OF OTHER CRITERIA

The capabilities of both the basic and logarithmic Poisson execution time models are superior to those of other published models. They are the only two models that

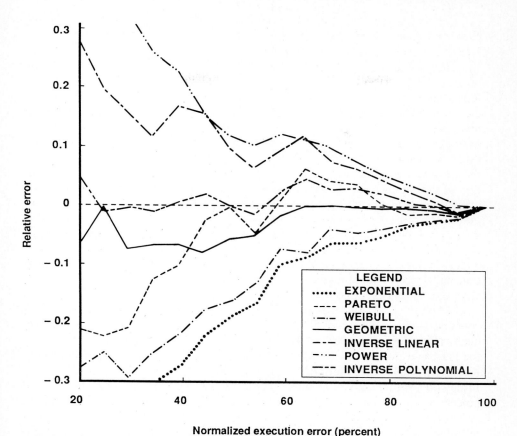

FIGURE 13.5
Median curves of relative error for seven model groups using the method of least squares.

model reliability in execution time and then use calendar time components to convert execution time quantities to calendar time. They readily yield present failure intensity. They also provide the expected date of reaching a specified failure intensity and the associated resource and cost requirements.

The basic execution time model has parameters that can be related to the characteristics of the software and the development process (although not with high accuracy at present). Thus it has prediction capability or the ability to project software reliability before execution. This capability does not appear to exist at present for models outside the exponential class of the finite failures category. Although models such as Jelinski-Moranda, Shooman, and Goel-Okumoto share this property with the basic execution time model, we use the latter because it incorporates the important concepts involved in the former models.

There has not been a general evaluation of all the assumptions on which the published models are based. Hence it would be difficult to draw any conclusions about their relative merits on this criterion.

In general, the published models seem to be widely applicable to most types of software products under various conditions. If the operational profile (set of input states experienced and associated probabilities) is highly nonuniform, then the decrement in failure intensity per failure experienced will tend to be nonuniform. In this case, models of class or family other than exponential (for example, geometric) may tend to fit better and yield better predictive validity. On the other hand, models are developed for programs that are stable in size, while most programs evolve as the result of the phasing of integration and the introduction of design changes. Musa and Iannino (chapter 15) have developed a method of compensating for changing size but model parameters must be related to program characteristics, particularly size. Hence we can use at present only the basic execution time model for the large class of programs that are changing in size.

In point of fact, the basic execution time model is the one that has been most widely applied to projects as development was proceeding. Hence, much information and lore is available about its use and convenient programs have been developed and refined to do the calculations.

Both the basic and logarithmic Poisson execution time models are simple in concept. Both have execution time components that are based on only two parameters. These parameters are readily interpretable as physical quantities, especially for the basic model. On the other hand, the Weibull and Pareto types have three parameters, and their physical significance is not as readily apparent. The Littlewood-Verrall general model uses Bayesian inference. Most software engineers and managers find this a difficult approach to comprehend. The analysis is frequently complex. The computer programs that implement the Littlewood-Verrall model are substantially more difficult to develop and debug, and the run times are sometimes several orders of magnitude greater than those of the two execution time models with maximum likelihood estimation.

13.5 RECOMMENDED MODELS

After considering the previous evaluations, it appears that the basic execution time model is generally superior in capability and applicability to the other published models. The basic and logarithmic Poisson execution time models are superior in simplicity. The logarithmic Poisson is second to the basic model, but superior to the others, in capability. The logarithmic Poisson is superior in predictive validity. Although the basic model is not as good as the logarithmic Poisson model in this respect, the difference is not significant after about 60 percent of the way through the test period. Thus these two models appear to be the two models of choice. One possible approach is to use the basic model for pretest studies and estimates and for periods of phased integration. Switch to the logarithmic Poisson model when integration is complete and the program is stable.

We have seen that many models have a prediction bias and that the direction and amount of this bias varies among them. If one of the techniques being investigated for reducing prediction bias is successful, the basic execution time model will probably become more important.

13.6 DISCUSSION: COMPARISON OF TIME DOMAINS

In this section, we will look at two time domains—execution time and calendar time—to determine which is best suited for expressing software reliability models. We use a flexible generic failure intensity function that can represent most published models, and fit it to failure data expressed in each of the time domains. We then compare the fits and examine how well trends are shown as a function of time domain. Consult Musa and Okumoto (1984a) for a detailed discussion.

13.6.1 Estimation of Failure Intensity

We will develop a method for estimating the failure intensity (expected failures per unit time) based on groups of failures. Suppose that we have observed m_e failures during $(0, t_e]$. Then, as discussed in Section 12.3, we can obtain the observed failure intensity for the lth subinterval $(t_{k \times (l-1)}, t_{k \times l}]$ by

$$
r_l = \begin{cases} \dfrac{k}{t_{k \times l} - t_{k \times (l-1)}}, & l = 1, \cdots, p-1 \\[4mm] \dfrac{m_e - k\,(p-1)}{t_e - t_{k \times (l-1)}}, & l = p \end{cases}
\tag{13.2}
$$

at time

$$
t_l = \frac{t_{k \times (l-1)} + t_{k \times l}}{2}.
\tag{13.3}
$$

Note that the r_l's are assumed to be independent of each other since subintervals are disjoint.

The failure data discussed in Section 13.2 are available as successive failure intervals in seconds for execution time and days for calendar time, respectively. The observation interval is partitioned at every kth failure occurrence time, so that there are at least k failures in each subinterval. As discussed in Section 12.3, grouping a small number of failures (a small value of k) will result in large variations in the estimated failure intensity while grouping a large number of failures (a large value of k) will result in too much smoothing. We have selected a group of five failures ($k = 5$) as a reasonable compromise in the following analysis. It should be pointed out that the use of different values of k was investigated. There was little effect on the results of the comparison. Although we may lose some information because of grouping failures, an advantage of the failure intensity approach is that we do not assume any specific model or distribution. This approach is useful, especially in analyzing a general trend or functional relationship of the failure intensity with respect to time.

We obtained the observed failure intensity using Equation (13.2), based on execution time and calendar time for each of 15 data sets. Figures 13.6 and 13.7 show plots of the observed failure intensity (marked points connected by a dashed line) for the data set T1 based on execution time and calendar time, respectively. They are useful for studying a general trend. For instance, for the system T1 there is a decreasing trend as a whole in the execution time data (see Figure 13.6). On the other hand, there are large variations in the calendar time data (see Figure 13.7) and hence, a trend is not so evident as for the execution time data. It appears likely that the daily usage of the program is both increasing rapidly and exhibiting

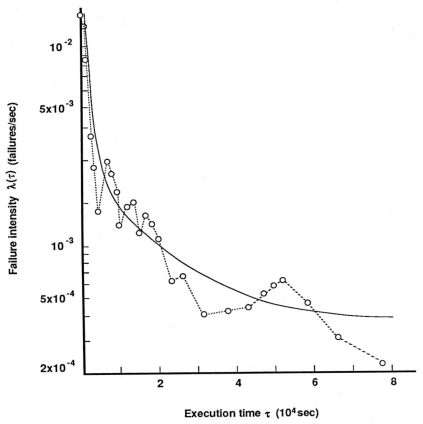

FIGURE 13.6
Failure intensity for system T1: data and fitted curve for execution time data.

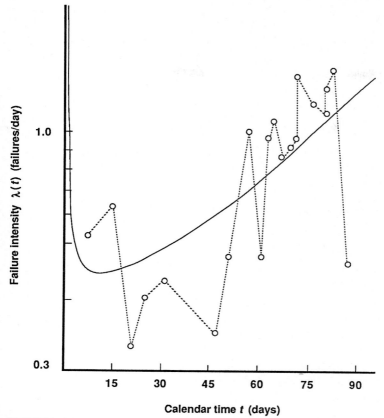

FIGURE 13.7
Failure intensity for system T1: data and fitted curve for calendar time data.

substantial variability, and that this is confounding the failure intensity picture. The failure intensity in calendar time is consequently generally increasing and highly variable.

In the following section we will discuss the procedure for fitting a generic function to the observed failure intensity.

13.6.2   Fitting the Observed Failure Intensity

Let $\lambda(t)$ be a theoretical failure intensity function of time t. In searching the data for possible trends we use the generic function

$$\lambda(t) = \alpha t^{\gamma-1} \exp(-\beta t^{\gamma}), \tag{13.4}$$

where α, β, and γ are real-valued parameters. It should be pointed out that the assumed function (13.4) is flexible. Depending on the values of the parameters, it can describe such cases for the failure intensity as a monotonically increasing or decreasing function or a unimodal function of time. The function represents the exponential and Weibull classes and it is also a good approximation of the Pareto class and the geometric and inverse linear families. Therefore, the function can represent most published models.

Figures 13.8 and 13.9 show the flexibility of the function. In Figure 13.8, where $\beta > 0$, the function is monotonically decreasing for $\gamma \leqslant 1$ or unimodal (first increasing and then decreasing) for $\gamma > 1$. On the other hand, in Figure 13.9, where $\beta < 0$, the function is monotonically increasing for $\gamma \geqslant 1$ or monotonically decreasing for $0 < \gamma < 1$. Finally, it can easily be seen from Equation (13.4) that the function will be time-invariant (that is, constant) when $\beta = 0$ and $\gamma = 1$.

We have shown the flexibility of the function given in Equation (13.4). It is also simple to work with. We therefore use this function to analyze trends in the observed failure intensity (t_l, r_l), $l = 1, \ldots, p$. We now develop a method that finds the estimates of the unknown parameters α, β, and γ using the least squares method.

Note that in tracking and predicting reliability status, software managers or engineers usually need a constant *relative* (rather than absolute) accuracy for MTTF and hence failure intensity. Therefore, we will minimize the sum of squares of the logarithms of the ratio of $\lambda(t_l)$ to r_l to estimate the unknown parameters. This approach also yields analytical simplicity.

Let ϵ_l represent the logarithm of the relative error of the lth data point. Thus, we have

$$\ln r_l = \ln \lambda(t_l) + \epsilon_l$$

$$= \ln \alpha + (\gamma - 1) \ln t_l - \beta t_l^\gamma + \epsilon_l, \tag{13.5}$$

where we obtained the last equality by substituting Equation (13.4) into the first. We can then find the estimates $\hat{\alpha}$, $\hat{\beta}$, and $\hat{\gamma}$ by minimizing

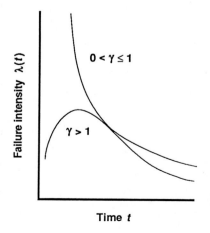

FIGURE 13.8
Shapes of the function $\lambda(t) = \alpha t^{\gamma-1} \exp(-\beta t^\gamma)$ **for** $\beta > 0$.

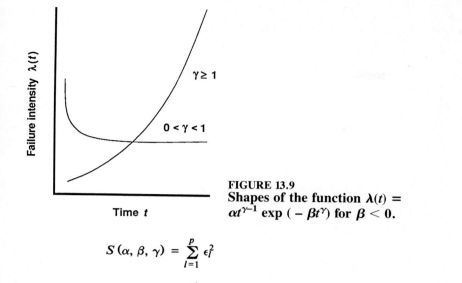

FIGURE 13.9
Shapes of the function $\lambda(t) = \alpha t^{\gamma-1} \exp(-\beta t^\gamma)$ for $\beta < 0$.

$$S(\alpha, \beta, \gamma) = \sum_{l=1}^{p} \epsilon_l^2$$

$$= \sum_{l=1}^{p}[\ln r_l - \ln \alpha - (\gamma - 1)\ln t_l + \beta t_l^\gamma]^2. \tag{13.6}$$

Equation (13.6) represents a nonlinear regression or a nonlinear minimization problem. Hence, we can find the estimates only through numerical procedures. There are several algorithms available that find the minimum of a nonlinear function. We used the procedure described in Appendix D to find $\hat{\alpha}$, $\hat{\beta}$, and $\hat{\gamma}$ for 15 data sets based on execution time and calendar time.

Table 13.3 summarizes the results for both execution time and calendar time. For illustration, consider the data set T1. The fitted curve, shown as a solid line in Figure 13.6, is a decreasing function of execution time (since $\hat{\beta} > 0$, $\hat{\gamma} < 1$). Similarly, we plot a fitted curve for the data set T1 based on calendar time in Figure 13.7. Since $\hat{\beta} < 0$, $\hat{\gamma} < 1$, the fitted curve (as shown in Figure 13.7) is first decreasing and then increasing. Using the results obtained in this section, we will investigate the appropriate time metric (execution time versus calendar time) for software reliability models in the following section.

13.6.3   Comparison of Execution Time and Calendar Time

We now compare the use of execution time with that of calendar time for software reliability models based on the regression analysis for 15 sets of failure data. The following two criteria are considered: estimated variance of regression errors and coefficient of multiple determination.

ESTIMATED VARIANCE OF REGRESSION ERRORS. To compare the fit for the two time domains, we assume that ϵ_l's are independently and identically distrib-

TABLE 13.3
A summary of regression analysis of log-failure intensity

System	Execution time			Calendar time		
	$\hat{\beta}$	$\hat{\gamma}$	R^2	$\hat{\beta}$	$\hat{\gamma}$	R^2
T1	0.2672×10^{-2}	0.5185	0.939[**]	-0.9190×10^{-1}	0.7181	0.465[**]
T2	0.4849×10^{-2}	0.3786	0.965[**]	0.1139×10^{-2}	1.726	0.442
T3	0.2948×10^{-1}	0.3142	0.992[**]	-0.7863	0.1022	0.849[*]
T4	0.9029×10^{-3}	0.7644	0.961[**]	0.4757×10^{-1}	0.7561	0.724[*]
T5	-0.4682×10^{-6}	0.7465	0.203[**]	-0.3453×10^{-1}	0.6070	0.063[**]
T6	-0.1010	0.3260	0.658[**]	-0.6879	0.2459	0.658[**]
T16	0.3072×10^{-3}	0.5654	0.906[**]	-0.7367	0.1310	0.862[**]
T17	0.9669×10^{-3}	0.4544	0.882[**]	0.1558×10^{-2}	1.250	0.564[**]
T18	0.2085×10^{-3}	0.5331	0.917[**]	0.5935×10^{-2}	0.7838	0.624[**]
T19	0.9476×10^{-4}	0.7921	0.996[**]	0.8499×10^{-2}	1.377	0.740
T20	0.8861×10^{-5}	0.7907	0.378[**]	0.1833×10^{-2}	1.388	0.262[**]
T21	-0.9702×10^{-1}	0.2326	0.835[**]	-0.5925	0.3038	0.334
T22	0.3606×10^{-3}	0.7185	0.627[**]	-0.6846	0.3048	0.383[**]
T23	-0.2210×10^{-2}	0.5373	0.397[**]	-0.4780	0.3791	0.197[*]
T25	-0.2391×10^{-2}	0.4949	0.619[**]	0.4983×10^{-2}	0.8576	0.364[**]

[*]Significant (95 percent)
[**]Highly significant (99 percent)

uted with a variance of σ^2. Since we estimated three parameters from p data points, the degrees of freedom are reduced to $p - 3$. We can then estimate the variance as

$$\hat{\sigma}^2 = \frac{S(\hat{\alpha}, \hat{\beta}, \hat{\gamma})}{p - 3},$$ (13.7)

which represents variation of the data points around the fitted curve. The smaller value of $\hat{\sigma}^2$ suggests the better fit.

Note that the estimated failure intensities have different units, that is, failures per second for execution time and failures per day for calendar time. Therefore, if the sum of the *absolute* errors were minimized for estimating the parameters, it would not make sense to compare the estimated variances for execution time with those for calendar time. In the regression analysis described in Section 13.6.2, however, we minimize the sum of the *relative* errors. Hence, we can compare the values of the estimated variance $\hat{\sigma}^2$ to decide which time metric yields the better fit.

Let $\hat{\sigma}_{ET}$ and $\hat{\sigma}_{CT}$ be the estimated standard deviations for execution time and calendar time, respectively. Figure 13.10 shows plots of $\hat{\sigma}_{CT}$ versus $\hat{\sigma}_{ET}$ for the 15 data sets. A point associated with any data set will fall in the upper-left area of the triangle if execution time models fit better than calendar time models, that is, $\hat{\sigma}_{ET} < \hat{\sigma}_{CT}$. It will fall in the lower-right area if calendar time models fit better ($\hat{\sigma}_{ET} > \hat{\sigma}_{CT}$). If both are almost equal, then the point will be close to the dashed line, that is, $\hat{\sigma}_{ET} = \hat{\sigma}_{CT}$. Only three points (T17, T20, and T25) out of the 15

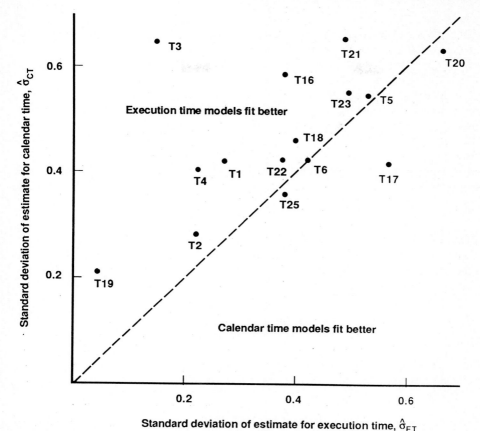

FIGURE 13.10
Standard deviations of regression error for calendar time and execution time.

points show superiority of calendar time to execution time. For the rest of the data sets execution time is shown to be either equivalent (T6) or superior (T1, T2, T3, T4, T5, T16, T18, T19, T21, T22, and T23).

It is of further interest to statistically determine, based on the results, whether there is a difference between paired values of the estimated standard deviation. The sign test is an extremely simple test that can be used for this case. It is useful for many such engineering cases when the underlying distributions are not known or are too difficult to determine. Since we don't use the magnitude of the difference between two values, this test is less powerful than a parametric test. This disadvantage is offset by the advantage of being quick and simple. We therefore use the sign test in the analysis.

The sign test is based on the binomial distribution, which involves analyzing pairs of data points based on the sign of the differences (that is, $\sigma_{ET} - \sigma_{CT}$). With a null hypothesis $H_0 : \sigma_{ET} = \sigma_{CT}$, it would be expected that the probability of a positive or negative difference is 1/2. Therefore, if H_0 is true, there should be nearly an equal number of positive and negative signs. If one sign appears a significantly small or large number of times for the size of the sample, then we reject H_0 since there is a significant difference between them. Note that we can apply the sign test only where there are no ties in the data. When there is a tie, the practice is to discard that piece of data and reduce the sample size by 1.

In comparing the paired values of $\hat{\sigma}_{ET}$ and $\hat{\sigma}_{CT}$ for each data set, there is only one tie and hence the sample size is $15 - 1 = 14$. The critical value for rejecting H_0 at the 90 percent confidence level is 3 [Lipson and Sheth (1973)]. Since the three points (T17, T20, and T25) were shown as $\hat{\sigma}_{ET} > \hat{\sigma}_{CT}$, we can conclude from the sign test at the 90 percent confidence level that execution time data can be fit significantly better than the corresponding calendar time data. Therefore, we can consider execution time as the appropriate metric for software reliability models.

COEFFICIENT OF MULTIPLE DETERMINATION. We now investigate whether a significant trend exists in the observed failure intensity using a coefficient of multiple determination R^2. It is defined as the ratio of the sum of squares resulting from the trend model to that from a constant model subtracted from 1, that is,

$$R^2 = 1 - \frac{S(\hat{\alpha}, \hat{\beta}, \hat{\gamma})}{S(\hat{\hat{\alpha}}, 0, 1)}. \tag{13.8}$$

Note that $\hat{\hat{\alpha}}$ represents the least squares estimate of α for the model with only a constant term, that is, $\beta = 0$ and $\gamma = 1$ in Equation (13.5). It is given by

$$\ln \hat{\hat{\alpha}} = \frac{1}{p} \sum_{l=1}^{p} \ln r_l. \tag{13.9}$$

Therefore, R^2 measures the percent of the total variation about the mean accounted for by the fitted curve. In other words, it is a measure of usefulness of the terms, other than the constant, in the models. The larger it is, the better the fitted equation explains the variation in the data.

For 15 data sets we compute the R^2 values from Equation (13.8) for the execution time and calendar time data and summarize the results in Table 13.3. It is observed that fitting curves to the model-free failure intensity estimates accounts for a greater percentage of variability about the mean when using execution time as compared to calender time.

To investigate whether a significant trend exists in the estimated intensity, we will test the null hypothesis H_0: $\beta = 0$ and $\gamma = 1$ against H_1: $\beta \neq 0$ or $\gamma \neq 1$ using the F-test [Litzau (1986)]. Since the degrees of freedom associated with $S(\hat{\hat{\alpha}}, 0, 1) - S(\hat{\alpha}, \hat{\beta}, \hat{\gamma})$ and $S(\hat{\alpha}, \hat{\beta}, \hat{\gamma})$ are 2 and $p - 3$, respectively, the quantities $[S(\hat{\hat{\alpha}}, 0, 1) - S(\hat{\alpha}, \hat{\beta}, \hat{\gamma})]/2$ and $S(\hat{\alpha}, \hat{\beta}, \hat{\gamma})/(p - 3)$ yield the estimated variances due to the two parameters β and γ and for the trend model of Equation (13.4), respectively. Then the ratio

$$F = \frac{[S(\hat{\alpha}, 0, 1) - S(\hat{\alpha}, \hat{\beta}, \hat{\gamma})]/2}{S(\hat{\alpha}, \hat{\beta}, \hat{\gamma})/(p - 3)} \tag{13.10}$$

should follow the F distribution with degrees of freedom 2 and $p - 3$ under the normality assumption of ϵ_i's. If the calculated value F from Equation (13.10) is greater than $F_{2,p-3;\alpha}$, which is the α percentile of the F distribution with degrees of freedom 2 and $p - 3$, we can be $(1 - \alpha)100$ percent confident that H_0 should be rejected (that is, there is a significant trend). The results will be said to be significant if H_0 is rejected at the significance level $\alpha = 0.05$ and highly significant if at $\alpha = 0.01$.

Table 13.3 summarizes the results from this significance test for 15 data sets, where * and ** indicate significant and highly significant. We observe that the fitted models are all highly significant for execution time. Hence, there is a significant trend in the failure intensity in execution time. Also note from the estimates that the fitted curves show decreasing trends since in most cases $\beta > 0$ and $0 < \gamma < 1$. Even for T5, T6, T21, T23, and T25, the curves are decreasing most of the time.

On the other hand, results for calendar time indicate that H_0 should be accepted half of the time (that is, $\beta = 0$, $\gamma = 1$). The trend model is not any better than the constant model in explaining the data. This means either:

1. We don't have the right model, or
2. Calendar time is a poor metric or independent variable for software reliability models.

Note that we have picked a flexible generic function, as given in Equation (13.4), which should represent many models of interest to us. We do not want more complex models (that is, more parameters). Therefore, the second statement appears to be the case. There is no structure or pattern to the failure intensity when expressed in calendar time.

The superiority of execution time has also been demonstrated by, among others, Trachtenberg (1985) and Hecht (1981).

13.7 SUMMARY

We have compared existing software reliability models by a set of criteria based on 15 sets of failure data collected from a wide variety of software development projects. It is recommended that two execution time models (the basic and the logarithmic Poisson models) be used by software engineers and managers for their application.

FOURTEEN

CALENDAR TIME MODELING

Up to now we have focused our attention on the theory of the execution time modeling of software reliability. This type of modeling characterizes and predicts the variation of failure intensity with execution time. However, projections of when failure intensity objectives will be met in terms of execution time are not too useful when talking with managers. For example, stating that a system will attain its reliability goal in 16.2 hr of CPU time is not helpful. Most managers want to know the date on which the objective will be reached. This is the motivation for developing a second component of software reliability modeling, that is, the calendar time component. This component can be used to characterize and predict the passage of calendar time with execution time. With it, projections of when failure intensity objectives will be met can be made in terms of calendar dates rather than execution time. Thus, it is seen that software reliability models with an execution time component *and* a calendar time component are the most desirable and useful for managers. Calendar time modeling will be described in detail in this chapter. We will include some review of the practical aspects of calendar time modeling presented in Chapters 2 and 5. This will enable us to present a fully integrated treatment here. We will focus on test periods, where calendar time modeling is most significant.

The concept of limiting resources is considered first. This is followed by a description and validation of a usage model for these resources. Then in Section 14.3 the relationship of calendar time to execution time is discussed in detail. The appropriate settings for the resource utilization parameters used in the calendar time component are discussed in Section 14.4. The practical aspects of the settings were discussed in Chapter 5. Section 14.5 concludes with some remarks on maximum likelihood estimation and confidence intervals for the number of calendar days required to reach a failure intensity objective.

14.1 LIMITING RESOURCE CONCEPT

The resources that govern the pace of testing for almost all software projects are:

1. failure correction personnel,
2. failure identification personnel, and
3. computer time.

Experience has shown that during the system test phase of a project of reasonable size, testing and failure correction are usually performed by different people. Thus, failure identification and correction personnel are considered as separate resources. Three different resources have been identified, but generalization of what follows to handle additional resources is readily possible. Figure 14.1 illustrates the typical interaction of these resources during the system test phase of a project.

The failure identification personnel are the members of the test team. Their functions are to run test cases and compare the test results against program requirements to establish the failures that have occurred. Also, part of their function is to generate a trouble or failure report giving all the pertinent facts about each failure identified. Their work does not include finding the fault causing a failure. Work associated with test planning and test case development is usually completed before the testing proper. Hence it does not ordinarily burden the failure identification personnel when that resource is limiting. The number of *available* failure identification personnel is denoted by P_I. The failure identification personnel do not always work full-time on the project. "Available" only means that they be able to do so given sufficient notice.

The failure correction personnel are the debuggers or developers available to repair the software. Failure correction is the process of determining the fault that caused a failure, removing the fault from the system, and proving that the failure no longer occurs. Correction is considered to include repeating the test that previously caused the failure and preparing change documentation during (not after) the test period. The number of *available* failure correction personnel is denoted by P_F. Available is used here in the same context as stated previously.

The computer facility represents the computer(s) necessary for the failure identification personnel and failure correction personnel to do their tasks. Computer time is the measure that is used for allocating computer resources. The available computer time is denoted by P_C. This quantity is measured in terms of prescribed work periods to put it on the same basis as personnel.

At any time the amount of work being performed by one of the resources will use that resource to the fullest. That resource is called the *limiting resource*. It determines how much calendar time is being used up with respect to execution

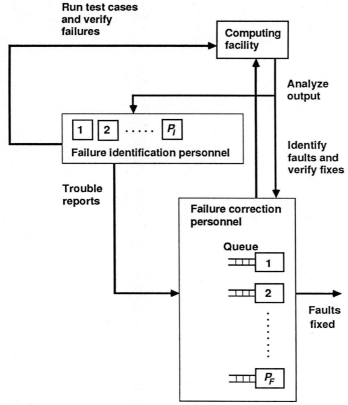

FIGURE 14.1
Failure queueing diagram for the system test phase.

time. The limiting resource concept forms the basis of calendar time component modeling.

To simplify the modeling process, we assume that the quantities of the available resources are constant from the point of use of the model through the period of prediction. It is possible to handle more complex patterns of resource availability. However, it does not seem to be worth the effort, since:

1. Constant or nearly constant resources during test are a common condition.
2. As will be seen shortly, the constancy assumption is necessary only to make schedule predictions simple. It must be true only for the period of prediction. Resource values can be changed for the next prediction.
3. If resources are not constant, an average value will give results that are a reasonable first approximation to reality.

14.2 RESOURCE USAGE MODEL

To relate calendar time to execution time we need to know how resource requirements are related to execution time. Experience and common sense suggests that all three total resource requirements may be closely approximated by a model of the form

$$\chi_r = \theta_r\tau + \mu_r\mu(\tau) , \qquad (14.1)$$

where r denotes a resource[1], χ_r is the expected resource requirement, θ_r is the average resource usage rate with execution time, μ_r is the average resource usage per failure, τ is the execution time, and $\mu(\tau)$ is the mean value function or expected number of failures by time τ. Note that resource usage represents a resource applied for a time period, for example, a person hr. The alert reader has probably observed that since the mean value function is a function of execution time the resource usage given by Equation (14.1) is actually a function of execution time only. It is also dependent on the execution time component of the software reliability model being used. Thinking in terms of expected number of failures *and* execution time was seen in Part I to be useful in gaining physical insight into what is happening. It also lets us obtain model-independent resource usage parameters. We will see in the next section that this model is a good representation of reality.

Often it will be necessary to work with the incremental or additional resource requirement $\Delta\chi_r$. This is given by

$$\Delta\chi_r = \theta_r \, \Delta\tau + \mu_r \, \Delta\mu(\tau) , \qquad (14.2)$$

where $\Delta\tau$ is the incremental testing time and $\Delta\mu(\tau)$ is the incremental number of expected failures.

Example 14.1. Let us take a closer look at the DATCOM project that was used as an example in Chapter 1. A total of $m_e = 180$ failures have been experienced in $\tau_e = 450.6$ CPU hr of testing. We will use an exponential-class model for our illustration. Applying the techniques of Chapter 12 to the failure time data we estimate the mean value and failure intensity functions to be

$$\hat{\mu}(\tau) = 199[1 - \exp(-0.005187\tau)]$$

and

$$\hat{\lambda}(\tau) = 1.032 \exp(-0.005187\tau) ,$$

respectively, where τ is measured in CPU hr. The failure intensity objective is 2×10^{-4} failure/CPU hr. We expect this to be reached at $\tau_F = 1648.1$ CPU hr of testing. This corresponds to (almost) $\mu(\tau_F) = 199$ failures having to be experienced.

---

[1] $r = C, F, I$ for computer time, failure correction personnel, and failure identification personnel, respectively.

The increment of resource requirements $\Delta\chi_r$ to reach the failure intensity objective is given by Equation (14.2). In this case $\Delta\tau = \tau_F - \tau_e = 1197.5$ CPU hr and $\Delta\mu(\tau) = \mu(\tau_F) - m_e = 19$ failures.

The resource usage parameters for this project are shown in Table 14.1. Two of the parameters μ_F and θ_I are a little unrealistic. The former is larger than normally expected; the latter smaller (see Table 14.4). All the parameter values have been picked so that we could illustrate certain features of calendar time modeling. Using these and the values found for $\Delta\tau$ and $\Delta\mu(\tau)$, we have for the additional amount of work required for failure correction,

$$\Delta\chi_F = \mu_F \, \Delta\mu(\tau) = 307.8 \text{ person hr.}$$

Similarly, the additional amount of failure identification work required will be

$$\Delta\chi_I = \theta_I\Delta\tau + \mu_I\Delta\mu(\tau) = 71.1 \text{ person hr .}$$

The additional amount of computer time required is

$$\Delta\chi_C = \theta_C\Delta\tau + \mu_C\Delta\mu(\tau) = 1235.5 \text{ hr .} \qquad \blacksquare$$

While the arguments presented in Section 2.3 make Equation (14.1) or Equation (14.2) plausible, the bottom line will be how well the model agrees with actual data. For this purpose, data on failure identification work, failure correction work, and computer time have been collected on four projects. One set of such data is shown in Table 14.2 for system T1 (see Table 13.1 for project characteristics). The data were collected weekly from each project member. Each person was asked to record his or her resource usages for the previous week in the categories shown in Table 14.2. Data were also recorded from project logs on execution time (in hours) for each week.

Estimates of θ_r and μ_r for each resource for each project can be obtained using linear least squares fits of the data by the resource usage model. In order for the following results to be model-independent it is necessary to approximate the value of the mean value function by the observed number of failures $m(\tau)$. Thus each incremental resource requirement is given, approximately, by

$$\Delta\chi_r = \theta_r \, \Delta\tau + \mu_r \, \Delta m(\tau) . \qquad (14.3)$$

This can be turned into a simpler form by dividing both sides by $\Delta\tau$. We have

TABLE 14.1
Resource usage parameters for
DATCOM project

r	μ_r	θ_r
F	16.2 person hr/failure	0
I	0.34 person hr/failure	0.054 person hr/CPU hr
C	2.0 CPU hr/failure	1.0

TABLE 14.2
Incremental resource usage data—System T1

Week	Execution time $\Delta\tau$ (CPU hr)	Failure identification work $\Delta\chi_I$ (person hr)	Failure correction work $\Delta\chi_F$ (person hr)	Computer time $\Delta\chi_C$ (CPU hr)	Failures identified	Failures corrected
1	0.00917	2	5	4	2	1
2	0.010	1.5	6	4.3	0	1
3	0.003	1	3.5	2	0	0
4	0.023	0.5	2.3	0.6	1	1
5	0.041	1	6.5	2.3	1	1
6	0.004	0.5	2.7	1.6	2	0
7	0.025	0.5	3.1	1.8	1	1
8	0.302	4	21.5	14.7	9	2
9	0.973	15	87.5	25.1	13	6
10	0.020	2	16	4.5	2	4
11	0.450	8.5	43	9.5	11	1
12	0.250	3.5	67	8.5	2	14
13	0.94	16	103	29.5	11	5
14	1.34	32.5	103.1	22	14	19
15	3.32	42	66	39.5	18	19
16	3.56	22	92.7	26	12	10
17	2.66	17	105.5	25.5	12	12
18	3.77	18.5	75.1	31.4	15	20
19	3.40	17	67.5	30	6	12
20	2.40	13	33	12.8	3	2
21	1.80	9	4.6	5	1	5
Total	25.3	227	914.6	300.6	136	136

$$\frac{\Delta\chi_r}{\Delta\tau} = \theta_r + \mu_r \frac{\Delta m(\tau)}{\Delta\tau}. \tag{14.4}$$

As a result of this transformation there is only one independent variable $\Delta m(\tau)/\Delta\tau$ and a new dependent variable $\Delta\chi_r/\Delta\tau$. The number of failures identified was used for $m(\tau)$ in fitting the failure identification work, while the number corrected was used for the failure correction work. Finally, the average of both these numbers was used for the computer time since the computer time involved both failure identification and correction.

We will first look at the need for each term of the resource usage model. In order to test whether θ_r or μ_r equals 0, the partial F test [see Neter, Wasserman, and Kutner (1983) for example] can be employed. Let $S(\hat{\mu}_r, 0)$ be the residual sum of squares when the θ_r term is omitted and $S(\hat{\mu}_r, \hat{\theta}_r)$ be the residual sum of squares when both terms are included. Then the statistic

$$(N-2)\left[\frac{S(\hat{\mu}_r, 0) - S(\hat{\mu}_r, \hat{\theta}_r)}{S(\hat{\mu}_r, \hat{\theta}_r)}\right],$$

where N is the number of data points, has an F distribution with 1 and $N - 2$ degrees of freedom. Large values of the statistic provide evidence against θ_r being equal to 0 or we can say that there is a need for the term. Critical values for this statistic can be easily determined for a given significance level from standard tables of the F distribution. Similar results apply for the parameter μ_r.

The values of the described statistics resulting from the least squares fits using Equation (14.3) are given in Table 14.3 for each resource for each system. It is clear from the critical values shown there that one cannot demonstrate any need for the θ_F term for failure correction work, that is, $\theta_F = 0$. The invariance of failure correction work with execution time is supported by data taken by Shooman and Bolsky (1975). One might think that failures occurring late in a test phase might be more complex and hence require more effort to correct. Apparently this supposition is false or there is a countervailing factor. One such factor might be increasing programmer experience with the system. The need for both terms for failure identification work and computer time appears to be highly probable.

Resource parameter values resulting from the least squares fit using Equation (14.4) for the four systems are given in Table 14.4. The term θ_F was set equal to 0 in fitting the equation for failure correction work because of the foregoing results. Both terms were used for the other two resources. It is believed that the differences in parameter values are mainly the result of the different skill levels of the teams involved (the largest team had nine people).

The resource usage model, using the estimated parameters, has been plotted against the resource usage data for all four systems. In general, the plots show good agreement between model and data. For example, Figures 14.2, 14.3, and 14.4 illustrate the fit between the model of resource usage and the data for system T1.

TABLE 14.3
Values of the statistic indicating the need for each term in resource usage fits

Resource usage		System			
		T1	**T2**	**T3**	**T4**
Failure identification work	μ_I	25.4	17.1	8.8	4.9
	θ_I	7.7	5.0	35.0	47.0
Failure correction work	μ_F	11.0	18.2	3.0*	4.0*
	θ_F	1.3*	0.26*	0.02*	0.02*
Computer time	μ_C	34.6	22.0	9.2	41.0
	θ_C	6.4	3.3*	27.0	33.0
(5%) Critical value		4.4	4.5	4.8	4.6

*These values do not exceed the 5 percent critical value.

TABLE 14.4
Resource usage parameter values

Resource usage parameters	System			
	T1	T2	T3	T4
μ_C (CPU hr/failure)	1.56	1.73	0.38	0.63
μ_F (person hr/failure)	4.42	6.88	0.58	0.68
μ_I (person hr/failure)	0.23	3.89	0.53	0.24
θ_C	4.80	1.73	1.06	2.13
θ_I (person hr/CPU hr)	9.92	3.24	4.77	5.70

14.3 CALENDAR TIME DETERMINATION

The rate of passage of calendar time with respect to execution time is related to the rate of resource usage with respect to execution time for a given limiting resource through the relation

$$\frac{dt_r}{d\tau} = \frac{1}{P_r \rho_r} \frac{\partial \chi_r}{\partial \tau} , \qquad (14.5)$$

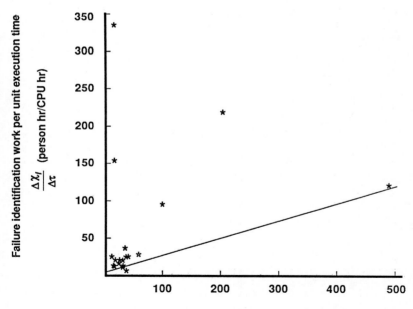

FIGURE 14.2
Failure identification work for system T1—model versus actual.

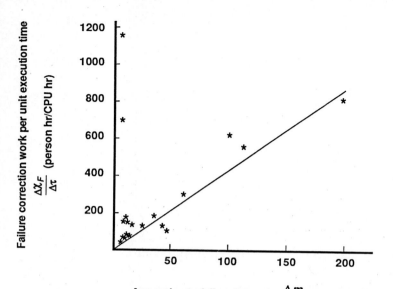

FIGURE 14.3
Failure correction work for system T1—model versus actual.

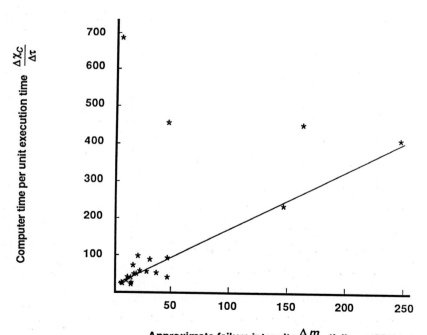

FIGURE 14.4
Computer time for system T1—model versus actual.

416

where $dt_r/d\tau$ represents the instantaneous calendar time to execution time ratio and ρ_r is the utilization of the rth resource. Note that $P_r\rho_r$ represents the *effective* amount of resource r that is available. We defer a discussion of resource utilization until Section 14.4. At any point in execution time one resource will be used at its limit. This resource will be the one that gives the largest value for the above ratio. Thus, the passage of calendar time is governed by the equation

$$\frac{dt}{d\tau} = \max_r \left[\frac{dt_r}{d\tau} \right].$$ (14.6)

Substituting Equations (14.1) and (14.5) into Equation (14.6) we have

$$\frac{dt}{d\tau} = \max_r \left\{ \frac{1}{P_r\rho_r}[\theta_r + \mu_r\lambda(\tau)] \right\}.$$ (14.7)

Figure 14.5 illustrates a typical form of the calendar time component. The instantaneous ratio of calendar time to execution time versus execution time for each resource is plotted. The ratio always has an initial value of $(\mu_r\lambda_0 + \theta_r)/P_r\rho_r$ and always approaches the asymptote given by $\theta_r/P_r\rho_r$. The thick dark curve represents the maximum value of the ratio. It is the one that governs the passage of calendar time.

The point, in terms of failure intensity, where a potential transition occurs from one limiting resource r to another s can be determined by equating $dt_r/d\tau$ and

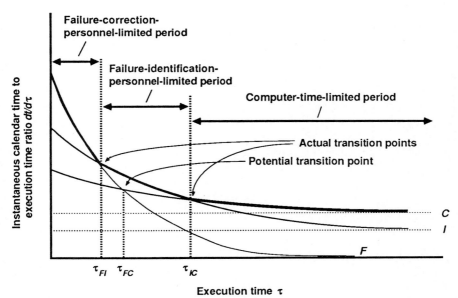

FIGURE 14.5
Typical execution time relationship among resource usages.

$dt_s/d\tau$. The potential transition points are given by

$$\lambda_{rs} = \frac{P_s \rho_s \theta_r - P_r \rho_r \theta_s}{P_r \rho_r \mu_s - P_s \rho_s \mu_r} , r \neq s . \qquad (14.8)$$

The independence of the failure intensities of the potential transition points with respect to the specific execution time model used should be particularly noted. This fact makes the construction of confidence intervals for calendar time predictions simple. This will be seen when we discuss confidence intervals in Section 14.5. Once again let us refer to Figure 14.5. The potential transition points given have been converted to execution times, that is, the potential transition between resource r and s occurs at time τ_{rs} (which corresponds to a failure intensity of λ_{rs}). The τ_{rs}'s *are* dependent on the execution time model employed. Limiting resources can be readily identified as the failure correction personnel for $0 \leq \tau \leq \tau_{FI}$, the failure identification personnel for $\tau_{FI} \leq \tau \leq \tau_{IC}$, and computer time for $\tau \geq \tau_{IC}$. We said "potential" transition. For an actual transition to occur, one of the resources of Equation (14.8) must be limiting. In the figure the potential transition at τ_{FC} does not occur because neither resource F or C is limiting at that point. This case is depicted in terms of failure intensities (rather than execution time) in Figure 14.6. This represents the most typical case encountered in practice.

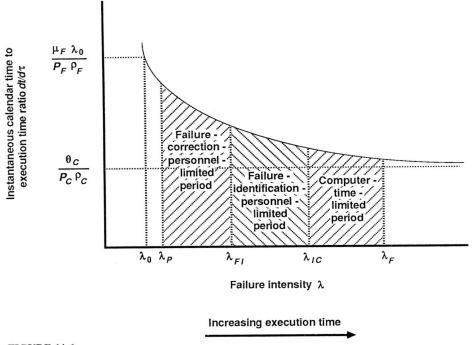

FIGURE 14.6
Typical failure intensity relationship among limiting resources.

Example 14.2. The numbers of available failure correction and identification personnel and the amount of available computer time along with their effective utilizations for the DATCOM project are given in Table 14.5. Using these data and those given in Table 14.1 the potential transition points (14.8) for the DATCOM example are

$$\lambda_{FC} = 0.037 \text{ failure/CPU hr},$$

$$\lambda_{IC} = -0.56 \text{ failure/CPU hr},$$

and

$$\lambda_{FI} = 0.00154 \text{ failure/CPU hr}.$$

Figure 14.7 shows a diagram that is useful in visualizing the situation. The stated potential transition points are shown.

We must now determine the resource that is limiting in each of the intervals $(0, \lambda_{FI})$, $(\lambda_{FI}, \lambda_{FC})$, and (λ_{FC}, ∞), the point λ_{IC} being ignored since it is negative. All we need to do to accomplish this is to determine the resource that gives the maximum value for the instantaneous ratio of calendar time to execution time for a particular choice of λ in each of the intervals. Thus, for example, for computer time this ratio is $(1 + 2\lambda)/2.48$. Evaluating for $\lambda = 0.001$ (which lies in the first interval), we have 0.404. Table 14.6 contains results for the other resources and intervals. Consideration of these results shows that computer time becomes limiting once the failure intensity drops to λ_{FC}. Otherwise, the failure correction personnel are limiting. Failure identification personnel never become limiting for this project. ∎

It can be easily shown that the increment of calendar time over a segment made up of just one limiting resource is given by

$$\Delta t_r = \int_{\tau_1}^{\tau_2} \frac{\theta_r + \mu_r \lambda(\tau)}{P_r \rho_r} d\tau, \tag{14.9}$$

where τ_1 and τ_2 define the boundaries for when the resource is limiting. Applying a change of variables from τ to $u = \lambda(\tau)$ in the integration results in[2]

---

[2] The change of variables is carried out for two reasons. First, it is more natural to speak in terms of failure intensity rather than execution time (for example, we use a failure intensity objective). Second, confidence intervals can be established directly using failure intensities.

TABLE 14.5
Resource quantities
and their utilizations
for DATCOM project

r	P_r	ρ_r
F	5.0	0.275
I	3.0	1.0
C	2.48	1.0

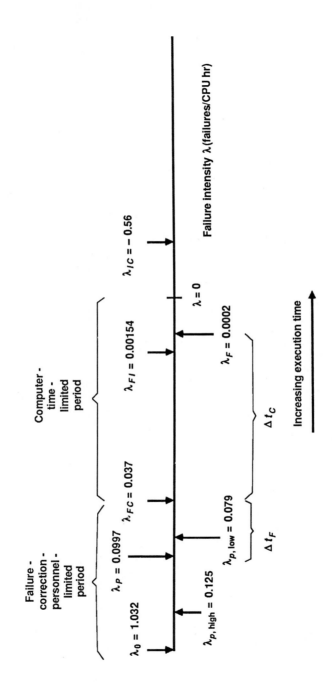

FIGURE 14.7
Ordering of failure intensities for DATCOM project.

TABLE 14.6
Instantaneous ratios of calendar time to execution time

Resource r	Failure intensity interval		
	$(0, \lambda_{FI})$ $(\lambda = 0.001)$	$(\lambda_{FI}, \lambda_{FC})$ $(\lambda = 0.01)$	(λ_{FC}, ∞) $(\lambda = 0.1)$
C	0.404	0.411	0.484
F	0.012	0.118	1.178
I	0.018	0.019	0.029

$$\Delta t_r = \frac{1}{P_r \rho_r} \int_{\lambda(\tau_1)}^{\lambda(\tau_2)} \left[(\theta_r + \mu_r u) / \frac{d\lambda}{d\tau} \Big|_{\lambda^{-1}(u)} \right] du , \qquad (14.10)$$

where λ^{-1} denotes the inverse of λ. This expression may look a little daunting but is usually easy to determine. For example, for an exponential-class model (see Table 12.5) $\lambda^{-1}(u) = -\beta_1^{-1} \ln (u/\beta_0\beta_1)$ and $(d\lambda/d\tau) |_{\lambda^{-1}(u)}$ is simply $-\beta_1 u$ and Equation (14.10) becomes

$$\Delta t_r = \frac{1}{P_r \rho_r \beta_1} \left\{ \theta_r \ln \left[\frac{\lambda(\tau_1)}{\lambda(\tau_2)} \right] + \mu_r [\lambda(\tau_1) - \lambda(\tau_2)] \right\} . \qquad (14.11)$$

As a second example consider a geometric-family model (see Table 12.5) where $\lambda^{-1}(u) = \beta_0 u^{-1} - \beta_1^{-1}$ and $(d\lambda/d\tau) |_{\lambda^{-1}(u)}$ is $-u^2/\beta_0$. Then Equation (14.10) becomes

$$\Delta t_r = \frac{\beta_0}{P_r \rho_r} \left\{ \theta_r \left[\frac{1}{\lambda(\tau_2)} - \frac{1}{\lambda(\tau_1)} \right] + \mu_r \ln \left[\frac{\lambda(\tau_1)}{\lambda(\tau_2)} \right] \right\} . \qquad (14.12)$$

For the case shown in Figure 14.6 the total calendar time required to achieve a failure intensity of λ_F is given as

$$\Delta t = \Delta t_F + \Delta t_I + \Delta t_C = \sum_r \Delta t_r , \qquad (14.13)$$

where Δt_F, Δt_I, and Δt_C are the increments of t corresponding to the change in failure intensity from λ_0 to λ_{FI}, λ_{FI} to λ_{IC}, and λ_{IC} to λ_F, respectively. A similar expression holds if we had started system test already and reached a failure intensity of λ_P. In the case shown Δt_F would be the increment of t corresponding to the change in λ from λ_P to λ_{FI}, the other terms of Equation (14.13) remaining unaltered.

In practice, many resource transitions are possible and it would be tedious to list them all. However, they may all be treated like the case we have considered.

Let's look at the general shape of the plot of calendar time against execution time (see Figure 14.8). This curve is composed of segments, each of which represents a period in which a different resource is limiting. Each segment represents the integral of the calendar time to execution time ratio with respect to execution time. This ratio decreases monotonically with execution time, hence the shape of the curve in Figure 14.8. The value of the ratio is the same at the boundaries between different limiting resource periods. Hence the plot of calendar time against execution time is smooth with respect to these boundaries and the boundaries are not evident.

Example 14.3. We will determine, using an exponential-class model, the amount of calendar time required to decrease the failure intensity from its current value of λ_P = 0.0997 failure/CPU hr to the objective of λ_F for the DATCOM project. We assume a 10.7 hr work day for this project.

The increment of calendar time required to reduce the failure intensity from λ_P to λ_{FC} is determined by the failure correction personnel resource (see Figure 14.7). Substituting the appropriate values[3] into Equation (14.11), where $r = F$, we have Δt_F = 13.3 days. Similarly, the increment of calendar time required to reduce the failure intensity from λ_{FC} to λ_F is determined by the computer time available. Thus, Δt_C = 38.5 days. The total calendar time required to achieve the objective is from Equation (14.13), $\Delta t_C + \Delta t_F$ or 51.8 days. Note that Δt_I is not included in the example because failure identification personnel never become limiting. ∎

---

[3] Assume β_1 = 0.005187/CPU hr (the maximum likelihood estimate).

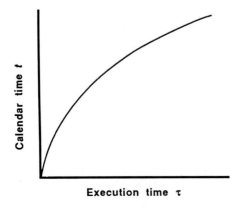

Calendar time t

Execution time τ

FIGURE 14.8
General shape of calendar time curve.

14.4   RESOURCE UTILIZATION

To fully specify the calendar time component the utilization of each resource during the period in which it is limiting needs to be determined.[4] The easiest of these utilizations to establish is that for the failure identification personnel. Here ρ_I may be set equal to 1 since utilization of this resource does not have to be restricted by any queueing constraints. There is usually no reason for available failure identification personnel not being fully used.

Determinations of failure correction personnel and computer time utilizations are somewhat more complicated. Each will be discussed in turn in the next two sections.

14.4.1   Failure Correction Personnel

Available failure correction personnel cannot always be fully employed during the failure-correction-personnel-limited period because of the unpredictable identification times of failures and inequality in load among the debuggers. Projects appear to naturally limit utilization of failure correction personnel to prevent an excessive backlog of failures awaiting correction from building up in any area of code. Such a backlog might hamper further testing in that area.[5] Note that the area of code will generally be associated with one responsible person.

The queueing constraints on each debugger will be modeled as a classical queueing system with random arrivals and random service. That is, both the identification of failures *and* the correction of failures are considered to be time-invariant Poisson processes in calendar time. We will look at each process (identification and correction) in detail to convince ourselves that this is an adequate representation of real data.

The Poisson process has two implications for the correction of failures. First, correction of a failure is independent of the correction of other failures. Secondly, the probability that a fault is removed during any time period of debugging effort is equal to the probability that it is removed in any other such time period. The latter is a good assumption, although it may somewhat overestimate the proportion of failures with short fix times.

The Poisson failure correction process also implies that the failure correction effort (in person hr) is exponentially distributed. To determine if the exponential distribution is a reasonable model for the distribution of failure correction times, consider the data shown in Figure 14.9. The data (representing 178 failure corrections) were taken from the unit debugging phase of a project and involved eight

---

[4]These utilizations are *maximum* figures that apply during the period in which the resource is limiting. At other times the resource utilization will have lower values.

[5]In measuring backlog we do not count failures whose correction is deferred for reasons other than availability of personnel to fix them.

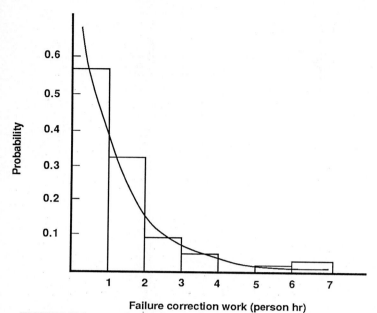

FIGURE 14.9
Exponential distribution of failure correction times.

programmers. All times are "direct effort" times, that is, no overhead factor has been applied to account for absence, training, meetings, or coffee breaks. The failure correction time distribution is compared with an exponential distribution with the same mean (that is, 1.185 person hr). They agree well and a chi-square goodness of fit test shows that the data are consistent with the assumption that they come from an exponential distribution.

It appears likely that in system test a constant component will be added to the distribution of time given. This component represents administrative overhead and retest requirements, and it is usually smaller than the mean time for the variable component [Herndon and Keenan (1978)]. It is not expected that this component will have any appreciable effect on the relationship between utilization and queue length.

For the identification of failures the Poisson process implies a constant arrival rate in calendar time for failures requiring fixing. It also requires random assignment of failures to the failure correction personnel.

Random assignment is a reasonable assumption since ordinarily no section of code (and the programmer responsible for it) is being favored in the testing process. If an evolving program is being tested, random assignment can still occur if each debugger has code in the part of the system that is under test. If this is not so, it may still be possible to handle this case by applying an appropriate correction based on the debuggers who are involved. For example, the number of debuggers can be corrected to the average number to whom failures can be assigned.

That the arrival rate of failures with respect to calendar time during the failure-correction-personnel-limited period is constant can be shown as follows. Let $\lambda(t)$ denote the failure intensity with respect to calendar time. An expression for $\lambda(t)$ can be obtained by taking the derivative of the mean value function expressed in terms of calendar time with respect to calendar time, that is,

$$\lambda(t) = \frac{d\mu(t)}{dt} . \qquad (14.14)$$

During the failure-correction-personnel-limited period t and τ are related by Equation (14.7) with $\theta_F = 0$, that is,

$$\frac{d\tau}{dt} = \frac{P_F\rho_F}{\mu_F} \frac{1}{\lambda(t)} , \qquad (14.15)$$

where we have inverted the differential and $\lambda(t)$ is the failure intensity expressed in terms of calendar time. We can now write

$$\lambda(t) = \left. \frac{d\mu(\tau)}{d\tau} \right|_{\tau(t)} \frac{d\tau}{dt} . \qquad (14.16)$$

The first differential when evaluated at $\tau(t)$ is just the failure intensity with respect to calendar time $\lambda(t)$. Substituting Equation (14.15) into Equation (14.16) we have

$$\lambda(t) = \lambda = \frac{P_F\rho_F}{\mu_F} . \qquad (14.17)$$

This can be seen to be constant provided ρ_F is (possibly maintained) constant.

Having provided some justification for the queueing model, we are now in a position to determine the utilization of the debuggers. The arrival rate of failures requiring correction to each debugger is λ/P_F and the service rate of each debugger for correction is seen to be $1/\mu_F$. The utilization factor is defined (in queueing theory) as the ratio of arrival rate to service rate or

$$\rho_F = \frac{\lambda\mu_F}{P_F} . \qquad (14.18)$$

The probability that a particular debugger has a queue of m_Q or more failures awaiting correction or being corrected is $\rho_F^{m_Q}$ in the steady state [see $M/M/1$ queueing system in Kleinrock (1975)]. The probability P_{m_Q} that no debugger has m_Q or more failures queued is

$$P_{m_Q} = (1 - \rho_F^{m_Q})^{P_F} . \qquad (14.19)$$

Therefore, we may assume with probability P_{m_Q} that no debugger has m_Q or more failures to work on at any given time by limiting ρ_F to

$$\rho_F = (1 - P_{m_Q}^{1/P_F})^{1/m_Q} . \qquad (14.20)$$

If we control ρ_F at the value given above, we will maximize effective manpower under the constraint of preventing excessive backlogs.

Use of the steady-state value of probability for queue length results in a small overestimate of time expended, since queues are actually shorter during the buildup transient. However, we also have assumed that identification and correction of failures are parallel processes. Correction, of course, always follows identification, so that there are intervals at the start and at the end of the test phase during which only one process is occurring. Thus our assumption results in a small underestimate of calendar time expended. It will be assumed that the two foregoing factors nearly cancel.

Figure 14.10 gives curves of utilization versus failure correction personnel for various values of queue length. The curves are constructed such that 90 percent of the queues that occur are less than the specified value. The topic of what queue length is most commonly encountered is currently a matter for further research (see Chapter 5 for discussion).

Example 14.4. Determine the utilization of the failure correction personnel that maintains the queue length so that it does not equal or exceed 3 with probability 0.9 for the DATCOM problem (use $P_F = 5$). From Equation (14.20) we have

$$\rho_F = (1 - 0.9^{1/5})^{1/3} = 0.275 .$$ ∎

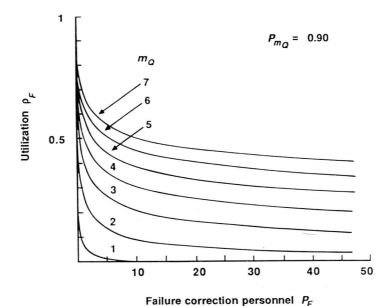

FIGURE 14.10
Failure correction personnel utilization.

14.4.2 Computer Time

The computer utilization factor ρ_C can be established in one of two ways depending on whether turnaround time or response time can be controlled or not. Typically for a small project that is using a general purpose computation facility, turnaround or response time cannot be controlled. Here ρ_C should be set to its measured value.[6] For a larger project or one that constitutes a major portion of the computer's load ρ_C may be controllable. If it is, then its value should be set to obtain "good" turnaround or response. Response is probably most important, since the vast bulk of the failure identification and correction activity is interactive. A good way of establishing ρ_C was briefly described in Section 5.2.2. Here we give an example of how one would actually go about calculating this value.

Example 14.5. Computer capacity is sometimes defined in terms of MIPS (millions of instructions per second). Suppose the projected workload level is estimated to be 10 MIPS. Then the required CPU capacity, if we control the utilization at ρ_C, is $10/\rho_C$ MIPS. For example, if we set the utilization to be 0.5, a 20 MIPS machine will be needed to handle the workload level. The cost to the company for computer capacity is assumed to be proportional to the capacity. The constant of proportionality is defined as k_1 and is the cost per MIPS per year. Thus, the yearly computing cost is

$$C_C = \frac{10k_1}{\rho_C} \,. \tag{14.21}$$

The cost of salary for the failure identification and correction personnel is assumed, for the sake of simplicity, to be proportional to the total waiting time. The constant of proportionality is defined as k_2. It is the cost per person per year. Let's assume that the total waiting time is given by the product of the average number of system users N and some function of the utilization ρ_C, that is, $h(\rho_C)$. The salary cost is

$$C_S = k_2 N h(\rho_C) \,. \tag{14.22}$$

Suppose a study was conducted in which it was shown that $h(\rho_C)$ is given by (see, for example, a $M/M/1$ queueing system [Kleinrock (1975)])

$$h(\rho_C) = \frac{\rho_C}{1 - \rho_C} \,. \tag{14.23}$$

Then the overall cost (hardware plus direct salary) to the company is

$$C_O = \frac{10k_1}{\rho_C} + \frac{k_2 N \rho_C}{1 - \rho_C} \,. \tag{14.24}$$

This cost can be minimized if ρ_C is set equal to

---

[6]If the wait time is much greater than the norm and it cannot be profitably used in other activities, then μ_F should be increased by the ratio of correction work time plus excess wait time to correction work time.

$$\frac{10k_1 \pm 3.16 \sqrt{k_1 k_2 N}}{10k_1 - k_2 N} \qquad (14.25)$$

Let k_1 = \$100,000/MIPS yr, k_2 = \$150,000/person yr, and the average number of users of the system be equal to 10. Then ρ_C = 0.45. By using a 22 MIPS machine the company will incur a minimum cost of slightly over 3.4 million dollars/yr. See Figure 14.11. ∎

14.5 CALENDAR TIME ESTIMATION AND CONFIDENCE INTERVALS

Point estimation and the generation of approximate confidence intervals for the additional calendar time required to reach a failure intensity objective is usually a straightforward process. It is best illustrated as follows. The calendar time duration for a segment made up of just one limiting resource for an exponential class

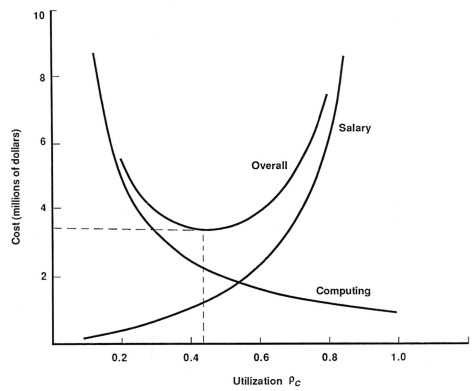

FIGURE 14.11
Variation of cost with computer utilization.

model is given by Equation (14.11) as

$$\Delta t_r [\beta_1, \lambda(\tau_1), \lambda(\tau_2)] = \frac{1}{P_r \rho_r \beta_1} \left\{ \theta_r \ln \left[\frac{\lambda(\tau_1)}{\lambda(\tau_2)} \right] + \mu_r [\lambda(\tau_1) - \lambda(\tau_2)] \right\}, \quad (14.26)$$

where the dependency of Δt_r on β_1 and the segment end points has been made explicit. Let us further assume that Figure 14.12 shows the ordering of the resource-limited periods. The maximum likelihood estimate for Δt, using Equation (14.13) and the invariance property of maximum likelihood estimators (Section 12.2), is given by

$$\hat{\Delta t} = \Delta t_F (\hat{\beta}_1, \hat{\lambda}_P, \lambda_{FI}) + \Delta t_I (\hat{\beta}_1, \lambda_{FI}, \lambda_{IC}) + \Delta t_C (\hat{\beta}_1, \lambda_{IC}, \lambda_F) . \quad (14.27)$$

Confidence intervals can be determined by considering each term of Equation (14.27) as a function of $\hat{\beta}_1$. If this function is strictly monotonic in $\hat{\beta}_1$, then straightforward substitution, as discussed in Chapter 12, can be used. Since λ_{FI}, λ_{IC}, and λ_F are fixed quantities, $\hat{\Delta t}_I$ and $\hat{\Delta t}_C$ are proportional to $\hat{\beta}_1^{-1}$ and therefore strictly monotonically decreasing in $\hat{\beta}_1$. The first term in Equation (14.27) must be considered more carefully because $\hat{\lambda}_P$ is also a function of $\hat{\beta}_1$. Using Equation (14.26) this term is

$$\hat{\Delta t}_F = \left(\frac{1}{P_F \rho_F \hat{\beta}_1} \right) \left[\mu_F (\hat{\lambda}_P - \lambda_{FI}) \right] . \quad (14.28)$$

The first multiplier above is clearly a decreasing function of $\hat{\beta}_1$. In Chapter 12 we saw that $\hat{\lambda}_P$ is a decreasing function of $\hat{\beta}_1$ and hence, the second multiplier is also decreasing in $\hat{\beta}_1$. Therefore $\hat{\Delta t}_F$ is strictly monotonically decreasing in $\hat{\beta}_1$. If we denote the lower confidence limit of β_1 as β_{low} and the upper limit of $\hat{\lambda}_P$ as $\lambda_{P,\text{high}}$ then the upper confidence limit of Δt can be written as

$$\Delta t_{\text{high}} = \Delta t_F (\beta_{\text{low}}, \lambda_{P,\text{high}}, \lambda_{FI}) + \Delta t_I (\beta_{\text{low}}, \lambda_{FI}, \lambda_{IC}) + \Delta t_C (\beta_{\text{low}}, \lambda_{IC}, \lambda_F) . \quad (14.29)$$

The lower limit of Δt as well as different orderings of resource-limited periods follows analogously. A similar approach can be used for geometric-family models.

Example 14.6. We have already determined the maximum likelihood estimate of Δt for the DATCOM project in Example 14.3. Further, suppose the 75 percent confidence limits for β_1 are determined to be (0.00444, 0.00594) and for λ_P to be (0.079, 0.125). The upper 75 percent confidence limit for Δt can be determined from Equations (14.28) and (14.29) with $\Delta t_I = 0$ as follows. During the failure-correction-personnel-limited period the failure intensity will decrease from 0.125 to 0.037 failure/CPU hr. Using these values in Equation (14.28) with $\beta_1 = 0.00444$ results in $\hat{\Delta t}_F = 21.8$ days. The failure intensity limits of the computer time limited period remain unchanged. Therefore, $\Delta t_C = 44.9$ days. Thus, the upper limit for Δt is 66.7 days.

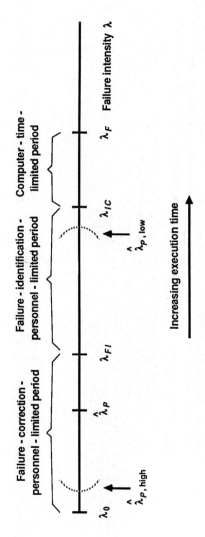

FIGURE 14.12
Ordering of transition points for calendar time example.

Since the lower limit for λ_P is greater than λ_{FC}, the lower limit for Δt is computed analogously as $\Delta \hat{t}_F + \Delta \hat{t}_C = 7.8 + 33.6 = 41.4$ days. ■

CASE STUDY 14.1
A LOOK AT THE PREDICTIVE VALIDITY
OF THE CALENDAR TIME COMPONENT

Data suitable to investigate the predictive validity of the calendar time component are known presently for the four systems: T1, T2, T3, and T4. To test the estimates made by the calendar time component, a failure intensity objective, independent of the model that will be used, must be supplied for each system. It seems reasonable to use an estimate of the failure intensity at the end of system testing for this objective. This estimate is made using the total elapsed execution time at the end of testing during which the last five failures were experienced. Once we have this value, it becomes a simple matter to estimate the amount of calendar time required to meet the objective, along with confidence intervals, at various points in time. The estimates can be directly compared to the known values.

The calendar time components of the basic and logarithmic Poisson execution time models will be considered in this study. The results given in Chapter 13 on the predictive validity of the execution time component suggest that the estimates from the logarithmic Poisson model are superior to those from the basic execution time model for systems T1, T2, and T3. The basic execution time model provides superior execution time estimates for system T4. The data for systems T2 and T3 and the estimates made by the logarithmic Poisson execution time model are shown in Figures 14.13 and 14.14. Shown in these figures is the estimated additional calendar time (solid curve) required to meet the failure intensity objective, as a function of the normalized execution time. The 95 percent confidence limits are shown as dashed curves. The actual data are plotted as dots. The goodness of fit is evident (the data always lie within the confidence bands). For system T4 neither calendar time component did a good job. The basic execution time model always underestimated the calendar time value while the logarithmic Poisson execution time model always overestimated it. System T1 provided a surprise in that the calendar time estimates from the basic execution time model were superior to those of the logarithmic Poisson execution time model, even though the latter model provides superior execution time estimates.

Obviously general conclusions cannot be drawn from such a small sample of systems. More data need to be collected for further study in this area.

14.6 SUMMARY

The calendar time component is a highly desirable feature for a software reliability model to possess. It allows one to relate the passage of calendar time to that of

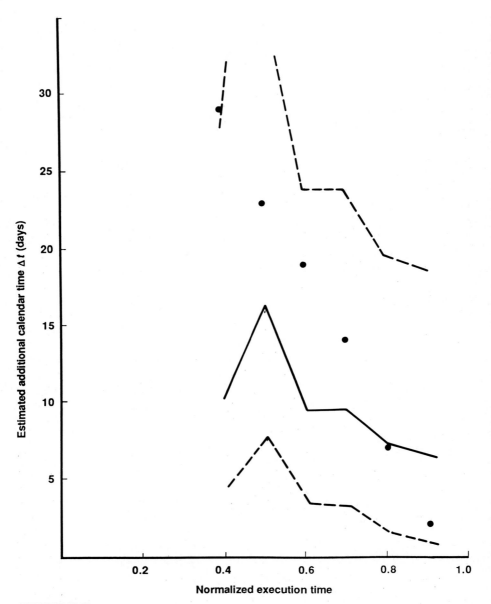

FIGURE 14.13
Additional calendar time for system T2—actual versus estimated (logarithmic Poisson model).

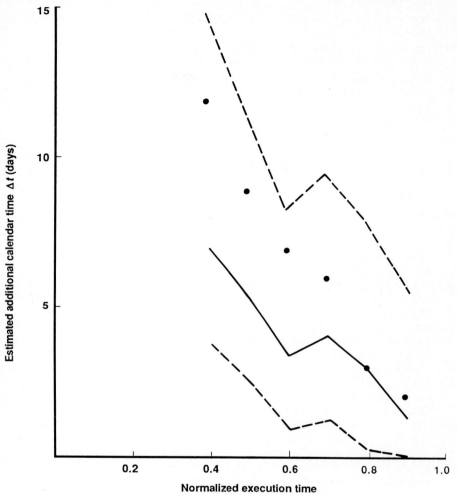

FIGURE 14.14
Additional calendar time for system T3—actual versus estimated (logarithmic Poisson model).

execution time. This component was described in detail in this chapter and illustrated using project data. Calendar time prediction requires knowledge of the planned and resource usage parameters. The setting of appropriate resource utilizations was also described in some detail. Calendar time estimation with confidence intervals was discussed for given failure data.

PROBLEMS

14.1 What improvement in schedule will be realized if the DATCOM debuggers work 50 percent overtime?

14.2 How many debuggers must be added to the DATCOM staff so that this resource is no longer limiting?

14.3 Suppose computer time costs $200/CPU hr and personnel salary is $35/hr. How much additional cost will there be for the DATCOM project if the present failure intensity of 0.0997 failure/CPU hr is to be reduced to 0.0002 failure/CPU hr?

14.4 A geometric-family model with $\beta_0 = 40$ failures and $\beta_1 = 1$/CPU hr has the following parameter values.

| Resource | Parameter | | | |
	μ	θ	P	ρ
C	4	2	6	1
F	4	0	5	0.275
I	4	0.5	2	1

Determine the expected amount of total resources required to achieve a failure intensity of 0.01 failure/CPU hr.

14.5 Determine the potential transition points and the limiting resource in each of the appropriate intervals for the data given in Problem 14.4. What is the total calendar time necessary to satisfy the objective? Assume a 10.7 hr work day.

14.6 What happens if $\mu_C = 12$ hr/failure and $\theta_C = 1.5$ hr/CPU hr in Problem 14.5?

14.7 Show for a project that has only one limiting resource that Δf_r is a monotonically decreasing function of $\hat{\beta}_1$ when a geometric-family model is used.

14.8 Suppose the 75 percent confidence interval for β_1 is (0.70, 1.2) after 750 CPU hr of testing and 265 failures. Determine Δt and its 75 percent confidence interval for the model in Problem 14.4. Assume the maximum likelihood estimate for β_1 is 1/CPU hr and a 10.7 hr work day.

14.9 An alternative way of showing that a Poisson process describes the identification of failures in calendar time is to show that the interarrival calendar times are exponentially and independently distributed. The probability density of T_i' conditioned on T_{i-1} is given by Equation (10.17). Under what condition will this distribution reduce to an exponential distribution independent of all the previous failure times? Assume that time is calendar time.

14.10 The alert reader has probably noticed that since in the resource usage equation (14.1) μ and τ are related, θ_r does not totally represent the resources expended per unit time. Similarly, μ_r does not totally represent the resources expended per failure. Derive these quantities for the basic and logarithmic Poisson execution time models.

FIFTEEN

FAILURE TIME ADJUSTMENT
FOR EVOLVING PROGRAMS

The reliability models discussed so far have assumed that the programs are stable and that all changes are the result of failure correction. In actuality, many programs evolve as noted in Chapter 6. As a result, the failure times that occur do not all come from the "same" program. One is attempting to estimate, from the failure times, the parameters of a model that should be changing to match the changing characteristics of the program.

Software reliability researchers have in general not dealt with this problem. This approach has sometimes resulted (at least for an exponential-class model) in two undesirable effects:

1. Present failure intensity tends to be underestimated in the early stages of system test, resulting in overly optimistic status evaluations. These are followed by long periods in which *apparent* progress is slight.
2. Completion date predictions are undefined or unstable.

Three methods for handling evolution have been described in Chapter 6. The theoretical background and details of one of these methods, failure time adjustment, will be described in this chapter. (The method was first presented by Musa and Iannino (1981) but has undergone considerable development since that time.) Section 15.1 reviews some necessary terminology. The adjustment method is described and developed at length in Section 15.2. Results for models of the Poisson and binomial types are then presented in Sections 15.3 and 15.4, respectively. The implementation of this method for the exponential class is also given for both

435

types of models. The basic execution time model, as you will recall, is included in the exponential class of the Poisson type. A practical application is described in Section 15.5.

Failure time[1] adjustment involves the transformation of the failure times experienced. This transformation results in the set of anticipated failure times that would have occurred for a stable program that was always in its final configuration. These times are then processed as they would be for a stable program. That is, the original estimation approach and computations for the particular model are applied to determine model parameters and quantities of interest to the software manager or engineer.

It will be seen that the specific adjustment to be made depends on the software reliability model to be employed. It appears that a model-independent adjustment procedure would be extremely difficult and probably impossible to develop.

Figure 15.1 shows the running histories of estimated software reliability parameters, based on simulated data for a program undergoing evolution during the system test phase.[2] Maximum likelihood estimates are shown by solid lines. The associated limits of the 75 percent confidence interval are shown by dashed lines. Horizontal dashed lines indicate the true value of the quantity plotted. The simulated data were based on the basic execution time model for a system with final values (that is, after all growth has taken place) of $\nu_0 = 200$ failures and $\phi = 0.005$/hr. The history of program growth is shown in Figure 15.2. As the reader can see from Figure 15.1, most of the estimates are useless. For example, the estimated total failures and completion date are essentially undefined throughout the test phase. The initial failure intensity is substantially underestimated. The present failure intensity estimate does not decrease until late in the project. Now consider Figure 15.3, which shows the same estimates after the failure data have been "adjusted." The predictions are vastly superior and significant over a much longer period of time. Being based on simulated data, these figures do not validate the "adjustment" approach for practical use. However, the potential benefits are clearly shown.

15.1   EVOLVING SOFTWARE CONCEPTS

Some definitions and concepts must first be reviewed. Two kinds of instructions will be distinguished. Instructions that were obtained from a thoroughly tested and developed operational system will be called *inherited instructions*. It will be assumed that there are no faults in this type of code or that the number is so small that they may be neglected, to a first approximation. Typically, this code is com-

---

[1]Possible extension to grouped data is given in Problem 15.4.

[2]Here, and elsewhere in this chapter, running history estimates are made on a continuous basis and not after the fact.

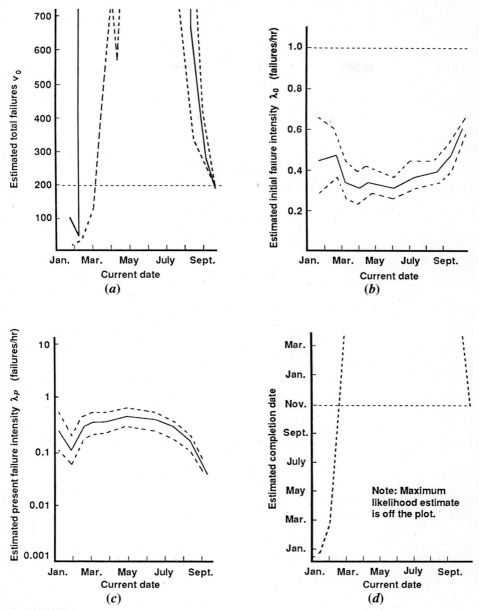

FIGURE 15.1
Estimated model parameters for unadjusted data. (*a*) Total failures. (*b*) Initial failure intensity. (*c*) Present failure intensity. (*d*) Completion date.

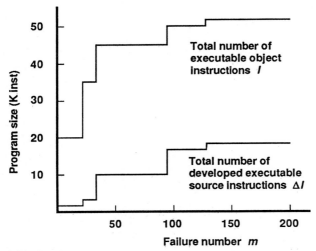

FIGURE 15.2
History of program growth for simulated example.

posed of complete, proven modules (for example, standard subroutines) or un-modified parts of such modules. Instructions that were designed and newly writter for the program or newly modified (that is, all other code) will be called *developed instructions*. This code will contain faults.

A collection of code forming a configuration for test or operation is known as a *stage*. A stage is characterized by the total number of deliverable executable object instructions I and the total number of deliverable developed executable source instructions ΔI. Note that I and ΔI are both cumulative values. They represent the state of the system as it actually exists.

A transition to a new stage is defined as occurring whenever I or ΔI changes. In practice there are many situations that have the effect of altering one or both of these values and thus causing a transition to a new stage. An important case, and the one considered in this chapter, is that of sequential evolution with pure growth. The process of pure growth always causes an increase in I or ΔI or both. This increase results from code being added to the current program configuration either as the result of the normal integration plan or a *requirements change*. The removal of code is not allowed under pure growth.

Figure 15.4 illustrates *sequential evolution* with pure growth. Here a section of code, A, is tested in isolation in the first stage of integration. After a certain amount of testing, another section of code, B, is integrated and both A and B are tested in the second stage. This procedure continues until the system is fully integrated. With sequential evolution only one path of evolution and hence only one stage can exist at any given time. Restricting ourselves to sequential evolution with pure growth does not result in a significant limitation, as noted in Chapter 6.

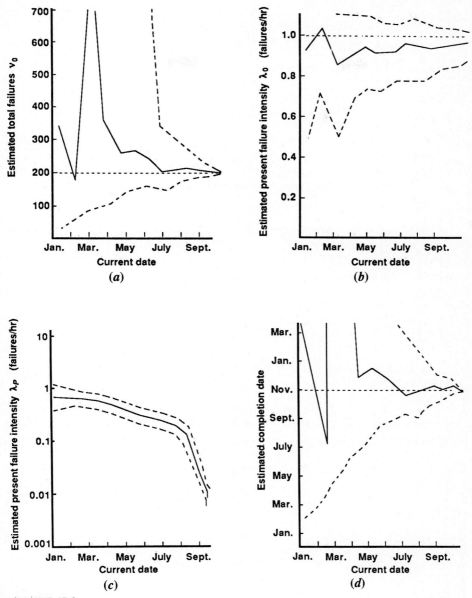

FIGURE 15.3
Estimated model parameters for adjusted data. (*a*) Total failures. (*b*) Initial failure intensity. (*c*) Present failure intensity. (*d*) Completion date.

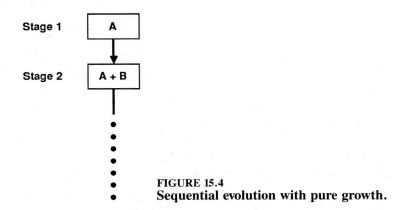

FIGURE 15.4
Sequential evolution with pure growth.

Violation of the pure growth condition causes a complication. If the condition is not met, then some code must have been removed. This code, while it was integrated, had two effects. First, it slowed down how rapidly the program cycled and hence lengthened the intervals between failures. Second, and more important, it might have contained the faults that were responsible for one or more of the failures that occurred. Thus, the failure time sequence does not correctly represent the failure behavior of the system with the code removed. Hence, to avoid any technical difficulties, the pure growth condition was incorporated.

15.2 BASIC INTERSTAGE FAILURE TIME ADJUSTMENT

The expected number of failures as a function of execution time follows a smooth curve for a stable program. Figure 15.5 shows one such curve. This represents the ideal and commonly assumed case from a modeling point of view. In the follow-

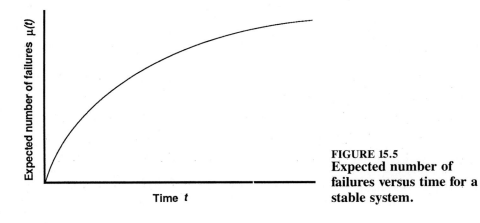

FIGURE 15.5
Expected number of failures versus time for a stable system.

ing sections we will look in some detail at what happens when there are two or three stages of integration. Generalization to a greater number of stages will then be straightforward.

15.2.1 Two-Stage Evolution

Consider what happens when there are two stages (see Figure 15.6). The expected number of failures as a function of time will follow a known curve during the first stage. The parameters of this curve will depend on the fault content and total amount of code being executed in the stage. The total amount of code generally affects how rapidly the program cycles or repeats and hence how rapidly the faults are encountered (only some encounters will result in failures). The fault content will generally be related to the amount of developed code. After a certain interval of execution t^* the remainder of the system is added. At this point the curve of expected number of failures against time switches to the one that would have occurred for a system in its final configuration. The curve, however, is time-translated. The amount of translation depends on the number of failures experienced during the first stage. Figure 15.6 illustrates the case where testing during the first stage lasts for a time t^*. This is expected to be equivalent to testing the entire system for a time $\tilde{t}^*$ based on the expected number of failures being the same.

The expected failures plot for this and other systems with multistage test phases will be a complex set of "model segments," with each segment representing the model under different parameter values. It makes sense to think in terms of a "virtual model" that would represent anticipated behavior if all the code were there. This is because we are interested principally in the behavior of the final program. The result is a change and movement of the model segments that yields a single, continuous model that is much easier to work with. Many approaches to do this are possible, including the use of a modified likelihood function. However, they all would almost certainly involve at least an implicit transformation of the failure times of one sort or another. The approach used here was taken because of the physical and conceptual appeal.

> **Example 15.1.** Let us be a little more concrete by using some numbers in our two-stage system. Table 15.1 contains the significant information for each stage. The last two columns are the parameters of the model that is assumed to be appropriate for this system. Here it is the basic execution time model. The values of the parameters were intentionally picked to amplify the difference between the two stages.
>
> During the first stage the mean value function $\mu_1(t)$ will be given by
>
> $$\mu_1(t) = 10\,[1 - \exp(-0.5t)]. \tag{15.1}$$
>
> Suppose testing during this stage lasts for 4.61 time units. Then we would expect, from Equation (15.1), 9 failures.
>
> Assume for the moment that we had started system testing using the configuration of the second stage. Since this is a two-stage integration we are in effect assuming that we had a stable system all along. Here the mean value function $\mu(t)$ *would*

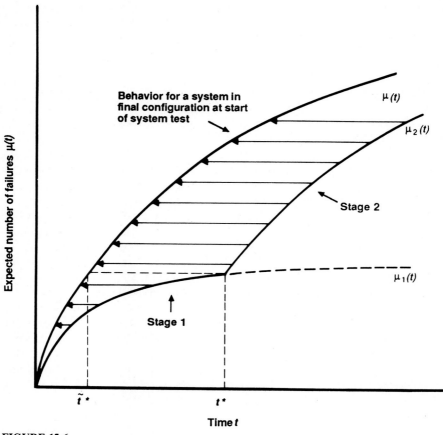

FIGURE 15.6
A two-stage example.

have been

$$\mu(t) = 250[1 - \exp(-0.05t)],\qquad(15.2)$$

and 9 failures would have occurred in 0.73 time units. Thus, we would expect the $t^* = 4.61$ time units spent during the first stage to be equivalent to $\tilde{t}^* = 0.73$ time units of testing on the stable system.

TABLE 15.1
Stage characteristics for two-stage example

Stage	I (K inst)	ΔI (K inst)	ν_0	ϕ
1	100	20	10	0.5
2	1000	500	250	0.05

When we go from the first to second stage of testing the mean value function $\mu_2(t)$ will follow a translated version of Equation (15.2). The amount of translation is given by $t^* - \tilde{t}^*$ or 3.88 time units. Thus, we can write

$$\mu_2(t) = 250\ \{1 - \exp[-0.05(t - 3.88)]\}, \quad t \geqslant 4.61. \tag{15.3}$$

∎

Denote the transformation Q_{12} that will take a value of t_i from a curve representing the first stage to the value of $\tilde{t}_i$ expected from the conditions of the second stage as

$$\tilde{t}_i = Q_{12}(t_i;\ I_1, I_2, \Delta I_1, \Delta I_2, \boldsymbol{\beta}_{(1)}). \tag{15.4}$$

The functional form that Q_{12} takes on depends on the specific software reliability model being used. In general, Q_{12} also explicitly depends on an estimate of the model's unknown parameters for the first stage (the vector $\boldsymbol{\beta}_{(1)}$), the known quantities of I_1, I_2, ΔI_1, and ΔI_2, and the time associated with each failure. The use of this transformation is illustrated in the following example.

Example 15.2. Consider once again the two-stage system used in Example 15.1. The values of I and ΔI for each stage are given in Table 15.1. Table 15.2 contains some "observed" failure times for our example (third column). These were constructed to follow a smooth pattern to eliminate the random effects that would otherwise be present and to have a more illustrative example.

As a result of testing during the first stage a total of 9 failures were experienced in 4.61 time units. Note that from Example 15.1 this is the expected number of failures. An additional 6 failures were experienced in 0.50 time units during the second stage. It will often be true that the rate at which failures are experienced will increase after a transition to a new stage. From this data we wish to estimate the parameters of the software reliability model being used for the final system, that is, the second stage.

The failure times that would have been expected from a stable system are shown in the last column of Table 15.2. There is, of course, a large difference between this data and the observed data (third column of Table 15.2). Using the latter data without any changes or adjustments would result in extremely poor, if not meaningless, parameter estimates from our software reliability model for the stable program.

Suppose we determine $\hat{\boldsymbol{\beta}}_{(1)}$, the estimates of model parameters for the first stage using the first 9 failures. Then we apply Equation (15.4) to each failure time in the interval $[0, 4.61]$. That is, we perform the calculations implied by

$$\tilde{t}_i = Q_{12}(t_i, 100K, 1000K, 20K, 500K, \hat{\boldsymbol{\beta}}_{(1)}), \quad i = 1, 2, \cdots, 9. \tag{15.5}$$

Now translating the failure times from the second stage by an amount equivalent to $t_9 - \tilde{t}_9$ results in the adjusted failure times shown in the fourth column in Table 15.2. It is clear that the transformation and translation procedure has resulted in failure data that are ideally suited for estimating the model parameters. ∎

The estimate of $\boldsymbol{\beta}_{(1)}$ used in the preceding example was the exact (correct) value. That is, $\hat{\beta}_0 = \hat{\nu}_0 = 10$ failures and $\hat{\beta}_1 = \hat{\phi} = 0.5$/time unit. Because we

TABLE 15.2
Time of failure data for two-stage example

Stage	Failure number	Observed data	Transformed data	Ideal data
			Time of failure	
1	1	0.21	0.08	0.08
	2	0.44	0.16	0.16
	3	0.71	0.24	0.24
	4	1.02	0.32	0.32
	5	1.39	0.40	0.40
	6	1.83	0.49	0.49
	7	2.41	0.57	0.57
	8	3.22	0.65	0.65
	9	4.61	0.73	0.73
2	10	4.69	0.82	0.82
	11	4.78	0.90	0.90
	12	4.86	0.98	0.98
	13	4.94	1.07	1.07
	14	5.03	1.15	1.15
	15	5.11	1.24	1.24

used these values the adjustment was perfect. In practice there will be random fluctuations in the observed failure data and therefore a certain amount of error in the estimated value of $\boldsymbol{\beta}_{(1)}$. The resulting transformed data will not be perfect, but they will still represent a vast improvement over not adjusting.

15.2.2 Three-Stage Evolution

Now consider a three-stage system as depicted in Figure 15.7. The expected number of failures versus time is made up of three segments, one for each stage. To transform these segments to what would have been expected for a stable system requires a two-step procedure.

The first step involves determining $\hat{\boldsymbol{\beta}}_{(1)}$ for the first stage as before and then adjusting the failure times of the stage by use of the function Q_{12}. After translating the failure times of the second and third stages by an amount equivalent to the difference between the experienced and adjusted final failure time of the first stage, the middle curve shown in Figure 15.7 results. The effects of the first stage of integration are removed from the data by this step. That is, the step converts the data into what they could be expected to be if the first stage had not been present. The failure data now look like they came from a two-stage system test plan.

The second step in the procedure is a reapplication of the first step. In this step $\hat{\boldsymbol{\beta}}_{(2)}$ is determined using the transformed data from the first stage and the translated data from the second stage. Define Q_{23} as the transformation taking a value of t_i from a curve representing the conditions of the second stage to the value $\tilde{t}_i$ expected from the conditions of the third stage. It can be written as

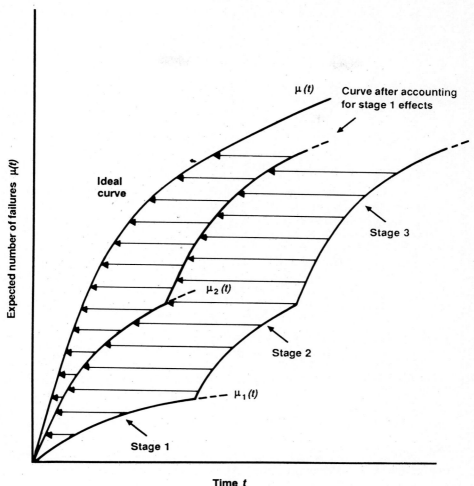

FIGURE 15.7
A three-stage example.

$$\tilde{t}_i = Q_{23}\ (t_i;\ I_2,\ I_3,\ \Delta I_2,\ \Delta I_3,\ \beta_{(2)}).\qquad(15.6)$$

We apply Q_{23} to all the failure times up to the end of the second stage and translate the data from the third stage. We have now removed the effects of the second stage from the data and are left only with data representing the conditions of the third stage. Note that the original data for the first two stages have been transformed to account for the effects of those stages. Data from the third stage have only been translated and are the only data actually experienced given the conditions of that stage. The result of this step is to make the data from the first two stages look like they came from the third stage.

Example 15.3. It is instructive to go through a three-stage example. Table 15.3 contains the stage characteristics. Once again, we will be using the basic execution time model. Table 15.4 contains the observed failure data and the results from the various steps of the transformation procedure. To keep the example simple we have limited the number of failures in each stage.

The first step of the procedure requires that $\hat{\boldsymbol{\beta}}_{(1)}$ be determined. Normally 3 failure times will be insufficient to derive accurate estimates for the unknown parameters but let's assume that we arrive at the values $\hat{\nu}_0 = 15$ failures and $\hat{\phi} = 0.5$/time unit.

Now we apply

$$\tilde{t}_i = Q_{12} \, (t_i; \, 100K, \, 500K, \, 100K, \, 300K, \, \hat{\boldsymbol{\beta}}_{(1)}) \qquad (15.7)$$

to the 3 failure times experienced during the first stage. The remaining failure times are translated by the amount $t_3 - \tilde{t}_3 = -0.24$ time unit. Since this amount is negative, the failure times from the second and third stages are *increased*. The results of this step are shown in the fourth column of Table 15.4. The fifth column of this table shows what ideal data from the second stage would look like. This step has removed the effects of the first stage.

The second step of the procedure can now be applied. Using the first 5 failure times in column 4 we have $\hat{\nu}_0 = 45$ failures and $\hat{\phi} = 0.1$/time unit. Now we apply

$$\tilde{t}_i = Q_{23} \, (t_i; \, 500K, \, 1000K, \, 300K, \, 800K, \, \hat{\boldsymbol{\beta}}_{(2)}) \qquad (15.8)$$

to these failure times. The sixth failure time is translated by the amount $t_5 - \tilde{t}_5 = 0.32$ time unit. Note that the value of t_5 used here is the value after the first step, that is, not the original value. Since the amount of translation is positive the sixth failure time is *decreased*. The results of this step are shown in the sixth column of Table 15.4 and can be compared with the data from a stable system given in the last column of the table. ∎

15.2.3 Generalization to More Stages

The examples given illustrate the key idea of the adjustment procedure. The idea is to transform failure times from one stage of integration into the anticipated values if the program had been in each of the succeeding stages. The generalization of Equation (15.4) or Equation (15.6) is

$$\tilde{t}_i = Q_{kl} \, (t_i; \, I_k, \, I_l, \, \Delta I_k, \, \Delta I_l, \, \boldsymbol{\beta}_{(k)}). \qquad (15.9)$$

TABLE 15.3
Stage characteristics for three-stage example

Stage	I (K inst)	ΔI (K inst)	ν_0	ϕ
1	100	100	15	0.5
2	500	300	45	0.1
3	1000	800	120	0.05

TABLE 15.4
Time of failure data for three-stage example

Stage	Failure number	Time of failure				
		Observed data	Results of step 1	Ideal data from stage 2	Results of step 2	Data from stable system
1	1	0.14	0.23	0.23	0.17	0.17
	2	0.29	0.45	0.45	0.34	0.34
	3	0.45	0.69	0.69	0.51	0.51
2	4	0.69	0.93	0.93	0.68	0.68
	5	0.93	1.17	1.17	0.85	0.85
3	6	1.11	1.35	—	1.03	1.03

This allows us to take a value of t_i from a curve representing the condition of the kth stage to the value $\tilde{t}_i$ expected from the conditions of the lth stage. Application of Equation (15.9) is straightforward.

Up to now we have considered cases where data from all stages of integration were available. What happens when we are currently testing in a stage and others are to follow? Say we are in the kth stage and that there will be a total of n stages. We apply the adjustment procedure for the first k stages. This results in failure times that look like they came from a stable program with characteristics of the kth stage. After doing this we next apply the transformation Q_{kn}. This effectively skips the stages without data. The result will be data that look like they came from the final program.

15.2.4   Transformation Specification

The transformation given by Equation (15.9) can be applied with any software reliability model with parameters that can be established from the software characteristics.[3] Specification of the transformation can be carried out in a general fashion by using the cumulative conditional distribution function of the failure times in each stage. To apply the following method, the functional form of the cumulative conditional distribution function for each failure time must be known and its inverse computable. For a specific software reliability model, this form will remain the same from failure to failure and stage to stage. However, its parameters will depend on the characteristics I and ΔI of the stage in which a failure occurs. Let $F_k(t_i \,|\, t_1, \ldots, t_{i-1}; \boldsymbol{\beta}_{(k)})$ and $F_l(\tilde{t}_i \,|\, t_1, \ldots, \tilde{t}_{i-1}; \boldsymbol{\beta}_{(l)})$ denote the cumulative

---

[3]For the models we discuss, the characteristics are I and ΔI, but a different set would be theoretically possible.

conditional distribution functions for the ith failure, given the conditions of stage k and stage l respectively. We note here that the $\tilde{t}_1, \ldots, \tilde{t}_{i-1}$ are not actually experienced but are computed using $t_1, \ldots, t_{i-1}$.

A straightforward approach exists that allows us to derive the transformation we seek. It is based on the repeated use of the probability integral transform[4] [Mood, Graybill, and Boes (1974)]. We first evaluate $F_k(t_i \mid t_1, \ldots, t_{i-1}; \boldsymbol{\beta}_{(k)})$ at the realization of the ith failure time (that is, at the experienced value of t_i). This evaluation results in a realization u of a random variable U that is uniformly distributed on the interval $(0, 1)$. Then, given this realization, $\tilde{t}_i = F_l^{-1}(u \mid \tilde{t}_1, \ldots, \tilde{t}_{i-1}; \boldsymbol{\beta}_{(l)})$ is a realization of a random variable that has the cumulative distribution function $F_l(\tilde{t}_i \mid \tilde{t}_1, \ldots, \tilde{t}_{i-1}; \boldsymbol{\beta}_{(l)})$. Hence the overall transformation is given by

$$Q_{kl}(t_i; \boldsymbol{\beta}_{(k)}, \boldsymbol{\beta}_{(l)}) = F_l^{-1}(F_k(t_i \mid t_1, \ldots, t_{i-1}; \boldsymbol{\beta}_{(k)}) \Big|_{\tilde{t}_1, \ldots, \tilde{t}_{i-1}; \boldsymbol{\beta}_{(l)}}). \quad (15.10)$$

This transformation cannot be used in practice since the failure data that are available when applying Q_{kl} are only enough to estimate $\boldsymbol{\beta}_{(k)}$ (and not $\boldsymbol{\beta}_{(l)}$).[5] Now the requirement that the software reliability model have parameters that can be established or predicted from the software characteristics comes into play. That is, the value that $\boldsymbol{\beta}_{(l)}$ might take on must be *predicted* from the *estimated* value of $\boldsymbol{\beta}_{(k)}$ and the characteristics of the program during stages k and l. Denoting the predicted value of $\boldsymbol{\beta}_{(l)}$ as $\boldsymbol{\beta}_{(l)}^*$ we can write

$$\boldsymbol{\beta}_{(l)}^* = g(\hat{\boldsymbol{\beta}}_{(k)}, I_k, \Delta I_k, I_l, \Delta I_l), \quad (15.11)$$

where g is a known (possibly vector) function. Substituting Equation (15.11) into Equation (15.10) will result in the practically usable form given by Equation (15.9).

In the following Sections 15.3 and 15.4 we will develop the specific form of Equations (15.10) and (15.11) for general Poisson- and binomial-type models. We will particularize this for the basic execution time and logarithmic Poisson models. The general approach illustrated could be used for other software reliability models, but many models do not have parameters that can be established from the software characteristics.

---

[4]The probability integral transform is a transformation that has the form of the cumulative distribution function $F(x)$ of a random variable X. Suppose we transform a set of values $\{Y_1, Y_2, \ldots, Y_m\}$ of a random variable Y of unknown distribution using function F. The transformed set $\{F(Y_1), F(Y_2), \ldots, F(Y_m)\}$ will have a uniform distribution if they actually follow the distribution F. Thus, you can assume different types of likely distributions for a random variable of unknown distribution. Each can be tested through transformation and checking for a uniform distribution.

[5]Note that if the failure data were enough to estimate $\boldsymbol{\beta}_{(l)}$ in addition to $\boldsymbol{\beta}_{(k)}$ there would be little need to use this procedure, or any other, for that matter.

15.3 POISSON-TYPE MODELS

The transformation given in Equation (15.10) can be determined for a general Poisson-type model by starting with Equation (10.15), that is,

$$F(t_i \mid t_{i-1}) = 1 - \exp\left[\mu(t_{i-1}) - \mu(t_i)\right]. \tag{15.12}$$

Thus, we have

$$F_k(t_i \mid t_1, \ldots, t_{i-1}) = 1 - \exp\left[\mu_k(t_{i-1}) - \mu_k(t_i)\right] \tag{15.13}$$

and

$$F_l(\tilde{t}_i \mid \tilde{t}_1, \ldots, \tilde{t}_{i-1}) = 1 - \exp\left[\mu_l(\tilde{t}_{i-1}) - \mu_l(\tilde{t}_i)\right], \tag{15.14}$$

where $\mu_k(t)$ and $\mu_l(t)$ are the mean value functions for the kth and lth stages, respectively. Note that $\mu_k(t)$ and $\mu_l(t)$ have the same functional form, but the specific nature in each case depends on the conditions of the respective stage.

Using Equation (15.13) and the inverse of Equation (15.14) with Equation (15.10) yields, after some algebra,

$$\tilde{t}_i = \mu_l^{-1}\left[\mu_l(\tilde{t}_{i-1}) + \mu_k(t_i) - \mu_k(t_{i-1})\right], \tag{15.15}$$

or equivalently

$$\mu_l(\tilde{t}_i) = \mu_l(\tilde{t}_{i-1}) + \left[\mu_k(t_i) - \mu_k(t_{i-1})\right]. \tag{15.16}$$

Example 15.4. Consider again the two-stage system used in Example 15.1. The fifth failure time had an observed value of 1.39 time units. Let's determine its adjusted value. Using the mean value function of the first stage given by Equation (15.1) we have

$$\mu_1(t_4) = \mu_1(1.02) = 4 \text{ failures}$$

and

$$\mu_1(t_5) = \mu_1(1.39) = 5 \text{ failures}.$$

Assume that the adjusted value of the fourth failure time is 0.32 time unit. Then we have from Equation (15.16) that $\tilde{t}_5$ is the solution of

$$\mu_2(\tilde{t}_5) = \mu_2(0.32) + 5 - 4,$$

where $\mu_2(t) = 250\,[1 - \exp(-0.05t)]$. Solving for $\tilde{t}_5$ in the above we find that $\tilde{t}_5 = 0.40$ time unit. ∎

For finite failures Poisson-type models, that is, those models that have $\mu(\infty) = \nu_0$, the pure growth condition is sufficient for the existence of a solution to Equation (15.16). For infinite failures Poisson-type models, that is, $\mu(\infty) = \infty$, the pure growth condition is not needed to solve Equation (15.16). In this latter case since both $\mu_l(\tilde{t})$ and $\mu_k(t)$ have values in the interval $(0, \infty)$ there will always exist a value of $\tilde{t}$ for given t that results in equality. However, in the former case both $\mu_l(\tilde{t})$ and $\mu_k(t)$ are bounded. If $\mu_k(t)$ has a value larger than the maximum value of $\mu_l(\tilde{t})$, no solution is possible. This cannot happen with pure growth. We now particularize the solution of Equation (15.16) for the basic and logarithmic Poisson execution time models.

15.3.1 Basic Execution Time Model

For this case the mean value function is given by

$$\mu(t) = \nu_0[1 - \exp(-\phi t)] . \tag{15.17}$$

Substituting Equation (15.17) for stages k and l into the solution of Equation (15.16) and manipulating we have

$$\tilde{t}_i = -\frac{1}{\phi_l} \ln\left\{1 - \frac{\nu_{0k}}{\nu_{0l}}[1 - \exp(-\phi_k t_i)]\right\}, \tag{15.18}$$

where ν_{0k} and ν_{0l} are the expected number of total failures in the kth and lth stages, respectively, and ϕ_k and ϕ_l are the constant per-fault hazard rates for the kth and lth stages, respectively.

We will now determine Equation (15.18) in terms of total object instructions and developed source instructions present in stages k and l, that is, we need to establish the relationship given by Equation (15.11). Total object instructions present affect the frequency of execution of the program and hence the hazard rate. Developed source instructions present affect the number of faults in the program, which influences the expected number of failures. We are always concerned only with deliverable executable code.

Consider first the per-fault hazard rate ϕ_k for the program in stage k. This is given as

$$\phi_k = fK , \tag{15.19}$$

where f is the linear execution frequency and K the fault exposure ratio. The linear execution frequency of the program is the ratio of average instruction execution rate r to program size in object instructions. Thus Equation (15.19) becomes

$$\phi_k = \frac{rK}{I_k} . \tag{15.20}$$

Similarly, the per-fault hazard rate ϕ_l for the program in stage l is given by

$$\phi_l = \frac{rK}{I_l} \,. \tag{15.21}$$

Combining Equations (15.20) and (15.21) we get

$$\phi_l = \frac{I_k}{I_l}\phi_k \,. \tag{15.22}$$

This allows us to *predict* ϕ_l by *estimating* ϕ_k.

The expected number of total inherent faults for a stage is assumed to be proportional to the total number of developed executable source instructions in that stage (see Section 5.1.1). Thus, we may write

$$\omega_{0l} = \frac{\Delta I_l}{\Delta I_k}\,\omega_{0k} \,, \tag{15.23}$$

where ω_{0k} and ω_{0l} are the expected number of faults in stages k and l, respectively.

Faults and failures are related through the fault reduction factor B, that is,

$$\nu_{0k} = \frac{\omega_{0k}}{B} \,. \tag{15.24}$$

Substituting Equation (15.24) and the similar expression for ν_{0l} in Equation (15.23) results in

$$\nu_{0l} = \frac{\Delta I_l}{\Delta I_k}\,\nu_{0k} \,. \tag{15.25}$$

Using Equations (15.22) and (15.25), our failure time transformation given by Equation (15.18) becomes

$$\tilde{t}_i = -\frac{I_l}{\phi_k I_k}\,\ln\left\{1 - \frac{\Delta I_k}{\Delta I_l}\left[1 - \exp(-\phi_k t_i)\right]\right\} \,. \tag{15.26}$$

Example 15.5. Once again consider our two-stage illustration and the information given in Table 15.1. Using failure data from the first stage we *estimated* the values $\hat{\nu}_{01} = 10$ failures and $\hat{\phi}_1 = 0.5$/time unit. These can be used with Equations (15.22) and (15.25) to *predict* the corresponding values, ν_{02} and ϕ_2 for the second and final stage. Thus,

$$\phi_2^* = \frac{I_1}{I_2}\,\hat{\phi}_1 = \frac{100}{1000}\,(0.5)$$

$$= 0.05/\text{time unit}$$

and

$$\nu_{02}^* = \frac{\Delta I_2}{\Delta I_1}\,\hat{\nu}_{01} = \frac{500}{20}\,(10)$$

$$= 250 \text{ failures}.$$

The failure time transformation (15.26) is given by

$$\tilde{t}_i = - 20 \ln \{1 - 0.04[1 - \exp(-0.5t_i)]\}. \qquad \blacksquare$$

The adjustment transformation given by Equation (15.26) is an approximation [because of Equations (15.22) and (15.25)] to the true adjustment desired.[6] One might argue that sensitivity of Equation (15.26) to the error in the approximation could make it better to forego the adjustment procedure. However, through many simulations in which deliberate deviations from Equations (15.22) and (15.25) were introduced, we have found that the adjustment procedure for the basic execution time model is robust. The procedure almost always yields results that represent an improvement in the estimated parameters for the final program over not adjusting.

15.3.2   Logarithmic Poisson
Execution Time Model

For this case the mean value function is given by

$$\mu(t) = \frac{1}{\theta} \ln (\phi t + 1), \qquad (15.27)$$

where $\phi = \lambda_0 \theta$. Substituting this for stages k and l into the solution of Equation (15.16) and manipulating we have

$$\tilde{t}_i = \frac{1}{\phi_l} \left[\left(\phi_k t_i + 1 \right)^{\frac{\theta_l}{\theta_k}} - 1 \right]. \qquad (15.28)$$

It now becomes necessary to relate ϕ_l to ϕ_k and θ_l to θ_k. At the present state of the art, the required relationships are not known. Thus, failure time adjustment has not been reduced to practice in this case. However, it appears that the logarithmic Poisson execution time model may have enough flexibility to handle evolution directly in an empirical fashion.

Note that evolution will probably affect the failure intensity scale and shape parameters β_1 and β_2 and the fault reduction factor decay parameter β_3.

15.4   BINOMIAL-TYPE MODELS

The failure time transformation for binomial-type models can be determined as follows. From Equations (10.33) and (10.37) we find the conditional cumulative density function for the ith failure time for stages k and l as

---

[6]True adjustment would be achieved if ν_k, ν_l, ϕ_k, and ϕ_l were all known precisely.

$$F_k(t_i \mid t_{i-1}) = 1 - \left[\frac{1 - F_{ak}(t_i)}{1 - F_{ak}(t_{i-1})} \right]^{u_{0k} - i + 1} \tag{15.29}$$

and

$$F_l(\tilde{t}_i \mid \tilde{t}_{i-1}) = 1 - \left[\frac{1 - F_{al}(\tilde{t}_i)}{1 - F_{al}(\tilde{t}_{i-1})} \right]^{u_{0l} - i + 1}, \tag{15.30}$$

where F_{ak} and F_{al} are the cumulative density functions per fault for stages k and l, respectively.

Using Equation (15.29) and the inverse of Equation (15.30) with Equation (15.10) yields, after some algebra,

$$\tilde{t}_i = F_{al}^{-1} \left\{ 1 - \left[\frac{1 - F_{ak}(t_i)}{1 - F_{ak}(t_{i-1})} \right]^{\frac{u_{0k} - i + 1}{u_{0l} - i + 1}} \left[1 - F_{al}(\tilde{t}_{i-1}) \right] \right\}, \tag{15.31}$$

where F_{al}^{-1} is the inverse of F_{al}. Unlike the transformation given in Equation (15.15) for Poisson-type models, Equation (15.31) does not have a simple interpretation.

Example 15.6. Consider an exponential-class binomial-type model. Here $F_a(t) = 1 - \exp(-\phi t)$ and Equation (15.31) becomes, after some simplification,

$$\tilde{t}_i' = \frac{\phi_k}{\phi_l} \frac{u_{0k} - i + 1}{u_{0l} - i + 1} t_i'. \tag{15.32}$$

Using Equations (15.22) and (15.25), with ν_0 replaced with u_0, we have the practically useful form

$$\tilde{t}_i' = \frac{I_l}{I_k} \frac{u_{0k} - i + 1}{\frac{\Delta I_l}{\Delta I_k} u_{0k} - i + 1} t_i'. \tag{15.33}$$

∎

15.5 AN APPLICATION

The adjustment procedure presented in Section 15.3.1 for the basic execution time model has been applied to a software project that underwent evolution. The project was a military software system involving eight programmers and 48,412 deliverable executable object instructions. Parts of the system were extracted from a previous system and appropriately modified. The history of program growth during the system test period is shown in Figure 15.8. The reader will note that this project experienced 20 stages in its testing phase. In addition, 163 test failures were experienced in 9994 CPU hr of testing.

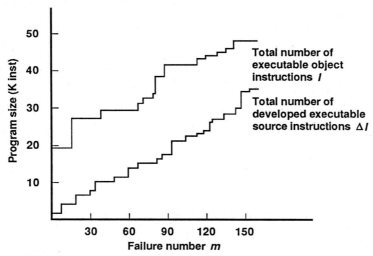

FIGURE 15.8
History of program growth.

Primary attention (by project managers) was paid to the basic execution time model estimates for the present failure intensity. Straightforward application of the model, ignoring the program evolution, causes an underestimation of the present failure intensity. This in turn leads to optimistic status evaluation.

The performance of the basic execution time model using unadjusted and adjusted data, as well as the logarithmic Poisson execution time model using unadjusted data will be illustrated next. We'll do this by looking at the relative error in the predicted number of failures at the end of testing at various points during the test phase.

The predicted number of failures at end of system test is given by $\hat{\mu}(t_e; m)$ where the maximum likelihood estimates for the unknown parameters are based on m failures. The relative error for this case is given by

$$\frac{\hat{\mu}(t_e; m) - 163}{163}. \tag{15.34}$$

The smaller the absolute value of the relative error, the better the predictive validity of the model and the more likely that the software reliability estimates made by the model are better.

Figure 15.9 shows the relative error as a function of m for the cases mentioned above. It will be seen that the basic execution time model, using unadjusted data, provides the worst performance. The basic execution time model, using adjusted data, provides, for the most part, a substantial improvement. The logarithmic Poisson execution time model also provides a substantial improvement over the (unadjusted) basic execution time model, thus supporting our argument given in Section 15.3.2. During the last quarter of the project the (adjusted) basic execution time model is the best performer.

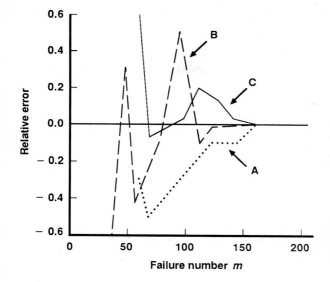

**FIGURE 15.9
Relative errors in predictions. A = unadjusted basic execution time model. B = adjusted basic execution time model. C = unadjusted logarithmic Poisson model.**

We should caution the reader that drawing general conclusions based on one set of data is dangerous. More experience with the procedures and models is required to obtain general results. However, the benefits that can be gained from failure time adjustment have been demonstrated.

Figure 15.10 shows the running history of estimated present failure intensity during the test period. The basic execution time model and both unadjusted and adjusted failure time data were used. The set of maximum likelihood estimates of the plotted quantity is shown in this figure. Based on the experience of the project personnel, it was felt that the adjusted curve more correctly estimated the failure intensity during the early part of the project. The failure intensity decreases steadily throughout the test phase as would be expected. The period of near-constant failure intensity found in the unadjusted curve does not occur.

The sometimes large effect that failure time adjustment can have on estimated quantities such as failure intensity is well illustrated by this application. That is, an order of magnitude difference exists between the failure intensities estimated using unadjusted and adjusted data. We should not be terribly surprised about this result. As we can see from Figure 15.8 this project underwent much evolution. About half of the total experienced failures occurred before half of the total developed code was integrated.

The raw failure interval data for the project as well as the adjusted data using the basic execution time model are presented in Table 15.5. Note that the final "negative" value denotes a failure-free interval.

15.6   EFFECT ON CALENDAR TIME COMPONENT

There may be some error (in addition to the normal statistical error) in the calendar time predictions. This can occur if there is delay in building the final program.

TABLE 15.5
Raw and adjusted failure interval data for a military software system

Failure number	Failure interval (CPU sec)	Adjusted failure interval (CPU sec)	Failure number	Failure interval (CPU sec)	Adjusted failure interval (CPU sec)	Failure number	Failure interval (CPU sec)	Adjusted failure interval (CPU sec)
1	320	42	57	19150	1330	113	21600	1250
2	14390	1697	58	2611	117	114	64800	3444
3	9000	1004	59	39170	2490	115	302400	11326
4	2880	311	60	55794	3100	116	752188	10541
5	5700	605	61	42632	2055	117	86400	469
6	21800	2155	62	267600	8366	118	100800	452
7	26800	2341	63	87074	1555	119	194400	42984
8	113540	6847	64	149606	17222	120	115200	19078
9	112137	3470	65	14400	1372	121	64800	8976
10	660	16	66	34560	3119	122	3600	465
11	2700	498	67	39600	3286	123	230400	23507
12	28793	5169	68	334395	18607	124	583200	25213
13	2173	381	69	296015	8025	125	259200	28476
14	7263	1264	70	177399	2782	126	183600	13061
15	10865	1863	71	214622	2171	127	3600	210
16	4230	717	72	156400	1038	128	144000	7295
17	8460	1420	73	166800	772	129	14400	618
18	14805	2437	74	10800	41	130	86400	3343
19	11844	1910	75	267000	745	131	110100	3474
20	5361	852	76	34513	3639	132	28800	3065
21	6553	1032	77	7680	772	133	43200	4301
22	6499	1770	78	37667	3603	134	57600	5222
23	3124	840	79	11100	1006	135	468000	26467
24	51323	12754	80	187200	13651	136	950400	14610
25	17010	3820	81	18000	1031	137	400400	1371

n			n			n		
26	1890	413	82	178200	8191	138	883800	168207
27	5400	1166	83	144000	4531	139	273600	16785
28	62313	12140	84	639200	8650	140	432000	12707
29	24826	4210	85	86400	442	141	864000	42875
30	26335	4108	86	288000	24501	142	202600	3708
31	363	56	87	320	20	143	203400	2618
32	13989	2039	88	57600	3468	144	277680	2367
33	15058	2090	89	28800	1597	145	105000	637
34	32377	4146	90	18000	955	146	580080	2021
35	41632	4687	91	88640	4251	147	4533960	1158
36	4160	433	92	432000	13056	148	432000	47869
37	82040	7289	93	4160	80	149	141200	36952
38	13189	977	94	3200	64	150	172800	751
39	3426	564	95	42800	804	151	86400	287
40	5833	948	96	43600	756	152	1123200	123048
41	640	104	97	10560	174	153	1555200	19080
42	640	102	98	115200	1700	154	777600	897
43	2880	818	99	86400	1064	155	1296000	255
44	110	32	100	57600	621	156	1872000	786398
45	22080	6090	101	28800	289	157	335600	25346
46	60654	15235	102	432000	11978	158	921600	24134
47	52163	11488	103	345600	4522	159	1036800	4318
48	12546	2558	104	115200	962	160	1728000	643
49	784	157	105	44494	3717	161	777600	777600
50	10193	2017	106	10506	833	162	57600	57600
51	7841	1519	107	177240	11846	163	17280	17280
52	31365	5792	108	241487	10910		−213120	−213120
53	24313	4191	109	143028	4457			
54	298890	34863	110	273564	41751			
55	1280	96	111	189391	11803			
56	22099	1627	112	172800	12126			

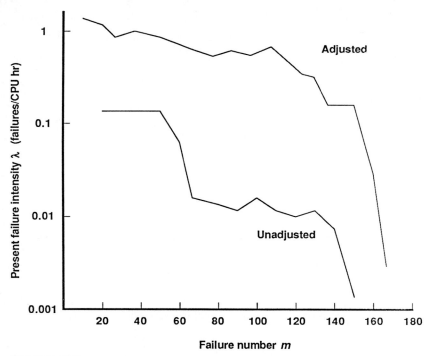

FIGURE 15.10
Estimated present failure intensity using both unadjusted and adjusted data.

However, if integration proceeds at a reasonable pace then the error will be small. For example, suppose we decide to stay in a stage until all or almost all of the failures that can occur in that stage are experienced. A large amount of execution time and calendar time will then be spent removing what may only be a handful of failures. This "extra" time is not accounted for in our calendar time estimates. If we had moved to the next stage a great many more failures would have been removed and substantial progress toward the failure intensity objective would have resulted. This is not to say that the extra time we spent while in the previous stage was wasted. It is probably better spent later when we are trying to close in on the failure intensity objective.

Deciding when to go from stage k to stage $k + 1$ can be based on the estimate of $\beta_{(k)}$. For example, if we are using a finite failures model and the estimated number of remaining failures is large, then further testing in that stage can be recommended. If the remaining failures estimate is small, then proceeding to the next stage may be appropriate.

15.7 SUMMARY

A method to allow for evolving programs in software reliability modeling has been presented. It is based on the cumulative conditional distribution function of the failure times. The method requires that we be able to predict the model parameters for a stage based on the estimated value of these parameters from the preceding stage. Most models, including the logarithmic Poisson model, do not have "predictable" parameters. A notable exception is the basic execution time model.

PROBLEMS

15.1 Develop the failure time transformation for the Schick-Wolverton model. Use Equations (10.22) and (15.31) and the fact that $z_a(t) = 2\phi t$ for this model.

15.2 Develop the failure time transformation for the Littlewood-Verrall model. For this model the cumulative conditional distribution function for the ith failure time is given by [Littlewood and Verrall (1973)]

$$F(t_i \mid t_{i-1}) = 1 - \left\{ \frac{\gamma}{\gamma + \ln \left[\dfrac{t_i - t_{i-1} + \xi(i)}{\xi(i)} \right]} \right\}^i ,$$

where

$$\gamma = \sum_{j=1}^{i-1} \ln \left[\frac{t_j - t_{j-1} + \xi(j)}{\xi(j)} \right] .$$

What problem(s) must be solved before failure time adjustment is reduced to practice for this model?

15.3 What happens to the failure time transformation when $\hat{\phi}_k = 0$ for the basic execution time model?

15.4 Show that Equation (15.16), with t_i and $\tilde{t}_i$ replaced with x_i and $\tilde{x}_i$, respectively, is a reasonable basis for transformation when using grouped data with a Poisson model. Note that x_i is the total recorded time at the end of the ith group and $\tilde{x}_i$ is its transformed or adjusted value.

15.5 In this problem we will look at an example of modeling evolving programs with a likelihood function that directly incorporates program growth. The model is the Jelinski-Moranda model, which we know is a binomial-type model with a constant per-fault hazard rate. The idea for what follows was taken, in part, from Moranda (1981) with notation changes made for consistency.

(a) What is the conditional probability density function for the ith failure time for this model and what restriction, if any, must be imposed on our estimate for u_0?

(b) Let:

ΔI_i = number of deliverable developed executable source instructions integrated at the occurrence of the ith failure,

I_i = total number of deliverable executable object instructions at the occurrence of the ith failure,

ω_I = characteristic fault density for all portions of the program (faults per line of developed source code), and

$\phi(i)$ = per-fault hazard rate at the occurrence of the ith failure.

What is the conditional probability density function for the ith failure time using this notation (express $\phi(i)$ in terms of final program characteristics)?

(c) Write the likelihood function at the time of the mth failure. What problem regarding our estimate of u_0 for the final program makes this approach unsatisfactory?

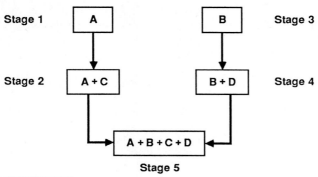

FIGURE 15.11
Parallel evolution.

15.6 Consider a case where testing of a program in its final configuration is performed by two *completely* independent test teams. We will need to combine failure time data from each team into a single sequence. This sequence can then be used in a procedure that deals with parallel evolution (see next problem). Find the interleaved sequence, given the following data. Assume that failures 3 and 5, experienced by team A, were the same as failures 4 and 2, respectively, experienced by team B. Note that no failure-free time has accumulated after the last failure of the first sequence while 100 failure-free time units have accumulated at the end of the second sequence. Although testing is performed on different machines, they are of the same type and have the same instruction execution rates.

	Failure time	
Failure number	**Team A**	**Team B**
1	9	3
2	21	27
3	25	100
4	45	111
5	117	129
6	267	180
End of test	267	280

15.7 Up to this point we have limited ourselves to sequential evolution. A more general case is *parallel* evolution where more than one path and hence stage can exist at any given time. Consider, as an example, the parallel integration plan shown in Figure 15.11. Here two paths (stages 1 and 2 and stages 3 and 4) are taken to the final stage (stage 5). Determine a procedure to account for the program size variation in this and similar cases. Note any requirements that must be fulfilled for the procedure to work.

FOUR

FUTURE DEVELOPMENT

T his concluding part of the book evaluates the current state of the art and practice of software reliability measurement and prediction. It discusses needs for further research.

SIXTEEN

STATE OF THE ART

In this chapter we will revisit each of the main application areas for software reliability measurement and prediction. We will evaluate the state of the art with respect to that application. Areas needing further research will be highlighted.

16.1 MEASUREMENT

We can measure software reliability in the operational environment now with excellent accuracy. Hence, use of failure intensity as a means for controlling change in operational systems or as a way of evaluating software engineering technologies is currently feasible [Musa (1979c)].

The quality of software reliability measurement based on testing depends on the accuracy of our knowledge of the test and operational execution environments. If you cannot represent the operational environment satisfactorily when testing, then you must compensate for the difference between it and the test environment. Also, there is a natural difference between the test and operational environments that results from eliminating redundancy in tests. Finally, there is the need to be able to estimate the change in failure intensity that would result from a changing operational environment. Methods for dealing with all these situations have been developed and discussed in Chapter 6. However, they need to be more widely applied and experience needs to be gained in their use. Given the current capability to measure software reliability during test, status monitoring and tracking of projects can be accomplished with a relatively good level of quality.

463

16.2   PREDICTION QUALITY

The quality of prediction of software reliability and other quantities associated with failure behavior is important, as many managerial and engineering decisions depend on it.

16.2.1   Using Parameter Estimation

The current quality of prediction of failure behavior in execution time based on parameter estimation could be characterized as good. Parameter estimation, of course, requires that the program be executed and failure data collected. Although the accuracy may be sufficient for many purposes, prediction frequently tends to be biased. That is, there appear to be consistent patterns among models of predicting values of failure intensity that are either too high (pessimistic) or too low (optimistic). In Chapter 13 it may be seen that finite failures category models tend to be optimistic. Note in Figure 13.4 that they underpredict the number of failures to be experienced at a future point in time. This may be the result of the estimator of the parameter total failures being biased. Infinite failures category models tend to be neutral or pessimistic. In addition, there is a fair amount of dispersion in the predictions (see Figure 13.3) in both cases. There is great potential benefit in techniques that would reduce the prediction bias and/or the dispersion. Improvement in predicting failure intensity would improve prediction of the dates for reaching various failure intensity objectives. Such predictions are important from project schedule and product marketing perspectives. Currently, there appear to be two general strategies for improving the situation, improving parameter estimation and improving prediction directly.

Joe and Reid (1985) have studied the estimation problem for an exponential-class binomial-type model. They note that it is surprisingly difficult to find an estimator that is unbiased in all situations. For values of total failures between 10 to 20, they found that the harmonic mean of the end points of the 50 percent likelihood interval for total failures was the most effective estimator. However, it appears likely that improvements in inference in determining model parameters and their confidence intervals may be possible. Investigation may be fruitful.

Current approaches to directly improving prediction of failure behavior [Littlewood, Ghaly, and Chan (1986)] focus on two possibilities, adaptive prediction and weighted averages of predictions from different models. One form of adaptive prediction may be visualized as "using" what Littlewood calls a "u-plot" as an indicator of prediction bias. A "core" model is used to predict the distribution of the failure time t_i, given as $F(t_i \mid t_{i-1})$. The core model can be any of the models we described in this book. First, the model parameters must be estimated from the known failure times $t_1, t_2, \ldots, t_{i-1}$. The prediction, denoted by $\tilde{F}(t_i \mid t_{i-1})$, is then made, using the model with the parameter values that have just been estimated. The actual failure time t_i is observed and transformed by using the probability integral transform corresponding to the predicted distribution:

$$u_i = \tilde{F}(t_i \mid t_{i-1}) \ . \tag{16.1}$$

Recall that the probability integral transform is the hypothesized cumulative distribution function of the data being transformed [Mood, Graybill, and Boes (1974)]. If the hypothesis is correct, then the transformed data u_i will be uniformly distributed. We make predictions on a step-by-step basis, starting with i at a value that gives a sample of reasonable size (perhaps 10 or 20). Thus we develop a set of independent u_i to be tested.[1]

The u-plot is constructed by first ordering the u_i in ascending order (assume there are m values). Then we plot a point corresponding to the first u_i on the horizontal axis and $1/(m + 1)$ on the vertical axis. The axes represent, respectively, the empirical and theoretical quantiles. We take as the next point the coordinate of the second u_i and $2/(m + 1)$. This is done for all m values. Figure 16.1 illustrates

---

[1] Note that we could make predictions for any fixed number of failures ahead in the future, not just one.

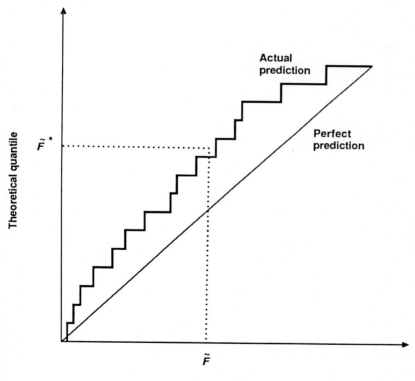

FIGURE 16.1
Sample *u*-plot.

the plot. Here the u-values are excessively small, indicating optimistic predictions.

The bias in the prediction is related to the distance between the u-plot and the perfect prediction line of slope 1. Before correcting for bias, we must first assure ourselves that any bias that exists is reasonably stationary. Consequently, we must check to see if there is any trend in the u_i data. One way to do this is to transform the u_i using

$$x_i = - \ln(1 - u_i) \, . \qquad (16.2)$$

This transformation yields independent unit exponential random variables if the u_i are independent and uniform. We can test for trend by testing for a homogeneous Poisson process [Cox and Lewis (1966)].

Assuming that the bias is stationary, an adjusted prediction $\tilde{F}^*$ can be developed by modifying the raw prediction $\tilde{F}$ as some function of the distance between the u-plot and the perfect prediction line. Preliminary results indicate that this adaptive prediction removes a substantial amount of the prediction bias experienced with models. It may reduce the differences in predictive validity experienced between models. This would increase the importance of other criteria in selecting a model.

The other approach to improving predictive validity, taking weighted averages of predictions from different models, also looks promising. The weights, for example, might be taken from some estimates of the bias like the u-plot. However, this approach may have more disadvantages than the adaptive approach. It appears likely to result in a loss of the capability to gain a physical feel for the model. Hence, it would be difficult to relate parameters to characteristics of the software and the software development process.

16.2.2   Using Parameter Prediction

Predicting software reliability from software product and development process characteristics needs the most work [Musa (1979c)]. However, it also offers great promise in terms of ultimate potential benefits, since it is crucial to system engineering studies and determines how well early planning decisions can be made. Such decisions often have the greatest impact on schedules and cost. When the program is not yet executable, we must predict the execution time component parameters from program characteristics rather than estimating them from failure data. For the basic execution time model, you require the number of inherent faults ω_0, the fault reduction factor B, the fault exposure ratio K, and the linear execution frequency f.

One approach to determining the number of faults (already discussed) is based on the size of the program. Data on the relationship between faults and size are beginning to accumulate but more are needed. There are evidently other variables that affect the number of inherent faults, and some possibilities are beginning to emerge. Complexity of the program would seem to be one. However, no one has been able to convincingly capture the concept of complexity in a simple metric and show that it improves the prediction of the number of inherent faults. We need to find a small set of readily measurable additional factors that improve the predictability of the number of inherent faults. Also, better ways of estimating size of a program in the requirements stage, before any code has been written, are required.

Initial data appear to indicate that the fault reduction factor B may be relatively stable across different projects, but more study is required. If it is not stable, we need to determine the project variables that have the most effect on it. Some possible variables were discussed in Chapter 5. The fault exposure ratio K may be dependent on the dynamic structure of the program and the degree to which faults are data-dependent. However, it is also possible that these effects average out for programs of substantial size. Knowledge of the value of this parameter is important if we are to obtain good absolute software reliability predictions. Obviously, further study is important.

Even if good absolute values for system engineering studies are not available, it is often possible to conduct studies involving relative comparison with reasonable results. Besides refining parameter prediction for the basic model, we need to establish whether it is practical to predict parameters for the logarithmic Poisson model.

16.2.3 Calendar Time

Prediction in calendar time is currently fair in quality [Musa (1979c)]. Calendar time prediction requires knowledge of the planned and resource usage parameters. We need to collect data on a number of projects to determine the values of the resource usage parameters and the extent to which they vary between different projects or classes of projects. If they do vary, a study of the factors that influence them should be undertaken.

16.3 EXTENSIONS AND APPLICATION

One area of possible extension of software reliability models, relatively unexplored, is to the unit test phase. Since failures occur in this phase and times of failure are available, it should be theoretically possible to do so. There are two principal problems that must be overcome:

1. small failure samples, and
2. relating unit tests to the operational profile.

The small failure sample problem can probably be handled by grouping together failures from the different units. The second problem appears far more difficult. Unit testing is generally performed from a structural or "white box" viewpoint. Tests are selected to maximize "coverage" of instructions, branches, or paths (best). It is difficult to determine which input state is being exercised by any given unit test. Furthermore, a unit test generally represents only a partial and incomplete test of the input state. Thus, it is difficult to determine what operational profile corresponds to a given set of unit tests. Hence, it is hard to establish whether such a set represents the operational environment. If it does not, it is difficult to establish what adjustments must be made to failure intensities.

The continuing application of software reliability models to actual projects is expected to build up a collection of techniques for handling various special situations. Also, some existing techniques may be refined. For example, it is desirable to determine how different projects classify failure severity and the proportions of failures that fall in each class. It would be helpful if we could verify with more certainty that the proportions tend to be stationary. A possible technique worthy of further investigation is the idea of limiting the range of data used for estimation of parameters when the system is undergoing substantial program design change. The value of this idea is not known nor do we know the optimum limit to the range.

It would be highly desirable if there were a single reliability-related metric that could actually be *measured,* rather than simply predicted, through all phases of the software life cycle. This poses a difficult problem. Failures appear to be the only entities that are closely related to reliability. Faults in code have some relationship with reliability, but reliability is also strongly influenced by the operational profile. You could define design and requirements faults by generalizing the concept of faults in code. Such faults are even more "distant" in their relationship with reliability in the sense that additional factors may intervene. Further, faults cannot be tracked against the same base, execution time, as failures. We might track them against some quantity like inspection effort (in person hr) but now we have the problem of different independent variables. Yet at present, faults are a quantity that is highly observable in the phases before execution. For example, requirements and design faults are detectable through such processes as requirements reviews and design inspections. Code faults can be found through code reading, either in desk checking or code walk-throughs.

Perhaps the most promising approach would be to use failures for all project phases. Then failures would have to be defined in terms of simulated execution during the early development phases. This would require executable requirements and design languages or a way of determining the fail set of every fault that is identified. Further, you would have to develop a good way of estimating execution time from the "time" recorded for simulated executions. However, if these problems could be solved, you would have the mechanism for looking at the entire software life cycle and allocating reliability improvement goals to each phase. Then "reliability risk" and challenge could be spread rationally across the phases, perhaps in a way to minimize reliability improvement cost.

Some of the techniques of software reliability are applicable to hardware design faults. Ascher and Feingold (1982) have pointed out the desirability of further investigating this possibility. This book has dealt with the question of reliability of programs. Reliability of data bases is becoming an increasingly important question. Little is known about this subject. However, artificial intelligence applications (particularly expert systems) greatly increase the impact of data base reliability (or the lack of it). Unlike programs, data base faults result from both structural error (misunderstanding the system requirements for the definition of the data base) and data entry faults.

There have been at least two interesting side benefits of software reliability modeling. The conceptual framework provided by a good model yields greater insight into the software failure process. The processes of defining just what constitutes a failure and of setting a failure intensity objective have both been salutary in stimulating customer and developer to communicate.

16.4 SUMMARY

In summary, the field of software reliability measurement and prediction has made substantial progress in the last decade. It cannot yet provide a standard cookbook approach for widespread application. There are several problem areas that need work. However, it is clearly beyond the pure theory stage and it can provide practical dividends for those who make the modest investment in time required to learn and apply it.

REVIEW OF PROBABILITY, STOCHASTIC PROCESSES, AND STATISTICS

The purpose of Appendix A is to review basic background material in probability, statistics, and stochastic processes. Many simple examples are used to help readers understand basic concepts. This appendix is primarily intended as background for Part III. Parts I and II introduce whatever background is needed as they go.

Section A.1 reviews basic probability theory. We first introduce probability concepts along with some probability laws useful for computing the probability of the occurrence of an event in association with other events. We then present random variables, probability distributions, mathematical expectation, and the moments of a distribution such as the mean and variance.

Section A.2 presents basic concepts of stochastic processes, which deal with a sequence of random variables varying over a period of time. We discuss a few simple forms of stochastic processes, such as a two-state Markov chain and a Poisson process.

Section A.3 reviews basic statistics. A basic problem of statistics is to make inferences about an unknown population parameter from the information provided by a sample selected from the population. We present methods for both point estimation and interval estimation. We also discuss the method of maximum likelihood for finding an estimator of a population parameter. Finally, we present simple regression analysis for estimating an inherent relationship among variables.

It should be pointed out that in this appendix we do not intend to provide comprehensive treatments of the topics. For those who wish to explore in-depth material, there are many standard textbooks available. Some of them are: Walpole and Myers (1972), Lipson and Sheth (1973), Roussas (1973), Rohatgi (1976),

Trivedi (1982), and Billinton and Allan (1983) on probability and statistics and Clarke and Disney (1970), Ross (1970, 1972), and Cinlar (1975) on stochastic processes.

A.1 BASIC PROBABILITY THEORY

A.1.1 Probability Concepts

Scientists conduct experiments to produce observations on measurements that will assist them in arriving at conclusions. The recorded information in its original collected form is referred to as *raw data*. The word *experiment* is used to describe any process that generates raw data. An example of a statistical experiment might be the tossing of a coin, which consists of only the two outcomes: head or tail.

A set whose elements represent all possible outcomes of an experiment is called the *sample space*, which we will denote by S. The sample space for the coin tossing experiment is $S = \{H, T\}$, where H and T represent head and tail, respectively. An element of a sample space is called a *sample point*. For a sample space that has more than two sample points, it is often possible to group together those points which can be called "success" and those which can be called "failure." An *event* is a subset of a sample space. In our example, both "success" and "failure" are events.

The word *probability* is used as a scientific measure of chance. It quantitatively defines the likelihood of any event resulting from a statistical experiment. Mathematically, probability is a numerical index that can vary between 0, which defines an absolute impossibility, and 1, which defines an absolute certainty.

The probability of any event is the sum of the probabilities of all elements in the event. In an experiment resulting in any one of N different equally likely outcomes, if exactly n of these outcomes correspond to event A, then the probability of event A is

$$P[A] = \frac{n}{N} .$$
(A.1)

Example A.1. Consider a coin and the probability of getting a head or a tail in a single toss. There are two equally likely outcomes (that is, $N = 2$). Therefore, the probability of getting a head or a tail is 1/2. ∎

Example A.2. Consider a coin which is tossed twice. Define a success to be the event that at least one head occurs. Otherwise, it is a failure. What is the probability of success? There are four possible outcomes resulting from the experiment (that is, $N = 4$). The sample space is $S = \{HH, HT, TH, TT\}$. Since the event is $\{HH, HT, TH\}$, the number of ways success can occur is three. Therefore, the probability of success is 3/4. ∎

A.1.2 Some Probability Laws

There are several laws that are useful for computing the probability of occurrence of an event in association with other events. A Venn diagram is a useful tool for understanding the basic concepts of the laws pictorially. We will briefly describe the laws using Venn diagrams. A Venn diagram is normally drawn as a rectangle which represents the sample space S. There may be two or more events, drawn by circles, within this space for which the probabilities must be computed.

The *union* of two sets A and B is the set of elements that belong to A or B or to both. The *intersection* of two sets A and B is the set of elements that are common to A and B. Symbolically, we write $A \cup B$ and $A \cap B$ for the union and intersection of A and B, respectively. In the Venn diagram in Figure A.1(a) the areas representing the union and intersection of A and B are shown. If two sets A and B have no elements in common, they are said to be *mutually exclusive* (see Figure A.1(b) for the corresponding Venn diagram).

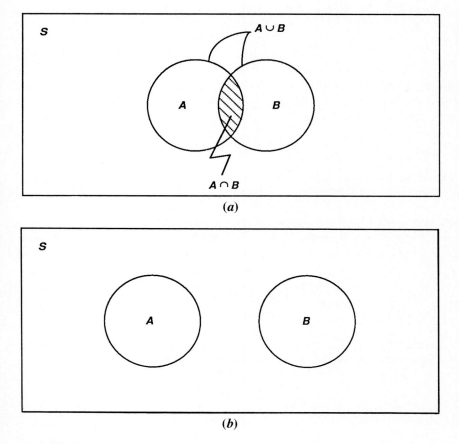

(*a*)

(*b*)

FIGURE A.1
Venn diagrams. (*a*) Union and intersection of A and B. (*b*) Mutually exclusive sets.

OCCURRENCE OF AT LEAST ONE OF TWO EVENTS. If A and B are any two sets, then

$$P[A \cup B] = P[A] + P[B] - P[A \cap B] . \tag{A.2}$$

If A and B are mutually exclusive, then

$$P[A \cup B] = P[A] + P[B] . \tag{A.3}$$

Example A.3. The probability that a student passes mathematics is 2/3, and the probability that he passes computer science is 4/9. If the probability of passing at least one course is 4/5, what is the probability that he will pass both courses? Let M and C denote the events "passing mathematics" and "passing computer science," respectively. Then, by transposing the terms in Equation (A.2) we have

$$P[M \cap C] = P[M] + P[C] - P[M \cup C]$$
$$= 2/3 + 4/9 - 4/5$$
$$= 14/45 . \tag{A.4}$$
∎

COMPLEMENTARY EVENTS. Two events are said to be *complementary* if when one outcome does not occur, the other must. We denote the complement of A by $\overline{A}$. Then, the probability of $\overline{A}$ is

$$P[\overline{A}] = 1 - P[A] . \tag{A.5}$$

Example A.4. When tossing a coin, the outcomes head and tail are complementary since $P[\text{tail}] = 1 - P[\text{head}]$. ∎

CONDITIONAL EVENTS. Conditional events are events which occur conditionally on the occurrence of another event or events. The probability of event A occurring under the condition that event B has occurred, denoted by $P[A \mid B]$, is defined by

$$P[A|B] = \frac{P[A \cap B]}{P[B]} \quad \text{for} \quad P[B] > 0 . \tag{A.6}$$

Example A.5. In Example A.3, the probability that a student will pass computer science, given that he has passed mathematics, is obtained as

$$P[C \mid M] = \frac{P[C \cap M]}{P[M]}$$
$$= \frac{14/45}{2/3} = \frac{7}{15} . \tag{A.7}$$
∎

SIMULTANEOUS OCCURRENCE OF EVENTS. If two events A and B can both occur, then

$$P[A \cap B] = P[A] \, P[B \mid A] . \tag{A.8}$$

Example A.6. To illustrate the use of Equation (A.8), consider a fuse box containing 12 fuses of which three are defective. If two fuses are selected at random and removed from the box in succession without replacing the first, what is the probability that both fuses are defective?

Let A and B be the events that the first and second fuses are defective, respectively. Then, the probability that the first fuse is defective is $P[A] = 1/4 \, (= 3/12)$. Under the condition that the first fuse is defective, the probability that the second fuse is defective is $P[B \mid A] = 2/11$. From Equation (A.8) we have the probability that both fuses are defective as $P[A \cap B] = (1/4)(2/11) = 1/22$. ∎

Two events A and B are said to be *independent* if the probability of occurrence of each event is not influenced by the probability of occurrence of the other, that is,

$$P[A \cap B] = P[A] \, P[B] . \tag{A.9}$$

If in Example A.6 the first fuse is replaced and the fuses thoroughly rearranged before the second is removed, then the probability of a defective fuse on the second selection is still 1/4. That is, $P[B|A] = P[B]$.

BAYES' RULE. The concept of conditional probability can be extended to consider the occurrence of an event A that depends on many mutually exclusive events $B_1, B_2, \ldots, B_n$. The Venn diagram with four such events (that is, $n = 4$) is shown in Figure A.2. The general procedure to obtain the probability of A, using the conditional probabilities, is given by

$$P[A] = \sum_{k=1}^{n} P[A \mid B_k] \, P[B_k] . \tag{A.10}$$

Hence, the conditional probability of each B_i given A is obtained as

$$P[B_i \mid A] = \frac{P[A \mid B_i] \, P[B_i]}{P[A]} . \tag{A.11}$$

This procedure is called *Bayes' rule*.

Example A.7. A certain item is manufactured by two machines. Machine 1 makes 60 percent of the requirement and machine 2 makes 40 percent. From machine 1, 90 percent meet a particular standard and from machine 2 only 80 percent. How many items out of every 100 produced will be up to standard? Given that an item is standard, what is the probability that it was made by machine 2?

Let A be the event that an item is up to standard. Also, let B_1 and B_2 be the events that the item is made by machine 1 and machine 2, respectively. Thus, we have $P[A \mid B_1] = 0.9$ and $P[A \mid B_2] = 0.8$. Applying Equation (A.10) yields

$$P[A] = P[A \mid B_1]P[B_1] + P[A \mid B_2]P[B_2]$$

$$= (0.9)(0.6) + (0.8)(0.4)$$

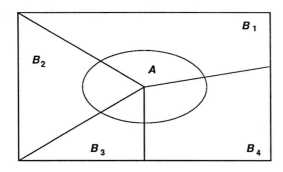

FIGURE A.2
Venn diagram showing the events A, B_1, B_2, B_3, and B_4.

$$= 0.54 + 0.32 = 0.86 .$$

Therefore, out of every 100 items produced $0.86 \times 100 = 86$ items will be up to standard. The probability that the item is made by machine 2 given that it was standard is given by $P[B_2 \mid A]$. From Equation (A.11) we obtain as

$$P[B_2 \mid A] = \frac{P[A \mid B_2] \, P[B_2]}{P[A]}$$

$$= 0.32/0.86 = 0.37 .$$ ∎

A.1.3   Random Variables

Often we are not interested in the details associated with each sample point in a statistical experiment but only in some numerical description of the outcome. A function that is associated with each element in the sample space and whose values are real numbers is called a *random variable*. We will use a capital letter, say X, to denote a random variable and its corresponding small letter, x, for one of its values. Each possible value x of X then represents an event, a subset of the sample space.

Example A.8. When a coin is tossed three times, there are eight sample points in the sample space. If one is concerned with the number of heads that fall, a random variable X, defined as the number of heads, will assign a value of 0, 1, 2, or 3 to each sample point. The possible outcomes and the values x of the random variable X are summarized as follows:

Event	x
HHH	3
HHT	2
HTH	2
THH	2
HTT	1
THT	1
TTH	1
TTT	0

∎

If a sample space contains a countable (or discrete) number of points such as in the case of the coin example, it is called a *discrete random variable*. On the other hand, if the sample points are uncountable (or continuous) such as heights, weights, temperatures, or life periods, we have a *continuous sample space* and a random variable defined over this space is called a *continuous random variable*.

A.1.4 Probability Distributions

A discrete random variable assumes each of its values with a certain probability. In tossing a coin three times, for example, the random variable X representing the number of heads takes the value 2 with probability 3/8 since 3 out of 8 equally likely sample points results in 2 heads and one tail.

Frequently it is convenient to represent all the probabilities of a random variable X by a formula. A function $f(x)$ of the numerical values x is called a *probability distribution* of the discrete random variable X if it represents the probability that the random variable X will take the value x, that is, $f(x) = P[X = x]$. Note that the summation of the probabilities must equal 1, that is,

$$\sum_x f(x) = 1 . \tag{A.12}$$

A further method of presenting data is to use the *cumulative distribution function*. We can find the cumulative distribution function as follows: Order the values of the random variable in ascending order. Starting with the smallest value, sequentially sum the probability of occurrence of each value up to some predetermined value. The cumulative distribution function $F(x)$ represents the probability of the random variable X being less than or equal to x. Mathematically, it is given by

$$F(x) = P[X \leqslant x] = \sum_{t \leqslant x} f(t) . \tag{A.13}$$

Example A.9. Consider the case of tossing a coin three times, as discussed in Example A.8. Let X be a random variable representing the number of heads that fall. The probability distribution and the cumulative distribution function of X are obtained as follows:

x	0	1	2	3
$f(x)$	1/8	3/8	3/8	1/8
$F(x)$	1/8	1/2	7/8	1

Figure A.3 shows plots of $f(x)$ and $F(x)$. ∎

A continuous random variable has a zero probability of being exactly any of its values. Consequently, its probability distribution cannot be given in tabular form. In dealing with continuous variables, $f(x)$ is usually called the *probability*

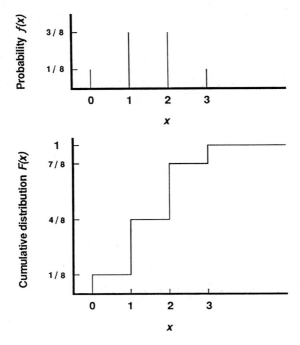

FIGURE A.3
Plots of the probability distribution $f(x)$ and the cumulative distribution function $F(x)$ in Example A.9.

density function. A probability density function $f(x)$ can be derived by differentiating the cumulative distribution function $F(x)$ of a continuous random variable X, that is,

$$f(x) = \frac{dF(x)}{dx}. \tag{A.14}$$

The cumulative distribution function $F(x)$ of a continuous random variable X with probability density function $f(x)$ is then given by

$$F(x) = P[X \leqslant x] = \int_{-\infty}^{x} f(u)\,du. \tag{A.15}$$

Note that the probability of the random variable X being between a and b is

$$P[a < X < b] = \int_{a}^{b} f(x)\,dx = F(b) - F(a) \tag{A.16}$$

In practice, it is often found that random variables follow one of many standard distributions. Typical standard discrete distributions are the binomial and Poisson distributions and typical standard continuous distributions are the normal, exponential, Weibull, and gamma distributions. We illustrate some of the standard distributions in the following examples.

Example A.10. An experiment often consists of repeated trials, each with two possible outcomes, which may be labeled *success* or *failure*. For instance, in testing items as they come off an assembly line where each test or trial may indicate a defective or nondefective item, we may choose to define either outcome as a success. Such an experiment is known as a *binomial experiment*. Each trial, resulting in a success with probability p or a failure with probability q ($= 1 - p$), is called a *Bernoulli trial*. If a binomial experiment consists of n independent Bernoulli trials, then the number X of successes in n trials is called a *binomial random variable*. The probability distribution of X is called the *binomial distribution* and is given by

$$f(x) = \binom{n}{x} p^x q^{n-x}, \quad x = 0, 1, \cdots, n . \tag{A.17}$$

The case of tossing a coin three times (discussed in Example A.8) is a binomial experiment with $n = 3$ and $p = 0.5$. The probability distribution $f(x)$ obtained in Example A.9 can be computed from Equation (A.17) for $x = 0, 1, 2, 3$. ∎

Example A.11. If a random variable X denotes the number of successes occurring during a given time interval or in a specified region, we obtain the probability distribution of X as

$$f(x) = \frac{\lambda^x}{x!} \exp(-\lambda), \quad x = 0, 1, \cdots, n , \tag{A.18}$$

where λ is the average number of successes occurring in the given time interval or specified region. This is known as a *Poisson distribution*. Figure A.4 shows $f(x)$ and $F(x)$ for a Poisson distribution with $\lambda = 1$.

The Poisson distribution is appropriate for describing random behavior in many applications such as in predicting the number of phone calls arriving at a given telephone exchange within a certain period of time, the number of automobile accidents occurring within a certain period of time, and the number of radioactive particles passing through a counter during a certain time interval. ∎

Example A.12. The most important probability distribution in the entire field of statistics is the *normal distribution*. Its graph, called the *normal curve*, is the bell-shaped curve that describes the distribution of so many sets of data that occur in nature, industry, and research. It is often referred to as the *Gaussian distribution*. The mathematical equation for the normal distribution depends on the two parameters μ and σ, its mean and standard deviation, and is given by

$$f(x) = \frac{1}{\sqrt{2\pi\sigma^2}} \exp\left[- \frac{(x - \mu)^2}{2\sigma^2} \right] . \tag{A.19}$$

Figure A.5 illustrates $f(x)$ and $F(x)$ for a normal distribution with the mean μ and the standard deviation σ. ∎

Example A.13. An *exponential distribution* has many applications in statistics, particularly in *reliability theory* and *queueing theory*. The time between customer arrivals, length of time of telephone conversations, and the life of electronic compo-

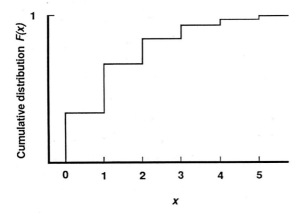

FIGURE A.4
Plots of $f(x)$ and $F(x)$ for a Poisson distribution with $\lambda = 1$.

nents are often assumed to follow an exponential distribution. Its probability density function is given by

$$f(x) = \frac{1}{\theta} \exp\left(-\frac{x}{\theta}\right), \quad x > 0, \tag{A.20}$$

where θ is the parameter representing its mean. Figure A.6 illustrates $f(x)$ given in Equation (A.20) and the corresponding $F(x)$. ∎

A.1.5   Mathematical Expectation

In practice, it is useful to describe the random behavior of a system or a set of data by one or more parameters rather than a distribution. This parametric description can be achieved using numbers, known as the *moments* of a distribution. The most important of these moments is the *expected value*, which is referred to as the *average (mean) value*.

The expected value of any discrete random variable may be obtained by multiplying each value of the random variable by its corresponding probability and summing results. For continuous random variables, the definition of mathematical expectation is the same with summations being replaced by integrals.

Let X be a random variable with probability density function $f(x)$. Then, the expected value of X is

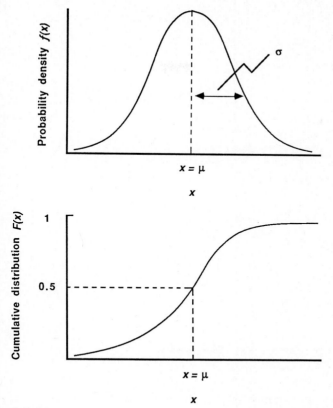

FIGURE A.5
Plots of $f(x)$ and $F(x)$ for a normal distribution with the mean μ and the standard deviation σ.

$$E[X] = \begin{cases} \displaystyle\sum_{x} xf(x) \text{ if } X \text{ is discrete} \\[2em] \displaystyle\int_{-\infty}^{\infty} xf(x)\,dx \text{ if } X \text{ is continuous} . \end{cases} \qquad (A.21)$$

Example A.14. In tossing a coin three times (as discussed in Examples A.8 and A.9), the expected value of the random variable X, representing the number of heads, is

$$E[X] = (0)(1/8) + (1)(3/8) + (2)(3/8) + (3)(1/8)$$
$$= 1.5 .$$ ∎

This simple example produces a result with practical implications. The expected number of heads is found to be 1.5, which is physically impossible to ob-

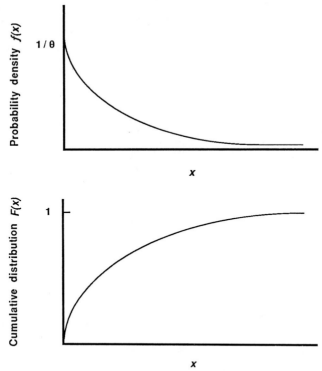

FIGURE A.6
Plots of $f(x)$ and $F(x)$ for an exponential distribution with the mean θ.

tain in a trial. Mathematical expectation is therefore not something that is expected in the ordinary sense but is only the *long-term average* as the number of trials is increased to infinity. This means that if the trial is repeated over and over again, there will, on the average, be 1.5 heads. Figure A.7 illustrates the long-term average.

A.1.6   Variance and Standard Deviation

Although the expected value is probably the most important parameter, the underlying shape of the distribution is lost when only this parameter is considered. The amount of spread or dispersion of a distribution is measured by the second moment about the mean, which is known as the *variance*.

Let $\text{var}[X]$ be the variance of a random variable X. Then, it can be shown (using the properties of mathematical expectation) that

$$\text{var}[X] = E[X - E[X]]^2$$

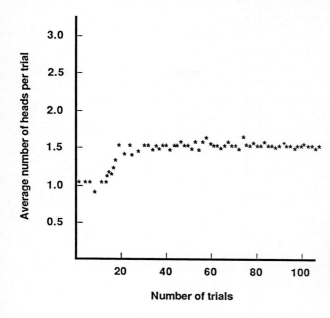

FIGURE A.7
Example of variation of the average number of heads in three coin tosses as the number of trials increases.

$$= E[X^2] - E^2[X] \,. \qquad (A.22)$$

The positive square root of the variance is a measure called the *standard deviation*. If the spread or dispersion of the underlying distribution is small, the values of the variance and the standard deviation are small (see Figure A.5).

In general, the kth moment about the origin of a random variable X with probability density function $f(x)$ is given by

$$E[X^k] = \begin{cases} \displaystyle\sum_x x^k f(x) & \text{if } X \text{ is discrete} \\[2em] \displaystyle\int_{-\infty}^{\infty} x^k f(x)\,dx & \text{if } X \text{ is continuous}. \end{cases} \qquad (A.23)$$

Example A.15. In Example A.14, we showed $E[X] = 1.5$. Now

$$E[X^2] = (0)(1/8) + (1)(3/8) + (4)(3/8) + (9)(1/8)$$

$$= 3 \,.$$

Therefore,

$$\text{var}[X] = 3 - (1.5)^2$$

$$= 0.75 \,.$$

The standard deviation of X is $\sqrt{\text{var}[X]} = 0.87$. ∎

A.2 BASIC STOCHASTIC PROCESSES

A.2.1 Definitions

We often encounter situations in which observations are made over a period of time and are influenced by change or random effects, not just at a single instant but throughout the entire interval. This situation is called a *stochastic* (or *random*) *process*. Some examples of a stochastic process are the daily variations in the size of a certain company's inventory, variations in the quality of the products of a factory, and variations in stock market activity.

A stochastic process is a sequence of random variables whose values may vary discretely or continuously with respect to time t. A stochastic process for which time is measured discretely or continuously is called a *discrete* or *continuous time stochastic process*, denoted by $\{X_n, n = 1, 2,...\}$ or $\{X(t), t \geq 0\}$ respectively.

The set of all possible values for the random variable $X(t)$ is called the *state space*. The value assumed by $X(t)$ is called the *state of the process at time t*. Changes of state are called *transitions*. A single sequence of observations of $X(t)$ is called a *realization* of the process. The foregoing is also true for discrete time stochastic processes.

If the state space of a stochastic process is discrete (or continuous), it is a *discrete* (or *continuous*) *state process*. In the following discussions we assume all state spaces to be discrete. These processes are frequently called *random chains*.

A.2.2 Two-State Markov Chain

Consider a discrete-time stochastic process $\{X_n, n = 1, 2,...\}$. If $X_n = i$, then the process is said to be in state i at time n. Suppose that when the process is in state i, there is a fixed probability P_{ij} that it will next be in state j, that is,

$$P[X_{n+1} = j \mid X_n = i, X_{n-1} = i_{n-1}, \cdots, X_1 = i_1]$$

$$= P[X_{n+1} = j \mid X_n = i]$$

$$= P_{ij} . \tag{A.24}$$

In other words, the conditional distribution of any future state X_{n+1}, given the past states $X_1, ..., X_{n-1}$ and the present state X_n, is independent of the past states and depends only on the present state. Such a stochastic process is known as a *Markov chain*. The probability P_{ij}, called a *one-step transition probability*, represents the probability that it will next make a transition into state j when in state i. Note that in the foregoing discussion we assumed that the transition probabilities P_{ij} are independent of time. In this case the process X_n is called a *homogeneous* (or *stationary*) process. In general, P_{ij} may depend on time, for which X_n is said to be *nonhomogeneous* (or *nonstationary*).

The simplest example of this process would be one in which the state space consists of only two states, which is called a *two-state Markov chain*. Consider a piece of equipment that can be in one of two conditions: running or under repair. We observe the condition of this equipment every hour.

Let $X_n = 0$ if the equipment is running at the nth observation and $X_n = 1$ if it is under repair. Assume that the equipment will fail during a 1 hr period with probability α and be repaired within 1 hr with probability β.

The one-step transition probabilities for the process $\{X_n, n = 1, 2,...\}$ are then given by $P_{00} = 1 - \alpha$, $P_{01} = \alpha$, $P_{10} = \beta$, and $P_{11} = 1 - \beta$ or in terms of a matrix

$$\mathbf{P} = \begin{bmatrix} P_{00} & P_{01} \\ P_{10} & P_{11} \end{bmatrix} = \begin{bmatrix} 1-\alpha & \alpha \\ \beta & 1-\beta \end{bmatrix}. \tag{A.25}$$

To study the behavior of the process, we wish to evaluate all probabilities of the form

$$P_{ij}^{(n)} = P[X_{k+n} = j \mid X_k = i], \quad n \geq 1, i, j = 0, 1. \tag{A.26}$$

This is the nth *step transition probability* representing the probability that the process in state i will be in state j after n additional transitions. The *Chapman-Kolmogorov equations* provide a method for computing these probabilities as

$$P_{ij}^{(n+m)} = \sum_{k=0}^{1} P_{ik}^{(n)} P_{kj}^{(m)} \tag{A.27}$$

or in the matrix form

$$\mathbf{P}^{(n+m)} = \mathbf{P}^{(n)} \mathbf{P}^{(m)}. \tag{A.28}$$

Hence, in particular,

$$\mathbf{P}^{(2)} = \mathbf{P} \, \mathbf{P}. \tag{A.29}$$

Example A.16. Suppose $\alpha = 1/5$ and $\beta = 3/5$. That is, the equipment will fail during a 1 hr period with probability 1/5 and be repaired within 1 hr with probability 3/5. Then, we obtain the one-step transition probability matrix from Equation (A.25) as

$$\mathbf{P} = \begin{bmatrix} 4/5 & 1/5 \\ 3/5 & 2/5 \end{bmatrix}.$$

Figure A.8 illustrates a realization of the X_n process. For instance, there is a transition from state 0 to state 1 at $n = 3$, indicating that the equipment failed at the end of the 3 hr period. The repair was completed within the next 1 hr period since there is a transition from state 1 to state 0 at $n = 4$.

A transition diagram is a frequently used tool to illustrate transitions among states, where each state is represented by a node and a transition is represented by a directed edge with the corresponding probability. Figure A.9 shows a transition diagram for the X_n process.

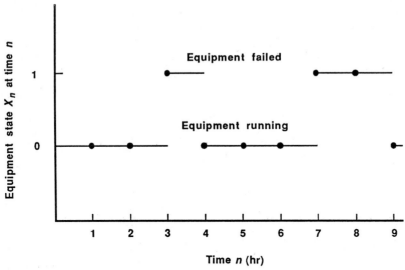

FIGURE A.8
A realization of the X_n process in Example A.16.

Using Equation (A.29), we obtain the two-step transition probability matrix as follows:

$$\mathbf{P}^{(2)} = \mathbf{P}\,\mathbf{P}$$

$$= \begin{bmatrix} 4/5 & 1/5 \\ 3/5 & 2/5 \end{bmatrix} \begin{bmatrix} 4/5 & 1/5 \\ 3/5 & 2/5 \end{bmatrix}$$

$$= \begin{bmatrix} 0.76 & 0.24 \\ 0.72 & 0.28 \end{bmatrix}.$$

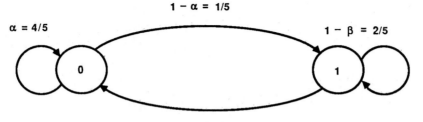

FIGURE A.9
A transition diagram for the X_n process in Example A.16.

Therefore, for example, the probability that the equipment is operating at the end of a 2 hr period, when it was initially operating, is $P_{00}^{(2)} = 0.76$.

Similarly, for $n = 3$,

$$\mathbf{P}^{(3)} = \mathbf{P}^{(2)}\,\mathbf{P}$$

$$= \begin{bmatrix} 0.76 & 0.24 \\ 0.72 & 0.28 \end{bmatrix} \begin{bmatrix} 4/5 & 1/5 \\ 3/5 & 2/5 \end{bmatrix}$$

$$= \begin{bmatrix} 0.752 & 0.248 \\ 0.744 & 0.256 \end{bmatrix}$$

Hence, the probability that the equipment is operating at the end of a 3 hour period is $P_{00}^{(3)} = 0.752$.

In Figure A.10 we plot the n-step transition probabilities against n. As n increases, the probability of being running or under repair tends to approach a fixed value, regardless of the initial conditions. ∎

We now focus attention on the behavior of the state probabilities $P_j^{(n)}$, the probabilities that the process is in state j at the nth observation, for large n. Let π_j be the limiting probability for state j, that is,

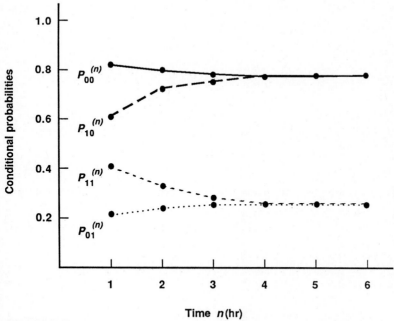

FIGURE A.10
Plots of the n-step transition probabilities versus n for the two-state Markov chain in Example A.16.

$$\pi_j = \lim_{n \to \infty} P_j^{(n)} , \tag{A.30}$$

which is often referred to as the *steady-state probability*. In designing a physical system, there are often "start up" effects that are different from what can be expected in the "long run." The "long run" behavior is described by the limiting probabilities π_j. The limiting probability π_j might be interpreted as the portion of time that the process will be in state j in the long run.

If $\pi_j = \lim_{n \to \infty} P_{ij}^{(n)}$ exists and is independent of the initial state, then π_j is the unique solution of

$$\pi_j = \sum_{i=0}^{1} \pi_i P_{ij}, \quad j = 0, 1 \tag{A.31}$$

and

$$\sum_{j=0}^{1} \pi_j = 1 . \tag{A.32}$$

Example A.17. In Example A.16 the steady-state probabilities are obtained as follows. From Equation (A.31)

$$\pi_0 = \pi_0(4/5) + \pi_1(3/5) ,$$

$$\pi_1 = \pi_0(1/5) + \pi_1(2/5) .$$

After rearrangement, these equations become

$$(1/5)\pi_0 - (3/5)\pi_1 = 0 ,$$

$$- (1/5)\pi_0 + (3/5)\pi_1 = 0 .$$

Since one equation is simply the negative of the other, the system gives only one condition, that is,

$$\pi_0 = 3\pi_1 . \tag{A.33}$$

Note that this is a probability vector, that is, the sum of its components equals 1. Thus

$$\pi_0 + \pi_1 = 1 . \tag{A.34}$$

Solving Equations (A.33) and (A.34) simultaneously yields $\pi_0 = 3/4$ and $\pi_1 = 1/4$. Hence, the long run portion of time the equipment is running is 75 percent, which is often called the *availability*. ■

A.2.3   Poisson Process

A stochastic process $\{N(t), t \geq 0\}$ in which $N(t)$ represents the number of "events" that occur up to time t is called a *counting process*. Some examples of counting processes are the number of customers who enter a particular store by time t, the number of long-distance telephone calls that have been made between two cities by time t, and the number of children who were born by time t.

A counting process is said to have *independent increments* if the numbers of events that occur in disjoint intervals are independent. For example, this means that the number of customers who entered a store between 8 A.M. and 10 A.M. [that is, $N(10) - N(8)$] is independent of the number of customers entering between 10 A.M. and noon [that is, $N(12) - N(10)$]. In other words, the future value of $N(12)$ depends only on the present state $N(10)$ and is independent of the past state $N(8)$. This is equivalent to the Markov property discussed in Section A.2.2.

A counting process is said to have *stationary increments* if the distribution of the number of events which occur in any interval of time depends only on the length of the interval. In the example of counting the number of customers entering a store, the assumption of stationary increments would be reasonable if there were no times of day (for example, a rush hour) at which people were more likely to enter the store.

A counting process $\{N(t), t \geq 0\}$ is said to be a *Poisson process* with rate λ if the following conditions are satisfied:

1. No events have occurred at time $t = 0$, that is $N(0) = 0$.
2. The process has stationary and independent increments.
3. The probability that an event will occur in a small interval Δt is $\lambda \Delta t + o(\Delta t)$.[1]
4. The probability that more than one event will occur in a small interval Δt is $o(\Delta t)$.

The Poisson process provides a good approximation to many real-world situations such as telephone traffic, orders to a factory, software failures, breakdown of machinery, arrivals on a queue, and insurance claims.

We now derive the Poisson process using the stated assumptions.

Let $P_n(t)$ be the probability that n events have occurred by time t. That is,

$$P_n(t) = P[N(t) = n] . \tag{A.35}$$

A differential equation for $P_0(t)$ can be derived in the following manner. For a small interval Δt we have

$$P_0(t + \Delta t) = P[N(t + \Delta t) = 0]$$

$$= P[N(t) = 0 \text{ and } N(t + \Delta t) - N(t) = 0]$$

---

[1]The function $o(\Delta t)$ is defined as $\lim_{\Delta t \to 0} (o(\Delta t)/\Delta t) = 0$.

$$= P[N(t) = 0] \, P[N(t + \Delta t) - N(t) = 0]$$

$$= P[N(t) = 0]P[N(\Delta t) = 0] \, , \tag{A.36}$$

where the last two equations follow from assumption 2. Combining assumptions 3 and 4 yields $P[N(\Delta t) = 0] = 1 - \lambda \Delta t + o(\Delta t)$. Hence,

$$P_0(t + \Delta t) = P_0(t)[1 - \lambda \Delta t + o(\Delta t)] \tag{A.37}$$

or

$$\frac{P_0(t + \Delta t) - P_0(t)}{\Delta t} = -\lambda P_0(t) + \frac{o(\Delta t)}{\Delta t} \, . \tag{A.38}$$

Letting $\Delta t \to 0$ we obtain the differential equation

$$\frac{dP_0(t)}{dt} = -\lambda P_0(t) \tag{A.39}$$

or equivalently

$$\frac{1}{P_0(t)} \frac{dP_0(t)}{dt} = -\lambda \, . \tag{A.40}$$

Integrating both sides yields

$$\ln P_0(t) = -\lambda t + C \, , \tag{A.41}$$

where C is the constant of integration. From assumption 1, $P_0(0) = 1$ and hence $C = 0$. Thus

$$P_0(t) = \exp(-\lambda t), \tag{A.42}$$

which is the probability of zero events by time t.

Similarly, for $n > 0$, we have

$$P_n(t + \Delta t) = P[N(t + \Delta t) = n]$$

$$= P[N(t) = n \text{ and } N(t + \Delta t) - N(t) = 0]$$

$$+ P[N(t) = n - 1 \text{ and } N(t + \Delta t) - N(t) = 1]$$

$$+ \sum_{k=2}^{n} P[N(t) = n - k \text{ and } N(t + \Delta t) - N(t) = k] \, . \tag{A.43}$$

Applying assumptions 2, 3, and 4 results in

$$P_n(t + \Delta t) = P_n(t)P_0(\Delta t) + P_{n-1}(t)P_1(\Delta t)$$

$$= (1 - \lambda\Delta t)P_n(t) + \lambda\Delta t P_{n-1}(t) + o(\Delta t) . \tag{A.44}$$

Thus,

$$\frac{P_n(t + \Delta t) - P_n(t)}{\Delta t} = -\lambda P_n(t) + \lambda P_{n-1}(t) + \frac{o(\Delta t)}{\Delta t} \tag{A.45}$$

and letting $\Delta t \to 0$ yields the differential equation

$$\frac{dP_n(t)}{dt} = -\lambda P_n(t) + \lambda P_{n-1}(t) \tag{A.46}$$

or equivalently

$$\exp(\lambda t) \left[\frac{dP_n(t)}{dt} + \lambda P_n(t) \right] = \lambda \exp(\lambda t) P_{n-1}(t) . \tag{A.47}$$

Hence,

$$\frac{d}{dt} [\exp(\lambda t)P_n(t)] = \lambda \exp(\lambda t)P_{n-1}(t) . \tag{A.48}$$

Substituting Equation (A.42) into Equation (A.48) with $n = 1$, we obtain

$$\frac{d}{dt} [\exp(\lambda t)P_1(t)] = \lambda \tag{A.49}$$

or

$$\exp(\lambda t)P_1(t) = \lambda t + C . \tag{A.50}$$

Since $P_1(0) = 0$, we have $C = 0$ and hence

$$P_1(t) = \lambda t \exp(-\lambda t) , \tag{A.51}$$

which is the probability of one event occurring by time t.

This can be substituted again into Equation (A.48) with $n = 2$, so that the system can be solved recursively. The general solution is given by

$$P_n(t) = \frac{(\lambda t)^n}{n!} \exp(-\lambda t), \quad n = 0, 1, \cdots . \tag{A.52}$$

Note that the number of events in time t has a Poisson distribution with mean λt and variance λt. The mean number of events per unit time is λ.

Example A.18. Customers arrive at a service facility according to a Poisson process with mean rate 5 per hour. It is assumed that none of the customers will leave the system. Suppose that the system was empty at 8 A.M. Find the following:

1. probability of having 7 customers in the system by 10 A.M., given that there were 3 customers at 9 A.M.
2. average number in the system at 9:30 A.M. and 11 A.M.

Let $N(t)$ represent the number of customers who arrive at the service facility by time t, where time is measured in hours from 8 A.M. Then, $N(t)$ is a Poisson process with $\lambda = 5$.

1. Since the Poisson process has independent and stationary increments, we have

$$P[N(2) = 7 \mid N(1) = 3]$$

$$= P[N(2) - N(1) = 4]$$

$$= P[N(2 - 1) = 4]$$

$$= \frac{\lambda^4}{4!} \exp(-\lambda)$$

$$= \frac{5^4}{4!} \exp(-5)$$

$$= 0.175 .$$

2. Since $E[N(t)] = \lambda t$, the average number in the system is $(5)(1.5) = 7.5$ at 9:30 A.M. and $(5)(3) = 15$ at 11 A.M.   ∎

There are other ways to characterize a Poisson process. Suppose that T_n represents the random variable corresponding to the time between the $(n-1)$th and nth events. In particular, T_1 is the time until the first event. Since the event $(T_1 > t)$ takes place if and only if no events occur in the interval $[0, t]$, we have

$$P[T_1 > t] = P[N(t) = 0]$$

$$= \exp(-\lambda t) . \tag{A.53}$$

Thus, T_1 has the cumulative distribution function

$$P[T_1 \leqslant t] = 1 - \exp(-\lambda t) \tag{A.54}$$

and the probability density function

$$f(t) = \lambda \exp(-\lambda t) . \tag{A.55}$$

This distribution can be recognized as the exponential distribution with mean $1/\lambda$ and variance $1/\lambda^2$.

By a similar argument, it can be shown that the times $\{T_n; n = 1, 2,...\}$ between events in a Poisson process are all exponentially distributed with the same parameter λ. This fact provides an alternative characterization of the Poisson process.

The exponential distribution has the unique property that, at any point in time, the time until the next event occurs is independent of the time elapsed since the occurrence of the last event. This property is usually referred to as "lack of memory" or "forgetfulness" of the exponential distribution.

Example A.19. In Example A.18, suppose a customer arrived at the service facility at 10 A.M.

1. What is the probability of the next customer arriving by 10:10 A.M.?
2. What is the probability of the next customer arriving before 10:10 A.M. and after 10:05 A.M.?
3. What is mean time to the next arrival?

Note that the times between events in the Poisson process are all exponentially distributed with the same parameter λ, where $\lambda = 5$ customer/hr. Let T represent the time to the next arrival since 10 A.M. Then,

1. $P[T \leq 10/60] = 1 - \exp[-(5)(10/60)]$
$= 0.565.$
2. $P[5/60 < T \leq 10/60]$
$= \{1 - \exp[-(5)(10/60)]\} - \{1 - \exp[-(5)(5/60)]\}$
$= 0.224.$
3. $E[T] = 1/\lambda$
$= 1/5$ hr or 12 min.   ∎

A.3. BASIC STATISTICS

A.3.1 Sampling Theory

Statisticians work primarily with numerical observations. The totality of observations relevant to anything of interest, whether finite or infinite, is called a *population*. The number of observations in the population is the *size* of the population, which may be finite or infinite. Some finite populations are so large that in theory they can be assumed to be infinite.

Each observation in a population is a value of a random variable with some probability function $f(x)$ of known functional form but depending on an unknown constant (or constants). Each such constant is called a *parameter*. A basic problem of statistics is to make inferences about the parameter from the information provided by a sample selected for the population. In order for inferences to be accurate, the sample should be representative of the population.

A *random sample* consists of the observations made independently and at random. We can obtain a random sample of size n from the population $f(x)$ by repeating the experiment that defines the population n independent times under the same conditions. Let $X_1, \ldots, X_n$ be a random sample of size n from the population $f(x)$. Then, its joint probability distribution is given by

$$f(x_1, \cdots, x_n) = f(x_1) \cdots f(x_n) . \qquad (A.56)$$

A value computed from a sample is called a *statistic*. The statistic would be expected to vary somewhat from sample to sample since many random samples are possible from the same population. Hence, a statistic is a random variable.

One of the most commonly used statistics for measuring the center of a set of data is the *mean*. If $X_1, \ldots, X_n$ represent a random sample of size n, the *sample mean* is defined by the statistic

$$\bar{X} = \frac{1}{n} \sum_{i=1}^{n} X_i \ . \tag{A.57}$$

A measure of variability can be represented by the *sample variance*, defined by the statistic

$$S^2 = \frac{1}{n-1} \sum_{i=1}^{n} \left(X_i - \bar{X} \right)^2 . \tag{A.58}$$

The *sample standard deviation*, denoted by S, is defined to be the positive square root of the sample variance.

The probability distribution of a statistic is called a *sampling distribution*. Some important sampling distributions of frequently used statistics are the *normal distribution, chi-square distribution, t distribution*, and *F distribution*. The standard deviation of the sampling distribution of a statistic is called the *standard error* of the statistic.

A.3.2 Point Estimation

An estimation of a population parameter may be given as a *point estimation* or as an *interval estimation*. A point estimate is a single value of a statistic. For example, the value $\bar{x}$ of the statistic $\bar{X}$, computed from a sample of size n, is a point estimate of the population mean.

The statistic that is used to obtain a point estimate is called an *estimator*. An estimator is not expected to estimate the parameter without error. An estimator is said to be *unbiased* if the sampling distribution has a mean equal to the parameter estimated. The basic problem of estimation is reduced to searching for an estimator that is unbiased and has the smallest variance.

A frequently used method of finding an estimator is the *method of maximum likelihood estimation*. The principle of maximum likelihood assumes that the sample is representative of the population and chooses as the estimate the value of the parameter that maximizes the probability density function.

Let $X_1, \ldots, X_n$ be a random sample of size n from the population $f(x;\theta)$, where θ is a parameter. Then, the joint probability density function is given by

$$f(x_1, \cdots, x_n; \theta) = \prod_{i=1}^{n} f(x_i; \theta) \ . \tag{A.59}$$

We will treat the x's as if they were constants and look at this joint probability density function as a function of θ denoted by $L(\theta \mid x_1, \ldots, x_n)$, which is called the *likelihood function*. If the likelihood function is maximized at $\theta = \hat{\theta}$, then $\hat{\theta}$ is called a *maximum likelihood estimate* (MLE) of θ.

It is convenient to work with the logarithm of the likelihood function. Since the logarithm is a monotone function, it suffices to maximize $\ln L(\theta \mid x_1, \ldots, x_n)$. If it is a differentiable function of θ, we obtain the *likelihood equation*

$$\frac{d \ln L(\theta \mid x_1, \cdots, x_n)}{d\theta} = 0 , \qquad (A.60)$$

whose root is the MLE.

In many important cases there is a unique MLE. Sometimes, however, the likelihood equation may be complicated and difficult to solve explicitly. In that case one may have to resort to some numerical procedure to obtain the estimate.

We will now apply the method of MLE to a couple of concrete examples.

Example A.20. Let $X_1, \ldots, X_n$ be a random sample from a Poisson distribution with a mean of λ [see Equation (A.18) for the probability distribution]. Then, we obtain the likelihood function as

$$L(\lambda \mid x_1, \cdots, x_n) = \exp(-n\lambda) \; \frac{1}{\prod\limits_{i=1}^{n} x_i!} \; \lambda^{\sum\limits_{i=1}^{n} x_i} .$$

Hence we have the log-likelihood:

$$\ln L(\lambda \mid x_1, \cdots, x_n) = -n\lambda - \ln\left[\prod_{i=1}^{n} x_i!\right] + \left[\sum_{i=1}^{n} x_i\right] \ln \lambda .$$

Therefore, from Equation (A.60) the likelihood equation becomes

$$-n + \frac{1}{\lambda} \sum_{i=1}^{n} x_i = 0 ,$$

which gives $\lambda = \bar{x}$. Thus, $\bar{x}$ is the MLE of λ. ∎

Example A.21. Suppose that $X_1, \ldots, X_n$ is a random sample from a normal distribution with a mean of μ and a variance of σ^2, where σ^2 is known [see Equation (A.19) for the probability distribution]. Then, we obtain the log-likelihood function as

$$\ln L(\mu \mid x_1, \cdots, x_n) = -n \ln \sqrt{2\pi} - n \ln \sqrt{\sigma^2} - \frac{1}{2\sigma^2} \sum_{i=1}^{n} (x_i - \mu)^2 .$$

The likelihood equation becomes

$$\frac{1}{\sigma^2} \sum_{i=1}^{n} (x_i - \mu) = 0 ,$$

which yields $\mu = \bar{x}$. Thus, $\bar{x}$ is the MLE of μ. ∎

A.3.3 Interval Estimation

An interval estimate of some unknown parameter, say θ, is an interval of the form $a < \theta < b$, where a and b depend on the point estimate $\hat{\theta}$ for the particular sample chosen and also on the sampling distribution of the estimator $\hat{\Theta}$. The interval estimate represents, by its length, the accuracy of the point estimate.

Different samples yield different $\hat{\theta}$ values and therefore produce different interval estimates of the parameter θ. Some of these intervals will contain θ and others will not. The distribution of $\hat{\Theta}$ enables us to compute the end points, a and b, so that any specified fraction $1 - \alpha$, $0 < \alpha < 1$, of the intervals computed from all possible samples contain the parameter θ. In other words, we are $100(1 - \alpha)$ percent confident that the computed interval contains the parameter θ. The interval computed from a particular sample is called a $100(1 - \alpha)$percent *confidence interval*. The fraction $1 - \alpha$ is called the *confidence coefficient*, and the end points, a and b, are called the *confidence limits*.

We will illustrate the method in the following. Suppose that a random sample of size n is selected from a normal population with mean μ and variance σ^2, where the variance is assumed to be known. Then, we can find a confidence interval for μ by considering the sampling distribution of $\overline{X}$.

It can be easily shown that $\overline{X}$ is normally distributed with mean μ and variance σ^2/n. Using the transformation

$$Z = \frac{\overline{X} - \mu}{\sigma / \sqrt{n}}, \tag{A.61}$$

the new random variable Z has a normal distribution with mean 0 and variance 1. This distribution is called a *standard normal distribution*. If we let $\kappa_{1-\alpha/2}$ denote the value above which an area of $\alpha/2$ is found (the κ values for given α are available in tabular form in most statistics books), we have

$$P[-\kappa_{1-\alpha/2} < Z < \kappa_{1-\alpha/2}] = 1 - \alpha. \tag{A.62}$$

Substituting Equation (A.61) into Equation (A.62), multiplying each term in the inequality by $\sigma/\sqrt{n}$, subtracting $\overline{X}$ from each term, and then multiplying by -1, we obtain

$$P\left[\overline{X} - \kappa_{1-\alpha/2}\frac{\sigma}{\sqrt{n}} < \mu < \overline{X} + \kappa_{1-\alpha/2}\frac{\sigma}{\sqrt{n}}\right] = 1 - \alpha. \tag{A.63}$$

Thus, for the mean $\bar{x}$ computed from the raw data, we can find the $100(1 - \alpha)$ percent confidence interval as

$$\bar{x} - \kappa_{1-\alpha/2}\frac{\sigma}{\sqrt{n}} < \mu < \bar{x} + \kappa_{1-\alpha/2}\frac{\sigma}{\sqrt{n}}. \tag{A.64}$$

REMARKS. For small samples selected from a non-normal population, it is generally difficult to obtain an exact confidence interval. However, for samples of size $n \geq 30$, regardless of the population distributions, sampling theory usually guarantees good results from the normal approximation. To compute a $100(1 - \alpha)$ percent confidence interval for μ, we assumed that the population standard deviation was known. Since this is not the case in general, we replace σ by the sample standard deviation s, provided $n \geq 30$.

Example A.22. Based on a random sample of 100 batteries in a large factory, we compute an average life of 394 days and a standard deviation of 46 days. Find 95 percent and 99 percent confidence intervals for the population mean.

The point estimate of μ is $\bar{x} = 394$. Since the sample size is large ($n \geq 30$), we can approximate the population standard deviation σ by $s = 46$. Note $\kappa_{0.975} = 1.96$. Hence, using Equation (A.64) for $\alpha = 0.5$, we find the 95 percent confidence interval for μ as

$$394 - (1.96)\left[\frac{46}{\sqrt{100}}\right] < \mu < 394 + (1.96)\left[\frac{46}{\sqrt{100}}\right] ,$$

which reduces to

$$385 < \mu < 403 .$$

Similarly, to compute a 99 percent confidence interval we find $\kappa_{0.995} = 2.575$ and hence the 99 percent confidence interval is

$$394 - (2.575)\left[\frac{46}{\sqrt{100}}\right] < \mu < 394 + (2.575)\left[\frac{46}{\sqrt{100}}\right]$$

or simply

$$382 < \mu < 406 .$$

Note that a longer interval is required to estimate μ with a higher degree of accuracy. ∎

A.3.4 Simple Linear Regression

Often in practice, there exists some inherent relationship among variables. It is of interest to develop a method for estimating the relationship among the variables. In general, there is a single *dependent variable* or *response*, that is uncontrolled in an experiment. This response depends on one or more *independent variables* that are often controlled in the experiment.

Simple linear regression analysis is a method for predicting, or estimating, the value of a single random variable Y from a single measurement x when certain conditions of linearity can be assumed. In many applied problems, a straight-line relationship can describe the dependence of one variable on another. There are usually three steps involved in the analysis:

1. preliminary examination of sample data,
2. estimation of a regression line, and
3. computation of confidence limits.

We will examine each step in more detail.

PRELIMINARY EXAMINATION OF SAMPLE DATA. In a linear regression analysis we must first conduct a preliminary examination of sample data to determine the validity of an assumption of linear dependence. Suppose that the data consist of a set $[(x_i, y_i), i = 1, \ldots, n]$ of n paired observations of measurement x and measurement y. Then the simplest method of examining the data is to develop a *scatter diagram* of the data by plotting the coordinates $(x_1, y_1), \ldots, (x_n, y_n)$ of the n paired measurements. The scatter diagram provides a visual display of the relationship of the data. If the points in the scatter diagram seem to fall along a line, there is an indication that values of y are, on the average, linearly dependent on values of x. Hence, the data are appropriate for a linear regression analysis.

ESTIMATION OF A REGRESSION LINE. If a preliminary examination of sample data suggests that it is reasonable to assume a linear dependence of Y on x, we postulate that the mean of Y is linearly related to x. Therefore, we have

$$E[Y] = \alpha + \beta x , \tag{A.65}$$

where α and β are parameters to be estimated from the data. Note that α and β represent the intercept and slope of the line, respectively. Hence, we can express the observation y_i as

$$y_i = \alpha + \beta x_i + \epsilon_i, \quad i = 1, \cdots, n , \tag{A.66}$$

where each ϵ_i represents a random variable with mean zero and the same variance σ^2. Note that ϵ_i is referred to as a *random error*. The most frequently used method for estimating the parameters is the *method of least squares*.

The principal use of the method of least squares is to determine the "best fit" of a linear function to the data $\{(x_i, y_i), i = 1, \ldots, n\}$. It minimizes the sum of the squares of the deviations between what we expect and what we actually observe. More precisely, we determine the parameters so that the *sum of squares of errors*,

$$S = \sum_{i=1}^{n} \epsilon_i^2$$

$$= \sum_{i=1}^{n} [y_i - (\alpha + \beta x_i)]^2 , \tag{A.67}$$

is minimized.

Differentiating S with respect to α and β, we have

$$\frac{\partial S}{\partial \alpha} = - 2 \sum_{i=1}^{n} (y_i - \alpha - \beta x_i) \tag{A.68}$$

$$\frac{\partial S}{\partial \beta} = - 2 \sum_{i=1}^{n} (y_i - \alpha - \beta x_i) x_i . \tag{A.69}$$

Setting the partial derivatives equal to 0 and rearranging the terms, we obtain the equations (called the *normal equations*)

$$n\alpha + \beta \sum_{i=1}^{n} x_i = \sum_{i=1}^{n} y_i \tag{A.70}$$

$$\alpha \sum_{i=1}^{n} x_i + \beta \sum_{i=1}^{n} x_i^2 = \sum_{i=1}^{n} x_i y_i . \tag{A.71}$$

The solutions of the normal equations are the *least squares estimates*, denoted by $\hat{\alpha}$ and $\hat{\beta}$, respectively. Equations (A.70) and (A.71) yield

$$\hat{\beta} = \frac{n \sum_{i=1}^{n} x_i y_i - \left[\sum_{i=1}^{n} x_i \right] \left[\sum_{i=1}^{n} y_i \right]}{n \sum_{i=1}^{n} x_i^2 - \left[\sum_{i=1}^{n} x_i \right]^2} \tag{A.72}$$

and

$$\hat{\alpha} = \bar{y} - \hat{\beta} \bar{x} , \tag{A.73}$$

where $\bar{x} = (1/n) \sum_{i=1}^{n} x_i$ and $\bar{y} = (1/n) \sum_{i=1}^{n} y_i$. Therefore, we obtain the estimated response $\hat{y}$ from the regression line as

$$\hat{y} = \hat{\alpha} + \hat{\beta} x . \tag{A.74}$$

COMPUTATION OF CONFIDENCE LIMITS. Having obtained a least squares estimate of the regression line, the next step of a regression analysis is the computation of confidence limits for the intercept, slope, or the regression line that are useful in evaluating the accuracy of the estimate.

In addition to the assumption that the random error ϵ_i in Equation (A.66) is a random variable with mean zero, we assume ϵ_i's to be independent and normally distributed with the *same variance* σ^2. Then, using the *residual*, that is the difference between the data and the regression line

$$e_i = y_i - \hat{y}_i$$

$$= y_i - \hat{\alpha} - \hat{\beta} x_i , \tag{A.75}$$

we can estimate the variance of the random errors as

$$\hat{\sigma}^2 = \frac{1}{n - 2} \sum_{i=1}^{n} e_i^2 , \tag{A.76}$$

which reflects the variation about the regression line. Note that we divide by $n - 2$ in Equation (A.76) because the substitution of $\hat{\alpha}$ and $\hat{\beta}$ for α and β in Equation (A.75) reduces the *degrees of freedom* by 2.

We will summarize the procedures for computing confidence limits for the intercept, the slope, the regression line, and the actual response in the following.

The derivation can be found in most statistics books [for example, Walpole and Myers (1972) and Rohatgi (1976)].

1. A $100(1 - \alpha)$ percent confidence interval for the intercept α is given by

$$\hat{\alpha} - \frac{t_{\alpha/2;\, n-2}\, \hat{\sigma}\, \sqrt{\sum\limits_{i=1}^{n} x_i^2}}{\sqrt{n\, S_{xx}}} < \alpha < \hat{\alpha} + \frac{t_{\alpha/2;\, n-2}\, \hat{\sigma}\, \sqrt{\sum\limits_{i=1}^{n} x_i^2}}{\sqrt{n\, S_{xx}}}, \qquad \text{(A.77)}$$

where

$$S_{xx} = \sum_{i=1}^{n} (x_i - \bar{x})^2. \qquad \text{(A.78)}$$

Note that $t_{\alpha/2;n-2}$ represents the $\alpha/2$ percentile of the t distribution with $n - 2$ degrees of freedom.

2. A $100(1 - \alpha)$ percent confidence interval for the slope β is given by

$$\hat{\beta} - \frac{t_{\alpha/2;\, n-2}\hat{\sigma}}{\sqrt{S_{xx}}} < \beta < \hat{\beta} + \frac{t_{\alpha/2;\, n-2}\hat{\sigma}}{\sqrt{S_{xx}}}. \qquad \text{(A.79)}$$

3. For each value x_0, a $100(1 - \alpha)$ percent confidence interval for the mean response $E[Y] = \alpha + \beta x_0$ is given by

$$\hat{y}_0 - t_{\alpha/2;\, n-2}\, \hat{\sigma}\, \sqrt{\frac{1}{n} + \frac{(x_0 - \bar{x})^2}{S_{xx}}} < E[Y]$$

$$< \hat{y}_0 + t_{\alpha/2;\, n-2}\, \hat{\sigma}\, \sqrt{\frac{1}{n} + \frac{(x_0 - \bar{x})^2}{S_{xx}}}, \qquad \text{(A.80)}$$

where

$$\hat{y}_0 = \hat{\alpha} + \hat{\beta} x_0. \qquad \text{(A.81)}$$

4. For each value x_0, a $100(1 - \alpha)$ percent confidence interval for a single response y_0 is given by

$$\hat{y}_0 - t_{\alpha/2;\, n-2}\, \hat{\sigma}\, \sqrt{1 + \frac{1}{n} + \frac{(x_0 - \bar{x})^2}{S_{xx}}} < y_0 < \hat{y}_0$$

$$+ t_{\alpha/2;\, n-2}\, \hat{\sigma}\, \sqrt{1 + \frac{1}{n} + \frac{(x_0 - \bar{x})^2}{S_{xx}}}. \qquad \text{(A.82)}$$

Example A.23. Consider the following data:

x	200	250	300	400	450	500	550	600	650	700
y	3	4	5	5.5	6	7.5	8.8	10	11.1	12

Assume that there is a linear dependence of Y on x and the regression line is $E[Y] = \alpha + \beta x$. Furthermore, assume that for each fixed value of x the distribution of Y is normal.

1. Find a least squares estimate of the regression line.
2. Find a 90 percent confidence interval for the intercept.
3. Find a 90 percent confidence interval for the slope.
4. Find a 90 percent confidence interval for the mean response at $x_0 = 300$.
5. Find a 90 percent confidence interval for a response at $x_0 = 300$.

For the data given, we first compute $\Sigma x = 4600$, $\Sigma y = 72.9$, $\Sigma x^2 = 238 \times 10^4$, and $\Sigma xy = 382 \times 10^2$. Hence, $\bar{x} = 460$ and $\bar{y} = 7.29$.

1. Using Equation (A.72), we obtain the estimate of the slope as

$$\hat{\beta} = \frac{(10)(382 \times 10^2) - (4600)(72.9)}{(10)(238 \times 10^4) - (4600)^2}$$

$$= 0.0177 .$$

We can find the estimate of the intercept from Equation (A.73) as

$$\hat{\alpha} = 7.29 - (0.0177)(460)$$

$$= -0.852 .$$

Therefore, the regression line is estimated from Equation (A.74) as

$$\hat{y} = -0.852 + 0.0177\, x .$$

Figure A.11 shows the regression line as a solid line along with the scatter diagram of the data.

2. Note that $t_{0.05;8} = 1.86$, $\hat{\sigma} = 0.619$ from Equation (A.76), and $S_{xx} = 26.4 \times 10^4$ from Equation (A.78). Then, we obtain a 90 percent confidence interval for the intercept α from Equation (A.77) as

$$-0.852 - (1.86)(0.619)\frac{\sqrt{238 \times 10^4}}{\sqrt{(10)(26.4 \times 10^4)}} < \alpha$$

$$< -0.852 + (1.86)(0.619)\frac{\sqrt{238 \times 10^4}}{\sqrt{(10)(26.4 \times 10^4)}} ,$$

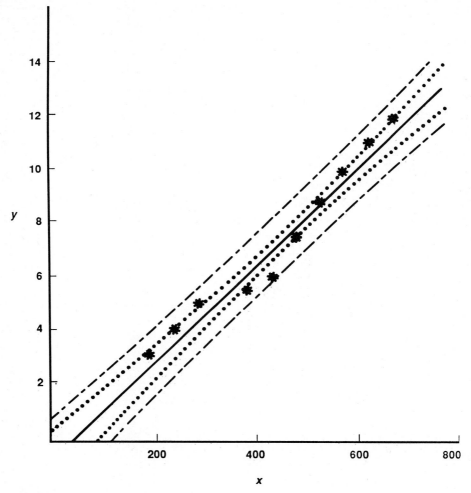

FIGURE A.11
Scatter diagram of the data, the regression line, and 90 percent confidence for $E[Y]$ and y_0 in Example A.23.

which simplifies to

$$-1.95 < \alpha < 0.24 \ .$$

3. We obtain a 90 percent confidence interval for the slope β from Equation (A.79) as

$$0.0177 - \frac{(1.86)(0.619)}{\sqrt{26.4 \times 10^4}} < \beta < 0.0177 + \frac{(1.86)(0.619)}{\sqrt{26.4 \times 10^4}}$$

or

$$0.0155 < \beta < 0.0199 .$$

4. With $x_0 = 300$, we compute the value of $\hat{y}_0$ from Equation (A.81) as

$$\hat{y}_0 = -0.852 + 0.0177(300) = 4.46 .$$

Therefore, we find a 90 percent confidence interval for $E[Y]$ at $x_0 = 300$ from Equation (A.82) as

$$4.46 - (1.86)(0.619)\sqrt{\frac{1}{10} + \frac{(300 - 460)^2}{26.4 \times 10^4}} < E[Y]$$

$$< 4.46 + (1.86)(0.619)\sqrt{\frac{1}{10} + \frac{(300 - 460)^2}{26.4 \times 10^4}}$$

or

$$3.95 < E[Y] < 4.97 .$$

Similarly, we compute 90 percent confidence intervals for the true average value of y at other values of x_0. Figure A.11 illustrates the intervals as dotted lines. Note that the confidence interval is minimized at $x_0 = \bar{x}$ and it increases as x_0 diverges from $\bar{x}$.

5. We can obtain a 90 percent confidence interval for predicting the actual value of y_0 at $x_0 = 300$ for some future measurement from Equation (A.82) as

$$4.46 - (1.86)(0.619)\sqrt{1 + \frac{1}{10} + \frac{(300 - 460)^2}{26.4 \times 10^4}} < y_0$$

$$< 4.46 + (1.86)(0.619)\sqrt{1 + \frac{1}{10} + \frac{(300 - 460)^2}{26.4 \times 10^4}} ,$$

which simplifies to

$$3.2 < y_0 < 5.72 .$$

Similarly, we compute 90 percent confidence intervals for the actual value of y_0 at other values of x_0 and plot them as dashed lines in Figure A.11. ∎

A.4 SUMMARY

Basic concepts in probability, statistics, and stochastic processes were reviewed to provide readers with background for Part III.

REVIEW OF HARDWARE RELIABILITY

This appendix will provide a summary of hardware reliability theory for software engineers and managers who are not familiar with this topic but must deal with software-hardware systems. A reliability study is concerned with random occurrences of undesirable events, or failures, during the life of a physical system. Since a failure phenomenon can only be described in probability terms, the definition of reliability depends heavily on probability concepts. The reliability of a system is defined as the probability that the system will adequately perform its intended function for a specified interval of time under stated environmental conditions.

Reliability evaluation using probability methods provides a quantitative measure of system performance. Hence it allows comparison between systems or provides a logical basis for reliability improvement in a system. We will define terms such as reliability function, expected life (or mean time to failure), hazard rate, and failure rate in Section B.1 and discuss some well-known reliability functions in Section B.2.

It should be pointed out that in this appendix we do not intend to provide a comprehensive treatment on the subject. For those who wish to explore in-depth material, there are many standard textbooks available. Some of them are: Mann, Schafer, and Singpurwalla (1974), Barlow and Proschan (1975), Lawless (1982), Ascher and Feingold (1984), and Shooman (1986).

B.1 DEFINITIONS

Let T be a random variable representing the failure time or lifetime of a physical system. Then, the probability that the system will fail by time t is

$$F(t) = P[T \leqslant t]$$

$$= \int_0^t f(x)dx \,, \tag{B.1}$$

where $F(t)$ and $f(t)$ are the cumulative distribution function and probability density function (or the failure density function), respectively. The probability of the system surviving until time t is

$$R(t) = P[T > t]$$

$$= 1 - F(t)$$

$$= \int_t^\infty f(x)dx \,, \tag{B.2}$$

where $R(t)$ is the *reliability function*. Figure B.1 illustrates the relationships among $f(t)$, $F(t)$, and $R(t)$. Note that the area under the failure density function $f(t)$ between 0 and t represents the probability of failure by time t, $F(t)$, while the area under $f(t)$ beyond t represents the probability of surviving beyond time t, $R(t)$.

The *expected life*, or the expected time during which the system will function successfully, is defined as

$$E[T] = \int_0^\infty tf(t)dt. \tag{B.3}$$

Another convenient method for determining the expected life is given by [see Lawless (1982) for example]

$$E[T] = \int_0^\infty R(t)dt \,. \tag{B.4}$$

When the system being tested is renewed through maintenance and repairs, $E[T]$ is also known as *mean time to failure* (MTTF).

Another useful concept in reliability theory is the *failure rate*. It is defined as the probability that a failure per unit time occurs in the interval, say $[t_1, t_2]$, given that a failure has not occurred before t_1. In other words, the failure rate is the rate at which failures occur in $[t_1, t_2]$. That is,

$$\frac{P[t_1 \leqslant T < t_2 \mid T > t_1]}{t_2 - t_1} = \frac{P[t_1 \leqslant T < t_2]}{(t_2 - t_1)P[T > t_1]}$$

$$= \frac{F(t_2) - F(t_1)}{(t_2 - t_1) R(t_1)} \,. \tag{B.5}$$

The *hazard rate* is defined as the limit of the failure rate as the interval approaches zero. If we redefine the interval in Equation (B.5) as $[t, t + \Delta t]$ and let

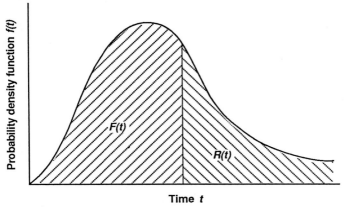

FIGURE B.1
Failure density function, cumulative distribution function, and reliability function.

$\Delta t \to 0$, we obtain the hazard rate at time t as

$$z(t) = \lim_{\Delta t \to 0} \frac{F(t + \Delta t) - F(t)}{\Delta t \; R(t)}$$

$$= \frac{f(t)}{R(t)} . \tag{B.6}$$

The hazard rate is an instantaneous rate of failure at time t, given that the system survives up to t. In particular, the quantity $z(t)dt$ represents the probability that a system of age t will fail in the small interval t to $t + dt$. Note that although there is a slight difference in the definitions of hazard rate and failure rate, they are often used interchangeably.

The functions $f(t)$, $F(t)$, $R(t)$, and $z(t)$ give mathematically equivalent specifications of the distribution of T. Expressions for $R(t)$ and $f(t)$ are given in terms of $z(t)$ by

$$R(t) = \exp[-\int_0^t z(x)dx] \tag{B.7}$$

and

$$f(t) = z(t) \exp[-\int_0^t z(x)dx], \tag{B.8}$$

respectively.

The hazard rate will change over the lifetime of a physical system. The hazard rate curve depicted in Figure B.2 exhibits all the characteristics of many

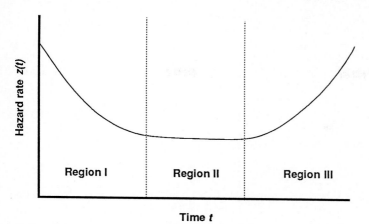

FIGURE B.2
Typical hazard rate of an electronic component as a function of age.

physical components. The shape is often referred to as a bathtub curve and can generally be divided into three distinct regions.

Region I, known by various names such as the debugging phase or infant mortality, represents early failures because of material or manufacturing defects or improper design. Quality control and initial product testing usually eliminate many substandard devices and thus avoid this higher initial hazard rate. In this region, the hazard rate decreases as a function of time.

Region II is known as the useful life period or normal operating phase and represents chance failures caused by sudden stress or extreme conditions. This is the only region in which the exponential distribution is valid. Region III represents the wear-out or fatigue failures and is characterized by a rapid increase in the hazard rate.

Distributions such as the gamma and Weibull distributions are often used to represent Regions I and III since these distributions have shape and scale parameters, the variation of which can create significantly different characteristic shapes. We will examine these distributions in more detail in the next section.

B.2 WELL-KNOWN RELIABILITY FUNCTIONS

B.2.1 Exponential Distribution

The exponential distribution is most widely known and used in reliability because of its great simplicity and applicability. The probability density function and cumulative distribution function are given by

$$f(t) = \lambda \exp(-\lambda t), \qquad \lambda > 0 \tag{B.9}$$

and

$$F(t) = 1 - \exp(-\lambda t) ,\qquad\text{(B.10)}$$

respectively, where λ is a parameter. Then, the reliability function is obtained from Equation (B.2) as

$$R(t) = \exp(-\lambda t)\qquad\text{(B.11)}$$

and the hazard rate is from Equation (B.6) as

$$z(t) = \lambda .\qquad\text{(B.12)}$$

Thus, the exponential distribution represents the constant hazard (or failure) rate λ. As discussed in Section B.1, the exponential distribution is valid only for Region II (that is, the useful life period or normal operating phase). Figure B.3 illustrates typical shapes for the probability density function, reliability, and hazard rate that can be produced for the exponential distribution. We can obtain the average life time or MTTF from Equation (B.3) or (B.4) as

$$E[T] = \frac{1}{\lambda} ,\qquad\text{(B.13)}$$

which is the reciprocal of the hazard rate.

B.2.2   Weibull Distribution

The Weibull distribution, in common with some other distributions such as the gamma distribution, plays an important role in reliability because of its great adaptability. Depending on the values of the parameters in its reliability function, it can be shaped to represent many distributions as well as shaped to fit many sets of data.

A special type of graph paper, known as *Weibull probability paper*, is readily available on which experimental data can be plotted. This paper is constructed in such a way that the parameters can be easily deduced from the plots.

The probability density function is given by

$$f(t) = \alpha\beta(\beta t)^{\alpha-1} \exp[-(\beta t)^{\alpha}],\qquad \alpha > 0, \beta > 0,\qquad\text{(B.14)}$$

where α and β are the shape and scale parameters. We can obtain the reliability function from Equation (B.2) as

$$R(t) = 1 - F(t)$$

$$= \exp[-(\beta t)^{\alpha}]\qquad\text{(B.15)}$$

and the hazard rate from Equation (B.6) as

$$z(t) = \frac{f(t)}{R(t)}$$

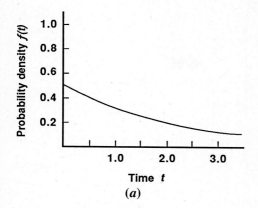

(a)

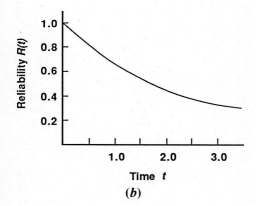

(b)

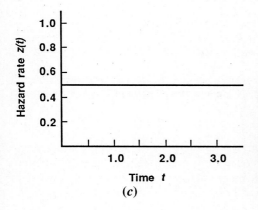

(c)

FIGURE B.3
Typical shapes for the probability density function, reliability, and hazard rate of the exponential distribution for $\lambda = 0.5$. (a) Probability density function. (b) Reliability function. (c) Hazard rate.

$$= \alpha\beta(\beta t)^{\alpha-1} . \tag{B.16}$$

Note that the hazard rate is a power function of t. It can be shown that the expected value is

$$E[T] = \frac{1}{\beta} \Gamma \left[\frac{1}{\alpha} + 1 \right] , \tag{B.17}$$

where Γ is the gamma function defined as

$$\Gamma (\gamma) = \int_0^\infty t^{\gamma-1} \exp(- t)dt . \tag{B.18}$$

Two special cases can be deduced from the Weibull distribution.

1. $\alpha = 1$
The hazard rate becomes a constant, that is,

$$z (t) = \beta . \tag{B.19}$$

Therefore, this is an exponential distribution with parameter β.

2. $\alpha = 2$
The hazard rate is linearly increasing with time, that is,

$$z (t) = 2\beta^2 t . \tag{B.20}$$

The corresponding probability density function and reliability function are given by

$$f (t) = 2\beta^2 t \exp[- (\beta t)^2] \tag{B.21}$$

and

$$R (t) = \exp[- (\beta t)^2] , \tag{B.22}$$

respectively. Note that this distribution is called the *Rayleigh distribution*. It is applied not only in reliability but also in noise problems associated with communication systems.

Note that the Weibull distribution can be made to fit or approximate many distributions. Figure B.4 shows typical shapes for the probability density function, reliability, and the hazard rate that can be produced for the Weibull. It is evident from the plots that $0 < \alpha < 1$ represents a decreasing hazard rate (as occurs in the debugging phase), $\alpha = 1$ represents a constant hazard rate (as occurs in the normal operation phase), and $\alpha > 1$ represents an increasing hazard rate (as occurs in the wear-out phase).

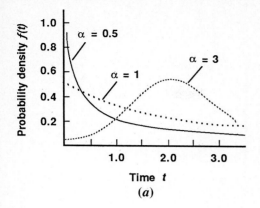

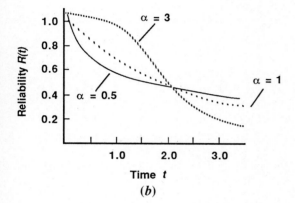

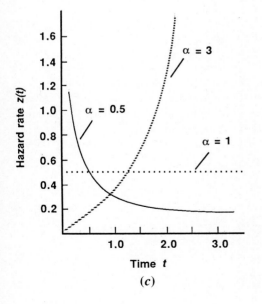

FIGURE B.4
Typical shapes for the probability density function, reliability, and hazard rate of the Weibull distribution for β = 0.5. (*a*) Probability density function. (*b*) Reliability function. (*c*) Hazard rate.

B.2.3   Gamma Distribution

The gamma distribution has similar properties to those of the Weibull distribution. It can be made to fit or approximate a wide variety of experimental data by varying the shape and scale parameters.

The probability density function is given by

$$f(t) = \frac{\lambda(\lambda t)^{\alpha-1}}{\Gamma(\alpha)} \exp(-\lambda t), \qquad \alpha > 0, \tag{B.23}$$

where α and λ are the shape and scale parameters, respectively. The reliability function is thus computed as

$$R(t) = \int_t^\infty \frac{\lambda(\lambda x)^{\alpha-1}}{\Gamma(\alpha)} \exp(-\lambda x) \, dx . \tag{B.24}$$

Note that the expected value is

$$E[T] = \frac{\alpha}{\lambda} . \tag{B.25}$$

Three special cases can be deduced from the gamma distribution.

1. $\alpha = 1$

   The probability density function becomes identical to the exponential distribution with parameter λ. The hazard rate is constant.

2. $\alpha = n$, where n is an integer

   The probability density function becomes

$$f(t) = \frac{\lambda(\lambda t)^{n-1}}{(n-1)!} \exp(-\lambda t), \quad n = 1, 2, \cdots, \tag{B.26}$$

   which is known as the *Special Erlangian* distribution. It should be pointed out that a sum of n exponentially distributed (with parameter λ) random variables can be expressed by this distribution. The Erlangian distribution has often been used to represent service times and interarrival times in queueing theory. The reliability function may be shown to be

$$R(t) = \sum_{k=0}^{n-1} \frac{(\lambda t)^k}{k!} \exp(-\lambda t) . \tag{B.27}$$

3. $\lambda = 1/2$ and $\alpha = n/2$.

   The probability density function becomes

$$f(t) = \frac{1}{\Gamma\left(\frac{n}{2}\right) 2^{n/2}} \, t^{(n/2)-1} \exp\left(-\frac{t}{2}\right) . \tag{B.28}$$

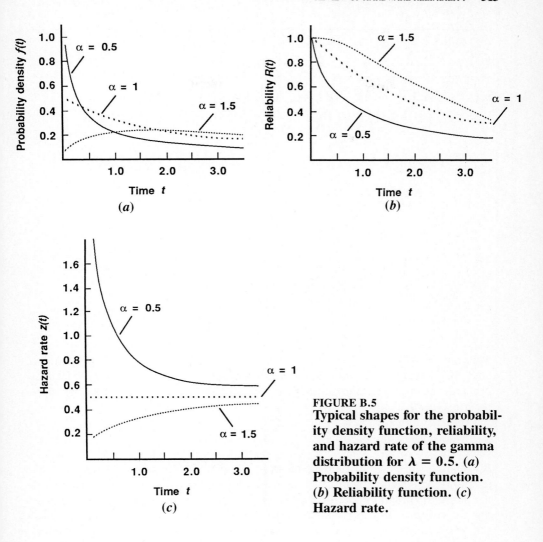

FIGURE B.5
Typical shapes for the probability density function, reliability, and hazard rate of the gamma distribution for $\lambda = 0.5$. (a) Probability density function. (b) Reliability function. (c) Hazard rate.

This is known as the *chi-square distribution* with n degrees of freedom, which is an important distribution used in statistical testing and construction of confidence limits. Figure B.5 shows typical characteristics for the probability density function, reliability, and hazard rate that can be obtained for the gamma distribution.

B.3 SUMMARY

We have provided a summary of hardware reliability theory. We introduced terms such as reliability function, expected life (or mean time to failure), hazard rate, and failure rate, and discussed some well-known reliability functions.

C

REVIEW OF SOFTWARE AND SOFTWARE DEVELOPMENT FOR HARDWARE ENGINEERS

This review will first cover computer hardware and architecture. It will then discuss the languages used for controlling computers and the system software that provides an improved human interface. Finally, the process of software development is outlined.

C.1 COMPUTER BASICS

A computer in the most general sense is a logical device whose operation is directed by a sequence of instructions called a program. Creating this sequence is the job of the programmer. Although many people think of computers as machines that do general purpose processing, the broad definition we have given is necessary because there are many special purpose processors as well. Virtually all computers work with binary numbers or *bits*. The basic hardware of the computer consists of logic circuitry that performs various Boolean operations on these bits such as "AND" and "OR."

The *instructions* that constitute a program are strings of bits that follow a definite format. Certain bits represent the operation or function to be performed and others represent the addresses in memory of one or more operands. The instructions combine operands in various ways and store the results in memory at specified addresses. Memory to store intermediate results is an important part of a computer, in view of the fact that the operations that can be performed are relatively simple ones. Almost all useful functions, when implemented on computers, require a series of machine instructions with intermediate storage of the results to

514

perform their tasks. Although instructions can perform operations at the bit level, in general they operate on larger entities. These include the *byte*, which consists of 8 bits, or the *word*, which can range between 8 and 64 bits. Word lengths of 16 and 32 bits are the most common.

Machine instructions are not necessarily the lowest level of programmable logical functions in the computer. In many computers, the instructions activate various logical functions in the machine through *microcode*. That is, the instructions are interpreted in terms of lower level logical primitives. Microcode permits the instruction repertoire of a computer to be changed either to add improvements or to tailor it to some special application.

Memory is frequently organized in a hierarchical fashion based on the time required to access it. For example, a machine may have a high-speed small semiconductor memory called a *cache*, which contains currently active or about-to-be-active instructions. The main memory will be a slower semiconductor memory or core memory, also directly accessible or addressable by the computer's processor. The machine will also have *secondary storage*, connected to the computer by a high-speed data channel. The secondary storage itself may be hierarchical. The most active files or data sets will reside on disk and the less active files on some sort of *mass storage system*.

The conventional computer, before the widespread application of integrated circuits, consisted of a processor, a main memory, secondary storage, and various peripheral devices. With the advent of inexpensive chips and computer-aided design of these chips, computer architecture began to diversify in many ways. For example, processing may be performed by several processors in a multiprocessor configuration. Peripherals, especially input-output devices, may, in effect, be specialized computers on their own. Many small computers may be connected together to form a *distributed processing system*. In a distributed system it is common for different functions or roles to be assigned to each computer or to groups of computers. Specialized machines may be provided for managing a data base. There are array or vector processors that process arrays (structured collections) or vectors of data with multiple processing elements. Computers may be configured into *networks* that, in effect, are loosely coupled distributed processing systems.

The process of programming first involves an analysis of the functions one wishes to perform. These are generally broken down into smaller and smaller subfunctions (the "top-down" approach) until one arrives at a level where the subfunctions are already implemented. This level may be at the level of machine instructions. It may also be at the level of previously programmed or *reusable* subfunctions. Obviously, the latter situation is preferable from the viewpoint of programming productivity. Consequently, it is often desirable when designing to develop general purpose subroutines. These can then be reused for many other situations.

Once the program has been prepared, it must be verified. Experience has shown that the complexity of even the simplest program is such that you can't be sure it will "work" in all circumstances without verification. By "work" we mean "perform the functions for which it was designed." Verification can involve checking of the program itself. However, it *always* involves testing the program by executing it for the functions it is required to perform. Checking of the program itself can be performed by several means. The program may be inspected by the programmer or a colleague for common flaws. You may step through the program as if simulating its execution for different cases. You might even attempt a correctness proof, which is a formal mathematical demonstration that the program functions to meet the requirements. Such a proof is generally quite difficult and may not be practical or economic.

C.2   COMPUTER LANGUAGES

As noted previously, the basic instructions in a computer consist of strings of bits. These are referred to as *machine language*. Machine language is difficult and tedious for the programmer to deal with. Therefore, *assembly languages* were developed early in the history of computers to provide a better human interface. An assembly language assigns more readily understood codes to operations instead of a string of bits. These are command names or their abbreviations such as "ADD" or "MUL." It also permits the programmer to assign names to locations in memory. Thus, assembly language is easier for programmers to understand and work with. An *assembler* (a computer program itself) translates the operation and operand symbols into the strings of bits of machine language that are needed to actually operate the computer. The assembly language program is called the *source program*. The binary program output by the assembler is called the object program. An assembler may generate an *object program* for the machine on which it is running or for a different target machine, in which case it is called a *cross assembler*.

Although assembly language was a substantial improvement over machine language, it was still far from being natural in terms of being suited to the way in which people usually think. The second step in improving the human interface was the introduction of *high-level languages*. These are languages that express operations in a form akin to formulas or equations. This is contrasted with assembly language, which is a series of single operations performed on one or more operands. High-level languages are translated into machine language by *compilers*. The process is called compilation. There are also programs called *interpreters* that accept statements written in high-level languages and translate them in real time to machine language statements that are immediately executed. Interpreters are useful for programs that are dynamic (that is, changing rapidly), such as sets of commands for a user who is interacting with a computer in real time. Interpretation, of course, is much slower than execution because of all the extra translation required. Hence, if a program is relatively stable, it is more efficient to compile it and then execute, rather than interpret it every time it is needed.

FORTRAN was the first of the high-level languages. It is still in wide use on many machines, although it lacks many of the features of the more modern languages. COBOL is commonly used in the business field. ALGOL is popular in Europe. BASIC and to some extent PASCAL are frequently used on personal computers. PL/1 is a powerful but correspondingly difficult to learn language that has many adherents. C is popular among scientific and university users. It is widely used in telecommunications applications. A new language, Ada, has been developed and is intended as a standard in the United States Department of Defense. In addition to the general high-level languages just mentioned, there are many specialized application languages. These have been developed for particular fields, such as APT for programming of machine tools and GPSS for simulation.

Current languages are but another step on the road toward a better interface between computer and human. The explosion of personal computers has resulted in new ways of commanding a computer. These include selecting operations from menus that are displayed on a screen. You may use graphic symbols that are highly evocative. For example, pointing to a picture of a file will store data. Pointing to a waste basket symbol will destroy the data. Investigators in artificial intelligence are carrying this movement toward more natural means of expression to machines even further.

C.3 SYSTEMS SOFTWARE

We have been talking about the bare hardware computer. In reality, users of computers interact with an extended machine, which consists of hardware plus systems software, that eases the job of working with the computer.

The most basic piece of systems software is the *operating system*. The operating system administers all the resources of the computer including the processor or processors, memory, secondary storage, and peripherals. It allocates these to users as they require them. One of its most basic functions is to load programs into the machine for execution. In larger machines it is common to use *multiprogramming*. That is, the programs of many users are loaded into the machine at the same time. Each is located in a different partition of the main memory and all share the processor. When a machine operates in the *batch processing* mode, each program in turn is commonly given control of the processor until it must wait for an input/output operation to be completed. The other common mode of operation is the *time-sharing* mode. In this mode, each program is allowed to run only for a limited slice of time, commonly much less than 1 second. This type of operation is necessary when users are working in an interactive mode. Response times to commands of users working interactively must be in the region of fractions of a second to be satisfactory.

Some operating systems implement a method of addressing storage called *virtual storage*. The amount of main memory that is available to a program at any given time is limited. It is generally less than the total size of the program and its data. The virtual storage concept allows the programmer to assign memory locations as if a very large memory were available for use. The virtual storage operating system then handles the paging of parts of the program and its data from secondary storage to main storage and back as the program parts and data are required for execution.

There are many other functions of operating systems including:

1. file management (management of secondary storage),
2. assigning and controlling priorities to different system users,
3. protecting user files so that only those persons designated by the user can read the files or write to them (this is a *computer security* function),
4. control of who has access to the machine by use of passwords and other security measures,
5. accounting and charging for usage, and
6. recording performance characteristics of the machine and its systems software so that it can be tuned for more efficient operation.

Compilers, assemblers, and interpreters are generally considered as systems software.

Data base management systems provide facilities for organizing data items (as contrasted with files) in a structured fashion into data bases. They furnish facilities for accessing the data items in various convenient ways, such as searching for data items with a field (part of a data item) having a specified "value." A "value" can be a number, a name such as "Zook," or a logical variable like "TRUE" or "FALSE." Graphics system software provides facilities for constructing common graphical figures (for example, curves or bar plots) and specifying their attributes (line texture and thickness, color, etc.). Diagnostic and debugging tools create environments in which a program can be executed in a controlled fashion and data needed for diagnosis of problems can be specified and recorded.

C.4   THE SOFTWARE DEVELOPMENT PROCESS

The development of software as a usable, marketable, profitable product (*software engineering*) is a considerably more complex undertaking than the development of a program that works. Several books have been devoted to this topic [Shooman (1983), Pressman (1982), and Myers (1976)]. It includes development of documentation, training, and other necessary support facilities. Ordinarily the program must be capable of evolving easily to meet changing user needs.

Frequently, the users of the software product are unsophisticated when it comes to computers. Thus the user-machine interface, or the way in which the user tells the machine what to do, must be carefully designed. It must be simple to learn. It must be easy to remember. It must work in a way that minimizes the risk of introducing wrong commands. When the program doesn't work properly, possibly due to user error, it must be easy to diagnose what went wrong. Finally, the program must not depend on the intelligent intervention of the user to help it over situations that may not have been considered beforehand. If a program is just written for yourself, it is often no great tragedy if you have not considered all the cases that can occur. You can simply handle the resulting problem in real time. But this is not true of software developed for a general user.

Most software products are too large and complicated to be produced by an individual. They involve a team of software engineers, sometimes one of substantial size. Thus software development frequently involves all the problems that can arise in "designing by committee." These problems are usually more severe than those involved in simply working together as a team to perform some task. To all the issues of group dynamics are added the communication difficulties of trying to think and create together. The foregoing considerations have been emphasized because a little programming is truly a dangerous thing. It is traditional for the programmer who takes on the responsibilities of the software engineer to find this out the hard way.

C.4.1 Design and Coding

As previously noted, software is built in a process of sequential steps that in general proceed from the top down, that is, from a few high-level concepts to many lower-level concepts. The lower-level concepts can either be instructions or standard software packages that are selected for use in this application. Although the software development process is sequential, it is also iterative. The process of filling in more detail often results in problems that make it necessary to modify some of the higher-order concepts. Also, although both hardware and software can evolve with time to meet changing customer needs or exploit new technology, software can do so somewhat more easily. While the hardware is often standard, software is readily tailored to a customer's needs, and it can be continually retailored as the customer's needs evolve. These evolutionary and adaptable aspects of software complicate the process of its development. They add to the iterative nature and thus the high degree of interactivity in the development process. Evolution tends to erode the integrity of the original software design. Continuing reintegration of high-level concepts and system testing is thus needed for software to a much greater extent than it is for hardware.

A software project starts either as the result of a customer requesting a product or marketing or technical personnel seeing an opportunity to develop a product that can be profitable. This product may be solely a software one but it is often a hardware-software system. In the "product opportunity" case, the concept of the product is developed, marketing analyses are done, and costs and potential profitability are investigated. Prospective customers may be consulted directly. The result of this is a system concept. The system concept, which can also emanate from a specific customer request, is further detailed by examining the functions the system must perform and the needs it must meet. The result is a requirements definition. The requirements definition for a large system may be hundreds of pages in size.

There is a great danger at this point that the requirements definition may not represent what the customer really wants. This can occur because the requirements definition is usually generated by the developer. It is easy for this to diverge from the customer's needs. This is particularly true because the requirements definition is often lengthy and technical in nature. The user frequently does not have the time or the background to understand it fully. Therefore, it is often desirable to express the requirements in a way the user can grasp. It is important that they be expressed in terms of the functions the user wants to accomplish. One way of doing this is to prepare a draft of the user manual that will ultimately be used for the operational program. An even better but more expensive way to communicate with the user is to prepare a *rapid prototype*. This is a model or "draft version" of the system that clearly exhibits the user interface and principal user functions. If the user then exercises the prototype in the same way as the final system would be employed in operation, valuable feedback can be generated for the developer.

The project now enters the design phase. Depending on the size of the project, you proceed through a hierarchy of designs until the system has been divided into detailed functions that can be assigned to individual software developers. Thus, the overall system may be divided into subsystems with the interfaces between subsystems being defined, subsystems divided into components, and so forth. Various design methodologies have been proposed to make this process more efficient and less prone to error. Many projects conduct *design inspections* in which the design is carefully examined by various people from different viewpoints.

Each of the programmers assigned to a detailed function then carries out the process of detailed design. This involves dividing the assigned function into modules and establishing the interfaces. The structure and format of the data are defined. The subfunctions in each module are outlined. Again, various design methodologies have been developed to help this process. Design languages have been developed for specifying designs. Some design languages have associated tools that check the design for completeness, consistency, and other important attributes.

When the detailed design is complete, the programmer proceeds to code the various modules, compile or assemble them, and test each of them as a unit. *Editors* are used to create and modify the code. Compilers or assemblers find many of the syntactic faults. *Syntactic faults* are violations of the syntactic structure of the language being used. A recent development is the syntax-driven editor, which guides the programmer in the construction of syntactically valid statements in the language being written. With this tool, programs do not have syntactic faults that must be corrected after compilation. Semantic faults cannot be automatically diagnosed. They must be found either through careful inspection of the code (by the original programmer or others) or through testing. *Semantic faults* are mistakes in meaning, such that the computer is not instructed correctly about one's desired action.

To conduct a unit test, the programmer must develop various *test drivers* to exercise each of the modules. Also, each programmer will utilize diagnostic or debugging tools, which represent another component of systems software. These tools build scaffolding around the executing program. They make it possible to, in effect, insert temporary changes into the program that make it stop at various points and print out the values of important variables. By wisely choosing the *breakpoints* and the variables to be printed, the programmer can verify correct operation of the program or isolate problems. Rapid isolation is a key to efficient debugging.

It is frequently common in the unit test stage to keep track of the *coverage* of the program. By "coverage" we mean the percentage of instructions (or better, branches or paths) that have been executed in the testing so far. Complete coverage is not usually attained, but coverage is a useful index of the thoroughness of testing. Note that complete coverage is a necessary *but not sufficient* condition for finding all the faults.

Editors and diagnostic and debugging tools form the programming environment. It is highly desirable that all parts of the programming environment be designed to function together, using commands and programmer interfaces that are consistent with each other.

C.4.2   Test

Once the modules have been developed and tested to a programmer's satisfaction, they are generally turned over to another individual or group that integrates them to form larger entities. Integration generally proceeds in a hierarchical fashion through component integration, subsystem integration, and finally, system integration. For a smaller system, system integration alone may occur. When you reach the level of system integration, the entire system is generally operated as a unit. Software is tested against inputs that represent what the program will encounter in actual operation. As you move from unit test to system test, there will be a transition from structural to functional testing. *Structural testing*, sometimes called "white box" testing, uses knowledge of the program structure to plan efficient tests. Test planning for structural testing requires the involvement of the programmer. *Functional testing*, often called "black box" or system testing, requires only knowledge of the system requirements. A user or system engineer can do the test planning for functional testing. In fact, it is probably best that one of them and not the programmer do it. Careful functional test planning is necessary to ensure that the operational environment is represented correctly, so that the testing of a program does truly represent its eventual use. Functional testing is sometimes divided into feature testing and load testing. *Feature testing* involves the testing of each program feature or function in sequence with as little repetition as possible. *Load testing* tries to represent the operational environment as accurately as possible with regard to relative frequencies of demand for various functions.

Also, the testing must be reasonably comprehensive. In theory, the program should be tested for every possible input state or set of input variables that can occur. In practice, this is impossible because the number of different input states is astronomical. Equivalence partitioning can be used to reduce this number. An *equivalence partition* or *equivalence class* is a set of similar input states that are believed to have the same failure behavior. Thus it is necessary to run only one input state to establish whether a fault is associated with the partition. The determination of equivalence classes is both an art and a gamble. You try to group functionally similar input states together, or states that appear likely to exercise the same program paths. But there is no guarantee that you have done this correctly! It is probably wise to occasionally execute more than one input state from an equivalence partition. Also, you must recognize that some inevitable uncertainty must remain about the thoroughness of the testing.

Some special techniques may be employed for the verification of critical systems such as nuclear power plants, defense systems, and air traffic control systems. Critical outcomes that must be avoided are enumerated (for example, reactor meltdown). A thorough analysis of all the sets of conditions that can lead to these outcomes, called a *fault tree analysis*, is made. Appropriate defensive actions are taken in the program to prevent these conditions from occurring [Leveson (1986)].

When system testing is complete, the system is generally delivered to the customer. The customer may require verification testing before accepting the product. Verification testing is generally either performed by the customer with the developer's help or by the developer under the customer's direction. Once a program has been accepted, it is said to be in the operational phase. In this phase, the software generally continues to evolve, as customers find through use of the system that certain improvements are necessary or desired. At the same time, there are generally some residual faults in the software that are causing it to fail in various ways. The customer will request that these be corrected. The principal activity after delivery is often referred to as one of *program maintenance*. But this term is somewhat misleading to people familiar with the concept of hardware maintenance. The maintenance of software does not involve a replacement of parts that wear out or the preventive replacement of parts that are likely to fail. Rather, it includes the improvement of both the reliability and the features of the software. Often it is required by functions that change as a customer's needs change. Also, changes may be necessary to handle changes in the hardware or software environments in which a program operates. And thus, it would probably be better if we used the term *software evolution*.

C.5   SUMMARY

Computing systems may be viewed as a functional hierarchy of logic and memory. The "lower" levels are simple in function and implemented in hardware. The intermediate levels may involve software, firmware (programs permanently recorded in memory that can't be changed), or complex hardware. The higher levels are sophisticated in function and generally implemented in software. The quality of the human interface generally improves as you approach the higher levels.

The software development process is complex, iterative, evolutionary, and fraught with potential for the introduction of faults. Developing software as a product is orders of magnitude more difficult than developing it as a personal tool. It is common for people who have learned to program to be deceived into thinking that they therefore know how to develop software products. As in any other branch of engineering, much training and experience are necessary to become a proficient and professional software engineer.

OPTIMIZATION ALGORITHM

Estimating the unknown parameters of a specific software reliability model will usually require the optimization of a particular function. For maximum likelihood estimation the log-likelihood function is to be maximized, while least squares estimation requires the minimization of the sum of squares function. Since this latter case is equivalent to maximizing the negative sum of squares function, we only really need an algorithm which performs maximization. Thus, in what follows, we will focus on maximum likelihood estimation.

Two basic methods can be considered, namely:

1. numerical root finding procedures for

$$\frac{\partial \ln L(\boldsymbol{\beta})}{\partial \beta_k} = 0, \quad k = 0, 1, \cdots, w, \tag{D.1}$$

and

2. searching schemes, both with and without use of gradient information.

Each of these methods will be briefly considered, in turn. The procedure which we have used with great success, not only on functions related to software reliability but in several other areas as well, will also be described. The books by Walsh (1975) and Beveridge and Schechter (1970) can be consulted for further details and references on optimization.

D.1   NEWTON-RAPHSON
ROOT-FINDING PROCEDURE

The direct algebraic solution of the system of nonlinear simultaneous equations defined by Equation (D.1) is usually impossible.[1] However, it is possible to use a numerical root-finding procedure for solving this system. The Newton-Raphson procedure [Carnahan and Wilkes (1973)] was chosen for this purpose. It is based on the first order Taylor series expansion of $U(\boldsymbol{\beta})$, where $U(\boldsymbol{\beta})$ is a $(w + 1) \times 1$ column vector with element k given by

$$U_k(\boldsymbol{\beta})^{\cdot} = \frac{\partial \ln L(\boldsymbol{\beta})}{\partial \beta_k} , \ k = 0, 1, \cdots, w . \tag{D.2}$$

Given a trial value $\boldsymbol{\beta}_t$ the vector defined above can be written as

$$U(\boldsymbol{\beta}) \approx U(\boldsymbol{\beta}_t) + H(\boldsymbol{\beta}_t)(\boldsymbol{\beta} - \boldsymbol{\beta}_t) , \tag{D.3}$$

where $H(\boldsymbol{\beta})$ is the $(w + 1) \times (w + 1)$ matrix with elements

$$H_{kl}(\boldsymbol{\beta}) = \frac{\partial^2 \ln L(\boldsymbol{\beta})}{\partial \beta_k \partial \beta_l} , \ k, l = 0, 1, \cdots, w . \tag{D.4}$$

Setting $U(\hat{\boldsymbol{\beta}}) = 0$ and solving Equation (D.3) for $\hat{\boldsymbol{\beta}}$ gives

$$\hat{\boldsymbol{\beta}} \approx \boldsymbol{\beta}_t - H^{-1}(\boldsymbol{\beta}_t)U(\boldsymbol{\beta}_t) , \tag{D.5}$$

where H^{-1} is the inverse of H. The right side of Equation (D.5) yields a new trial value for $\boldsymbol{\beta}$. The process is repeated until successive $\boldsymbol{\beta}$ estimates agree to a specified tolerance on an element by element basis.[2]

The procedure has two attractive features. First, if the method converges it will do so very rapidly. Secondly, convergence to a solution of Equation (D.1) is assured if the initial estimate for $\boldsymbol{\beta}$ is close enough to $\hat{\boldsymbol{\beta}}$. While this latter trait is desirable, it also represents the main drawback of the method. The region of feasible values for $\hat{\boldsymbol{\beta}}$ is usually infinite in scope. Thus, if we lack a good way of guessing an initial estimate close enough to the solution, the method will more often than not diverge. This problem becomes more severe as the number of unknown parameters which must be estimated increases.

---

[1]The best we can realistically hope for is to solve these equations for a subset of the parameters (in terms of the remaining parameters). The remaining parameters are then estimated using numerical methods.

[2]In our current implementation convergence occurs when all elements of two successive $\boldsymbol{\beta}$ estimates differ in absolute magnitude by less than 10^{-6} and are within 0.1 percent of each other.

D.2 NELDER-MEAD
SEARCHING PROCEDURE

Several good searching schemes using gradient information are available. Chief among these are Fletcher and Powell's (1963) descent method and Fletcher and Reeves' (1964) conjugate gradient method. Perhaps due to the particular form that Equation (D.1) can take on, especially in the context of software reliability modeling, neither of these methods display suitable convergence in practice. In fact, investigations indicated that searching schemes incorporating gradient information are not particularly well suited for the problem at hand.[3]

Searching schemes not using gradient information can also be used. Chief among these is the Nelder and Mead (1965) simplex procedure. This method possesses many desirable properties:

1. it is conceptually simple and therefore easily tailored to meet special needs,
2. it is easy to program (all the computations are trivial), and most important,
3. it is very robust and always converges to at least a local minimum.[4]

The main drawback is that the method lacks any form of acceleration, per se, and therefore tends to be slow.

D.3 RECOMMENDED MAXIMIZATION
PROCEDURE

We are left with a choice between the fast and sometimes diverging Newton-Raphson method and the often slow, but always converging Nelder-Mead method. Given that a choice must be made, we would choose the latter method, since an expensive (in terms of CPU time) answer is probably better than none at all. Of course, we are not restricted to one or the other method and it turns out that a combination of the two provides a very robust, moderately fast, procedure. The procedure is illustrated in Figure D.1. Our strategy is to use the simplex procedure to improve the estimate of the solution until it is close enough to the roots of Equation (D.1) for the Newton-Raphson method to converge. When the simplex procedure is called, it is allowed to improve the current estimate for β but not to converge completely. That is, the time spent in the simplex procedure is limited to just a few iterations. The improved estimate is then used by the Newton-Raphson procedure. If this procedure converges then we are done. Otherwise, the simplex pro-

---

[3]Divergence is an even greater problem for these procedures than it is for the Newton-Raphson procedure, particularly when two or more parameters must be estimated simultaneously.

[4]The procedure is used to minimize a function. Therefore, instead of using ln $L(\beta)$ you use $-\ln L(\beta)$.

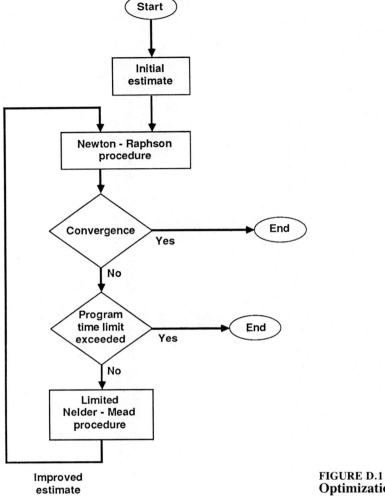

FIGURE D.1
Optimization algorithm.

cedure is allowed to improve the estimate for β some more and the process repeats itself.

The initial estimate of the solution is made by the procedure. As we have seen it no longer matters how close this initial estimate is to the correct solution because the combined procedure will always converge. Of course, the better the estimate, the faster convergence will take place. In the absence of anything better, the procedure will automatically pick a trial solution at random. In Chapter 12 we showed that maximum likelihood estimation for both the exponential class and geometric family of Poisson models is centered around the single parameter β_1. From practical experience it turns out that an excellent choice for an initial guess for β_1 is t_e^{-1}. This value almost always results in the initial convergence of the Newton-Raphson procedure. When the procedure is being used for one of these models it will automatically choose $\beta_1 = t_e^{-1}$ for the initial solution.

Sometimes the derivatives (first and second) required by the Newton-Raphson procedure are difficult to determine because of the analytical forms involved. When this occurs a special option of our procedure can be used which bypasses the Newton-Raphson routine. Then, just the simplex procedure is employed.

D.4   SOME CONCERNS

As with any other maximization procedure, some care should be exercised to ensure that a global maximum and not a local one has been found. Further, we should make sure that the procedure did not accidently locate a minimum.

This latter concern has not been a problem for two reasons. First, since we are mostly concerned with one-parameter scaled mean value functions the sign of $[\partial^2 \ln L(\boldsymbol{\beta})]/\partial\beta_1^2$ can always be checked to ensure that a maximum has been found. Secondly, the Nelder-Mead part of our procedure virtually guarantees that the estimate moves toward a maximum.

The former concern can be a problem when using a small sample to estimate multiple parameters simultaneously. Here it is a good idea to have the procedure pick several different starting values (perhaps chosen randomly) and use the best [that is, leading to the largest value of $\ln L(\boldsymbol{\beta})$] estimate obtained. Once the sample size reaches about 25, multiple solutions to Equation (D.1) are rare.

SUMMARY OF FORMULAS FOR APPLICATION

E.1 FAILURE INTENSITY-RELIABILITY (FOR CONSTANT FAILURE INTENSITY)

$$R(\tau) = \exp(-\lambda\tau)$$

$R(\tau)$ = reliability
λ = failure intensity
τ = execution time

E.2 BASIC EXECUTION TIME MODEL

E.2.1 Execution Time Component

Failures experienced (expected)

$$\mu(\tau) = \nu_0 \left[1 - \exp\left(-\frac{\lambda_0}{\nu_0}\tau\right)\right]$$

Present failure intensity

$$\lambda(\tau) = \lambda_0 \exp\left(-\frac{\lambda_0}{\nu_0}\tau\right) \qquad \lambda(\mu) = \lambda_0\left(1 - \frac{\mu}{\nu_0}\right)$$

Reliability

$$R(\tau' \mid \tau) = \exp\left\{ - \left[\nu_0 \exp\left[-\frac{\lambda_0}{\nu_0}\tau \right] \right] \left[1 - \exp\left(-\frac{\lambda_0}{\nu_0}\tau' \right) \right] \right\}$$

Additional failures to failure intensity objective

$$\Delta\mu = \frac{\nu_0}{\lambda_0} \left(\lambda_P - \lambda_F \right)$$

Additional execution time to failure intensity objective

$$\Delta\tau = \frac{\nu_0}{\lambda_0} \; \ln\left(\frac{\lambda_P}{\lambda_F} \right)$$

Relationship between parameters

$$\frac{\lambda_0}{\nu_0} = B\phi$$

B = fault reduction factor
μ = failures experienced (expected)
$\Delta\mu$ = additional failures (expected)
τ = execution time
τ' = execution time measured from the present
$\Delta\tau$ = additional execution time
λ_0 = initial failure intensity
λ_P = present failure intensity
λ_F = failure intensity objective
ν_0 = total failures (expected)
ϕ = per-fault hazard rate (constant)

E.2.2   Calendar Time Component

$$\frac{dt_r}{d\tau} = \frac{1}{P_r \rho_r} \left[\theta_r + \mu_r \lambda_0 \exp\left(-\frac{\lambda_0}{\nu_0}\tau \right) \right]$$

t = calendar time
τ = execution time
r = index of limiting resource (C = computer time, F = failure correction personnel, I = failure identification personnel)
P_r = resource quantity
ρ_r = resource utilization

θ_r = execution time coefficient of resource usage
μ_r = failure coefficient of resource usage
λ_0 = initial failure intensity
ν_0 = total failures (expected)

E.2.3   Parameter Prediction

Inherent faults

$$\omega_0 = \omega_I \, \Delta I$$

Total failures

$$\nu_0 = \frac{\omega_0}{B}$$

Linear execution frequency

$$f = \frac{r}{I}$$

Initial failure intensity

$$\lambda_0 = fK\omega_0$$

ω_0 = inherent faults
ω_I = inherent faults per developed source instruction
ΔI = developed executable source instructions
ν_0 = total failures
B = fault reduction factor
f = linear execution frequency
r = instruction execution rate
I = executable object instructions
λ_0 = initial failure intensity
K = fault exposure ratio

E.3   LOGARITHMIC POISSON EXECUTION TIME MODEL

E.3.1   Execution Time Component

Failures experienced (expected)

$$\mu(\tau) = \frac{1}{\theta} \ln (\lambda_0 \, \theta \tau + 1)$$

Present failure intensity

$$\lambda(\tau) = \frac{\lambda_0}{\lambda_0 \, \theta \, \tau + 1} \qquad\qquad \lambda(\mu) = \lambda_0 \exp\left(-\theta\mu\right)$$

Reliability

$$R(\tau' \mid \tau) = \left[\frac{\lambda_0\theta\tau + 1}{\lambda_0\theta(\tau' + \tau) + 1} \right]^{1/\theta}$$

Mean time to failure

$$\Theta(\tau) = \frac{\theta}{1 - \theta} \, (\lambda_0\theta\tau + 1)^{1 - \frac{1}{\theta}} \qquad (\theta < 1)$$

Additional failures to failure intensity objective

$$\Delta\mu = \frac{1}{\theta} \, \ln\left(\frac{\lambda_P}{\lambda_F}\right)$$

Additional execution time to failure intensity objective

$$\Delta\tau = \frac{1}{\theta} \left[\frac{1}{\lambda_F} - \frac{1}{\lambda_P} \right]$$

μ = failures experienced (expected)
$\Delta\mu$ = additional failures (expected)
τ = execution time
τ' = execution time measured from the present
$\Delta\tau$ = additional execution time
λ_0 = initial failure intensity
λ_P = present failure intensity
λ_F = failure intensity objective
θ = failure intensity decay parameter
Θ = mean time to failure

E.3.2   Calendar Time Component

$$\frac{dt_r}{d\tau} = \frac{1}{P_r\rho_r} \left[\theta_r + \mu_r \, \frac{\lambda_0}{\lambda_0 \, \theta \, \tau + 1} \right]$$

t = calendar time

τ = execution time

r = index of limiting resource (C = computer time, F = failure correction personnel, I = failure identification personnel)

P_r = resource quantity

ρ_r = resource utilization

θ_r = execution time coefficient of resource usage

μ_r = failure coefficient of resource usage

λ_0 = initial failure intensity

θ = failure intensity decay parameter

E.4 RESOURCE REQUIREMENTS

$$\Delta\chi_r = \theta_r\ \Delta\tau + \mu_r\ \Delta\mu$$

$\Delta\chi_r$ = resource quantity

θ_r = execution time coefficient of resource usage

μ_r = failure coefficient of resource usage

$\Delta\tau$ = additional execution time

$\Delta\mu$ = additional failures

GLOSSARY OF TERMS

We have tried to make this glossary of terms reflect present standard usage. In most cases it is in conformance with *The IEEE Standard Glossary of Software Engineering Terminology* [IEEE (1983)], which is also an ANSI (United States) standard. Consequently, the terminology used in describing historic works in the field may not always be the same as that used in the works themselves.

availability: expected fraction of time during which system or component is functioning acceptably

calendar time: chronological time, including time during which a computer may not be running

category: model characteristic that relates to whether total number of failures is finite or infinite

class: model characteristic (finite failures category) that relates to the form of failure intensity as a function of time

clock time: elapsed time from start to end of program execution, including wait time, on a running computer

common-cause failures: failures arising from the same cause and hence unlikely to be independent of each other

computer utilization: fraction of clock time the processor is executing

concurrent: consisting of components that function at the same time

confidence bound: one limit of a confidence interval

confidence interval: range of values within which a parameter is expected to lie with a certain confidence *coverage*: sum of probabilities of occurrence of input states tested

data element: scalar quantity such as a numerical value, logical variable, character string, or abstract data type

data item: associated set of one or more data elements

deterministic: possessing the property of having only one value at a given time

deterministic testing: testing in which all selection of runs has been planned and prescribed in advance

developed code: new or modified deliverable executable instructions

discrepancy: difference between actual value of output variable, resulting from a run, and the value prescribed by the requirements

environment: operational profile

equivalence partition: set of input states that appear likely to be similar in that a given fault will result in a failure no matter which input state is activated

evolving program: program that is changing for reasons other than correction of failures

execution time: CPU time or time spent by processor in executing a program

expected value: mean of a random variable

exponential distribution: a specific probability distribution

fail set: set of input states that produces failures for a fault at a point in time

failure: see "software failure"

failure intensity: failures per unit time, the derivative with respect to time of the mean value function of failures

failure interval: time between failures

failure severity: classification of a failure by its operational impact

failure time: accumulated elapsed time at which a failure occurs

failure type: conjunction of input state and discrepancy

family: model characteristic (infinite failures category) that relates to the form of failure intensity as a function of expected number of failures experienced

fault: defective, missing, or extra instruction or set of related instructions that is the cause of one or more actual or potential failure types

fault exposure ratio: proportionality factor that relates failure intensity with the rate at which faults would be encountered if the program were executed linearly

fault reduction factor: net reduction in faults per failure experienced

fault-tolerant: incorporating design features to protect against effects of defects

grouped data: failure data in the form of number of failures in some interval

hazard rate: probability density (per unit time) of failure given that failure has not occurred up to the present *homogeneous*: possessing characteristics that do not vary with time

inference: the process of making a model specific, based on data that have been collected

inherent fault: fault associated with original software product (whether new or modified) at completion of coding

inherited code: deliverable executable instructions that are reused from a previous application (this code is usually well debugged)

input space: the set of all possible input states for a program

input state: set of input variables for a particular run

input variable: any data item that exists external to a run and is used by the run

least squares fit: a method of fitting a curve to data in which the parameters of the curve are determined so as to minimize the sum of squares of deviation of the curve from the data

limiting resource: the resource that controls the relationship between execution time and calendar time

maximum likelihood estimation: a form of parameter estimation in which those parameters are selected that maximize the possibility that the data that have been observed could have occurred

mean: the average value of a random variable, where the values that a random variable can have are weighted by the associated probabilities

mean time to failure (MTTF): expected value of the failure interval

mean time to repair (MTTR): expected value of the time required to restore to normal operation

mean value function: function that expresses the average value of the number of events experienced by a random process at each point in time

nonhomogeneous: possessing characteristics that vary with time

operational mode: one possible operational profile (among two or more) in which program can operate; mode is usually a function of installation or time

operational profile: the set of all possible input states (input space) with their associated probabilities of occurrence

output state: set of output variables for a particular run

output variable: any data item that exists external to a run and is set by the run

parameter: a quantity that, when specified, gives specific form to the general form of a model

parameter estimation: the process of establishing parameter values for a model, based on data

parameter prediction: determination of parameter values from characteristics of the software product and the development process

planned parameter: calendar time component parameter relating to resource quantities available and their utilizations, readily determinable from project person responsible

Poisson: a particular probability distribution and random process

predictable parameter: parameter whose value can be determined from properties of the software product and development process

prediction of parameter values: see "parameter prediction"

prescribed work period: the amount of time (usually specified in hours) per calendar time unit (usually per week) the average project member can work upon request

probability: the fraction of occasions on which a specified value or set of values of a quantity occurs, out of all possible values for that quantity

probability density: probability per unit variation of random variable

probability distribution: the set of probabilities corresponding to the values that a random variable can take on

program: a set of complete instructions (operators with operands specified) that executes within a single computer and relates to the accomplishment of some major function

random: possessing the property of having more than one value at one time, each occurring with some probability

random process: a set of random variables arranged by some other variable (usually time)

random testing: testing where selection of input states is random with selection probabilities equivalent to operational profile probabilities

random variable: a variable that possesses the property of randomness (see "random")

regression test: a test case or run that repeats an input state that was previously executed

resource usage parameter: calendar time component parameter that describes resources required for functions such as failure identification and correction

robust system: system that handles unexpected input states in a way that minimizes performance degradation, data corruption, and undesirable output states

run: a subdivision of the execution of a program, usually based on the accomplishment of a user-oriented function (during test, often called a "test case")

sampling with replacement: selecting from a population, with the states that are selected being returned for the possibility of being selected again

sampling without replacement: selecting from a population, with the states that are selected being eliminated from the possibility of being selected again

sequential: consisting of components that function one after another

software failure: departure of program operation from requirements *software reliability*: probability of failure-free operation of a program for a specified time in a specified environment

software reliability model: general form for characterizing software reliability or a related quantity as a function of failures experienced or time

stable program: program in which code is unchanging, with program neither evolving nor being repaired

stage: period of execution during which total code and developed code remain constant

statistically significant: sufficiently different to be attributable to cause, not random fluctuation

testing compression factor: ratio of execution time required in operational phase to execution time required in test phase to cover the input space of the program

total failures: number of failures that will occur in infinite execution time

type: model characteristic that relates to distribution of failures experienced

uniform: all possible values or selections occur with equal probability

utilization: proportion of time a resource is used

GLOSSARY OF NOTATION

A uniform set of symbols has been adopted in this book for clarity and consistency. They may differ from the symbols used in the original works. The symbols listed here are those used frequently throughout the book. Any departures from the definitions noted here are special exceptions necessary for clarity that are defined when they occur.

For random quantities, the random variables themselves are denoted by upper case letters and the observed values are denoted by lower case letters unless otherwise noted. Random variables denoting time can be modified by adding the subscript "i" or any integer to indicate the ith failure or the failure number denoted by the integer. In addition, a prime ($'$) indicates a difference (for example, interfailure time in the case of τ').

Other general conventions which are used are: the caret ($\hat{\ }$) denotes estimate and the tilde ($\tilde{\ }$) denotes an adjusted, transformed, or predicted value. Model parameters are generally denoted by β_k, but special symbols will be assigned for parameters with important physical meaning. The reuse of the same β_k in different models does not imply any relationships. Finally, vectors are denoted using bold type.

When looking up a symbol with a numeric subscript, note that the subscript will often be indicated in the glossary with a generic symbol such as i or k. Similarly, if the subscript is C, F, or I, look for the generic subscript r.

a	Fault index when used as a subscript
B	Fault reduction factor (average ratio of rate of reduction of faults to rate of failure occurrence)
C	Computer time when used as a subscript; otherwise, testing compression factor
$E[X]$	Expectation of X or mean of random variable X
f	Linear execution frequency r/I; failure probability density function $dF(t)/dt$
f_a	Failure probability density function per fault
$f(t_i \mid t_{i-1})$	Conditional density function for t_i given t_{i-1}
F	Cumulative failure probability function or probability that failure time is less than or equal to t; failure-correction personnel when used as a subscript
F_a	Cumulative failure probability function per fault
F_k	Cumulative failure probability function for stage k
$\tilde{F}$	Predicted cumulative failure probability function
$F(t_i \mid t_{i-1})$	Conditional cumulative distribution function for t_i given t_{i-1}
$F_k(t_i \mid t_{i-1})$	Conditional cumulative failure probability function for t_i from stage k given t_{i-1}
$g_a(t)$	Density function of time to remove a fault
$G_a(t)$	Cumulative distribution function of time to remove a fault
i	Index indicating sequential number of a failure event, $i = 1, 2,...$
I	Failure-identification personnel when used as a subscript; number of deliverable executable object instructions in the program when used with failure time adjustment; otherwise, expected or Fisher information
I_k	Number of deliverable executable object instructions for stage k
I_O	Observed information
I_S	Number of inherent source instructions
j	Alternate for i
k	Generic index for use with other than failure times (for example, component or stage number)
K	Fault exposure ratio
l	Alternate for k
L	Likelihood function
m	Number of failures experienced
m_e	Number of failures experienced at time t_e
m_l	Number of failures experienced for lth subinterval
m_Q	Bound on number of failures allowed to queue up for correction by any debugger

$M(t)$	Random variable denoting number of failures experienced by time t
$N(t)$	Random variable denoting number of faults removed by time t
p	Total number of subintervals
p_k	Probability of occurrence of input state k
p_{kl}	Transition probability (from component k to component l)
$P_{\min}$	Probability of occurrence of rarest input state
P_{m_Q}	Probability that no debugger has m_Q or more failures to work on at any given time
P_r	Available quantity of resource r where $r = C, F, I$
$P[E_1]$	Probability of the event E_1
$P[E_1 \mid E_2]$	Probability of the event E_1 conditioned on the event E_2
$P_m(t)$	Probability that m failures have been experienced by time t
q_{kl}	Probability of failure occurring during transition from component k to l
$q(t)$	Expected number of failures remaining by time t or $E[Q(t)]$
Q_I	Total number of input states
Q_P	Total number of components
Q_X	Code expansion ratio or ratio of object to source instructions
$Q(t)$	Random variable denoting number of failures remaining at time t
r	Resource when used as a subscript; otherwise, average instruction execution rate
r_l	Observed failure intensity for the lth subinterval
R	Reliability or probability of failure-free operation
R_k	Reliability of component k
$R(\tau_i' \mid \tau_{i-1})$	Reliability following $(i-1)$th failure
s	Alternate for r
S	Sum of squared errors
t	Cumulative calendar or generic time (realization when this time is a random variable)
t_e	A specific deterministic time denoting the end of failure data
t_i	Time of ith failure
t_l	Time at midpoint of lth subinterval
t'	Calendar or generic time since last failure (realization when this time is a random variable)
$\bar{t}'$	Average failure interval or t/m
t_i'	Failure interval following $(i-1)$th failure
$\tilde{t}_i$	Adjusted failure time
T	Random variable denoting cumulative generic time
T_i	Random variable denoting time of failure i
T'	Random variable denoting generic time since last failure
u_i	Realization of a uniformly distributed random variable
u_0	Inherent faults for binomial-type model

$U(t)$	Random variable denoting number of faults remaining at time t
$\text{var}[X]$	Variance of X
w	Index of last element in $\boldsymbol{\beta}$
x_l	Time at end of lth interval
X	Generic random variable
y_l	Cumulative failures at end of lth interval
y_l'	Number of failures in lth interval
Y	Generic set (subscript used to denote a particular set)
Y_l	Random variable denoting number of failures in lth interval
Y_D	Set of observations
z	Hazard rate or realization of hazard rate
z_a	Hazard rate per fault
z_k	Hazard rate for stage k
$z(t_i' \mid t_{i-1})$	Hazard rate for ith failure interval, given that time t_{i-1} has elapsed at the $(i-1)$th failure
Z_a	Hazard rate per fault that is a random variable
Z_i	Hazard rate that is a random variable
α	Shape parameter when used with a gamma distribution; overtime fraction when used in calendar time component; otherwise, confidence level
β_{high}	Upper confidence limit for β_k
β_k	Model parameter (Note: The same symbol used in different models does not imply any relationship between their parameters.)
β_{low}	Lower confidence limit for β_k
$\boldsymbol{\beta}$	Set of model parameters (individually denoted $\beta_0, \beta_1, \beta_2,\ldots, \beta_w$)
$\boldsymbol{\beta}_A$	Set of model parameters without β_0 (that is, $\beta_1, \beta_2,\ldots, \beta_w$).
Γ	Gamma function
Δm	Increment of failures experienced
Δt	Additional calendar time (especially, amount associated with reaching failure intensity objective); small time interval
Δt_r	Calendar time interval for limiting period of resource r where $r = C, F, I$
ΔI	Number of deliverable developed executable source instructions
ΔI_k	Number of deliverable developed executable source instructions for stage k
$\Delta \mu$	Increment of expected failures (especially, number associated with reaching failure intensity objective)
$\Delta \tau$	Increment of execution time (especially, amount associated with reaching failure intensity objective)
$\Delta \chi_r$	Increment of resource r where $r = C, F, I$
$\Delta \mu_l$	Expected number of failures in the interval (x_{l-1}, x_l) or $\mu(x_l) - \mu(x_{l-1})$
$\Delta \mu_r$	Expected number of failures during resource r period

$\Delta\tau_r$	Execution time interval for the resource r period
$\Delta\chi_{rr}$	Usage of resource r during its limiting period
ϵ	Random error
$\eta(t)$	Expected number of faults removed by time t or $E[N(t)]$
θ	Failure intensity decay parameter of logarithmic Poisson execution time model
θ_r	Execution time coefficient of resource usage where $r = C, F, I$
Θ	Mean time to failure (MTTF)
κ_3	Coefficient of skewness
$\kappa_{1-\alpha}$	$(1 - \alpha)$ percentile of a standard normal distribution
λ_k	Component failure intensity
λ_{rs}	Potential transition point between different resource-limited periods
λ_t	Failure intensity in clock time
λ_τ	Failure intensity in execution time
λ_F	Failure intensity objective
λ_P	Present failure intensity λ_0
γ_0	Initial failure intensity
$\lambda(t)$	Failure intensity function $d\mu/dt$
μ_{kl}	Mean duration spent in component k before going to component l
μ_r	Failure coefficient of resource usage where $r = C, F, I$
$\mu(t)$	Expected number of failures experienced by time t or $E[M(t)]$
ν_0	Expected failures experienced in infinite time
ξ	Scale parameter of a gamma distribution
ξ_k	Alternate for β_k
$\boldsymbol{\xi}$	Alternate for vector of model parameter $\boldsymbol{\beta}$
ρ_k	Probability of control residing in component k
ρ_r	Utilization of resource r during its limiting period where $r = C, F, I$
ρ_C	Average utilization of computer
σ	Error standard deviation
τ	Cumulative execution time (realization when execution time is a random variable)
τ_k	Cumulative execution time (realization when execution time is a random variable) for stage k; the execution time for a run corresponding to input state k
ϕ	Model parameter representing constant per-fault hazard rate; per-fault hazard rate at zero time; with a numerical subscript, an alternate for β_k
ϕ_k	Per-fault hazard rate for stage k
χ_r	Requirement for resource r where $r = C, F, I$
ψ	Psi (digamma) function
ω_I	Inherent fault density (with respect to source instructions)
ω_0	Number of inherent faults

$\omega(t)$	Expected number of faults remaining at time t or $E[U(t)]$
$A <-> B$	Statement A implies statement B and conversely
$\Pi_{i=1}^{k} a_i$	$a_1 a_2 \ldots a_k$ (product notation)
(t_1, t_2)	Open interval between t_1 and t_2 (does not include end points)
$[t_1, t_2]$	Closed interval between t_1 and t_2 (includes end points)
$\binom{n}{k}$	Binomial coefficient $= n!/[k!(n-k)!]$

H

PROBLEM SOLUTIONS

CHAPTER 1

1.1 First, the term "software reliability" is in general use, like it or not. However, we have deliberately decided to promote the usage further to emphasize compatibility of software and hardware reliability calculations and their joint use in computing system reliability. It is true that software doesn't wear out. "Software reliability" is really a measure of confidence in the design. Design confidence could be estimated for hardware systems. It usually isn't, because wear-out phenomena tend to swamp out design defects for most hardware systems.

1.2 First, a random model of behavior is just like any other model, an *approximation* to reality. The question is not whether the model is perfect but whether it is better than other (for example, deterministic) models. Hardware failures are not purely random. They do have deterministic causes that could be found given enough time and technology. We view hardware failures as random because it is easy to do so and this model is sufficient for making the predictions we find necessary.

There are a large number of ways in which *humans* fail and introduce faults into software. It is easiest (and satisfactory for prediction purposes) to model this behavior as a random process. Furthermore, the *use* of software systems (and hence the determination of which faults will cause failures) often is best modeled by a random process. You might even say that a deterministic view of software failure makes no sense. If you could inexpensively predict the failures that would be encountered in a particular usage, why wouldn't you correct the underlying faults?

1.3 Manipulation of the failure intensity estimate is possible. You must know at least one input state that fails and one that succeeds. You then select them in the proportions you desire. However, we aren't really interested in behavior of the program for an artificial set of tests. We are concerned with the typical environment of inputs (usually randomly sequenced) that will normally be encountered. Manipulation of tests for hardware is possible and just as unreasonable as for software. For example, you can obtain a very large failure intensity for most automobile tires by running them over a set of spikes.

1.4 Suppose people do learn the weaknesses of a system and avoid them rather than request the software designer to correct them. This acceptance is equivalent to a redefinition of the system requirements. Incidentally, there is no reason why usage of the remaining functions should not be regarded as a random process.

1.5 That depends. One essential is that the level of coverage be much closer to 1 than the reliability being measured. The other is that the probabilities of selection in test be the same as in operation (or the differences be known so you can compensate for them). If these conditions are satisfied, repeated runs do no harm except that the efficiency of testing is degraded.

1.6 Yes and no. A change in the environment is likely to result in more failures if the program has not been tested in the changed environment. However, failures can also occur in a familiar environment. It should be pointed out that hardware failures are also likely to increase when the environment changes. The increase may be less noticeable because of the failures that are constantly occurring due to wear-out.

1.7 In general, yes, but the answer is more complicated than that. When we speak of hardware reliability, we usually mean *physical* reliability or the probability that a system will survive physical failure mechanisms. Software reliability refers to design reliability or the probability that the system is free from behavior that departs from the system requirements. Both types of reliability are dependent on the usage of the system. However, systems are often built so that they are physically tolerant to a wide range of uses. Hence physical reliability may not be as susceptible to changes in usage as design reliability is.

The reliability of a hardware system is really dependent on both physical reliability and design reliability, although only the former is usually considered. The reliability of a software system is dependent only on design reliability.

1.8 Often, where recovery consists of a system reload plus perhaps a data base recovery, the time for the reload (and recovery, where applicable) is the MTTR. This is analogous to a hardware system where units are replaced by spares and later repaired. The actual software debugging and correction time doesn't normally apply, because the system would not be shut down while this activity was in process.

1.9 It means that enough runs must be made such that the sum of the probabilities associated with those runs in the operational phase approaches 1.

1.10 Yes. Your method is approximately equivalent to the assumption. The random selection of input states during test is usually done with the probability of selection of a particular input state proportional to the probability of selection it is expected to experience in use. Random selection will then result in an ordering of tests that is approximately the same as the order of their probability of occurrence.

CHAPTER 2

2.1 *Objective of 10 failures/CPU hr.* For the basic execution time model:

$$\Delta\mu = \frac{\nu_0}{\lambda_0} (\lambda_P - \lambda_F) = \frac{120}{20} (20 - 10) = 60 \text{ failures},$$

$$\Delta\tau = \frac{\nu_0}{\lambda_0} \ln \frac{\lambda_P}{\lambda_F} = \frac{120}{20} \ln \frac{20}{10} = 6 \ln 2 = 6(0.693) = 4.16 \text{ CPU hr}.$$

For the logarithmic Poisson execution time model:

$$\Delta\mu = \frac{1}{\theta} \ln \frac{\lambda_P}{\lambda_F} = \frac{1}{0.025} \ln \frac{50}{10} = 40 \ln 5 = 40(1.609) = 64 \text{ failures,}$$

$$\Delta\tau = \frac{1}{\theta} \left[\frac{1}{\lambda_F} - \frac{1}{\lambda_P} \right] = \frac{1}{0.025} \left[\frac{1}{10} - \frac{1}{50} \right]$$

$$= 40 (0.1 - 0.02) = 3.2 \text{ CPU hr.}$$

Note that the additional failures required are approximately the same but the additional execution time is somewhat less for the logarithmic Poisson execution time model.

Objective of 1 failure/CPU hr. For the basic execution time model:

$$\Delta\mu = \frac{\nu_0}{\lambda_0} (\lambda_P - \lambda_F) = \frac{120}{20} (20 - 1) = 114 \text{ failures,}$$

$$\Delta\tau = \frac{\nu_0}{\lambda_0} \ln \frac{\lambda_P}{\lambda_F} = \frac{120}{20} \ln \frac{20}{1} = 6 \ln 20 = 6(3.00) = 18 \text{ CPU hr.}$$

For the logarithmic Poisson execution time model:

$$\Delta\mu = \frac{1}{\theta} \ln \frac{\lambda_P}{\lambda_F} = \frac{1}{0.025} \ln \frac{50}{1} = 40 \ln \frac{50}{1} = 40 (3.91) = 156 \text{ failures,}$$

$$\Delta\tau = \frac{1}{\theta} \left[\frac{1}{\lambda_F} - \frac{1}{\lambda_P} \right] = \frac{1}{0.025} \left[\frac{1}{1} - \frac{1}{50} \right]$$

$$= 40(1 - 0.02) = 39.2 \text{ CPU hr.}$$

Note that as failure intensity objectives get smaller, the additional failures and execution time required to reach them become substantially larger for the logarithmic Poisson than the basic execution time model.

2.2 Usually most but not all failures result in the correction of the faults that caused them. We actually estimate failures rather than faults required to reach the failure intensity objective. The terminology "failures that must be experienced" is intuitively awkward but necessary for strict accuracy.

2.3 Convert the reliability level to a failure intensity objective. Then find the additional failures from Equation (2.9) or (2.10), depending on model used, or by running a software reliability estimation program.

2.4 Not necessarily. It approaches $\theta_r/P_r\rho_r$, which can be greater or less than 1.

2.5 You are missing one very important concept. The spacing between faults in "instruction space" is not the same as the spacing between failures in "execution space." The reasons for this are twofold:

1. Except in very trivial cases, code is not "straight line" but has many loops and branches.
2. Even if code were "straight line," the state of the machine will most likely not be constant and hence the fault associated with an instruction may or may not be exposed at one particular execution of the instruction.

Experience to date has shown that intervals between failures typically represent cycling through the program a large number of times. The picture you paint depends on all the faults being uncovered in one cycle through the program, which just doesn't happen in practice. With multiple cycles, the fault density *is* reduced when the first fault is corrected. *On the average* the failure intensity will decrease. Thus the failure intensity *does* change as testing progresses.

CHAPTER 4

4.1 The event diagram for the configuration is shown in Figure H.1. Note that the position of the mainframe operating system is in *series* with all the other components. It is *not* in each of the two parallel branches representing the mainframe hardware reliability. This is because the two programs are identical copies of each other. A failure occurring in one copy would have occurred in the other copy as well. Since these two software components are not independent of each other in regard to failure behavior, redundancy does not improve reliability. Let R_x be the required reliability for the mainframe operating system. Applying combinatorial rules for concurrently functioning components, we obtain:

$$0.90 = 0.99 \ (0.95) \ [1 - (1 - 0.98)^2]R_x,$$

$$0.90 = 0.9401 \ R_x,$$

and therefore

$$R_x = 0.9573.$$

4.2 The application programs are not considered (in effect, they can be viewed as having a reliability of 1). The calendar time failure intensities for the operating and time sharing systems will be 0.01 and 0.005 failure/hr, respectively. These numbers do not change if one processor should fail. The prime shift reliabilities are found to be 0.905 and 0.951, respectively. The combined reliability of the two processors is found as 0.9999. Combining all the "series" elements, we find an overall system prime shift reliability of 0.856.

4.3 Suppose you expect that the compiler will be reliable by the time you finally recompile the program before delivery to the customer. Then do not count failures due to bad compilation when making estimates of program failure intensity or reliability. If it will probably still be unreliable, you may wish to make your estimates twice, with the compiler-caused failures *included* in one estimate and *excluded* in the other. You

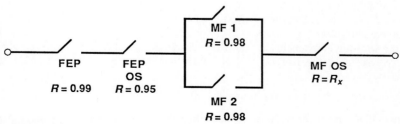

FIGURE H.1
Event diagram.

will then have a range of failure intensities or reliabilities with the extreme values representing a reliable compiler and an unreliable one.

4.4 You can continue testing or restart. It doesn't matter. If degraded data cause another failure, then the second event is really part of the first failure and shouldn't be counted again. However, if the system is required to recover from the first failure by cleaning up the data, the second failure is counted because it represents a failure of the *recovery mechanism*.

4.5 No, as far as we can determine. On the projects that have been observed to date, no correlation has been seen between complexity or subtlety of fault and phase of the test period.

4.6 Usually not. But suppose you are estimating failure intensity based on all failures, and deriving failure intensities for different failure severity classes from it by use of average proportions of severities. Then you may be temporarily overestimating the severe failure intensity just after the severe failures have been removed. However, the estimate will be correct in the long run. We should remark that your experience is *not* typical. Most projects do not have any correlation between severity and point in the test phase.

4.7 Yes, to some extent, *for that particular interval*. Reloads generally occur either just after a failure (to clean up the system) or randomly with respect to failures (routine periodic reloads). For any sample of failures of reasonable size, the effects tend to average out, so the estimation of failure intensities is reasonable. In any case, we never try to predict *individual* failure intervals. Note that if the frequency of reload is changed substantially on a long-term basis, this could conceivably result in a different failure intensity.

4.8 Yes, but this usually occurs less than 5 percent of the time. If in doubt, be consistent. Classify the failure as nonsoftware if it doesn't reappear on a rerun with all software and with known nonsoftware inputs exactly the same.

4.9 A system or component is *fault tolerant* if it operates satisfactorily in the presence of faults [defects that would cause failures (that is, unsatisfactory operation) if not counteracted]. "Hardware" and "software" fault tolerance refer to the source of the faults. Software components may be hardware-fault-tolerant or software-fault-tolerant or both. Hardware components are often hardware-fault-tolerant but usually not software-fault-tolerant. Software is said to be *robust* if it responds to nonfunctional inputs in a way that minimizes performance degradation.

4.10 Not directly, since test driver failures are not considered to be failures of the system being tested. Occasionally, test driver failures are so substantial that they result in a distortion of the operational profile being executed. Then the reliability measured for the system being tested may be in error.

4.11 No. We have repeated failures, just as if the software were executed on the same machine for the same input states. Whether the repetitions should be counted depends on circumstances and the objectives you have in collecting your data. This has been covered elsewhere.

4.12 Since the software components are not being repaired, the relationship between reliability R_k and failure intensity λ_k for component k is found from Equation (2.13) to be

$$R_k = \exp(-\lambda_k t) \ .$$

Note that time has been expressed generically. Using Equation (4.1) we have the overall system reliability

$$R = \prod_{k=1}^{Q_P} \exp(-\lambda_k t) = \exp\left[-t \sum_{k=1}^{Q_P} \lambda_k\right],$$

where Q_P is the number of components. But this is of the form

$$R = \exp(-\lambda t),$$

where λ is the system failure intensity. Hence

$$\lambda = \sum_{k=1}^{Q_P} \lambda_k.$$

4.13 Yes, as long as it is a requirement for that software component. Note that in this case the fault may be complex and distributed throughout the software component, since it relates to insufficient speed of execution.

4.14 If the only system requirement is to process work, the answer is "no." Failures relate only to external behavior of the system, not internal malfunctions.

4.15 No. You can interpret "requirements" as "user needs." Then if program operation departs from user needs, a failure is recorded. This interpretation may be the most useful and practical one from the customer's viewpoint. However, it does pose some legal and contractual problems. Most contractors will probably insist that the customer assume the responsibility for requirements faults and will not agree to counting their operational effects as failures.

4.16 In general, don't count them in test but do in the operational phase.

4.17 These failures should not be counted nor should execution time spent in unit test. Unit test involves testing only a small part of the software. Here you would have a retrogression, since a substantial part of the system would already have been in test. Suppose that the ratio of faults corrected in unit test to failures experienced in system test is relatively constant. Then you could adjust for the extra faults being corrected from unit test by increasing the fault reduction factor B.

CHAPTER 5

5.1 (b), (c), and (e). Note that testing in which the planning of tests depends on the results of previous tests can be inefficient. This approach typically lengthens the critical path of the schedule. It can also result in underutilization of the test team and even the debuggers. In addition, the resultant tests that are run may differ substantially in operational profile from those that would be encountered in operation, since test results are controlling.

5.2 Infinity and 0, respectively.

5.3 Yes. You will probably get the same results as for software in the operational phase.

5.4 Yes. You can predict the failure intensity to be expected by backing up in the test phase by the number of failures outstanding. Estimation of parameters and calculation of various quantities of interest are performed at this point.

5.5 Yes. You could rederive the maximum likelihood estimation formulas to account for missing or unknown data and change the supporting computation programs accordingly, but that would not be worthwhile. Picking failure times randomly within the period to which they are limited (for example, day or week) will give better results than assuming that the data are completely missing.

5.6 Yes, nothing prevents it. In practice, however, if the subsystems are *too* small, estimates made may have wide confidence intervals for a large part of the test period. Hence they may be of limited value. If calendar time predictions are to be accurate, you may wish to use resource parameter values that are either measured or adjusted to apply to the particular individuals involved.

5.7 No.

5.8 It could. It is best to subtract the delay from all the failure times before processing them.

5.9 No. There may be faults found and fixed indirectly as the result of correcting failures found during test. We may subtract the average number of such faults from the number of new faults spawned. The net remainder is used in computing the fault reduction factor *B*.

5.10 This computer time should not affect execution time intervals between failures, since these relate to the execution of the program that is to be delivered *only*. However, the analysis program could expend a limiting resource. If so, it must be accounted for by the calendar time component of the model.

5.11 Nothing, except your conception of what should happen. The prediction of total failures is dependent on the trend in failure intervals, not the total number. If the failures removed were near the start of test, you could have a failure interval trend that increases more slowly, yielding an increase in the total failures predicted.

5.12 The estimated total failures will be infinite. Note that the fault reduction factor *B* will be 0, so that the actual number of faults can be finite.

5.13 If the user determines that some failures are not to be corrected (either by direct order or by what is paid for), the specification has been effectively changed. The system behavior in question is no longer unacceptable. Thus the failure has been redefined out of existence. Once this category of failures has been removed from consideration the number of faults that can be corrected does relate to the number of failures identified.

5.14 Only the computer time and failure identification personnel resources can be simultaneously limiting. The following relationships between parameters must occur for this to happen:

$$\frac{\mu_C}{\mu_I} = \frac{\theta_C}{\theta_I} = \frac{P_C \rho_C}{P_I}.$$

5.15 As long as there is some repair effort (that is, the fault reduction factor *B* is not 0), all faults will ultimately be eliminated from the program. The interval between failures will approach infinity. Thus it is possible to have a finite number of failures in infinite time.

5.16 We experience and can readily count *total* failures. The best measure of the degree to which the software is repaired, with the resultant change in failure intensity, is *net* (not total) faults corrected.

5.17 It is assumed that each person involved in failure identification can run and examine the results from any test that is made. Failure correction personnel are assumed to work only on failures that have been attributed to their respective design areas. If a person has enough background to work at either failure identification or failure correction, depending on where staff is required, that person should be included in *both* counts. This might sound like duplication, but remember that, except in rare circumstances (see solution to Problem 5.14), only one resource at a time can be limiting.

5.18 No, because they do not directly constitute a limiting resource. Of course, the amount of support available may affect the environment in which the project operates, so that the resource usage parameters may be a function of the support level. That is, a higher level of support may reduce the amount of work done by the failure identification and failure correction personnel for each failure or per unit execution time.

5.19 No. They must all be available if needed (or suitable replacements must be provided, where "suitable" implies that the overall average skill level of the group remains the same). However, they will usually be far from fully employed in the latter part of the system test phase. Hence for practical purposes we can transfer some to other projects, with infrequent demands made for correction of failures in their programs.

5.20 Establish the maximum number of hours the computer can be used by your project each week. Subtract items such as maintenance time and down time. The result is hours of availability, which should be expressed in terms of prescribed work periods.

5.21 No. The ρ_C and ρ_F factors that are supplied as inputs relate to utilization during the computer-limited and failure-correction-personnel-limited periods, respectively, and are *maximum* figures. Each will have lower values during the other two periods.

5.22 An overhead factor should be applied to the parameters μ_F, μ_I, and θ_I. The overhead factor provides an allowance for training, vacations, absences, and administrative activities. A typical value is 1.67 (equivalent to the assumption that 60 percent of a person year is effective work time). This results in lengthening of all calendar time estimates to account for overhead activities on an *average* basis. You cannot, of course, predict the time of correction of a particular failure with any decent accuracy. The time required is a random variable. Also, the particular person who must do the correction *can* be sick or on vacation.

5.23 Change them. You may notice a "jump change" in many of the quantities you are monitoring as a result, but your predictions should henceforth be more accurate.

5.24 Usually not. The field test period is often a computer-time-limited one. Then only computer resource parameters need be known.

5.25 Yes. This can be handled in two ways:

1. You can reduce the number of available failure identification personnel by an amount proportional to the size of these activities relative to total test activities.
2. If the activities require work proportional to the amount of testing (execution time) or the number of failures or both, the resource expenditure parameters μ_I (failure identification work per failure) and θ_I (failure identification work per unit execution time) can be adjusted to reflect them.

5.26 Yes, a somewhat longer queue would probably be permissible. A modular-by-function program would be tested in a modular fashion, and a failure in one function would have little impact on another. Thus there would be less effect on the work of another program or on other work of the same programmer as a failure queue lengthens.

5.27 Note that you are really estimating *observable* failure intensity and the observability has suddenly changed. You might view this in the same light as a program being tested in a new environment. This violates the general assumptions of software reliability models, to some extent, but the effects are usually not serious. A new crop of failures will occur. Behavior will be analogous to behavior occurring when a substantial number of design changes are made at one time.

5.28 Let r_1 and r_2 be the instruction execution rates of the "failure identification" and "failure correction" computers, respectively. View all quantities as being referred to the failure identification computer. Then the failure correction computer can simply be considered as an additional computer resource with prescribed work periods P_{C_2} which adds an effective

$$P_{C_2} \frac{r_2}{r_1}$$

prescribed work periods to the original resource P_{C_1}.

5.29 Remember you are estimating what the initial failure intensity *must have been*, not what the present failure intensity is now. You *will* usually see an increase in present failure intensity. However, the occurrence of a number of short time intervals between failures indicates the proportion of faults that has been removed is not as high as we thought. In other words, the present failure intensity does not represent as much progress from the initial failure intensity as we had believed. This means we must have been overestimating the initial failure intensity.

   Note that the situation described will happen when a number of design changes are made, introducing new faults. The present failure intensity will rise, but the estimate of initial failure intensity will drop.

5.30 After a fashion. Later predictions are approximations to reality. Hence we can use them as a standard against which quality is measured, but only to a degree. We can check the execution time component parameters in this way, since they should be constant if there are no perturbing circumstances. A convenient way to do this is to use plots of the quantities against execution time. Project horizontal lines from the confidence limit boundaries at the point whose predictions are to be checked. If these are, for example, 75 percent confidence limits, then 75 percent of the points spanned by the succeeding confidence intervals should lie within the horizontal lines. This may be checked by comparing the ratio of the area inside the confidence intervals *and* the horizontal lines to the area inside the confidence intervals.

5.31 Providing that the quality of the estimation is good, they (particularly the total execution time plot) can be considered as an indication of the stability of the software. The plots should be horizontal in a stable situation. A rising plot usually indicates that design changes are introducing additional faults into the system and thus prolonging the completion time.

5.32 This time is *not* execution time. It represents failure identification time for the person (or persons) examining the data. If the same computer is used as that used for failure identification and correction, it also represents computer time expended.

5.33 Yes. Add 4 days to the predictions.

5.34 Yes. Test cases required would be determined by execution time expended in test. Treat the test case generation capability as an additional limiting resource.

5.35 We may include regression tests with the rest of the tests we are running. We can merge all the failure data, as long as the frequencies of the test cases match the operational profile.

5.36 Yes. The machine speed affects the linear execution frequency f.

5.37 Perhaps in absolute but not in relative terms. The effect mentioned is counteracted by the fact that the accuracy with which failure intensity can be estimated is increasing with execution time. This results from a larger sample of failure data being available. Software reliability models have at least two parameters, with associated accuracies. Both affect the geometry of the interaction of the failure intensity curve with the failure intensity objective. Therefore, a simple geometric analysis of this situation is not feasible. Instead, let's look at an example from an actual project (T1 in Table 13.1). Using the basic model, estimates of hours of execution time required to reach various failure intensity objectives were made, along with the 75 percent confidence intervals. Results are indicated in Table H.1. Note that the absolute size of the confidence interval increases as the failure intensity objective decreases, but the relative size *decreases*.

5.38 Since there will be 200,000 object instructions, the linear execution frequency f of the program will be $333,333/200,000 = 1.67 \text{ sec}^{-1}$ or $6,000 \text{ hr}^{-1}$. Note that inherent faults $\omega_0 = 300$. Hence initial failure intensity λ_0 is given by $\lambda_0 = fK\omega_0 = 6000(1.67 \times 10^{-7})(300) = 0.3$ failure/CPU hr, where K is the fault exposure ratio.

5.39 The computer utilization factor is set to reflect the *available*, not actual, level of utilization. If the users of the computer in question have their usage carefully scheduled, a reasonable value might be 1. If demands for service are essentially unscheduled and hence random, utilization must generally be held in the range of about 0.5 to 0.8 for reasonable turnaround.

If turnaround requirements are stringent, the utilization should be set near 0.5; average, 0.65; not stringent, 0.8. However, you may wish to set the value at the value that minimizes overall development costs, as described in Chapter 14.

5.40 Failure correction work required per failure. Almost all projects are in the failure-correction-personnel-limited period at the start of system testing. Most remain in this period for most of system test. Some (particularly those released with a moderate failure intensity remaining) stay in the period for *all* of system test. It is desirable to collect data on all limiting resources, since all limiting periods can occur. However, you can take a calculated risk that a particular resource other than failure correction personnel will never be limiting. You then do not collect resource expenditure data for it, if the collection is particularly difficult or burdensome.

TABLE H.1
Execution times of reaching various failure intensity objectives, basic model, project T1 [Table 13.1]

Objective (failures/CPU hr)	Execution time to objective (CPU hr)	
	Estimate	75% confidence interval
0.05	23.0	18.0–29.5
0.01	36.1	29.5–44.6
0.005	41.7	34.4–51.1
0.001	54.8	45.9–66.3
0.0001	73.5	62.4–88.0
0.00001	92.2	78.8–109.7

5.41 Yes, and the obvious generalizations of the calendar time component of the execution time theory should be made, unless one of the four resources can be considered to be nonlimiting. This is often the case with computer time for failure correction.

5.42 Generally not. Its effect is to place a time delay into the test and debug process that may be added to predicted completion dates.

5.43 Determine how many groups of such people exist (where any member can correct the failure) and the average group size. To determine the utilization factor, use the number of people and increase the acceptable queue length by a factor equal to the average group size.

5.44 You don't have to and should not. By finding more faults through code reading, you will reduce the failure intensity more rapidly than would normally be the case. The failures will be farther apart and the estimation process will automatically take care of this.

5.45 The parameter can be greater than 1 because computer time is used for more than testing. For example, recorded data must be processed and printed, and this requires computer time proportional to the length of the period of execution.

5.46 Note that each of these machines represents a separate resource. Thus we should apply an obvious generalization of the calendar time component of the execution time model. There will be three computer resources rather than one. Computer resource expenditures will be accounted for in three separate categories.

There can be as many as five resource-limited periods (three computer and two personnel) in this situation. Transition points between these periods and the calendar time to execution time ratio in each period may be computed in the same way as for the case of three resources.

5.47 No. Only the time used for general system testing by the failure identification (test) team that is devoted to initial failure identification. Additional selective testing undertaken to verify the existence of the failure or collect data on it is not counted. We do not count time required to diagnose the fault causing the failure. Neither do we count time needed to show that the failure has been corrected. Although we don't count these times as cumulative execution time, we do count them in determining computer resources used.

CHAPTER 6

6.1 It could do either. It would tend to increase if the simulator didn't adequately represent the environment. It would tend to decrease if you have underestimated the testing compression factor. Note that the software simulator itself may have failures due to faults, but you shouldn't be including these with the system you are testing. If the simulator itself represents deliverable software (for example, for system exerciser purposes), an estimate of its independent failure intensity may be desirable.

6.2 Yes. When applying software reliability measurement to monitoring system test, you will probably have a shorter test period because there will be fewer faults to remove. However, it seems likely that there will always be a substantial system test period before the release of any software product. It will always be necessary to run the code through a number of functional tests.

6.3 Yes, use a double randomization procedure. First choose the length of the period by picking a random number (uniformly distributed) from the range of possible period lengths. Then pick another random number that represents the location of the failure within the period. The following example may be illustrative.

Tester A runs tests for 3 hr following the previous failure with no new failures. Tester B, who keeps poor records, follows with more tests and experiences a failure, but does not record the time of the failure occurrence or the length of test. It is known, however, that the test period ran somewhere between 1 and 9 hr.

First, select a random number in the range 1 to 9 to establish the length of the period; assume that 3.7179 is selected. We now have the failure occurring sometime between 3 and 6.7179 hr since the last failure. Select another random number to fix the failure location. Assume that it is 6.3036. We have a failure interval of 6.3036 hr and 0.4143 hr of failure-free testing that follows it. This information may ordinarily be used directly in a software reliability estimation program.

The foregoing procedure will yield more accurate results than ignoring the failures and test periods that are not accurately recorded. An estimate of the inaccuracy in any derived quantity can be obtained by computing the quantity using the extreme values of the possible ranges of the unknown failure intervals.

Note that the first step of the procedure will prove useful in establishing the length of a failure-free test period that is uncertain.

6.4 Only if we can characterize the changes as the addition of a new subsystem(s), so that it can be combined with the previous subsystem using combinatorial rules for reliability. If not, then it is best to work with both pre- and post-change data together. The larger sample size generally means that perturbations in estimated quantities resulting from changes are reduced, and recovery from the perturbation is faster.

6.5 No. Ignore the second and following occurrences of the same failure, just as you would for faults not yet fixed in single site testing.

6.6 As noted in the solution to Problem 6.5, eliminate from consideration failures that reoccur at the field site but have already been detected at the development site. The data can then be merged as you do for multiple sites with the same release. If design changes have been introduced in the later release, then the situation is similar to that of design changes being introduced at a single site. However, the effects are somewhat moderated for the period during which failure data are being merged from the different releases. For example, a sharp increase in estimated total failures due to new faults introduced with the design changes will be "softened" and occur more gradually due to the overlap. Since this problem assumes few new features, their effect will be neglected.

6.7 By "actual environment more severe than test environment" we really mean that a substantial part of the input space of the operational phase was not or could not be covered in test. It's best that the test environment realistically represent the operating environment of the program. You can't expect to obtain good reliability predictions without a well-planned testing effort. (You couldn't do this with hardware either.) However, suppose you can estimate the probability of selection of that part of the input space that was not covered and the failure intensity for that part. Then you can estimate overall failure intensity using Equation (6.17).

6.8 First determine whether the versions are substantially different. Two versions are different if the code of one contains appreciable additions and modifications with respect to the other. If they are not substantially different, we can merge the failure data from the two directly. If they *are* different, the techniques of failure time adjustment or breakdown into subsystems should be considered for combining the data.

Sometimes it may be possible to directly merge failure data from different subsystems, with acceptable error occurring in the estimations based on the data.

If one version has repaired faults that have not been repaired in other versions, the reoccurrence of failures due to these faults should not be counted.

6.9 The approach is best illustrated by an example. Assume two testers with the following test and failure patterns indicated for a particular day:

Tester 1	Tester 2
8:00 A.M. Start test	
8:36 A.M. Failure A	
	9:00 A.M. Start test
	9:15 A.M. Failure B
9:40 A.M. Failure C	
10:00 A.M. End test	
	10:24 A.M. Failure D
	11:00 A.M. End test

Total execution time accumulated is measured as follows:

Time	Execution time (min)
8:00 A.M.	0
9:00 A.M.	15
10:00 A.M.	45
11:00 A.M.	60

The utilization for each hour is readily found from the above table to be:

Time	Utilization
8–9 A.M.	0.25
9–10 A.M.	0.5
10–11 A.M.	0.25

Since both testers are running on the same system we compute:

$$\text{execution time to failure A} = 36(0.25) = 9 \text{ min}$$
$$\text{execution time between failures A and B} = 24(0.25) + 12(0.5) = 12 \text{ min}$$
$$\text{execution time between failures B and C} = 28(0.5) = 14 \text{ min}$$
$$\text{execution time between failures C and D} = 20(0.5) + 24(0.25) = 16 \text{ min}$$
$$\text{execution time from failure D to end of test} = 36(0.25) = 9 \text{ min}$$

Thus the execution time intervals between failures are given by:

Failure	Execution time interval from previous failure (min)
A	9
B	12
C	14
D	16
end of test	9

If the two testers were testing different subsystems and we wanted to keep the failure data separate (to get subsystem reliability estimates) we could proceed as follows. Note that execution time measured between 9 and 10 A.M. is for both subsystems. Thus it must be allocated. The utilizations for each subsystem for each hour are

	Utilization	
Time	Subsystem X	Subsystem Y
8–9 A.M.	0.25	
9–10 A.M.	0.25	0.25
10–11 A.M.		0.25

We would compute for subsystem X:

$$\text{execution time to failure A} = 36(0.25) = 9 \text{ min}$$
$$\text{execution time between failures A and C} = 64(0.25) = 16 \text{ min}$$
$$\text{execution time from failure C to end of test} = 20(0.25) = 5 \text{ min}$$

For subsystem Y we would calculate:

$$\text{execution time to failure B} = 12(0.25) = 3 \text{ min}$$
$$\text{execution time between failures B and D} = 72(0.25) = 18 \text{ min}$$
$$\text{execution time from failure D to end of test} = 36(0.25) = 9 \text{ min}$$

The execution time intervals for the two subsystems are:

Subsystem X		Subsystem Y	
Failure	Execution time interval from previous failure (min)	Failure	Execution time interval from previous failure (min)
A	9	B	3
C	16	D	18
end of test	5	end of test	9

6.10 Yes. Weight clock time by an estimate of utilization. A good approximation of the utilization in any time period is given by the ratio of current users to maximum feasible users, multiplied by the utilization that corresponds to this maximum.

6.11 You shouldn't assign a trend because you do not know what the trend is (form) or what its parameters are.

CHAPTER 7

7.1 Each system experiences, on the average, 0.1 failure/week. Total failures will average 60/week or 12/day, requiring 6 service persons. Each doctor will require an average of 5.2 calls/yr at $200 each. Applying the profit margin to the annual cost of $1040 yields a contract fee of $1248.

7.2 The basic execution time model will be applied here, since we want to relate failure intensity to number of faults.

Consider first the situation without design reviews. We compute a value of $\nu_0 = \omega_0 = 400$ failures, using the program size and average fault density. Since initial failure intensity $\lambda_0 = 10$ failures/CPU hr, we have

$$\Delta\mu = \frac{\nu_0}{\lambda_0}(\lambda_P - \lambda_F) = \frac{400}{10}(10 - 0.1) = 396 \text{ failures}$$

and

$$\Delta\tau = \frac{\nu_0}{\lambda_0} \ln \frac{\lambda_P}{\lambda_F} = \frac{400}{10} \ln \frac{10}{0.1} = 40 \ln 100 = 184 \text{ CPU hr}.$$

The resource expenditures will be identical to the requirements, since no resources are allowed to be idle. Now

$$\chi_C = \mu_C\Delta\mu + \theta_C\Delta\tau$$

$$= 0.5(396) + 2(184)$$

$$= 566 \text{ CPU hr},$$

$$\chi_F = \mu_F\Delta\mu$$

$$= 6(396)$$

$$= 2376 \text{ person hr},$$

and

$$\chi_I = \mu_I\Delta\mu + \theta_I\Delta\tau$$

$$= 3(396) + 5(184)$$

$$= 2108 \text{ person hr}.$$

The cost of system test will be

$$\$1000 \, \chi_C + \$50 \, (\chi_F + \chi_I) = \$1000 \, (566) + \$50 \, (4484)$$

$$= \$790,200 \ .$$

Now, consider the case *with* design reviews. Since the programs are of the same size and executed on machines of the same speed, they will have the same linear execution frequency f. Since they are similar in type also, K may be assumed to be the same. Thus, $fK = \lambda_0/\omega_0 = \lambda_0/\nu_0 = 0.025$ is the same also. We have $\nu_0 = \omega_0 = 300$ failures and

$$\lambda_0 = fK\omega_0 = 0.025(300) = 7.5 \text{ failures/CPU hr}.$$

Hence

$$\Delta\mu = \frac{\nu_0}{\lambda_0}(\lambda_P - \lambda_F) = \frac{300}{7.5}(7.5 - 0.1) = 296 \text{ failures}$$

and

$$\Delta\tau = \frac{\nu_0}{\lambda_0}\ln\frac{\lambda_P}{\lambda_F} = \frac{300}{7.5}\ln\frac{7.5}{0.1} = 173 \text{ CPU hr}.$$

We have

$$\chi_C = \mu_C\Delta\mu + \theta_C\Delta\tau$$

$$= 0.5(296) + 2(173)$$

$$= 494 \text{ CPU hr},$$

$$\chi_F = \mu_F\Delta\mu$$

$$= 6(296)$$

$$= 1776 \text{ person hr},$$

and

$$\chi_I = \mu_I\Delta\mu + \theta_I\Delta\tau$$

$$= 3(296) + 5(173)$$

$$= 1753 \text{ person hr}.$$

The cost of system test *with* reviews is

$$\$1000\,\chi_C + \$50(\chi_F + \chi_I) = \$1000(494) + \$50(3329)$$

$$= \$670,450.$$

Thus the saving in system test costs from design reviews is $119,750. The design reviews require a total of 380 person hours of time, which costs $19,000. Thus the design reviews are cost effective, producing a net saving of $100,750.

7.3 (*a*) For the logarithmic Poisson execution time model

$$\Delta\mu = \frac{1}{\theta}\ln\frac{\lambda_P}{\lambda_F}$$

$$= \frac{1}{0.05}\ln\frac{10}{0.1} = 20\ln 100 = 20(4.61) = 92 \text{ failures}$$

and

$$\Delta\tau = \frac{1}{\theta}\left[\frac{1}{\lambda_F} - \frac{1}{\lambda_P}\right]$$

$$= \frac{1}{0.05}\left[\frac{1}{0.1} - \frac{1}{10}\right] = 20(9.9) = 198 \text{ CPU hr}.$$

Hence

$$\chi_I = 2(92) + 3(198)$$

$$= 778 \text{ person hr},$$

$$\chi_F = 6(92)$$

$$= 552 \text{ person hr},$$

and

$$\chi_C = 1(92) + 1.5(198)$$

$$= 389 \text{ CPU hr}.$$

(b) No, somewhat less. Note that $\Delta\tau$ is approximately doubled but increases logarithmically. Thus the resource increase will be between a logarithmic increase and a linear increase for changes in failure intensity objective.

7.4 We compute a value of $\nu_0 = \omega_0 = 500$ failures, using the program size and average fault density. The linear execution frequency, determined by dividing object instruction execution rate by number of object instructions, is 2.5 CPU sec^{-1} or 9000 CPU hr^{-1}. Hence, $\lambda_0 = fK\omega_0 = 9000(2.222 \times 10^{-7})(500) = 1$ failure/CPU hr. Now

$$\Delta\mu = \frac{\nu_0}{\lambda_0}(\lambda_P - \lambda_F) = \frac{500}{1}(1 - \lambda_F) = 500(1 = \lambda_F)$$

and

$$\Delta\tau = \frac{\nu_0}{\lambda_0}\ln\frac{\lambda_P}{\lambda_F} = \frac{500}{1}\ln\frac{1}{\lambda_F} = -500\ln\lambda_F.$$

The resource expenditures will be identical to the requirements, since no resources are allowed to be idle:

$$\chi_C = \mu_C\Delta\mu + \theta_C\Delta\tau$$

$$= 0.5\left[500 - 500\lambda_F\right] + 1\left[-500\ln\lambda_F\right]$$

$$= 250 - 250\lambda_F - 500\ln\lambda_F,$$

$$\chi_F = \mu_F\Delta\mu = 5\left[500 - 500\lambda_F\right]$$

$$= 2500 - 2500\lambda_F,$$

and

$$\chi_I = \mu_I\Delta\mu + \theta_I\Delta\tau$$

$$= 2\left[500 - 500\lambda_F\right] + 4\left(-500\ln\lambda_F\right)$$

$$= 1000 - 1000\lambda_F - 2000\ln\lambda_F.$$

The cost of system test will be

$$\$1000\,\chi_C + \$50(\chi_F + \chi_I) = \$250,000 - \$250,000\lambda_F - \$500,000\ln\lambda_F$$

$$+ \$50\left[3500 - 3500\lambda_F - 2000\ln\lambda_F\right]$$

$$= \$425,000 - \$425,000\lambda_F - \$600,000\ln\lambda_F\,.$$

The number of failures during operation will be the total operating lifetime multiplied by failure intensity, or $4000\,\lambda_F$. Hence the cost of failures will be $\$40,000,000\lambda_F$. The expression for the sum of these costs,

$$\$425,000 + \$39,575,000\lambda_F - \$600,000\ln\lambda_F,$$

is of the form

$$a + b\lambda_F - c\ln\lambda_F.$$

A simple minimization using calculus yields

$$\lambda_F = \frac{c}{b}\,.$$

Thus we obtain a value of 0.01516 failure/CPU hr for the failure intensity objective that minimizes system life cycle costs. The cost of system test and operational failures for this value is $3,538,000.

To determine the duration of system test, note that since there is only one limiting resource period, we have $\Delta\chi_{FF} = \Delta\chi_F$ and

$$t = \frac{\Delta\chi_F}{P_F\rho_F}\,.$$

Since no debugger can have more than 2 failures, with 90 percent probability, no debugger can have 3 *or* more with that probability. Thus the utilization factor is

$$\rho_F = \left[1 - P_{m_Q}^{1/P_F}\right]^{1/m_Q} = (1 - 0.9^{1/25})^{1/3} \approx 0.16\,.$$

Hence

$$t = \frac{\Delta\chi_F}{P_F\rho_F} = \frac{2500 - 2500\lambda_F}{25(0.16)} = 625 - 625\lambda_F\,.$$

At the minimum cost point, the system test period will require 616 hr or 77 days, each 8 hr long.

The reliability of the software for one day (8 CPU hr) of operations, assuming the failure intensity objective of 0.01516 failure/CPU hr is attained, is given by

$$R = \exp\left(-\lambda\tau\right) = \exp\left[-8(0.01516)\right] = 0.886,$$

where τ is the period of operation and λ is the failure intensity. This figure can be combined with reliabilities of hardware components to give overall system reliability.

7.5 Note that each installation will have an operational life of 10,000 CPU hr. The total number of failures over all installations will be $50{,}000\lambda$, where λ is the failure intensity. The cost impact of operational failures is $\$5{,}000{,}000\lambda$.

Using the table that was furnished, the following table can be constructed:

Failure intensity objective (per 100 CPU hr)	Operational cost(K\$)	System test cost(K\$)	Total cost(K\$)
1	50	1585	1635
2	100	1490	1590
3	150	1440	1590
4	200	1400	1600
5	250	1360	1610

Minimum cost occurs at about 2.5 failures/100 CPU hr.

At the high and low ends of system test cost we have:

Failure intensity objective (per 100 CPU hr)	Operational cost(K\$)	High end		Low end	
		System test cost(K\$)	Total cost(K\$)	System test cost(K\$)	Total cost(K\$)
1	50	1840	1890	1230	1280
2	100	1710	1810	1160	1260
3	150	1650	1800	1100	1250
4	200	1600	1800	1070	1270
5	250	1560	1810	1040	1290

Note that the minimum cost occurs at 3.5 and 3 failures/100 CPU hr, respectively. Thus the range of values of failure intensity objective is 2.5 to 3.5 failures/100 CPU hr.

7.6 The normalized failure time is 5. With no failures experienced, Figure 7.9 shows that the objective has been met with high confidence.

7.7 The base program had 500 faults at the start of system test. Since $B = 1$, $\nu_0 = 500$ failures.

The number of failures experienced during test was

$$\Delta\mu = \frac{\nu_0}{\lambda_0}(\lambda_P - \lambda_F) = \nu_0\left[1 - \frac{\lambda_F}{\lambda_0}\right]$$

$$= 500 \left[1 - \frac{0.06}{2} \right]$$

$$= 500(0.97)$$

$$= 485 \text{ failures}.$$

Since $B = 1$, 485 faults have been corrected and 15 remain. The modification will add 10 faults, making a total of 25 remaining.

The failure intensity in the operational phase is proportional to the faults remaining, hence

$$\lambda = \frac{25}{15} \ (0.06) = 0.10 \text{ failure/CPU hr} .$$

Thus the impact of modifying the code is to increase the failure intensity from 6 to 10 failures per hundred hours.

7.8 Yes. It can provide information on the present reliability of each subsystem. To decide on priorities for testing, you will also need information on the relative criticalities of the functions implemented by the subsystems and knowledge of how system failure is related to failures of the individual subsystems.

7.9 The entire fraction, during the failure-identification-personnel-limited segment, since failure identification personnel (unlike failure correction personnel) utilization is 1. The overtime cannot be profitably used when other resources are limiting. During the failure-identification-personnel-limited segment, a fraction of overtime to regular time of α will reduce elapsed calendar time by the factor $1 + \alpha$. The cost will be increased by a factor that is the product of α and the fractional increase for premium pay (typically 0.5).

7.10 The inefficient program will give a failure intensity that is realistic for that program. The system engineer must interpret failure intensity in the light of all other system characteristics, particularly performance, in establishing the quality of a particular implementation. For example, consider an airline reservation system that handles 10,000 reservations/CPU hr and has a failure intensity of 1 failure/CPU hr. It may be superior in quality to a system that handles 1,000 reservations/CPU hr and has a failure intensity of 0.5 failure/CPU hr. In a case such as this it may be useful for comparison purposes to transform time units to functional units. In other words, the systems have 0.1 and 0.5 failure/1000 reservations, respectively.

7.11 Not necessarily. You must take account of different cost impacts, perhaps due to different repair costs for the components.

7.12 The effects of "better testing" on the variation of failure intensity with time are illustrated in Figures H.2 and H.3.

Good test planning will increase the rate at which failure intensity decreases with execution time. Such planning will ensure that the most frequently occurring input states during operation are tested first. If faults are associated with these input states, the related failures will occur early. Thus failure intensity reduction will be rapid. Good test planning will also minimize inefficient duplicate activation of input states.

Proper execution of tests, with appropriate recording of relevant information, will maximize the value of the fault reduction factor B that can be attained. This will ensure that the rate of decrease of failure intensity with execution time is the maximum possible.

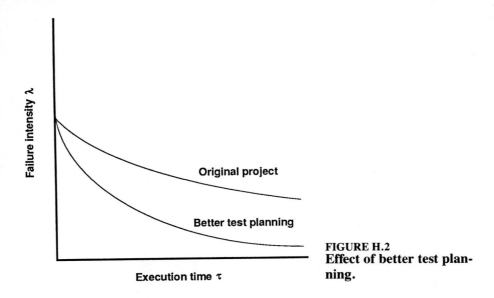

FIGURE H.2
Effect of better test planning.

7.13 This is really an "evaluation of software engineering technology" problem *except* that the technology in general cannot be evaluated. You can only evaluate the effect of the particular audits for the particular program in question. This must be done by a comparative test of the program with and without audits. The test must be sufficiently extensive that the part of the operational profile covered totals up to a high probability.

7.14 Yes. Plot the logarithm of the failure intensity function, given by

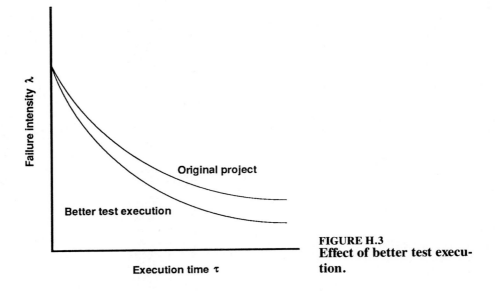

FIGURE H.3
Effect of better test execution.

$$\ln \lambda = \ln \lambda_0 - \frac{\lambda_0}{\nu_0} \tau .$$

You will note that it is a straight line (Figure H.4). Hence it is easy to project the model and read off execution times corresponding to various failure intensity objectives.

CHAPTER 9

9.1 Coverage is not used because:

1. The total number of segments is extremely large and impractical to compute for large programs.
2. Failure also depends on the machine state that exists when a segment is traversed.
3. The coverage measure does not take account of the relative frequencies of execution of the different segments.

9.2 It is true that "instructions executed" would be computer-independent, but is usually not as easy to measure as execution time. Also, it is not compatible with hardware reliability metrics.

9.3 The reason is a rather fine distinction. As you know, a "failure" is an operational manifestation of a "fault." It represents a departure from "satisfactory" operation. The fault is the actual software defect that is causing the failure. When a failure occurs, the associated fault doesn't always get corrected (for example, information about the failure may be insufficient for diagnosis). We use the term *failure* correc-

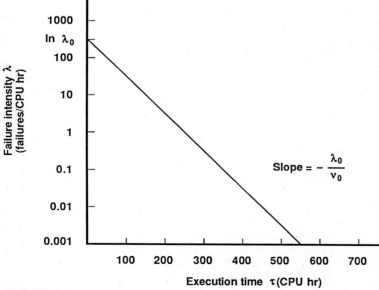

FIGURE H.4
Failure intensity for basic model, plotted on logarithmic scale.

tion personnel because these people not only diagnose and correct faults but also examine the failures identified to see if fault correction is possible. Hence they take action on or "correct" in one fashion or another all failures.

9.4 Yes.

9.5 The number of faults in a program *does* vary with the environment. If the environment is limited (few possible input states), it is possible that the program may execute without failure forever. In that case, there are no faults. However, with a more extensive set of input states, there are likely to be failures and hence faults causing them.

9.6 Failure intensity is the time derivative of expected failures. Failure density is the time derivative of the probability that the failure interval is less than or equal to some value.

9.7 Incorrect or inconsistent requirements differ from the requirements that were intended. Hence they contain faults, which may result in failures.

9.8 Yes.

CHAPTER 10

10.1 First, consider the case for $m = 0$. From Equation (10.4) we have

$$\frac{P_0(t+\Delta t) - P_0(t)}{\Delta t} = - \lambda(t) \, P_0(t) + \frac{o(\Delta t)}{\Delta t} , \tag{H.1}$$

which yields the differential equation for $\Delta t \to 0$

$$\frac{dP_0(t)}{dt} = - \lambda(t) \, P_0(t) . \tag{H.2}$$

Equivalently, we have

$$\frac{1}{P_0(t)} \frac{dP_0(t)}{dt} = - \lambda(t) . \tag{H.3}$$

Integrating both sides of Equation (H.3) yields

$$\ln P_0(t) = - \mu(t) + C , \tag{H.4}$$

where C is the constant of integration. From assumption 1 we have $P_0(0) = 1$ and hence $C = 0$. Thus, the desired expression for $P_0(t)$ is given by

$$P_0(t) = \exp[- \mu(t)] . \tag{H.5}$$

Now, consider the case for $m > 0$. Using a similar technique as above, we obtain the differential equation as

$$\frac{dP_m(t)}{dt} = - \lambda(t) \, P_m(t) + \lambda(t) P_{m-1}(t) . \tag{H.6}$$

After rearranging Equation (H.6) and multiplying both sides by $\exp[\mu(t)]$, we have

$$\exp[\mu(t)]\left[\frac{dP_m(t)}{dt} + \lambda(t)\,P_m(t)\right] = \lambda(t)\,\exp[\mu(t)]P_{m-1}(t)\ . \qquad \text{(H.7)}$$

Hence,

$$\frac{d\left\{\exp[\mu(t)]P_m(t)\right\}}{dt} = \lambda(t)\exp[\mu(t)]P_{m-1}(t)\ . \qquad \text{(H.8)}$$

Substituting Equation (H.5) into Equation (H.8) with $m = 1$, we obtain

$$\frac{d\left\{\exp[\mu(t)]P_1(t)\right\}}{dt} = \lambda(t) \qquad \text{(H.9)}$$

or

$$\exp[\mu(t)]P_1(t) = \mu(t) + C\ . \qquad \text{(H.10)}$$

Since $P_1(0) = 0$, we have $C = 0$ and hence

$$P_1(t) = \mu(t)\,\exp[-\mu(t)], \qquad \text{(H.11)}$$

which is equivalent to Equation (10.5) with $m = 1$.

This can be substituted again into Equation (H.8) with $m = 2$, so that the system can be solved recursively. It is evident that the general solution is given by Equation (10.5).

10.2 First, consider the case for $m = 0$. From Equation (10.24) we have

$$\frac{dP_0(t)}{dt} = -u_0 z_a(t)P_0(t) \qquad \text{(H.12)}$$

or equivalently

$$\frac{1}{P_0(t)}\,\frac{dP_0(t)}{dt} = -u_0 z_a(t)\ . \qquad \text{(H.13)}$$

Integrating both sides of Equation (H.13) yields

$$\ln P_0(t) = -u_0 \int_0^t z_a(x)\,dx \qquad \text{(H.14)}$$

or

$$P_0(t) = \exp\left[-u_0 \int_0^t z_a(x)\,dx\right]$$

$$= [1 - F_a(t)]^{u_0}, \qquad \text{(H.15)}$$

where the last equality was obtained using Equation (10.22). Note that Equation (H.15) is equivalent to Equation (10.25) with $m = 0$.

Now, consider the case for $m > 0$. After rearranging Equation (10.24) and multiplying both sides by $[1 - F_a(t)]^{-(u_0-m)}$, we obtain

$$[1 - F_a(t)]^{(u_0-m)} \left[\frac{dP_m(t)}{dt} + (u_0 - m)z_a(t)P_m(t) \right]$$

$$= (u_0 - m + 1)z_a(t)P_{m-1}(t)[1 - F_a(t)]^{-(u_0-m)} \quad \text{(H.16)}$$

Hence,

$$\frac{d\left\{ [1 - F_a(t)]^{-(u_0-m)}P_m(t) \right\}}{dt}$$

$$= (u_0 - m + 1)z_a(t) \, P_{m-1}(t) \, [1 - F_a(t)]^{-(u_0-m)} . \quad \text{(H.17)}$$

Substituting Equation (H.15) into Equation (H.17) with $m = 1$ yields

$$\frac{d\left\{ [1 - F_a(t)]^{1-u_0} P_1(t) \right\}}{dt} = u_0 z_a(t)[1 - F_a(t)]$$

$$= u_0 f_a(t) . \quad \text{(H.18)}$$

Integrating both sides, we obtain

$$[1 - F_a(t)]^{1-u_0}P_1(t) = u_0 F_a(t) \quad \text{(H.19)}$$

or

$$P_1(t) = u_0 F_a(t) \, [1 - F_a(t)]^{u_0-1} \quad \text{(H.20)}$$

which is equivalent to Equation (10.25) with $m = 1$.

This can be substituted again into Equation (H.17) with $m = 2$, so that the system can be solved recursively. It is evident that the general solution is given by Equation (10.25).

10.3 Consider the conditional distribution of T_i given $M(t_e) = m_e$, where $i > m_e$. Using Equations (10.12) and (10.32), we obtain

$$P[T_i \leq t \mid M(t_e) = m_e] = P[M(t) \geq i \mid M(t_e) = m_e]$$

$$= \sum_{j=1}^{u_0} \begin{bmatrix} u_0 - m_e \\ j - m_e \end{bmatrix} [F_a(t \mid t_e)]^{j-m_e}[1 - F_a(t \mid t_e)]^{u_0-j}. \quad \text{(H.21)}$$

Let $R(t_i' \mid t_{i-1})$ be the conditional reliability of T_i' given $T_{i-1} = t_{i-1}$, that is,

$$R(t_i' \mid t_{i-1}) = P[T_i' > t_i' \mid T_{i-1} = t_{i-1}] \,. \tag{H.22}$$

Since the event $T_{i-1} = t_{i-1}$ is equivalent to $M(t_{i-1}) = i - 1$, we have

$$P[T_i > t_i \mid T_{i-1} = t_{i-1}] = 1 - P[T_i \leqslant t_i \mid T_{i-1} = t_{i-1}]$$

$$= 1 - P[T_i \leqslant t_i \mid M(t_{i-1}) = i - 1] \,. \tag{H.23}$$

Note that for $m_e = i - 1$, Equation (H.21) is the sum of binomial probabilities except for one term. Hence,

$$P[T_i \leqslant t_i \mid M(t_{i-1}) = i - 1] = 1 - \left[1 - F_a(t_i \mid t_{i-1})\right]^{u\sigma - i + 1}. \tag{H.24}$$

Substituting Equation (H.24) into Equation (H.23) yields

$$P[T_i > t_i \mid T_{i-1} = t_{i-1}] = [1 - F_a(t_i \mid t_{i-1})]^{u\sigma - i + 1}. \tag{H.25}$$

CHAPTER 11

11.1 Recall that the per-fault hazard rate for a Weibull-class, binomial-type model is given by (see Section 11.1.1)

$$z_a(t) = \phi\gamma t^{\gamma - 1} \,. \tag{H.26}$$

We obtain the corresponding per-fault probability density function as

$$f_a(t) = z_a(t)\exp[\, -\int_0^t z_a(x)dx\,]$$

$$= \phi\gamma t^{\gamma - 1} \exp(-\phi t^\gamma) \,. \tag{H.27}$$

Substituting Equation (H.27) into Equation (11.3) yields the failure intensity as

$$\lambda(t) = u_0 f_a(t)$$

$$= u_0 \phi\gamma t^{\gamma - 1} \exp(-\phi t^\gamma) \,. \tag{H.28}$$

Therefore, we can find the desired expression, where $\xi_0 = u_0\phi\gamma$, $\xi_1 = \phi$, and $\xi_2 = \gamma$.

The corresponding per-fault cumulative distribution function is obtained as

$$F_a(t) = 1 - \exp\left[-\int_0^t z_a(x)dx \right]$$

$$= 1 - \exp(-\phi t^\gamma) \,. \tag{H.29}$$

Hence, substituting Equation (H.29) into Equation (11.2) yields the mean value function as

$$\mu(t) = u_0 F_a(t)$$

$$= u_0[1 - \exp(-\phi t^\gamma)] . \tag{H.30}$$

If we solve Equation (H.30) for t, we have

$$t = \left[-\frac{1}{\phi} \ln (1 - \frac{\mu}{u_0}) \right]^{1/\gamma} . \tag{H.31}$$

Substituting Equation (H.31) into the failure intensity function of Equation (H.28) yields the function in terms of μ as

$$\lambda(\mu) = u_0 \phi \gamma t^{\gamma-1} \exp(-\phi t^\gamma)$$

$$= u_0 \phi \gamma \left[-\frac{1}{\phi} \ln \left(1 - \frac{\mu}{u_0} \right) \right]^{(\gamma-1)/\gamma} (1 - \frac{\mu}{u_0}) . \tag{H.32}$$

We can easily verify that this expression is the desired form, where $\phi_0 = \gamma \phi^{1/\gamma}$, $\phi_1 = u_0$, and $\phi_2 = (\gamma - 1)/\gamma$.

11.2 Recall that the per-fault hazard rate for a Pareto-class, binomial-type model is given by (see Section 11.1.1)

$$z_a(t) = \frac{\beta_2}{t + \beta_1} . \tag{H.33}$$

The corresponding per-fault probability density function is obtained as

$$f_a(t) = z_a(t) \exp \left[- \int_0^t z_a(x)dx \right]$$

$$= \beta_1^{\beta_2} \beta_2(t + \beta_1)^{-\beta_2-1} . \tag{H.34}$$

Substituting Equation (H.34) into Equation (11.3) yields the failure intensity as

$$\lambda(t) = u_0 f_a(t)$$

$$= u_0 \beta_2(t + \beta_1)^{-\beta_2-1} . \tag{H.35}$$

Therefore, we can find the desired expression, where $\xi_0 = u_0\beta_1^{\beta_2}\beta_2$, $\xi_1 = \beta_1$ and $\xi_2 = \beta_2 + 1$.

The corresponding per-fault cumulative distribution function is obtained as

$$F_a(t) = 1 - \exp \left[- \int_0^t z_a(x)dx \right]$$

$$= 1 - \beta_1^{\beta_2}(t + \beta_1)^{-\beta_2} . \tag{H.36}$$

Hence, substituting Equation (H.36) into Equation (11.2) yields the mean value function as

$$\mu(t) = u_0 F_a(t)$$

$$= u_0[1 - \beta_1^{\beta_2}(t + \beta_1)^{-\beta_2}] . \tag{H.37}$$

If we solve Equation (H.37) for $t + \beta_1$, we have

$$t + \beta_1 = \left[1 - \frac{\mu}{u_0}\right]^{-1/\beta_2} \beta_1. \tag{H.38}$$

Substituting Equation (H.38) into Equation (H.35) yields the function in terms of

$$\lambda(\mu) = u_0 \beta_2 (t + \beta_1)^{-\beta_2 - 1}$$

$$= u_0 \frac{\beta_2}{\beta_1} \left[1 - \frac{\mu}{u_0}\right]^{1+1/\beta_2} , \tag{H.39}$$

which corresponds to the desired form. Note that $\phi_0 = (u_0^{-1/\beta_2})\beta_2/\beta_1$, $\phi_1 = u_0$, and $\phi_2 = 1 + 1/\beta_2$.

11.3 For an inverse polynomial family model, MTTF is given by

$$\Theta(i) = \beta_0 + \beta_1 i^2 . \tag{H.40}$$

Substituting Equations (11.57) and (11.58) into Equation (H.40) yields

$$\frac{1}{\lambda(t)} = \beta_2 + \beta_1 [\mu(t)]^2 \tag{H.41}$$

and further substitution of Equation (9.6) yields

$$\left\{\beta_0 + \beta_1[\mu(t)]^2\right\} d\mu(t) = dt . \tag{H.42}$$

After integrating both sides, we obtain

$$\beta_0 \mu(t) + \frac{\beta_1}{3} [\mu(t)]^3 = t + C , \tag{H.43}$$

where C is the constant of integration. Since $\mu(0) = 0$, we have $C = 0$. It is shown [Beyer (1976)] that for $\beta_0 > 0$ and $\beta_1 > 0$, this equation will have one real root and two conjugate imaginary roots. The real root is given by

$$\mu(t) = 3 \xi_0 \left[\sqrt[3]{t + \sqrt{t^2 + \xi_1}} + \sqrt[3]{t - \sqrt{t^2 + \xi_1}}\right] , \tag{H.44}$$

where $\xi_0 = (18\beta_1)^{-1/3}$ and $\xi_1 = 4\beta_0^3/9\beta_1$. Differentiating by t yields the desired expression.

11.4 For the geometric de-eutrophication model, MTTF is given by

$$\Theta(i) = \frac{1}{\lambda_0 k^{i-1}} . \tag{H.45}$$

Using Equations (9.6), (11.60), (11.61), and (H.45) this is reduced to the following differential equation:

$$\frac{d\mu(t)}{dt} = \lambda_0 k^{\mu(t)-1} . \tag{H.46}$$

Let $k = \exp(-\theta)$. Then, we have

$$\frac{d\mu(t)}{dt} \exp[\theta\mu(t)] = \lambda_0 \exp(\theta) . \tag{H.47}$$

Integrating both sides yields

$$\exp[\theta\mu(t)] = [\lambda_0\theta \exp(\theta)]t + C ,$$

where C is the constant of integration. Since $\mu(0) = 0$, we have $C = 1$. Hence, the mean value function is

$$\mu(t) = \frac{1}{\theta} \ln \{[\lambda_0\theta \exp(\theta)]t + 1\} . \tag{H.48}$$

Therefore, we can obtain the failure intensity as

$$\lambda(t) = \frac{\lambda_0 \exp(\theta)}{[\lambda_0\theta \exp(\theta)]t + 1} ,$$

which is equivalent to the desired form with $\xi_0 = \lambda_0\theta \exp(\theta)$ and $\xi_1 = \lambda_0\theta \exp\theta$.
   The other desired form can be found in the differential equation of (H.46), where $\phi_0 = \lambda_0/k$ and $\phi_1 = -\ln k$.

CHAPTER 12

12.1 The conditional likelihood based on grouped data is given by Equation (12.125) while that for failure time data is given by Equation (12.32). A comparison of the two shows that since $m_e = y_p$ and $t_e = x_p$, we need to show that

$$\lim_{p \to \infty} \prod_{l=1}^{p} [\mu(x_l) - \mu(x_{l-1})]^{y'_l}/y'_l! = \prod_{i=1}^{m_e} \lambda(t_i) .$$

As $p \to \infty$, the quantity $x_l - x_{l-1} \to 0$ and y'_l will be either 0 or 1. Thus we have

$$\lim_{p \to \infty} \prod_{l=1}^{p} [\mu(x_{l-1} + \Delta x) - \mu(x_{l-1})]^{y'_l}/y'_l =$$

$$\lim_{p \to \infty} \prod_{i=1}^{m_e} \frac{\mu(x_{i-1} + \Delta x) - \mu(x_{i-1})}{\Delta x} \cdot \Delta x ,$$

where we have used the fact that there are only m_e values of y'_i which equal 1. Since in the limit x_{i-1} is indistinguishable from x_i and both are equal to t_i we obtain

$$\lim_{p \to \infty} \prod_{i=1}^{m_e} \frac{\mu(t_i + \Delta t) - \mu(t_i)}{\Delta t} \cdot \Delta t = \prod_{i=1}^{m_e} \frac{\partial \mu(t_i)}{\partial t} = \prod_{i=1}^{m_e} \lambda(t_i) .$$

The extra Δx factors were ignored since they are not a function of the data or the unknown parameters.

12.2 The sum in Equation (12.27) can be simplified by using the approximation

$$\sum_{i=1}^{m_e} \frac{1}{\hat{u}_0 - i + 1} \approx \int_{\hat{u}_0 - m_e}^{\hat{u}_0} \frac{dx}{x} = \ln \left(\frac{\hat{u}_0}{\hat{u}_0 - m_e} \right) .$$

The likelihood equation for u_0 then becomes

$$\ln [1 - F_a(t_e)] + \ln \left(\frac{\hat{u}_0}{\hat{u}_0 - m_e} \right) = 0 ,$$

or, after solving for $\hat{u}_0$ we have

$$\hat{u}_0 = \frac{m_e}{F_a(t_e)} .$$

12.3 A more accurate approximation for the sum in Equation (12.27) is given by Davis (1962) as

$$\sum_{i=1}^{m_e} \frac{1}{\hat{u}_0 - i + 1} \approx \psi(\hat{u}_0 + 1) - \psi(\hat{u}_0 - m_e + 1) ,$$

where ψ is the Psi function. Kelley (1979) showed that

$$\psi(x + 1) = \ln (x + 1/2)$$

is a good approximation. Thus,

$$\sum_{i=1}^{m_e} \frac{1}{\hat{u}_0 - i + 1} \approx \ln \left(\frac{\hat{u}_0 + 1/2}{\hat{u}_0 - m_e + 1/2} \right)$$

and solving Equation (12.27) for $\hat{u}_0$ we obtain

$$\hat{u}_0 = \frac{m_e}{F_a(t_e)} - \frac{1}{2} .$$

Since $\hat{u}_0$ is rounded to the nearest integer we would expect to overestimate by no more than 1 failure using Equation (12.33). This is a small price to pay for the ease of computation.

12.4 The conditional likelihood function, $L(\beta_1|m_e)$, will have a maximum for a positive value of β_1 if the slope of the function at the origin is positive. That is, the function must be increasing as it crosses the origin from left to right. The slope of $L(\beta_1|m_e)$ follows that of $\ln L(\beta_1|m_e)$. For the exponential class we start with the left-hand side of Equation (12.54), that is,

$$\frac{\partial \ln L(\beta_1 \mid m_e)}{\partial \beta_1} = m_e \left\{ \frac{\exp(\beta_1 t_e) - \beta_1 t_e - 1}{\beta_1[\exp(\beta_1 t_e) - 1]} \right\} - \sum_{i=1}^{m_e} t_i .$$

Concentrate on the term within the braces. Applying L'Hopital's rule [Crowell and Slesnick (1968)] twice it can be verified that the term approaches $t_e/2$ as β_1 approaches 0. Thus, the condition that must be satisfied for a positive $\hat{\beta}_1$, is

$$\frac{m_e}{2} t_e > \sum_{i=1}^{m_e} t_i .$$

For the geometric family we start with the left-hand side of Equation (12.57) and use the approximations $(1 + x)^{-1} \approx 1 - x$ and $(1 + x) \ln (1 + x) \approx x(x + 2)/2$. With these approximations we have

$$\frac{\partial \ln L(\beta_1 \mid m_e)}{\partial \beta_1} \approx \frac{m_e}{\beta_1} - \sum_{i=1}^{m_e} t_i - \frac{2m_e t_e}{\beta_1 t_e (\beta_1 t_e + 2)}$$

$$= \frac{m_e}{\beta_1} - \sum_{i=1}^{m_e} t_i - m_e t_e \left[\frac{1}{\beta_1 t_e} - \frac{1}{\beta_1 t_e + 2} \right]$$

$$= - \sum_{i=1}^{m_e} t_i + \frac{m_e}{2} t_e .$$

Thus, the condition that must be satisfied for a positive $\hat{\beta}_1$ is the same as the one for an exponential-class model. The condition for both models is the same as that given in Case Study 12.1 for reliability growth.

12.5 Start with Equation (12.42). As β_1 approaches 0 the exponential in the denominator approaches $1 - \beta_1 t_e$. Thus, $L(\beta_1 \mid m_e) \to m_e!/t_e^{m_e}$. Now look at Equation (12.56). Here the logarithmic term approaches $\beta_1 t_e$ so that once again $L(\beta_1 \mid m_e) \to m_e!/t_e^{m_e}$.

12.6 For the exponential class we see from Equation (12.53) that as $\hat{\beta}_1$ approaches 0, $\hat{\beta}_0$ approaches $m_e/\hat{\beta}_1 t_e$, which is unbounded. However, the product $\hat{\beta}_0\hat{\beta}_1$ is seen to approach the constant m_e/t_e, which represents the observed failure intensity. As far as the model is concerned, $\lambda(t)$ approaches the constant value m_e/t_e, and we have a stationary process. Analogous results hold for the geometric family.

12.7 The unconditional probability density function of T_i is given as the derivative of Equation (10.13) with respect to t_i. Thus,

$$f(t_i) = \frac{dP[T_i \leq t_i]}{dt_i} = \lambda(t_i) \exp[-\mu(t_i)] \sum_{j=1}^{\infty} \left\{ \frac{[\mu(t_i)]^{j-1}}{(j-1)!} - \frac{[\mu(t_i)]^{j}}{j!} \right\} .$$

It can be easily verified that the value of the sum is $[\mu(t_i)]^{i-1}/(i-1)!$ so

$$f(t_i) = \frac{\lambda(t_i)[\mu(t_i)]^{i-1} \exp[-\mu(t_i)]}{(i-1)!}$$

12.8 Replacing t_e with t_m and m_e with m in Equation (12.46) and dividing by $f(t_m)$ results in the conditional likelihood function

$$L(\beta \mid m) = \frac{(m-1)! \prod_{i=1}^{m-1} \lambda(t_i)}{[\mu(t_m)]^{m-1}}.$$

Comparison of this result and Equation (12.51) shows that the resulting estimation is the same except that a sample, in effect, has been "lost" in preassigning the number of failures. This sample can be viewed as being required to set the time of test, the remaining samples are then treated as before.

12.9 The conditional likelihood can be obtained by dividing Equation (12.120) by the probability that the observed number of failures occurred during the pth interval. This probability is seen to be equal to the product of the probability that y_{p-1} failures occurred by time x_{p-1} and the probability that an additional y_p' failures occurred during the last interval, that is,

$$P[M(x_{p-1}) = y_{p-1}] \, P[M(x_p) - M(x_{p-1}) = y_p'].$$

Using Equation (12.119), the above expression becomes

$$\frac{[\mu(x_{p-1})]^{y_{p-1}}}{y_{p-1}!} \cdot \frac{[\mu(x_p) - \mu(x_{p-1})]^{y_p'}}{y_p'!} \exp[-\mu(x_p)],$$

and carrying out the division operation we have

$$L(\beta \mid p) = y_{p-1}! \prod_{l=1}^{p-1} \frac{\dfrac{[\mu(x_l) - \mu(x_{l-1})]^{y_l}}{y_l!}}{[\mu(x_{p-1})]^{y_{p-1}}}.$$

Comparing with Equation (12.125) we see that, here too, a "sample" has been lost, except this time the sample corresponds to the last interval of data.

12.10 From Equation (10.33) we have, after substituting Equation (10.26) and parameter changes,

$$F_a(x_l \mid x_{l-1}) = \frac{\Delta\mu_l}{u_0 - \mu(x_{l-1})}$$

and

$$\frac{\partial F_a(x_l \mid x_{l-1})}{\partial \beta_k} = \frac{[u_0 - \mu(x_{l-1})]\dfrac{\partial \Delta\mu_l}{\partial \beta_k} + \Delta\mu_l \dfrac{\partial \mu(x_{l-1})}{\partial \beta_k}}{[u_0 - \mu(x_{l-1})]^2}.$$

Substituting these in Equation (12.106) and manipulating we obtain

$$
\frac{\partial \ln L\,(u_0,\, \beta_A)}{\partial \beta_k} = \sum_{l=1}^{p} \left\{ \frac{y_l'\, \dfrac{\partial \Delta \mu_l}{\partial \beta_k}}{\Delta \mu_l} + \frac{y_l'\, \dfrac{\partial \mu(x_{l-1})}{\partial \beta_k}}{u_0 - \mu(x_{l-1})} \right.
$$

$$
\left. - \frac{u_0 - y_l}{u_0 - \mu(x_l)} \cdot \frac{\partial \Delta \mu_l}{\partial \beta_k} - \frac{(u_0 - y_l)\Delta \mu_l\, \dfrac{\partial \mu(x_{l-1})}{\partial \beta_k}}{[u_0 - \mu(x_l)][u_0 - \mu(x_{l-1})]} \right\}
$$

By requiring that $\mu(x_l) = y_l$ for all l and noting that $\Delta \mu_l = y_l'$ under these conditions, we obtain Equation (12.108).

12.11 The derivative of $\hat{\lambda}(t)$ with respect to $\hat{\beta}_1$ is from Equation (12.91)

$$
\frac{d\hat{\lambda}(t)}{d\hat{\beta}_1} = \left\{ \frac{m_e \exp(-\hat{\beta}_1 t)}{[1 - \exp(-\hat{\beta}_1 t_e)]^2} \right\} \left\{ 1 - t\hat{\beta}_1 + \exp(-\hat{\beta}_1 t_e)[(t - t_e)\hat{\beta}_1 - 1] \right\}
$$

Since the first term is always positive we need only consider the second term. Denote this term as q and let $t = \gamma t_e$ and $x = \hat{\beta}_1 t_e$. Then $q = 1 - \gamma x + \exp(-x)[(\gamma - 1)\, x - 1]$. Consider the initial failure intensity. This is given when $\gamma = 0$ or $q = 1 - (x + 1)\exp(-x)$. Taking the first derivative of q with respect to x we have $dq/dx = x \exp(-x)$. Thus, q has a *minimum* value of 0 at $x = 0$. Since q is never negative the estimator of the initial failure intensity is an increasing function of $\hat{\beta}_1$. Consider next the present failure intensity. This is given when $\gamma = 1$ or $q = 1 - x - \exp(-x)$. Here $dq/dx = -1 + \exp(-x)$. Thus q has a *maximum* value of 0 at $x = 0$. Since q is never positive, the estimate of the present failure intensity is a decreasing function of $\hat{\beta}_1$. The future failure intensity is given when $\gamma > 1$. Here $dq/dx = -\gamma + [\gamma - (\gamma - 1)x]\exp(-x)$. The second term is always less then γ when $x > 0$ and always greater than γ when $x < 0$. Thus q has a maximum value at $x = 0$ and the future failure intensity is a decreasing function of $\hat{\beta}_1$.

12.12 The derivative of $\hat{\lambda}(t)$ with respect to $\hat{\beta}_1$ is from Equation (12.96)

$$
\frac{d\hat{\lambda}(t)}{d\hat{\beta}_1} = \frac{m_e}{[(1 + \hat{\beta}_1 t)\ln\,(1 + \hat{\beta}_1 t_e)]^2} \left[\ln\,(1 + \hat{\beta}_1 t_e) - \hat{\beta}_1 t_e \left[\frac{1 + \hat{\beta}_1 t}{1 + \hat{\beta}_1 t_e} \right] \right]
$$

Here q becomes $\ln(1 + x) - x(1 + \gamma x)/(1 + x)$ and arguments similar to those used in Problem 12.11 can now be applied.

12.13 We know from our discussion in Chapter 10 that there is a finite probability of $T_i = \infty$ so that $E[T_i] = \infty$. As an example consider $i = 1$. From the result of Problem 12.7 we have

$$
f\,(t_1) = \beta_0 \beta_1 \exp(-\beta_1 t_1)\, \exp\{-\beta_0[1 - \exp(-\beta_1 t_1)]\} \qquad 0 \leqslant t_1 < \infty
$$

On integrating $f(t_1)$ between $(0, \infty)$ we obtain $1 - \exp(-\beta_0)$. Thus $f(t_1)$ is an improper density function. The missing mass, that is, $\exp(-\beta_0)$, is the probability that $T_1 = \infty$. In general $P[T_i = \infty] = \exp(-\beta_0) \sum_{j=1}^{i} (\beta_0)^{j-1}/(j - 1)!$.

12.14 By substituting Equations (12.6) and (12.7) in our solution to Problem 12.7 we have

$$f(t_i) = \frac{\beta_0^i \beta_1}{(i-1)!} \frac{[\ln (1 + \beta_1 t_i)]^{i-1}}{(1 + \beta_1 t_i)^{\beta_0 + 1}}, \qquad 0 \leqslant t_i \leqslant \infty .$$

The expected value of T_i is given by

$$E[T_i] = \int_0^\infty t_i f(t_i) dt_i$$

Through the repeated use of integration by parts it can be shown that

$$E[T_i] = \frac{1}{\beta_0 \beta_1} \sum_{j=1}^{i} \left[\frac{\beta_0}{\beta_0 - 1} \right]^j$$

and using $\Sigma_{j=1}^n a^j = a(1 - a^n)/(1 - a)$ we arrive at our answer. The condition $\beta_0 > 1$ comes about from convergence requirements.

12.15 Substituting Equations (12.6) and (12.7) in Equation (12.52) we have

$$f(t) = \frac{\beta_1}{(1 + \beta_1 t) \ln (\beta_1 t_e + 1)}, \qquad 0 \leqslant t \leqslant t_e .$$

Therefore,

$$E[(\beta_1 T + 1)^{-n}] = \frac{\beta_1}{\ln (\beta_1 t_e + 1)} \int_0^{t_e} (\beta_1 t + 1)^{-n-1} dt$$

$$= \frac{1}{n \ln (\beta_1 t_e + 1)} [1 - (\beta_1 t_e + 1)^{-n}] .$$

12.16 Starting with Equation (12.61) we have

$$\frac{\partial^2 \ln L(\beta_1 \mid m_e)}{\partial \beta_1^2} = \frac{1}{\beta_1^2} \left[\sum_{i=1}^{m_e} \left(\frac{1}{\beta_1 t_i + 1} \right)^2 - 2 \sum_{i=1}^{m_e} \left(\frac{1}{\beta_1 t_i + 1} \right) \right]$$

$$+ \frac{m_e t_e^2 [\ln (1 + \beta_1 t_e) + 1]}{[(1 + \beta_1 t_e) \ln (1 + \beta_1 t_e)]^2} .$$

By using the results of Problem 12.15 and some manipulation we easily arrive at Equation (12.74).

12.17 The Laplace transform of Equation (12.71) is

$$f_t(s) = \frac{\beta_1}{1 - \exp(-\beta_1 t_e)} \int_0^{t_e} \exp[- (\beta_1 + s)t] dt$$

$$= \frac{\beta_1}{1 - \exp(-\beta_1 t_e)} \frac{1 - \exp[- (\beta_1 + s)t_e]}{s + \beta_1} ,$$

and hence the Laplace transform of the probability density function of X is

$$f_X(s) = \prod_{i=1}^{m_e} f_{t_i}(s) = \left[\frac{\beta_1}{1 - \exp(-\beta_1 t_e)} \right]^{m_e} \left\{ \frac{1 - \exp[-(\beta_1 + s)t_e]}{s + \beta_1} \right\}^{m_e} .$$

The numerator of the second term can be expanded by using the binomial theorem [Mood, Graybill, and Boes (1974)]. Carrying this out

$$f_X(s) = \left[\frac{\beta_1}{1 - \exp(-\beta_1 t_e)} \right]^{m_e} \sum_{j=0}^{m_e} \binom{m_e}{j} (-1)^j \frac{\exp[-(\beta_1 + s)jt_e]}{(\beta_1 + s)^{m_e}} .$$

This is easily inverted to

$$f_X(x) = \left[\frac{\beta_1}{1 - \exp(-\beta_1 t_e)} \right]^{m_e} \sum_{j=0}^{m_e} \binom{m_e}{j} \frac{(-1)^j}{(m_e - 1)!} u_{jt_e}(x) (x - jt_e)^{m_e-1} \exp(-\beta_1 x),$$

where

$$u_c(x) = \begin{cases} 0, & x < c \\ 1, & x \geq c \end{cases}.$$

An alternative derivation based on characteristic functions is given by Bain and Weeks (1964).

Bain, Englehart, and Wright (1977) give a beta approximation to $f(x)$ that can be used for moderate m_e.

12.18 The cumulative density function is

$$F_X(x) = \int_0^x f_X(q) dq =$$

$$\left(\frac{\beta_1}{1 - \exp(-\beta_1 t_e)} \right)^{m_e} \frac{1}{(m_e - 1)!} \sum_{j=0}^{m_e} \binom{m_e}{j} (-1)^j \int_0^x u_{jt_e}(q) (q - jt_e)^{m_e-1} \exp(-\beta_1 q) dq .$$

Set s equal to the nearest integer greater than or equal to x/t_e. After eliminating $u(q)$ and a change of variables the above becomes

$$F_X(x) = \left(\frac{\beta_1}{1 - \exp(-\beta_1 t_e)} \right)^{m_e} \frac{1}{(m_e - 1)!} \sum_{j=0}^{s-1} \binom{m_e}{j}$$

$$(-1)^j \exp(-\beta_1 jt_e) \int_0^{y-jt_e} y^{m_e-1} \exp(-\beta_1 y) dy .$$

This last expression may be expressed as a sum of chi-square variables.

12.19 The skewness, κ_3, is by definition, the third moment about the mean. That is,

$$\kappa_3 = E\left[\left(\frac{\partial \ln L(\beta_1 \mid m_e)}{\partial \beta_1} \right)^3 \right]$$

which Bartlett (1953) showed was equivalent to

$$\kappa_3 = 3 \, \frac{\partial I(\beta_1)}{\partial \beta_1} + 2E\left[\frac{\partial^3 \ln L(\beta_1 \mid m_e)}{\partial \beta_1^3}\right].$$

The third derivative of the log-likelihood function [starting with Equation (12.68)] is

$$\frac{\partial^3 \ln L(\beta_1 \mid m_e)}{\partial \beta_1^3} = \frac{2m_e}{\beta_1^3} - \frac{m_e t_e^3 \exp(-\beta_1 t_e)}{[1 - \exp(-\beta_1 t_e)]^3} \, [1 + \exp(-\beta_1 t_e)].$$

The right-hand side above is also equal to $E[\partial^3 \ln L(\beta_1 \mid m_e)/\partial \beta_1^3]$. Furthermore it can be shown that

$$\frac{\partial I(\beta_1)}{\partial \beta_1} = -\frac{\partial^3 \ln L(\beta_1 \mid m_e)}{\partial \beta_1^3}$$

and hence κ_3 becomes Equation (12.73).

12.20 In order for a pole to exist we require that

$$\int_0^{t_e} z_a(x; \beta_1) \, dx = 0.$$

Differentiating both sides with respect to t_e we have the condition $z_a(t_e; \beta_1) = 0$ or after substituting Equations (10.20) and (10.28), $\lambda_1(t_e; \beta_1) = 0$ for a binomial-type model. The same result applies for a Poisson-type model. Note that the solution is valid since $z_a \geqslant 0$.

12.21 For the exponential class our formula requires that $\beta_1 \exp(-\beta_1 t_e) = 0$, which in turn has as its only solution $\beta_1 = 0$. Thus a pole exists at the origin. For the geometric family we require $1/(1 + \beta_1 t_e) = 0$. This leads to a pole at $-1/t_e$.

The pole at the origin causes a problem because it is within the permissible range of β_1 for the exponential class. The pole at $-1/t_e$ does not cause a problem because it is at the left boundary of permissible β_1 values for the geometric family.

12.22 The probability that a chi-square distributed random variable with one degree of freedom is less than or equal to 3.84 is 0.95. Therefore, a 95 percent confidence interval for β_1 can be found as the set of values giving $-2 \ln [L(\beta_1 \mid m_e)/ L(\hat{\beta}_1 \mid m_e) \leqslant 3.84$. These values turn out to lie in the interval $(0.271 \times 10^{-4}, 0.430 \times 10^{-4})$. This interval is almost identical to the interval given in Example 12.4.

12.23 Proceeding as in Problem 12.22, we find the approximate 95 percent confidence interval for β_1 to be $(0.133 \times 10^{-3}, 0.533 \times 10^{-3})$ which agrees favorably with the interval given in Example 12.5. It is worth mentioning that the interval for β_1 we would get using the normal approximation given by Equation (12.12) which is known not to be correct is $(0.089 \times 10^{-3}, 0.433 \times 10^{-3})$. This does not agree well with the previous two intervals.

12.24 The information expected from a sample of size m_e for an exponential-class model is given by Equation (12.69). It can be easily verified that the second term within the brackets approaches 0 as t_e approaches infinity. In addition the value of m_e under these conditions will approach v_0 or u_0. Thus, the expected information approaches v_0/β_1^2 or u_0/β_1^2.

The analysis is a little more complex for the geometric family. We start with Equation (12.74) and replace m_e with its mean value, $\beta_0 \ln (1 + \beta_1 t_e)$. Now with repeated use of L'Hopital's Rule for each term of Equation (12.74) it is straightforward to show that the expected information approaches $\beta_0/2\beta_1^2$.

The variance of $\hat{\beta}_1$ is inversely proportional to the expected information. Thus, we see that the accuracy of our estimation approaches a fixed limit, beyond which we cannot go no matter how much additional testing is performed.

12.25 Let the constant failure intensity be λ. Then the likelihood function for λ using failure time data is given by Equation (12.46) or

$$L(\lambda) = \lambda^{m_e} \exp(- \lambda t_e) \, ,$$

where we made use of the fact that $\mu(t_e) = \lambda t_e$. The maximum likelihood estimate for λ is given by m_e/t_e. The expected information is m_e/λ^2. The likelihood function for λ with grouped data using Equation (12.120), is

$$L(\lambda) = \prod_{l=1}^{p} \frac{\lambda^{y_l}(x_l - x_{l-1})^{y_l}}{y_l} \exp(- \lambda x_p) \, .$$

The maximum likelihood estimate for λ is y_p/x_p and the information is y_p/λ^2.

The information content is the same using either type of data collection so it does not matter how we gather the data. Use whichever form is easiest to implement.

12.26 Set the mean value function equal to m_e and solve for ν_0, that is, $\nu_0 = m_e/[1 - \exp(-\beta_1 t_e)]$. Now for fixed m_e we see that the skewness increases as m_e approaches ν_0.

CHAPTER 14

14.1 Here the effective number of available debuggers is $1.5 P_F = 7.5$. The new potential transition points become $\lambda_{FC} = 0.0572$ failure/CPU hr and $\lambda_{FI} = 0.0023$ failure/CPU hr. A quick check of the calendar time to execution time ratios shows that computer time is limiting for failure intensities below λ_{FC} and debuggers are limiting for failure intensities greater than λ_{FC}. Proceeding as we did in Example 14.3 we find that $\Delta t_F = 6$ days and $\Delta t_C = 41.9$ days. The total required calendar time is 47.9 days. When compared with the nonovertime value of 51.8 days we see that little has been gained.

14.2 Failure correction personnel will no longer be limiting if the transition point λ_{FC} is equal to the present failure intensity of 0.0997 failure/CPU hr. That is, we must solve for P_F in

$$0.0997 = \frac{P_F(0.275)}{40.176 - P_F(0.55)} \, .$$

The solution is found to be $P_F = 12$. This means that an additional 7 debuggers are required.

14.3 Additional resource requirements are given by Equation (14.2). For each resource these are

$$\Delta\chi_C = \Delta\tau + 2\Delta\mu ,$$

$$\Delta\chi_F = 16.2 \ \Delta\mu ,$$

and

$$\Delta\chi_I = 0.054 \ \Delta\tau + 0.34 \ \Delta\mu .$$

Multiplying by the cost factors and summing gives us

$$C = 201.89 \ \Delta\tau + 978.9 \ \Delta\mu ,$$

where C is the cost. Since $\Delta\tau = 1197.5$ CPU hr and $\Delta\mu = 19$ failures the total additional cost will be about \$260K.

14.4 The failure intensity for a geometric family model is given by Equation (12.7). Setting this equal to the objective and solving for the expected time results in $\tau = 3999$ CPU hr. Using the mean value function given by Equation (12.6), the expected number of failures will be about 332. Thus,

$$\chi_C = (2)(3999) + (4)(332) = 9326 \text{ CPU hr} ,$$

$$\chi_F = (4)(332) = 1328 \text{ person hr} ,$$

and

$$\chi_I = (0.5)(3999) + (4)(332) = 3327.5 \text{ person hr} .$$

14.5 The potential transition points in this case are $\lambda_{FC} = 0.1486$ failure/CPU hr, $\lambda_{IC} = 0.0625$ failure/CPU hr, and $\lambda_{FI} = 0.275$ failure/CPU hr. By using Equation (14.7) we find that computer time is limiting for $\lambda \leq \lambda_{IC}$, failure identification personnel for $\lambda_{IC} < \lambda \leq \lambda_{FI}$, and failure correction personnel for $\lambda > \lambda_{FI}$. The amount of calendar time can be determined from Equation (14.12). Thus, the amount of time required to reduce the initial failure intensity of 40 failures/CPU hr to λ_{FI} is $\Delta t_F = 54.2$ days. The amount of time to reduce the failure intensity from λ_{FI} to λ_{IC} is $\Delta t_I = 22.6$ days. Lastly, the amount of time required to reduce the failure intensity from λ_{IC} to λ_F is $\Delta t_C = 109.2$ days. The total time is $\Delta t_F + \Delta t_I + \Delta t_C = 186.0$ days.

14.6 Here the calendar time to execution time ratio for computer time and failure identification personnel is identical. Therefore, both resources are simultaneously limiting.

14.7 Start with Equation (14.12). Since there is only one limiting resource, $\lambda(\tau_1)$ will be the present failure intensity λ_P and $\lambda(\tau_2)$ will be the failure intensity objective λ_F. Thus Equation (14.12) becomes, after substituting the maximum likelihood estimate of β_0 from Equation (12.55),

$$\Delta\hat{t}_r = \left[\frac{m_e}{P_r\rho_r \ln{(1 + \hat{\beta}_1 t_e)}} \right] \left[\theta_r \left[\frac{1}{\lambda_F} - \frac{1}{\hat{\lambda}_P} \right] + \mu_r \ln\left(\frac{\hat{\lambda}_P}{\lambda_F} \right) \right]$$

The first multiplier above is clearly a decreasing function or $\hat{\beta}_1$. In Chapter 12 we saw that $\hat{\lambda}_P$ is a decreasing function of $\hat{\beta}_1$ and hence, the second multiplier is also decreasing in $\hat{\beta}_1$. Therefore $\Delta\hat{t}_r$ is monotonically decreasing in $\hat{\beta}_1$.

14.8 The maximum likelihood estimate for λ_P is given by Equation (12.98) as 0.0533 failure/CPU hr. An approximate 75 percent confidence interval for λ_P, using the substitution principle and Equation (12.98), is (0.0519, 0.0563). From Problem 14.5 we know that the project is computer-time-limited for failure intensities below $\lambda_{IC} = 0.0625$ failure/CPU hr. Thus, $\Delta \hat{t} = \Delta \hat{t}_C = 105.4$ days. Additionally, the 75 percent confidence interval for Δt is (102.0, 112.9) days.

14.9 Expanding $\mu(t)$, the calendar time mean value function, in a Maclaurin series we have

$$\mu(t) = \lambda(0)t + \frac{t^2}{2} \left. \frac{d^2\mu(t)}{dt^2} \right|_{t=0} + \cdots ,$$

where $\lambda(0)$ is the initial failure intensity in calendar time. It should not be confused with the parameter λ_0. Suppose the second and following terms in the above series can be ignored. Then we have $\mu(t) \approx \lambda(0)t$. Substituting into the conditional distribution of T_i', we have

$$f(t_i' \mid t_{i-1}) = \lambda(0) \exp[- \lambda(0)t_i'] .$$

That is, T_i' is exponentially distributed independently of the previous failure times. Our approximation is valid if t is, say, an order of magnitude less than $2\lambda(0) \, d^2\mu(t)/dt^2]_{t=0}$.

14.10 Substituting Equation (11.21) with $B = 1$ and Equation (11.41) into Equation (14.1), we obtain for the basic execution time model

$$\chi_r = \theta_r \, \tau + \mu_r \nu_0 \, [1 - \exp(- \phi\tau)] ,$$

and for the logarithmic Poisson execution time model

$$\chi_r = \theta_r \, \tau + \frac{\mu_r}{\theta} \, \ln \, (\lambda_0 \theta\tau + 1) .$$

Taking derivatives with respect to τ, we obtain for the resource expenditures per unit time

$$\frac{d\chi_r}{d\tau} = \theta_r + \mu_r \lambda_0 \exp(- \phi\tau)$$

for the basic model and

$$\frac{d\chi_r}{d\tau} = \theta_r + \mu_r \lambda_0 \, \frac{1}{\lambda_0 \theta\tau + 1}$$

for the logarithmic Poisson execution time model. Note that in both cases the initial resource expenditure per unit time is $\theta_r + \mu_r \lambda_0$. The resource expenditure resulting from failures decreases with time. For large values of time, the expenditure approaches θ_r per unit time as an asymptote. In other words, in the late stages of testing, most of the cost results from the many hours of test required.

If we solve Equation (11.21) with $B = 1$ and Equation (11.41) for τ and substitute the results into Equation (14.1) we obtain for the basic execution time model

$$\chi_r = -\frac{1}{\phi} \theta_r \ln\left(1 - \frac{\mu}{\nu_0}\right) + \mu_r\mu$$

and for the logarithmic Poisson execution time model

$$\chi_r = \frac{\theta_r}{\lambda_0\theta}\left[\exp(\theta\mu) - 1\right] + \mu_r\mu.$$

Differentiating with respect to μ, we obtain for the resource expenditures per failure

$$\frac{d\chi_r}{d\mu} = \mu_r + \frac{\theta_r}{\phi}\frac{1}{\nu_0 - \mu}$$

for the basic execution time model and

$$\frac{d\chi_r}{d\mu} = \mu_r + \frac{\theta_r}{\lambda_0}\exp(\theta\mu)$$

for the logarithmic Poisson execution time model. Note that in both cases the initial resource expenditure per failure is $\mu_r + \theta_r/\lambda_0$. The resource expenditure resulting from failures increases with number of failures, eventually approaching infinity for the logarithmic Poisson execution time model. It is thus seen that the cost of identifying and correcting a failure becomes greater as testing proceeds.

CHAPTER 15

15.1 From Equation (10.22) and $z_a(t) = 2\phi t$ we have $F_a(t) = 1 - \exp(-\phi t^2)$. Thus

$$F_{ak}(t) = 1 - \exp(-\phi_k t^2)$$

and

$$F_{al}(t) = 1 - \exp(-\phi_l t^2).$$

Substituting the above expressions and Equations (15.22) and (15.25) into Equation (15.31) we arrive at

$$\tilde{t}_i = \left[\frac{I_l}{I_k}\frac{u_{0k} - i + 1}{\frac{\Delta I_l}{\Delta I_k}u_{0k} - i + 1}(t_i^2 - t_{i-1}^2) + \tilde{t}_{i-1}^2\right]^{1/2}$$

15.2 For this model,

$$F_k(t_i \mid t_{i-1}) = 1 - \left\{\frac{\gamma_k}{\gamma_k + \ln\left[\dfrac{t_i - t_{i-1} + \xi_k(i)}{\xi_k(i)}\right]}\right\}^i$$

and

$$F_l(\tilde{t}_i \mid \tilde{t}_{i-1}) = 1 - \left\{ \frac{\gamma_l}{\gamma_l + \ln\left[\dfrac{\tilde{t}_i - \tilde{t}_{i-1} + \xi_l(i)}{\xi_l(i)}\right]} \right\}$$

where

$$\gamma_k = \sum_{j=1}^{i-1} \ln\left[\frac{t_j - t_{j-1} + \xi_k(j)}{\xi_k(j)}\right]$$

and similarly for λ_l.

Substituting these expressions into Equation (15.10) yields

$$\tilde{t}_i - \tilde{t}_{i-1} = \xi_l(i) \left\{ \exp\left[\gamma_l \left(\left\{ \frac{\gamma_k}{\gamma_k + \ln\left[\dfrac{t_i - t_{i-1} + \xi_k(i)}{\xi_k(i)}\right]} \right\}^{-1} - 1 \right) \right] - 1 \right\}$$

To use this transformation, it is necessary to know both the functional form of $\xi(i)$ and how it depends on the total amount of code and the number of inherent faults. This latter quantity may be related to either the amount of developed code or some complexity metric. The adjustment has not been reduced to practice for the Littlewood-Verrall model since this relationship is not currently known.

15.3 Starting with Equation (15.26) and applying L'Hopital's rule we have

$$\tilde{t}_i = \frac{I_l}{I_k} \cdot \frac{\Delta I_k}{\Delta I_l} \, t_i$$

The case $\hat{\phi}_k = 0$ represents a stationary Poisson process with a linear mean value function. The adjustment merely changes the slope of the mean value function.

If all the code is developed, that is, there is no inherited code, then $I_l = \Delta I_l$ and $I_k = \Delta I_k$, and the transformation becomes $\tilde{t}_i = t_i$.

15.4 Denote the probability of observing y_i failures by time x_i for stage k as $h_k(x_i, y_i; \boldsymbol{\beta}_{(k)})$. Proceed in a manner analogous to that used for failure time data. Set this probability equal to the equivalent probability for stage l, that is, $h_l(\tilde{x}_i, y_i; \boldsymbol{\beta}_{(l)})$. Thus, using Equation (10.5), $\tilde{x}_i$ is given as the solution to

$$\frac{[\mu_k(x_i)]^{y_i}}{y_i!} \exp[-\mu_k(x_i)] = \frac{[\mu_l(\tilde{x}_i)]^{y_i}}{y_i!} \exp[-\mu_l(\tilde{x}_i)]$$

or equivalently, $\mu_k(x_i) = \mu_l(\tilde{x}_i)$.

15.5 (a) Using Equation (10.38), and $z_a(t) = \phi$ yields

$$f(t_i \mid t_{i-1}) = (u_0 - i + 1)\phi \exp[-\phi(u_0 - i + 1)(t_i - t_{i-1})].$$

In order for this equation to be a valid density function we require that $u_0 \geq i$, where i is the number of failures experienced. This is a perfectly natural and acceptable restriction.

(b) A constant value for $\phi(i)$ was assumed in Moranda (1981). In our approach [compare with Equation (15.22)] we write $\phi(i) = (I/I_i)\phi$, where I is the total number of executable object instructions in the final program. The number of failures at risk when the ith failure occurs is given by the product of the amount of developed code present and the characteristic fault density, that is, $\Delta I_i \omega_I$. Thus,

$$ f(t_i \mid t_{i-1}) = (\Delta I_i \omega_I - i + 1) \frac{I}{I_i} \phi \exp \left[\frac{I}{I_i} \phi (\Delta I_i \, \omega_I - i + 1) \, (t_i - t_{i-1}) \right] . $$

(c) Here the likelihood function would be

$$ L(\phi, \omega_I) = \prod_{i=1}^{m} f(t_i \mid t_{i-1}) . $$

The estimate of u_0 for the final program is $\hat{u}_0 = \Delta I \hat{\omega}_I$, where ΔI is the amount of developed code in the final program. To insure that the density function given in (b) is not negative, we need to place the restriction that $\Delta I_i \hat{\omega}_I - i \geq 0$ or $\hat{\omega}_I \geq \max_i (i/\Delta I_i)$. This is similar to the condition $u_0 \geq i$. It guarantees that the estimate of the total number of failures possible ($\Delta I_i \omega_I$) is at least equal to the number of failures experienced at any time. This in turn places an artificial restriction on $\hat{u}_0$. For example, suppose a project has the failure history shown below:

i	ΔI_i
1–5	1K
6–12	4K
13–20	10K

We have $\hat{\omega}_I \geq 10^{-3} \max(5, 3, 2) = 5$. If $\Delta I = 10K$ then $\hat{u}_0 \geq 50$. Imposing this restriction does not seem reasonable. It is possible that additional failures will not occur. This would mean $u_0 = 20$. The problem comes about because ω_I captures the average or expected behavior. An unusually fault-ridden section of code (especially if integrated early on) can impose an unwanted restriction for u_0. In our example the first stage is a culprit. Every failure experienced during this stage increases the restriction on u_0 by 10.

15.6 Since failure 3 of the first sequence occurs before failure 4 of the second sequence, the latter failure is ignored. Similarly, failure 5 of the first sequence is to be ignored. The procedure is to sum the concurrently running times. Thus, the first failure of the interleaved sequence occurs after 6 time units; 3 from each test team, before a failure occurs. The second failure of the interleaved sequence occurs after 12 time units, 6 from each test team, before the next failure occurs. Continuing in this fashion we have:

Failure number	Failure time
1	6
2	18
3	42
4	50
5	54
6	90
7	200
8	258
9	360
10	534
End of test	547

Of the 12 total failures experienced only 10 are distinct, so that the interleaved sequence has only 10 failures. Also the failure-free execution time accumulated at the end of the interleaved sequence is not 100 but 13 time units.

15.7 First $\boldsymbol{\beta}_{(1)}$ and $\boldsymbol{\beta}_{(3)}$ are estimated using the failure time data from stages 1 and 3, respectively. Then, the failure times of stage 1 are adjusted to the conditions of stage 2 and those of stage 3 are adjusted to the conditions of stage 4. Estimates of $\boldsymbol{\beta}_{(2)}$ and $\boldsymbol{\beta}_{(4)}$ are now made. Failure times from stages 1 and 2 (also 3 and 4) can now be adjusted to stage 5. Finally, when making predictions based on stage 5 the technique (given in Problem 15.6) for combining failure interval sequences should be employed. In order for this procedure to be valid, the two integration paths must be completely independent. The general applicability requirement can be stated as follows. The failure time adjustment procedure may be applied to each path provided each path undergoes only pure growth and is independent of the other paths. That is, each path can be treated as a separate sequentially integrated system.

To determine whether the failure time adjustment procedure may be applied to a particular integration plan, one should do the following. Draw the integration diagram for the plan. Now, consider all the paths from all the initial stages to the final stage, where the final stage usually represents the completed system. For the plan used in this problem there are two initial stages (1 and 3) and two paths (1, 2, 5 and 3, 4, 5).

When determining $\boldsymbol{\beta}$ for a stage, two possibilities exist, based on the number of paths that lead to the stage. If only one path leads to a stage, then nothing special need be done. If more than one path leads to a stage then, before estimating $\boldsymbol{\beta}$ for the stage, the technique for combining failure time sequences (adjusted to the stage in question) should be applied.

RECOMMENDED SPECIFICATIONS FOR SUPPORTING COMPUTER PROGRAMS

Designing a software reliability estimation support program can be a time-consuming task. This appendix has been written in order to provide you with some guidance. The basic structures described here can handle most situations, though some customizing may be necessary.

Four computer programs that are most useful in the application of software reliability theory were identified in Section 5.3.1. These were the tabular, plotting, simulation, and log conversion programs. Each of these will be discussed in the following sections.

I.1 TABULAR AND PLOTTING PROGRAMS

The tabular program provides a snapshot of system status and the plotting program provides a running history of system status. It is generally a good idea to have two separate input files. The first file contains model and, in the case of plotting programs, plot control parameters. Examples of model parameters would be the resource usage parameters, the testing compression factor, and the amounts of available resources. Plot control parameters are used to determine which plots are to be drawn, what confidence level should be shown in the plots, whether or not there should be a grid, and so on. Many of the parameters in this file should have standard default values. Others are sometimes not needed. For example, if you just want a table, the plot parameters can be omitted.

The second file contains the actual failure data. Various formats are possible depending on whether the failure data are time data or grouped data. As an example, consider the case of failure interval data. One workable format consists of the following sequence per record:

1. execution time interval between the present and previous failure experienced in testing,
2. the number of days from the start of testing on which the present failure occurred (optional),
3. the number of instructions integrated (optional), and
4. the number of instructions of developed code integrated (optional).

We have generally found the following outputs useful:

1. a listing of parameters with their associated values,
2. an echo of the input failure data,
3. a listing of the adjusted data, days from start of test, and associated numbers of the failures in columnar format, in the situation where failure times are adjusted to account for a program that is changing in size,
4. program error and warning messages (if present),
5. a listing of plot messages and diagnostics (if present),
6. results in tabular format, and
7. results in graphical format.

The format of the third output should be compatible with the input failure data file. This allows the user to use the result as input to other software reliability programs. This is particularly useful when using software reliability programs that do not perform failure time adjustment.

A typical program structure is shown in Figure I.1. The first thing done is to read the data from the two input files. The data are checked and error flags are set so that appropriate messages can be printed in the output routine. The errors detected will abort all or part of the calculation, as appropriate.

The next step is to determine if a tabular or graphical output has been requested. Suppose tabular output is the case. Then a check is made to see if failure time adjustment is required. If so, then the failure adjustment routine is called. This routine implements the procedure given in Chapter 15. Once the failure data is adjusted a maximization routine is called to calculate $\hat{\beta}$ via maximum likelihood (or some other procedure). Equations given in Chapter 12 and the procedure described in Appendix D will be used in the maximization routine. Once $\hat{\beta}$ is determined we move to a routine which computes all of the derived quantities using equations from Chapters 12 and 14. The final step is to output all the files described earlier.

Now suppose graphical output has been requested. A loop on the failure number is started. For each iteration of this loop the following calculations are performed. A check is made to see if the failure data should be adjusted. If so, the pro-

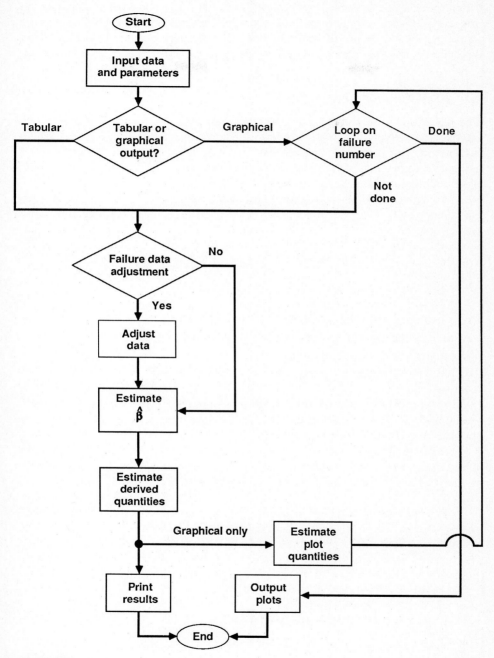

FIGURE I.1
Basic program structure for tabular and plotting programs.

cedure in Chapter 15 is used. As before, $\hat{\beta}$ is determined and used to calculate the quantities requested in the plot(s). The results are saved for final plotting and the loop is continued. When all of the failure data have been exhausted, the plots and any other appropriate information are outputted.

I.2 SIMULATION PROGRAM

The simulation program computes schedule and cost as a function of one of several parameters you choose to vary. Two modes of operation are useful: test-phase and pretest. In the test-phase mode the execution time component parameters are estimated from actual data, along with confidence levels to express bounds. In the pretest mode the parameters and bounds are both input.

As with the tabular and plotting programs, the use of two separate input files is recommended. The first file contains model and plot control parameters. Many of these parameters are the same as those in the previous programs. Additional parameters include the cost of computer time and personnel, predicted values of β_k, $k = 0, \ldots, w$, along with low and high bounds for these values, and the parameter which is to be varied.

The following outputs have been found useful:

1. a listing of parameters with their associated values,
2. echo of the input failure data (if test-phase mode is used),
3. program error messages, and
4. plots of schedule or cost against a selected parameter.

A typical program structure is shown in Figure I.2. The first thing done is to read data from the two input files. The input routine functions exactly the same as the one used for the previous programs.

After input processing has been completed a test is made to see if the test-phase or pre-test mode has been selected. If the former is the case a maximization routine is called to calculate $\hat{\beta}$ along with upper and lower bounds (confidence limits).

A print routine is called to handle any of the first three outputs mentioned above. Then a loop is begun on the parameter being varied. For each value of the parameter an estimate of project cost or completion date is made and saved. When the loop is finished the plot is generated and the program terminates. An additional loop can be included if more than one plot at a time is desired.

I.3 LOG CONVERSION PROGRAM

The final program is the log conversion program which calculates failure intervals for use in the other three programs. Three input files are recommended. The first consists of event entries. The second consists of control parameters which dictate

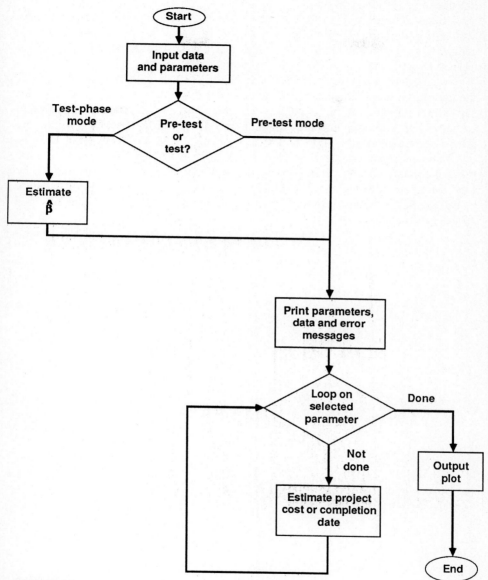

FIGURE I.2
Basic program structure for simulation program.

how the events are to be processed. The third is optional and contains a previously calculated set of intervals.

Separate event entries for the start of the test, the end of the test, a run duration, a stop duration, program growth specification, and a failure should exist. A provision to allow specification of window start and end times should be made in case an event is known only within a window.

The control parameters should give the user some selection capability over the data to be used for interval calculation. For example, one might have entries for several programs in the input file. The user may exclude event entries from a subset of the programs and may exclude all data before a certain start time and after a certain end time.

The program structure is relatively simple in this case. An input routine reads the data from the various input files and checks the data for validity. If no fatal errors are detected, a routine which performs the failure interval calculation is called. The program terminates with the output of the failure intervals to a specified file.

REFERENCES

Adams, E. N. 1980. "Minimizing Cost Impact of Software Defects," IBM Research Division, Report RC 8228 (35669).

Adams, E. N. 1984. "Optimizing Preventive Service of Software Products," *IBM Journal of Research and Development*, **28**(1), pp. 2–14.

Akiyama, F. 1971. "An Example of Software System Debugging," *Information Processing 71*, North-Holland, New York, pp. 353–359.

Albin, J. L., and R. Ferreol. 1982. "Collecte et Analyse de Mesures de Logiciel," (in French), *Technique et Science Informatique*, **1**(4), pp. 297–313.

Anderson, T., and P. A. Lee. 1981. *Fault Tolerance: Principles and Practice*, Prentice-Hall, Englewood Cliffs, NJ.

Angus, J. E., J. B. Bowen, and S. J. VanDenBerg. 1983. "Reliability Model Demonstration Study," Rome Air Development Center, Technical Report RADC-TR-83-207, Rome, NY.

Ascher, H. E., and H. Feingold. 1982. "Repairable Systems Reliability: Future Research Topics," (E. Langer and J. Moltoft, Editors), *Reliability in Electrical and Electronic Components and Systems*, North-Holland, Amsterdam, pp. 81–88.

Ascher, H. E., and H. Feingold. 1984. *Repairable Systems Reliability: Modeling, Inference, Misconceptions and Their Causes*, Marcel Dekker, New York.

Bain, L. J., M. Englehart, and F. T. Wright. 1977. "Inferential Procedures for the Truncated Exponential Distribution," *Communications in Statistics—Theory and Methods*, **A6**(2), pp. 103–111.

Bain, L. J., and D. L. Weeks. 1964. "A Note on the Truncated Exponential Distribution," *Annals Mathematical Statistics*, **35**, pp. 1366–1367.

Bardsley, I. 1984. Unpublished communication.

Barlow, R. E., and F. Proschan. 1975. *Statistical Theory of Reliability and Life Testing Probability Models*, Holt, Rinehart and Winston, New York.

Bartholomew, D. J. 1963. "The Sampling Distribution of an Estimate Arising in Life Testing," *Technometrics*, **5**(3), pp. 361–374.

Bartlett, M. S. 1953. "Approximate Confidence Intervals," *Biometrika*, **40**, pp. 12–19.

Basili, V. R., and D. H. Hutchens. 1983. "An Empirical Study of a Syntactic Complexity Family," *IEEE Transactions on Software Engineering*, **SE-9**(6), pp. 664–672.

Basili, V. R., and B. T. Perricone. 1984. "Software Errors and Complexity: An Empirical Investigation," *Communications ACM*, **27**(1), pp. 42–52.

Basin, S. L. 1973. "Estimation of Software Error Rates via Capture-Recapture Sampling: A Critical Review," Science Applications Report, Palo Alto, CA.

Bates, G. E. 1955. "Joint Distributions of Time Intervals for the Occurrence of Successive Accidents in a Generalized Polya Scheme," *Annals Mathematical Statistics*, **26**, pp. 705–720.

Becker, R. A., and J. M. Chambers. 1984. *S: An Interactive Environment for Data Analysis and Graphics*, Wadsworth, Belmont, CA.

Belady, L. A., and M. M.Lehman. 1976. "A Model of Large Program Development," *IBM Systems Journal*, **15**(3), pp. 224–252.

Bendick, M. 1976. "Error Rate as a Management Tool," Computer Sciences Corporation, Report of June 8, 1976.

Beveridge, G. S. G., and R. S. Schechter. 1970. *Optimization: Theory and Practice*, McGraw-Hill, New York.

Beyer, W. H. 1976. *Standard Mathematical Tables*, CRC Press, Cleveland.

Billinton, R., and R. N. Allan. 1983. *Reliability Evaluation of Engineering Systems: Concepts and Techniques*, Plenum Press, New York.

Boehm, B. W. 1981. *Software Engineering Economics*, Prentice Hall, Englewood Cliffs, NJ.

Box, G. E. P., and G. C. Tiao. 1973. *Bayesian Inference in Statistical Analysis*, Addison-Wesley, Reading, MA.

Brooks, F. P., Jr., 1975. *The Mythical Man Month*, Addison-Wesley, Reading, MA.

Budd, T. A., R. J. Lipton, R. A. De Millo, and F. G. Sayward. 1979. "Mutation Analysis," Department of Computer Science, Research Report 155, Yale University.

Burington, R. S., and D. C. May. 1970. *Handbook of Probability and Statistics with Tables*, 2d ed., McGraw-Hill, New York.

Card, D. N., V. E. Church, and W. W. Agresti. 1986. "An Empirical Study of Software Design Practices," *IEEE Transactions on Software Engineering*, **SE-12**(2), pp. 264–271.

Carnahan, B., and J. O. Wilkes. 1973. *Digital Computing and Numerical Methods*, Wiley, New York.

Cheung, R. C. 1980. "A User-Oriented Software Reliability Model," *IEEE Transactions on Software Engineering*, **SE-6**(2), pp. 118–125.

Cinlar, E. 1975. *Introduction to Stochastic Processes*, Prentice-Hall, Englewood Cliffs, NJ.

Clarke, A. B., and R. L. Disney. 1970. *Probability and Random Processes for Engineers and Scientists*, Wiley, New York.

Cox, D. R., and P. A. W. Lewis. 1966. *Statistical Analysis of Series of Events*, Methuen, London.

Cox, P. R. 1981. "Specification of a Regression Test for a Mini Computer Operating System," *Performance Evaluation Review*, **10**(1), p. 29.

Crow, L. H. 1974. "Reliability Analysis for Complex, Repairable Systems," (F. Proshan and R. J. Serfling, Editors), *Reliability and Biometry*, SIAM, Philadelphia, pp. 379–410.

Crow, L. H., and N. D. Singpurwalla. 1984. "An Empirically Developed Fourier Series Model for Describing Software Failures," *IEEE Transactions on Reliability*, **R-33**(2), pp. 176–183.

Crowell, R. H., and W. E. Slesnick. 1968. *Calculus with Analytic Geometry*, Norton, New York.

Currit, P. A., M. Dyer, and H. D. Mills. 1986. "Certifying the Reliability of Software," *IEEE Transactions on Software Engineering*, **SE-12**(1), pp. 3–11.

Dale, C. J. 1982. "Software Reliability Evaluation Methods," British Aerospace, Report ST26750.

Davis, H. T. 1962. *The Summation of Series*, The Principia Press of Trinity University, San Antonio.

Dhillon, B. S. 1983. *Reliability Engineering in Systems Design and Operation*, Van Nostrand Reinhold, New York.

Downs, T. 1985. "An Approach to the Modeling of Software Testing with Some Applications," *IEEE Transactions on Software Engineering*, **SE-11**(4), pp. 375–386.

Draper, N. R., and H. Smith. 1981. *Applied Regression Analysis*, Wiley, New York.

Duane, J. T. 1964. "Learning Curve Approach to Reliability Monitoring," *IEEE Transactions on Aerospace*, **AS-2**(2), pp. 563–566.

Duran, J. W., and S. C. Ntafos. 1984. "An Evaluation of Random Testing," *IEEE Transactions on Software Engineering*, **SE-10**(4), pp. 438–444.

Endres, A. 1975. "An Analysis of Errors and their Causes in System Programs," *Proceedings 1975 International Conference on Reliable Software*, Los Angeles, pp. 328–329. Also *IEEE Transactions on Software Engineering*, **SE-1**(2), pp. 140–149.

Feuer, A. R., and E. B. Fowlkes. 1979. "Some Results from an Empirical Study of Computer Software," *Proceedings Fourth International Conference on Software Engineering*, Munich, Germany, pp. 351–355.

Fletcher, R., and M. J. D. Powell. 1963. "A Rapidly Convergent Descent Method for Minimization," *Computer Journal*, **6**, pp. 163–168.

Fletcher, R., and C. M. Reeves. 1964. "Function Minimization by Conjugate Gradients," *Computer Journal*, **7**, *pp. 149–154.*

Fries, M. J. 1977. "Software Error Data Acquisition," Rome Air Development Center, Technical Report RADC-TR-77-130, Rome, NY.

Gilb, T. 1977. *Software Metrics*, Winthrop, Cambridge, p. 28.

Goel, A. L., and K. Okumoto. 1978. "An Analysis of Recurrent Software Errors in a Real-time Control System," *Proceedings ACM Conference*, pp. 496–501.

Goel, A. L., and K. Okumoto. 1979a. "A Markovian Model for Reliability and other Performance Measures," *Proceedings National Computer Conference*, pp. 769–774.

Goel, A. L., and K. Okumoto. 1979b. "Time-Dependent Error-Detection Rate Model for Software Reliability and other Performance Measures," *IEEE Transactions on Reliability*, **R-28**(3), pp. 206–211.

Grant, E. L., and R. S. Leavenworth. 1980. *Statistical Quality Control*, McGraw-Hill, New York, p. 559.

Gremillion, L. L. 1984. "Determinants of Program Repair Maintenance Requirements," *Communications ACM*, **27**(8), pp. 826–832.

Halstead, M. H. 1977. *Elements of Software Science*, Elsevier, New York.

Hamilton, P. A., and J. D. Musa. 1978. "Measuring Reliability of Computation Center Software," *Proceedings Third International Conference on Software Engineering*, Atlanta, pp. 29–36.

Hecht, H. 1977. "Measurement, Estimation, and Prediction of Software Reliability," *Software Engineering Technology—Volume 2*, Infotech International, Maidenhead, Berkshire, England, pp. 209–224.

Hecht, H. 1981. "Allocation of Resources for Software Reliability," *Proceedings COMPCON Fall 1981*, Washington, DC, pp. 74–82.

Herndon, M. A., and N. T. Keenan. 1978. "Analysis of Error Remediation Expenditures During Validation," *Proceedings Third International Conference on Software Engineering*, Atlanta, pp. 202–206.

Howden, W. E. 1980. "Functional Program Testing," *IEEE Transactions on Software Engineering*, **SE-6**(2), pp. 162–169.

Hudson, G. R. 1967. "Program Errors as a Birth and Death Process," System Development Corporation, Report SP-3011, Santa Monica, CA.

Iannino, A. 1979. Private communication to J. D. Musa and B. Littlewood.

Iannino, A., J. D. Musa, K. Okumoto, and B. Littlewood. 1984. "Criteria for Software Reliability Model Comparisons," *IEEE Transactions on Software Engineering* **SE-10**(6), pp. 687–691.

Inglis, J., F. Gray, Jr., D. M. Kane, and M. K. Kaufmann. 1986. Unpublished work.

Institute of Electrical and Electronics Engineers. 1983. *IEEE Standard Glossary of Software Engineering Terminology* (Standard 729-1983), IEEE, New York.

Jelinski, Z., and P. B. Moranda. 1972. "Software Reliability Research," (W. Freiberger, Editor), *Statistical Computer Performance Evaluation*, Academic, New York, pp. 465–484.

Joe, H., and N. Reid. 1985. "Estimating the Number of Faults in a System," *Journal of the American Statistical Association*, **80**(389), pp. 222–226.

Jones, C. 1986. *Programming Productivity*, McGraw-Hill, New York.

Kapur, K. C., and L. R. Lamberson. 1977. *Reliability in Engineering Design*, Wiley, New York.

Keiller, P. A., B. Littlewood, D. R. Miller, and A. Sofer. 1983. "On the Quality of Software Reliability Prediction" (J. K. Skwirzynski, Editor), *Electronic Systems Effectiveness and Life Cycle Costing*, NATO ASI Series, **F3**, Springer-Verlag, Heidelberg, pp. 441–460.

Kelley, C. S. 1979. "Accurate Approximations to the Polygamma Functions," *Quarterly of Applied Mathematics*, **37**(2), pp. 203–207.

Kendall, M. G., and A. Stuart. 1961. *The Advanced Theory of Statistics*, vol. 2, Hafner, New York.

Kleinrock, L. 1975. *Queueing Systems*, vol. 1, Wiley, New York.

Knight, J. C., and N. G. Leveson. 1986. "An Experimental Evaluation of the Assumption of Independence in Multi-Version Programming," *IEEE Transactions on Software Engineering*, **SE-12**(1), pp. 96–109.

Koch, H. S., and P. Kubat. 1983. "Optimal Release Time of Computer Software," *IEEE Transactions on Software Engineering*, **SE-9**(3), pp. 323–327.

Kremer, W. 1983. "Birth-Death and Bug Counting," *IEEE Transactions on Reliability*, **R-32**(1), pp. 37–47.

Laner, D. 1985. Commentary on War, Public Television series.

Langberg, N., and N. Singpurwalla. 1985. "A Unification of Some Software Reliability Models," *SIAM Journal on Scientific and Statistical Computing*, **6**(3), pp. 781–790.

Laprie, J. C. 1984. "Dependability Evaluation of Software Systems in Operation," *IEEE Transactions on Software Engineering*, **SE-10**(6), pp. 701–714.

Lawless, J. F. 1982. *Statistical Models and Methods for Lifetime Data*, Wiley, New York.

Lawson, D. J. 1983. "Failure Mode, Effect, and Criticality Analysis," (J. K. Skwirzynski, Editor), *Electronic Systems Effectiveness and Life Cycle Costing*, NATO ASI Series, **F3**, Springer-Verlag, Heidelberg, pp. 55–74.

Leveson, N. G. 1986. "Software Hazard Analysis Techniques," (J. K. Skwirzynski, Editor), *Software System Design Methods*, NATO ASI Series, **F22**, Springer-Verlag, Heidelberg, pp. 681–699.

Lipson, C., and N. J. Sheth. 1973. *Statistical Design and Analysis of Engineering Experiments*, McGraw-Hill, New York.

Littlewood, B. 1976. "A Semi-Markov Model for Software Reliability with Failure Costs," *Proceedings Symposium on Computer Software Engineering*, Polytechnic Press, New York, pp. 281–300.

Littlewood, B. 1979. "Software Reliability Model for Modular Program Structure," *IEEE Transactions on Reliability*, **R-28**(3), pp. 241–246.

Littlewood, B. 1981. "Stochastic Reliability-Growth: A Model for Fault-Removal in Computer-Programs and Hardware-Design," *IEEE Transactions on Reliability*, **R-30**(4), pp. 313–320.

Littlewood, B., A. A. Ghaly, and P. Y. Chan. 1986. "Tools for the Analysis of the Accuracy of Software Reliability Predictions," (J. K. Skwirzynski, Editor), *Software System Design Methods*, NATO ASI Series, **F22**, Springer-Verlag, Heidelberg, pp. 299–335.

Littlewood, B., and J. L. Verrall. 1973. "A Bayesian Reliability Growth Model for Computer Software," *Journal Royal Statistical Society-Series C*, **22**(3), pp. 332–346.

Littlewood, B., and J. L. Verrall. 1974. "A Bayesian Reliability Model with a Stochastically Monotone Failure Rate," *IEEE Transactions on Reliability*, **R-23**(2), pp. 108–114.

Litzau, J. T. 1986. Private communication to J. D. Musa.

Lloyd, D. K., and M. Lipow. 1977. *Reliability: Management, Methods, and Mathematics*, 2d ed., published by the authors, Redondo Beach, CA.

McCabe, T. J. 1976. "A Complexity Measure," *IEEE Transactions on Software Engineering*, **SE-2**(4), pp. 308–320.

Mann, N. R., R. E. Schafer, and N. D. Singpurwalla. 1974. *Methods for Statistical Analysis of Reliability and Life Data*, Wiley, New York.

Martz, H. F., and R. A. Waller. 1982. *Bayesian Reliability Analysis*, Wiley, New York.

Meinhold, R. J., and N. D. Singpurwalla. 1983. "Bayesian Analysis of a Commonly Used Model for Describing Software Failures," *The Statistician*, **32**, pp. 168–173.

Mendis, K. S. 1981. "Quantifying Software Quality," *Proceedings American Institute of Aeronautics and Astronautics*, pp. 300–308.

Miller, A. M. B. 1980. "A Study of the Musa Reliability Model," M. S. thesis, University of Maryland.

Miller, D. R. 1986. "Exponential Order Statistic Models of Software Reliability Growth," *IEEE Transactions on Software Engineering*, **SE-12**(1), pp. 12–24.

Mills, H. D. 1972. "On the Statistical Validation of Computer Programs," IBM Federal Systems Division, Report FSC-72-6015, Gaithersburg, MD.

Misra, P. N. 1983. "Software Reliability Analysis," *IBM Systems Journal*, **22**(3), pp. 262–270.

Mittermeir, R. T. 1982. "Optimal Test Effort for Software Systems," (E. Lauger and J. Moltoft, Editors), *Reliability in Electrical and Electronic Components and Systems*, North-Holland, Amsterdam, pp. 650–654.

Miyamoto, I. 1975. "Software Reliability in Online Real Time Environment," *Proceedings 1975 International Conference on Reliable Software*, Los Angeles, pp. 194–203.

Mood, A. M., F. A. Graybill, and D. C. Boes. 1974. *Introduction to the Theory of Statistics*, McGraw-Hill, New York.

Moranda, P. B. 1975. "Predictions of Software Reliability During Debugging," *Proceedings Annual Reliability and Maintainability Symposium*, Washington, DC, pp. 327–332.

Moranda, P. B. 1981. "An Error Detection Model for Application During Software Development," *IEEE Transactions on Reliability*, **R-30**(4), pp. 309–312.

Mosteller, F., and J. W. Tukey. 1977. *Data Analysis and Regression*, Addison-Wesley, Reading, MA.

Motley, R. W., and W. D. Brooks. 1977. "Statistical Prediction of Programming Errors," Rome Air Development Center, Technical Report RADC-TR-77-175, Rome, NY.

Musa, J. D. 1975. "A Theory of Software Reliability and its Application," *IEEE Transactions on Software Engineering*, **SE-1**(3), pp. 312–327.

Musa, J. D. 1979a. Private communication to B. Littlewood.

Musa, J. D. 1979b. "Software Reliability Data," report available from Data and Analysis Center for Software, Rome Air Development Center, Rome, NY.

Musa, J. D. 1979c. "Software Reliability Modeling—Where Are We and Where Should We be Going?," *Proceedings Fourth NASA Software Engineering Workshop*, Goddard Space Flight Center, Greenbelt, MD, pp. 239–249.

Musa, J. D. 1979d. "Validity of Execution Time Theory of Software Reliability," *IEEE Transactions on Reliability*, **R-28**(3), pp. 181–191.

Musa, J. D. 1985. "Software Engineering: The Future of a Profession," *IEEE Software*, **2**(1), pp. 55–62.

Musa, J. D., P. A. Hamilton, and R. B. Hollander. 1983. "Program for Software Reliability and System Test Schedule Estimation—Revised for Staged Failure Interval Adjustment—Program Documentation," available through J. D. Musa.

Musa, J. D. and R. B. Hollander. 1983. "Program for Software Reliability and System Test Schedule Estimation—Revised for Staged Failure Interval Adjustment—User's Guide," available through J. D. Musa.

Musa, J. D., and A. Iannino. 1981. "Software Reliability Modeling—Accounting for Program Size Variation due to Integration or Design Changes," *ACM SIGMETRICS Performance Evaluation Review*, **10**(2), pp. 16–25.

Musa, J. D., and K. Okumoto. 1983. "Software Reliability Models: Concepts, Classification, Comparisons, and Practice," (J. K. Skwirzynski, Editor), *Electronic Systems Effectiveness and Life Cycle Costing*, NATO ASI Series, **F3**, Springer-Verlag, Heidelberg, pp. 395–424.

Musa, J. D., and K. Okumoto. 1984a. "A Comparison of Time Domains for Software Reliability Models," *Journal of Systems and Software*, **4**(4), pp. 277–287.

Musa, J. D., and K. Okumoto. 1984b. "A Logarithmic Poisson Execution Time Model for Software Reliability Measurement," *Proceedings Seventh International Conference on Software Engineering*, Orlando, pp. 230–238.

Myers, G. J. 1976. *Software Reliability: Principles and Practices*, McGraw-Hill, New York.

Myers, G. J. 1979. *The Art of Software Testing*, Wiley, New York.

Nelder, J. A., and R. Mead. 1965. "A Simplex Method for Function Minimization," *Computer Jour-*

nal, **7**, pp. 308–313.

Neter, J., W. Wasserman, and M. H. Kutner. 1983. *Applied Linear Regression Models*, Richard D. Irwin, Inc., Homewood, IL.

Okumoto, K. 1985. "A Statistical Method for Software Quality Control," *IEEE Transactions on Software Engineering*, **SE-11**(12), pp. 1424–1430.

Okumoto, K., and A. L. Goel. 1978a. "Availability and Other Performance Measures of System Under Imperfect Maintenance," *Procceedings COMPSAC*, pp. 66–71.

Okumoto, K., and A. L. Goel. 1978b. "Classical and Bayesian Inference for the Software Imperfect Debugging Model," Rome Air Development Center, Technical Report RADC-TR-78-155, Rome, NY.

Okumoto, K., and A. L. Goel. 1980. "Optimum Release Time for Software Systems Based on Reliability and Cost Criteria," *Journal of Systems and Software*, **1**(4), pp. 315–318.

Ostrand, T. J., and E. J. Weyuker. 1982. "Collecting and Categorizing Software Error Data in an Industrial Environment," New York University. Technical Report 47.

Pressman, R. S. 1982. *Software Engineering: A Practitioner's Approach*, McGraw-Hill, New York.

Presson, P. E. 1981. "A Study of Software Errors on Large Aerospace Projects," *Proceedings National Security Industrial Association Conference on Software Technology and Management*, Alexandria, VA.

Putnam, L. H. 1976. "A Macro-Estimating Methodology for Software Development," *Digest of Papers: Fall COMPCON 1976*, Washington, DC, pp. 138–143.

Ramamoorthy, C. V., and F. B. Bastani. 1982. "Software Reliability—Status and Perspectives," *IEEE Transactions on Software Engineering*, **SE-8**(4), pp. 354–370.

Rohatgi, V. K. 1976. *An Introduction to Probability Theory and Mathematical Statistics*, Wiley, New York.

Ross, S. M. 1970. *Applied Probability Models with Optimization Applications*, Holden-Day, San Francisco.

Ross, S. M. 1972. *Introduction to Probability Models*, Academic, New York.

Roussas, G. G. 1973. *A First Course in Mathematical Statistics*, Addison-Wesley, Reading, MA.

Rubey, R. J., J. A. Dana, and P. W. Biché. 1975. "Quantitative Aspects of Software Validation," *IEEE Transactions on Software Engineering*, **SE-1**(2), pp. 150–155.

Rudner, B. 1977. "Seeding/Tagging Estimation of Software Errors: Models and Estimates," Rome Air Development Center, Technical Report RADC-TR-77-15, Rome, NY.

Saunier, P. 1983. "Fiabilité du Logiciel: Quelques Remarques Tirèes d'une Expérimentation de Trois Modéles à Taux de Panne," (in French), *L'Industrie Face a la Qualité du Logiciel*, Belvedere, Toulouse, France, Oct. 20–21, 1983, pp. 257–290.

Schafer, R. E., J. F. Alter, J. E. Angus, and S. E. Emoto. 1979. "Validation of Software Reliability Models," Rome Air Development Center, Technical Report RADC-TR-79-147, Rome, NY.

Schick, G. J., and R. W. Wolverton. 1973. "Assessment of Software Reliability," *Proceedings Operations Research*, Physica-Verlag, Wurzburg-Wien, pp. 395–422.

Schick, G. J., and R. W. Wolverton. 1978. "An Analysis of Competing Software Reliability Models," *IEEE Transactions on Software Engineering*, **SE-4**(2), pp. 104–120.

Schneidewind, N. F. 1972. "An Approach to Software Reliability Prediction and Quality Control," *1972 Fall Joint Computer Conference, AFIPS Conference Proceedings*, **41**, AFIPS Press, Montvale, NJ, pp. 837–847.

Schneidewind, N. F. 1975. "Analysis of Error Processes in Computer Software," *Proceedings 1975 International Conference on Reliable Software*, Los Angeles, pp. 337–346.

Shanthikumar, J. G. 1981. "A State- and Time-Dependent Error Occurrence-Rate Software Reliability Model with Imperfect Debugging," *Proceedings National Computer Conference*, pp. 311–315.

Shen, V. Y., T. J. Yu, S. M. Thebaut, and L. R. Paulsen. 1985. "Identifying Error-Prone Software—An Empirical Study," *IEEE Transactions on Software Engineering*, **SE-11**(4), pp. 317–324.

Shooman, M. L. 1972. "Probabilistic Models for Software Reliability Prediction," (W. Freidberger, Editor), *Statistical Computer Performance Evaluation*, Academic, New York, pp. 485–502.

Shooman, M. L. 1983. *Software Engineering*, McGraw-Hill, New York.

Shooman, M. L. 1984. "Software Reliability: A Historical Perspective," *IEEE Transactions on Reliability*, **R-33**(1), pp. 48–55.

Shooman, M. L. 1986. *Probabilistic Reliability: An Engineering Approach*, McGraw-Hill, New York, 1968. Updated and reprinted, Krieger, Malabar, FL, 1986.

Shooman, M. L., and M. I. Bolsky. 1975. "Types, Distribution, and Test and Correction Times for Programming Errors," *Proceedings 1975 International Conference on Reliable Software*, Los Angeles, pp. 347–357.

Shooman, M. L., and S. Natarajan. 1976. "Effect of Manpower Deployment and Bug Generation on Software Error Models," *Proceedings Symposium Computer Software Engineering*, New York, pp. 155–170.

Shooman, M. L., and A. K. Trivedi. 1976. "A Many-State Markov Model for Computer Software Performance Parameters," *IEEE Transactions on Reliability*, **R-25**(2), pp. 66–68.

Snyder, D. L. 1975. *Random Point Processes*, Wiley-Interscience.

Stover, R. E., Jr. 1977. "A Statistics Collection Package for the JOVIAL J3 Programming Language," Rome Air Development Center, Technical Report RADC-TR-77-293, Rome, NY.

Sukert, A. N. 1976. "A Software Reliability Modeling Study," Rome Air Development Center, Technical Report RADC-TR-76-247, Rome, NY.

Sukert, A. N. 1979. "Empirical Validation of Three Software Error Prediction Models," *IEEE Transactions on Reliability*, **R-28**(3), pp. 199–205.

Sunohara, T., A. Takano, K. Uehara, and T. Ohkawa. 1981. "Program Complexity Measure for Software Development Management," *Proceedings Fifth International Conference on Software Engineering*, San Diego, pp. 100–106.

Takahashi, N., and Y. Kamayachi. 1985. "An Empirical Study of a Model for Program Error Prediction," *Proceedings Eighth International Conference on Software Engineering*, London, pp. 330–336.

Thayer, T. A. 1976. "Software Reliability Study," Rome Air Development Center, Technical Report RADC-TR-76-238, Rome, NY.

Trachtenberg, M. 1985. "The Linear Software Reliability Model and Uniform Testing," *IEEE Transactions Reliability*, **R-34**(1), pp. 8–16.

Trivedi, K. S. 1982. *Probability and Statistics with Reliability, Queuing, and Computer Science Applications*, Prentice-Hall, Englewood Cliffs, NJ.

Wagoner, W. L. 1973. "The Final Report on a Software Reliability Measurement Study," Aerospace Corporation, Report TOR-0074(4112)-1.

Walpole, R. E., and R. H. Myers. 1972. *Probability and Statistics for Engineers and Scientists*, Macmillan, New York.

Walsh, G. R., 1975. *Methods of Optimization*, Wiley, New York.

Walston, C. E., and C. P. Felix. 1977. "A Method of Programming Measurement and Estimation," *IBM Systems Journal*, **16**(1), pp. 54–73.

Watson, I. A. 1981. "Review of Common Cause Failures," National Centre of Systems Reliability, Report NCSR R27.

Weiss, D. M. 1981. "Evaluating Software Development by Analysis of Change Data," University of Maryland Computer Science Technical Report TR-1120.

Yamada, S., M. Ohba, and S. Osaki. 1983. "S-Shaped Reliability Growth Modeling for Software Error Detection," *IEEE Transactions on Reliability*, **R-32**(5), pp. 475–478.

AUTHOR INDEX

A

Adams, E. N., 108, 208
Agresti, W. W., 115
Akiyama, F., 115, 116
Albin, J. L., 116
Allan, R. N., 472
Alter, J. F., 116
Anderson, T., 84n
Angus, J. E., 116, 131
Ascher, H. E., 468, 504

B

Bain, L. J., 578
Bardsley, I., 80
Barlow, R. E., 504
Bartholomew, D. J., 310
Bartlett, M. S., 332, 333, 579
Basili, V. R., 115, 116, 119, 121, 122
Basin, S. L., 114
Bastani, F. B., 31, 238
Bates, G. E., 311
Belady, L. A., 119
Bendick, M., 116
Beveridge, G. S. G., 523
Beyer, W. H., 571
Biché, P. W., 116
Billinton, R., 472
Boehm, B. W., 116, 137
Boes, D. C., 315, 325, 326, 332, 335n, 360, 368, 377, 381, 448, 465, 578
Bolsky, M. I., 138, 139n, 414
Bowen, J. B., 116, 131

Box, G. E. P., 371
Brooks, F. P., Jr., 55
Brooks, W. D., 115, 116
Budd, T. A., 109

C

Card, D. N., 115
Carnahan, B., 524
Chan, P. Y., 464
Cheung, R. C., 232
Church, V. E., 115
Cinlar, E., 255, 365, 472
Clarke, A. B., 472
Cox, D. R., 146n, 310, 466
Cox, P. R., 110
Crow, L. H., 243, 249, 251, 292, 395
Crowell, R. H., 574
Currit, P. A., 108

D

Dale, C. J., 31
Dana, J. A., 116
Davis, H. T., 179, 234, 573
De Millo, R. A., 109
Dhillon, B. S., 95
Disney, R. L., 472
Downs, T., 35
Duane, J. T., 292
Duran, J. W., 108
Dyer, M., 108

601

SUBJECT INDEX